A Life To Enjoy

by

John Reeve

About the author:

John Reeve was born in Woking in 1931, enjoyed a conventional middle-class education during which time the family moved to the Cornish countryside. He then joined the Royal Navy.

After twenty years in the Navy he moved on to a quieter, more settled life in Watford, working for Kodak at their Harrow factory. He is now fully retired and still lives in Watford.

A Life To Enjoy

by

John Reeve

Published by
Mediaworld PR Ltd
Best Books Online

Acknowledgements

To my wife Patricia who spent ages with the proof reading, checking accuracy and suggesting different names for one or two people about whom I have been somewhat critical.

Also to Greg Child, our family pedant, who checked and corrected many minor inaccuracies.

To Stephen Webb who took the lovely picture of us at the Scottish Country Dance.

And to my many friends who have read excerpts and have enthusiastically encouraged me to complete the book.

Finally to Margaret Smith of Mediaworld who, with great patience, has guided me through the revision process of getting the book ready for publication.

Dedication

This book is dedicated to my family who feature in these pages. Most especially it is to my wife Patricia who has put up with me spending weeks shut away in what I grandly call my computer room, emerging only when I sense it must be time for another meal.

Contents

Colour Pictures
(after page 344)

Part I

Bachelor

1

Anstruther — An Awakening

My life started to look up when we had a visit from Anstruther, who had become our unofficial family 'adviser' during that lull in 1945 after my father was demobbed. We were all sitting quietly one day after Sunday lunch when he appeared on our doorstep.

"What are you going to do?" he asked father as he settled himself in father's armchair. "You won't be going back to work in London will you, not after all you've said these last years?"

Father looked uncomfortable. He hadn't told us children what was in his mind. We both assumed he would return to his work in a London import-export clothing agency as soon as it was up and running again, catching the same 8.04 morning train from Byfleet to Waterloo, returning on the 4.58 afternoon train, five and a half days a week with a half day for golf on Saturday afternoon. Sunday was the family day (which usually meant gardening for father while us children ran around frantically helping and generally getting under his feet). It was a comfortable routine and very predictable.

I liked Anstruther. He led a far from routine life operating from a lovely house in Redbourn on the far side of London. My sister Jane, three years my senior, had stayed with him and his family since leaving school at fifteen, and now, a few years later, was considered to be fully trained in the management of a smallholding. I, too, had stayed there for a few days and it was this exciting visit that probably opened my eyes to the existence of an alternative and much more interesting way to make a living than travelling to London each day.

Father was over-age for front line military service when the war began in 1939, but was given a staff job at the War Office. He looked after an elderly general and sat at a desk in the outer office pushing red tape around. One day the door opened a crack and a genial sun-tanned middle-aged man appeared. He was shortish, built fairly comfortably and dressed in a somewhat shabby major's uniform. He sported a moustache which could do with a trim and had a far from military bearing. Father thought he was in urgent need of a smart refresher from one of the more sadistic RSMs.

"Anstruther," said the man with a smile, holding out a hand and, nodding at the closed inner door. "Is he in?"

"Yes, but... do you have an appointment?" Father got to his feet.

Anstruther was across the room and opening the inner door before father could stop him. "Hallo, Bobo," he said, disappearing into the inner sanctum.

"For God's sake, what the hell are you doing here?" The general's raised voice was far from welcoming. Anstruther reappeared after a few minutes, nodded genially at father and departed. The general strode out and growled at father:

"Don't listen to his excuses, he is never, never to come into this office. Clear?"

But he did, of course. Every few months Anstruther would creep around the door, give a cheery wave to father and march into the general's office unannounced, always with the same reception. Over time he and father got to know one another well and that was when father discovered some people were having a very different war to others.

It turned out Anstruther was the general's brother-in-law, who considered him a bad influence on everybody. "Don't know where he got his bloody uniform, but he has no right to call himself a major. Ought to be given a proper job."

My sister Jane left school in the middle of the war at a time when bombs were raining down on London every night, with only one thought as to what she wanted to do—work with animals. Over lunch one day father and Anstruther discussed how best to get her fixed up. Anstruther had a suggestion.

"Let Jane come and live with us at Redbourn," he'd said. "I'll teach her to ride, milk a cow and look after our hens. She'd be a wonderful asset. Then, when this lot is over she'll know whether it's a passing infatuation or whether she really does want to work with animals."

And so it came about. Jane went to Redbourn and settled in happily. Some months later it was suggested I go and join her for a week.

Looking back to those unsettled times it is difficult to imagine now just what a problem it was to safely transport on his own an eleven year-old boy from Byfleet, twenty miles south of London to Redbourn twenty miles north, without travelling through the middle of town during the blitz. To this day I remember the trip so well. I took the scenic route. On a lovely spring day I set out from home on my first trip alone, caught a bus the few miles to Weybridge from where I was able to take a service launch up the Thames to Windsor. From Windsor it was another bus ride through the village of Denham and on to Rickmansworth, Watford and through to St. Albans where I met Jane and we travelled the last few miles together in yet another bus. It took all day and I enjoyed every moment. The sun shone, birds sang, the countryside looked lovely and there was no traffic on the small winding roads that the bus took. We could have been in a different country to the war-scarred environs south of London.

Jane had changed. Part of the deal had been for Anstruther and his wife to give her the 'finishing school' treatment, and Jane was now a lady and looked like one. She lectured me on how I was to behave when I arrived and I tried my best to remember all I had been taught from my mother. Mother occasionally taught dancing and deportment herself. She never had much success with me, but then children seldom take much notice of their parents and I was no exception. By the time Jane and I arrived at the house I was expecting someone like a despotic headmaster.

The Anstruther house, Greyfriars, is on the edge of Redbourn common; a lovely rambling place originally three cottages that had been knocked into one. Thus there were doors everywhere, with changes of level in unexpected places and several staircases. It was a wonderful house to explore and full of lovely furniture and all sorts of knick-knacks. Every room contained a hidden loudspeaker from which the muted voice of the BBC Home Service would sound at pre-arranged times throughout the day, starting at 7.00 a.m. when it was decreed the household should rise.

Anstruther's lifestyle hadn't been too disrupted by the war. With enormous foresight he had laid up stocks of sugar and one or two other imported essentials before food rationing was imposed, and was virtually self-supporting in everything else—a far cry from our own urban family who, like most people, had to plan very carefully in order to get enough to eat. He achieved this by turning his business, a floral plant nursery, into a market garden from which he supplied fruit and veg to shops in Berkhamsted and Hemel Hempstead (that would have been 'Old Hemel'—not the new town of today which is virtually all post-war). To deliver his produce from the market garden near Harpenden, he had acquired an ideal vehicle at minimum cost: a 1920s Rolls Royce hearse, scarcely altered from its original role and still retaining the engraved glass side panels. With the back full of produce, he would purr quietly along the empty Hertfordshire lanes looking down benignly on any passer-by.

When we arrived at Greyfriars, Jane introduced me solemnly to Anstruther and his wife of whom up to this time I had only heard the most extraordinary stories. I was about to see whether they were all true. I was allocated my own room along the corridor from Jane's.

"Don't be alarmed if the bust on that plinth in the corner starts to talk first thing in the morning. There's a loudspeaker inside it. The Home Service, seven o'clock news. Oh, and be careful of the loo seat in there," she nodded her head at an open bathroom door. "That talks too sometimes."

We set about exploring the rest of the house. Several closed doors were 'no go' areas for us children. In the course of the tour we came across a number of dogs, more than I had ever seen in one house before. On arrival I had noticed a sign "CAVE CANUM" on the gate leading onto the common and had asked Jane what it meant. "Beware of the dog, silly," was her withering reply. My schoolboy Latin was somewhat rudimentary and I was indignant to be put down like that. Maybe the notice was necessary, though whether the postman understood Latin was another thing. Dogs everywhere.

"Seven altogether," Jane told me as we toured around. "They're all safe except Fritz who doesn't come into this part of the house. When you meet him, just don't upset him. He has a very quick temper. And he bites and asks questions

3

afterwards. He's the only black and white one, but one of the smallest and with a terrible bark. Earns his keep guarding the house against opportunist German parachutists." She looked at me to see how much I was taking in. "Seriously, little brother, I'd just avoid him if I were you, and don't be tempted to give him a kick. He can move a lot faster than you." I wasn't sure I was going to like living here. Dangerous dogs and talking busts...

"This is where his bedroom is."

She pulled open a door that swung outwards across the passage and latched into another doorframe. The bedroom was now connected via the passage to the next room, a dressing room, with a bathroom beyond. "If you do come this way during the afternoons, you might find him having forty winks. Just a warning— he tends to lie on the bed naked."

"Have you seen him naked, then?"

"Oh yes. First time, it was a bit of a surprise. Not a very pleasant sight. Nothing to be alarmed about, though, I'd trust him not to get too familiar."

"But...." I thought all this extraordinary. What would our parents think if they knew?

We continued our tour. Jane pointed out that although all the doors had latches, with some of them the latch was kept in the up position by means of a wedge, and these doors had pneumatic door closers instead. This was so they could be nudged open by a dog. The dogs had learnt that when a door closed behind them, it was possible to leave the room by another door and proceed round the house, clockwise, so to speak, thus never getting trapped in any room and never getting blamed for leaving a door open. I thought this a sensibly ingenious arrangement and proceeded to check it out for myself, finding several rooms and corridors that seemed to have no other purpose than to be on the dogs' circulatory route.

Anstruther had retired to his office somewhere and I was summoned by his wife to give her a hand with preparations for supper. Jane disappeared to milk the cows, promising to let me help her next morning. I entered the kitchen, a wonderfully exciting place full of bits and pieces I had never seen before and could only guess at their meaning. Mrs Anstruther was a delightful person and treated me like another adult (though with hindsight I realised this was all part of the 'development' training which Jane had received and which was missing at home). She patiently got me to do things, telling me just enough to get started and leaving me to use my initiative to work out how to do them. Food shortages of the sort we experienced at home just didn't seem to feature here. It was another world.

I told the story of my mother who recently had two guests for lunch. A meagre pie was divided between us with some left over for 'seconds'. The guests politely declined a second helping and before they changed their minds (which they might well have done, judging by their hungry looks) mother said; "Oh good. There'll be just enough for tomorrow" and quickly took the unfinished pie out to the kitchen. That's how it was then. Nobody thought such behaviour was bad manners. We were all hungry most of the time.

In the morning Jane collected me early, and we set off on bicycles for the meadow just beyond the railway line where two cows were kept. Milking was done crofter style, with the cow in the field, still grazing, while Jane on her three-legged stool attempted to milk into an open bucket without the cow moving on and kicking over the bucket. These were a couple of lovely docile Guernseys who knew what was expected, and generally they behaved well. With two brimming buckets, one dangling from each handlebar, riding the bike back to Greyfriars was not really practicable, so we walked. No traffic of course, yet this was the main London to Holyhead A5 that in a few years time would be so congested as to be virtually unusable.

There were various outbuildings at Greyfriars, one of which went under the grand name of the Dairy. Here was a milk cooler and slate shelves on which stood cheeses wrapped in muslin in various states of maturity. It had a lovely smell which reminded me of the Byfleet Sainsbury's grocery shop. Jane showed me how she cooled and strained the milk and set it aside in settling pans for the cream to rise, ready for skimming off to make butter with.

There were also stables in one of which stood the pony Jane was allowed to ride. She would spend hours happily mucking out and grooming. The harness room next door smelt of Neatsfoot and leather and all the harness shone with the care and attention it received.

A picture had arrived which was to be hung in one of the passages. Anstruther beckoned to me to follow him outside, and led the way to a door at the end of the house, which I hadn't noticed earlier. Inside was a wonderful Aladdin's cave, a sturdy workbench with shelves above containing hundreds of tobacco tins, all labelled with pictures of their contents. He asked me what he should use to support the picture and patiently explained how to decide on a suitable fastening to suit the wall. We went to have a look at the wall, uneven whitewashed plaster over cob. A beam ran along at ceiling height. "We'll hang it from that," he said. "This plaster is very soft and it would be safer to use the beam. What sort of hook shall we use?" Together we returned to the workshop and chose a suitable fixing. Then with the tools needed and a chair to stand on I was the one who did the fixing. A simple thing perhaps, but it was the first time I had ever been encouraged to take the initiative and I did so under subtle instruction without realising this was all part of Anstruther's training. At home father, who was all fingers and thumbs and hopeless with any tools, would have called in a Mr Fixit who would arrive next day on his bicycle. It would never have occurred to father to think I might be able to do anything and I probably never thought of it myself.

As a gesture to the war effort there were cabbages and rhubarb growing among the flowers in the garden. Anstruther asked whether I'd like to meet Ransome, his lawnmower. How does an eleven-year-old boy answer an apparently serious question from such a man? He led me round to the back where a sheep, tethered to a stake, was cropping the grass to a beautiful bowling green finish.

"See the shape of this bit of lawn? Ransome can get at all of it from either this position, or if I move the stake over here…" He heaved out the stake and pushed it down into a hole at the other end, "… now she can cover this other half. And all without getting at the flowers. What do you think of that then, eh?" The trouble was, he always invited me to comment on anything he showed me, and it was difficult sometimes to say anything sensible about some of them. I muttered something about it being a good idea. He then showed how all the other small lawns were similarly shaped. "Ransome covers the lot in a week and then we start again," he said.

"What about the winter when grass isn't growing?"

He beamed. "Then she spends her time in the meadow with the cows. Eventually we have her for dinner and the following spring get a new one."

I was so shocked I couldn't reply to that. Not true, surely? He gave nothing away.

I accompanied Anstruther to the market garden near Harpenden. The stately Rolls purred down little country lanes and in the back were bags of stable manure and a box full of papers and files. When we arrived I was let loose to explore the gardens while he disappeared into the office to sort out the orders. Later we loaded up some boxes and made a delivery to the shop in Hemel Hempstead. I loved being allowed to do all the lifting and carrying under Anstruther's direction, and I think he enjoyed giving the orders.

One evening while we were all sitting in front of the log fire there was a quiet knock on the front door. Fritz leapt into frenzied action, but one quiet word from Anstruther reduced him to a quivering cowering bundle, poised to leap at whoever might enter should he be needed. The door was opened to a tall, very tall as he was wearing his helmet, policeman. Anstruther asked him in, much to Fritz's consternation, and the policeman removed his helmet and stood on the threshold awkwardly while Anstruther disappeared with Fritz into the kitchen, to reappear a moment later without Fritz but with a brown paper parcel which he handed over. I had never seen a uniformed policeman inside a private house before and was vaguely surprised that without his helmet he was just an ordinary man underneath; moreover he looked unbelievably pleased at the sight of the parcel which had the familiar shape of a trussed fowl. The prospect of a square meal must have been too much to control the happy gleam in his eye as he thanked Anstruther and bade us goodnight. One or two other instances like this occurred during my visit and I began to realise that living in the country had a number of advantages at times like these, and bartering was one of them. One just needed something to barter with and most country folk were clearly more fortunate than us townies in that respect.

It must have been on some other visit to Greyfriars that Jane warned me about another visitor staying for a day or two. This was Anstruther's younger sister, Joyce, and I was told to be on my best behaviour since Joyce was very important. My memories of that meeting are faded now, but to me she seemed a very pleasant lady, though a bit distant. I believe she was going through some upset at the time, but I never knew what. It was only much later that I discovered she was a famous author, one whose best-selling book Mrs Miniver had been adapted to make a film that enjoyed a huge circulation both in Britain and America, where it was made and first shown. Joyce's pen name was Jan Struther—a play on J. Anstruther. Needless to say she became known, especially in America, as

'Jan' and her real name Joyce was only used by family at home. Not by me, I hasten to add: I would never address an adult by their first name. Not in those days.

Greyfriars: Anstruther's rambling house in Redbourn

2

Early Days

My whole outlook on the world was seriously blinkered by two major aspects of my life—I was born and brought up in a family which had clear ideas about which layer of society it thought it was positioned, and I drifted along in it, quite content to believe one did not mix with the layer below, only above (and that was done only with very great care). The other aspect was my schooling at a series of private boys' schools designed to ensure I would never be tempted to become involved with 'the wrong sort'. Consequently with this restricted upbringing I missed out on a whole side of life—some good, some admittedly awful. It wasn't until I went to university that I realised just how innocent and naïve I was.

So I drifted through the 'thirties happily unaware of much outside my protected environment, no doubt to the relief of my parents. My father had come from relatively humble stock, a family who were clearly 'in trade' in a prosaic way, and he was a little ashamed of this though he wouldn't dream of admitting it. He referred to it as his 'business', which was, in fact, concerned with importing and exporting cloth. When he bought clothes he examined the cloth with a real expert's eye which must have been a giveaway to the tailor, but it did mean he always bought well, and was always very well turned out.

He met my mother on the dance floor. Father's name was Sidney, a name he hated. Mother's was Dorothy, but she was called Eve by many of their friends after an occasion during a dancing evening when she was introduced to somebody who misheard 'Reeve' as 'Eve'. Father was promptly dubbed Adam, which he much preferred to the dreaded Sidney. Mother's family used to run a teashop in Hove, and mother herself had been taught to dance by none other than the famous Mrs Worthington, of whom Noël Coward had something to say. The dancing was all part of what young ladies of the day would be taught as part of the finishing process, and mother herself undoubtedly had the necessary graces to mix with society at any level. She in turn taught deportment and dancing in a small way and even tried to get me on the floor, but I was at the gangling youth stage when she tried, so it was somewhat unsuccessful. About the only bit I remember was how to enter a room, closing the door behind me without turning my back on the occupants. Later she corrected my loping slouch, teaching me to walk elegantly with a straight back and good footwork—something I still do to this day when I remember.

I was born in Woking in 1931 in a little house called Jasmine Cottage. I remember my birthplace through a dreamy memory filter. It was all deliciously 1930s, roses round the door (and no doubt lots of jasmine too, but I wouldn't have known what that was), a slippery brick path leading to the gate which had a rose arch over it. The road was called Park Road East (now just Park Road) with gas lamps and a grass verge between the gravel footpath and a pot-holey unmetalled road. The only wheeled traffic belonged to the tradesmen most of whom delivered with their horse-drawn vehicles. For the milkman this was by far the best way as his horse knew exactly where to stop, and he completed his rounds quicker than all the others. The various horses cropped the grass at the roadside while their owners were calling, thus solving the problem of keeping the verges neat. When the coalman delivered, he came with a great cart pulled by an enormous shire horse which to me, a little three year old, seemed to rear up into the sky. Meat and groceries were delivered by a youth on one of those tradesman's bicycles with a small front wheel below a huge basket. This was in the days when ladies out shopping had everything delivered.

In 1934 we moved from Woking to West Byfleet, three miles away but to a larger house. This was 'Woodcombe' one half of a three-storey semi in Madeira Road conveniently close to a good golf course which father patronised on Saturday afternoons. He had arrived.

~*~

As I said, father was not a handyman and so throughout the days we lived at Woodcombe a series of 'little men' turned up, usually on a bicycle, to do small jobs around the home. It might be fixing a fence panel, some decorating, planing a sliver off a sticky door or—the first priority when we arrived: to put bars across the opening windows of the new children's room. Yes, we had a nursery. We children, too, had arrived.

There were three of us in those early days at Woodcombe. The eldest was Gillian, aged nine, then three years younger came Jane, and I was three years younger again, the baby of the family as my sisters would frequently point out. Early faded photographs exist showing us all playing together on the huge back lawn at Woodcombe (years later I revisited the house and found the lawn had shrunk to miniscule proportions, such are the distorted memories of young children). I would hate to see the family album come out because in it were pictures of us all playing including some of me rolling around naked on the family tartan rug, sporting a curly quiff which made me look quite ridiculous. Jane and Gillian always fell about laughing whenever they came across such pictures, leaving me squirming with embarrassment.

Nine-year-old Gillian to a small boy of three was a fairy-like beauty whom I worshipped. She remained a somewhat ethereal image in my small mind, ever so grownup and sophisticated, and would show me all sorts of hiding places in the garden where she assured me fairies hid, as she had definitely seen them. I was entranced and would spend ages creeping about hoping that one day I too might see one, although I was told little boys seldom saw fairies—only little girls.

With the nursery came Lawrie, a lovely lady who joined the family specifically to look after us children. The nursery became her special domain, and Lawrie loved us and treated us with a kindness and affection it would be difficult to better. It was a happy period indeed. Lawrie, for all her adult demeanour was in fact only nineteen when she came to us. Nineteen seemed a very adult age indeed, and we respected her authority without question.

My two sisters, Gillian (10) and Jane (7) shortly before Gillian caught pneumonia

Lawrie's arrival meant that mother was able to resume her dance teaching, something that had been on the back burner ever since her children were born. Our sitting room had a polished wood floor, and on dancing days the furniture was pushed against the wall, the rugs rolled up and out came the Victor Sylvester gramophone records, to be played upon a large floor-standing radiogram fitted with heavy turntable and a big metal pickup that used steel needles. When mother's students arrived we were not allowed downstairs and had to play 'quiet' games in the nursery.

As the baby of the family I had more than my fair share of Lawrie's attention, since my elder sisters went to school each day. Lawrie and I went for walks along the towpath of the nearby Basingstoke Canal on which many working boats travelled, each pulled by a heavy horse plodding along the towpath. I would frantically wave to the boatmen who would wave back and shout a greeting (probably more to Lawrie than me). We also walked on the golf course that was quiet and little used during the week, and on nearby heathland which had sandy paths all over it with gorse scrub for me to hide behind.

Not much more than a year later Gillian fell ill with a heavy cold which turned to a fever and confined her to bed. The doctor's daily visit was followed by serious discussions with mother and father in the hall before he left. Gillian had contracted pneumonia. Some time later a nurse appeared and looked after Gillian when we had to go out. An oxygen cylinder arrived and stood ominously by the bed with a tube leading to a mask, which Gillian held to her face when breathing became too laborious. It was impressed upon me that she was very ill, and the illness would have to take its course. We crept about the house quietly and everyone seemed very worried. There came a time when I was only allowed to visit Gillian in her bedroom for a short time when she felt up to it. Throughout all this dark period I never saw her suffering and she always smiled and seemed happy to see me. One day an ambulance came and she was taken away. Mother went too and only occasionally seemed to be at home after that. Then one morning mother called Jane into her room to talk to her. Jane came out a little later with tears streaming down her face and then I was called in. I was frightened we had done something terrible to upset mother, it now being my turn to be chastised. Mother sat in a little chair in her bedroom looking very distressed. She told me Gillian would not be coming back, that God would be looking after her from now on. I would have to be a brave boy and not get too upset. I didn't feel upset, and I left the room wondering why this seemed so serious. God always sounded such a wonderful person and surely Gillian was in very good hands? I was just four-years-old.

Father caught the same train for the 24-mile journey to London every morning where he spent the day at his office. This involved him wearing his suit and highly polished shoes, which he meticulously cleaned the night before. His immaculate bowler hat would be brushed with a special curved brush kept in a drawer in the hallstand, along with his gloves. To complete the apparel he had a folded copy of the Daily Telegraph for reading on the train and a rolled umbrella which no London businessman would be without. Attired thus he would kiss mother goodbye then us children, call out to Lawrie and be gone. The walk to the station took six minutes and he would arrive at the foot of the steps to the 'up' platform just as his train could be heard rumbling overhead. His run up the steps and into the same compartment of the same carriage giving a cursory nod to the same passengers was all done on autopilot, timed to perfection. Just occasionally there would be a stranger sitting in the compartment, possibly in his seat, and this would cause considerable upset. Once he even had to stand in the corridor all the way to London and was still talking about it when he came home that night. On Saturdays father came home early and had lunch at home. Then the afternoons would be spent either on the golf course or maybe looking after the garden. We had a small vegetable patch that he tended meticulously and grew many of the vegetables we ate. At the bottom of the garden was a fence beyond which a steep embankment dropped down to the main Southern Railway line—all four tracks of it. I would love to spend time with my little friend from next door standing on the bottom wire and holding onto the top one while we watched the great steam locomotives come thundering past, hauling their carriages full of pipe-smoking passengers on their way to or from London; passengers seen each day but never spoken to. Sometimes the train would be on one of the outer lines and travelling much more slowly for these were the 'slow' lines and these trains would stop at West Byfleet station just out of sight. Their passengers seemed different to the ones in the fast trains, for they were surely people one might see on Saturdays at the golf club, people like father.

Woodcombe had a small kitchen at the back with a scullery opening off it and beyond that a larder. The kitchen seemed large to me, but it must have been tiny really, as there was only room for a cupboard and a kitchen range down one side.

The range was coal-fired of course and its purpose was to heat the water. There was a separate gas cooker, an early 'Main' standing on cast iron cabriole legs with interesting taps just inviting to be turned. It had four rings and an oven and was a new innovation for us. Mother did the cooking, but I dimly recollect the kitchen had another inhabitant. This was somebody who helped mother around the house, did most of the cleaning, and had a 'comfortable' chair in one corner of the room. She had her own rag mat to alleviate the hardness of the quarry-tiled floor in this part of the house. Along the ceiling was a row of ten bells, hung from large spiral springs and operated by wires that disappeared into the wall behind them. Beside each bell was a label, which showed from which room the bell had been operated, and it was this person's job to answer these bells when required. She was, of course, the maid and a new status symbol for our family now that we lived in this larger house. When mother had guests and we were all in the sitting room, she would turn the bell handle beside the fireplace when it was time for the maid to come in to draw the curtains or make up the fire. One of the rooms that had a bell handle was the bathroom, and I used to feel a slight tingle whenever I touched it while sitting in the bath. Years later when I was beginning to understand a little about electricity, I realised there was probably a potentially lethal insulation fault from an electric cable to the unprotected bell wire which caused this, but no one in the house paid much attention at the time.

The weekly wash was a major event for us all, when one of the grownups would spend all morning at the deep earthenware sink pummelling around in the soapsuds. We had a splendid hand-operated mangle with rubber rollers that was carried out into the yard on fine days, and I was allowed to attempt to turn the great handle. I well remember the smell of the rollers, a smell of rotting rubber like an old hot water bottle. The clothes would emerge almost dry and were just shaken out and put up on a line behind our shed. Ironing took a long time using a series of heavy cast-iron flat irons, which were placed on the top of the kitchen range to reheat between items. Some of father's shirts and collars had to be starched and they looked very fine after this process.

The larder beyond the scullery was a lovely place to explore. In place of glass in the window it had a zinc gauze fly screen, and was always very cold, so cold in fact that in hard winter weather some of the icy air blowing in through this air inlet used to be blocked off. There were slate shelves on which stood all the food that nowadays goes in the fridge, and above this were narrower shelves stacked with boxes and tins all out of my reach. In really hot weather, our milk bottles would be stood in an earthenware bowl half filled with water and covered by a damp cloth. The bowl was placed in front of the air vent to catch any air movement; this would usually chill the milk well enough to prevent it turning sour before the end of the day.

If keeping cool in summer was a problem it was nothing to the difficulty in keeping warm in winter. Houses built in the twenties had no insulation at all, not even in the roof. The windows were single-glazed and rather draughty, there was no central heating and the only means of keeping warm was to have a proper fire. In the dining room we had a freestanding anthracite stove with little doors that closed across the front of it with mica panels through which one could see the red heat. This kept my parents' bedroom over it tolerably warm as well. In the sitting room and our nursery we had an ordinary coal fire that burnt smoky sulphurous fuel, and that was it. Any other heating was provided by electric radiators that had one or two bars with a reflector of some kind behind to throw the heat out. They were plugged in to an unearthed two-pin socket using ordinary flex that sometimes became frayed or chewed by the dog. There was nothing to stop little fingers from touching the red-hot bars and getting a nasty burn. I only did that once. Up on the top floor there were two more bedrooms and a walk-in attic space in which was the cold-water tank. This was just under the roof so, not surprisingly, in cold weather all the nearby pipes were liable to freeze which would involve a visit by the local plumber while we went without water until he had finished replacing a section of pipe.

One day it was announced Jane and I were to go for a holiday with Lawrie to visit her home in Kent. This was very exciting for Lawrie's parents lived in the country. The journey involved travelling to Borough Green, near Sevenoaks, and then catching a local bus to a place called Comp. Lawrie's parents, Daddy Lawrence and Mummy Lawrence, were ever so old. There was also Joyce Lawrence who had a long pigtail and was Lawrie's elder sister. They lived in a farmhouse called Comp Corner that butted against the side of the road at a crossroads. There were outbuildings and two oast houses and a huge chicken shed where hundreds of brown hens were kept at night. During the day they were let out and would peck about in the nearby field looking for insects. Joyce looked after the hens, Daddy Lawrence also helped outside and Mummy Lawrence spent most of the day in bed in a lovely sunny room overlooking the farmyard. She had a wireless by her bed, an ominous looking thing wired up to a big accumulator under the table and another wire leading to a switch screwed to the windowsill. From here a bare wire went out through the window frame and was strung across the yard from two tall posts.

Jane and I shared a room over the large farm kitchen. The wide floorboards had gaps in them in places and it was possible to see through to the people walking past below. The floorboards creaked as we walked about and it was all very different from our modern suburban house in Byfleet. The kitchen was a wonderful place. Alongside one wall stood a huge range, with ovens and rings all fed from an oil supply that came from a nearby tank. Various controls had to be adjusted to keep the burner flames correct, and there always seemed to be someone tending something on that range. The kitchen smelt of paraffin and lovely cooking smells. Joints of ham and sides of bacon hung from big steel hooks in the ceiling dimly visible in the gloom. At one end of the kitchen were hung coats and all along the floor below were Wellington boots. In the corner stood a table with numerous egg boxes stacked on it. A superb paraffin lamp with a pump-up brass reservoir topped with a gas mantle provided the main illumination. When lit, involving a complicated procedure that only special people could cope with, it hissed comfortingly and gave off a brilliant white light. This lamp was carried into the back room in the evenings or to the separate dining room. Most rooms were otherwise lit by the more ordinary oil lamps sporting a wick which had to be trimmed and adjusted every day. There were no lamps outside the main rooms—we found our way about by means of a flickering candle. In spite of its strangeness, Comp Corner was a welcoming, friendly place and the many dark corners held no terrors for me. I was too young to know about or be frightened by ghosties and ghoullies…

Meals were taken in the dining room next to the kitchen and up a couple of steps. How odd to have steps between rooms! Daddy Lawrence, who had a big moustache, made loud sucking sounds as he slurped his soup, which I found fascinating. I didn't really like getting too close to him as he exuded a rather strange, pungent odour interspersed with the normal adult tobacco smell.

This was my first visit to a house with no electricity and I found it really exciting. Not surprisingly my main memories of Comp Corner are the smells. Paraffin and cooking aromas downstairs, damp smells in the bathroom, strange scented smells from Mummy Lawrence's room and the smell of freshly laundered sheets and towels in one of the other rooms. Outside it was a whole new range of scents: a lovely warm mousey smell from the chicken house, wonderful fresh hay in the hayloft, a rather nasty whiff from the oast house where Joyce would sit knee-deep in feathers plucking and preparing innumerable chickens for market, and evocative aromas from the bins containing chicken pellets and crushed corn.

I was given the privileged job of collecting eggs from the nest boxes every morning. Fat dozy birds, quietly cooing, would hardly stir as my little hand groped beneath them to find the warm freshly laid egg. I was given a basket, lined with a cloth into which this egg would be reverently placed, and I must have pestered Joyce relentlessly several times a day for permission to have just another look in case more had been laid since my last collection.

Jane and I were introduced to an elderly couple who lived in a house down the lane. Here there was a special attraction—a real piano! Mr Rogers would play and both he and his wife sang to us. Then one day when we visited, Mr Rogers opened a small door in the front and inserted a roll of paper with holes punched all over it. He then sat back with his arms folded while the keys in front of him depressed on their own and the piano played by itself. I must have seen a piano before in someone else's house, an instrument that was not to be touched, but this was something special. Not only could it be made to play by itself from the magic roll, but I would sit on the stool, my little hands on the keys, and was allowed—indeed, encouraged—to bang away to my heart's content. This was the first musical instrument I had seen in action and from this moment my interest in music probably began.

There came a day when Jane was away with Joyce somewhere, and Lawrie was busy indoors, and I found myself alone. In fact, I felt lonely. Why was mother not here? She would surely find the farm as interesting as I had. I had to find her and bring her here to see it all. I knew how to find her, of course, for had I not come to Comp on the bus, and the bus had come from down that road? It would take me a while to get home, but if I started off now, then I could be back again with mother before too long. So off I set, walking as quick as my little legs would carry me towards Borough Green, carefully keeping in to the side of the road in case anything came along. I was starting to get tired by the time I met the first vehicle approaching. The driver stopped and called out to me. I recognised him as the milkman, and he asked whether I'd like a ride on his milk float. "No thanks," I replied, for he was travelling back the way I had come, and that would only delay my getting home. Nevertheless, he climbed down, came over and scooped me up and sat me down beside him. "Just a short ride" he said reassuringly, and within a few minutes we were back at Comp Corner where he took me into the kitchen.

What a fuss! Everyone had been out searching, and they were now discussing where to look next. Joyce's bicycle, which I hadn't seen before, was outside the door preparatory to a wider search. The Rogers were there with bicycles and everyone seemed very worried. I was in deep trouble; apparently they all thought I had been trying to run away. Grownups were sometimes so silly.

~*~

I started school, actually a kindergarten where Jane had first gone. I didn't last there long as I was continually in trouble for pinching another little boy (so Jane told me years later). It seems most unlikely since I was a retiring little chap generally happier in the shadow of someone else, but mother was always right so it must have been so.

After that I joined Jane at the local school just down the road from Woodcombe. It was really a girls' school, but they accepted very small boys up to the age of about seven if they had elder sisters there. So I found myself in a mixed class with a motherly teacher who introduced all sorts of subjects completely new to me. The most exciting times, which I remember so well to this day, were the lessons taken by the headmistress, who taught Divinity. We had been told to be on our best behaviour in her class, but the warning was unnecessary. She described Palestine in biblical times, brought alive by recounting her own visits to that country. We were in the presence of a Traveller, someone who had been abroad and spoke from experience, not just from reading books. And it was magical; we all sat on the edge of our seats, enthralled.

I don't remember much about my first school. The older girls were fairly tolerant of us little ones and we didn't have a lot to do with them really. One of them who lived nearby walked me home one day. It was a week or two before Christmas and I was enthusing about what Father Christmas would bring. The terrible truth emerged. She informed me casually that there was no such person as Father Christmas.

I burst into tears and ran all the way home to confront mother. Was it true? Was there really no Father Christmas? For the first time I saw mother look flustered, while she attempted to explain that there was, but, well, no, not actually a real Father Christmas…. My world fell apart. Not only was there no Father Christmas, but much more importantly mother had been withholding this truth from me. I felt frighteningly vulnerable. What other things were also not true? I

15

was distraught.

I remember a special treat when mother took Jane and me to Woking by train, then after visiting one or two shops we all trooped into a huge dark room with rows of seats. In front of us a moving scene appeared. I couldn't understand how it moved, and rushed up to the front to see where the bottom of the scene had disappeared to, only to find everything went very fuzzy when so close, leaving me perplexed. I cannot have been very old at this, my first visit to a cinema, but soon afterwards we went again to see Walt Disney's Dumbo which had just been released. After watching this I ran round the house with my arms out making whooshing noises, but was quite unable to fly like Dumbo. Later came a proper stage show, probably a local pantomime, and then the real thing, Cinderella at a London West End theatre. I developed an interest in the theatre to the extent that I built a model theatre out of a cardboard box, made curtains that pulled back and forth with a string, and even had lighting provided by a torch. I needed an audience for my shows, so any visitor would be dragged up to my playroom to be sat in front of my theatre in a hard chair while I provided organ music to open the show, humming in time to my playing on a cinema organ console made from Minibrix, a rubbery forerunner of Lego (I used to mix up cinema and theatre at this time, but both required an audience, so it didn't matter which I did).

The local Byfleet church was a bare modernish building with a cold atmosphere, which none of us liked. When we went to church, which was not every week and only if the weather was dry, we preferred the little church at Pyrford. This was not only extremely old, rather dark inside and smelled of damp hymnbooks but had a nice vicar who preached what father called a 'meaty' sermon, long and thought-provoking. Pyrford was about a mile and a half away down Coldharbour Lane, which started off at the Byfleet end as a proper road, but had become a quiet country lane by the time we arrived at the church. We always walked, firstly along a proper pavement, but further on when the road narrowed and there was no pavement we walked in the centre of the road, and on the way we passed a farm which had a sickly sweet smell which I was told was silage. Naturally we dressed in our best clothes for church, mother pointing out to me as she helped me struggle into clothes that I knew meant no larking about, that it was important "because God will be there, and we must look our best for Him." Sometimes we also walked to Pyrford to picnic at the edge of the River Wey meandering through water meadows, a lovely quiet spot, but that didn't involve dressing in our best.

Later we did have a car. It was a small Morris with running boards, a starting handle and a canvas hood; a tourer. It was kept in the tiny garage behind the house which it filled, and would be pushed out sometimes to be washed and polished. Very occasionally we all climbed in and father would take us for a drive. Such drives were only undertaken for special visits, those where it was not practicable to go by train or bus. The big occasion was the annual holiday to Selsey. This was a long journey involving much preparation and packing, with a big leather trunk and several suitcases strapped onto a luggage rack at the back. Father spent a long time tinkering with spanner and oilcan under the bonnet before he deemed everything was ready for the departure.

After half an hour or so we would be bowling along the Hogsback beyond Guildford, a town I had only ever visited before by train when accompanying mother to some shops there. We would be in new country, pioneering country, with hills and open fields and several other cars on the road. Jane and I would keep up a non-stop cry of "I can see the sea!" until we were told to be quiet; the sea was a long way beyond the next set of hills.

Eventually we went through a large town with a market cross at the intersection of two main roads. It was full of people all dressed very casually, some of them without hats even, and seemed a very long way indeed from home. Chichester sported not only a cathedral, but one with a separate bell tower. The other attraction was the factory in the middle of the town where visitors could go round and watch white-overalled workers making Shippams Paste, something we had for tea at home. In Chichester we sensed something altogether more attractive. I realised it was the new smell, a distinct salty tang in the air which only meant one thing. We really must be very near THE SEA! Shippams could wait. Jane and I started up our "I can see the sea" at full blast, and then we were skirting Pagham Harbour near the coast and could actually see the sea as we entered Selsey.

Usually we took a bungalow called Sunny Corner near the beach. The moment we arrived we would rush down to see the magical sea, and run along the lovely sandy beach kicking our sandals off on the way. Oh what delights!

Sometimes we were joined by another family and my memories are of various grownups sitting about on the beach with dark glasses and deckchairs while us youngsters built sand castles, were in and out of the sea all day, and sat shivering wrapped in sticky salty towels eating banana and jam sandwiches (my favourite!) all gritty with blown sand. What heaven!

On one of our visits when I must have been about five, father took us all to Navy Days in Portsmouth. The highlight for me that day was boarding an enormous battleship, all gleaming brass and shiny paint, where a smart sailor dressed in white with a blue collar looked after me. I particularly wanted to see the engines, and he took me down lots of metal ladders and through great steel doors until we stood on a platform at the top of a vast, brightly lit and spotlessly clean space. I had no idea what a ship's engine should look like, except that it must be huge if it was to push the great ship through the sea, but all I could see looking down were large metal-covered lumps—no moving parts anywhere! Back on deck I met up with the others and we explored the upper deck, with its scrubbed teak planking and tremendous gun turrets. It was wonderful and I decided right then to join the Royal Navy the moment I was old enough.

On one of our later visits to Selsey when I must have been about seven and Jane was into pony books, a riding school for children was discovered nearby. Jane had several lessons there, and I joined her on one or two occasions. The establishment was run by a large and somewhat grubby woman who would be sitting up in bed when we arrived. We entered her rather smelly bedroom and, with other children who had also booked in, would discuss who was to ride which pony. Then, while we went off with the helpers to harness them up, the woman would stagger out of bed and clamber straight onto a large steed which she rode side-saddle. This was my first experience of sitting on a horse (it could hardly be described as riding) but I wasn't frightened and actually quite enjoyed it, mainly because I was doing something Jane was capable of, though my mount was a demur little pony while Jane's was bigger and friskier.

I would often accompany mother to her favourite department store in Woking where she bought most of her clothes. This could be a bit tedious for she took ever such a long time trying on everything, but there were compensations. On arrival she was welcomed by a floorwalker who offered a chair while she explained what she was looking for. The store had lots of dark polished wood shop fittings, with racks and shelving all over the place, leaving little room for customers to wander around. I was intrigued by the way the assistant dealt with the money, for there were no cash registers (such things would probably have been considered rather vulgar in such a store). When the time came to pay, an invoice was laboriously written out, figures checked and agreed with the customer and a method of payment decided upon. The invoice together with the payment was then placed inside a spherical wooden ball, the top screwed on and the ball placed inside a cage, to be hoisted up to the ceiling by the assistant pulling a string. From here the ball left the cage, dropped onto a couple of slender rails and began to roll down a gentle slope, eventually disappearing through a hole at the back of the shop from where the accounts department operated. A few minutes later the ball would reappear from another hole higher up and trundle back down a different set of rails to the counter. Inside would be the invoice, now stamped PAID, together with the change. Nobody could explain how the ball found its way to the correct counter, but it never made a mistake. While mother was trying on clothes behind a curtain as the assistant outside called out "Perhaps madam would like to try the beige model with the fringed hem?" or some such, I could happily spend all morning, neck craned, following the wooden balls around the shop. One day the floorwalker led me through a door to the other side of that mysterious wall to see what happened to them, where a number of clerks sitting at desks around the room opened the shells and dealt with their contents.

We bought most of our groceries from Summers, a proper grocery shop. Here there were several counters, each manned by an assistant wearing a brown dustcoat, who took the order. Mother again would be offered a chair while she ran through her list. It was always half a pound of best butter, as if the shop would ever stock anything other than best, indeed! And the order invariably ended with "half a pound of broken biscuits, please." Biscuits would be in one of the large Huntley and Palmer biscuit tins that were lined up along the front of the counter, with glass-panelled lids so one could see the contents. Tea came from a foil-lined plywood tea chest, of the sort used afterwards by every furniture removal firm, and indeed, we had one or two at home, still smelling of tea, where we kept things under the stairs. Loose items such as sugar and rice came out of a sack, to be scooped up, weighed and poured by means of a shiny brass funnel into a brown paper bag, a label written out and stuck on the side. As each item was dispensed, the details were entered into mother's account book, and the total recorded for payment at the end of the month. Actual cash was not used at the time. It took a long while to dispense a few groceries and mother needed that chair.

A few doors down was J.S. Sainsbury selling cold meats and cheese. This was a small shop with marble-topped counters manned by assistants wearing striped blue-and-white aprons and panama-style hats. Hanging from the ceiling would be chickens, a pheasant or two, rabbits and maybe a duck or goose. None of these would be plucked; however oven-ready birds would appear when we wanted one. On the counter were cheeses, cut with a wire cutter from huge muslin-wrapped blocks, and also various butters which were scooped from a lump moulded between a couple of ribbed wooden butter bats into a neat rectangle, then wrapped in greaseproof paper. Across on the other side of the sawdust-covered tiled floor was the cold meat section. Here was a bacon slicer, expertly operated by the chief dispenser (he had a different hat to the others) also the hams, huge orange breadcrumb-covered marsh hams with soft white fat. Ham, tongues and other cold meats, would be cut with a long parallel-sided knife employed specially for that purpose. Each assistant had a steel dangling from his belt with which he put a keen edge on his knife from time to time. The smell in this shop was really lovely.

When it came to uncooked meat, our butcher sold wonderful cuts of British beef, lamb and pork, and he also had chickens and rabbits hanging from hooks behind his counter. He, too, had a steel dangling from his belt and he also wielded a fearsome cleaver for slicing cleanly through a large joint. His apron was deep blue and he wore a straw boater, unlike the fishmonger next door whose apron was white and his hat was a starched cotton hat with a brim. We collected our fish, wrapped in lots of newspaper, but meat would always be delivered. The delivery boy rode a proper 'butcher's' bicycle with thick tyres and a small front wheel over which was a huge basket for carrying all his orders.

One year we went to a different resort for our summer holiday. We went by train and after what seemed all day we finally arrived at Southwold where we stayed in a boarding house on the front. First impressions were not good: Southwold didn't have a sandy beach (I thought at the time all seaside places had sandy beaches) and therefore there was nothing to do. Father sneaked off birdwatching once or twice while mother dragged Jane and me round the shops and then discovered a Punch-and-Judy man. Southwold's unique attraction, of course, is the famous lighthouse right in the middle of town, the first I had seen. Selsey had no such edifice. I wanted to know how far away Selsey was; could we walk there along the beach, perhaps? A map had to be drawn for me, but there was no sand to draw it on, not in Southwold. The resort had a pond with rowing boats and little sailing dinghies for hire. I enjoyed trying to row a boat and managed to cope after a fashion with what seemed to me enormously heavy sweeps, though in reality they must have been little lightweight oars, for the boat would only have been tiny. Father preferred the sailing boats and while I splashed about by myself struggling with the oars, he and Jane zoomed around having great fun. When it was my turn to go with father I quickly realised sailing was frighteningly dangerous—the boat leaned over so far I was certain we would quickly fill up and sink, and I screamed to be put ashore while father tried to reassure me. Jane, watching from the bank, just laughed. Little did I remotely believe that I would one day find sailing to be my favourite sport.

In those days it was normal for people to go to work on Saturday mornings, the 'weekend' starting at lunchtime on Saturday. Father's habit was to play a round of golf on a Saturday afternoon leaving Sunday for the family; often church in the morning and an outing of some sort in the afternoon. We were not a particularly adventurous family—few people in those days were—so our outing would take the form of a local walk. On special occasions the car would be brought out and we might venture as far as the countryside around Guildford, country that my parents knew well. Father was somewhat old-fashioned and had lots of quaint habits and expressions that I took for granted. When he wished to leave the conversation he would say rather darkly, "Well! Must go and see a man about a dog..." before striding off purposefully out of the room. I never discovered who this man was or what it had to do with a dog.

The next year father announced that the family would spend two whole months at Selsey. We would be staying at a different house, and he would only be able to come for the usual two weeks, and apart from that would just come down at the weekends. We would be having somebody else to live at Woodcombe while we were away. All this was announced as if it was a most serious turn of events, and to an eight-year-old boy this seemed very odd. Surely it was wonderful news. Jane was not so sure, and mother shared father's concern.

The year was 1939.

~*~

The glamour of a two-month holiday in Selsey soon wore off once we arrived. With father back at work and mother on her own with the two of us and no help, we didn't spend so much time on the beach, and were not allowed to wander too far on our own. We had our bicycles, but mother didn't have one so we really only cycled up and down the road outside the house. I still managed to fall off mine quite often and seemed to spend a lot of time with bandaged knees or elbows. The treatment at that time was to apply liberal quantities of iodine to a fresh graze, which hurt intensely. A newly acquired pair of roller skates added to the number of collisions with a hard pavement. Roller-skating certainly drew attention to uneven paving stones, but going bump-bump-bump along these was preferable to trying to skate on sand-covered tarmac. I think the skates must have been very cheap ones with poor or non-existent bearings, for I never persevered with them.

Whenever father came down, he listened to every news broadcast, and he and mother would discuss the 'situation'. If things developed we might have to leave Selsey, but would not be able to return to Woodcombe until much later. What would we do? I tried to understand what was likely to happen if the country went to war, as my parents talked about what was going on in Europe at that time. I felt it was all a long way from England and didn't understand why they worried so much. And then one day the announcement came.

Britain was at war with Germany.

Almost at once a new phenomenon emerged—big silver barrage balloons appeared floating in the blue sky over Portsmouth to the West. I looked out to sea half expecting to see a fleet of German battleships heave over the horizon, but nothing came. In fact nothing happened at all. Father returned to London, and life carried on as usual. Soon he was back again, and then we were all on our way home. Holidays would become just a memory now.

Woodcombe's tenants were still there, so we found another house, not far from Jasmine Cottage in Woking. This one was a 300 year-old thatched cottage called, appropriately, The Old Cottage. It was timber framed with brick infill, and had a lovely winding brick path from the front gate. We would stay here until the end of the year by which time it was hoped the tenants at Woodcombe would have moved on. They were a mother and two daughters who had come over from India for the summer, and because of the outbreak of war the husband was to remain in Bombay in some important Government job. They were marooned for the time being.

It was while we were at The Old Cottage that we had a visit from my senior uncle, who was blind and seemed very old indeed (he was, in fact only three years older than father, but was not fit and seemed considerably older). Father said proudly that my uncle was an author, but later I discovered his only book was one on ship models that had been privately printed. I don't remember much about him except that he stayed on in the evening and crept up to my bedroom with my parents to say goodbye after I had supposedly gone to sleep. Through flickering eyelids I sensed his nearness and then heard a clink. As soon as the door closed behind them I opened my eyes to discover a shiny half-crown on my bedside table. Untold riches! What a wonderful uncle! Uncle Bernard had a skill that was singularly lacking in father: he was able to negotiate all the doors in The Old Cottage without banging his head, no doubt due to acute hearing developed as a result of his blindness that enabled him to sense the proximity of obstructions. Father banged his head on every door lintel every time he went through one and never learned. He would recoil with a "damn and blast!" clutching his forehead while we children would try not to snigger.

The families were not very close, and although father was one of three boys, we very seldom met my uncles. Bernard lived in Cheam, so that was not so very far away. After this one visit I never met him again, and only once or twice met his daughter Shirley, my only cousin. Twenty years later he was living in a home, sharing a room with two other elderly men when he knocked over a glass of whisky, which ignited when one of them lit a cigarette. Moments later the bed was alight. The fire quickly gained hold causing considerable damage. All three of them sustained severe burns and were taken to the Roehampton Hospital burns unit. This was reported on the local London news early next morning which I heard whilst staying with my other uncle, Ted, in nearby Surbiton. We took Ted over to the hospital and waited. An hour later he emerged extremely shaken, and for twenty-four hours Bernard's life was teetering in the balance. He finally died as a result of his burns, a poor lonely man.

Father told us he was about to be called up, although he was considered too old for front line service (he was 45) and would probably be given a desk job at the War Office in London thereby releasing someone younger. He had been in the Army in the first World War and survived a quite terrible time in the trenches and at Gallipoli, returning home with an MC, the rank of Captain and some appalling memories about which he never spoke, although he would tell stories of embarking in a troopship with the regimental horses hoisted aboard one at a time from rope slings. Old sepia photographs showed him in jodhpurs standing by his field gun. I was glad he was now too old; serving overseas didn't sound at all pleasant.

A few days later he came home in his new khaki uniform, studded with polished brass buttons and wearing a shiny Sam Browne belt. He wore his First World War medal ribbons and the insignia of Captain; on his lapels the bronze Royal Artillery regimental badge. I was so proud to see this glittering figure and to think that this was our own father! Instead of his umbrella he now carried a short stick. Every morning before setting off for London he would polish not only his shoes but also the leather Sam Brown, and the Brasso came out for cleaning every one of the buttons. He must have been the smartest officer of all time.

Mother had come to know the tenants now living at Woodcombe. Their eldest daughter was going to live in the Bahamas (she subsequently married over there and remained) and the youngest, Freda, who was a few years older than Jane, would be starting work soon and probably moving away from the area. Their mother, Mrs Stones, was on her own at Woodcombe with her little black Scots terrier, Scotty, unsure where to live while the war was on; this was during the period when everyone said it would be over by Christmas. As time went on it became apparent that the war would be a protracted affair and it was eventually agreed that we would all move back to Woodcombe while Sally Stones remained there, occupying the room that had been our nursery. She would become a permanent P.G. At this time there was a general exodus from the London area, with child evacuation in full swing, and people in large houses with room to spare were concerned about having evacuees foisted upon them. Far better to fill the house with one's friends, and Sally Stones was a lovely easygoing person with whom we struck up a fine rapport. Our stay at The Old Cottage, fun as it was to live in such an old house, was over. The winter of 1939-40 was memorably cold for us, living in such a draughty abode with only a cooking range in the kitchen and a log fire in one of the rooms as the sole source of heat.

Back in Byfleet small things were changing. The *Walls* 'Stop-me-and-buy-one' ice cream tricycle, so much a part of my pre-war life, was one of the first to quietly disappear. Bananas, famously, were the next. Other things became in short supply all around us. We realised—too late—we would probably have to adopt a survival strategy and plan for hard times ahead, but no one quite knew what was going to happen. All we could see ahead was a dark blank wall with no opening. Food rationing was introduced and immediately the realities of war hit everyone. Overnight, luxury foods disappeared off the shelves and so began a long belt-tightening time which certainly benefited the overweight, but made life difficult for most people.

Other things did not change for a while. Father still caught the 8.04 a.m. train from West Byfleet station every morning, and still sat in the same carriage amongst the same fellow passengers, most of them also in uniform. But he met lots of new people now that he had temporarily escaped from what must have been a dreary job. One of these was a cheerful hail-fellow-well-met character called Colonel Jennings, or Jorrocks to his friends. He lived in Woking on the edge of Chobham Common and had two sons, Tony who was a couple of years older than me and David, a year younger. I could cycle to their house and used to play with the boys on Chobham Common. Their mother was a somewhat frail lady very immersed in the Catholic Church and a complete contrast to her hearty husband, who preferred beer and boisterous nights out with the boys. Tony was at a Catholic boarding school near Bristol and so it was usually David with whom I played, but I did find him a bit young for the sort of games I enjoyed.

My parents felt it was time for me to go to a preparatory school, and they had been recommended the prep school for Clayesmore, situated in Charlton Marshall in deepest Dorset. It had two special attractions: firstly it was cheap, well—just cheap enough to fall into their price range, and secondly it was way out in the sticks, well away from built-up areas which were considered a target for the enemy bombs expected at any minute. I was to be a boarder and would have to leave home - an exciting prospect. I looked forward greatly to starting. As the time drew near, mother daringly made several daytime telephone calls to the school to discuss the finer points of my arrival. Our telephone was one of those heavy stands like a table lamp, with a separate earpiece. It had no dial—one lifted the earpiece from its bracket and this switched it on. A distant voice then said "Operator" and one shouted out the name, or number if one knew that, and waited for some time while the operator struggled to make the connection. Mother was terrified with the whole procedure while I stood beside her, behind the door of our cloakroom where the telephone had its own table, and admired her skill in managing this thing without father being present.

I had to go to London with mother where we bought items of school uniform from Forsyth's, the school outfitters in Regent Street. We were amazed that I needed so many things, and items such as football boots were completely new to me. No long trousers, though. The day I would wear long trousers was still many years off.

Father lectured me on the importance of good mixing with other boys. "You will meet all sorts of boys at your school," he said. "You are at an impressionable age and must be careful to observe which boys may be a bad influence on you, and avoid them; at least, take care not to copy any of their bad habits. Try to make friends with the really nice ones and endeavour to emulate them, for that will stand you in good stead when you grow up. I hope that by sending you to a public school, there won't be many of the wrong sort of boy to influence you." Even at that tender age, it crossed my mind that the 'wrong sort of boy' might well have been sent by his parents in order for him to latch onto 'better' boys and do exactly what father was proposing, but forbore to mention that.

And so, one day in the summer, not yet aged nine, I stood on the platform at Woking with mother awaiting the school train which was to stop and pick me up on its way from London to Dorset. How important I felt, attired in my uniform, my cap on my head and a porter beside us with my school trunk! The train arrived, a man alighted, introduced himself and shook hands, and I leapt aboard into a carriage full of identically dressed little boys all rushing about and shouting. I just remembered in time to wave goodbye to a very quiet mother now alone on the platform. The next chapter in my life had begun.

I'd misunderstood a few things. It wasn't a school train, but the normal Waterloo to Exeter express (which was why it didn't stop at our local West Byfleet station three miles up the line) and it wasn't exclusively for us boys—we only had a couple of reserved compartments. The man was Mr Davis, one of the masters charged with the unenviable task of keeping us all together and out of trouble. By the time we'd been on the train for an hour the excitement of meeting lots of other boys had begun to wear off, and I was missing mother. I hadn't fully realised that by starting school in the summer term I would be joining a lot of boys who had been there for two terms already and therefore all knew one another. It didn't take them long to decide I was no great shakes and from then on they ignored me. I was finding just how cruel boys can be to one another.

Eventually we pulled into Templecombe, a little junction where we had to change to another train. This involved a whole hour to wait and would tax Mr Davis's controlling skills to the limit. We explored every room on every platform, ran up and down all the stairs and across every bridge, obediently but reluctantly kept off the track itself, rushed to whichever platform a stopping train arrived at and examined all the luggage on every handcart everywhere on the station. We made friends with a frightened week-old calf tethered to one of the seats and with a luggage label tied round its neck, and pestered the ladies in the station buffet for something to eat (we had no money, of course). We tried unsuccessfully to prise the lid off a full milk churn, and generally kept all the station staff on their toes (in those days a small station such as this employed a whole range of people to look after passengers and goods) until at long last we heard our train arriving at a side platform. It came in, three or four elderly carriages clanking and bucking, laboriously pulled by a tired-looking tank locomotive. This was the Somerset and Dorset line (known by all as the Slow and Dirty line, though perhaps not in those days) and a great comedown after the sleek express which had transported us thus far.

Mr Davis now had a new problem as there were more of us than could be seated in one compartment and this was a train whose carriages had no corridor. He solved it by keeping the noisiest ones with him and putting the rest in several compartments, a few in each. On our own we immediately behaved much better, and at each of the many stops Mr Davis walked purposefully up and down the platform making sure we really were all behaving and would make no attempt to alight on the other side. Thus we proceeded at a dignified rural pace with much puffing and clanking, stopping at every tiny halt along the way to pick up or discharge the occasional passenger and quite a lot of parcels, milk churns, a bicycle or two and various other packages all to be delivered to outlying parts of the locality. We were without doubt truly in the country now. After many stops and passing lush meadows, meandering streams and some lovely beech hangers, we eventually stopped with a sigh at Charlton Marshall, yet another small country halt. Mr Davis ran down the train telling us all to get off, a man appeared and began to offload our luggage onto a hand truck and the guard stood importantly by the exit gate ready to collect our tickets. We had arrived.

In fact we were actually at the school, for the railway line cut through the grounds. It was but a short walk through some woods and there we were, a crocodile of small boys led by an exhausted schoolmaster relieved that none of his charges had gone astray, and followed by the man pulling the handcart with our luggage. Several people were waiting to greet us, and the new boys—there were three of us—were segregated and taken through to a large entrance hall with polished mahogany doors leading off on all sides. Like many small boarding establishments, Clayesmore Preparatory School was housed in what had once been a rather imposing manor house together with its outbuildings. We were shown into a splendid drawing room dominated by a grand piano and were soon being introduced to Mr Everett, the headmaster.

I had no preconceptions about the headmaster except that I expected him to be old, frightening and very authoritative. He was none of these, was quite a lot younger than father and I took to him immediately. None of us had attended the school for an interview. Travelling in wartime was becoming quite difficult, and it would have been considered unnecessary for my parents to bring me along for both sides to eye one another up before I had been accepted by the school.

Matron appeared. She was all the things the matron of a boys' boarding school should be—large, rather plump, kindly, about the same age as our mothers, unflappable, comforting, reassuring and competent. She took us off, pointing out as we left the drawing room that this was an area of the school that was strictly out of bounds, except when specifically invited there. I had never been anywhere 'out of bounds' before and wasn't too sure what that meant. We went up a somewhat tatty back staircase and shown our dormitory at the top of the main building. There were four beds, the three of us plus one other who had yet to arrive. Matron showed us our lockers, explained where everything was to go, and gave the younger one (I was not quite the youngest) help with unpacking while keeping an eye on us other two.

In the course of the next couple of hours the rest of the boys arrived, a further sixty or so by bus, another train and one or two in cars or taxis. The noise level in the school began to rise as they greeted one another and I began to feel quite scared amongst all these larger lads who were so manly and self-assured.

The school briefing to new parents, those details discussed in the telephone calls my mother had made, had been very thorough. I found I had all the right things in the right quantity and nothing that wasn't needed; so important for a little boy away from home for the first time. The friendly greeting did much to allay my fears and for the first time I began to feel a little less nervous and therefore happier. Perhaps school would be quite fun once I had got to know all these people.

We quickly settled into a routine. I remember the bathroom, all lead pipes and an ancient bathtub on legs; the school lavatories, some of them with mahogany seats in the old part of the house, modern ones in the new wing and all of them smelling slightly as a result of boys who had 'missed'; the rows of basins in the washrooms and the bare echoing corridors. The school dining room, one of the big rooms opening off the main hall, contained five long tables with benches either side. Every boy had his own pot of jam, which was the only concession towards indulgent eating. Food by now was rationed, and this meant there were a lot of things that could not be got, either because they were unavailable or because of the price. I was discovering some fundamental rules about housekeeping in wartime.

I began to know the staff. Most able-bodied people were now on active service which left us with a motley bunch of teachers and helpers, some fairly old, some a bit lame, some just plain incompetent, but all of them kind and trying their hardest to bond us into a happy team. The school's edict was that a happy boy is a receptive one and will cooperate. I wasn't aware how sensible this edict was until years later when I was subject to a quite different kind of discipline, but more of that later.

My special friend for most of the time at Clayesmore was a boy called Yeo. (Amazingly, I didn't know his first name was Julian until much later; but then it was the custom to call one another by our surnames. It certainly avoided the confusion where everyone has the same common first name.) Yeo was a Dorset lad and spoke with a lovely country dialect, had a wonderful knowledge of wildlife and I learnt much from him. Just about everyone else came from a town, and I felt I didn't belong so much with them; strange really, as West Byfleet even in the thirties was quite urban with streetlights and metalled roads. I was always happier out walking in the country and here we were, in really deep country, and I had a country friend to go around with.

There was one member of staff who stood out from the rest. He wore a tweed jacket, smoked a pipe and was another countryman. His name was Mr Household and he taught geography and history and ran the scout troop. On Sundays he would lead a walk out in the country and point out all sorts of interesting things. From him we learnt a huge amount about natural history without realising this was really teaching by stealth. Yeo and I were always at the front hanging on every word Mr Household said. From him I learnt the differences between jackdaws, crows and rooks, the different sorts of fungi, why certain plants thrived on the chalky soil while others did not, and he was invariably the first to spot a rabbit or fox or even a stoat. His walks were always enjoyable and we never noticed the miles we tramped. Not so with some of the other boys. They hated walking anywhere and tried to avoid having to come.

I couldn't wait to join the cubs. Our art and botany mistress, Miss Jenkins, was the Akela and we met in a clearing in the woods outside the scout hut. This was actually one of the classrooms scattered about the grounds with a room opening off it where all the paraphernalia relating to scouts and cubs was stored. We learnt to erect a tent and light a fire safely, how to walk intelligently through the woods—basic fieldcraft, I suppose. We learnt to tie knots, to hoist the scout flag and to salute as it made its jerky way to the top of the flagpole.

Miss Jenkins looked upon me very kindly as I was the only one in her art class who had any aptitude with a pencil. To this day I remember and practise her tip for drawing a straight line without using a ruler (one looks at the end point where the line is to finish rather than the tip of the pencil as it wavers along the paper). After I'd been at the school for several terms I discovered she lived in a tiny cottage in the village, so called in to see her one Sunday and was asked to stay for tea. What a treat! To enter a private house whilst at boarding school was unheard of. None of the other staff encouraged us to ask about their lives outside the school, and apart from those who 'lived in' I never found out where the others went to after lessons.

Of the rest of these staff I have only hazy memories. There was the bald man with a grating voice who attempted to teach us Latin. He was extremely shortsighted and didn't notice—or pretended not to notice—when we played him up. Latin was a dreary subject especially when taught by a bored man well past retirement age who had no rapport with small boys. Had he been able to make the subject interesting I'm sure we would have behaved much better. As it was I remember one boy who lit a cigarette and this was passed round the giggling class for everyone to take a puff without this master apparently noticing. I never mastered Latin and to this day any benefits it might have bestowed upon us were lost on me, though I have since learnt the Latin names for many plant species. Mr Everett himself never taught my class. We would see him striding purposefully about always clutching an armful of books, and would sometimes meet him marching to or from his bungalow which was through the woods near the railway halt. It was only in my last year that I joined in a debating group that he chaired and discovered the need for another talent I failed miserably to exhibit—thinking on my feet. Fortunately debating was an evening entertainment rather than a school subject and any thoughts he may have had about this crass little lad never appeared on my school report.

All too soon in my first term I caught chicken pox and had to spend a whole week confined to my dormitory. I didn't feel particularly ill, nor did I get the sort of spots that cause problems. Of the four of us in our little dormitory on the top floor, three went down with it almost on the same day and the fourth two days later. One was a fair-skinned boy with ginger hair and the sort of skin that reacted very badly, each spot turning into a revolting weeping pustule. Matron fussed over him, rubbing calamine everywhere to ease the itching, but she didn't have time to worry about the rest of us. It was a summer with a prolonged heat wave, so being confined to our dormitory was frustrating. Outside the big sash window a shining lead roof shimmered in the heat, and we leant out to scratch our names in the soft lead.

In the next few years I also caught mumps whilst at school, much to the relief of mother and father who were only too pleased not to be anywhere near! One term most of the school went down with scarletina, I think it was, but while they were suffering, surrounded by a busy matron and a helper whom she'd recruited to assist, I quietly just became ill, and was put in the same isolation room as the others. Eventually the doctor diagnosed glandular fever, which put them all into a bit of a panic, for apparently that could be extremely serious and no one was quite sure how best to treat me. I was made to stay in bed in spite of feeling not too bad at all, and had to inhale a friar's balsam vapour twice a day which I really rather liked. I was six weeks getting over that, eventually being allowed up to walk about and recover my strength. Apart from the usual infectious diseases we were a healthy bunch on the whole, matron's nursing skills being required only seldom. One incident we all witnessed concerned a slightly mentally subnormal young man who used to do some gardening from time to time. He was working just outside our classroom window one day, when he suddenly fell to the ground twitching all over and foaming at the mouth. We crowded round the window fascinated at this display, especially when the school cook of all people appeared from nowhere, sat on him, crammed a handkerchief in his mouth, constraining him until the fit was over. In a few minutes he got up, none the worse for this experience, and she led him away. We resumed our seats while the teacher made the most of this opportunity to explain her understanding of how our brains can sometimes get disturbed in this way. For the next few days we would all look at one another very carefully to see whether there were any signs of an imminent brain disorder.

Mr Household would invite a group of boys of an evening to his room across the courtyard, where we would sit around the log fire while he made himself comfortable in the only upholstered chair and read from Rudyard Kipling's Just So Stories. He had a lovely reading voice, rather like Uncle Mac on the BBC Children's Hour, and we would be transported to mysterious places such as the great grey green Limpopo River to discover how the elephant got his trunk. Sometimes it was The Jungle Book, and there we would be, creeping about in the forest, watching out for Shere Kahn and making friends with all the other animals. Occasionally it was a ghost story, and one evening after listening to The Monkey's Paw we were terrified to leave the bright fire and venture across a dark courtyard to return to the main house and the comfort of our beds.

On Sundays the whole school attended the village church for matins. Boys from the school formed the treble section of the choir, kept in order by stern elders in the row behind or across the aisle who achieved this with a fierce finger-wagging scowl if too much fidgeting took place. I sang in the choir, from which we took it in turns for one lucky lad to enjoy spending the service in a tiny space behind the organ with the job of keeping the organ pumped up. In theory this was simple: all one had to do was keep an eye on a little weight dangling from a string, and when the weight rose up to near a painted mark on a beam, one heaved a handle up and down which worked a bellows to recharge the air reservoir. There was quite a latitude, so one's attention could safely wander for a minute or two, long enough to watch the antics of a spider as it busied itself wrapping up its prey. During the sermon, the organ would be switched off and the reservoir slowly emptied so that one had to jump to it as soon as one heard the parson start his peroration "and now to God the Father…" indicating he would at any moment announce the last hymn. Half a dozen pumps and the reservoir became sufficiently charged to enable the organist to play the introduction provided he didn't have too many stops open. One day I saw a lovely little mouse and was so absorbed by his antics that I hadn't noticed during a loud organ passage the weight rise swiftly above the danger mark, but I quickly realised fast action was needed as the organ began to wheeze and slowly die. I leapt to my feet, scuttled across to the pump handle knocking over a small stool and began to pump for all I was worth. From a near-death rattle the poor organ now went into fibrillation, the sound pulsing uncontrollably until the organist shut off all the stops and then restarted in a suitably sepulchral manner. During that brief lull I could hear the choirboys (who should have been singing at the tops of their voices to drown out this sorry lapse) laughing and giggling behind their hymnbooks. Trouble was not far away. At this point I realised I was cornered; there was no way out after the service was over without passing the organist's console and he could move a lot quicker than me. I trembled with fear wondering whether he had another side to him than the quiet fatherly manner he had thus far shown me. Would I soon find out?

I must have been lucky. The organist was engrossed in conversation with a gushing lady as I at last crept out from the organ loft like my church mouse and scuttled away as fast as my little legs would carry me. Only the vicar, guarding the west door to catch every member of his congregation as they emerged, gave me a withering look but was unable to do more as he, too, was surrounded by worthy ladies of his parish.

It was not until evening that Matron mentioned it while we were getting ready for bed and some of us were having their nightly spoonful of cod-liver oil.

"Do you think I should give some of this to the organ," she said. "It seemed to have a rather wheezy cough this morning, didn't you think?" But she was laughing and so with immense relief I laughed too, and that was that.

The church was opposite the school entrance, sandwiched between the road and the River Stour, a lovely clean chalk stream that at this point meandered gently near the road to the next village at Spetisbury. There were trout in this stream, and Yeo said he could catch one without a rod by lying on his tummy dangling a hand in the water. He spent ages doing this, but never succeeded in catching anything, probably due to his impatient audience not giving him time to settle down quietly. One or two old men fished the river along these parts and a water bailiff looked after the stretch, shouting dire warnings about not getting too close to the bank if he saw one of us on that side of the road.

You will gather that we must have had considerable freedom to wander about at will. That road which is now the busy trunk road from Blandford to Wimborne was no more than a narrow country lane in those days, with scarcely any traffic on it. Charlton Marshall was still a tiny hamlet, with no modern buildings, and although in theory we were constrained to the school grounds, this was not strictly enforced; nor need it have been, for we were recognised by our uniform wherever we went, and children were safe amongst adults. On one occasion in my second or third year I decided I would like to visit Badbury Rings, an ancient monument about five miles away. I had discovered this on the map we used to practise our scout orienteering skills (though it didn't have a long name like that in those days) and I had learnt quite a lot about maps in my geography lessons and about early man, so Badbury beckoned. It was a bright summer Sunday and I was granted permission to walk there with two friends. We kept to the lanes all the way and stopped at an isolated house when we got thirsty, where we were given, not only a drink but also some lovely apples. We arrived, explored the Rings and came back tired, hungry and very pleased with ourselves. We never knew that several friends of the Everett's whose farms were on the way had monitored our progress, and Mr Everett himself had set out on his bicycle to cover an area just beyond Spetisbury not otherwise covered.

If all this seems a long way from war-torn Britain and the London blitz, then you would be right. The school did have an air raid shelter of sorts, and we practised using it a few times, but rural Dorset was of little concern to the Luftwaffe who had more important targets to interest them. Mr Everett was telephoned when it was thought an air raid might happen, and he had a hand-cranked siren which he clamped to the handlebars of his bicycle. With this he set off wobbling through the village steering with one hand and cranking with the other, though nobody took a lot of notice. The school, however, had to assemble in a long underground passage beneath the main building until the enemy aircraft had passed overhead. I remember one brilliant summer's day looking up in the sky and seeing tiny birdlike creatures like silverfish weaving about with the sun glinting from them as they turned. It was only after watching for a minute or two that someone realised we were witnessing a high altitude dogfight, with about a dozen fighters trying with some success to scatter a large number of enemy bombers. They were so high we couldn't hear any sound, except occasionally a faint plopping from cannon fire. "There'll be shrapnel, I expect," observed one lad. We all collected shrapnel if ever we could find any, though this was always in the holidays—never in Dorset! After we had been watching for some time, a member of staff came out to see what was going on, and spoilt the fun by rushing us indoors and down to the gloomy basement passage.

One day we did hear a low flying aircraft (not a common sound in rural areas, unless one was near an airfield). It came low over the school, and moments later we heard a most definite sound of an impact as it came down on the other side of the hill. It was a damaged fighter and the pilot had been killed. We were forbidden to leave the school grounds and everyone was rather quiet for some days.

The school grounds gave us plenty of space to run around without breaking bounds. Not only did we have the area immediately around the school buildings, but beyond our two playing fields was the railway line, where it crossed the school grounds on an embankment. Beyond the railway was the 'park', an open area accessed by a path under a bridge. It would be a challenge to attempt to cross over the line itself, for we could always hear if a train might be coming. The fun here was to elude a particularly fierce track maintenance man who patrolled these parts, and who seemed to inhabit a small shed built of old railway sleepers. Like many such huts, this one had a large whetstone outside used for sharpening various tools. Needless to say we boys, who all owned a penknife or sheaf knife, used the railwayman's whetstone for sharpening these lethal weapons. We came to know what his working hours were, and found it easy to avoid being caught. It was also quite fun to place a penny on the line when we heard a train approaching, and to watch from the nearby woods as the engine ran over it, flattening the coin into a useless copper disc.

The park beyond the track had beech woods round three sides of it, and a herd of cows grazed in the middle. These cows were milked in a parlour near the station, and we would sometimes visit at milking time to watch. It was all hand milking, of course, and would take the cowman over an hour to milk the small herd. Nearly all the milk was sold locally and the school obtained its milk from here. I was fascinated watching these huge amiable beasts calmly munching hay whilst giving milk. Up in the park we collected dead branches to build a bonfire and in the ashes baked potatoes which we'd scrumped from a nearby field. These were eaten with relish, as we were always hungry of course. Our food was sparse but nourishing, and not very interesting. Rationing had meant the disappearance of all the interesting foods, and it would often mean we filled up on slices of thick bread cut from a 'standard loaf'—a boring grey-brown concoction baked from semi-refined flour. Onto this we scraped a rather unpleasant unsweetened chocolate spread, peanut butter or some other spread. The one luxury—our pot of jam—had to last all term, so was used very sparingly. Heavy suet puddings with unsweetened custard poured over them filled us up at lunchtime (and ensured we didn't pester cook for second helpings). No wonder we enjoyed our baked potatoes up in the park.

Amongst the dead wood were several large pieces so rotten they were almost reduced to sawdust. In them crawled huge stag beetles, and we would each claim one and endeavour to make them race each other, but the beetles weren't very sporting and crawled off before the starting gun was fired. With our knives we fashioned crude pipes from bits of soft wood, and used hollow elder twigs for the stem, filling our pipe with sawdust and puffing away to emulate our elders. It was a red-letter day when someone found a discarded dog end and we were able to mix this with the sawdust to impart a more realistic 'tobacco' flavour. It was very tempting to steal a cigarette from a carelessly left packet on some teacher's desk, but nobody dared risk this. So far as I was concerned, this experimentation with smoking was so horrible I never went for it seriously, and to this day I can claim I've been a non-smoker since the age of ten.

On Sunday evenings we had no prep, but instead had to write a letter home. My very first letter when I started at school was written about the time when the full shock of being away from home had hit me between the eyes, and much later mother told of receiving this tear-stained scrawl imploring her to take me away, I was so unhappy. Fortunately she had been prepared for this, but even so it was a worry for her and made her miserable for a while. By about three weeks into the term my letters would be full of what we had been up to and I sounded much

31

happier.

In the school dining room, which doubled as an assembly area, there was an upright piano. Miss Jenkins was the pianist and sometimes allowed me to play the elderly piano, taught me a few chords, explaining why some sounded right and others discordant; very basic stuff, but it sowed the seed of a music interest. She taught me how to read music and demonstrated some simple tunes. On the wireless at that time was a regular Home Service programme called 'Music While You Work' with a catchy signature tune, which I found I could play (with one finger), and for days I must have driven the staff to distraction while I banged out this melody. I even managed to write it down on some manuscript paper Miss Jenkins gave me, and the next Sunday took it to church and asked the organist to play it at the end of the service instead of some of the sombre churchy pieces he usually played. He did actually play it, but wrapped up in such a manner that only I recognised it! He was very long suffering, but understood children.

At the end of term there was a school concert, held in the dining room. Any type of live show was exciting to a generation brought up before the days of television, and this was certainly fun. One impromptu sketch put on by two country yokels, alias the Headmaster's wife and Mr Household, both thinly disguised with bits of straw in their hair and—in Mr Household's case—a lovely old scarecrow jacket, featured the song "There's an 'ole in me bucket, dear Liza, dear Liza…" sung in a thick Dorset dialect, accompanied by Miss Jenkins on the old piano. I loved it, particularly witnessing serious adults performing knockabout acting.

Visits at half term (which was a long weekend with no lessons on Saturday morning) were not really practicable because of travelling problems, though mother did manage to come on one occasion. With another boy whose mother was also visiting I walked to Blandford to meet her at a hotel where she had arrived earlier off the train and the four of us had a real lunch, a wonderful experience after school meals. Then we all four walked back to the school for our mothers to be shown around. We walked a lot in those days.

One term we had a new master, Mr T. He wore a somewhat threadbare town suit in which he looked out of place wandering about the school premises. He was quite young and we wondered why he had not been called up until he told us he had a medical condition which wouldn't allow him to be on active service. He taught us French and made it more interesting than the master whom he replaced. He would often sit around out in the afternoons after lessons chatting to the boys in the school yard, the only master to get the remotest bit familiar. Some of the boys shied away, but I found him quite pleasant to talk to and it was a change to converse with an ordinary adult. He was unused to the country and when he accompanied the school on one of the Sunday walks he wore thin town shoes quite unsuitable for the somewhat muddy roadside. His room was a few doors down from Mr Household's room in a row of cottages at one end of the school yard and one day he asked me in. He possessed a portable typewriter which he said he would teach me to use, and several times I went along for informal lessons trying to manage to get my fingers on the right keys while he stood behind me, patiently guiding me along. Even at that young age I intuitively sensed I might be playing with fire to allow Mr T to give me this private tuition, was somewhat unsettled by it and backed off with relief. Evidently I was not the first Mr T had approached. He left at the end of that term to be replaced by a new French teacher.

I've mentioned our country walks and the scouts, but not sports. The reason for this is that I have never enjoyed team games, mainly because they all seem to involve a ball, and I soon found out at school that I was unable to coordinate properly when it came to assessing where a ball was or how fast it was going. Do they call it a 'lazy eye'? Consequently I was soon regarded as useless, and had to be found a position way out in the outfield when we played cricket, so that if a ball perchance came my way I would have plenty of time to put down the daisy chain I was engrossed in, run hopefully towards the ball which by this time would be rolling gently along the grass, and endeavour to stop it and—horror of horrors—somehow get it back to the wicket keeper with everyone on the pitch all shouting at me to hurry up. Throwing a ball was also one of my non-achievements and my attempts to hurl the thing vaguely in the right direction were not very successful. Overarm throwing was out of the question as my weedy little arms never mastered the technique, and underarm throws usually resulted in the ball disappearing into the sky only to thud down moments later just in front of where I was standing. In the meantime the other fielders would be screaming at me while the two batsmen rushed back and forth clocking up runs while laughing their heads off. It was so humiliating and I hated playing, but school sports were considered good for one's development and therefore compulsory.

Rugby was played in the winter terms, and that was even worse. Lightweight for my age, I could run quite well so could have made a passable three-quarter, always provided I had a ball to run with. This would normally arrive by chance when I happened to be standing at the spot where one of the players—from either side—happened to kick it. This nasty muddy thing then generally hit me; I would bravely grab it and start to run as fast as possible. Needless to say, within moments I was being pursued and my escape cut off by thundering great heavyweights who hurled me to the ground, trod on me with their studded boots for good measure, then made off into the distance leaving me worryingly injured. Just occasionally I would get the ball when only yards from the line, so was able to transport it there with safety and score a try. That would be a rare event and worth the ridicule of a mock accolade; a wonderful moment, but all the same I would still have preferred to be nowhere near a playing field. Once someone thought I might be better as hooker, since I was so light. There I would find myself linked to a hefty thug either side of me as we engaged with a similar threesome of the opposing team. Then while this scrum formed an arch with me in the middle with my arms pinioned, the ball was thrown in and my face, inches from flailing boots, was pressed into the muddy ground. It was a couple of years later the penny dropped, and only then after I had been severely admonished for not copying something down from the blackboard correctly. It was discovered I was shortsighted and couldn't see. I had to have spectacles from then on, and made a great play of taking them off when required to play rough games, groping my way around myopically hoping someone would realise. Eventually they did, and I joined that small group of non-participators scorned by the rest of the school. Interestingly, though, I found during this time I could do something none of the other boys could and that was to recognize a familiar figure walking a couple of hundred yards away—too far off to be seen clearly even with good sight, but recognise them I did. In birdwatchers' parlance this would be called 'giss' (pronounced 'jiz', meaning general identification by sight or sound). What I had done was to notice how people walk a bit lop-sided, or have a hunched back, or swing their arms in an unusual way, or lean forward. Everybody has various mannerisms like this to some extent and evidently I was observant enough to have noticed such habits and associate them with the person exhibiting them. The rest of the sports-mad crowd never noticed a thing and could not approach my skills in this direction. Unfortunately this didn't count towards anything useful in other people's eyes, so it was disregarded. I remained the school nincompoop.

Boarding school had its compensations, the main one being that eventually term ended and we went home. Excitement mounted a couple of weeks before term end, and conversations turned to what we would do in the holidays. Many boys lived near to each other and so would be seeing one another, but it seemed nobody lived anywhere remotely near me. Never mind—I would soon be home amidst the family and it would be a relief not to have to compete the whole time. Matron and her helpers packed furiously, the last lessons were held, the last morning dawned, the last meal eaten. The crocodile formed up and we headed for Charlton Marshall station.

~*~

Back at home things were changed. Sally Stones had become an auxiliary nurse at Addlestone hospital, and she drove a Baby Austin car to get her to work. She had also acquired a title by virtue of being the wife of Frederick Stones, still out in Bombay, who had received a knighthood. She was still the same, though, still delightful and a wonderful person to have living with us. My mother had joined a group of ladies practising first aid in a house down the road. Wounded patients were hard to come by, so I was quickly recruited to help out. By this time my scouting knowledge had become quite good, and I think I knew more about splints and bandaging broken limbs than they did!

Father was working very long hours and came home exhausted every evening except those days when he did ARP duty on the roof of the War Office and didn't come home at all. On other days I would run down the road to meet him at the station and walk back with him. He didn't say a lot about the London blitz that he had to endure; though we listened assiduously to the news every day and terrible pictures appeared in the daily newspapers.

I often did the shopping for mother, who was not the most organised person and would run out of something during a cooking session. Off I would go on my bicycle and buy it for her. With rationing in full spate we were always on the lookout for anything 'off ration' which usually meant something slipped into the shopping bag from under the counter. Presumably because of my innocent looks I would occasionally come home with some sausages or fish, which the grownups failed to get, so this was a popular job for me which I enjoyed. Father had dug up his precious rose bed and planted vegetables, magnificent produce to my eyes, which tasted wonderful. In general, though, I was always hungry whether at home or at school. For most people food was never plentiful unless one produced one's own, and even then there were strict rules about what one could do with it. Due to paper shortages no purchases were wrapped, so one had to take one's own secondhand bags. Fish, though, was wrapped in newspaper, but even that was not plentiful as newspapers during the war were very much slimmer than they were before.

Next to the attic space in which was the cold water tank we had a tiny bath, used in the days when there would be a maid sleeping in, but was now kept permanently filled with cold water in case we had to deal with an incendiary bomb that might land on us. We also had a bucket on each landing filled with dry sand, and a stirrup pump was kept handy too. These pumps were designed to put out a minor fire, using a sparing amount of water, and were operated by putting the suction end of the pump into a bucket of water while the operator stood with one foot on a bracket or stirrup to stabilise things, whilst pumping a handle up and down with one hand and directing a hose with the other. I doubt whether they would have been any good except for a very minor event, but they gave us reassurance. Wherever we went we also carried our brown cardboard box containing a gasmask, again more for reassurance than anything else. Many people were convinced Germany would never again employ mustard gas as a weapon since the retaliatory consequences would have been very real, so they used their gasmask boxes as a sort of overflow handbag.

A lot of families installed a 'Morrison Shelter'—a portable metal framework under which they slept at night in case the ceiling fell in as a result of a bomb. Others built a semi-underground construction in their garden, digging out a deep hole, installing a corrugated iron structure in the hole, with steps leading down into it, and covering the whole lot with several feet of spoil from the hole. It was a massive undertaking, and depending on one's competence, could result in a cold, damp tunnel into which the entire household would have to creep when the air raid siren sounded off at night. Many people became resigned to nightly disturbances, and slept regularly in these shelters. Father reckoned we'd all fetch up with rheumatism if we went down that route, and one of his 'little men' had told him some people were having one of their downstairs rooms reinforced to withstand a collapsing roof above, and recommended we had that done. When I came home I found big timbers had been erected across the ceiling of our little cloakroom, and mattresses installed. The space under the stairs had been cleared, and a mattress just fitted in there. When there were night raids, we would all tramp downstairs and attempt to get to sleep again in one of these cramped spaces.

We often went to the cinema in Woking, maybe as much as once a week. Jane's film star heartthrob at the time was the handsome Scottish actor, Bruce Seton, so if there was a film showing which had him in the cast, Jane just had to go. Father told us of a war office acquaintance who'd been bombed out and the man who had been lodging with him was having to find somewhere else to live. He said he would be bringing this man down at the weekend for the day. Apart from saying that his name was Gordon, he, didn't say much more. On the Saturday he came in through the door with not one, but two strangers. One was Gordon, the other—a friend of Gordon's—was none other than Bruce Seton himself. I'd never before seen Jane so overcome. She blushed, stumbling for words, couldn't stop herself grinning continuously, and talked of nothing else for weeks afterwards. I don't remember what happened to Bruce later, but his companion Gordon Jackson, also in the film business, went on to work in television after the war and became a household name some years later when he starred in Upstairs Downstairs.

Jane told me about an ack-ack emplacement on our hallowed golf course, and took me along to have a look. Sure enough, a part of one of the fairways had been fenced off and, amongst some gorse scrub at one end there were now some 'temporary' buildings and a khaki-coloured shiny gun with a huge searchlight nearby, both covered with a net for camouflage. Several uniformed soldiers were wandering about and there were 'Keep Off' notices displayed around the fence. One of the soldiers waved at Jane and beckoned us to the edge of the fence so they could have a chat. They were probably bored out of their minds at this time, and any passers by, even a couple of children, were a welcome distraction. I was greatly excited to be allowed so near what was undoubtedly a real gun, with real ammunition nearby. I'd have something to tell the boys at school next term!

One of my favourite outings from home was to cycle a few miles to the Fairey Aviation airfield near Woking, and lie amongst gorse and heather on the rise beside the grass runway, watching Tiger Moth biplanes take off and land. I think this was a pilot training establishment, but I was never sure. The other nearby airfield active at this time was my father's beloved Brooklands. In his younger days he used to race cars on the banked circuit, and told me about thundering around in a heavy Bentley roadster at speeds exceeding eighty miles an hour or even faster. He had a photo of himself sitting at the wheel of one of these powerful monsters, wearing goggles and a leather helmet with ear flaps, and he looked very dashing. Photos in those days were mostly 2¼ by 3¼ inches in size, black and white of course, and with none too good definition, but that didn't stop us being able to enjoy them.

The banked circuit was now disused with tufts of grass becoming established in the cracked surface. The centre of this circuit contained a Vickers aircraft factory and a short runway, tiny by today's standards, where Spitfires could land or take off.

I'd found another friend in Byfleet whom my parents approved of. He was Peter, a boy my own age who lived with his parents in a flat above the local Barclays Bank. The flat extended over the shop beside the bank with its entrance door between the two premises opening onto the street. He wasn't a very adventuresome lad, and all we did together was play indoor games. Still, it provided another outlet for my energies. I would leave my bike propped up beside the bank when I visited without securing it in any way. I didn't possess a padlock for it, indeed nobody locked up bicycles wherever they left them. People were honest. About a year into the war the occasional bomb would land somewhere near us, usually dropped by a German bomber on its way home after a London raid. Late one evening we heard the unmistakeable "crumph" accompanied by a rattling of our windows and realised we'd had one drop quite near. Early next morning I cycled about wondering where it had landed, to find the shop next to the bank simply wasn't there any more. Peter's bedroom had been over that shop and just as I was beginning to panic, I saw Peter himself running towards me, a big smile on his face.

"I was in the sitting room with Mum and Dad," he told me, "and then we heard this noise followed by a loud rumbling from across the corridor. We rushed out to see what had happened, opened the door to my bedroom and there was nothing there! Nothing. Just a drop down with dust everywhere and a horrible smell. We couldn't see a thing. Dad rushed downstairs and out into the street to find my bed sticking out from under a pile of tiles and wooden beams just over there, where the shop had been."

"Wow! Lucky you weren't in bed." I looked up at the neatly closed door to Peter's bedroom ten feet up in the wall above the rubble. It had been a near escape.

"I'd been in bed and asleep, but then woke up," he said. "I just felt I wanted to see if Mum and Dad were still up, so went in to see. I don't know why."

The bomb was apparently quite a small one and had gone down through the roof not exploding until it hit the ground, blowing out the front and back of the shop. This had caused the floor above and the roof to collapse. Peter had had a very lucky escape. This was not the first time I'd talked to people who had felt impelled to do something unusual, only to find they had avoided a nasty accident thereby. We often hear of people missing their train for some reason, and the one they should have caught is involved in an accident. Our guardian angels must be watching.

3

Holidays and More Schools

Throughout the war years my parents did their best to ensure we had at least one holiday each year, choosing safer places than our beloved Selsey. Father wasn't always able to get the time off, although he did try to be with us for at least part of the holiday.

Our first wartime holiday was a complete change. With father promising to follow in a few days, mother took Jane and me on the train to Criccieth in north Wales. Our guesthouse was a few yards from the sea where we were warmly welcomed by a big blousy lady with a delicious Welsh accent and immediately made to feel at home. The sun came out, and in no time at all Jane and I were running about on warm golden sands while mother took up her usual position, sitting on a rug above high watermark where the sand was dry and soft, and providing us with a base at which to leave towels and deposit shells. Behind the town rose the distant Snowdonia mountain range, beckoning as mountains do, and war-torn London seemed in another world.

We found even nicer country a mile or so further west along the shore, with sand dunes and open country behind and still with a glimpse of the Snowdonia massif in the distance. Only the single-track railway line was there to remind us that we were anywhere near civilisation. This remained our favourite spot, and was good for butterflies, which seemed to be everywhere. Father joined us and we explored Portmadoc, the nearest place of any size, and saw the Festinniog narrow gauge railway that wound its way down from the Snowdonia slate quarries. All too soon the week was over and there we were, standing outside the guesthouse with our luggage packed, waiting for the station taxi. Criccieth has always remained for me a friendly sunny little place, quiet and welcoming. Alas, I'm afraid there are few places nowadays that still retain the memories of our childhood.

The next holiday, in the spring of 1942, was completely different again, and was my first introduction to the county I now always think of as 'home'. We went to Cornwall. This was a break of a week or so, just father and me aged eleven. I believe Jane had gone to stay with Anstruther for an early visit there, and it was mother who couldn't get away this time. Father and I went to London and crossed to Paddington station once again, this time to board the night train to the West Country. This was at the height of the blitz, with few trains and those that did run were overcrowded. Father pulled rank and managed to get the station RTO personnel to secure two seats for him, and we pushed our way to our two precious seats through crowds of passengers on the blacked-out train lit only by feeble blue lights. Eventually the train pulled out of Paddington in the dark, in the rain, with an air raid just starting. At Reading half an hour down the line, enough people got off for there to be a few empty seats, and not long after that I was able to lie down and get some sleep. I vaguely remember in my dreams a distant west-country voice calling out "Bristol Temple Meads". Travelling by train at night was not easy, for all station name boards had been taken down in order to confuse the enemy, so one had to be very sure where one was before alighting, difficult at the best of times, but doubly so at night. The next thing I remember was wakening to find we were dashing along right by the beach, plunging in and out of tunnels at Dawlish. The sun was just coming up, and my excitement knew no bounds. Opening the window, I stuck my head out and took great draughts of clean salty sea air, gulls screeching overhead, my happiness complete. This is the scenery depicted in the Great Western Railway posters of the time, usually with the Cornish Riviera Express thundering along in its chocolate and cream livery, and is surely some of Brunel's finest railway engineering.

We turned inland. A Devonshire voice called "Newton Abbot", then we set off once more with a second locomotive up at the front, both of them pulling with all their might, while further back we could just hear the complementary "chump chump chump" of the two engines behind the quieter creaking and clunk-clunking of our own carriage as we pulled ever so slowly up a steep incline through flowering rhododendrons right beside the track. The red Devon soil here was hidden by rock and lush grasses, ferns and patches of primroses.

On to the city of Plymouth with its slate roofs and granite or whitewashed buildings waking up to another day, then we slowed to a near walking pace to cross the Tamar over Brunel's famous wrought iron bridge at Saltash. Father reminded me we had now left England and entered Cornwall, a county so remote that the local people would exclaim they were "travelling to England" when they meant they were visiting Plymouth for a day's shopping.

I remember a line of tropical-looking palm trees (actually cordyline australis) on the platform at Par station, with the milky-blue sea behind, the sea coloured by runoff from china clay pits way up in the hills. Then a few more miles of green undulating country passing little stone-banked meadows grazed by huge brown South Devon cows, before crossing the viaduct at Truro, looking down on its homely cathedral nestling amongst the smaller town buildings. It was time to change to another line.

The connecting train to Falmouth stood waiting at a siding and left as soon as we were safely aboard. Then it was a few stops down to Falmouth, over muddy creeks full of boats and birds and eventually into Falmouth terminus, the sea on one side, and Falmouth docks with its cranes and big ships on the other. At the Greenbanks Hotel, nestling right at the water's edge, we enjoyed a huge breakfast of bacon and eggs sitting in the restaurant bay window with a panoramic view over Penryn Creek to the little village of Flushing across the water. It was then but a step to the quay where the St. Mawes ferry waited.

Crossing the Carrick Roads to St. Mawes, passing great ships at anchor in the roads awaiting their turn at the docks, was magical. The twin castles of St. Mawes and Pendennis built by Henry VIII to keep the French at bay, guarded the approaches, while the lighthouse perched on St. Anthony's point gleamed white in the sunshine. By now the horrible start to our journey in the rainy night of London's blitz seemed a million miles away. Surely we must be beyond the reaches of the war?

We were to stay right on the sea front in the home of Geoffrey and Gwen Marreco, and here was Mr Marreco himself, wearing a jaunty yachting cap and a navy blue blazer, standing on the quay to welcome us as we stepped off the ferry. The Marrecos were old family friends from Woking days, the first of a number of our friends to find their way down to Cornwall. Their house was called 'The Old Court House', a tiny house with a slate roof brushed with cement to hold it all together in the fierce gales experienced in these parts, and cream-painted uneven rubble walls. Inside it was low ceilings and slate floors and a creaky staircase to the semi-attic bedrooms above. Mrs Marreco stood at the open door to greet us and show us around. Our bedroom had a little diamond-paned casement window looking out across the estuary to a stand of Scots Pine on Carricknath point with St. Anthony's lighthouse beyond, surely the most photographed view of all. That night when I went to bed I was surprised to see a light burning intermittently from the lighthouse, seeming very bright in an otherwise blacked out night. Apparently this operated at reduced brightness and could not be seen from far out at sea. The front door that opened direct onto the road was always hooked open during the day, with just a wicket gate to keep passing dogs out. Nobody locked anything in these parts, and visitors would just call out a greeting and come in. Everybody was welcome.

The people of St. Mawes live with one foot in a boat. Boats are in people's blood, the sea the reason the village is there. Its situation is superb, with the St. Anthony peninsula providing shelter from all except the prevailing south-westerlies, and even those winds tempered somewhat by the Lizard peninsula stretching south only five miles beyond the harbour entrance. Almost immediately another couple, the Roses, invited father and me to join them for their weekly shopping outing. There was no bus from St. Mawes, so shopping in the market town of Truro was not feasible in these times of petrol rationing, in fact not many people in St. Mawes had a car. A shopping trip meant crossing to Falmouth, and in the case of the Roses this meant sailing over. We clambered aboard a tiny dinghy which Mr Rose rowed with short stabbing strokes quite unlike the sleek river rowing I'd seen until now, and came alongside their boat, a comfortable cabin cruiser with a single gaff-rigged mainsail and a couple of headsails.

I had changed since my terrifying experience in the boat pond at Southwold.

By now I had read most of the Arthur Ransome books, indeed had read Swallows and Amazons so many times I could quote great chunks of it. I knew from his book We Didn't Mean to go to Sea just how to rig and sail the boat I was now sitting in and was dying to have a go. When I asked if I could steer father laughed and said I'd never been in such a boat before, but Mr Rose, noticing how I had usefully helped prepare for sailing, said "Let him have a go, we can't come to any harm", and to my delight I was soon clutching the silky smooth varnished tiller and could feel the boat respond and the sails pull as we picked up a breeze. I think father was surprised and quite impressed that I was able to tack close to the wind without difficulty, and was soon giving orders for him to pull in the mainsheet a bit, or let out the jib a little. It was exhilarating. We crossed the two and a half mile stretch of Carrick Roads in no time, and tied up at Customs House Quay in Falmouth for our shops. Falmouth in those days catered for local people; there were no tourists. With our purchases aboard, we sailed home with the wind behind us, a truly marvellous way to go shopping!

Father couldn't understand how I had managed to sail the boat, and didn't believe me when I said I'd learnt it all from the Arthur Ransome books. Teaching by stealth! Children's books aren't like that anymore. Father had tried to bring me up on adventure books from his own boyhood, but I found them just too tedious. It was Arthur Ransome for me, usually Jane's cast offs. She was now into pony books.

It was a lovely spring that year, made even better in the Cornish mild air, and father stripped off and lay out in the sun on a couple of occasions. Slightly dark-skinned anyway, he just loved the sun and very quickly became tanned, to the envy of most people who just went red when they sunbathed. Cornish sun is extremely strong, and those two sessions sent him several shades browner. Geoffrey Marreco had arranged with one of the mackerel fishermen to take us out to sea one day, so in the morning we met up with Leslie and his fishing boat down at the quay, and chugged out to the harbour entrance amidst the smell of diesel fumes and fishy bilge water. The boat had a for'd half-cabin, an open well deck with the thumping engine under a wooden cover amidships, and carried a small brown mizzen sail abaft the rudder which enabled Leslie to tend his lines without having to steer all the time. Across the harbour from Carricknath to Black Rock and beyond to Pendennis Castle on the Falmouth side was an anti-submarine boom, a heavy steel mesh suspended from large buoys and extending to near the bottom. It had an entrance 'gate' in the deepest part of the channel, which was normally kept open, and we had to go through this to get to the open sea beyond. We headed for the mackerel grounds a mile or so offshore and cast out four lines, set with spinners, while we chugged along gently at a slow pace. For several hours we kept with a shoal and must have landed some hundreds of big plump fish along with the occasional garfish and other species that Leslie would give to lobster fishermen when he returned in exchange for a lobster or two. By mid afternoon we had a big enough catch for Leslie's local market, pulled in our lines, opened the throttle and turned for home. While we were nearing the boom entrance there was a sudden cacophony of sirens and klaxons from an army gun emplacement on the top of St. Anthony's at the same time as a motor torpedo boat came racing across from Falmouth riding high on a huge bow wave, and out through the boom entrance. Leslie slowed his engine and veered in towards the shore.

"Us'll be stuck out 'ere for a while," he said calmly, as we watched. "That klaxon be for we to keep out the way."

We didn't have to wait long to find out what all the fuss was about. Suddenly round the headland screamed a sinister E-boat travelling at some forty knots. We could clearly see the crew huddled on the bridge as they sped past. A harbour launch had by now succeeded in pulling the boom closed after the motor torpedo boat had hurtled out through the entrance. Then followed an exciting chase, the E-boat turning right round and heading out to sea with the MTB in hot pursuit. Not long afterwards came the muffled sound of gunfire from the far side of St. Anthony's head as the E-boat came within the arc covered by the battery, but they were too fast and would have been well away by the time the guns had found the range.

The MTB returned, more slowly now, and the boom was opened for it. We were given a signal to follow it through, and the launch waited until we were safely inside before it closed the boom again. I was so excited I forgot I'd been starting to feel seasick earlier. What a story to tell the lads back at school! No one would believe it. And I'd seen real Germans hell bent on attacking us! Wow!

Gwen Marreco was waiting for the boat when we returned, along with about twenty other people and more coming all the while, every one of them carrying a plate. Fresh mackerel was a super addition to the meagre wartime rations, as I found out about an hour later when we sat down to the feast. Full of salt air and tired out by all the excitement, I slept well that night.

At Christmas time that same year our family booked in for a Christmas holiday at a little hotel on the edge of Dartmoor. Taking a holiday in the winter was a new venture for us, and we looked forward to it. We all felt desperately in need of a break by now. Once more we took the GWR train, this time alighting at Ivybridge a few miles short of Plymouth. From here a small, elderly bus took us north over the railway line we had just come down, and along the narrowest of lanes up a steep incline. West Country lanes are generally bounded by dry stone walls topped with lush vegetation, so sitting up in the bus we could see over the top as we brushed the grassy banks on both sides. It was a couple of miles to the hamlet of Harford—just a few houses, a farm and a church. The 'farm' had been converted to a ramshackle hotel called, appropriately, the Bullaven Farm Hotel. It comprised a collection of buildings built in the local Delabole slate and an extension or two of cheap timber-framed structures clad with asbestos-cement sheets, all arranged around three sides of a yard. 'Hotel' was rather a grand description for such a place, but it did have the great advantage of being right out on the moors, was warm and friendly, had good food and comfortable beds. Fleeing from war-torn London, this was a haven indeed.

The hotel obtained its electricity from a generator just down the hill, powered by a small hydroelectric plant built across a stream. Nearly every evening the lights would start to get dimmer and dimmer until somebody groped their way down the hill with a torch in one hand and cleared debris away from a grating upstream of the plant. Then the turbo would pick up speed once more and the lights perked up. We never discovered where the hotel water supply came from, but almost certainly it was from the same stream.

I joined Jane and father with their riding one day. My mount seemed huge and I felt very unsafe sitting so far up from the ground. We trotted off, and then Jane's horse broke into a canter and mine followed. I had no idea how to control it and before long had lost both my stirrups and began to slip back off the saddle until I was bumping up and down on its rump. A moment later with a kick of its heels it had me off, and promptly cantered off to join the others. Father was miles ahead by this time having a wonderful gallop on the open moor, and it was Jane who came back for me. I felt bruised and very sorry for myself. The next day, Jane's mount gave birth to a lovely long-legged foal, much to everyone's surprise, as the owners didn't even know she was pregnant.

On Christmas Day we all went to the little Harford church. The small congregation were huddled in winter coats, with one or two other visitors from the hotel. The parson, an elderly man, shuffled up to his pew casting a malevolent eye in the direction of the few outsiders present. After a mumbled introduction he announced a hymn and the equally elderly organist produced an introductory few bars from his out-of-tune organ.

"You're playing the wrong tune," called out the parson.

"No I hain't," replied the organist.

"Yes, you are! The tune's meant to be number 44 in your red book."

"I always plays number twelve for this one." He played a few bars. "There," he said, turning round to the congregation. "That's the one you like, hain't it?" The congregation looked back at him in silence.

"Thought so," said the organist, and before the parson could say anything else, he opened up with full swell, and we all joined in, except the parson who sulked in silence.

The hotel had managed to find food for a splendid Christmas lunch that went on half the afternoon. In the evening someone organised party games for us all. My memories of that holiday are mainly the way in which everyone there all joined in together like a house party.

~*~

Clayesmore Preparatory School was limited by the size of its premises as to how many boys it could accommodate, and as the main feeder school for Clayesmore School proper, situated in the village of Iwerne Minster on the far side of Blandford, it had been the custom for boys to progress to the senior school in their twelfth year rather than the more normal thirteenth. Thus the time at my first boarding school was all too brief, though it seemed a long time to me. At the end of the summer term in 1944 all the boys in the senior year took exams, all who wanted to go on were deemed to have passed, and we were told we would transfer at the start of next term to the senior school.

At this time father was in America enjoying the freedom of a country far from the war with plentiful food in the shops and no blackout. After Britain, he found it unbelievable. Sure, the Americans were in the war with us, but for the American people at home not much had changed. Father wrote guarded letters about "enjoying being there" but not telling us a lot. He would enclose a packet of Wrigley's chewing gum in his letters inviting the censor to take one piece, and we would receive the letter with one piece missing, so presumably the censor had taken his share. Sometimes the packet wasn't opened, and we wondered whether the censor just didn't like chewing gum or whether the letter hadn't been through the censors. Either way, these letters were eagerly jumped upon, mother reading them out to us while Jane and I enjoyed our piece of gum. It wasn't much, but sweets had long since disappeared from the shops together with every other little luxury. With the arrival of the school's letter about me moving up, mother flew into a panic. It had never been their intention for me to go on to the senior school, and she wasn't sure whether we could afford it. Without father to talk to she had no one to consult. Eventually she decided I would go for a term or two, at least until I had reached the common entrance age of thirteen. That the quiet of Dorset was a safer place than Byfleet was no doubt a consideration.

By this time the flying bomb, the 'doodlebugs' as we knew them, were coming over every day and quite a few landed in Surrey, twenty miles short of their London target. These fiendish devices were essentially simple pilotless aircraft containing a large bomb set to explode when they landed and with a most basic control system, cheap to make and simple to launch, and could be sent over in daylight. Some were intercepted by our own fighters, who would fly alongside and tip them over by nudging their wings, but although this put them off course, they still landed somewhere. Besides, we needed all our precious fighters for more important matters. We had staying with us during the doodlebug period another of father's war office friends. This was a Brigadier Kennedy, a Scotsman living at the time in a bedsit in London who worked at the war office on the scientific side. He came home with father one night after sharing air-raid warden duties the previous night on the roof of the war office with father, on the very night a bomb had demolished his bedsit. After that near escape he spent the rest of the war with one or other of his friends. How we found room to fit him in I never knew, but we did. He was very jittery and worried about his family living in Gloucestershire. It was not until after the war we discovered he had been involved in one of the 'Wheezers and Dodgers' schemes for getting the doodlebug's engines to cut out early, and thereby land in the comparative safety of the Surrey countryside rather than in London. But some of them landed near us instead, so no wonder he was nervous. They were a psychological weapon as much as anything, made more menacing by having an easily distinguishable phut-phutting engine sound which, when you heard it stop, you knew that within half a minute it would land and explode not far away. I remember looking out of the window at home one day and seeing one fly overhead. I called out to mother to come and have a look, but she yelled at me to get down under cover.

"It's quite okay, Mummy," I called back. "The engine's still going so it won't land yet."

Brigadier Kennedy, or "DV" as we called him after his initials, wore tartan trews and a navy blue forage cap with two tabs at the back and looked very smart. He told us one evening he had been walking along Regent Street that day when a car stopped, a policeman appeared from nowhere and asked the few pedestrians to stand to one side, whereupon the Queen got out to walk across the pavement into one of the shops. She noticed him as she passed, stopped and said, "I don't suppose you've had much chance to do any fishing lately." DV was astonished. He'd spoken to the Queen several years previously while salmon fishing in the Dee, and she'd stopped then and chatted about fishing. Yet she'd recognised him dressed in uniform, in quite different circumstances and remembered that occasion. Impressive.

DV had also been to America, with a liaison job in Washington. He told of being followed around by small boys calling out "Gee, fancy pants!" After the war I believe he went on to become vicar of Moreton-in-the-Marsh parish church.

But back to school: I was amongst friends when I started at the big school, as our entire class had transferred together. Like many such schools, the premises were once a minor stately home set in rolling acres of parkland. The stable block had been converted to classrooms, the main building had tacky extensions at the back of it and the whole lot suffered from neglect, due probably to the war as much as anything.

As a new boy I was in line for being selected to be a prefect's 'fag', strangely considered an honour, presumably because it conferred privileges to offset the undoubted labours involved. To my delight I was duly selected, not by one of the glamorous sporty prefects, a cluster of whom ran the disciplinarian side of the school allowing the teaching staff to get on with the job of teaching, but by a lesser individual called the library prefect with the task of running quite a good well-stocked school library. He had a small study leading off the library which it was my job to look after. There I was expected to keep the place clean and tidy, polish his shoes and provide mugs of tea or whatever was on the go. He was a good mentor, kind and thoughtful, and never took advantage of me but was also somewhat distant and a bit of a bookworm himself unlike me. However, having the envious rank of prefect this gave him unrestricted entrée to the holy of holies—the Head of School's private room, and wherever he went, so I could go too. Thus I rubbed shoulders with the top people and loved it. You might think that such exalted seniors would strut around in identifiable clothes, but no. Everyone in the school wore a grey flannel shirt and grey shorts, with a grey pullover enlightened by the school colours around the Vee collar. It was long grey socks too, with school-coloured garter tabs. There was a school cap, the same as the one I had at prep school, but nobody ever wore it. Only on special occasions were some older boys who possessed any long trousers allowed to wear them.

Meals at Clayesmore were ghastly. Vegetables had virtually disappeared off the menu altogether, meat portions were miniscule and tough (old goat, probably, if the rumours were to be believed), potatoes were plentiful but always lumpy and overcooked with black bits in them. Sometimes we had reconstituted dried potato that was so badly prepared that in spite of our hunger it was a struggle to eat. Fruit was unheard of and puddings especially unappetising. A particularly nasty pudding was an unsweetened suet creation with the occasional currant, which we called arbuckle after a grossly obese strip cartoon character of that time. It was cooked in a large trough-shaped tin with a hinged lid, so that when it emerged from the kitchens and the lid opened, the slimy evil-smelling concoction sat there making us want to puke. Unsweetened custard spooned over the top made it just about bearable to a starving youngster, but only just. Of my time at Clayesmore, that is the memory which has lasted the longest. It was soon whispered around the dormitory that a house in the village could provide an untold feast for just threepence. The house, it appeared, was the home of the village baker, and although we never actually met him, we did meet his wife who held an open kitchen to any boy calling. At break time each morning she had supplies of hot crusty mini cottage loaves, which she split crosswise, spreading a large spoonful of golden syrup on the hot doughy inside. Golden syrup, inexplicably, was fairly easily obtained. Nearby a shop sold hot pork pies, and although these were delicious, they were reserved for high days since they cost sixpence. So to offset my memories of the horrible arbuckle I also have happy recollections of sprinting down to the village most mornings for my golden syrup butty.

I started biology, a subject in which I had a real interest since I could see the connection between much of what we learnt in class with what I had encountered out on my walks. It was taught by another spinster lady whom we respected. In fact we respected most of the teachers, maybe because we were growing up but more probably because the fear of a prefect's cane was always there if we were reported misbehaving.

I also started physics and chemistry lessons. French was taken by a Mr Bateman who spent most of his time changing spectacles, with one pair for reading, one for blackboard work and another for glaring over the top at the class. The reading pair had a string round the back so they hung on his chest while he was wearing one of the others. I was intrigued by him because mother had bought my own spectacles from a chain called G.C. Bateman, and I wondered whether our French teacher might be anything to do with that company. He had at some time lived in France himself and, as if to drive home the point, always wore copious amounts of a heady after-shave. He spoke in a splendid sounding French accent with wild arm movements and Gallic shoulder-shrugging which he tried to teach us to emulate, showing us pictures of the mouth of a person spouting French vowels. At the prep school our French master never attempted to teach spoken French, finding it quite enough to cope with just the grammar.

The school had an open-air swimming pool in which we were expected to bathe naked. I was dreadfully self-conscious about stripping off in front of the others, especially since the pool was only protected on three sides by hedges, the fourth side being open to any passer-by. I soon got used to it, although when the matron occasionally stopped by I quickly wrapped a towel round me. One boy, far older, always got an erection when he undressed much to everyone's amusement, but he laughed as much as they did, so avoided being teased. If matron noticed she certainly ignored it.

The school padre who taught divinity and one or two other subjects was an easy-going middle-aged bachelor, with a room over the science laboratories reached via an outside staircase and a balcony. He was interested in astronomy and several boys collected on the balcony on fine nights to look through his powerful telescope and join in the subsequent discussions afterwards in front of his fire. I went along for a while but soon found the mathematics beyond me, and with memories of Mr T, I also suspected his true motives.

We had a scout troop of sorts but it was without a good leader and I never pursued it. Scouting was one activity I really missed from the prep school and Mr Household's wonderful inspiration was undoubtedly the most lasting influence from my early schooldays. Instead, the school had an Army Cadet Unit, but I was not old enough to join that. Besides, it was nothing like the same as scouting.

In the winter terms we again played rugby, and as the rest of the teams in which I played consisted of the same boys I had endured whilst at the prep school, the severity of the games was not much different. One big change was the actual field on which we played. Being the most junior year in the school, not unnaturally we were allocated the worst field. This was little more than a meadow; indeed it was at one end of a meadow that was grazed the rest of the week by a herd of cows. We felt really stupid walking down to the field (which was also the furthest away) with one of us carrying a shovel. Even with careful removal of every cowpat, I usually managed to get my face pushed into the remnants of one. Being a little older now, the team I played in nearly equated with some prep schools' 1st XV, and I was once mysteriously picked to play in a team against Salisbury Cathedral Choir School. Now this was just great fun. Not only did we enjoy the adventure of a coach trip across to Salisbury, an hour or sos journey away, but the home team looked after us really well, and after the game (which, predictably, we lost) we were given a marvellous tea and shown round the school, then went across to the cathedral where the boys showed us the vestry where they kept their surplices, before being allowed to stay on for evensong with those same rugger-tackling fiends now looking and sounding angelic in the choirstalls.

~*~

Father returned home early in 1945 and my parents set about finding a 'better' school for me to go to. Although the V2 rockets were an even more terrifying occurrence than the doodlebugs, appearing as they did without any warning at all, they did not seem such a threat to us in Byfleet. My parents felt the advantage of being cast away in the safety of deepest Dorset was not compensation enough for the dubious quality of the school I attended. My school reports were none too good, I was picking up some nasty habits—bad manners and suchlike—and my parents felt I would do better elsewhere. Nearby family friends were related to one of the housemasters at Bradfield College, near Theale in Berkshire. Perhaps I would be able to go there? We went to discuss the possibilities with them. Lady Locock (her husband, Sir Charles, was a hereditary baronet, stone deaf and walked about like an actor in a Whitehall farce) gave me a good going over and declared that Cecil Bellamy, the housemaster in question, would probably assess me and I might be able to go to his House. Normally one would have taken the common entrance exam but Clayesmore did not prepare its thirteen year olds for this, so the back door method would need to be employed. The telephone was used once again, and this time I was asked to visit for the day.

With much trepidation and a lot of warnings about good behaviour I took various trains cross-country to Reading, a sort of zig-zag trip most of the way to Guildford and then back to Wokingham before heading the other way once more to Reading. Then it was a bus for the last part. Bradfield is the name of the village, the school being founded in 1850 by the vicar of the time who, it was said, did so in order to get boys for his choir. Once started, with three houses in the main part of the school around a lovely hammer-beam roofed central hall, it quickly grew, more houses being added as the need arose. By 1945 there were seven altogether scattered about the village, and the village itself grew to support the school. When the bus turned off the Pangbourne road at a sign that simply said 'Bradfield', I felt I was going somewhere very special indeed.

I found my way to the Bellamy's private wing, tacked onto the end of one of the original Houses, to be greeted by the most delightful couple one could wish to meet. I endeavoured to be on my very best behaviour hoping my terror was not too obvious. I sat at the shiny polished table in their dining room, and given some papers to write, a sort of mini-common entrance exam. Then we had a break for lunch after which I struggled with another exam. But Cecil Bellamy was kindness itself, and after glancing at the final paper I'd written, reassured me that in spite of some obvious problems I would be the sort of boy he would be able to bring along, and he would like me to join.

And so it was. Once again I would be joining a new School in the summer term, a term ahead of the main entry. There was a wonderful optimism in the air. Father was home, mother obviously hugely relieved that she no longer had to take the major decisions without help, the war in Europe was almost over, I had been accepted at this wonderful school to which my parents now admitted they'd thought I had no chance of being accepted, the sun shone and the relief was too good to be true.

Jane had now enjoyed several extended stays with the Anstruthers. She had also hitched-hiked with Freda Stones all the way to Braithwaite in Cumberland for a holiday, and had come back with tales of being looked after by hopeful lorry drivers and helped by all sorts of people to whom, nowadays,

Jane with Holmbury Robert's Boy. Jane was never far from one of her animals.

one would give a very wide berth. She'd loved it all, and wanted to spend each summer up in the mountains. They'd walked to the top of Skiddaw (no mean feat for Freda who was enormously heavy, unlike Jane who was slim, fit and pretty tough).

Later, on the strength of her work with Anstruther, she applied and was accepted for a job looking after a herd of cows at Holmbury St. Mary in Surrey. This turned out to be a prestigious herd of pedigree Guernseys, part of the Guinness empire, and 'looking after' meant just that. She milked the entire herd by hand twice a day, swept out the cowshed and milking parlour, drove a tractor, kept everything in a spick and span condition in keeping with such important animals and lived over the shop in the house of the farm manager. She even managed some riding occasionally. I went to visit her while she was there. It was a true model farm, money no object (except when it came to her wages). During her time there she had to take the pedigree bull, Holmbury Robert's Boy, to the Reading Show. He went by train, and was disembarked from a siding a couple of streets away from the showground. Jane led him down the quiet residential road without a thought, and it was only when she stopped to do up her shoelace while the bull waited quietly for her to finish, that it occurred to her that the place seemed strangely deserted. She then noticed faces at windows, looking out in some alarm. She picked up his rope and led him off, wondering what all the fuss was about. Also during her time with the herd she took a couple of cows to the Dairy Show at Olympia where she virtually lived for several days alongside her charges, with the excitement of speaking to the Queen when the Royal family toured the show.

~*~

I started at Bradfield one day ahead of the beginning of term, and met up with two other new boys who would be joining Army House, as Bellamy's house was called. Paul Brader and Tony Clover were clearly high flyers in comparison to me, but we got on well enough. Our first night was easy going, the calm before the storm. Boys then arrived in dribs and drabs all next day, and by teatime the place was teeming with noisy lads all wanting to know what everyone else had been doing in the holidays. The three of us were each given a 'nurse', our mentor for the next two weeks. In that time we had to learn the school rules—and there were plenty of them—also learn the school hymn by heart, the special lesson from the Prayer Book and a school poem. We had to visit every House and every classroom, meet a number of masters and boys of various sorts, and generally become absolutely familiar with all manner of things needed to get along there. At the end, our head-of-house prefect would test us, and if we failed then it was our mentor who received a punishment. Needless to say, my nurse kept me at it without letup.

The headmaster at this time was Colonel John Hills, who came to Bradfield after having been an Eton housemaster. He was a smallish man, upright with a military bearing, dapper, always immaculately dressed in a black jacket and pin-striped trousers, a wing collar with white bow tie, highly polished black shoes and, except during the afternoons, wore a smart uncreased MA gown and mortar board. He strode about with gown flowing out behind, and left one in no doubt about his importance. He lived with his wife and two teenage horse-mad daughters in a brick and timbered house on the corner of Bradfield crossroads, just across the road from Army House, so we saw him frequently whenever he swept through the main entrance into School. In comparison with the HM, all other masters appeared shabby. He commanded an undue amount of 'personal space' around him, and I wondered what would happen if that was encroached upon, for example, if one had to cram into a lift with him. He affected an Edwardian manner of speech, referring to his daughters as "gels" and their horses as "hosses".

Bradfield was known as a 'classics' school, not so much because it neglected the maths and science side but, strangely, because of a huge depression in the school grounds located in thick woodland quite near the crossroads, which the school had recognised many years previously as an opportunity. The bowl-shaped depression, deep into the underlying chalk, was about twenty metres deep and fifty metres across. With not too much effort this had been the basis for building an amphitheatre with a large wooden Greek-style covered stage at one end, and seating for an audience upwards of 500, around a circular 'orchestra' in front of the stage. The audience, each supplied with an essential cushion as they entered, sat on concrete steps around this area. The front of the stage structure was fashioned in classical Greek style with a huge proscenium arch, and to add realism a smoking incense burner was positioned in the centre of the orchestra. Every year the school put on a play which parents and the public could attend, one year in four the play being one of the Greek classics, performed in Greek, while a Shakespeare play would be put on at other times. Cecil Bellamy, or 'CB' as he was universally called, was producer excelsis of these wonderful performances, which occupied all the main players' spare time for much of the summer term. CB's other talent was choral singing, and he was the school choirmaster. He also taught, of course, but I was never in any of his classes.

My Latin master, a Mr Neat, much older than the other staff, had been gassed during the First World War, leaving him with a thin reedy voice. He was philosophical about the members of his class unable to enjoy learning such a language, and reckoned most pupils showed leanings towards either the classics, or to mathematics and science, and that this showed at quite an early age. Something to do with the type of brain we have. Nobody had propounded such a comforting theory to me before, and it certainly fitted my own experience. I was hopeless at all languages, was rather indifferent to history (which I put down to having a poor memory for strings of facts, but was probably because it was taught so unimaginatively), managed well enough with the two English subjects, and loved art, geography, maths and the sciences—all the practical subjects. I am naturally curious about how and why everything is as it is, the fundamental enquiring mind of a science-oriented person. I would quote Kipling's poem:

I have six faithful friends, who taught me all I knew.
Their names are How and When and Where,
and Why and What and Who.

I sat in Mr Neat's class while he covered the blackboard with impossible words, only ever involving the Latin lovers to comment on this or that. Occasionally he would patiently explain something to us 'mathematicians and scientists' but otherwise leave us to yawn through the lesson, coping as best as we could. I liked Mr Neat.

Some masters were far less forgiving. Mr Moulsdale, a form master and housemaster of one of the up-the-hill houses, terrified all his class by hurling chalk, blackboard rubbers, books or any other missile that came to hand with unerring accuracy at any boy who failed to understand immediately what he was wittering on about. If the boy had not been paying attention, then he would be subjected to a torturing bout of hair pulling. Friends of mine who endured this treatment said he was more forgiving with those who could play good cricket— a sport at which he himself excelled. No doubt that explained why he threw things so devastatingly well.

Most of my peers considered me a bit of a misfit, a bit dim. Not only did I dislike sport, but didn't shine in anything initially. I came to believe this myself, and wondered whether anyone realised how I had managed to come to Bradfield when it was most unlikely I could ever have passed the Common Entrance exam. However, it did mean I was put in the bottom class for most subjects and these tended to have the most understanding teachers.

During that first term I made no proper friends, though we all rubbed along well enough together. If there were any misfits, they were tolerated; bullying was not. Paul Brader was bright, went into a higher class for maths, which was his best subject, and excelled on the cricket field. As such, he was immediately accepted, and was the envy of everybody else. Tony Clover's sports and school subjects were different to mine, and we were never together. Boys who had joined at the start of the academic year two terms earlier had already formed their friendships treating the three of us as junior to them, and it was not considered the done thing to relate to such inferiors. I chummed up with some boys in my various classes but who were at different houses, so a close friendship with such people was not easy; one was really constrained to the boys in one's own house. The juniors were all liable to fagging, and after our first two weeks, the three of us enjoyed that dubious privilege.

The first year boys at Army House occupied the two dormitories at the top of the building on the third floor. Each of us had a narrow iron-framed bedstead with a thin mattress and a couple of inadequate blankets, and a chest for keeping all our clothes. We were to find in wintertime these rooms could get almost lethally cold, as some of the sash windows had blocks nailed to them preventing the last three inches from being closed. Down the middle of the dormitory was a line of old-fashioned washstands, and any water left in the bowls overnight sometimes froze solid by morning. Mysteriously the bathroom and lavatories on this floor never froze up. All the plumbing was in lead, including drinking water supplies, and the bathroom had lead-lined floors with a single bath and a shower. Each morning when the bell rang throughout the building we would have to endure a cold shower, albeit a very quick one, before we were deemed fit to face the day. To ensure this sadistic experience was not bypassed, a house prefect would be present in the bathroom to check us off as we came in. Then we dressed, quickly made our still-warm beds and clattered down the stone stairs for breakfast across the schoolyard in the big hall.

One reached this through a massive oak door called 'snakers' because of the elaborate snake design of its hinges. The hall itself was a magnificent panelled barn-like room with a lovely hammer beam roof, hung with gloomy portraits of previous disapproving headmasters or scenes of imaginary 19th century landscapes.

After breakfast there was time, briefly, for that essential daily visit to the loo, a most inhibiting experience for Army House boys, who were not expected to use the limited facilities in the house itself during the day but to cross the yard to a row of outside lavatories called, unsurprisingly, 'freezers'. There one sat, in a damp, draughty cubicle, trying to perform before time ran out and the bell started to ring for morning chapel.

As one of CB's choirboys I quite enjoyed chapel. We would assemble in the vestry, don a simple white surplice, then after a brief prayer from the chaplain us trebles importantly led the small procession into chapel from a side door, with the tenors and basses following and the chaplain bringing up the rear. CB sang tenor and there were two other members of staff in the choir. Everybody else in the school entered chapel by the west door at the far end, and sat in wide pews, twelve to a side, with staff in rather grander pews with arms, one step above floor level around the sides and rear of the chapel. Last to come in would be the HM, who sat at the back so all the boys could feel his eyes boring into the backs of their heads.

The school music master played the rather splendid organ, and we had lots of descants and solo parts for the choir, which I enjoyed. Daily chapel was all over in 15 minutes, but on Sundays there would be full Morning Prayer and a meaty sermon. This would be preached either by the chaplain or sometimes by the HM who rather fancied himself as a preacher, and occasionally by a visiting cleric. Sometimes the visitor would be a somewhat dry local vicar, or occasionally we had a lively charismatic speaker who gave a wonderful oration that had us sitting on the edge of our uncomfortable pews. One such was a brown-habited monk who was magnificent, and—alas—showed up all the others. Once a year the Bishop of Oxford would take a confirmation service. On Fridays we had extended chapel which started a little earlier so that the whole congregation could practise some pieces that would be coming up on the following Sunday. The choristers would already be privy to these so we would show off our expertise.

Many years later Noggin, a contemporary of mine who had been at Harrow, recounted how they, too, had a weekly practice service. Theirs was on Thursdays, took the place of normal morning prayers, and only involved some of the boys that did not include him. He was late finishing breakfast one day, stopped someone and asked, "What day is it?" When being told it was Thursday, he replied "Oh good, I can have a george" (the Harrow term for having a crap), whereupon Thursdays became dubbed St. George's Day and he was thereafter regarded as the rather strange boy who only went once a week…

Next to Army House was a level area that had once been a grass tennis court. During morning break, which lasted for twenty minutes or so, all Army House boys had to assemble in this area and spend ten minutes doing physical jerks, simple warm-up exercises to combat the effects of sitting in a classroom all morning. We also had time for tea and a piece of dry currant bread. All the school bread was baked in the bakery, just across the yard. We would pass this in the mornings on our way to freezers, and lingered on the way back to take in the appetising aroma wafting out of the open door, where pies, tarts and other lunch items requiring to be baked would also contribute to the smells. The baker, whose name was Carter, took pity and sometimes one was lucky enough to come back clutching a bun or some such in one's unwashed hands. The school also employed a carter, called Baker. True! He led a lovely shire horse pulling an open cart on his rounds of the school and village. In those times just after the war when nobody had any petrol, this was a most useful conveyance.

Within a few weeks of starting at Bradfield the war in Europe was over. Naturally I expected bananas to reappear in the shops immediately, but nothing actually changed at all, except that somehow the sun shone brighter, and a happy future now seemed probable. Cricket was in full swing, Paul Brader, blond, good-looking and confident, strode out to the wicket in his whites and started to send sixes all over the place. If I, the despair of any team captain, had to play I would surely be sent to a remote part of the outfield in the hope that other fielders would be able to stop all balls that might be heading in my direction, and when it came to batting, well—hopefully the game would be decided one way or the other before it was my turn to bat. So I spent my summer afternoons making daisy chains in the outfield and being shouted at occasionally by all those gods running around where the action was. At weekends it was better, for Saturday afternoons were generally match days and the likes of me were released to do our own thing. The River Pang ran alongside the school boundary. A lovely clean chalk stream full of fish with dragonflies zinging about overhead, this river was really delightful. With a friend, I used to walk up to what I took to be its source a couple of miles away near Stanford Dingley where it emerged from a series of bubbling springs. There were also attractive woods to explore, where we would often see foxes, stoats, weasels, lots of rabbits and sometimes a swooping diurnal owl. Greathouse Wood, one of my favourites, which was absolutely silent with no signs of ever having been desecrated by human intervention, now has the M4 slicing right through the middle of it. Whenever I drive along that stretch of motorway I am reminded of those halcyon times.

The summer term ended with the usual exams, after which there was about a week of far more relaxed work. The school play involved a lot of people, some of whom were needed for rehearsals during the day as well as performances in the evenings, so not much relaxation for them. The play that first year was Shakespeare's Henry IV Part 1, and I'm ashamed to say that the only lines I can quote are the very first "If music be the food of love, play on...." delivered by the senior actor of the day, lying back on a pile of cushions while a scratchy orchestra plucked away on lutes. I would remember more of future plays when I myself became involved.

Most of the boys travelled home by train. On this occasion the Mountain graciously condescended to come to Mohammed, in the form of two Great Western Railway booking hall staff who set up shop in one of the classrooms to sell us tickets. This took place on the afternoon after our end-of-term special lunch, a wonderful gargantuan feast with second helpings all round. The distance from Hall to the classroom was about a hundred yards, and the last ones to arrive might be in a queue for an hour or longer. Therefore, the moment the valedictory grace was said, several hundred boys leapt up and tried to leave the room all at the same time, to sprint the short distance. The booking clerks had a heavy cylindrical date stamping machine that authenticated the card tickets, which they laboriously wrote out by hand using indelible ink. One wrote the ticket details while the other looked up the cost in a grubby dog-eared book and took our money. Then the first one stamped the ticket and handed it over. Before the next customer was attended to, a record had to be entered in another dog-eared book. The whole operation took a few minutes. Multiply that by the hundreds of boys in the queue, and the advantages of that mad dash to be among the first soon became apparent, in spite of the stomach pains occasioned after such a heavy meal.

And then it was "Goodbye, see you next term!" as we piled into the several buses waiting out in the road, and were off. One could feel the whole school heave a sigh of relief as we departed for home and freedom.

4

The Big Move

A week or so into the summer holidays brought about the visit from Anstruther, described at the start of this book. Father was still in the Army, though he had been promised his discharge fairly soon.

"Well, what are you going to do?" repeated Anstruther to father.

"I'd like something different, but I'm not trained for anything else," said father, somewhat wistfully.

"Well, what would you like to do—what do you really enjoy?" Anstruther knew the answer to this, of course.

"Gardening, golf, sailing, that sort of thing. But none of that will keep the wolf from the door."

"And you, Dorothy?" Anstruther turned to mother.

"Oh, I don't come into it!" said mother, almost shocked, "Adam's the breadwinner."

"But you do, my dear. You are a team. Now is your opportunity to enjoy life, both of you!"

"Well, I suppose it's dancing and entertaining, meeting people and that sort of thing," said mother.

Jane and I sat listening on the sidelines with great interest. Never before had we been present at such a moment for our adult parents. Suddenly they seemed vulnerable, unsure. Anstruther turned to us. "A team," he repeated to us, "This is essential for a successful family venture. Wouldn't you agree?"

"Hey," said father, "Who said anything about a family team? Jane has her own interests and John's still at school!"

"And your interests, Jane?" said Anstruther, looking at her, "Something to do with animals, maybe?" He glanced around the room, beaming at us all. We waited. He pulled a torn piece of newspaper from his pocket and began to read.

"For sale. Manor House with eighteen acres of land. Suitable for small hotel. Ruan High Lanes, Cornwall. £4,500. Apply bla-bla-bla... There you are! Sell Woodcombe and emigrate to Cornwall!"

"But… I know nothing about hotels," exclaimed father. "No. Ridiculous idea."

"Lots of sailing, eh?" Anstruther turned to mother. "Dorothy? Ridiculous idea?"

"It's a lovely idea. Pie in the sky, of course! But I could just see myself entering a drawing room full of guests, having a sherry with them and then announcing a lovely dinner ready in the dining room next door." She smiled dreamily.

"There you are!" said Anstruther. "Seriously, this could be a family venture. You, Adam, run the establishment and indulge your hobby of gardening by converting some land to growing crops for the house. Jane, you will look after all the animals, a couple of cows, pigs, a few hens, all for the house. You, Dorothy, could do what you just said, and be the catering and social manager. What a time you'd have with that. No rationing, living off the land. Wonderful fresh gourmet food. They'd come knocking at the door from miles. Couldn't fail."

"John." He turned to me. "Your job will be to keep the establishment in good order, screw back the odd hinge, paint the gutters, fix the tiles. That'll keep you out of mischief in the holidays!" I recalled my first visit to Greyfriars when I'd helped Anstruther hang a picture. He'd remembered how I enjoyed practical things like that.

"Ridiculous," said father, "No money. I wouldn't get much for Woodcombe, and I've virtually no savings. No. Lovely idea, Douglas, but not for us. Sorry." He looked a little reflective. Anstruther noticed, but didn't comment.

In the next few days as father's demob date approached, we spoke often about Anstruther's ludicrous idea for us all. Would it be possible? The Jennings family came over for drinks.

"Splendid idea!" roared Jorrocks, "I'll join you. Look after the bar. Take the guests out. Do the books and all that. Why not?" He tipped back his whisky. Muriel Jennings looked aghast. Go and live way out in the wilds of Cornwall… But the seed was sown and met fertile soil.

A few more days, and plans developed. We found Ruan High Lanes on the Ordnance Survey map, a military map overprinted with purple gridlines which father had acquired from the War Office. A little hamlet, a road junction really, and a mile down a lane there it was: 'Polsue' marked clearly on the map.

"Only five or six miles from St. Mawes, you see!" pointed out father. "Sailing. We'd have a boat. Everyone down in those parts needs a boat."

"We could catch our own mackerel!" I cried out delightedly.

Anstruther visited again. He had the sale details. The house had been requisitioned at the start of the war and had lain virtually empty for five years, with an elderly couple occupying just two rooms on the ground floor. It 'needed some repairs.' An Estate agents' disguised warnings went unheeded. Jorrocks poo-poo'd them all. He was a Sapper and professed to have knowledge about such matters, which father certainly didn't.

"We'll need some builders to put right all the little things, of course," he said. "We'll have to set aside a few thousand to get ourselves up and running. Furniture, of course. Have to start off with second-hand stuff. Can't buy new furniture at present."

Father and Jorrocks visited the house and came back elated, at least Jorrocks did. Father was secretly dismayed by the state of everything, but Jorrocks' enthusiasm won him over. Actually what really won him over was the thought of a new life three hundred miles away from London. Their visit had been on a beautiful summer's day and the neglected garden was full of pink and blue hydrangeas all flowering their hearts out. There were wonderful opportunities there as well as 'challenges'. There was something to look forward to. He persuaded himself they would be able to cope. He didn't want this to slip away, to be left with a shattered dream and the prospect of that 8.04 train to London every day. They put in an offer and it was accepted.

~*~

Back at school I was now a second year boy, which conferred some minor privileges such as being allowed to use certain paths banned to first year boys. I was in the next dormitory, a smaller and nicer one. 'The Kember', as matron was known, treated me in a less motherly way, no doubt all part of the calculated process of weaning her charges off maternal dependence, and I was given a new boy to 'nurse' for his first couple of weeks. The House captain, Barlow, had left and his place taken by the next in line, and we had three new house prefects. Everybody had moved on.

At Bradfield games were the thing. Nothing else was so important to the public school ethic as playing games. Team games. Everyone pulling together. Eventually I managed to escape by discovering cross-country running. This was really enjoyable, and I loved running along the Berkshire country lanes and along tracks, getting ever muddier, to return to soak in a hot tub with just the other runners for company. Running only took half as long as playing soccer, so we enjoyed a blissful half hour or so with the changing rooms to ourselves. Best of all, running was considered an okay sport, and therefore respectable. The changing rooms at Army House occupied the basement. Here each boy kept his essential tuck box, containing books, sweets or biscuits, items too precious to be left in one's locker up in the common room. There were also a couple of coat hooks and spaces for our shoes. Next to this was the calorifier, a noisy hissing tank with pipes and valves around it, secured behind a cage. It was always warm in here and ideal for drying wet clothes pegged to the caging or hanging from hot pipes. The shower space was next to that, with four showers either side of a tiled area, each one above a foot-deep hipbath. It was in these that we enjoyed our post games hot bath. Finally there was a bank of urinals that usually stank horribly, and were visited from time to time by the janitor who poured hydrochloric acid into them in an attempt to dissolve the evil smelling deposits. It was in the changing rooms that boys noticed the effect of puberty on their chums as each of us developed at different rates. One lad, clearly well supplied with testosterone, developed in a spectacular fashion and once invited others to handle it "for a small fee". He was quickly put down by a nearby prefect and there was no more of that. Any reference to sex, especially any inclination towards homosexuality came under the heading of 'filth', to be firmly suppressed. Anybody actually caught indulging in such pursuits was liable to swift but covert dismissal, and this indeed happened to a couple of boys elsewhere in the school during my time. Nevertheless, there was inevitably an undercurrent of sexual attraction between various individuals, not surprising in such a closed community. Bellamy's own daughter Jean, several years older than us, singularly lacked any sex appeal even to the most rampant of post-puberty boys, and the HM's two daughters though attractive, were just too remote for anyone to speak to. And that was it. No girls. It had to be accepted. The school tried some stilted social functions with Down House, a girls school a few miles away, but I was never involved.

After several weeks I damaged my Achilles tendon during one of my runs, and was temporarily off sport. There was no such thing as access to a physiotherapist, nor was the local GP who occasionally visited the school invited to have a look. The Kember told me to pull myself together, and to this day I have a weakness in one leg, which returns after a spell of running. I joined the no-hopers, a small group of Army House boys considered too uncoordinated to be safe anywhere on a sports field. While the others were kicking balls around our task was to convert dead trees into manageable sized logs for Bellamy's own use and our common room open fire, an essential wintertime addition to the meagre heating. We had a rickety sawhorse and several rather blunt two-handed saws. The operation needed three people, one at each end of the saw and one sitting astride the log being sawed in order to stop everything falling over. We then took turns to split the sawn off disc with an axe. I was quite good at splitting, having become proficient at axemanship in the Clayesmore Scouts; however, these logs, gleaned from nearby woods, generally had an impossibly convoluted grain. I am sure we became far fitter attacking all this wood than the rest of Army House down on the sports fields, but it took a long time getting those logs sawn and split! On one occasion the HM came past, stood and watched for a moment then came over to offer some advice. This was the first time any of us had spoken to him or been so near. He was without gown or mortarboard, but still wore the pinstripe trousers, black jacket and white bow tie. Close up one could smell expensive after-shave.

"Here, let me demonstrate." He had a clear clipped voice rather like Noël Coward. Taking the axe from me he addressed the log. "Now, aim here, a foot below where the contact point is. That way it will hit the log at greater speed. It's the impact that does the splitting. Weight of axehead times the speed. Watch." With that, his small feet encased in their highly polished shoes lifted off the ground as he took a huge swing, the axe cleaving the log neatly in two. We were impressed, especially at his knowledge of mechanics—not bad for a classics man.

Pleased with himself he allowed a slight smile, handed back the axe saying, "Now you have a go!" I swung the axe while the HM stood to one side, hands on hips. The others tried. No luck. HM then cleanly split another log. I noticed there were now specks of white sawdust on his shiny shoes. I also noticed CB standing some way off, grinning broadly. That evening when he came round the dormitory before lights out as he often did for a social chat, he commented on our new coach.

"I can see you'll soon be in the log-splitters first eleven after your private tuition."

The weekly letters from home now had news of our own house sale. It was all going very fast. We had an interested buyer who made an offer that we accepted, and was now itching to move in. Father worried about not pitching the price high enough, but the agent insisted he had achieved the quick sale he needed, and this was the main thing. We would be moving in time for Christmas, all being well. I could hardly wait.

At the end of term, I only had to catch a local train to Reading. Then it was a different platform, the down platform for my connection. I was to catch the westbound express, GWR's most prestigious train, The Cornish Riviera Express. It pulled in, a huge 4-6-2 shiny locomotive hauling twelve to fourteen sleek coaches with a restaurant car in the middle, all in the GWR livery of chocolate and cream. I just loved that first daytime trip down to Cornwall. I studied the mileposts as we shot past, all the stations we swept through with a "watch-out!" whistle from the locomotive. This train wasn't going to stop just anywhere. It was the Cornish express, travelling non-stop down the direct line to Exeter, none of this scenic route through Bristol. Oh no!

"Exeter St. Davids! Exeter St Davids! Change 'ere for Barnstaple. Next stop Plymouth," came the Devonshire announcement as we pulled in. We were important, no doubt about it. Other trains could wait in a siding if we came. The Cornish Riviera Express had the reputation for always being on time. We crawled over Brunel's wrought iron bridge across the Tamar and were in Cornwall. From here the train deigned to stop from time to time. "Liskeard, change here for Looe", quick stops at Bodmin Road, Lostwithiel, "Par, change for Newquay!" the Cornish voices calling down the platform. Then St. Austell, and into Truro.

Father had acquired a car and met me on the platform at Truro. He was dressed in navy blue baggy trousers with mud on them, and an old jersey. As he greeted me and we got in the car he was almost as excited as I was. The car, an elderly Ford shooting brake, was ideal for the shopping trips and load carrying. Truro is twelve miles from Polsue if one goes over the King Harry Ferry, fourteen all the way round by road. He'd already done his shopping and we travelled to Polsue the long way as the ferry wasn't running. Ruan High Lanes is in the middle of the Roseland Peninsula, a lovely part of south Cornwall and even lovelier in the immediate post war period with very little traffic around. At the hamlet we turned off onto a tiny lane between high banks, just wide enough for the car. A mile down a hill and up the other side and there was the imposing gateway on our left. We crunched down a curving gravelled drive between rhododendrons and swung round to stop in front of a white painted Georgian house. Mother stood at the door, her arms out. While father put the car away, mother took me through a large impressive hall with dark mahogany polished doors opening off it and a grand staircase going up at the back, dividing at a half landing on which I recognised our old grandfather clock. We went through a door, along a dark passage a few yards to a huge kitchen where Jane was busy at a sink.

"Hallo, little brother," but no kisses. Jane was not the demonstrative type, certainly not with young brothers. "Lots of jobs for you to get stuck into."

We had tea in the kitchen sitting around the big scrubbed table, the warmest room in the house by virtue of a large double-fronted Aga. Under the table was a dog basket occupied by our own wire-haired terrier, which answered to the name Judy. By now it was dark and father had lit a paraffin mantle lamp that gave out quite a good light accompanied by a comforting hiss. It was like Comp all over again. Way out here in the country there was no gas, no electricity and no mains water or sewerage. We were on our own, and a long way from the comfortable urban conveniences of Byfleet. Exploring outside would have to wait until morning. I listened while they took it in turns to tell me all that had been done so far. Brambles covered most of the house when they arrived, some of them going right over the roof. Dry rot had been discovered in several areas, and the builders were working on it now, cutting out and removing all infected timbers, spraying fungicide everywhere. The floor in one of the front rooms was rotten and here one could stand on the bare earth under the house and look straight up to chinks of light coming through the roof slates two floors above. A complete window frame had been taken out of one of the back downstairs rooms, and the mild night air blew in and rattled the door. In spite of the gaps, before going to bed my parents carefully locked both front and back doors out of habit from their urban days. "A bit of repair here and there" had become a major internal rebuild and would cost thousands. Father was worried about how he would pay. Where were the Jennings? Not here yet? Coming at Easter. Wasn't Jorrocks going to oversee all the repairs, then? He'd visited a couple of times apparently, was now trying to sell his own house at Chobham, and was in the process of buying a small place in St. Mawes for Muriel and himself to live. No, they wouldn't be living with us at Polsue. I was rather glad. It meant we would have the place to ourselves in the off-season, just the family.

I recognised other furniture from Woodcombe spread sparsely around, the old dinner gong—a beaten brass drum hanging between two ivory tusks on an ebony stand was in the hall, and our one or two precious rugs which father cherished so much lost here in this vast old building. I had been given a bedroom in the front of the house, one that would be a guest room once things were organised. I slept well that night with the soft west-country air wafting in through the window, the utter silence of the countryside—until about four in the morning when a barking dog from a farm a mile away woke me up. Guests would later have that same experience: they couldn't sleep because it was so quiet.

In the morning I explored everywhere. Our water came from a covered spring just in front of the house, overflowing into a pond surrounded by trees. The name "Polsue" means the house by the pool. It was lovely soft water, pure and really nice to drink. We pumped it up to a tank above the kitchen by a simple pump attached to the wall outside our back door, operated by turning a huge hand wheel. Every day someone had to give the wheel a couple of hundred turns to supply sufficient water to last the day. Also in the small back yard between a large log store and the coal bunker (anthracite for the Aga) was a Lister stationary engine coupled to a 50-volt generator. Around the sides of this engine room stood twenty-five large lead-acid cells, each about a foot high. This was the electricity supply for a simple lights-only system around the house. The engine was in pieces when I first saw it, but was expected to be working by the time we opened for guests in the summer. There were only two lavatories in the house when we moved in, disgorging into a septic tank at the bottom of the orchard. The house had been built as a manor house in early Victorian times, with a large stable block set fifty yards to one side. This comprised a yard with a building running across the back of it with a central room complete with fireplace and a little loft room above, a pair of loose boxes on either side, and beyond each of them a large coach house. A narrow passage ran down beside the central room to the cowshed behind. Here was a series of linked buildings with a midden to one side, chicken houses the other and a large woodcutting shed with apple store over it at the back. Jane took me round explaining how they would upgrade the cowshed by concreting the earthen floor, install proper feeding troughs and partitions, and build a couple of pigsties. Beyond the stables a track led down from the road to our bottom field, the biggest at six acres, with a stream running down one side. There was a neglected copse at the end full of fallen trees and brambles, which would no doubt provide us with plenty of firewood in the coming years.

To one side of the house was attached a crumbling conservatory which father had great plans to restore for tomato growing, then some attractive lawns, a flat area which had once been a tennis court, and a path leading down to the stream again and our 'dell', a euphemism for a jungly area which had once been a lovely streamside garden. Now it was overrun with bamboos, an enormous gunnera on the edge of a dammed section of the stream, and several exotic trees (years later we discovered some banana trees half buried there). This is a right of way, leading across the stream over a little bridge and up the hill on the other side to Penhallow farm, our nearest neighbour. Half a mile beyond Penhallow and over another hill is Pendower beach, a gorgeous sandy bay. At the back of our house a retaining wall with steps led up to our remaining two fields, one of them a two acre field which father planned to convert to his market garden, and the other just a small patch with twenty or so apple trees. There was an acre or two of beech woodland between the house and the lane with the drive bisecting it, a rookery in the tops of the beeches. The whole establishment emanated a friendly welcome, only tempered somewhat by the slightly unsettling spooky atmosphere imparted by the non-stop cawing of rooks.

Jane and I walked through the dell, and over to Penhallow to collect milk. The farm was very basic, just a traditional Cornish farmhouse, cobbled yard all round, with several sheds and byres. The farmer, Willie Thomas, was crossing the yard as we arrived. Willie wore gumboots and shorts, summer and winter, and farmed his hundred acres with two lovely shire horses. Nothing had changed on his farm for fifty years and we were so fortunate that two of his fields sloped down to our stream, so that they formed the major part of the view from the Polsue front windows. When Willie worked his fields, we enjoyed the magical sight of the two great horses pulling a plough with Willie clumping along behind. Like several cottagers in the locality, we'd obtained our own bottles and caps, taking the clean empties along each day and collecting full ones, half full of cream, for Willie milked the big South Devon cows which gave milk with a 10% butterfat content. That milk was as organic as it could be, for no chemical had ever been used on his farm, and the cows lived on the pasture year round, never even being fed concentrates. We stopped for a long chat, for Willie was never rushed. His father, now in his eighties, appeared from the farmhouse and joined in while I, enjoying the unadulterated Cornish dialect as you will only find spoken by people who have never travelled nor rubbed shoulders with incomers, tried to remember the form of their speech so that I could attempt to emulate them. The true Cornish are Celts, broad shouldered and of medium height, generally dark complexioned with blue eyes. All Willie's family were like this, though Willie himself was painfully thin. How he survived we never knew, for it must have been backbreaking subsistence farming. Never, ever, did Willie take a day off and he lived till he was really old.

We headed back with our two bottles, plus some new laid eggs, Jane chatting away about plans for our menagerie of animals that would, hopefully, include a horse. From the hill one could see a dip with the blue of Gerrans Bay and could certainly smell the salty air in the breeze. There was always a breeze in these parts with nothing between us and America, as we were continually reminded around the house with the trees whispering to each other. Only at night did it go really quiet, uncannily so. I had to remind myself this was December, and here we were out walking without a coat, feeling the warm sunshine, and with grass still actively growing beside the path. The Cornish soil, reddish clay-rich, peppered with broken shale and lumps of blue-pink limestone, was so different to the gravelly stuff back at home. But, what was I thinking? This is home, for goodness sake. I broke into a run at the thought, Jane chasing me, the milk bottles clinking in their metal carrier.

The field flanking our other boundary belonged to Trenestrall, a small farm with just a few hundred acres down a side road on the other side of our lane. It was farmed by Jim Eva, never seen out of a leaky pair of wellie boots. He was a bit grander than Willie Thomas in that he employed a cowman. His wife kept poultry and it was rumoured Jim and his wife had not spoken to one another for ten years or more. I can't believe this was so, since they were such nice individuals, though I never actually saw them together, except once when I was with a group of people helping Jim harvest his corn, and his wife appeared at lunchtime with a basket of pasties and a gallon can of tea. At corn harvesting time Jim drove his Fordson Major tractor, the cowman sat on the reaper-and-binder at the back trying to keep it working while four of us followed behind with pitchforks collecting the sheaves as they came off the back of the binder, throwing two outer rows in to join a central, bigger, row all ready for a fifth person to build traditional stooks, each containing a dozen sheaves. As the area of uncut corn dwindled to a small square in the centre of the field the rabbits began to make a run for it. Out came the guns and if we were lucky there would be free-range rabbit casserole for dinner. The stooks stood all autumn, until one day in the early winter we carted them to Jim's yard where his elderly thrashing machine thundered all day long, producing sackfuls of corn, a huge amount of straw which would be made into stacks nearby, and a pile of chaff which got everywhere, especially down the back of one's neck. I loved these harvesting days, the camaraderie of the team of helpers, mostly local people from the nearby hamlets of Treworthal and Treworga, and the sheer hard work. Nowadays a half-million pound combine would deal with a field like Jim's in a matter of hours.

Jim was really a 'marster man'—a practical multi-trade artisan, more an engineer than a farmer. He had a full-size rusting sawmill in his yard, on which he sawed chestnut timbers for making all his own farm gates and parts for farm carts. His tractor fuelled by TVO needed a delicate touch to get it started, which only Jim seemed able to give it. He also had a motorboat moored at St. Anthony's opposite St. Mawes, in which he and his dog went fishing from time to time. He was a delightful neighbour, one of the best.

Opposite the gate to Polsue was a little cottage in which lived an elderly couple, the Gartens. Our arrival was a great help to them, for there were no other houses nearby, and some tradesmen who would not normally come down the lane would now do so, and call on them as well. What tradesmen? Well there was the newspaperman. He arrived in a little van about lunchtime, which he parked outside the Garten's cottage. He then darted through the woods near our side gate, collecting a stick, which he kept just inside to ward off any wild dogs he might encounter. Then there was Mr Pedlar. He ran the sub post office-cum-village shop at Ruan High Lanes, and also did the local postal deliveries on a heavy old bicycle correctly dressed in his GPO peaked cap. This service was wonderful, for not only did he open our back door and place any mail in a box we kept inside, but would take any letters waiting there for posting, and if some were unstamped he came on into the kitchen and told us how many stamps he'd had to put on them so that we could pay on our next visit to the shop. If there was a parcel to be delivered which was too big for his bicycle, he phoned us so that we could call in sometime. He, of course, guessed very accurately what might be in the parcel so that he could tell us whether it might be urgent or not. He was one of the best purveyors of local news, always so essential to country folk. New tradesmen who hadn't previously visited the Gartens now included the fishmonger Hunkin, a large man wearing a white coat and reeking of fish, who always greeted one with a shake of a wet fishy hand. He delivered fresh fish landed at Mevagissey that same morning, the finest and freshest fish imaginable. Hunkin also happened to be the brother of the then Bishop of Truro, but you would never guess it. Our butcher, who also operated out of the back of a van, had a shop in Veryan. He obtained a lot of his meat from local sources, which he either collected direct from the farm or was brought to him on the hoof. There was a meat marketing board, which operated strict controls when we first moved down to Cornwall, so I don't know how he complied with those. The quality of his meat was the finest, only surpassed once or twice a year when he obtained his meat from us!

~*~

All too soon the holidays were over, and it was back to school once more. The art master, Mr Liddell, had discovered I could draw and had a sense of colour, so he gave me a great deal of help. Only one or two boys in each class showed any promise, the others just having to be kept under control, so he was always pleased to find a new protégée. As School Certificate time loomed nearer, those of us taking art for a subject were given a lot of coaching.

"I never have a failure," he said confidently in his peculiar drawl, a voice we all imitated when out of earshot. "You will get a distinction, Reeve, if you can just master this," as he proceeded to demonstrate some technique. He was always right, all his pupils getting either a distinction or a credit pass. We wondered whether he took their finished work home to 'improve' it before sending it on to the examiners.

Next to the art schools was the geography department. This was under the control of a wild one-eyed man, Captain 'Hal' Halstead, ex-professional soldier who took an active part in running the school JTC, and whom it was rumoured kept a tin trunk under his bed full of explosives and guns. I never saw that side of him, but I did enjoy his classes. There was a huge epidiascope in the classroom, on which he could project maps onto a screen over the blackboard, the only visual aid used in the whole school. The maps had big chunks of red on them, these defining the British Empire, still at the time a large part of the world. I was intrigued that the east and west sides of the Atlantic looked as if they had once been joined together, but when I asked whether that could have been so, the suggestion was firmly poo-poo'd. We learnt very little about how our planet evolved, and I don't remember hearing any explanation about why the magnetic pole was different to the true pole nor why it moved about. The earth's fluid mantle was hinted at—after all, most of us had read Conan Doyle's Professor Challenger's attempt to dig down into it, and that's what volcanic lava is. Geography was really confined to the physical and political parts of the world as they existed at the time. Much later on, when I was a sixth former and able to devote one or two lessons a week to a 'fun' subject, I took a lightweight course in meteorology, a subject that interested me affecting as it did my outdoor life at home. I did well at geography, probably because of my ability for spatial interpretation. Drawing in the art classroom next door employed some of those same skills. It was Mr Liddell who commented to me one day that I would probably end up as an engineer.

"Whenever I ask you to explain something, boy, you reach for pencil and paper. You find it easier than words." He was quite right. I do tend to sketch anything that needs explaining. And I have always enjoyed maps, ever since the prep school days when we learnt map reading in the scouts. Orienteering, as they like to call it nowadays, has never been a problem for me, and when I am out in the country I see in my mind a map of where I am going.

Right from the beginning our curriculum included separate lessons in biology, physics and chemistry, but I did not persevere in biology, which was a shame. I am afraid I never really clicked with the somewhat dreary biology teacher. Physics was my favourite academic subject, for I could immediately understand what each physics subject was about. My quest for 'why' was answered at every turn. It also went hand in hand with applied mathematics which I enjoyed for the same reason. The physics master never seemed to be quite in touch with his class, which was a pity as I was so keen to get on and impatient whenever he had to restrain some boy or other and thereby waste our time. The senior chemistry master, Leslie Price, was a superb teacher, though sadly I wasn't in his class until the sixth form. He also had only one eye, though unlike Hal Halstead who wore a pirate-like black eye patch, Price's non-seeing eye just stared vaguely to one side. There was the story of three new boys sitting in a row in his class:

"What's your name?" enquired Price of the first one.

"Jones, sir," said the second.

"I wasn't talking to you, Jones," said Price turning to him.

"I wasn't speaking, sir," said the third.

Mr Price always called us 'gentlemen'. He once said that if you treat boys as adults, they will behave appropriately, and he must have been right for nobody ever took advantage of him; important for a science teacher surrounded as he is by potentially dangerous chemicals and equipment.

However, Mr Price generally only took the 'A' stream, so I was not taught by him until I was in the sixth form. Chemistry for me was taught by Mr Patchett, a genial man who chose to be totally unobservant of our misdemeanours in class. He never admonished anyone for not paying attention, leaving it to the keener members of his class to shut them up when the rowdiness became too great. Even so, it was a great temptation to play pranks on the poor man, the favourite being to choose a moment when he had a splendid experiment up and running on his demonstration bench, with a Bunsen burner hotting up some lethal-looking brew in a flask. Then one of the boys at the back of the laboratory would connect a tube from his local gas pipe to the nearby water supply and turn both taps on together. Usually the results were most spectacular as the Bunsen flame on the bench was suddenly replaced by a jet of cold water, causing the flask to shatter spilling its possibly corrosive contents all over the teacher's notes. At the end of class he would leave the room, still genially smiling, the tails of his MA gown adorned by now with test-tube clamps which flapped behind him as he sailed down the road on his bicycle.

The most boring subject after Latin was history. The teacher for this was just a boring person, colourless with no personality and no imagination. His idea of teaching history was to make us recite dates by rote, and to copy bits out of his textbook onto the board for us to copy down in turn into our school books; hardly an efficient use of time for either the teacher or his pupils. I didn't discover how wonderful a subject history could be until years later I attended some superb lectures on Naval history given by a Cambridge don, who had us sitting on the edge of our seats almost clamouring for more. After that in the boring stakes came French, boring for me because it was a language, for which I have this mental block. English literature was one step up on French, and English grammar one step up again. English was taught by my form master, Mr Coulson, another somewhat colourless man about whom I can remember little. Divinity I found neither interesting nor boring; I just accepted it as part of my general education. Only later did I regret not learning anything about comparative religions, which would have been so useful in today's world. One of my more boring subjects (so boring I don't even remember what subject it was) was taught by an exceptionally shortsighted master with powerful pebble-lensed spectacles. In order to relieve the tedium, we discovered by trial and error that beyond the third row he could see very little, and wondered whether it would be safe to cut class if one's seat was beyond that. Nobody had the nerve to put it to the test. Somebody sitting near the window found he could employ a small piece of mirror to reflect a beam of sunlight onto the blackboard, and gave us a lot of fun baiting this unfortunate master with a phantom chalk mark which the poor man chased around the board with his duster, trying to rub it out.

After my first year I was taught mathematics by a big rubbery man, a Welshman with the unforgettable name of Owen Roby Jones. He had two chins and perhaps another one or two more at the back of his neck, and he rolled along as he walked. He was an ex-army man and was in charge of our JTC when he appeared on Wednesday afternoons in major's uniform, tapping his thigh with a swagger stick as he bounced around. He had the rich bass voice of a true Welshman, and sang in our choir drowning out all the other basses. Hal Halstead avoided the parades we had to attend, each house having its own platoon with one of the senior boys of JUO rank shouting at us to dress by the right or stand still. The other JTC official was our Quartermaster. This old professional with the Great War medal ribbons lived in the armoury, a brick hut by the side of the Army House tennis court, with a miniature rifle range behind it. He looked after all the firearms and taught shooting. He must have done this pretty well for Bradfield always fielded a most successful team at Bisley. I never saw the Quartermaster out of uniform, so perhaps that was all he had to wear. I quite enjoyed shooting on the miniature range, one of the few skills I was better at than my peers. Not so much fun was learning all about the Bren gun. This clumsy piece of equipment was far heavier to lug around than one's rifle, and we seemed to spend all our time taking the long-suffering thing to pieces and then trying to get it back together again.

Several years into my time at Bradfield my physics master, who enjoyed sailing, started up a naval section, and about twenty boys thankfully escaped from all the shouting parades and spent their JTC afternoons being taught to sail dinghies on the peaceful Thames at Pangbourne, much to the amusement of the Nautical College lads whom they met on the river. By this time I had been promoted sergeant and was in line for becoming a JUO myself, so I didn't bother to move over, especially as by now I probably had more experience than the sailing instructor himself.

The winter term ended with a school mini-marathon, every boy partaking whether he liked it or not. Although I still suffered from Achilles tendon problems, I found I was able to run provided I didn't flex my left ankle too much, which meant I had to limp slightly. The six mile run was off-road, over muddy fields and tracks, and finished by splashing across a pond behind the geography building, hauling oneself up a six foot weir by means of a rope placed there for that purpose, then jumping into the shallow river Pang to cross to the finishing line on the other side. On the day of the run all the village girls crowded this area for it was well known that the white cotton shorts we wore for running became virtually transparent when they got wet, and their unfortunate owners had to run past an appreciative crowd of fans in as dignified a way as possible.

In the spring of my second year came the big freeze. This was 1947, the year when serious snow came in February and a thaw didn't set in until April. The parts of the school I lived in were quite inadequately heated, and we were continually cold. We crunched around in this snow, kicking it off our shoes when we entered any building so that there was always a mucky puddle just inside every entrance, but there were great compensations for such weather, for all field sports had to be abandoned. Another activity was born that kept us fit: tobogganing. The meadow behind the science laboratories had a good slope, and this quickly acquired an icy surface providing a near lethal run for an assortment of homemade toboggans. I loved it. Again, you see, here was something I could do, not involving some horrible ball nor requiring me to strain my bad Achilles tendon. At the bottom of the field one had to bring one's toboggan to a hasty stop before crashing into the gate that led on to the Bucklebury road. Sometimes boys abandoned ship at the last minute leaving their empty toboggan to slip under the gate at high speed, across the road, and down a lane on the far side. It was not long before we would leave the gate open, post a sentry (the bus and an occasional car used that road) and it was then possible to hurtle straight across and get another hundred yards of fun. If anything came, the sentry closed the gate abruptly, and one had to execute a swift stop, usually not very safely.

This meadow was the scene of another memorable incident at school after it had reverted to its normal use as a pasture for the long-suffering neighbouring farmer's herd of milking cows, and it involved Mr Patchett, my chemistry master. One autumn term round about the lead up to November the fifth he arranged to give an evening lecture on explosives. Needless to say he had a full house, the small lecture theatre packed until there was no more standing room. He demonstrated all sorts of ways to make a good bang, his object, I think, to try to inculcate a need for care and safety involving any such experimentation. However, he chose to start his lecture in a most spectacular way by sweeping into the room with a "Now, boys, I propose to talk about explosives" then promptly throwing a switch, whereupon there was a searing flash outside accompanied by an enormous bang which rattled every window in the building, frightening the life out of us. A smell of cordite wafted in through the window.

Somebody called out, "Please, Sir, there's a herd of cows out there", whereupon Mr Patchett blanched convincingly and said, with some hesitation, "Oh, I didn't know." I think he did though, because the farmer had put his cows into in a different meadow that night. Mr Patchett's reputation had a nice boost after that, and we spent the rest of the lecture paying rapt attention. Inevitably various private experiments resulted from that occasion. A friend had secreted a number of unused blank cartridges from JTC field days that we prised open, tipped out the cordite, and made our own little devices. Mine was to drill a hole down the centre of a broomstick, fill it with cordite then plug the hole tightly. To detonate this I drilled a small hole through the side, threaded a piece of fuse wire through and by means of a long length of flex, connect this to the mains. I pushed the stick into the ground outside CB's sitting room window late one evening, ran the flex back to my study not so far away, plugged it in and switched on. The bang was nothing like so spectacular as my crazy chemistry master's but it certainly had the effect of waking up CB. However quick he was to look out of his window he never found anything, for I would hastily pull the remnants of the wire back through my own window, and the broomstick—well, that would split clean down the middle and the two halves hurtle into the air, never to be seen again. Fortunately I soon tired of this somewhat dangerous activity.

A quieter side of my life revolved around the Music Schools. In his younger days father had known someone who would be called upon to play the piano at any party they happened to attend, and thought what a marvellous gift that must be. He was anxious for me to be taught to play, especially as he knew of my attempts at Clayesmore. So I was enrolled for a lesson every Tuesday taken by a useless peripatetic teacher with a serious addiction to the weed. There were a dozen or so little cells over the bakery opposite Army House, each one housing an upright piano and room for a second chair but not much more. I would fight my way through the tobacco smoke into one of these fug holes and be put through my paces by this man who, I am afraid, didn't teach me anything. He kept the window tight shut and turned up the radiator full blast, so half an hour of that was quite enough to endure. Having instrument lessons also entitled one to make use of a very comfortable, carpeted music room with armchairs and a lovely old gramophone with a huge horn. Here one could sit and doze off in the company of boys of different ages from various Houses, listening to the classics. From time to time someone would have to re-sharpen the thorn needle, but I believe the machine had an electric motor to operate the turntable, so at least it didn't require winding up. My memories are that the sound was quite good, but then that was before the days of the LP.

One of the other pupils from my own house was a boy called Fry, the elder of two brothers whose father was leader of the Reading Symphony Orchestra. I got to know him quite well because he, too, learnt the piano, but as he was two years my senior we were both really breaking the socialising mores of the day. His father was prevailed upon by the school to invite the Reading Symphony Orchestra to give the occasional concert in Big Hall, generally light classics which I enjoyed. I also sang treble in a performance of Handel's Messiah one year and entered a singing competition where I had to sing 'How Beautiful are the Feet…' from that oratorio. On one occasion the BBC graciously decided to record one of the Big Hall concerts and set up their recording studio a nearby classroom. This took all day, unloading and humping massively heavy equipment, arranging microphones all over the hall and running festoons of wire across to the recording room. Notices appeared saying "SILENCE—Recording in Progress". I was more interested in this than the concert itself, and must have got under their feet while

I hung around asking questions and trying ineffectually to help. During the extensive microphone tests that took place prior to the recording, several acetate master discs were cut, and I was given one or two. I still have them to this day, the wavy sound on them scratchy and thin. I thought the life of an engineer in the BBC must be very glamorous, giving an entrée to almost anywhere, and wondered whether that might be a good career to go for.

Round about this time I had—what was for me—a frightening experience. I had been wandering around in one of the common rooms in Army House when I started seeing jagged flashes of light, and the periphery of my vision began to disappear. The flashes of light became more intense and the centre of my vision disappeared entirely. Every migraine sufferer will instantly recognise this as the 'aura' that often precedes a migraine attack. My mother would sometimes suffer from migraine, and would take an aspirin and retire to bed for a few hours. Now it was my turn. Quite suddenly the searing headache came on and I had a desperate need to lie down and shut my eyes. I did this and was asleep almost instantly, waking a little later with the headache completely gone and my vision restored to normal. The Kember told me to report to her if I ever experienced this phenomenon again, and just once more I did so.

Outings from school were virtually non-existent, unless we organised our own. One older boy in Army House, Stephen Bailey-Reynolds, was a railway buff able to quote the name and number of every locomotive, knew which train went where and when—a sort of talking Bradshaw, and organised a trip for some of us to visit the carriage works at Swindon. I also joined a small party invited to visit Reading sidings where we drove up and down a quiet piece of line on the footplate of a sizable engine each taking turns to operate the steam valve, the brake and, of course, the whistle. Wonderful! Bailey-Reynolds' great achievement was to be able to recite and spell out in full all 55 letters of that most famous railway station name, Llanfairpwllgyngyllgogerychyrndrobwllllantysi-logogogoch. A Welsh-man himself, he would recite the station name in a rich bass Welsh voice, lovely to hear.

~*~

A huge amount had happened at Polsue during my previous term at school. The place hummed with expectancy. Jorrocks had settled in to his bungalow high on the outskirts of St. Mawes and came over every day to oversee progress and do those engineering things he excelled at. We had applied for an electricity supply to be brought over from the main road a mile away, though it would be a year before we could get this installed, and in the meantime our generator was now running reliably. A water diviner had marched around our top field and declared there was water there, and a borehole had been dug, a 'Climax' wind-driven water pump installed over it at the top corner of the field with a 10,000 gallon reservoir beside it, water being piped down to the house, the stables and a standpipe in the top field. The builders had finished and moved elsewhere. We had decorated in their wake, and now more furniture was starting to arrive. Father had employed a dour Cornishman, Dick Harris, a young local man freshly demobbed, who was as strong as an ox and did all the labouring work in our two-acre field, now being planted up with crops for the market garden. We also had another invaluable worker, young Rudi, a quiet German POW who was brought over each day from a nearby encampment. Although the war had been over for many months, there were still German and Italian POWs who, pending repatriation, were employed wherever they could be useful. Rudi came from farming stock and enjoyed his outdoor work with us. Having been indoctrinated about fraternising with Germans during the war, I was unsure how to behave sharing morning tea breaks with Rudi, but he took the initiative and was the perfect gentleman. Those morning tea breaks were memorable for me as the outdoor workers (Father, Jane, Rudi and me when I was at home) sat down at the kitchen table and chatted. Later, when we had guests, we polished off the surplus toast left over from breakfast, by this time soft and leathery, which we spread liberally with gorgeous beef dripping, all salty and yummy.

Our stable area had been refurbished and we would soon be getting a couple of piglets and in due course a couple of South Devon cows. Jane was already looking after twenty or so pullets, bought as day-old chicks from a hatchery in Sticker. She also had a couple of muscovy ducks she'd taken a fancy to, who were behaving very much as if a family might be imminent. Mother was getting occasional help in the kitchen from Mrs Buckingham, a lovely old lady from Treworthal who, in spite of her name, was as Cornish as they come and had never been further afield than Truro in her life. She greeted me like a visitor from another continent.

"What 'tis like, up in t'England, Jarn," she asked me, and listened with disbelief and a shaking head when I told her about all the people, noise, trains and houses. "I don' know as us would like that," she muttered. " 'Tain't be for we."

At the back of the house was a stone-flagged 'back' kitchen that had been a sort of scullery-cum-laundry. It had an enormous fireplace with a granite lintel that they had uncovered when stripping out a tatty cupboard. We converted this room to a little bar, and had an iron backplate cast with a Royal Artillery badge in the centre behind the fireplace. The chimney had been cleared and we would have a log fire in this room to add a bit of character. We'd found a high-backed settle in a local sale and a number of Boer war mementoes that came down from father's side of the family were hung on the wall. In the corner, we had stripped out a copper (now polished up and in use as a log box) and in its place fitted a bar counter, while Jorrocks had built shelves and was already starting to collect bottles, optics, glasses and bar-top trivia to set the place off. Father was worried—this time by his concern that if ever we made any profit, Jorrocks would surely drink it all. It was all very well for him, father would say, with Muriel in St. Mawes with the money, but the Reeve family had to depend on a profitable venture for our living.

Father had discovered a metal AA shield that had once hung on the wall beside the gate, with ' AA** Hotel' on it, and another similar sized shield with 'Polsue Manor Hotel' painted on it in an Old English Typeface. Briefly before the war Polsue had been a small hotel, but it must have been very simple. Mrs Eva told us how one morning someone from the house rushed down and desperately asked, "Have you any eggs. I must have half a dozen now!" Then, seeing some in a box, grabbed them and hurried off.

"I told 'er them be ones that hadn't hatched; must be many weeks old, but 'er says them'll do. Must have something for breakfast!"

I repainted both the signs and left them ready for putting up when the first guests were due. We'd started a reservations diary, and were taking one or two bookings resulting from an advertisement father had placed in The Sunday Times. We hoped to tick along through June and early July, then by the time the school holidays began we expected to have risen sufficiently up the learning curve to cope with maybe fourteen guests, sleeping in seven of the bedrooms which were now nearly ready.

A second bathroom had been installed, also a men's cloakroom near the bar. One of the back rooms had slate shelves and a perforated zinc screen across the window, and had been whitewashed all ready to become a walk-in larder. We had ordered a large refrigerator, a piece of equipment not many people were used to at that time, but essential if we were to cater properly.

That holiday for me went very quickly, with carpentry jobs, door locks to have new springs fitted, painting of course, errands to run all over the place, everybody needing another pair of hands somewhere. In no time the holidays were over and I was once again aboard the Cornish Riviera Express bound for Reading and Bradfield.

By the time I next went home (yes, Cornwall was my home and memories of the eleven years I lived in Byfleet were fast receding) we had opened, albeit in a fairly small way. I was met at Truro by Jane this time, newly qualified with her driving licence. I found her in the parcels office being chatted up by two station staff. Jane had a lovely bubbly personality and attracted all the local men wherever she went. On the way home she told me there were two families staying, with five children between them, also two couples. Mother was coping in the kitchen but hardly ever had a chance to sit down and was getting very tired. Clearly she would need help there. Jane herself was doing most of the housework, helped by another woman from Treworthal who came in the mornings. I would have to behave very well because father had been getting all twitchy about looking after the guests properly, and—Oh yes! We were getting a boat. A St. Mawes One Design, a sixteen foot half-decked boat. Father wanted me to go over to Falmouth with him to collect it.

This was wonderful news. I had hardly dared believe we would actually own a boat, and I thought of nothing else as I rushed around at home seeing all the new things. The two cows had arrived; Bella, a very big-boned large dominant one and Heather, a lightweight in-calf heifer. The two piglets had also arrived and a lot of excitable noises came from their sty. During the day Jane let them have the run of the midden, which now had quite a lot of straw in it. The cows had been put in our bottom field, and came up to the cowshed when called each day at milking times, Bella to be milked and Heather who just accompanied her. In the house the front part had become out of bounds to me until the middle of the day when the guests were out, and I duly met these guests in the bar that first evening. The two families had joined up and would walk down to Pendower beach each day, while the two couples had also joined up and, as one of them had come by car, were spending their days looking at local sights and just enjoying the countryside.

When we were on our own, father and mother told me about their mysterious visitor. One day soon after they had opened there had been a phone call from a man in London wanting to book a room for one night to check us out for a possible family visit. Father had met him at Truro, brought him back and shown him around, even suggesting he might like to get up early in the morning and join Jane at the milking. The man was very quiet and appreciative, and said he envied our new lifestyle and reckoned we would be certain to make a success of it as we were so enthusiastic and eager to please. The fresh country food was certainly a big attraction (Britain in the post war years still being in the grip of very severe food rationing, stricter even than during the war itself). After a big bacon-and-egg breakfast he went off with father to pay his bill and then admitted he would be happy to take on our account if we were interested. Oh, and his name incidentally was Ashley Courtenay. Father had written to him some weeks earlier when having difficulty with the wording of our small Sunday Times advertisement. Ashley Courtenay then asked my parents what sort of people they wanted to have come and stay at Polsue.

"People like us, I suppose," said mother, "Then we would know what they would like and how to look after them."

"Good. I was hoping you'd say that," agreed Ashley Courtenay, "I shall word the advertisements so that people who respond will be just like yourselves. Now that was my main reason for spending a night with you. I know you now and will be able to do as you ask. You'd be surprised how just one word can alter someone's idea of a place. I have about a dozen words to either win them or lose them."

And that's how it went. From then on for the next ten years a discreet advertisement would appear here and there, sometimes as part of the main 'Ashley Courtenay Recommended' display advertisement, and sometimes just by itself, generally in either The Sunday Times or sometimes The Daily Telegraph. And the people who came were just like us. We knew exactly what they would like and tried to provide it. A spin-off we hadn't thought about was that our guests were also like each other, and it was this that was largely responsible for them coming back year after year. The houseful of guests all behaved as if part of a house party, would assemble after breakfast and share cars to the beach, coming back for lunch in each others cars, would all get on together, and at meals would often mix up the tables and sit wherever they wanted. Everyone spoke to everyone else across the room, and the atmosphere couldn't have been less 'hotelly'. I think we surprised Ashley Courtenay about how well this worked, and it all began unintentionally, certainly by us. Of course, from time to time we had the occasional person, usually someone on their own, who felt out of place and unwilling to join in, but not often.

Being only a temporary visitor myself, I had a different room each time I came home. In the closed season, it would be one of the main guest bedrooms, seldom the same one twice, since they all had a paint-and-maintenance period, usually my job. During the season, I might have to sleep anywhere. Sometimes it would be a mattress on the floor in father's little office, later I took over the attic room in the stables, and later still I had a curtain across the passage leading to my parents' room with my bed and a chair behind it. As for Jane, she too had to move out of the house in the summer, and had a small caravan in a sunny part of the garden, which she made really rather nice. One year I found I had been allocated the spare room of the Garten's house across the road from our front gate, but the next year that room had overflow visitors in it. For the crucial seven weeks of the summer holidays we had to fill every possible space with visitors in order to have sufficient income to coast through the winter.

Father and I went over to Falmouth to pick up the boat. It belonged to Jennifer Holman of the mining family, and it must have been one of the last to be built before the war. She met us off the ferry at the Prince of Wales pier and rowed us out to the mooring where the boat waited. It was beautifully built, painted red with a cream deck. These boats had a sliding gunter rig in those days which meant the mast was relatively short, and there was a short bowsprit to carry the jib, normally left set permanently on a roller reefing gear. Altogether twelve of these boats had been built (we had "12" on our sail) though one or two had been lost over the years. All had been built by local boat builder Frankie Peters, whose yard was up the Percuil River at Polvarth in St. Mawes. I had seen them out occasionally, but had never seen them race together on Thursday evenings, a St. Mawes institution I was to get to know well. The boat was called 'Kestrel' and sailing her home was a delight with a gentle breeze on our quarter as she scudded along with us both sitting out on the deck. Father let me

Me aged about 15 happily sailing at St Mawes

take the helm for some of the way, and I practised going about and tried some tacking while we were in the Carrick Roads. We tied up to a mooring off Stone Quay, a small jetty on the tip of Polvarth point that belonged to the St. Mawes Sailing Club, from where our friend Geoffrey Marrecco waited for us with his dinghy to take us ashore.

So began my love affair with the sea. Whenever I was at home I was either out sailing, taking guests out, down at Stone Quay or across the river on the St. Anthony's side repairing moorings or just splashing about in our little pram. I'd quickly learnt to row this pram using short strokes lifting the oars well clear of the water, as one has to do when rowing in choppy water. I became adept at sculling a boat with a single oar in the transom cutout and waggling it to and fro like I'd seen the local ferrymen doing, though propelling a pram along this way wasn't easy. I also learnt to sail the boat single-handed, though not at first. During that first summer holiday I met a family living on the front at St. Mawes by name of Tracey who also owned a St. Mawes one-design amongst other boats. They had two teenage girls, Belinda and Mary, also a young toddler. The father, Christopher, would spend much time shut away in his writing shed in the garden working on some book, while his much younger wife sailed everywhere in a dashing style, winning all the races and very much one of the St. Mawes set. One day I had a panic call from Mrs Tracey. Was I available that evening to crew for her in the local race? Yes, I was. Jane ran me over to St. Mawes straightaway, and Mrs Tracey and I rushed down to the beach in front of their house, scrabbled aboard her dinghy, which she rowed frantically over to where her own one-design was moored. The races had already started and the five-minute gun for our class was imminent. We were still setting sail when I was ordered to cast off, leaving the dinghy on the buoy, moments before the gun went. Had we still been on the mooring, we would not have been eligible to take part. We made haste to the starting line while I was still adjusting the sails at Mrs Tracey's directions, crossing it just as the starting gun went. There were eight or nine of us in this race and it was ten minutes or so later, when we had achieved a comfortable lead over the others that I was able to explain that I hadn't raced before, nor was I very competent as yet.

"You're doing well, John. Do just as I ask, that's all you need worry about. You're a good lightweight crew. Just what we need tonight. Bring that jib in a whisker. That's fine, sit out a bit more. Fine." She looked about her continuously, watching for wind flurries on the water, keeping an eye on the rest of the fleet, watching to see how the class in front of ours was getting on, checking the set of our sails constantly, and finding time to talk to me about Kestrel and everything else, all at the same time. We tacked a lot, making use of every bit of extra wind, keeping out of the flood tide wherever we could, getting upwind when the breeze picked up a little. Soon we were amongst the boats in the class ahead of ours. Two exhilarating hours later we creamed over the finishing line to the satisfying sound of a gun. We had won. I learnt more from that one race than from any amount of reading books or attending classes or from father's patient but inadequate coaching.

Back at home father told me the Traceys had lived overseas for many years while Christopher was in the diplomatic service, first in the Sudan and later at Tripoli where he was the big cheese. They had started a sailing club in Tripoli for the British residents and years later when I called in to Tripoli I found the clubhouse still there, tatty and unloved, with a faded trophy panel on the wall. Most of the names on it were Traceys. They sailed International fourteen footers then, and still had one of these boats in their St. Mawes garage, one in which they'd won some important championship race before the war, and there were photographs of them with their boat together with such luminaries as Peter Scott and Stewart Morris. After that first time I raced on Thursday evenings whenever I could raise a crew, usually one of the guests, but occasionally it would be Belinda. Belinda was lovely. To a gauche fourteen year old, she was everything. Blue-eyed with lovely blonde hair and a peaches-and-cream complexion. I just adored her, but was far too naïve to know how to cement such a friendship, terrified I might say or do something which might drive her away, so I did nothing. My parents approved of this friendship, since the Traceys fitted their 'nice to know' category. But it was a year or two yet before I really discovered what girls were for!

A retired colonel with his wife and daughter stayed a couple of times, and were considered suitable to 'know'. Their name was Chetwynd-Stapleton, and they lived in a rather snooty private estate in Weybridge called Whiteley Village where Colonel Chetwynd-Stapleton was the warden and chief administrator. With their daughter, Jean, who was about twelve years my senior, they were staying at Polsue as I reached that excruciating age when I fell in love for the first time, so Jean was the target. She took it very well, probably rather amused by my clumsy but inadequate attempts to control my passion. She gave me a gentle kiss full on the lips as the terrible moment came when they had to depart, leaving me in a whirl. Mother secretly enjoyed watching this blossoming, but never told me at the time.

Then there was the local girl from Treworthal who came during the peak season to help do the rooms in the mornings. I caught up with her in the airing cupboard where I clumsily kissed her. There were no inhibitions on her part, and it was probably me holding back from sheer fright and a terrible guilt, which saved the day on that occasion.

One year the Portscatho amateur dramatic society put on some production in the village hall, and I wandered along to see whether I might join in. They needed someone to look after the backstage work, so I built some scenery and installed a light or two. As this was just a one-off production, I built everything on the cheap. And I mean real cheap. Lighting was a row of 200-watt lamp bulbs with large biscuit tins for reflectors, some of which were on dimmers. On the strength of what I learnt in one of my physics lessons I made two dimmers from a couple of salt-glazed soil pipes, setting a plug of concrete in the bottom and standing them upright. In the bottom I put a copper plate, connected to a wire via a switch to the nearest mains socket. I filled the pipe with seawater, added a bit of extra salt for luck and into this dangled another copper plate, which I connected to the other pin on the mains socket. Nothing was earthed because there were no metal parts to earth anything to. To prevent electric shock, I raised and lowered the dangling plate with a piece of string over a pulley, and when I first dipped it into the brine, there was a satisfactory hissing sound and the lights came on dimly, getting brighter as I lowered the plate. I set this up a couple of days before the first performance but by the time the show was due to start, I noticed water had seeped through the concrete plug at the bottom and spread across the floor. Furthermore I think it must have been a bit 'live' because I could feel a tingle when I went too near. How I survived without getting electrocuted heavens only knows, and it just shows what you can get away with if you are as ignorant as I was, enjoying the protection of a benevolent guardian angel. Fortunately the two shows went off before anything blew up. There was meant to be a nice fire which one of the actresses had to warm her hands by, so I achieved the effect of this by illuminating her face with a flickering red light which looked quite effective. At one point in the play this lass had to exit on my side of the stage from which there was no way out except by creeping across the back behind the furniture on the set. Therefore she spent fifteen minutes or so alone with me until her next entrance. There's not a lot you can do when a girl is plastered with stage makeup, and is concerned about going on stage within minutes, but we did hold hands, really for the fun of doing so with her parents just a few feet away on the other side of a cardboard wall!

But my chief love, which developed slowly with continued approval from both sets of parents, was the adorable Belinda. We often went sailing, just the two of us, and I remember one time after we'd put Kestrel back on her mooring which was across the Percuil river hard on the far shore, when we lay down in the bottom of the boat and spent a blissful half hour just enjoying one another's proximity. Sure, there was a bit of fondling, but nothing more intense than that. This was the early fifties and such freedom was not de facto then.

Belinda and Mary went to Sherborne School for Girls, and were away at various other times, so then I was alone once more with nobody of my own age around. During this period I became briefly entangled with a lass from St. Mawes who worked incredibly hard in her parent's holiday business, only getting brief moments off during the evenings. I think she was as desperate as I was and certainly more experienced than anyone I had come across at that time. We enjoyed frantic spells standing on the granite steps leading down from the road to the harbour, just below the wall where it was unlit. Nobody much ever walked about at night then, so it wasn't as obvious as it sounds. Then while I was away at school again, she was carried off by a highly eligible suitor with loads of money and comfortable prospects and is now mistress of a stately home. Such is life.

We tried the nearest church at Philleigh, but didn't feel at home there. The church was one of three looked after by the vicar, one Bobby Mossop, whose main church was at Ruan Lanihorne. I remember one Sunday kneeling at the altar rail while he was administering communion and noticed that under his cassock he was wearing muddy gumboots. Whilst waiting my turn, I couldn't help also noticing the soles of the shoes of other communicants kneeling in front of me. All were muddy and most had holes or patches. I remembered when I was younger, mother's insistence that I should always wear my newest shoes when going to church. Obviously that advice was not heeded in these parts. Maybe God was more forgiving with country folk. We eventually found a charismatic vicar at Portscatho, and ex RAF man, so went there. Our nearest pub was next to the Philleigh church. It had its regulars who were all 'locals'. We, of course, were not locals, even though we lived in the area. We were very definitely incomers and were never allowed to forget it. Only after some thirty years did our family really become integrated, by which time I had flown up country again. One year a film crew came down to film Treasure Island, complete with a square-rigger, pirates, the lot. They had a base at King Harry, where the boats were kept overnight, and once filming was finished for the day the cast headed straight for Philleigh's pub. Robert Newton was the actor playing Long John Silver and frightened the life out of me as well as most of the locals. He would drink prodigious amounts of beer and buy drinks for everyone, until he became roaring drunk and then the fights began. The landlord reckoned the custom, good as it was, didn't really help his meagre profits at the end of the day by the time the damage was paid for, but it did put him on the map. During filming, the square-rigger (which was a largish yacht complete with engine and a made-up superstructure) would potter up and down outside St. Anthony's, and I would sail as close as I was allowed to. They had a platform built out from the side of the boat on which the large camera was mounted. From here they filmed unfortunate sailors being made to walk the plank. This part of the West Country has often been used as a location purporting to be in some exotic tropical region, but I always think the giveaway is the colour of the sea, and of course I recognize individual rocks and such features.

It was back to school again for another term, hearing from my friends there all the things they had been up to during their holidays, mostly happenings in and around London, or holidays abroad. No one had been as far west as Exeter, it seemed. My sort of life sounded as strange to them as theirs did to me.

Term did not always end on the same day of the week. When it ended on a Wednesday I would be met at Truro by either father or Jane who would be visiting the market that day. If it was on a Friday, then there was the thrice-weekly Portscatho bus I could catch, getting off at Ruan High Lanes. This was a most useful bus, as it also carried parcels and often when mother needed something from Truro she would phone up and ask the shop to put it on the bus. This bus passed near to Tregony, a village about halfway, but did not go up the extremely steep hill into Tregony itself, any passengers having to manage that last quarter mile on foot. On one occasion the driver stopped at the bottom of the hill as usual, called out if anyone wanted to get off, saying he was a bit early so would take them up the hill, and meet any new passengers on the way perhaps. We went grinding up this hill in bottom gear all the way to where it opens out to a wide bit of the village where he could turn round. Actually he did this because he had run out of ciggies, and wanted another packet from the village shop there. There's country buses for you!

5

Polsue

Time went by and we settled into a routine at Polsue. In the next few years, there were a number of changes. Firstly Jorrocks became bored and sold his share of the venture, fortunately before he'd quite drunk all the profits. He was replaced by a retired naval man, Commander Stocker, who had spent his retirement gratuity on buying his partnership. He was a single man, much more businesslike, but with no experience of business. Consequently he worried even more than father as he saw his share of Polsue not growing at all, while the Reeve family enjoyed far greater benefits; at least our whole family was living fairly well.

We took in one or two permanent guests, bachelors needing somewhere to live. The first to settle in was Ian Main, living on family money made from the manufacture of gas cookers before the war. He was ten years older than Jane, but nevertheless took a great fancy to her, but Jane held him at arm's length, much preferring Cornish farmers at that time. (Jim Eva amused us all by saying " 'Er been putting they calves out to grass again, proper 'ansome, they be". Jane always wore extremely short shorts in summertime, which didn't go unnoticed.) Another naval man, a retired captain, 'Robbie' Robinson, and one-time friend of Commander Stocker, arrived and settled into his 'cabin' thereby occupying a further guest room. His particular interest was knocking into shape the ornamental part of the gardens, something we never had much time to attend to. He spent weeks down in the dell, trying to tame the bamboo forest, all the while discovering new treasures, rare tropical shrubs and trees.

After a year or so, Commander Stocker, who never really enjoyed our way of life out in the country, lost his nerve and decided he would do better to invest his money elsewhere so he sold up. Father then went it alone with a loan from the bank, and from that day on we never looked back. Father still worried, of course, probably more than ever, but at least we were no longer answerable to anyone other than ourselves.

Our two South Devon cows were the usual breed for these parts as they were tough and withstood the mild winters without the need to be brought inside. Both Heather and Bella had regular calvings. One calf we kept while the others went the way of most farm animals surplus to needs, sometimes to our Veryan butcher. The two pigs grew up and went the same way. The arrangement in the early strict rationing days was that we were allowed to retain one side of bacon for ourselves, the rest of the animal having to be sold to the meat marketing board. I was the one who collected our side of bacon from the Truro factory one time, and I remember standing at the entrance looking at a long line of bacon sides hanging from hooks down the length of this huge warehouse, while the white-aproned man worked his way down, reading each label. I kept shouting at him "It's the fourth from the bottom" and he kept ignoring me. Eventually he got to the one I just knew was ours, and, sure enough, it was. It looked so different to all the others, plumper, richer looking, just better quality. It had to be: our pigs lived off the fat of the land, or rather the best hotel leavings, plus concentrates and skimmed milk. They made the most marvellous bacon I have ever tasted. There was another aspect to meat quality in which we firmly believed, and that was a freedom from stress. Animals brought up almost as members of the family were more content. The only time they were put under stress was probably the day they went off to market when the lorry driver might whack them on the backside as he walked them up the ramp into his transporter. The first time this happened Jane was standing beside him and she was so incensed she turned round and whacked him! After that, transporter drivers were more circumspect.

When, later, we had control of the actual slaughter, which happened with pigs that our local butcher came over to deal with on the premises, the animal was not subjected to stress at all, right up until the moment the humane killer trigger was pressed. There is no doubt in my mind that meat from such animals tastes infinitely better. Another aspect, of course, was that our animals were totally organic, fed with the minimum of locally-grown concentrates and no antibiotics or hormone growth promoters.

Jane had found lots of mice running around the stable area, so had obtained a cat to look after them. Needless to say the cat soon became two cats, then several. A pregnant cat would craftily keep out of the way until her kittens were born and sufficiently grown up to introduce them, without us taking offence. How can one possibly contemplate culling such adorable little things? But we had to be hard hearted. When the cat population reached about a dozen, a cull took place to reduce the number back to about four again. This never happened when I was at home so I didn't enquire how it was done. One cat, wiser than the rest, became 'indoor cat' spending its days asleep under the kitchen table, occasionally coming out to wind itself round the legs of the guests. None of the rest were allowed indoors, and kept strictly to the stable area. They caught, not only mice, but also the occasional rat and often a rabbit or two. We only fed the indoor one; the others had to earn their own keep. One always had to be careful not to leave a bucket of milk unguarded just in case.

The central room in the stable block had become the dairy. Here Jane carried her buckets of milk, pouring them through a strainer and the milk cooler into a churn, keeping back about a gallon a day for house use. This gallon would be put out in large shallow settling pans, about a pound of thick cream being lifted off each pan after twenty-four hours. The cream was then heated in a large basin on top of a pan of water on the Aga, and the result was the most wonderful crusty deep yellow Cornish cream imaginable. We ate it with our pudding every day, as did the guests, and in winter when father had porridge for breakfast, a tablespoon of Cornish cream went on that too. We made butter, of course, using a lovely old wooden butter churn picked up in a farm sale, but never had much success with cheese as we were unable to give it the right keeping conditions. We also enjoyed endless free-range eggs, plentiful corn-fed poultry, a duck or two, and wonderful fresh organic produce from the market garden. And all this in the late forties and early fifties when food rationing was still pretty severe. No wonder we never had problems filling the house during the season.

Our guest season had settled into the period between Easter until the end of September, drifting into October if we had enough bookings then. Outside that time it was unlikely we would have sufficient bookings to warrant fully staffing the house, so we developed other pursuits. Our orchard burst into a blaze of yellow in January each year as thousands of daffodils appeared. We found a market for these with a Covent Garden wholesaler, and later with another in Stoke-on-Trent. Jane went off to the Scillies to learn all about marketing daffodils and her place was taken by Eva, a dreamy ex-land army girl who was a superb artist. She loved the land and happily combined looking after our growing menagerie with her painting. While she was with us she did a huge mural on the blank white wall of the bar, depicting us all—cows included—in a lovely rural scene with the house just showing behind great sweeps of flowering rhododendrons. Thereafter this became a favourite conversation piece, ideal for new guests to comment upon while getting to know us all.

In St. Mary's Jane stayed with the postmaster and his wife in Hugh Town with a lovely harbour view from her bedroom window, extending her visit to over a year. I sent her letters addressed simply to 'Jane Reeve, Isles of Scilly,' which was sufficient as all the islands' mail was sorted by her host. Jane discovered a lot about daffodil growing and advised us we could never approach the Scillonians' success with our venture, since that especially mild climate which they enjoy is necessary to obtain those early season higher prices. Nevertheless we kept it going for most of our time at Polsue, also growing wallflowers, which were packed and marketed in the same way. When we first started, mother, father and anyone else around would spend all day picking bunches of flowers just coming into bloom, place them up to their necks in assorted buckets of water for the rest of that day, then pack them in the evening ready to be driven to Truro to catch the night train. Buckets would stand all over the place and my mother would get backache with all the lifting and bending, and gooey water would drip everywhere from the cut stems. Father went to visit a professional flower grower somewhere north of Truro, coming back with ideas for a more factory-like approach to the preparation and packing. I was given the job of getting some big sheets of zinc, then available, from which I soldered up several foot-deep tanks.

These were reinforced around the top with strips of wood, then stood on trestle stands running down one side of our packing shed (one of the coach houses). I made a framework of lathe strips spaced a couple of inches apart, to fit over the tanks just an inch or so above the water level. These frames stood on legs spaced so that they could either be placed down into a tank with the slats just clear of the water, or stood above a tank for the flowers to drain. The procedure was for pickers to bring up box loads of flowers, which were then dropped into the slatted frames, the whole frame was then lowered into a tank for a deep overnight drink. Next morning the packing team lifted the full frames out to drain, then made up bunches of dozens in a homemade jig where the flowers were dropped in, flower side down, in four rows of three so that they displayed well, a couple of elastic bands put round the stems, then packed into the shallow flower boxes and held in place by a wooden stretcher that had metal points at each end. Finally the box was tied with a special flowerbox knot (a knot I use to this day for all sorts of things). The wholesaler supplied us with his labels, so each box looked very professional when we'd done. By late afternoon we would have up to fifty boxes that completely filled our vehicle. A trip to the parcels office at Truro station, where we had an account and where we soon came to know all the staff by their first names, and the job was done. There was a dedicated overnight flower train in those days. This went on for about a month, by which time flowers from other sources were forcing prices down, and it was no longer worth us marketing our own. Instead, mother would fill our house with huge displays, the scent filling every room overcoming the all-pervading damp smell that was in the building fabric.

On one occasion I had been gathering piles of daffodils while mother was indoors doing the displays, collecting her flowers from the front doorstep where I left them. Mother, her back to the open door, hearing a noise behind her and conscious of the light being blocked out by someone at the door, called out to me. No reply. She turned round to find Bella, several daffodils dangling from her drooling mouth, standing in the entrance looking around with interest, her eye alighting hopefully on the new display. Mother screamed (she never really came to like cows) so Bella sauntered off to find something else to eat. Both Bella and Heather would escape from their meadow from time to time, Bella taking the initiative and heading up the track to the road, from where she could then come down the drive to the front of the stables. They had learnt we kept our store of turnips in one of the looseboxes, and had worked out how to get there. Having arrived in the garden, there were all sorts of other things that appealed, much to the fury of Robbie who would shout and wave his arms at them, but this was the first time Bella had ever thought to try her luck in the house.

Sometimes we reared a lamb that Jim Eva let us have, one whose mother had either died, or was unable to look after for one reason or another. These lambs soon became rather too tame after enjoying being bottle-fed, and when they started on solid food, preferred Robbie's hydrangeas to eating grass. It was very difficult treating as a crop a pet animal with a name to which it answered (sometimes); something a hardened farmer must do. I'm afraid those lambs fetched up on the guest's dining table, but we couldn't bring ourselves to enjoy them. Sometimes the lamb from Jim was not on the hoof. It all started in the very early days; I remember opening the door to him late one evening.

"John," he began, "I s'pose the Major couldn't spare a poor 'ole Cornish farmer a cigarette or two, could 'ee?" Jim, addicted to cigarettes, couldn't buy sufficient for his needs and knew we had an allocation for our guests. Father produced a packet of a hundred and Jim's eyes lit up.

"Er, could 'ee help us out with this," producing a package from behind his back. "Er mother died and us was left with a problem." Inside the package was a beautiful half side of best lamb, extremely welcome. Jim was a wonderful neighbour in many ways especially in the early days, and we would pay him back however we could, generally by producing helpers at harvest time. These were recruited from eager-to-help guests who found this a nice change from the beach.

In February it was Cornish broccoli time. We grew these in rows in the market garden, packing them straight into boxes, six to a box, on the flat tractor trailer. At the end of the day, these too would fetch up at Truro station. The overnight train, dubbed at the beginning of the season as the "daffodil express" was now known as the broccoli train. This train service was actually the mail train, but it had special provision for carrying Cornish produce for Covent Garden and other main markets, with a couple of passenger coaches tagged on for the few night travellers. On one occasion Jane accompanied our consignment all the way to the wholesale marketplace and on to the final customer, noting how the price rocketed up as it went. We received hardly anything for all our work growing, picking, packing, transport to the station and freight charges, and in just a few hours the price would rise threefold in the hands of the various middlemen. It was very disheartening.

Cornish broccoli ('cauliflower' to the customer) the finest, freshest quality possible, was killed off overnight when the Italians began flying in plastic-wrapped produce at a cheaper price. Many Cornish growers were left with fields of unsold broccoli onto which they put their cows, much to the delight of the cows. The British housewife, as ever, fetched up with a foreign product which, although it looked nice on the greengrocer's shelf, was not a patch on the real Cornish produce. It was a hard lesson to learn: quality only sells to the few. We then grew wallflowers and stocks, which sold very well, again to the same wholesalers who took our daffodils, and we packed them in the same way.

We had a bungalow built on the edge of our land alongside the main gate. This was for Dick Harris and his family, planning permission only being granted because Dick was classified as an agricultural worker. Building materials were in really short supply at this time, and so were good builders. We used the same team who converted the main house when we moved in, a firm from nearby Portscatho more at home with this type of concrete block construction. We also employed tree surgeons to cut down some of our more dangerous trees, and to clear the space where the bungalow was to be built. 'Surgeons' was hardly an appropriate name for these men, who used brawn rather than brain when tackling any job. They employed explosives to get out the last of the big roots, detonating an enormous charge which went off in a most spectacular fashion with a noise like a high-explosive bomb, sending bits of tree root and stones hundreds of feet into the air. Jane was riding Silver up the drive nearby when this first happened, and not surprisingly he bolted. An hour later an extremely angry Jane returned to give these cowboys a dressing down which I'm sure they would remember for a long time. Not long afterwards the boss man was injured whilst attempting to haul a tree trunk out of our woods with a steel cable and winch, when the cable parted, whipping back and knocking him off his tractor. Traditional roofing slates for the bungalow were difficult to obtain, so we specified Canadian cedar shingles instead. Father had seen this type of material when he was in Canada during the war and liked it. This was one of the first uses in Cornwall of wood shingles for a proper house, though they had been used for gazebos and suchlike. Twenty years later they looked just fine, the roof still completely watertight. Being very light they needed far less substantial roof timbers, thereby bringing down the cost appreciably.

The daily flower run to Truro station became rather a drudge, and as soon as I was seventeen I obtained my driving licence and did the run whenever I was at home. I first drove a car when I was about sixteen, out with some guests who, on leaving the main road at Ruan High Lanes, asked whether I'd like to drive the last mile or so. Of course I was in that driving seat as quick as a flash and drove jolly well, so I thought... A little later on I drove a pre-war Daimler which belonged to another set of guests, with the early preselector gears, and became fairly proficient at placing a car well on the road without having to worry about managing a clutch. Later, we bought a new van, this one being a strange little Jowett with a two-cylinder engine which made the front of the car waggle from side to side in time with the engine speed, noticeable at tickover revs. This had a crash gearbox and one had to get the engine speed absolutely correct for the road speed otherwise the gearbox made a painful metallic squawk of protest when engaging gear. At the time many big vehicles like three-tonner trucks (yes, they were the 'big' vehicles of the day) had this type of gearbox, and managing one was an art in itself. It required double-declutching when changing down, and waiting for the revs to slow down when changing up. I got the hang of it fairly soon, and it was in the Jowett that I presented myself for my driving test in Truro.

The examiner was very wary when he saw I was proposing to take my test in a commercial vehicle and wanted to check our insurance before risking himself in the passenger seat, explaining that he was involved in an accident nearly every week when testing new drivers; a fine way to destroy one's confidence before we'd even started! However, he cheered up when he saw that the vehicle was the one with the crash box, quite a joke car even at that time. I drove him round Truro with great panache and thought I'd done ever so well, not crashing the gears once. He tested me on traffic lights by asking questions about sequencing. We couldn't try the real thing, because there weren't any lights any nearer than Plymouth. Finally he asked a few more questions, and then wrote up his notes. Handing me the 'failed' certificate he explained that I had twice failed to stop absolutely at a stop sign. With a "that'll cause him to realise he doesn't know it all" smirk on his face he got out and walked off. Devastated, I drove off (on my own) to find father who said he'd be waiting at Jennings, the wholesale grocers. He thought I would easily pass, and was as upset as I was. He needed the extra driver! A few weeks later I tried again, taking the greatest care to stop at the two stop signs, and passed.

When Jane returned from the Scillies and took over the farm animals once more, Eva moved on somewhere else. Jane had many tales to tell about the laidback slow life in the islands, still living in the twenties. Generally their visitors would go over on the original 'Scillonian' steamer, a few really intrepid ones risking the trip in an elderly De Havilland Rapide, a canvas-sided biplane with a quiet petrol engine which fluttered along very restfully at about sixty miles an hour. It was all most relaxing, so Jane told us after having tried it one time, but a bit alarming when the aircraft went flat out up the runway and arrived at the end having not quite reached flying speed. The subsequent drop over the cliff edge did the trick. I never really believed Jane's stories, as she was prone to tremendous exaggeration. She told us there were no car licence plates on St. Mary's, nor were they necessary since everyone knew who owned the few cars there were. Consequently, no tax discs were displayed, and far from locking their cars, most drivers left them with the key still in the ignition. As there was no crime, nobody worried. Street lighting was non-existent, so when Jane came home after dark on her bicycle, it was a bit of guesswork knowing where to steer. It sounded fun, even nicer than the Polsue area, and I looked forward to visiting the Scillies one day.

Father learned to select his guests. Initially he'd eagerly accept anyone who wanted to come, but occasionally someone would stay who caused no end of trouble, which simply didn't make it worth our while. One such was a strange man who spent a month with us one March. He was from the Abel-Smith dynasty, mysteriously on his own with no wish to join in anything or be sociable in any way. It was a lovely mild spring that year, ideal for getting about, but he spent all day in his room pacing up and down. What irked father was that he kept his electric fire on continuously, even when he came down for meals. Father reckoned the extra cost of electricity used up all the meagre profits. We wondered whether he was fleeing from something or somewhere, lying low until the fuss died down; or maybe he was an author trying to clear his mind of other distractions. We never found out. One day he paid his bill and vanished, never to be heard of again. Quite often we would have guests that intrigued us, and this was part of the fun of operating such an establishment. Early on, we'd had a booking for a couple who were very insistent about having our only room with a double bed. Honeymoon couple, we naturally thought. They arrived on a motorbike with sidecar, two immensely tubby young people swathed in all-weather biking gear with clumpy boots. They had eyes only for one another and kept us in stitches with their behaviour. On their first morning it was my turn to do the early morning teas, and when I knocked on their door there was a "come in!" followed by lots of giggles. Opening the door, there on the floor was the mattress with the two of them sitting up, the sheet pulled up to cover their nakedness, and bits of splintered bed framework stacked against the wall. It must have been a somewhat energetic night. I had to repair the bed with reinforced brackets later that day. During their stay they had several letters addressed to 'The Reverend and Mrs …'.

When the guest season started in earnest, we needed extra help in the house. We already had Mrs Buckingham, great on her malapropisms, complaining about "a constable stream of pots and pans". She did sterling work cleaning the misshapen vegetables that came from the garden, and coped with all the washing up by hand. One of us used to accompany her home to her cottage in nearby Treworthal if she worked on into the evenings, and it was on a brilliant clear night when father walked her home, commenting on the stars which were so clear, that she made the unforgettable remark "I'd like to see one of them things close up". We had installed a second, very large, earthenware sink, with a wooden plinth for her to stand on because she was on the short side, also it helped her feet. Mother's feet, though, became swollen with all the standing, and she was eventually obliged to get someone to do the cooking. We tried one or two 'professional' cooks, none of whom were up to much, then we found a slick young man, well trained with a reasonable pedigree who arrived with his own set of knives and a proper chef's white coat, and he got us out of trouble. He was good, indeed too good. We couldn't understand how we had landed such a good cook. One morning he wasn't around, and father eventually found him in bed, blind drunk, with one of father's precious gin bottles empty beside him. Within half an hour a taxi arrived and he was bundled in and sent packing in a most dramatic fashion.

This bit of drama couldn't have happened at a worse time. It was early in August, the house was full, everybody was working extremely hard, and mother was exhausted. There was nothing for it but for her to turn to and take up the cooking again. At the time we had a couple of scallywag builders repairing our conservatory that had shown signs of imminent collapse. They were sitting in the kitchen enjoying a mug of tea on the day the cook left, and one of them, George, an ex-army sergeant, sympathised with mother over her predicament.

"Can you cook, then?" asked Mother.

"'Corse I can cook," snorted George, and from that moment he donned an apron and spent the next five years cooking the most wonderful meals, leaving his mate to finish the conservatory single-handed, while mother resumed her role as lady proprietress.

All our animals had names, of course, except for the hens that never lasted long enough as a rule. There was one exception and that was Screwy. This was a mentally defective hen that refused to lay eggs, so eventually after several warnings it was consigned to the same fate as our cockerels. Jane had just administered its execution (a quick neck-wring) and had started to pluck her when Screwy suddenly leapt up and scuttled off round the back of the hay loft, her neck now noticeably longer and a bit bent. Amazingly she seemed none the worse for this treatment and Jane didn't have the heart to try again. Screwy lived on for several years, developing a character that only such animals can. She eventually discovered how to lay eggs, always doing so whilst perching on the edge of the pigsty, much to the delight of the two pigs who realised what was about to happen and jostled for prime position below her, mouths open, squealing with anticipation.

I'd heard of fowls recovering from having their necks wrung, and it happened a second time, though with a bigger bird. In the early days it was difficult to obtain a turkey for Christmas, so we settled for goose. I went with Jane to the farm near St. Just to pick up the bird, selecting one from the noisy flock scrabbling around at our feet. The farmer grabbed it, wrung its neck and popped it into a sack. We put the sack on the back seat of the Land Rover while we drove home. Halfway home a head appeared between us, looking ahead in an interested way to see where we were off to, and showing every signs of enjoying the drive. It received a reprieve, of course, and spent several years stalking the yard behind the stable block attacking everybody it came across by inflicting a painful peck in the fleshy part of their calf. All except father, that is. It seemed to realise that father had the power to order its demise if it bit him. Eventually, in a forgetful moment it did bite him, rather unwisely just a week before Christmas, and received the thumbs down for its trouble. After that we no longer kept any geese, much to my relief. We did, however, always have Muscovy ducks. These are a good choice for a smallholding such as ours, requiring very little looking after. They lay tasty eggs and eventually eat well (by which I mean we enjoy eating them). They were always popular with the guests, as whenever Mrs Muscovy had a young family she would lead them in single file across the drive to the pond in front of the house with Mr Muscovy bringing up the rear. Out would come the cameras to capture this ooh-ah sight.

Vehicles in the forties and fifties had engines which needed to be 'decoked' every 1,000 miles or so. With our frequent trips to Truro, around thirty miles for the round trip, we would clock up 1,000 miles in a month. The car servicing was initially carried out by Truscott's garage at Ruan High Lanes. Mr Truscott and his wife lived next door, with an entrance that opened out onto the road beside two ancient hand-operated petrol pumps. If we needed petrol, one or other of them served us or, if no one was at home, one of the garage hands did the honours. Usually this was a little man called Ginger by virtue of his red hair. He also serviced our car and I never saw him out of a filthy oil-sodden pair of dungarees, with a fag end stuck to his lower lip, even when operating the pump. Later when we became extremely well known we were allowed to operate the pump for ourselves, entering the amount taken in the book on the Truscott's kitchen table, and leaving the right amount of petrol coupons under the paperweight. At the end of the month we paid the bill.

About this time I became interested in having my own proper wireless set, and read an article in some magazine about building one from a kit. I bought the kit by mail order, Mr Pedlar delivering it on his bicycle. The wireless worked off the mains electricity supply which had now been installed, but up until then, if I wanted to hear any broadcasting, it was a question of an old battery set, the batteries being a low tension accumulator, which was recharged by Ginger every so often along with various car batteries, and a high tension battery which Truscotts also sold.

Our coal was delivered by one of the Chenoweths. They were a family with fourteen children who lived in a pair of semidetached cottages opposite Truscott's garage at Ruan High Lanes, spilling out onto the road with toys and tricycles from time to time. Mrs Chenoweth, all twenty stone of her, stood at the door bawling orders, whilst the eldest girl looked after the youngest child, the second eldest looked after the next youngest, and so on. The older boys went with their father on the delivery runs. However, the local coal-carrying champion of the region was not a coalman at all but a wiry farmer from Tregony, who won the race from one end of a particular field to the other with a hundredweight of coal on his back. One year for a joke Jane was challenged to take him on and, being Jane, she did so and won. She also entered for the next race, which thus became greatly enlivened with all the young toughies determined to make sure she wouldn't pull it off a second time. But she did. After that she enjoyed heroic status, for no one had really liked the fallen champion.

In the autumn of that same year Jane went to the Isle of Wight to stay for a couple of weeks with some ex-visitors, and whilst bathing in the Solent she contracted polio. This was before the days of a polio vaccine, and the first we knew about an outbreak anywhere was a week or so later after she was back at home and back at work when she said she felt a bit 'fluey and went to bed. In the evening she tried to get up and her legs went from under her. Next morning our GP visited and guessed what it might be. Within the hour she was on her way by ambulance to the austere Isolation Hospital on the outskirts of Truro. This establishment was unable to do anything other than keep the polio victims in strict isolation (there were now several patients, the number growing daily) and to offer palliative treatment. We were not allowed to visit, but had to leave any offerings at the hospital entrance. Jane could not write to us in case the paper the letters were written on might be 'hot', and we had to rely on verbal assurance from the staff that she was okay. This was a most traumatic few months for us all. Eventually, just before Christmas, she was moved to the Royal Cornwall Infirmary on the other side of town, and then we were able to see her again. What a reunion! Jane was far, far better, but still extremely weak and thin. She had lost all her muscle tone and at one time when her chest muscles weakened it had been touch and go whether she might have to be put into an iron lung. She was now to start a long series of physio sessions to get her fit enough to be discharged. Even in this state she was the one who enlivened the ward with a Christmas spirit, going from bed to bed, cheering the other patients, in the true Jane spirit. What a sister! She recovered more or less completely, but was never again the beefy girl I had known. No more coal carrying.

We were fortunate that during this time Eva was able to return to look after the animals, and she stayed until Jane was fully better, then landed a job as art teacher in a very exclusive posh girls' school near Bracknell. A few years later when I happened to pass the entrance to this school in my funny little vintage car, on an impulse I turned in and drove up the immaculate gravel drive and parked in front of an imposing grand house. I seemed to cause quite a stir as I clambered out (the cars I had at that time were ones which one had to clamber out of, since they were open two-seaters without doors) and asked for Eva. She arrived a few minutes later almost unrecognizable in a smart tweedy suit, to quickly shoo me round the back amongst the kitchen debris, concerned that if seen with an acquaintance of such an obviously undesirable type, her new image might be devastated.

The summer holidays were far and away my favourite. I was often asked to take guests out in Kestrel, sheer pleasure for me as usually they had no wish to be in charge of the boat, merely enjoying being sailed around in it. As I really loved being in the driving seat (with an opportunity to show off, if I am honest) that suited both sides admirably. I would take them out to Carricknath and maybe out past the lighthouse, or perhaps we would sail up the Carrick Roads to Mylor or Restronguet. Sometimes if the tide was right we would get as far as King Harry Ferry, past big silent hulks—surplus merchant ships lying at a mooring waiting to be sold to a breakers' yard. One year a few naval vessels were also moored here, among them the frigate HMS Amethyst, shortly after she famously ran the blockade down the Yangtze River under the command of Commander Kerrans. On several occasions we would see the author Howard Spring sailing his boat, always alone, and exchanged a solemn wave. This was as it should be, for we were right in "Howard Spring Country", the setting for the Cornish parts of several of his books. On one occasion we were out sailing when word went around that the tea clipper Pamir, a magnificent four-masted barque, was coming round the Lizard on its way to her final docking at Falmouth, the last of the great ships that raced one another from Australia. We didn't see her very clearly, but our friend Dennis Edmonds took the photograph I reproduce here.

The Tea Clipper *Pamir* rounding The Lizard

My do-it-yourself interests were always expanding—difficult in the late forties since materials were still hard to obtain and it was years before shops catering for DIY enthusiasts had started up. One person I met on the water quite often was a quiet man who lived with his young son in the little hamlet of Bohortha, on the St. Anthony peninsula opposite St. Mawes. He had built a largish aluminium rowing boat that sat high in the water making it very easy to row. I visited him at home and we discussed plans and designs. I decided that I, too, would build such a boat. Surprisingly sheet duralumin was readily available; it was just timber for the frames that one couldn't get. I solved the problem by obtaining old railway sleepers, sawing out usable parts on a homemade circular sawbench. I spent a lot of time sharpening the saw, which kept striking flints embedded in the sleeper surfaces, sending sparks all over the place. Eventually I finished the framework, clad it with duralumin fastened every inch or so with brass screws, painted it all with a Cerrux yacht paint obtained direct from the manufacturers by mail order, and we had a grand launching ceremony from the jetty at St. Anthony's. It was hugely successful; the boat was a delight to row. Being nearly twelve feet long she sat level even with four people aboard, the transom just clear of the water. Furthermore it was possible to propel the boat with a single scull over the stern without it weaving from side to side. It was only a year or two later I learnt about electrolytic reactions, so when paint began to wear off anywhere near a brass fastening, the aluminium nearby corroded into holes! They do say that one learns from one's mistakes, and I have never again made such a fundamental error and hope I never will.

One summer a family with two youngsters about my age came to stay. If they weren't out, the boy, Christopher, would bury his head in a book while his younger sister, Robinetta, would search me out (quite easy—I was always to be found in the flower packing shed, or what I called my 'workshop') and tease me. She was a hefty girl a year younger than me, infinitely stronger, and her technique was to grab me round the waist and squeeze like a boa constrictor. This was agonizingly painful and held thus, she commanded me to kiss her, or tell her the meaning of some four-letter word, or anything else she thought might embarrass me, not releasing her hold until I had to do as bidden. I'm sure I learnt a lot more from her than ever she did from me, and often wondered whether my parents would have been shocked had they known that this girl, definitely from a 'nice to know' family, was leading me astray under their noses.

For some years father grew early potatoes in a fenced-off section of our grazing meadow. We ploughed a few dozen furrows with the Trusty Tractor, the market gardener's machine of the time, basically a seven horsepower engine mounted over a couple of wheels with long handlebars which the operator heaved on while walking behind. It could have a single furrow plough, a harrow, cultivator, or a seat bolted on the back, and required a strong man to control it. It certainly needed every bit of my puny strength but I enjoyed using it. The idea was to grow a ton or two of earlies and get these to market by about mid June, when prices were guaranteed. After then the crop might be bigger but the prices would come tumbling down. Father worried about which day to lift them to obtain the best price. Eventually he would make his decision, and announce in the bar that tomorrow would be potato-lifting day and anyone was welcome to spend a day on the land helping. Amazingly this often worked and we would have eight or ten helpers bent over all day lifting spuds by hand in exchange for free drinks and excruciating backache. For weeks after that the area would be scrumped for missed potatoes. Eventually the pigs would be put on the site to clean it up, something they were most efficient at.

This early potato crop was only worthwhile when prices were guaranteed, but the government changed the system so it was no longer profitable to grow these earlies for market. Instead, having now got this part of the field under cultivation, father tried several other crops. One year he grew corn, which would save us having to buy it for our stock, but the little bit of land we grew it on was far too small for Jim Eva to come along with his reaper and binder. I learnt to use a scythe, not easy when the ground is lumpy and stony. In those days short-stalked cereals hadn't been developed, and in the windy parts of the county most corn crops would be flattened by a combination of wind and rain, making them impossible to harvest any other way than by hand. The combine harvester was only just coming in and only then on the corn prairies of East Anglia. So our corn venture was short lived and we used the land partly for turnips (for the cows) and partly for our wallflower crop. Eventually this, too, ceased to do very well, so the area was finally put down to grass once more. Once again we bought in our corn, generally 'sedge'—a mixture of oats and barley—from one of the farmers. This was kept in big galvanised bins in the stables, except for a sack at a time that Jane took along to a farmer in Treworthal who had a corn-crushing machine. Crushed corn was fed to the cows as a supplement, with added molasses and anything else Jane reckoned they might need.

Jane noticed the corn seemed to go down rather fast and as our market garden helper, Dick, kept some hens at the back of his house, began to wonder what he fed them on. One night she tied down the corn bin lid with a fine thread, and in the morning, hey presto! It had been broken. A couple of nights later it happened again. Father himself was a most honest person and wouldn't tolerate anyone who failed to come up to his standards, but Dick was an essential worker. He didn't want to shop him nor upset him too much. He took guidance and was advised to accept that this sort of thing happens with such people, and to turn a blind eye. Uneasily father did so for a while, but late one evening on his way home after taking the dogs for their evening walk, both dogs rushed into the shrubbery barking and snarling at something. Next day Dick was limping, and when our terrier Judy appeared with father, she uncharacteristically went for him. Father then chose to confront Dick with what we already knew, telling him to stop stealing our corn immediately or he would have to inform the police; a reasonable action to take, you might think, but unheard of in the quiet Cornish country at that time. An animosity grew up between the two of them and eventually Dick found another job and moved out. The story had a happy ending, for we found casual help quite easily for the market garden, and Dick's now empty cottage was converted into four extra rooms for guests.

Father caught another petty thief, but this time it was a policeman! He was an overweight passed-over inspector who strutted about the Truro streets being unnecessarily officious to everyone (such as telling father to move on when he parked the Land Rover on a narrow bend outside Jennings' retail grocery shop). At that time we took our produce in to a wholesale fruit and veg merchant on the outskirts of town, and one day father and I were unloading the boxes and when he went in to the office with his invoice I stayed outside and noticed this inspector wandering about with a basket, quite openly helping himself to this and that. He took one of father's broccolis out of a box, leaving a conspicuous gap, and when father returned with the manager to check off the boxes, he noticed it too. I nodded in the direction of the inspector who by now was moving off, and father almost exploded. The manager quickly said this only happened once a week or so, and he regarded it as the inspector's perks for allowing him to leave his lorries parked in a constricted area outside. As soon as he returned home father telephoned the Chief Constable whom he knew, leaving him with little alternative but to admonish his wretched man, after which we were unmercifully harassed whenever we tried to park anywhere in Truro. One day I had left the Land Rover outside Jennings as usual and on my return saw the inspector with his back to me standing by the driver's door, unnecessarily waving traffic past this unfortunate 'obstruction'. I crept up to the back of the car, in over the tailgate (all Land Rovers at that time were driven around with the canvas back flap permanently rolled up) slipped into the driver's seat, then started the engine and roared off before the inspector had time to turn round.

~*~

Father had spent so many years worrying about commercial survival that he had worried himself into having a duodenal ulcer. This gave him constant pain and as a result he became very fractious and his fuse, always a bit on the short side, now became dangerously short. This was a pity, as it interfered with my enjoyment at home. I was not the most understanding of sons, and probably deserved all I got.

He had been persuaded to buy a couple of stocks of bees that were installed in our upper orchard. It was a good idea in that the honey we extracted was a most useful addition to the Polsue food supplies, indeed father had a spoonful of beautiful honey along with the spoonful of Cornish cream on his porridge each morning. I can assure you, that and the full cream milk make any porridge unforgettably wonderful. However, when it came to looking after the bees, father was not the best person for the job. He had little patience, panicked if a bee stung him when he was inspecting the honey supers, and one day upset the bees so much that they went for him, lots got under his veil and he was extremely badly stung, in fact so badly that he had to be helped back to the house and into bed for some days. A local beekeeper was called in to calm the bees down and put the top back on the hive. That same local beekeeper was later offered the complete stocks of bees, hives included.

Father was having more and more trouble with his teeth, many of which were by now missing. Eventually it was decided he should have the remaining ten or so extracted and be fitted with a full set of dentures. This was done by our Truro dentist at a time when I was at home, so I was able to drive him there. He had the job done under gas, and I collected him afterwards and had to remain there for an hour before he was able to stand unaided and get down the steps into the car. He was only partly conscious on the way home and was in bed for some time after that, then could only manage sloppy food for the next week, after which his new dentures were fitted and he was a changed man, happy again and with a lovely smile once more. Recently, when I told my own dentist about this he didn't believe me.

In wintertime we often laid our boat up at Benny's yard near the St. Just in Roseland church. There is a gravel sand bar that half crosses the little creek just there providing a wonderful sheltered spot for boats. At the back of this Benny had his yard where he built all sorts of craft. He had a homemade plank-steaming apparatus consisting of a large cast iron pipe closed at one end which was propped up at an angle, into which he would pour a couple of bucketfuls of water. Around the base of this he lit a fire and waited. Planks to be softened up for bending would then be lowered down the pipe on the end of a piece of rope, and a bung put over the end to retain the steam. After half an hour or so, one of Benny's men would extricate the softened plank which could then be bent round the ribs of the boat he was building and nailed into place with long copper nails, the protruding ends being clenched over. Lovely traditional boatbuilding and so much nicer than the smelly fibreglass craft of today.

At the top of the hill, a signpost read 'church and bar'. During the war American servicemen would hopefully turn off down the lane, only to call out "Gee, where's the saloon" when they got to Benny's. On one occasion I was standing down there talking to Benny when some visitor with a sailing dinghy approached him to ask advice about the choppy seas that were getting up, receiving the immortal reply "Thee can go out if 'ee like, but it bain't no good for we."

Years later I was down there when I recognised something familiar about a sailing dinghy drawn up on the bar. A couple with two small children were just about to launch it when I realised it was my old aluminium boat which I'd sold several years previously when I reckoned it was in imminent danger of falling to pieces. I rushed down the beach in some alarm to see whether I could be mistaken but no, it was my original homemade boat all right, with a slot cut in the inadequate keel for a dagger board to go through, rudder pintles fitted on the transom, and a little mast. And there they were with two young children, no lifejackets, about to venture out into the Roads. I chatted for a bit, not admitting my involvement with the boat's origins. Yes, they had bought the boat when they were visiting a few years previously, yes, it was a lovely boat to sail, and no, it didn't corrode too much if kept well painted. I pushed them off and waved as they set out intrepidly for the deep water and with some concern, staggered back up the beach.

Some time after, the RAF vicar at Portscatho had moved on to be replaced by one whose sermons father didn't enjoy so much, so we searched around. We heard about Dr Barnaby, an elderly theologian who had retired to St. Mawes and was taken on as curate. The vicar had two churches, the parish church at St. Mawes and the one at St. Just in Roseland, across the road from which was his huge vicarage. They would take it in turns to take the service at each church. Dr Barnaby preached a cracking good sermon that drew a large congregation, which must have been galling for the vicar whose congregation at the other church was much smaller. The vicar drove from St. Just to St. Mawes for his morning service there, meeting a goodly proportion of his congregation heading the other way to hear his curate, but he took it all in good humour. A Mrs Montgomery who lived in an imposing house at Polvarth, near Frankie Peters' boatyard, considered herself socially superior and therefore the leading lady of St Mawes. She attended church in order to be seen, and expected to sit in the front pew with her husband obediently beside her. She always followed the vicar, because he was the vicar, not because she preferred one service more than the other. On one occasion I had attended the St. Just service on a day the vicar was there. Last to arrive came Mrs Montgomery, progressing regally up the aisle nodding graciously to anyone she thought she might know, followed dutifully by her husband. When the sermon began Mr Montgomery, settled into his pew, and was soon fast asleep. After some minutes the sound of his heavy breathing and the occasional snort could be heard right at the back of the church. Eventually this became too much even for Mrs Montgomery. She gave him a prod and said in a loud stage whisper, "James! James, wake up!" James sat up and looked about him. "James, he can't go on much longer, can he?"

The vicar, standing in the pulpit just above them, turned a bright pink, quickly brought his sermon to a close, and announced the last hymn. As we all filed out saying our good mornings to him outside the porch he behaved as if nothing had happened. He was a very understanding vicar.

Father, 'Robbie', Commander Stocker and mother

6

Final Schooldays and Afterwards

As I rose up through the school my life became more pleasant. Each term I was allowed those little things which enable one's status to be recognised by lesser individuals, for example as a fourth-termer I was allowed to go around with the top and bottom button of my sports jacket undone. Needless to say, nobody ever did those buttons up once they reached that status. The worst one was being allowed to go around with one's hands in one's pockets, not a smart habit at any time and to see every boy in the school except the juniors walking around thus looked so sloppy. Certain privileges, generally those awarded to house prefects, were extremely useful, such as being able to use certain routes around the school which saved time. The ultimate privileges were reserved for school prefects, that small bunch of elite toffee-nosed gods, generally just the head boy of each house, who walked shamelessly on the grass in the quad, even when the grass was sopping wet, just to elicit envy amongst their juniors. It was really all a bit silly, but it meant a lot at the time to most boys. Needless to say if there was an activity forbidden to some, then that became a challenge to the more adventuresome to see if they could enjoy it without being found out. The head of Army House in my penultimate year was Martin Stevens, a small fresh-faced boy who thought a lot of himself and clearly revelled in poncing around, head in air, looking important. A few years later I came across an illustrated article in a magazine picturing him dressed up like our HM in immaculate academic garb, guiding American visitors around Oxford's colleges. It takes all sorts...

We attended an annual JTC camp on army property near Burghfield, not so far away. This meant spending several days of our summer holidays dressed up in unspeakably uncomfortable prickly, khaki serge battledress, wearing blister-inducing hobnail boots, and carrying round a tiresome Lee-Enfield .303 rifle. We slept, twelve to a bell tent, and were harassed from the crack of dawn until after dark by a series of sadistic regular army NCOs, all with raucous uncouth voices.

We washed (when essential to do so) in a draughty ablutions tent with boys from several other schools, and ate pretty disgusting food slopped into our aluminium mess tins by sweaty fat cooks. I can't think why I agreed to go, unless it was under threat. The only enlightening episode I choose to remember occurred on my final camp when we were out on some sort of manoeuvre. There we were, lying prone in a muddy patch of heathland with some army umpire hurling thunderflashes around when I saw a terrified rabbit bolting towards where I was lying across its run. I'd discovered that the stub of my pencil just fitted nicely down the barrel of my rifle which had a blank cartridge loaded, so it was the work of a moment to raise the rifle, take aim and shoot the rabbit clean between the eyes. It spun over in the air and landed in front of me, seriously dead. When the whistle blew at the end of this 'game', we stood up and fell in to march back to our camp. Someone noticed I was carrying a dead rabbit in one hand, the back legs of which I had threaded, one into the sinews of the other, to make a convenient carrying handle like the best poachers of the day. The other boys were impressed, and the army staff so astonished they didn't do more than tut-tut.

Which leads me on to poaching... I had a friend in one of the in-college houses by name of Roger Butters, a lad full of fun and with scant regard for authority. His father owned a cardboard manufacturing mill beside the railway near Thatcham, he lived fairly near and knew the local countryside well. We used to go around nearby woodlands where he promised to show me how to poach, and told me about an apocryphal occasion not long previously when he was creeping through Lord Benyon's property at six in the morning, on the lookout for pheasants to have a go at. Lord Benyon owned most of the land between Bradfield and Theale, had a country pad at Englefield Park over the hill, was a respected College benefactor, and therefore someone not to be upset. Roger was just getting out some corn laced with aniseed, a sure way to lure a pheasant almost anywhere, when he became aware of a movement in the scrub a few yards away. To his astonishment he found himself looking straight into the eyes of an equally astonished and slightly embarrassed Headmaster, attired in scruffy camouflaged clothing. They stared at one another for a short moment, then both hastily retired behind cover. Roger fled back to college as soon as he had reached the lane and waited expectantly all day for the dreaded summons. It never came. When next he saw the HM, the HM looked straight past him, unseeing. Roger respected him for that.

I only had direct contact with the HM on a few occasions. He took the course of catechism classes in preparation for confirmation, when every week six of us spent an hour in his study at his house. This was a lovely room with a large open fireplace, exposed beamed roof, and walls lined with books. A few nice pieces of antique furniture and several really comfortable chairs were scattered about. His class was excellent, and well taught. On another occasion I had done something particularly naughty for which the punishment was 'six from the Head'. He was reputed to wield a painful swing with a thin bendy cane and I can vouch for the truth of that. The other time was when we were being prepared for going out into the wide world at the end of our school time, and involved compulsory attendance at a 'facts of life' session in one of the classrooms. Presumably he was unable to find a volunteer to give this talk, so had to do so himself. None of us learnt anything new for it came ten years too late, but we were fascinated by his ideas on how often one should do 'it', and what would happen if one did 'it' too often or not often enough. And how to take precautions was put over in a clipped, matter of fact way that seemed quite at odds, coming as it did from the oh-so-correct dapper man pacing up and down in front of us. Just as well the talk took place so near the end of our last term. After that talk I looked on the HM in a different light.

Teaching staff became more amenable as one grew up, all except for a few who played for safety and remained aloof, keeping a safe social distance from any boy. In Army House CB acquired a youngish assistant housemaster, Philip Stibbe, who joined in about my third year. He was a most charming person, would come into one's study just for an adult chat, and brought into my life an adult social side that was otherwise missing. I regretted not being in a class that he taught.

My physics teacher was another likeable man, and I was occasionally invited to his house to have tea with him and his wife at a weekend. We chatted about sailing, where I discovered that although he looked after the naval section of the JTC, he had no inborn affinity with the sea such as I had quickly acquired from living beside it, but had learnt everything from books. His respect for the sea came from fright rather than understanding, which at least ensured his charges were reasonably safe, although he held them on far too tight a rein for my liking.

Each year there was a speech day held in the summer term, usually sometime near half term so that parents could take their charges off somewhere. I never had parents visiting on these occasions since by that time they were working flat out at Polsue. One boy in an in-college house whose name was Cohen, was teased about his parents who appeared, usually in a smart Rolls, at a time when very few cars were on the roads and most parents made it by bus. His father wore a black coat with an astrakhan collar, and his mother, small and very dark-complexioned, was expensively dressed and bejewelled. We asked him what his parents did.

"Ah, my father, he is in zee business," would come the reply.

When, a year or two later, his parents appeared in a somewhat tatty car, we commented on that.

"Ah, but business 'eez not so good!" We fully expected the parents to arrive on creaky bicycles the following year, but business must have looked up, for they were back to the Rolls again, this time with a chauffeur. The poor little chap had his father's nose and was small and tubby, no good at games, but no doubt would grow up to use that nose successfully for 'zee business'.

Various luminaries, preferably old boys, gave the speeches on these occasions, and one such was Admiral of the Fleet Lord Fraser of North Cape, who had enjoyed a distinguished naval career. He arrived in full uniform, sporting a white cap cover, which was something I hadn't seen during the drab war years. I looked at this rather small figure on the platform and wondered whether I would ever go down that road for a career.

My schooldays were beginning to run out. In my final year CB made me a house prefect, though I would never rise higher than that, since Tony Clover who joined with me in 1945 was chosen to head the house. This satisfied me entirely, since I preferred to keep my head below the parapet and let others take all the responsibilities and receive the brick-bats that generally went with them. Higher School Certificate exams loomed. My school subjects in the sixth form were Physics, Chemistry, Maths, and one or two pleasant optional ones such as meteorology for which I would not be taking an exam. In our last term, I also became heavily involved with the school play, not as a thespian—heaven forbid!—but as a backstage technician. In the previous year I had been the assistant stage electrician, so I had a little experience. This time I would be the stage electrician. The play was Hamlet, the lead role being taken by John Bennett, an Army House boy who had grown his hair long over several months especially for the role. He was far and away the school's best actor, very gifted, and went on to a stage career after leaving school, though I only saw him in later years in one or two TV commercials.

Rehearsals for Hamlet started at the beginning of the summer term, the performances being given during that relaxing lull between the end of exams and the end of term. But for those taking part, the busiest time was actually just as exams were at their height. My role was to have total responsibility for lighting, from discussing lighting plots with the set designer (a West End professional, friend of CB's and an old boy), ordering the hired equipment from Strand Electric, taking delivery of a furniture van full of heavy equipment, installing it, and operating it throughout. I was working under CB of course, but he gave me a pretty free hand. The theatre had never been designed for evening performances, and there was no provision for any lighting. Sure, there were lights backstage to see one's way around a windowless area, but no proper power supply. I worked out we would be using quite a lot of power with anything up to thirty 1000 watt lights on at a time, so we had to lay in a temporary cable and fuse box, inadequate but all that the school was prepared to pay for. A large outdoor auditorium meant there was nowhere for front of house lights to be positioned clear of the audience sitting higher up at the back. We solved this by having several long-throw de-focussed spots behind the audience, about 150 feet away (and needing 150 feet of cable to each one).

On the great day the equipment arrived I was in my element. Huge 'acting area' floodlights were hoisted aloft and secured behind the thirty foot high proscenium arch, the masses of weighty cables being led all over the place ending at a heavy manual switchboard and dimmer arrangement, at stage left. Relays hadn't been heard of and all electrical requirements were manually controlled at full voltage on full power. My opposite number, the stage manager, had his control centre opposite, at stage right. It consisted of a desk on which his marked copy of the script sat, and a bank of battery-operated cue light switches. His lifesaving communications was a hand-cranked army field telephone, rigged up between him and CB, who sat in splendour in a deckchair halfway back in the audience. If he wanted to contact me he had to use a messenger. It took us all day to install the lights, fitting them with coloured gelatines as specified on the lighting plot, and angling each one to the required position. We used an eerie green spot to illuminate from below, the face of Bailey-Reynolds who played Hamlet's Ghost. The school carpenter put the finishing touches to our scenery, with me and others helping to make things and generally getting in his way. Then the scene painters got to work, myself among them of course. After that we had lighting rehearsals, where I made up my lighting plot. This consisted of a hard-cover exercise book with a page from the script inserted between each page of the book, underlined wherever lighting cues were required. I wrote in switchboard control changes that had to be set up after each cue, all ready for the next one. By turning a handle on the end of my switchboard I was able to bring up or take down any light by any preset amount. To do so at the right time meant following the script slavishly, listening to every diffused word heard from the other side of the scenery. After attending many rehearsals, I got to know the entire script fairly well and could quote great chunks of it, hearing in my head the voices of the actors declaiming.

We had two matinees, with lighting hardly required at all, but used nevertheless in case visibility went down due to heavy cloud, and three evening performances when it slowly got dark round about act two. It was very exciting hearing a live audience out there, the sound of all the talk and rustling as they arrived and waited expectantly, sitting on those hard little cushions with nothing to lean back against. No padded tip-up seats in Grecian times! Eventually came the whirr-whirr of CB's field telephone, the stage manager called out "Five minutes, please"; the tension rose and so did the butterflies.

Backstage technicians are considered by actors 'a necessary evil', a term I was often to hear throughout my career, but at least the stage manager and the

The Bradfield Greek Theatre. With Shakespeare plays much of the action took place on stage so the seats at the extreme sides would not be used.

lighting engineer were treated as essential members of the team, and therefore grudgingly respected; right up until the last few minutes of the final performance in my case. I'd been having troubles with the overloaded main fuse box getting extremely hot, and had succeeded in swapping the main fuse for a fresh one from time to time during low power demand moments of the play. On this occasion I was quietly watching while the words "Let four soldiers carry Hamlet to his grave…" wafted in from the stage when there was a loud report from this fuse box and all the lights went out, followed by silence broken a moment later by a frantic whirr-whirr of CB's phone and muttered curses as the four soldiers groped their way down the steps carrying a dead Hamlet. Fortunately the play ends just about there, and the orchestra managed the final strains of their music from memory. By the time I had flicked out the red-hot fuse holders and put in fresh ones, the play was over, house lights being all that was needed to help the audience find their way out of the arena. CB was furious, and it was not really the best time to remind him that my request for a proper power supply had been turned down.

A couple of days after I sat my final exams, the master responsible for careers advice fell into step beside me as I walked through the school.

"What are you going to do, Reeve, when you leave?"

"I don't know, Sir," I replied. This was true. I hadn't really given it a lot of thought.

"Going on to Oxford, are you?"

"No, Sir."

"Oh. Doing something in the City, perhaps?"

"No, Sir."

"Dear me. Church, then?"

"No, Sir."

"Well, have to think of something, won't we!"

That was the last time I saw him. Bradfield wasn't very good at careers advice in those days. Hopefully today's pupils get something better.

And so I arrived home with the happy prospect of summer holidays ahead, but not looking beyond that. Something would turn up as it always did.

At the end of my last term at Bradfield I went home as usual wondering how soon I would be called up for National Service, an unpopular two-year spell in the armed forces which all school leavers were subjected to at that time, provided they passed the medical. I was horribly fit so being called up was inevitable. Most of my contemporaries had gone up to Oxbridge, which meant they could defer their National Service until afterwards, by which time—with luck—it would have been abolished. I made enquiries about getting a university grant, only to discover I should have thought about this a year earlier, besides, Cornwall's allocation of grant money was pitifully small and might well only be granted to locally educated children. Father was no help, not realising careers advice wasn't taken care of at Bradfield. His attitude was that he'd spent so much giving me a good education, it was now up to me.

Robbie suggested I should join the Royal Navy, pointing to an advertisement in his Daily Telegraph saying the new Electrical Branch was recruiting would-be officers. Remembering my visit to Portsmouth Navy Days when I was about five, I agreed with him, so sent off for an application form, filled it in and waited. I received an invitation to present myself at the Admiralty for a two-day interview. I arrived at the Admiralty in Whitehall on the appointed day, joining about eight other hopefuls most of whom had been preparing for this interview for months, swotting up on Naval history and inventing convincing stories about their abilities. They all seemed a lot bigger than me, and considerably more worldly-wise. Frightfully important people in smart suits kept pushing past us as we waited in the foyer. I felt apprehensive and distinctly unprepared for the day ahead, as well I might have been. Nobody spoke to me, though they all chatted in a manly way to one another. I wanted to go home. Eventually we were led upstairs and the interviews began. After an introductory session, we went singly from room to room, being seen by various strange men who gave no clue as to who they were. I gathered that there was a senior Electrical Officer, also a co-opted headmaster, a psychologist and one or two other people. Then after lunch we went in one by one for the Board interview—I entered a room with a huge table in it, six men sitting down one side facing a single empty chair on the other. I was asked to sit in the chair. It felt like being invited to sit in the electric chair. Across the green baize tablecloth I looked at six pairs of eyes all boring into me, giving nothing away. My hands were sticky with sweat. I was terrified, and quite unprepared for the first question, which should have been obvious to any ordinary person:

"Why do you want to join the Navy?"

I muttered something about enjoying sailing around at home. The questioning went on, and well before they'd finished with me I reckoned I'd blown it.

At the end of the afternoon, we were each given a rail travel warrant and taken down to the main entrance where a smart blue minibus waited. A uniformed driver took us to Victoria station for the train to Brockenhurst, where another uniformed driver met us and took us off into the New Forest, eventually arriving at the main gate of Exbury House, a Rothschild mansion with the famous gardens. I was impressed. Clearly the Royal Navy did things in style, and I felt angry with myself for not coming prepared for the interview. I had been given a taste of what could be, but had fluffed it.

We had a quiet evening, just the interviewees together, wondering whether the implacable staff serving us at dinner were actually spies checking to see whether any of us ate peas with our knives. Next morning the Board arrived and we were all ushered into a gymnasium where there was a sort of obstacle course. Each of us in turn had to assume the leader role, with the others as his team. The task was to cross a river represented by two lines on the floor, with the aid of various bits of apparatus, and also to take across with us some heavy objects which would require the use of blocks and tackle. I had never heard of the Earl's Court annual Field Gun Competition between various Naval Commands, something the others seemed to know about and which would have been of considerable assistance to me, not understanding at all what was expected. The object, of course, was that each of us was to demonstrate our ingenuity and leadership potential, qualities singularly lacking in me. I got across the river successfully because I am quite athletic and good at this sort of thing, but had difficulties getting the others over and couldn't understand why they seemed to be so obtuse. The penny didn't drop that they were doing this on purpose to show me up in order to further their own chances. I was so naïve that I had never heard of hidden objectives.

After this fiasco, the final trauma was for us all to sit round a table and discuss who we would have to throw out of a hot air balloon to prevent it plummeting to the ground, the choice being the Archbishop of Canterbury, the First Sea Lord (he'd be quite safe), some captain of industry and a prominent politician. While we discussed this, the Board members sat around the side of the room enjoying it all. Then it was, "Thank you, gentlemen. We'll let you know," and back to London with another rail warrant.

I slunk around at home, miserably awaiting the inevitable letter, hardly daring to admit to my father I knew what the contents would say. He'd been going round telling everyone I was about to become an officer in the Royal Navy, something I was cut out for and would excel at.

The letter came within the week. After he'd recovered, father said he would apprentice me to HTP Motors in Truro, if I really wanted to become an engineer. I started at the bottom as an assistant in the Stores. A young man in the neighbouring village gave me a lift each way in his tatty van, for which I handed over £1 a week out of my meagre £3 wages. Father said I ought to contribute to my living expenses now that I was working, but thankfully didn't press this because he still required my share with looking after Polsue's maintenance and taking guests out when required. So began the most mind-numbing and useless year's work I have ever endured which I have no intention of boring you with in these pages. Suffice to say I still recall vividly the smell of rubber tyres, oil and cellulose paint which pervaded all my clothes. I did learn all about Messrs Hosking, Trevithick and Polkinghorne, Cornish mining engineers whose initials were the HTP of the Truro garage, and it was while working there, reversing a new red delivery van into the stores bay, that I had my first biff when I misjudged the gap, denting the corner of the van. I had to see the garage manager about that, and he gruffly told me to be more careful in future. Next day I looked guiltily towards the new van, parked outside, and to my astonishment there was not the slightest sign of any damage. Only by bending down and sniffing around the area could I detect the whiff of new cellulose paint. They'd done a good job there in the paint shop. It would never do for the garage delivery van to be seen with a dent; that would have sent out a poor image indeed. The year at HTP Motors was only tempered by the best year ever for meeting people and sailing.

It so happened that in this year we had a vicar and his three daughters staying, one called Faith and the other two, well, they had to be Hope and Charity though those were not their real names. At the time I was without a girl friend, Faith and I got on well, so we quickly developed what nowadays is called a relationship, within the confines of two sets of ultra watchful parents. Faith was keen to go quite a long way and I was keen to lose some of my innocence, so the prospects were promising. One evening she came over to my room after dinner (at this time my room was the attic space over the dairy in the stable block) and we started in on some clumsy fumbling. Faith had changed into a dress with a zip all the way down the back to make things easier, and I was just getting to work on this, becoming almost helplessly excited as I did so, when we heard irate cries of "John!" and the purposeful tread of father marching in our direction. "John, are you there?" The footsteps halted outside in the yard. We looked at each other. Tomorrow then?

That was as far as we ever got. And all father wanted was someone to man the bar while he had a sit down, but Faith's parents kept a closer eye on her after that, and two days later they were off home. We wrote to one another for some years afterwards, but our friendship had no further opportunity to blossom.

When Polsue first started up, we had tried opening for Christmas, but only for a couple of years. The difficulty keeping such a big house warm enough with no central heating, even in Cornwall, just wasn't worth it; besides during the off season we had no staff, and the family needed leisure time to recover. So we moved into the front of the house once the last guests had gone and lived grandly in the lovely large rooms. It was during the winter father and mother were able to take some holiday; not the best time for holidaying since most places at home were closed for the winter and they could not afford to go abroad, nor were tour operators really geared up for overseas holidays then. Usually it meant going 'up country' and staying with my uncle Ted in Surbiton, a convenient setting off point for a day's shopping in London. Mother, being short and stout, always had a clothes problem, and found it easier to find what she wanted in one of the big London stores. Later she discovered a boutique in Truro that sold attractive clothes for her, but alterations were always needed before they would fit properly. Father dreaded her visits to such places. Mother always returned clutching one or two large packages, biding her time to tell father how much they had cost. The longer she waited the more twitchy father became.

In the spring the St. Mawes Sailing Club opened the season with a grand day out for everyone. This consisted of a free-for-all race across the starting line off the St. Mawes quay and sailing over to Manaccan Creek, just beyond the entrance to the Helford River. On arrival our times were recorded, and for the return trip we would start, slowest boat first, so that we all arrived home again at about the same time. All the boats would have as many crew as they could comfortably take, since this was not a proper race as such, and we would have an hour or two picnicking on the beach in front of the little hamlet of St. Anthony (a different St. Anthony) which was a wonderful suntrap. This always took place in May, and the weather always seemed to be perfect, sunny with a gentle force three breeze. Idyllic.

As the summer wore on, with the demands of our guests my parents retreated into the house more, unable to escape for long. One fine August day Belinda, Mary and I entered Kestrel for a one-design race organised by the Falmouth

Yacht Club as part of Falmouth Week, starting over at Penryn. This was just for fun, really. The three of us had started out just for a sail that day since it was a lovely afternoon with a fresh wind that needed a three-man crew to keep the boat on an even keel. It was only when we were halfway across the Carrick Roads that we saw groups of identical boats sailing about and realised it was regatta day, we thought it would be fun to take part and arrived at the start just in time to enter for the St. Mawes O.D. class. Off we sped after a particularly lucky start when most of the others had gone over the line before the starting gun went, thus having to turn round and re-start. This put us right up at the front of the fleet. Most of the boats had taken in a reef, but we found we could cope with the extra weight of a third crew member, and in no time we were way out ahead. It was only really at this point that we realised how seriously the other competitors were taking the race, always something I avoid because it's less fun if it gets too serious. We creamed back after rounding the furthest buoy to meet the others still on their way out, frantically beating back and forth watching one another like hawks. By this time we were all three sitting in the back of the boat enjoying a cup of tea, with the thermos and cups arrayed on the deck beside us, and chatting away unconcerned. The more we enjoyed it the faster we went, the more the rest of the fleet panicked and the more they fell behind. We finished the race half a mile ahead of the nearest boat, sailed to the committee vessel to give them our details, only to discover it had been a special race and we had won a lovely big prestigious cup. I was given a certificate and asked to come over for the prize-giving at the weekend. Father didn't believe this until I brought the cup home, where it spent its year grandly displayed on the bar counter, a conversation piece for him to tell everyone I was one of the best helmsmen in the area.

The St. Mawes Sailing Club was certainly the social centre of the village. At that time it had no premises of its own, which didn't matter too much in the summer when everyone was out on the water, and from time to time repaired to one of the hotels in the evening. In wintertime they had occasional dances or similar events organised by the Traceys of course, which I always enjoyed. These usually took place in the Ship and Castle Hotel, the proprietor of which was a cheery little chap called Moseley, always anxious to be loved which he seldom was, especially by the tradesmen to whom he generally owed money. He had his own social occasion in the winter off-season by way of an egg-nog party, at which he dashed around dispensing bonhomie and plentiful drinks, delighted to be in favour for once. We had friends who stayed at his hotel one summer and recounted an incident that I can well believe. It was August at the height of the season with all the guests in the dining room waiting for breakfast to appear. There were noises going on behind the swing doors leading to the kitchens, but no sign of any service. After a considerable wait by which time guests were beginning to get restive, the doors suddenly swung open with a crash and out marched the chef followed by all his kitchen staff. He stomped through the dining room waving his arms, shouting, bumping into tables, eventually disappearing out of the far door and out of the hotel.

Close behind ran a whimpering Moseley bent over in a pleading stance calling out, "Come back. All eez forgiven. Pleez! I beseech you!"

"No! Is final. Is too far!" a faint cry from beyond the far door.

Moseley followed it, "Pleez! I double your wages. I give you all zee money! Pleez!"

"No!"

Moseley disappeared, only to reappear a moment or two later in a frantic state, and started to rush round the tables putting down pots of tea indiscriminately, muttering to everyone, "I am so sorry. A leedle problem with zee staff. Soon have eet fixed."

Ten minutes later the chef and his retinue came back in, the waiters reappeared with hot breakfasts, and Moseley came into the room all smiles. "Eez a wonderful chef, but so temperamental!" Later that week their table waiter told our friends all the staff were owed several weeks wages only half of which had been paid as a result of the incident.

The bar of the Ship and Castle was beneath the restaurant, a popular place with all the visitors, though the locals usually preferred the nearby Victory Inn. The whole of one wall had been painted by local marine artist Charles Pears, with a lively nautical scene depicting all the St. Mawes sailing boats milling around at the start of one of the weekly races. Kestrel was there, so also was Charles' own ketch, a lovely old vessel with tan sails and a black hull, not racing but creeping along by the far shore. Round the back of the Ship and Castle was the covered hotel garage where the more wealthy visitors could book a space for the duration of their stay. By squeezing between the cars and climbing over old oil drums and boat trailers one could reach a door at the back which gave onto a small room where the St. Mawes barber operated. From time to time father and I would get our hair cut there. One day I was waiting for my turn, seated between two elderly men I didn't recognize, when father looked in to see if I would soon be finished. Afterwards he commented on the good company I was keeping, saying that one of the men was Lord Falmouth and the other one General Costin.

There were three other hotels in St. Mawes at that time plus one or two guesthouses. Two of the hotels were impossibly upmarket but extremely nice if one had a deep enough pocket. Father, who was regarded by Moseley as a fellow hotelier, never thought of Polsue as a hotel—it was a country house, a home from home, run by a family for families. Certainly not a hotelly hotel.

Those families, of course, all had healthy appetites which was what we liked. Days down on the beach or walking the coastal paths left them ravenous by mealtimes, and we prided ourselves on ensuring everyone had generous helpings of only the best food. Mother had devised several special dishes she could create with the constrictions of the day. One in particular, I remember, was her 'paradise pudding' comprising bananas, prunes, apricots or peaches, with a sponge top, finished off with a soft meringue topping and a huge dollop of Cornish cream. My wife still makes it today but without that cream, alas.

~*~

With Robbie's help I prepared in earnest for another go at the Naval Selection Board in August. He taught me a lot about Naval traditions, a little bit of basic Naval history and introduced me to various people so I could do some name-dropping if the opportunity arose. He told me the qualities he would look for if he were selecting an officer for his own ship. I also had a big advantage over the other hopefuls—I had experienced it all before. Once again I applied and once again I was asked to attend at the Admiralty in Whitehall.

This time things couldn't have been more different. I had confidence, supreme confidence. Almost too much confidence. I stood around in the Admiralty foyer while all the important-looking dark suited men dashed in and out of the building, feeling I was as good as they were. I met the other applicants, most of whom reminded me how I must have looked this time last year, and felt lots better. We started our visits from room to room, having one-on-one interviews. I asked the first one whether he was the psychologist.

"Good heavens, no! I'm the technical man. Want to know if you can tell me the difference between volts and amps." We'd started well. We then proceeded to chat about sailing and he envied me having access to sailing from St Mawes. He told me he had holidayed on the Helford River.

The next person was obviously the headmaster. He had all the signs of a professional teacher, and had me talking about school subjects, particularly Physics, which he soon found was my favourite subject. He didn't say much himself, nor did he encourage me to chat away. I wasn't too sure how I got on with him.

Then it was into a room where a small man came running across waving two trilby hats, one green and one brown. "Which one do you prefer, Sir!" he cried. I looked at them both, thinking what a strange bloke this one was. Green hat. Brown hat... Brown hatter. Queer. Heavens! I'd nearly fallen into a trap. Quickly I said I thought the green one was a much nicer hat and waited with relief while he wrote something in his little book. This must be the psychologist, and I was wondering whether he'd become a bit affected by his own patients when he produced a tape measure and approached me with a gleam in his eye. I backed off.

"Just a few measurements, Sir."

"Tell me," I blurted out, "Are you the psychologist?"

"Good gracious me, Sir. No! I'm the Gieves Tailor. Have to measure you up for the uniform, you know. Only three weeks after they announce the results to when we have you properly kitted out. Start stitching as soon as we hear! Now then, Sir, we'll just get the inside leg measurement." He decorously slid one hand up my crutch while I stood wondering whether I'd stumbled into Alice in Wonderland and any minute the Queen would burst in demanding my head.

I saw the last man in the line. He sat in a gloomy room with heavy net curtains obscuring the window. Two empty teacups stood on the table, and the room smelt of mothballs. I was still recovering from my experience with the tailor from Gieves that I forgot to ask this one who he was, but by process of elimination he must have been the wretched psychologist, if indeed there was one.

I felt well prepared for the main interview with the whole Board after lunch. They sat in a line across the table from my solitary chair, the three I'd seen individually now joined by two new faces, one of whom introduced himself as the Chairman. The Gieves tailor was not there. No doubt he had dashed back to his shop to get out his scissors. The interview seemed to go on for a long time, but I felt fairly happy I had done all right. It was only as I got up to leave that I realised that from under the table I had been clutching nervously at the green baize tablecloth, so that it now had a series of creases all radiating out from that position.

The journey to Brockenhurst and on to Exbury House was just the same as last year, but this time all us candidates were getting on like a house on fire with nobody behaving like the competitive bunch last year. I had kept quiet about having been through all this before, thinking the fewer people who knew the better. We had peas with our dinner once again and no one ate them with his knife, but we had a few laughs about the inscrutable staff that no doubt had hidden microphones and cameras.

Next morning in the gymnasium I endeavoured with difficulty to take no active part in the crossing the river game, but only to give instructions to the others. In the end I joined in, but then that's me. I am the practical rather than the tactical kind, and just hoped I'd be forgiven this once. I was better prepared also for the throwing someone out of the balloon discussion, wading in the moment we had our brief with a "Well, gentlemen, which of them would not be missed?" and for a heady few minutes everyone excitedly deferred to me as a sort of chairman until, with impatience, they bypassed me and argued amongst themselves. But I had done it, just briefly. It was the first time I had ever chaired anything, and remembered the debates Mr Everett had organised at Clayesmore Prep School when I discovered thinking on my feet was not my strong point. It still wasn't my strong point.

Ten days later an official OHMS letter arrived. It started "You are hereby appointed Cadet, Royal Navy, and are directed to report to H.M.S. Britannia, Royal Naval College Dartmouth on…" A rail warrant was enclosed, and I was instructed to only take with me an overnight bag, all uniform and everything else being provided the next day. I'd done it!

Father forgot his ulcer for a while and told everybody in the bar that evening about his clever son. Robbie bought me a gin and tonic, a drink he assured me I would soon come to enjoy (to this day I hate the stuff). I joined the Navy in September 1950.

7

I Join the Royal Navy

I changed trains at Newton Abbot for the Torquay line, and met some of the others on the last leg of the journey, that superb run down to Kingswear station with the River Dart on one's right, the Royal Naval College rising majestically above the town; a stirring sight. To my delight, most of the people I had met at the interview had also been accepted, an unusual occurrence, and possibly explained why the interview had gone so well. We had some fun-loving charismatic people there who swept the rest of us along with them.

At Dartmouth we were met by a petty officer who herded us into an open backed naval truck for the half mile grind up to the college. In addition to the electrical entry there were engineers, supply and seamen cadets. First impressions were like a new school except that it was spotlessly clean with shiny floors, glistening polished brasswork, the grounds tended like those of a stately home, no expense spared. We were Special Entries, the name for post-school entries joining after Higher School Certificate. As such we were allocated to the Benbow Division. All other Divisions at Dartmouth were for the ordinary 13-year old entries, or Darts as they were called. Needless to say we worldly-wise ones looked down on the Darts. We were to spend only one term at Dartmouth after which the senior Darts and ourselves would leave to join the Training Cruiser, an elderly vessel built in 1927 and converted to a Cadet Training ship only three years previously. We were each issued with day uniform, comprising navy blue trousers and heavy blue cotton shirts, 'Number 8s' as we came to know them. Over the shirt we wore a navy blue jersey, very similar to the traditional Guernsey, and to top and tail it were good quality leather shoes and a cap with a white cover and officer's gold cap badge. When it rained we wore heavy oilskin jackets that were cold, stiff and uncomfortable. Such items as pyjamas, underclothes, handkerchiefs and socks were also provided, together with a tin trunk with our name painted on it to put everything in. After a week or two our Gieves 'No 5' uniform turned up along with a good quality Burberry raincoat. The No 5 jacket had four brass buttons signifying officer status, with a white tab on each lapel to denote our miserable rank of cadet. To round everything off we were issued with a seaman's knife, a massively heavy folding knife with a marlinspike at the other end, made of a steel that went rusty as soon as it sniffed salt air. The Navy, always slow and careful about adopting new ways of doing things and new materials to do them with, had not yet decided stainless steel would be a preferable alternative to the rusting sort. It took yachtsmen to show them that. I cherished my peak cap. To me, a peaked cap denoted authority, and made me realise more than anything else that I had at long last graduated from being a mere boy.

Our days were spent being transformed from rough schoolboys into elegant young Naval Officers, learning to march rather than slop along, to salute smartly anything that moved, to learn fundamental seamanship, navigation, engineering, boatwork, teamwork, working with ropes and sails. Apart from the universally disliked parade ground bashing I loved it all. There was a quiet Lieutenant Commander in charge of our Division, with a couple of assistant officers who did most of the classroom work. Then we had three chief petty officers, splendid salt-of-the-earth types, who knocked us into shape and taught the practical things like tying knots, or anchorwork (done on some magnificent models). We were spared any domestic chores such as cleaning or painting, there being a huge staff of civilians, many of them retired Naval people, who kept the establishment shining from top to bottom.

It was impressed upon us that as a group of responsible young men, academically well qualified, we could be brought up to speed quickly in all the non-academic activities that the Darts had been immersed in for the previous four or five years, and were expected to outshine them. A tall order, indeed.

The day started at the unearthly hour of 6.30 by one of the CPOs clumping round our dormitories shouting "Rise and Shine! C'mon, hands off cocks, on socks!" Ten minutes later we had to fall in on parade outside in the dark, which barely gave time to wash and dress. No late arrivals were tolerated. We soon learned to shave at night, and leave our clothes at the ready to leap into when we tumbled out of bed in the morning. The dormitories, known as chest flats, were large, with about twenty beds (which we had to call bunks) down each side, each one with a chest at the bottom and a chair at one side. The cadet next to me was a coloured lad by the name of De Silva, a Singhalese. There were several other Commonwealth Navy cadets, South African, Australian, New Zealand, Burmese and Canadian. One morning I awoke early to see De Silva unrolling a small coloured prayer mat on the floor beside our two beds, expertly check the alignment with his pocket compass, then proceed to say his morning prayers with much bending and straightening. I hadn't seen many coloured people before, certainly never witnessed a Muslim at his prayers. I had a lot to learn.

The morning parade was just a roll call after which one group was marched off to the gym for some energetic leaping about followed by a swim in the nuddy in the huge indoor pool; popular if it was cold and raining outside. Another group went down a steep path through the woods to Sandquay, an extensive boat pound on the River Dart, to learn to handle the heavy Naval boats; both sailing, also rowing—or 'pulling' as it is more descriptively called. Handling 32-foot cutters with a displacement of about a ton was heavy work, with every likelihood of being banged on the head by a metal block, or getting one's foot snarled in a thrashing rope. All ropes were made of coarse fibres, some of them of a softer hemp, and a few of coir. All were stiff and rough to handle when soused in salt water. We also learned to sail the slightly less heavy whaler, a narrower boat with a canoe stern, faster and more responsive than a cutter. Both these craft had heavy loose-footed canvas sails with a sliding gunter rig, in order that all spars were of a length that could be stowed within the boat. They were designed, of course, as ships' boats, which would be hoisted in davits. Sailing was taught by numbers in a most laborious way which took all the fun out of it. Whereas I would normally shout to my crew "Pull the jib in a bit!" we were expected to respond to the helmsman calling out something absurd like "Aft foresail!" Meaningless. It took me some time to get the hang of it. Still, the sound of water clop-clopping under the forefoot was the same whether it was a Naval whaler or our own boat at St. Mawes, and I was happy.

We also sailed in the afternoons, recreational sailing, less formal. I sailed the clinker built Naval fourteen-footer whenever I had the opportunity. With just two of us they went very well, and we even enjoyed a few races, but the river was not a patch on open sea sailing, with too much cover from overhead trees, muddy water and a strong tide or stream to contend with. There were also some Firefly twelve-foot dinghies belonging to the Darts that were not for our use at all, but one day I persuaded the duty officer (who that day happened to be our Divisional Officer, Lieutenant Commander 'Cokey' Cole) if I could take one out.

"Can you sail?" he asked, meaning was I at home sailing dinghies outside the Dartmouth environment. "Yes sir, I live by the sea and have my own boat."

"Very well. If you can sail one boat you should be able to sail anything. Like riding a bicycle. Off you go then."

I quickly rigged a Firefly, leapt in and scudded across the river. This was wonderful! With a fresh breeze I managed to get her up on the plane for a while. I was hailed from the shore to be smartly admonished for not taking a crew. Only senior Darts who had passed some test were allowed to take a Firefly out single-handed. Oh well, it was fun while it lasted.

Another cadet, Peter Walwyn, aided and abetted by Joe Snow, were with me when seven of us were detailed to man a cutter one morning. We had been assured that a cutter is so heavy it is impossible to capsize; a foolish remark, but what a challenge! Peter reckoned we should be able to turn one over if we all sat on the lee side and held both sails tight in as a squall hit us; with any luck she would broach to and provide some entertainment. We tried this across on the other side of the river and succeeded beyond all expectations, sinking the boat to the point where it only just stayed afloat due to the buoyancy tanks. A furious CPO came over in a rescue boat and towed the wallowing cutter home, a job that took ages, while we happily sat and shivered. The staff thought us incompetent, having no idea we'd done it on purpose.

The Britannia Royal Navy College dominates the Dartmouth skyline.
Notice how few small craft there are. Nowadays this is an overflowing marina.

Breakfast awaited by the time we had recovered from these exertions and cleaned up. Mealtimes were the only time we met the Darts, apart from on the parade ground in front of the College. Meals were presided over by Miss Buller, a wonderful catering lady loved by everybody and a Dartmouth Institution remembered fondly by every officer in the Royal Navy. She saw her task as ensuring everyone ate plenty of good nutritious food to enable them to survive the rigours of the day, and walked about from table to table making sure we didn't hold back. She seemed to have an unrestricted budget with access to unlimited off-ration food which, to the Benbows all of whom had endured stringent food rationing at their boarding schools for years, was manna indeed. We really didn't need to be encouraged.

Our days were filled with non-stop instruction, some in the form of formal lessons sitting behind a desk, others much more practical such as throwing a heaving line a distance of fifty feet without it snarling and falling short. Then there was the marching... Oh dear! I didn't mind the shouting and all the bull. I'd met that at Bradfield in the JTC, and just had to adjust to drill without stamping my feet army-fashion, and to learn how to salute the Naval way. What I dreaded was being put in charge of a group of cadets and doing the shouting myself, something in which we all had to take turns. I have a quiet voice and found the very act of raising it was enough for it to fade away altogether. The other cadets who were being marched up and down on my orders quickly discovered this, and as soon as I started them off they lengthened their pace and shot off at great speed out of my vocal range. While I watched helplessly, trying to get some words out, a patient instructor standing behind me and no doubt raising his eyes to heaven barked the immortal "Say something, lad, even if it's only goodbye!" All through my Naval career I suffered from this shortcoming, and it wasn't until many years after I left the Service when I took up public speaking in a small way that I learnt how to project my voice to be heard at the back of a hall.

There was a .22 miniature rifle range, something I quite enjoyed. Like Bradfield, the rifles used were sleeved .303 Lee Enfield rifles, so I was at home with these. Field sports were not really part of the Benbow curriculum, it being thought more important to get properly immersed in river activities as much as possible, so this suited me well. We did have one or two half-hearted cross country runs, mostly on very muddy woodland paths, and I even enjoyed those.

The College possessed a Naval picket boat, a splendid craft of about 45 feet in length, with twin diesel engines in a separate engine room below the raised cockpit. The formal crew for this was a skipper assisted by two hands who manned boathooks when coming alongside, and handled ropes when casting off. With twin outward turning screws, it was an ideal introduction to handling larger craft and enabled us to put into practice what we had learnt in the classroom about the way in which a ship's stern will initially kick to one side when starting off with no way on. We learnt how to make the boat travel sideways using this technique, something that looks very impressive, but nowadays overtaken by bow thrusters fitted to most ships designed for manoeuvrability. One Sunday four of us were allowed to take this picket boat up the Dart to Totnes and back. It was just before high tide so there should be plenty of water, though following the chart was necessary if we were to keep in the channel as the boat drew several feet. Naturally I assumed the skipper role, joined by three of my chums, and we had a wonderful outing, cruising up this lovely river. Somewhere off Ashprington Point I suddenly realised the boat was moving rather slowly in spite of churning up an appreciable stern wave, when someone pointed out we were pushing through soft mud showing only a foot or so below the surface. We had got the times wrong when computing the time difference between high tide at the entrance and high tide at Totnes, and were aground. Within moments the tide had receded a bit more with every likelihood of stranding us on a soft mud bank for the next twelve hours, with no food or drink and the prospect of being in serious trouble when we got back. We went astern on both engines, rocking the boat for all we were worth, and eventually began to move. A minute later we were back in deep water. Phew! Regrettably we had to abandon our visit to Totnes, and turned back, sadder but wiser. We still enjoyed having command of our own ship, taking it in turns to carry out smart boat drill which would have pleased our instructors no end had they been there to see us.

In a classroom down amongst the boatsheds at Sandquay we had lessons in basic engineering. These were taken by a soft-spoken Scottish lieutenant by name of Burn, whom we all took to immediately. On the blackboard he drew immaculate engineering sketches of screws and threads, gears with involute teeth, taught us the theory of energy derived from steam pressure and how to maximize this by reducing pressure to a vacuum, and many safety aspects of handling high pressure or high temperature machinery. One or two of the class were to become engineering officers, so took this in their stride though it must have been new for them as well. I was destined to be an electrical officer, so it was expected I would do better in electrical subjects. In the event I won the prize for the best engineering paper, much to the delight of my other electrical mates and the chagrin of the engineering ones.

At weekends, we usually had 'free' time when some people went down to the nearby Floating Bridge pub by the vehicular chain ferry. That was not my scene however, and I wanted to escape from the college and just explore nearby country. I was about drift off when I was stopped by one of the staff: "Where do you think you're going, lad?" I received a lecture reminding me I had joined the Royal Navy, which meant I was on duty 24-hours a day, seven days a week. Any time I wished to be absent was a privilege that would only be granted when 'the exigencies of the Service' allowed. A salutary admonition and something that I hadn't appreciated. Gosh.

We learnt a whole new culture. The Navy is steeped in tradition in which new recruits are expected to immerse themselves. From the moment we arrived, we adopted a nautical slant to everything. My first visit to the town of Dartmouth was not until a few weeks into the term, and required me to sign a book and be inspected before proceeding ashore. The fact that we weren't afloat so how could we be proceeding 'ashore' was not explained. Naval shore establishments are usually referred to as stone frigates and, well, one goes ashore there from. The internal walls of the College buildings were bulkheads, the ceilings deckheads. We walked around on the deck, and lavatories were known as the heads. When I retired from the Navy many years later, I still used these terms to the amusement of non-Naval people. Even today I use the proper terms for cordage, never referring to it as string or whatever, and wouldn't dream of using an incorrect knot for the purpose.

Part of the Benbow training involved a few days at sea in a real warship. The one allocated to us was HMS Burghead Bay, a bay class frigate with reciprocating engines (known by the cognoscenti as 'up and downers'), and on the appointed day there she was, anchored in the Dart just below the floating bridge ferry. College boats took a party of us out to her and almost immediately I received my first lesson in sailor-speak. You must remember most of us had enjoyed a very protected education, spared the descriptive language of the common man, and here was I, standing on the quarterdeck of this frigate looking at a sailor with a bucket and scrubber, washing salty deposits off the smart grey superstructure. He bent down to dip up some more water only to find his bucket had 'walked' while his back was momentarily turned. Hurling his scrubber down on the deck he shouted, "Fuck! Some fucker's fucked me fuckin' bucket," and then for good measure, "Fuck it!" Turning on his heel he stumbled off to find someone else's. I looked at the others disbelievingly. Is this what sailors are like then?

Burghead Bay smelt like all Naval ships—a mixture of paint, heavy oil fuel, heads and a whiff of cooking cabbage. Horrible when you first encounter it, but wonderfully nostalgic when one first steps aboard after a long spell ashore. Terse commands started to emanate from the Tannoy; "fo'c'sle party fall in", "Special Sea dutymen fall in". Burghead Bay had her visitors safely aboard and was about to sail. (There you are, I find myself using the term 'sail' without questioning how ridiculous this sounds over a century after the last ship had any sails...)

We stood at the back of the open bridge watching while the captain walked about giving orders, the first lieutenant spoke into the Tannoy, the navigator rushed from side to side taking bearings and checking our position, and a couple of sailors kept an eye open for small boats that might dare to cross our bows. A rumble from beneath us and a gush of water churned out at the stern. We began to turn and in moments she was moving through the moored boats in Dartmouth harbour heading for the open sea as the last traces of mud were sluiced off the anchor, a comforting chumping sound coming from below. As soon as we cleared the Heads we felt a gentle Atlantic swell, unnoticed by the ship's company who were showing us around and giving us minor tasks to do. I gazed with awe down a hatch at the sight of huge piston rods threshing backwards and forwards, glistening with oil. A blue-dungareed petty officer wandered about with a handful of cotton waste wiping this and that, oil smudges on the top of his cap that we looked down upon. We were able to enjoy being on the upper deck for most of the time while the ship steamed east along the lovely Devon and Dorset coasts heading for Portland. We entered the huge harbour and dropped anchor. More tasks; the inevitable cleaning, tidying up and suchlike. In groups we gathered round the chart table while the ship's navigator explained something about chartwork, showing us how he had plotted a course enabling Burghead Bay to steam safely through the breakwater entrance without hitting anything. I slept on a campbed in some tiny space with several others, unable to sleep properly with all the ship's noises. In the morning we sailed for Plymouth, and again I stood on the open bridge as we left, certainly the best place to see everything. No sooner had we rounded Portland Bill than we found ourselves in the teeth of a strong westerly that had the ship bucking about. Within half an hour most of us were feeling distinctly queasy, and for the rest of the day we huddled miserably on deck with our backs to the warm funnel. At long last we approached Plymouth breakwater, the motion eased and we all felt better. Our entry was to be formal 'entering harbour' where the ship's company man the upper deck, so we joined in, getting our first view of this most lovely harbour. We went alongside in the dockyard at Devonport and were allowed ashore for a few hours.

This was my first visit to Plymouth. I was completely unprepared for the devastation caused by enemy bombing, and slightly surprised that five years after the end of the war nothing much seemed to have been done to rebuild the city. Though I had now lived at Polsue just 60 miles to the west for several years, I'd never been into the middle of the city before, only passing through in the train. The whole of the centre was almost completely flattened with only an occasional building still standing, or so it seemed. Somebody had recommended Lockyers as a good place for a meal (miraculously our appetites had quickly recovered the moment we entered calm water), and we found it amongst a few unscathed buildings. After eating, it was back to the ship since nobody had any money to spend on visiting a pub afterwards—probably just as well. Another horribly uncomfortable night followed, trying to sleep on the camp bed with no mattress, amid noise, lights and smells. Blearily I stumbled on deck at the crack of dawn, the ship on her way back to Dartmouth, rolling around in a heavy swell with big seas building beneath us. Never was I more pleased to see the welcome sight of the River Dart open in front of us as we steamed passed the castle to our anchorage.

The next sea trip was nothing like so traumatic. This time the whole Benbow Division went out for just the day in a proper ship, something nice and huge, impervious to the vagaries of Atlantic swells. She was HMS Illustrious, a splendid Fleet aircraft carrier lying off Torquay. A naval tender ferried us out, coming alongside her huge grey side. A few faces watched from the deck above from where a single gangway had been lowered. We clambered up, saluting as we came over the side, once more becoming immersed in the same shipboard smells, our ears bombarded by the roar from ventilation outlets and incomprehensible 'pipes' from the Tannoy. Illustrious hadn't anchored, so the moment we were aboard she steamed off into the Channel. We split into parties of six, each in the charge of a midshipman, and the entire day was spent crawling all over the ship having everything explained in detail. It was an exhausting day, but hugely enjoyable. Towards the end of our day we had a chance to watch some flying, huddled together on a space beside the funnel known as the 'goofing platform'. This looked down on the huge flight deck from several decks above, hopefully far enough above to be safe should an aircraft come to grief whilst landing and plough into the island.

To watch a whole squadron of aircraft landing one after the other at less than one-minute intervals is an experience one never forgets. Not until the last one was safely aboard did the barrier come down and it was possible to tow the machines back onto the huge lift that took them down to the hangar below.

Part of becoming a Naval Officer concerned what one might call the 'ambassadorial' duties expected of one when visiting a foreign port, or indeed, when entertaining foreign visitors to our own shores. They included social niceties such as being a competent host, having the ability to make conversation and making one's guests feel relaxed. These are skills nowadays lacking with so many people, more's the pity. We had one or two parties at Dartmouth, which we attended, not to enjoy ourselves so much as to learn the technique; a bit of teaching by stealth here. One 'skill' we were taught was dancing, not that enjoyable when one's partner is a two-left-footed bloke since there weren't any girls at the college in those days. Popular at the time was Scottish Country Dancing, so we learnt to do some of the very basic dances such as the Eightsome Reel, the Dashing White Sergeant and the Gay Gordons. These were taught to us by Lieutenant Burn, who for the occasion wore a splendid creation consisting of his mess undress down to the waist, with a colourful kilt below.

The term drew to its close, a busy term filled with enjoyable activities, one that confirmed for me that I had done the right thing in joining the Royal Navy. With £8 in my pocket, pay accumulated through the term at 2/6d a day, I felt rich indeed. We said goodbye to Dartmouth and headed off to our various homes. We would meet again after Christmas at Devonport Dockyard for the first of our two terms aboard the training cruiser, HMS Devonshire.

Back at home once more I felt I had grown up, was independent, had at last something of real interest to chat to my parents about. Father noticed a difference straightaway.

"You don't slouch any more, John. Do you realise that?"

"Oh, don't I?" I thought for a moment. Maybe bashing around the Dartmouth parade ground had done some good after all.

"And another thing. You're much more confident."

Oh, did I feel it! The folks at home were already starting to look part of a previous life. Wasn't I about to sail across the Atlantic while they carried on here?

~*~

I wasn't at all sure what HMS Devonshire would be like. I eventually found her amidst cranes alongside in one of the basins, an elderly cruiser of some 8,000 tons with three raked funnels, built here at the Devonport Yard in the twenties. Hordes of dockyard workers in shapeless brown dungarees swarmed all over her. These men all carried something like a drill or a welding torch—a sort of badge of office, and spent much time standing around in small groups discussing how they might tackle some activity, working out how to do so with minimum expenditure of effort. Also milling around the ship were lots of young men in blue dungarees wearing officers' caps. These, I realised, were the senior cadets now starting their second spell aboard. I was back to being a junior once again. I threaded my way through all the bits and pieces on the jetty and started to clamber up the nearest gangway, to be told smartly it was for officers only; I was to use the other one. Clearly there were officers and 'officers'. I was allocated to the maintop division, one of four, with a large messdeck on the starboard side of the ship one deck down.

The Royal Navy training cruiser HMS Devonshire

Everything belonging to maintop division had a splodge of green paint on it, to differentiate it from the fo'c'sle division (red), foretop division (yellow), or quarterdeck division (blue). Thus ownership of every walkable item such as a bucket or scrubber could be traced. My messdeck had tables and benches, seating room for about fifty cadets, but no bunks. In the corner was a large cage—the hammock netting, in which a pile of hammocks was stowed. Later I drew my own hammock, blanket and pillow from the stores and received instructions on how to roll it up, securing the roll with a special hammock lashing using marline hitches. This is a tricky hitch to use since there are two ways of tying it, and Murphy's Law always ensured I used the wrong one.

The senior cadets showed us new boys around the ship, and within twenty-four hours we had completed our 'shakedown', even starting to feel at home. Devonshire seemed hopelessly overmanned, as in addition to 300 cadets on board she also had a skeleton crew of conventional lower deck sailors, who could have run the ship quite well without our presence. However, ours was a learning role, we did a lot of things in tandem, had daily theory classes in addition to all the practical work, and learnt a tremendous lot in an extremely short time. The hours were long, and at sea would include night watches, leaving us feeling permanently deprived of sleep which was made much worse by all the fresh air and the ship's motion. We could sleep whenever we weren't standing up and, I'm afraid, this included during lectures.

It took two days to complete storing ship, largely a manual task involving lines of cadets manhandling boxes from where they were dumped on the upper deck by a dockside crane down to the storerooms below. Eventually the last dockyard man left the ship to the relief of everyone aboard. Dockyard workers are not the cleanest of individuals, would leave mucky footmarks wherever they walked, oily fingermarks on everything they touched and had a revolting habit of spitting all the time. They also smoked continuously and had never heard of such a thing as an ashtray. It took three days to get the ship clean.

We sailed in the morning. Leaving the dockside and locking through from the basin to the Hamoaze with all the attendant warp-handling activities and organisation was a new experience for us cadets, so as many as possible were involved. At least a dozen cluttered up the bridge getting under the regulars' feet, with another dozen on an open bridge above playing a mock secondary role under instruction. The fo'c'sle was full of men even though no anchorwork was needed. A small harbour tug had entered the basin and assisted as we left the dockside to align ourselves with the narrow entrance of the basin lock. Teams of dockyard riggers took various warps offered them by the sailors above, wrapping them around large capstans on the dockside, while a bowler-hatted foreman controlled all dockside activities with nothing more than a whistle and a wave of an arm. Throughout all this, constant orders came over the Tannoy while us new boys gazed in wonder from one thing to another, conscious it would be our turn next time. Soon the ship was heading down the Hamoaze and out to sea, smart cadets lining the upper deck in our best uniforms.

Maintopmen had a space in the starboard waist where we fell in every morning, to be addressed by our chief petty officer, and by our divisional officer. We also had a 'schooly', appointed to the division. Ours was a charming lieutenant by the name of Mike Moreland, who wore the blue band between his gold stripes that identified him as an instructor officer. Mike was a bit of an enigma, much older than most lieutenants and sported some Eighth Army medal ribbons amongst the general service ones on his chest. He had served with Montgomery in Africa and

Me taking a sunsight

the invasion of Italy, only joining the Navy after obtaining his degree when the war ended. He was a wonderful person, full of interesting stories to tell and an excellent instructor. His speciality was navigation, a subject schoolies normally taught since it involved a lot of complicated mathematics working out the ship's position from the sun or stars by means of a sextant and an accurate timepiece. Every day at noon sightings would be recorded by groups of cadets dotted all over the upper deck, the ship's position being recorded as anywhere within a thousand miles or so of the correct one, often in such bizarre spots as the middle of the Sahara desert. If we were in sight of land, then it was eyes down at every binnacle around the ship, to take a bearing on any prominent object that could be seen. Coastal navigation was much more fun, and one of my favourite pursuits. I had done some of that in a small way whilst pinpointing the best mackerel grounds off St. Anthony's Head.

We were on our way to the West Indies, nowadays surely one of the favourite areas for cruise liners. We were no cruise liner, but there were a couple of compensations that cruise liner passengers would have given their eye teeth for—we were being paid to go on this cruise, and we were to visit a string of wonderful islands before the days of tourism, islands that normally only ever saw the occasional trading schooner. The anticipation was tremendous.

But first we had an unpleasant obstacle to overcome. This unwieldy high-sided cruiser was heading straight for the notorious Bay of Biscay, and it was January. The memory of my short trip in Burghead Bay was still painfully clear, and already, on our first day out from Plymouth, I realised our ship was quite the wrong shape to take a rough sea without protest. She had once been fitted with four huge eight-inch gun turrets, but three of these had been removed at her conversion, leaving her higher in the water and considerably more tender than originally designed. The gales hit us a day later and we spent four days in the Bay, the ship rolling twenty degrees or so, more or less hove-to in a heavy swell that imparted a horrible corkscrew motion. Almost to a man we became violently seasick and quite unfit for anything. We lay around the upper deck in oilskin-clad heaps wishing the world would end, while the one or two cadets unaffected by the motion walked about munching bacon sandwiches and laughing at us all. It was quite the most miserable four days I can remember, and unfortunately I can remember it very well even after half a century! Then, suddenly, I discovered I could keep down an ice cream without puking, the sun came out, I could venture below deck for long enough to have a wash and shave, and I was over the hump. It was a beastly experience I wouldn't wish on anyone, but the next time we went to sea, the nausea was not so bad, and eventually I was more or less unaffected, though after a long spell ashore I still get that light-headed dry throat feeling on my first day out, which I can nowadays control; and, of course, there are now plenty of motion sickness drugs one can take.

We kept watches. Ten minutes before our duty watch started, we would be woken up and blearily left our nice warm hammocks for the cold windy deck above. The boring job was to be detailed for seaboat's crew—eight or ten of us spent the watch huddled in the ship's waist beside a whaler secured above us in the davits; ready in case anyone fell overboard. Other jobs were more pleasant: watch-keeping on the bridge being a popular one. Even more popular on a cold winter's night was watch-keeping below in a machinery space. The engine room was okay, and one spent the watch chatting to a 'stoker' petty officer who stood beside the engine room telegraph indicators, near to big handwheels controlling steam to the main engines. His job was to keep the engine revolutions at the correct speed and respond to any orders from the bridge. He had one or two minions who visited every bit of working machinery to ensure it was operating correctly, and my job was to crawl around noisy vibrating machines taking readings, reporting back anything untoward. Next door in the boiler room was not quite so pleasant; actually if I am honest I found it a little scary. To start with, the boiler room space was pressurised, so one had to pass through an airlock to enter or leave. The temperature in this huge space was unbearably hot, so one wore nothing except a pair of pants beneath one's overalls. Also the noise from the enormous steam-powered turbo fans was tremendous, making conversation out of the question. I would clamber down slippery steel ladders, along metal gratings, eventually reaching the centre of operations—the metal deck in front of the boilers. Here one had the benefit of the incoming air blast, so it was a little better. The stoker PO responded to demands of the main engines in the next space by adjusting the boiler pressure. He did this by altering the speed of the big turbine-driven fans, and keeping the fuel supply to each boiler at the required pressure to ensure correct combustion. His success at doing this was instantly recognised on the bridge by whether any smoke appeared from the funnels. Each boiler had a door with a small spyhole through which one could peer at the raging furnace inside, extremely conscious of the searing heat only inches away. One was also aware that the steam being produced was at an extremely high temperature and pressure, which made it frighteningly lethal should there be any accident. A spell in the boiler room was exhausting and it took me half an hour to recover from the heat and noise. I felt sorry for the stoker PO and his minions (known as 'steam beetles') who virtually lived in such spaces whenever we were at sea. One of the duties of a bridge watch-keeper or seaboat's crew was to keep the other members of his watch supplied with pusser's 'kai': a horrible-sounding concoction which was warming and surprisingly acceptable on a cold night. It was made by shaving into slivers with one's rusting seaman's knife a block of unsweetened cooking chocolate. This would be done on a table top or similar, the resulting shavings being scooped up and placed in a large aluminium jug. Add to this a tin of condensed milk and some sugar, half fill the jug with cold water and the first stage was complete. One would then carry this gungey mixture down to the engine room, carefully negotiate the slippery steel steps to deck level, request permission from the watch-keeper PO to have some steam, then go round the side of one of the low pressure turbines to where a small copper pipe emerged. I think this was for taking off samples of feed water for analysis, but it was a convenient source of low pressure steam for our purpose. One would put the pipe into the jug and switch on, whereupon steam bubbled gently into the mixture, hotting it up and at the same time diluting the contents with condensed steam. The result was a most welcoming drink, albeit with a little oil in it and slightly tainted with the chemicals, mainly ferric chloride, used to control boiler feed water acidity. The metal mugs it was dispensed into were also nice to warm one's hands on, though the chipped edges both cut and burnt one's lips. One of our number reappeared from his visit to the engine room one night ashen-faced, his kai jug empty.

"Where's our kai!" we wailed, "Don't tell us you've spilt it".

"Gone. It just vanished as I was hotting it up. All I got was a furious bollocking from the stoker PO for polluting his feed water. Says he'll put me on a charge."

It wasn't entirely his fault. At the moment he was about to bubble steam into the jug someone altered the engine revs and for a moment there was a vacuum instead of a positive pressure in the line. Our kai was now circulating forever around the boilers and engines.

Every day it became warmer. Oilskins were discarded, as were our heavy blue jerseys. Then, one day, we discarded winter clothing altogether, moving into tropical rig. For the cadets this meant the same old blue cotton shirt, but we wore blue shorts and sandals. Flying fish leapt out of the way as our bows cut through their shoals, dolphins occasionally caught up with us and cavorted about in the bow wave zooming back and forth playing 'last across' with the old lady. I have happy memories of the night watch on Devonshire's bridge, a few of us chatting together with the professionals, a full moon shining across the sea, the hum of ventilation fans the only sound except for the rhythmic swish of our bow wave as we dipped into the swell. Idyllic moments, these. We even tried doing an eightsome reel one evening, hands joined as we circled round on the quarterdeck; not easy on a moving deck which might have shifted sideways by the time one landed, resulting in a twisted ankle perhaps.

But Devonshire was a working Naval ship, she wasn't all fun! Every morning the dreaded bugle call sounded reveille at some impossibly early hour, we tumbled out of our hammocks, stowed them away, and fell in on the upper deck where, barefoot, half an hour would be spent scrubbing decks. She had lovely sun-bleached white teak decks, which were hosed down by our trainer petty officer while we followed behind with long-handled deck scrubbers scrubbing for all we were worth. At the end of the run the petty officer would call "about turn, scrub aft" or "scrub for'd," and we'd go back the other way. Every so often the decks needed a better clean than could be obtained with plain water, and then it was down on hands and knees with the holystone. Only plain seawater was used for the teak decks, a commodity with an unending supply. From time to time it was deemed necessary to wash salt encrustation off the paintwork, when fresh water would be employed, a bucketful being meted out with care. About this time a new wonder substance was being introduced into the Navy, a thick brownish oily-looking liquid which was added to the water if there was oil to be washed off which wouldn't respond to the soft soap solution then in use. This came in one gallon cans called 'Teepol', an industrial detergent and the first anyone had seen, soon to be used for washing dishes and anything else that was greasy. It was a concentrated harsh chemical devoid of any scent or refinement to make it pleasant to use, and would degrease one's hands so effectively that they quickly became chapped.

The scourge of everyone's life was the ship's Executive Officer, 'Ajax'. He was everywhere, ensuring the ship from top to bottom was as clean as an operating theatre. Needless to say he was feared and disliked by all, something he seemed to revel in.To me he appeared to be one of those tiresome people one meets in all walks of life who are devoid of any humour, very 'pusser', interested solely in the highest standards of the Service, regardless how unpleasant this might be for everyone else. I suppose he was good for us, but we all felt we could have done without his standards. One particular person really upset him and that was the schoolie attached to the Foretop division, one Instructor Lieutenant Brett-Knowles, a bearded rangy man 6ft 6in tall. BK was an electronics boffin in uniform and as such utterly incomprehensible to Ajax. As we approached within a couple of hundred miles of the Windward Islands on our way to Trinidad, it was decided to drop one of our cutters with a crew of eight and for it to sail on alone to the nearest one, Barbados, where we would pick it up in a day or two. For safety reasons it was obviously necessary for the ship to know where it was at all times, and the Captain was proposing to rely on our radar for this, since he intended to be no further away than hull down below the horizon. BK had other ideas, of course, and proceeded to rig up aerials around the quarterdeck to make it possible for the cutter to have two-way radio contact as well. BK was in the middle of this when Ajax arrived with a cry of "Mr Knowles, get off my quarterdeck!" BK actually got his way and the cutter set off with a radio aboard which was probably very sensible and certainly a comfort for the crew who suddenly found themselves alone in the Atlantic watching their mother ship sail away over the horizon.

This might sound a somewhat foolhardy venture, but we were in the southeast trade winds, so there wasn't very much risk really. In the event we picked them up two days later none the worse except for over-exposure from a relentless sun. Certainly the crew had something to tell the folks at home.

Once we'd recovered the cutter we didn't call in to Barbados at that time, since we were due to do so a week or two later, but headed straight off for Trinidad. Port of Spain, Trinidad's capital and only port, has a lovely big harbour and it was intended we moor ship there. This is one of those complex evolutions no ordinary seaman would dream of attempting unless they were having to remain in a poor anchorage for a protracted stay. It involves dropping two anchors spaced some distance apart, the anchor cables being connected to the ship via a heavy unmanageable apparatus known as a mooring swivel. This device prevents the two cables from becoming twisted should the ship swing right round, and has to be let down from one hause pipe and hauled up through the other several times while anchor cables are 'broken', shackles inserted, the mooring swivel connected and the anchor reconnected to the other end of it, the whole operation being repeated for the second anchor cable.

So it was with some anticipation that we all looked forward to entering our first port of the cruise. Early next morning we awoke to find the ship close under Trinidad's mountainous north coast, intriguing tropical smells wafting out to us. Dressed in our best whites, cadets manned the ship's side as we entered the bay even though there was no one near enough to see us. Grubby brown pelicans plummeted into the sea around us, surely the clumsiest fishers one ever saw, but extremely successful for all that. Several rusty tramps rode at anchor off Port of Spain, but further out a clear space was available for our mooring game. I watched most of it from the cadet's bridge, the one above the real bridge where the action was. Our job up there was to take bearings on just about everything and 'fix' the ship's position on our chart. The fo'c'sle was crowded with cadets, clouds of rust rose up in the air as cables rattled in and out of various holes and the CPO in charge bellowed orders to everyone in sight. Eventually one of the anchors hit the bottom in the desired place and our Union flag was broken out at the jackstaff, timed by means of complicated flag signals to the quarterdeck where at the same moment a huge white ensign was hoisted at the ensign staff replacing the 'sea' ensign—a small somewhat tatty flag normally flying from the yardarm. Most of us by this time had fallen out, leaving the anchor party struggling for the next hour to finish their mooring. I'm sure all this must have looked wonderful to any watchers, but we were a mile from the shore, and the only people I noticed were a couple of dirty fishermen in a small open boat who never look our way at all. While all this was going on a large rusty tanker came in, passing us a few hundred yards off. There was only one man visible, whom I could clearly see at the wheel on the bridge. The tanker slowed right down, he left the bridge, sauntering along the walkway to the bows where he could be heard banging away at the anchor slip. Then came a rattle as the anchor dropped, the man now standing behind the capstan controlling the rate at which it fell while the ship still moved forward slowly, eventually coming to a stop and swinging round. He then went back to the bridge area and disappeared inside. The whole operation had taken just a few minutes. I glanced for'd at our own fo'c'sle. About twenty cadets were just securing the last items prior to being dismissed. We had arrived.

I don't remember much about that visit to Trinidad. It was my first visit abroad, and the memories are of noise, colour and dirt, and of a wonderful sandy beach fringed with palm trees. We had arrived during carnival time, so that explained the noise of course. But I think we only had one trip ashore and that was when some of us were taken by bus to Marracas Beach for an afternoon. Marracas then was an unspoilt tropical paradise and I have a photograph of me, skeletally thin in those days, posing with some local boys.

The quarterdeck division had to rig a heavy awning over their precious quarterdeck once we had entered harbour. This became another one of those 'evolutions' of which the Navy seem to be so fond, and involved most of the division 'cheesing down' the loose ends of ropes into flat coils after a weary half hour spent heaving an extremely heavy bundle of damp canvas over the various ridge wires. Naval ships had wire ropes here and there, notably the guardrails (which have to be struck down flat on the deck when at action stations), the ropes being of galvanised steel. However new they were, they always seemed to be verging on going rusty, so would be liberally wiped with linseed oil in an attempt to keep off the salt water. It meant one never put a hand on a guardrail or this mucky mess would get all over one's clothes (and we wore immaculate white sometimes). When rigging the awnings, any linseed oil that hadn't hardened had to be wiped off the ridge ropes with a handful of cotton waste, since the rust marked the cotton awning permanently.

Before leaving Trinidad the ship's officers held a party on the quarterdeck, all our motorboats being required to ferry the guests from shore. I didn't get involved in this one as boat crews only needed a few of us.

We set sail next morning after a protracted effort at unmooring ship which seemed to take half the morning and led to a lot of banter between the fo'c'sle officer and the foretop one. These two were always at each other in what they liked to call a healthy competitive spirit, and on one occasion when after entering harbour we were kept waiting ages by the fo'c'sle party before being allowed to fall out after manning ship, the foretop officer complaining "What on earth are you doing up there in the bows?" to which the reply came "I'm anchoring my part of the ship. What are you doing with yours?"

Back at sea again for just a few hours we headed for the first island of the Windward chain, Grenada. Here we dropped anchor right in front of the harbour entrance to St. George's, the capital. I loved Grenada. It was smallish, lush and green round the edges with a pleasant mountainous ridge running down the middle, and seemed quiet and reasonably prosperous. All these islands have their main town on the western, sheltered side while the unsheltered eastern side is generally battered by the trade winds that blow continually. It meant we could ride peacefully at anchor with sufficient breeze keeping the ship facing the same way all the time, and a flat sea with no swell. We launched all our boats, which was the job of the two top divisions. First we had to swing out from the ship's side a long wooden boom and secure this at right angles by means of guys. From the boom hung rope ladders and ropes from the end of which our boats could be secured, three big motorboats or cutters on either side, and several dinghies in a 'trot', one behind the other. To get aboard one had to walk along the boom holding onto the topping lift, climb down one's chosen rope ladder, then pull up a boat by heaving on its painter until it was possible to jump in without getting wet. There might be quite a current flowing, so one had to take great care. The boat officer would watch one's progress from the deck above, and there was usually a boat's crew not far away who could man a powerboat and effect a rescue if one did fall in.

The ship organised a number of races with whalers and the fourteen-foot dinghies. I entered a dinghy race and recruited from our division a lightweight friend, Jim Bowen, to crew me. We jumped aboard, rigged the dinghy which was none too easy with the boat snatching about on the end of its painter, fixed on a couple of darning wool 'telltales', one on each shroud, to tell me where the wind was, and off we went. We soon discovered the two of us were not heavy enough to keep the boat upright in the fresh breeze we found further out, so had to spill wind out of the mainsail. Other entrants on seeing how we were getting on decided to take in a reef to make their boats more manageable. I had already ignored the first precautionary rule—in doubtful conditions shorten sail before setting out rather than wait until one has found out what the weather is like out there. Taking in a reef while out on a choppy sea in a dinghy can be difficult, and I decided not to try.

The starting gun went and we sped off, soon getting the dinghy almost planing where she shot ahead of the rest of the fleet. It was exhilarating but also rather worrying, as we would have to go round a buoy about a mile downwind then beat back home in this fresh breeze, now gusting force five or six. Fortunately Jim was a competent crew and I was just lucky, so when we rounded the mark and began a series of long tacks, I tried to sail closer to the wind than I would normally do, thereby not having to spill so much wind to keep upright. It meant we theoretically went slower, but this was not noticeable in these conditions. It also meant we sailed several points closer to the wind than anyone else and so completed the course with fewer tacks. Another competitor, one of the officers, was a naval sailing champion, so I was anxious to do fairly well against him. We crossed the finishing line a good half-mile ahead of the rest of the fleet, much to our surprise, and had the boat back on the boom and unrigged by the time the last competitor came in. This race carried a prize, the Crispin Cup, which I am looking at now as I write.

My divisional officer was delighted, but the glory was soon forgotten. A distraction had been taking place while the race was in progress. One of the chiefs had been fishing off the quarterdeck on the far side of the ship and succeeded in catching a huge shark. It was hoisted out of the water on the little davit normally used for the starboard gangway, and must have been all of ten feet in length. The word 'sharkskin' may suggest a snazzy type of cloth to some people, but to me it will always mean something quite different. After all the photographs had been taken, this enormous fish was brought aboard and set upon eagerly by one of Ajax's seaman POs who in no time at all had skinned it, cutting the skin into pieces about six inches by four. Sharkskin is like a coarse grade of wet-and-dry sandpaper, extremely robust, and for the rest of the cruise was used in place of holystone for just about every cleaning job. The rest of the fish went back over the side where all its cousins soon devoured it.

With a couple of friends I went ashore in Grenada. Nobody had any money, so there was not much to attract us in the town, therefore the three of us decided to walk northwards up the west side of the island, along a quiet grassy path with fresh green herbage and wonderful tropical scents; a welcome change from shipboard smells and noises. We eventually came to an old colonial style house with a balcony covered in frangipani and bougainvillea, set back in a well-tended garden. One of us, John Daly, announced we would pay a visit to these ex-pats; they'd be sure to welcome us! The result was we were invited to tea and scones by an extremely kind lady who was indeed most welcoming. By this time the ship had lain off St. Georges for three days, so the whole island knew all about us. She told us there had been some unrest amongst the local people who felt they were being unjustifiably exploited by their English employers, one of whom was her husband. A British warship lying offshore might have a sobering influence on them.

Back on board we found that the captain had been discussing the civil unrest with the governor, wondering whether Devonshire could help in any way, and it was decided to attempt to show a bit of strength. As we had no actual strength not being an operational unit, he meant bluff. A couple of open-backed trucks were borrowed, filled with cadets in combat gear carrying rifles, and driven round the island's roads all day. Meanwhile the ship weighed anchor and slowly circumnavigated the island with its eight-inch gun trained ashore. This seemed to have the desired effect, and when we finally left Grenada all was peaceful.

The next stop was Barbados where we anchored off Bridgetown. This time I went ashore with a group of people to be shown round one of the sugar plantations at the southern end of the island. This was an eye-opener for me, not realising that sugar cane like all canes is a grass, and a lethally sharp-edged one at that. The way to handle it was to set fire to the crop at harvest time, the flames racing through the field, rapidly burning off all the dry husky outer part without damaging the sugar within. The result was a much safer crop to handle albeit a filthy dirty one. It was then cut by hand with machetes and brought to the refining sheds on hand-pushed trucks running on a rickety railway track. There it was crushed and boiled up, strained and put into huge tanks. A highly paid magician then watched over it until the exact moment when he deemed it right to start the crystallisation process. If he had judged correctly, sugar would be crystallised out at the correct size. I think it was exported in this semi-refined state to be further refined once it reached the UK. At that time there was no beet sugar grown at home, cane sugar being the only type imported, and it was incredibly cheap. West Indian wages were appallingly low, but the laid back lifestyle made it possible to exist, the employers arguing that if the men were paid any more they would spend it all on drink and be no good for work.

After this visit, the rest of my shore time was spent relaxing at a beachside bar, where a jetty ran out to enable the barman to hand swimmers their rum-and-orange cocktails without getting his feet wet. Bliss. I was enjoying a spell away from the ship with no sailing for a change.

After Barbados we sailed back to the Windward Islands chain past St. Lucia (without stopping) and on to Antigua. On the way we passed several large trading schooners, part-square riggers plying between islands, and a lovely sight to behold. On the lee side of the island chain the winds are generally on the beam and steady, ideal for these craft. At Antigua, where I was not free to go ashore, a party landed to go round to Nelson's English Harbour and tidy it up. Before the days of tourists, the harbour had become very run down. Nowadays it is a beautifully kept museum of Nelson's time. It was while anchored off Antigua that my maintop companions got into serious trouble one day. Someone had the idea of baiting the huge gulls that perched noisily on the boat boom just outside our gunroom scuttle (porthole). They devised a game whereby a gull would be made to take off by a sudden jerk on the forestay line tied to the boom from further up the ship. Then, as it was about to land again, a piece of ham fat tied to a length of string would be lobbed out of the scuttle. The gull hastily grabbed this, swallowing it before another gull could snatch it away, whereupon it was the work of a moment to pull in the string complete with gull on the end. Drawn to the ship's side by all the raucous gull screaming, the officer of the day on deck above was just in time to see a gull disappearing inside, and sent his petty officer down to find out what was going on. The PO opened the gunroom door to find three frightened gulls flying awkwardly round the room, their enormous five foot wingspan clattering against the bulkhead. Now, nobody had told us of the nautical man's belief that gulls are the souls of drowned sailors and must be respected, so three cadets found themselves up on a charge.

Being on a charge involved attending Commander's Table in the morning. Ajax would stand behind the mahogany lectern glowering at the offender being marched in by a regulating petty officer. With a "Left-right-left-right. Offender, 'Shun! Off cap," the poor man was brought up to the table, stood to attention to face the unfriendly scowl of Ajax at close quarters, a somewhat irritated stare from his own divisional officer on one side and a smug look from the prosecuting officer with a clipboard on the other. The charge was read out.

"Well?" invited Ajax.

Whatever one said, a punishment of some sort would be awarded, so it was generally best to think up a suitable excuse for one's momentary lapse of obedience. This was difficult in the case of the three gull-baiters, and they received Ajax's full wrath, then sent packing with extra cleaning to be done during the dogwatches in the days ahead.

On our last day at Antigua we had a visit from the local steel band, who gave us a colourful concert on the quarterdeck with enough noise to be heard back on shore. Most of us had a go on the highly polished drums, converted from humble oil drums cut in half.

Our final visit was to tiny Beef Island, one of the Virgin Islands, a British dependency set apart from the main Virgin Islands group, and uninhabited. Here we all went ashore for a 'banyan', Navyspeak for a beach party and barbecue. We swam and sunbathed all day but discovered the other side of such tropical paradises: some cadets stepped on sea eggs, breaking off the spine tips which then remained buried in the soles of their feet where they festered. Not nice. Also the water had a large number of rather nasty jellyfish floating about including Portuguese men-of-war. My photographs don't show these things any more than the tourist brochures do. Still, the banyan was a great success even though it did take hours to get everybody back on board again, several days to get rid of all the sand and weeks before one's feet were healed.

Returning across the Atlantic was an anticlimax after all this, but we were ready for home after a few months in the tropical West Indies. The weather was benign all the way with the Northeast trade winds behind us for much of the time. Devonshire's economical cruising speed was about twelve knots. Apart from a smudge of cloud on the horizon one day which somebody said was Madeira, we saw nothing all the way across.

We were headed for Gibraltar, our last port of call before home. Waking one morning there was the unmistakeable smell of land. Africa. A faint haze on our starboard side was all we actually saw of the great continent, and then the coast of Spain appeared on our port side. An hour or two later we rounded a headland and there was the magnificent sight of the Rock of Gibraltar rearing 1,400 feet up in the pink morning sunshine. Entering harbour was to be one of those tiresome events when we all had to don our best uniforms (we were back in 'blues' by this time) and line the ship's side. All, that is, apart from some of the hands who were preparing ropes and hawsers for coming alongside. Naval ships always come alongside a jetty with their bows facing out to sea in case a quick getaway is required, so as we were to come alongside port side to, the port seaboat was to be lowered before we entered the harbour so that it could be used during our stay in port. A group of cadets were getting into this boat to prepare for lowering when one of them on being instructed to "Check the pins"—a command given to ensure the safety pins that prevent the boat being slipped from the davits prematurely were indeed doing their job. However, all he was meant to do was ensure the pins were not taking a load, but he actually took one out to prove the point. At this precise moment someone else stumbled and grabbed at the first thing that came to hand which happened to be the apparatus for releasing the boat. The boat immediately slipped at one end only, to be left hanging vertically from one of the davits, the crew being hurled into the sea without warning. A tremendous panic ensued, the bridge sounded off six short blasts of the siren—the signal for Man Overboard, the captain put the ship hard a-port thereby swinging the stern away from the cadets in the water, while the other seaboat was made ready to effect a rescue. All this happened on the far side of the ship from where I was standing, so I missed all the fun. Fortunately nobody was seriously injured, but one of my chums, Antony Corfe, was badly shaken by his experience and was twitchy for days afterwards. The main injury was hurt to our pride, for doing something like this is not a very dignified way to enter harbour, not at all professional.

I enjoyed Gibraltar. I climbed to the top, saw the famous Barbary apes, went round the back to see the extraordinary water catchment structure, and visited some of the catacombs open to visitors. Most of the Rock was in the hands of the military at this time and strictly out of bounds, even to a sister armed Service. Several of us visited La Linea over on the Spanish side, a procedure that involved walking across the airfield runway to the border post, where we were waved through into a strip of no-man's-land. Then there was much form-filling and invented hassle at the Spanish border fifty yards on before we were allowed through by officious Spanish border police, with a lot of pretence reluctance and no welcome. We must have been issued with a paper pass of some sort, for we possessed no passport in those days. We sat outside in the sunshine drinking cheap sherry and being opportuned by small boys trying to polish our shoes or sell us their sisters. John Holmes, John Daly and myself took up the offer of visiting an 'exhibeesh' (just for the educational experience, you understand). We were led through dodgy back streets to a Certain House where we were met by a Madame wearing a housecoat with pockets full of jangling assorted coins of several currencies. She whistled up half a dozen well endowed but rather grubby looking women for us to choose from. John Holmes expertly selected two and we sheepishly followed them into a sordid back room where they proceeded to undress and have simulated sex with one another, then invited us to go further with them if we'd like to. I found the whole business somewhat distasteful and was glad we were all somewhat skint (as usual) so even had there been any temptation it wouldn't have been possible to satisfy it. Safely back in Gibraltar again we finished our day at the cinema watching some cowboy film whilst quaffing cheap sherry which we'd bought in La Linea.

Whilst in Gibraltar we had to paint ship. This didn't mean just giving it some paint here and there; we did that all the time, and there was always the smell of wet paint somewhere. No, this was Paint Ship, an evolution. Three months at sea had resulted in rusty streaks and patches here and there, and she no longer looked smart. This would never do for returning home in the full public glare. The whole ship's company was required, and involved unearthing masses of scaffold boards normally kept somewhere down in the bilges. The boards had cross members bolted at each end, so that they could be slung over the ship's side with the cross members holding them far enough off the side for someone to sit on the board, legs dangling, and wield a paintbrush. With two of us sitting on a board, a pot of paint between us and wielding a sticky three-inch paintbrush, we lowered ourselves down from ropes secured to a guardrail stanchion. From time to time we needed to lower ourselves a bit more in order to paint the next section, so had to employ careful teamwork to keep the plank level. This involved each of us untying the rope that had been secured around our end of the plank, and lowering the two ropes together. A boat would be cruising up and down in the paint-speckled water to retrieve an occasional dropped paintbrush, somebody's hat, sometimes a whole paintpot and—on one occasion—a complete painter who somehow fell off backwards. It took all day to paint the entire ship's side from deck level to the waterline, followed by cutting in a smart black boot-topping and the ship's identification number on each side. By the end of it most cadets had painted much of themselves as well. Messy business, but the ship looked lovely.

Leaving Gibraltar at last on a glorious sunny morning we headed out into the Atlantic once more, sailing close enough to the Spanish coast to catch a glimpse of Cape Finisterre and the Cantabrian mountain ranges behind, the realisation that at long last we really were on our way home, next stop Plymouth. Once more we headed into the Bay of Biscay with its inevitable steep seas and howling wind, but now worldly wise and impervious to the ship's bucking motion. Two days later we awoke on a grey morning to see Plymouth Breakwater ahead and proudly lined the rail for the run past the Hoe and Drake's Island. With a wonderful end of term feeling we came alongside once more, looking hopefully for any faces we might recognise on the jetty below.

In fact it was all a bit of a letdown initially. Shore leave was granted, but we had to be back on board before midnight. Next morning the ship was once again swarming with grubby dockies spitting their way round our lovely clean decks and by lunchtime Devonshire had settled down to a couple of weeks in Dockyard hands, her boilers extinguished, electric cables, water hoses, ropes of all sorts, festooned across from the jetty, the life gone out of her, a hulk once more. Two days later we went on leave, by which time we'd all forgotten how to put on a rolling gait as we walked along the jetty to waiting buses.

~*~

Our second cruise in Devonshire was completely different. To start with I was now a senior cadet and felt greatly superior to the pink-faced youngsters that were having their first cruise in the ship. We arrived a couple of days ahead of the new ones so that we could get ourselves organised before having to look after them. The Darts among them already knew a lot more at this stage than we did, and they seemed to take life very seriously. Probably due to the influence of some of my immediate contemporaries I had by this time learned to enjoy life, without getting too serious about it. I'm sure one lives longer that way.

When we left the Hamoaze and passed the breakwater this time we headed east up the channel, our eventual destination Norway. However, the first stop was to Torquay where we anchored in the bay for several days. It was glorious weather and the ship had been challenged by the Babbacombe Sailing Club in the next bay to a dinghy race. I managed to get into the team and we were taken round in one of the ship's boats to meet our hosts. We were to sail Firefly dinghies, the lightweight twelve footers in which I had enjoyed a single outing whilst at Dartmouth. There wasn't really enough wind to sail them fast, but it was a good day for all that, even though our hosts thrashed us; not surprisingly since they were all experienced Firefly sailors who knew their own bit of water well. After the race we repaired to the clubhouse to await our return boat. By the time it arrived three of us were so enjoying the hospitality that we elected to make our own way back to the ship later. Quite a bit later, in fact several hours and many beers later, I found myself standing on the Torquay jetty waiting for the next liberty boat. At this point I realised the three of us were still in our sailing kit while all the other waiting cadets were correctly dressed for going ashore, wearing their Naval blazers and that ridiculous trilby hat we were all issued with when we joined. The hat was compulsory 'in case we had to salute somebody or return a salute' which meant doffing it. I have never become used to hat etiquette and could never manage without feeling a proper prat, but now I also realised I would be unable to give an appropriate salute under the gaze of the Officer of the Day as I stepped aboard at the top of the gangway. I realised something else: we were none of us legally 'ashore' at all, having left the ship for sailing recreation and thereby missed the libertymen's inspection and handing in our leave cards. I boarded Devonshire with nonchalant bravado assisted by having indulged a little too freely at the Sailing Club, but it was no good. I was in the rattle. Next morning the three of us were up at Ajax's table and given three days stoppage of leave.

Fortunately this had little effect on me because next day I was on duty and the day after that, our last, boat's crew so wouldn't be entitled to leave anyway. Better still, I had been allocated to cox one of the fast motorboats, FMBs for short, which were great fun to drive. They had powerful twin engines and a planing hull, capable of speeds of about fourteen knots. One always drove them at full speed because when not on the plane they became rather uncontrollable and difficult to steer. I took over my duties after lunch and spent much of the afternoon with my two crewmen who managed the lines and boathooks, running trips between the ship and Torquay harbour. Inside the harbour we had an audience of holidaymakers standing along the top of the harbour wall, so we performed our boat drill impeccably, enjoying showing off. In the evening I did several runs taking the ship's officers ashore, and then I was called to take the PMO and a couple of his cronies off for some prestigious function. The PMO was a rather tubby pompous Surgeon Commander who came down the gangway attired in mess dress complete with a magnificent boat cloak lined with red silk fastened around his neck with a gilt chain. That and the brass hat made him look more pompous than ever. He sat on the high seat aft of the cabin with his two chums, one either side, while I drove him at full speed through the harbour entrance with great panache, to a stir of interest from the gawping onlookers. With nicely judged timing I shut the throttles hoping to bring the boat skating to a perfect stop at the steps. I had been practising this manoeuvre all afternoon, so reckoned I had it perfected. Unfortunately I had forgotten that if one slams the throttle shut too quickly, how suddenly the boat can fall back into the water, turning into an unmanageable wallowing log. In fact the boat slowed down so fast that the PMO, who had just started to get up from his seat, was catapulted forward where he hurtled straight into the cabin to finish up face down on the deck at the feet of the more junior officers. A loud cheer and burst of applause from the laughing watchers above greeted him as he emerged, red-faced and furious.

I'm afraid I spoilt his entrance somewhat and received one of those "I'll get you for this" scowls as he muttered some admonishment through gritted teeth and did his best to ascend the steps in as dignified a way as possible. I was so put out that we were nearly back at the ship before I realised several other ship's boats were stationary, their coxswains standing at the salute. Too late, I glanced ahead to see the white ensign slowly descending. I, too, stopped and in the ensuing silence heard the sound of our band playing 'Sunset' while everyone on the quarterdeck stood to attention at the salute.

This time I not only had more leave stopped, but received five days spud-bashing punishment as well. Every evening while the rest of the troops were enjoying their free time I would be up in the spud locker with another defaulter peeling pounds of potatoes for chips.

Our next stop was Bridlington. I found it cold and grey, a far cry from sunny Torquay. The North Sea always seems to be grey or even brown whenever I venture to that side of the country. Once again I was boat's crew, but this time as a lowly bowman on one of our big pinnaces fitted with a fiendish steering arrangement known as a kitchen rudder. Standing on the jetty holding on to the painter while the coxswain fought with the little handle he had to turn to get the boat to go astern, I was suddenly aware of a couple of Yorkshire ladies looking at me in my shorts.

"'Ee, look at them loovely legs!" and the next moment one of them began caressing the back of my thigh.

After two days we moved on, this time on the way to Rosyth just above the Forth Bridge. On the approach to the Forth estuary one passes Bass Rock on the port side. There it was, a huge extinct volcano plug, a cloud of gannets overhead, gannets plunging into the water all round us, the rock itself white with thousands more nesting gannets. Our captain, himself a keen birder, turned the ship to sail close by and sounded off the siren to see the effect it might have. From my spud-bashing eyrie just under the mast I had a grand view of all these magnificent birds. I'd seen them off Nare Head when out fishing with Jim Eva, but never in such numbers.

Half an hour later we sailed beneath the Forth Bridge, with me still peeling those never-ending potatoes, wondering how much clearance there was above our topmast. We stayed at Rosyth for several days, but it was only on the last day that my stoppage of leave was over, and on that day I was on duty watch so never did get ashore. It would have been my first visit to Scotland, too.

After Rosyth, Devonshire sailed for Kristiansand in southern Norway. This was special, our first visit to a truly foreign land, and we received countless talks about the Scandinavian way of life, their history, particularly Norway's occupation during the war, and yet more reminders about how to behave. After all, were we not ambassadors for our country? Did the lower deck sailors get such briefings? I don't think so. Royal Navy sailors always behave well abroad, though they do sometimes have a little too much to drink.

We tied up at the far end of an extremely long jetty, having threaded our way past lots of little islands, each with its private jetty and a few white-painted houses. This time I was to go ashore and on the pipe "Libertymen fall in, in the starboard waist," paraded in my grey flannel trousers, blue blazer with the Naval crest on the breast pocket, smartly polished shoes and the insufferable trilby hat. We had our lecture about shore behaviour, handed in our leave cards, and awaited our turn to be allowed ashore.

The procedure was for ship's officers to go ashore as they wished, cadets would be allowed ashore a little later, followed by Chiefs and POs, and ten minutes after that, the rest of the ship's company. We were still walking serenely down the long jetty, looking hopefully at a cluster of blonde Norwegian beauties waving from behind the barrier a hundred yards ahead, when we heard pounding feet behind us. It was the junior rates, dressed alluringly in their square rig, with blue collar and bell-bottom trousers. Within moments every one of them had paired up with a girl and vanished. We cadets arrived at an empty gate, thwarted. In ones and twos we found our way into the town, looked around, did some window shopping, and felt shunned by the populace. Not so the young sailors, though. We saw several all drinking in bars surrounded by gorgeous girls having the time of their lives. That's life. In the ensuing days some cadets bragged about the good time they had enjoyed at Kristiansand, but nobody believed them.

Our next visit was to steam up the Sogne Fiord which penetrates over a hundred miles into the heart of this mountainous part of Norway. We sailed up the fiord for a full day, gaunt mountains rising on both sides dwarfing our ship. We ventured up one or two side turnings to give our navigators some practise with their coastal navigation, and generally to have a look round. The water became still and very dark, and we did some sums in ship design and water density to prove we were floating lower in the water as we progressed, so that by the end of the day we were afloat in totally fresh water with a foot more draft and not a trace of salt anywhere. Needless to say, Ajax's merry men considered this a good opportunity to hose the salt off everything, which they proceeded to do with gusto, brackish-smelling water getting everywhere. In the evening we emerged from the gorge-like fiord shaded from the summer sun, to an open bay at the top, to drop anchor in front of the little ski resort of Flåm. From here I had the opportunity to take a trip in a small train which zig-zagged up on a toothed railway track to Myrdal where it joins the main Bergen line, and spent a few hours gazing across an immense glacier with a 4,000 foot mountain behind. Here we had a meal in a spotlessly clean restaurant, with a beautiful pine floor finished in clear high-gloss varnish.

After a couple of days, it was back to sea again. On the way down the fiord we took a right turn and tried weaving our way through a different set of islands, again for the benefit of the navigation class who found themselves having to plot our course on the charts. This is done by studying the chart for the deep water channels, sandbanks, etc, (no problem in a deep Norwegian Fiord!) then pencilling in a suitable course to give the widest berth to any possible obstruction. If the ship has to execute any turns then a curve is drawn on the chart, its radius depending on the ship's intended speed and the amount of helm used. It takes the ship a length or two after helm is applied before she alters course, so a pencil mark is made on the chart at the point where the helm is put over. Lines are then drawn through that mark to suitable landmarks ashore, and the bearings of those objects recorded beside each line by means of parallel rulers measuring off the bearing from the compass rose printed on the chart. The chart is now marked up with a series of straight lines, each connected to the next by radii. With this information to hand, all the navigator has to do is to take bearings continuously as the ship goes down the intended course, calling out when it is time to change direction to the next course. Provided allowance is made for any strong tides, then it should not be possible to go aground. This is where one starts to touch wood, because ships do go aground from time to time, and you might well wonder why.

To everyone's surprise (but probably not the Captain's) we rounded a bend on this new route to find a high voltage electricity cable stretched across the fiord, looking very near to the water at its lowest point.

"Well, shall we get under it safely? Navigation class?" asked the Captain.

The class thought hard, and one of them suggested it could be checked if someone climbed the mast with a sextant and measured the vertical angle between the top of the mast and the lowest point of the catenary. If it was above the horizontal, then we had positive clearance.

"Excellent idea," said the Captain. "Off you go, then!"

"What, me, Sir?" exclaimed the suggestor, wishing he hadn't opened his mouth.

"Yes, you. What do you have to do before climbing the mast?"

"Switch off the radar, Sir?" ventured the hapless volunteer.

"Correct." The Captain nodded at his officer of the watch who telephoned down to the radar office, also to the wireless office. In a few moments a couple of sailors appeared with brass keys which they handed over to him.

"All clear to go aloft, Sir" called the officer of the watch, hanging the keys on a board kept there for that purpose.

Our volunteer set off, and in a few moments returned to report that there was a positive angle of several degrees, but that he had measured it from a point ten feet below the masthead as he couldn't get any higher. There then followed a frantic bit of trigonometry on a page torn from the signal pad before it was pronounced safe to go under. By this time we were within a few cables of the wire. The Captain, remarkably unconcerned, nodded and sure enough we passed under with plenty of room.

I've described these episodes in quite some detail, as it was typical of the sort of activities we got up to on the training cruiser, from which we learnt a great deal in a fun, practical sort of way.

Our next port of call was Tromsø. My geography of these parts is not good, and I didn't appreciate quite where Tromsø was. We steamed north for a day or two, north of the Arctic circle, and a further day's steaming beyond that almost to latitude 70° north, passing countless enticing small islands until eventually we headed up a large fiord leaving the open sea behind us. Tromsø is on an island, probably best known by the British as the place where the German pocket battleship Tirpitz holed up, and was eventually sunk by Royal Naval frogmen whilst still at anchor, the first great success by these courageous men. We had lectures on the action. Stirring stuff. Tromsø island is situated at a narrow part near the entrance resulting in fast tideflows. The only boats we lowered were the big pinnaces used for getting ashore, as this stop was mainly an opportunity for everyone to enjoy a visit to a foreign port. I met up with a family who invited me to their home, modern furniture, glistening shiny wood floors with a few bright rugs, comfortable in a cold sort of way. It was a bit of a struggle as their command of English was somewhat limited and my Norwegian was, well… non-existent. By this time we'd all heard of beautiful blonde Scandinavian girls who enjoyed free love, so I was intrigued to see what materialised when the daughter was introduced. She was indeed beautiful and blonde, but alas, not an inkling of a desire for free love! I returned to the ship late that night in the midnight sunshine a little disappointed, but not really surprised.

Whilst at Tromsø I had the opportunity to take a trip in an elderly Sunderland flying boat of the Norwegian Air Force. We boarded her from one of our boats while she sat on the water tied to a buoy not far from the ship. Being a Service aircraft there were no frills inside, no insulation or soundproofing. Several of us squeezed into the cabin amongst electronic equipment, each with a small, and somewhat scratched Perspex window to see out of. I noticed quite a lot of water sloshing around under the duckboards and wondered how long this old girl could be left safely unattended on its mooring without filling up and sinking. When the engines started the noise was deafening, but this was nothing to the crashing just under our feet as the hull began to hurtle through the water. In a few moments we lifted gracefully up into the air, banked over a tiny Devonshire beneath us looking for all the world like a model toy, and circled over Tromsø town, the upturned keel of the ill-fated Tirpitz clearly visible in the water beyond. The aircraft climbed laboriously for half an hour or more to reach a comfortable cruising altitude, then settled down to fly inland over the mountains. We were not that far from the borders of Sweden, also Finland, and I wondered whether I was looking down on either of those countries. The scenery was bleak—range upon range of snow-covered mountains, the occasional glimpse of deep black fiords between, cold and forbidding. This was midsummer, for goodness sake, so what would it be like in December? Inside the unheated aircraft I gratefully accepted the loan of a padded jacket, and wished I had gloves as well. Coming down again, the crew warned us not to be alarmed as we touched down on the water, which can sometimes be a little bumpy. This was an understatement. Not only was there a noise like a machine gun going off beneath us, but I could see the metal bottom of the hull flexing with each wave. I had visions of hitting a big one and the seaplane tipping forward onto its nose. I must admit I was quite relieved when we came to rest at last, the door opened, and we stepped out into a waiting ship's boat with the next consignment anticipating their turn.

We crossed the North Sea once more and to provide a little more education, the ship returned via the Orkneys, steaming through Scapa Flow after we'd had lectures on the scuttling of the German Fleet there at the end of the Great War. It was a cold, windy day when we did this, with a light rain from a heavy overcast sky, what the Scots call 'a fine, soft day'. Personally I found it dreary beyond belief, and had no wish to linger in such a place. I was to think otherwise on a return visit many years later.

After that we came down the western side of the UK and visited St. Mary's in the Isles of Scilly. I was keen to see all those places Jane had told me about, but our visit would not allow more than a couple of hours ashore, and I used this to go for a leg-stretch with my friend, Alan Witt, where about all we were able to do was take the coastal walk round The Garrison and Peninnis Head areas. The main purpose of the visit was to have some sailing races amongst ourselves, and also with the St. Mary's sailing club using their Redwing one-design class boats. These are West of England Redwings, a Bermudan rigged 14-footer not unlike the Naval dinghy but sleeker, lighter and faster, and not to be confused with Solent Redwings which are more like Dragons. Fun as these races were, I was frustrated at being anchored in such a heavenly spot without the opportunity to explore. The wonderful island of Tresco was only a mile away, yet we couldn't land!

This was our last port of call before returning to Plymouth and saying goodbye to dear old Devonshire.

8

Cambridge

I said goodbye to Devonshire with mixed feelings. Looking back at the poor old thing alongside in Devonport Yard, she certainly showed her age. The three raked funnels and high main deck looked grossly out of place compared to some of the sleek modern warships nearby. Sure, there were forgettable times like having to clean the heads, endure being shouted at by Ajax and his ilk as though I were an idiot, and all the unnecessary things we were made to do. But there were also many sublime moments that I savoured. Moments such as a night watch on her open bridge watching the moon's reflection on the water as we steamed quietly along in the tropical trade winds, alone with one or two others while the ship's company slept below. Her old-fashioned lines with high deckheads built for service in the tropics before the days of air conditioning made her a far more comfortable vessel to live in than today's claustrophobic ships, and her white teak decks with soft fibres and no chance of a splinter were a pleasure to walk upon in bare feet. She was from a past era indeed. But after two cruises in her I had learnt so much, had caught up and overtaken my school contemporaries who hadn't been privileged to serve in one of HM ships. I was ready to move on.

I now had something else to look forward to. Those of us who were to be electrical engineers would shortly join HMS Collingwood, a cluster of wartime buildings surrounding a large parade ground between Fareham and Gosport in Hampshire, the Electrical Branch's alma mater, a 'stone frigate' we would call home for several years. The Branch's founder, Lord Louis Mountbatten, responsible at the end of the war for splitting off the electrical part of the Engineering Branch, had the foresight to realise the electrical and electronics side would grow fast and quickly become a speciality in its own right. To give the new branch a proper foundation, a group of officers would join each year and be given a good university education in electrical engineering before finishing off their training at Collingwood. These were the 'Long Course' entrants, and for the last few years these lucky men had enjoyed three years at Cambridge reading for the Engineering Tripos. I was in Long Course 6, surely the best one yet! Some of the others said they had only joined the Navy in order to get to Cambridge, but only one of them succeeded in leaving it again immediately afterwards. More of that anon.

But first some leave (yes, I no longer took 'holidays' —from now on any such time was called Leave). I waited for the summons from Their Lords Commissioners of the Admiralty. It came a week later:

"You are hereby appointed Midshipman and are directed to report for your duties at H.M.S. Collingwood on…"

And so the twenty of us who'd been dispersed around the training cruiser came together once more, sporting a thin green stripe on our sleeves, one step up the ladder. The white tab below a small brass button on our lapels that denoted a cadet's rank was now replaced by a white square. However, Collingwood at this time was a busy place, full of courses coming through from other branches for an electrical acquaint, also National Servicemen, and many others. LC6 was allocated a wooden hut a little distance from the main wardroom in which we had two dormitories with an ablutions section in between. It was like being back at school again. However, we could make as much noise as we liked here and were left very much to our own devices. The only disadvantage was that the ship's Executive Officer had his detached house just along the road next to our block so we had to watch out for him. But he was completely different from Ajax, being an electrical man like ourselves and with no sadistic streak, but nevertheless had his role which included discipline throughout the establishment. Our Divisional Officer and mentor was Lieutenant Jim McClune, a quiet and delightful Scottish man with a dry sense of humour. I'm afraid we gave him rather a lively time, but he accepted this as normal youthful high spirits and supported us very well. We attended classes in some fundamental electrical engineering subjects, and were bussed into Portsmouth Dockyard to attend the apprentice school there in order to learn how to use our hands. This involved making a test piece consisting of a metal plate with a square hole in it about two inches across, then filing down a block of steel into a square so that it would fit in the hole whichever way it was turned, in other words it had to be a perfect cube with right-angled corners and every face filed absolutely flat. This is not as easy as it sounds, and took days to do. I chummed up with another LC6 member, David Brooke, who was extremely good at this sort of thing. Fortunately for me he had lots of help and advice to give and we got along well, soon becoming inseparable. This was the 'Noggin' I referred to briefly in an earlier chapter and so called because when he was a baby he was so very small. He was a wonderful friend to me all through my early time in the Royal Navy while we were still together. He'd attended engineering classes whilst at Harrow so all this filing business was no trouble for him at all.

The Royal Navy had acquired a couple of large twelve-metre windfall yachts, one of which, the Wal, was kept at the MTB base at Haslar in Gosport. Collingwood people had chartered her for a weekend and I heard about this in time to join as crew. She had bunk accommodation for ten, and needed that size crew for hoisting and trimming the huge sails. We left Gosport on a Friday evening after work, and I had my first experience of manoeuvring a really large yacht without the benefit of an auxiliary engine. The ebb tide gushes out of the hole between Dolphin and Sallyport at about six knots, and ramming a huge metal buoy at that speed would be no joke, therefore good seamanship was essential. We had professional and experienced people aboard so I had no worries. Sailing over to Cherbourg, crossing the shipping lanes at night, was interesting to say the least. I had my turn on watch, taking the wheel and steering a compass course with the wind on one's cheek, keeping the sails trimmed by instinct more than anything, and found the experience most enjoyable. We entered Cherbourg next morning without mishap, tying up beside a trim little yacht also from Britain. Talking to the owner later, a crusty ex-RAF man, I discovered he was the editor of Yachting World, the recognised top sailing magazine of the period, and someone who believed in correct old-fashioned values and behaviour when it came to cruising around. He was not over pleased to have a bunch of potentially disruptive Naval types lying alongside, but took it in good spirit and I hope we behaved properly. On the Sunday when we were due to sail back to Gosport, it was blowing a gale and there was no way we could safely leave harbour. Most of us went walking a mile or two inland to savour the French countryside, and it was not until evening that the wind eased sufficiently to set off. The passage home was fast and uncomfortable, but Wal was built for such conditions and rode the waves well. On entering Portsmouth harbour, which has to be done rather fast in order to overcome the tidal stream, a sharp left turn into Haslar Creek is necessary, then rapidly the sails have to be dropped. Only a hundred yards up the creek we then had to turn into our berth alongside one of the MTB jetties, right beside Haslar footbridge. This meant taking the way off the boat without the benefit of engines, so we deployed the old custom of throwing a sea anchor over the side. This acted like a really good brake, and brought us down to a slow walking pace enabling the turn into her berth to be made safely without overshooting and fetching up on the mud. This is altogether an extremely difficult manoeuvre to achieve with such a large craft relying entirely on the wind.

On arrival the Customs launch came alongside to check us out, asked whether we had anything to declare and accepted everyone's assurance that nobody had more than the one permitted bottle of wine. As they were about to depart, a boat came past rather fast so that Wal rolled in its wash, which set up a suggestive sound of wine bottles clinking under our feet in the bilges. The Customs men were not officially amused, and suggested we might care to drink all the wine in excess of our allowance before we left the boat. Just across from Wal's berth was a moored cabin cruiser, the owners of which were dashing up and down the companionway with buckets, which they proceeded to empty over the side. Something didn't look quite normal, and then I realised the buckets had nothing in them.

"What are you doing?" we called out.

"*Calor* gas leak!" came the answer. *Calor* gas being heavier than air will sink to the bottom of a boat, and will sit there waiting for the first lighted match to be dropped. Potentially a very nasty situation, and one that Johnny and Fanny Cradock experienced many years later when they suffered a *Calor* gas explosion out in their boat in the Mediterranean.

News came through about our colleges. Every year the Admiral heading up the Electrical Branch, no less, would visit Cambridge doing the rounds of the colleges trying to place the twenty new long course members. One college would take a bright one with no strings, another would only take a mediocre one provided they could have a bright one as well, a third would want someone who could row or play rugby and weren't too fussed about their academic ability. So the wheeling and dealing went on for a couple of days until we were all placed. I found I had been provisionally entered for Fitzwilliam, then a small college opposite the Fitzwilliam Museum with no traditional buildings, and only a few yards from the engineering faculty in Trumpington Street. We were now invited by the individual colleges to attend for an interview, which would involve an overnight stay. I travelled by train as usual (for which I was provided with a railway warrant), forewarned about the odd layout at Cambridge station whereby there is just the one platform long enough to accommodate three trains at once, one behind the other. Fitzwilliam put me up in lodgings close by the college, where I was given a claustrophobic room filled by a huge brass bedstead with a somewhat fusty feather mattress, in which I slept very well. The interview itself was cursory; I doubt whether either side learnt much about the other, but it was a formality that had to be observed. I was handicapped by not having passed any Latin exams, then an entry requirement, so maybe that explained why I didn't get placed in one of the grander colleges.

In due course we left Collingwood for a few days leave, after which I took the train for Cambridge loaded with all my gear. I had been allocated lodgings in Devonshire Road which sounded reasonable enough, but when I asked the taxi driver to take me there, he looked at me rather oddly then drove all of a couple of hundred yards before depositing me in front of a mean terrace house which had a fine uninterrupted view over the Cambridge railway sidings. I should have realised town planners tend to give attractive road names to the less salubrious parts of town, as if that will improve them; otherwise why are there so many Acacia Avenues everywhere? The landlady, Mrs Smudge, welcomed me somewhat warily. A professional Cambridge landlady, she'd met students of every type in her business life and must have wondered if I'd turn out to be as bad as some of them. The bedroom was small and tatty, but I also had use of 'the front room' which I would share with another student. This was equally tatty, with a heavily net-curtained window looking out onto the blank wall of the sidings. Already I could hear the clanking of railway trucks behind that wall and the unforgettable steamy railway smell pervaded everything. Where was the Cambridge with all those magnificent colleges and lofty spires? The answer emerged: a couple of miles away. I knew all about the need for a bicycle—that was one thing I'd learnt from my interview visit—so had brought my bicycle with me. Actually, it was Jane's cast off bike that had lain unused in the back of the Polsue cowshed ever since we moved there. Mrs Smudge said it would have to stay in the hall and pointed out the rubber mat placed there on which it could drip oily mud. I'd been told the number, so before leaving home had carefully painted 'F143' on the rear mudguard to identify it as a Fitzwilliam bike. She commented rather sniffily that she only took in students who were clean and well-behaved, which was a bit rich as her premises didn't look good enough for a student who wished to remain clean…

Actually, after that first shock had sunk in, I found her all right. She supplied a comfortable bed, somewhere to retire away from the hurly-burly of university life, and a cooked breakfast every morning. She lived in the back room and never interfered, well—hardly ever. All this for £14 a term. Digs in Cambridge were tremendously variable, anything from humble premises such as Mrs Smudge's to magnificent rooms in part of a grand house in a posh part of town, and one paid accordingly. As a midshipman, my pay had risen a teeny amount, but every penny was precious. A month or two later I opened my first bank account with a deposit of £5 at Barclays Bank round the corner in Mill Road, and was probably better off than a student depending on his grant alone; at least I was actually earning by this time.

Later that first day another freshman appeared. He was to have the other bedroom and would share the front room with me. Geoff Barge was an architectural student whose home was in Kendal. He'd already completed three years structural engineering at Nottingham University and would now read architecture for a further three years. Mrs Smudge's premises were rather a comedown for him, but fortunately we got on so well together and this made up for a lot.

I set off on my bike to explore. In term time bicycles far outnumbered cars in Cambridge, and traffic was obliged to respond accordingly, by which I mean it was comparatively safe to cycle everywhere without being mown down. Students weren't allowed to have cars there, not that many students would have been able to afford to do so, probably a very good thing. Cars just didn't have a chance. I found Fitzwilliam, and met John Holmes, another member of LC6 who had also joined that college. Together we searched out Heffers bookshop, the most important shop in this university town, where we bought a street map and the Students' Handbook, an essential reference for freshmen listing every conceivable club, society, sport, and any other activity one could ever wish to indulge in. No mention of lectures; perhaps one didn't have time for those. I bought a suitably tatty second-hand gown which I would need when dining in Fitzwilliam, but Engineering was one faculty that did not require one to wear a gown for lectures, presumably because of the risk from too much whirling machinery for it to be safe doing so. I then met Tim Woodfin, a member of LC5 now starting his second year, who gave me masses of help settling in. It was all too easy to join everything in sight and one had to be really selective if one was to be able to attend lectures and do some work as well. Engineers had four lectures nearly every day, which was reckoned to be a pretty full schedule; students reading for some of the arts subjects only attended one or two lectures a week.

Noggin was at Peterhouse, a small and very ancient college a little further down Trumpington Street, one of the most intimate. Being irritatingly bright he was on a fast stream thereby completing his degree work in two years, leaving the third year for specialising in a chosen sub-discipline. However, about half of us dropped to a somewhat lower level, only obtaining a pass degree at the end of our time. We quickly discovered the academic side of Cambridge life could be swamped by the social life, and were soon immersed in every conceivable activity imaginable. The Naval authorities gave us a free hand and didn't seem too perturbed about this. At the end of our three years they wanted well-rounded Naval Officers with a broad, technically oriented education. Such men would head up departments manned by the real hands-on engineers, the artificers, specialists in their particular equipment.

Early on at Fitzwilliam I was approached by a student who asked whether I'd like to meet David Shepherd, Captain of cricket and a university blue. To any normal sports-mad person such an invitation would have been unbelievably wonderful, but I'm afraid I wasn't all that bothered. I went along anyway, joining a roomful of people all eager to set eyes on this god and maybe even shake his hand. It turned out, of course, to be a religious recruiting ploy, an invitation to join CICCU, the Cambridge Inter-Collegiate Christian Union. I don't remember shaking David Shepherd's hand, but I did meet Malcolm Seymour there with whom I became good friends and remained so during my time at Cambridge. Many of the Fitzwilliam students at this time were from overseas, sent at great expense by their countries to acquire an essential background towards one day becoming leaders in their country. I wonder how many of those I brushed against in the tiny JCR would later be seen on our television screens waving their arms around or maybe standing behind the Queen in a Heads of Commonwealth group portrait? There were one or two other students who seemed to make more noise than was warranted by a single person. One such was a young man by name of Norman St John Stevas whom I sometimes met when collecting my mail. I never discovered what he was reading, but it certainly wasn't one of the sciences. I found arts people to be so different from what I would think of as the practical ones, but this didn't matter since our paths seldom crossed.

My parents, still living in the past (the twenties) had said I must take ballroom dance lessons. Ballroom dancing was the way to meet nice people. Well, they would say that, wouldn't they! I actually thought about it, and one day ventured along to the Dorothy Café to inspect the venue where tea dances took place at regular intervals. It had a large hall above the café proper, with a genuine sprung floor—one suspended on chains, the whole contraption creaking and flexing when a group of people got going on it. I looked at this highly polished slippery surface and got cold feet. Surely the only people to venture on such a floor would be top-notch toffee-nosed experts? I looked elsewhere. Somebody said they'd gone along to an old time dancing club and enjoyed it. They persuaded me to go with them to the City Hall one Saturday when Sydney Thompson and his Old Time Dance Orchestra were playing. I'd heard Sydney Thompson on the radio, and the idea sounded great, so off I went and thoroughly enjoyed myself (though my parents would probably have thought such gallivanting was a bit downmarket). Several weeks later at another such dance, my companion at that time said how boring it all was.

"Good heavens, why do you say that?" I exclaimed.

"It's all so predictable. That awful mincing voice," he nodded at the stage, "and these same old dances, and the same dreary women."

I was taken aback. Being an engineer in a faculty of some 900 other engineers with only one woman amongst them, I was starved of female company. I glanced round the room. They all looked okay to me.

"Now, what you really want to try is Scottish Country Dancing. Now that's good. Real fun. Demanding. Have to concentrate all the time. Intricate footwork, not like all this … shuffling around." He looked around the floor. "Gorgeous girls too…" A dreamy expression came over his face and he smiled to himself.

"Okay. When do we go?"

He sat up. "Splendid. Next Tuesday, 7.30. Milton Road School. See you there!"

Milton Road School had a good hall to dance in, with a floor that was neither too slippery nor hard, but there was no sign of my Old Time companion. There were a lot of kilts around and a number of people were speaking with strong Scottish dialects. I introduced myself to someone who seemed to be organising things and told them I was a beginner.

That first evening was terrifying in that every single thing was completely new; I hadn't appreciated the footwork is so precise and complex, nor did I understand what the instructor meant by all the names he gave to various figures. My galumphing around doing the Eightsome Reel on Devonshire's quarterdeck hadn't prepared me for this. But I was given patient encouragement, enjoyed the evening, and decided to come again. The girls were certainly much more lively, but most seemed to have permanent partners. I would have to persevere. Cycling back home in the dark I hummed some of the catchy tunes and reckoned this sort of dancing would do very nicely if I could get up to speed.

I was intrigued by one of the clubs advertised in the Students Handbook, which was the Cambridge University Cruising Club or CUCrC for short, with premises down a little lane beside the Round Church in Magdalene Street. I decided to explore the CUCrC and discovered a largish wooden hut set out like a saloon bar with trophies and photographs all round the walls. I was greeted by the resident barman, a lovely individual with a barman's endless fund of anecdotal stories who, noticing my college scarf, asked whether I knew one of the regulars, Rodney Hill. This was another Fitzwilliam man whom, coincidentally, I had met only the previous evening. The barman produced an excellent cup of coffee saying "Have this one on the house, Rodney will probably be here shortly." This was a lovely welcome, so I stayed.

The barman told me a story, the one about the little boy who loved playing with his mother's makeup, something she forbade him to do. One day his mother said she was just popping out for a little while and he was to play quietly and not open the door to any strangers. The moment she had gone he ran into her bedroom and soon had her powder puff and lipstick out. Busying himself in front of the mirror he failed to hear voices downstairs and it wasn't until there were footsteps on the stairs that he realised he was about to be caught red handed. He just had time to hide in the large walk-in cupboard before the door opened and in came his mother accompanied by a strange man. Peering through a gap in the door he watched wide-eyed as the stranger and his mother took off all their clothes and began to do all sorts of things together. He was so absorbed he nearly didn't hear the front door close followed by the unmistakeable sounds of his father coming upstairs. Just as he was wondering what would happen next, the cupboard door opened and slammed shut and there beside him was a sweaty, panting man with an armful of clothes standing there in the dark. The two of them stayed there in silence for a few moments, then the little boy thought he ought to say something to the panting stranger. "It's dark in 'ere, innit," he said. There was a loud gasp.

"What are you doing here?" hissed the stranger, and then "You're not to say anything. Understand?"

The boy nodded in the dark.

"Here," whispered the stranger, "Here's a pound. You can keep that if you don't breathe a word. Remember, not a word to anyone."

The next Sunday the little boy and his parents went to mass as usual. When the collecting plate came round the little boy put the pound note in it.

"Where did you get that?" snapped his father accusingly.

"Not saying," said the boy.

"Where did you get it? Tell me."

"No."

"Right," said his Dad. "If you won't tell me, you'd better tell him," and with that he propelled the little boy towards the nearby confessional. The boy hadn't been in one of these before. He sat there in the gloom for a moment and was suddenly conscious of a movement beyond the grill. He spoke, "It's dark in 'ere, innit," he said.

There was a sharp intake of breath and a familiar voice said "I told you: you're not to say anything."

Rodney arrived and we discussed sailing interests. Rodney had been in the RAF for his National Service, and had sailed their boats. His approach to sailing was to try to understand the technical aspects of how a sail propels a boat through the water, aerofoils, wind angles, drag and a whole lot of design features which I had never considered before. By the time we'd finished this conversation and several coffees later I realised I had missed my next lecture. He invited me to crew with him the following Sunday at St. Ives where the CUCrC kept some Fireflies.

St. Ives is on the River Ouse, at this point running fast and wide. The club had a boatshed on the bank where about eight Fireflies were kept. I was pleased to meet these little dinghies again as they were great fun to sail. However, I had never before sailed on a river (whereas Rodney had never sailed on the open sea) so we had a lot to learn from one another. We got on well, had lunch at the hotel nearby overlooking the river, and spent the afternoon sailing in a number of informal races. Rodney had a little van that he used to get to St. Ives, so that was a great help. One day I was asked by Jack Knights, at that time the club chairman, whether I would crew his Firefly the coming Sunday when we had a series of races against some other club. Jack was a phenomenally clever dinghy sailor and had me jumping about just as Mrs Tracey did all those years ago. He kept the tiller constantly on the move, sensitive to every tiny nuance of wind speed or direction, and when the wind almost died away told me to sit right up for'd so that the stern came completely out of the water, only the tip of the rudder immersed, thereby presenting the minimum of wetted surface to maximise our speed. We won the race by brilliant tactics, and I like to think I learnt a few tricks that day. The Club's president, Stewart Morris, visited from time to time, usually for a few free beers on his way through Cambridge to some event further north.

The lectures I attended all had a practical interest for me, and I soaked up the information but not in the academic way expected by my tutor. This was a very serious and patient man, Percy Hammond, who shared his tiny tutorial room with a large blowsy lecturer by name of Nelson who was on a couple of year's sabbatical from English Electric. (A few years later I noticed a Lord Nelson was Chairman of English Electric; the same man). At our weekly sessions Percy patiently went through the academic details endeavouring to get me to take it all in—necessary if I was to pass exams, and couldn't have been nicer. Our head of faculty, Professor Baker, lectured on structural engineering and out of interest I went along to one of his lectures where he outlined his proposals for cantilevering a road deck on either side of the Forth Bridge, thereby doing away with the need for a separate road bridge. His ideas were too advanced for the stodgy government advisers of the time, who eventually went for the more conventional suspension bridge we have today.

Percy's immediate boss was Professor Moulin, a true academic living several planes higher than ordinary folk, whom I found impossible to understand. Fortunately he seldom lectured to us undergraduates, so all we saw of him was this elderly gentleman, muttering to himself, who drifted about unseeing, with odd socks and unpolished shoes, his mind on greater things. He was a brilliant electrical engineer, but not the sort of lecturer I needed!

The other charismatic academic I remember vividly was a chemist. This was Professor Sir Lawrence Bragg, the colourful faculty head of the Cavendish Laboratories in Pembroke Street, who invited our year to his annual lecture for engineers. I attended a packed lecture theatre to listen to a riveting talk on the effects of temperature on the physical properties of various substances. He started off by smashing a squash ball into rubber splinters by whamming it with a hammer (having dipped it first into a bath of liquid nitrogen) and went on from there. Wonderful stuff. Would that all lectures could be half as good.

One day Rodney Hill asked me to help him out on the other river—the River Cam. This relatively small river, known as the River Granta until it meanders into town, emerges over a weir beyond Magdalene College as the navigable Cam until it eventually joins the Great Ouse below Waterbeach. It is the river on which the University does all its rowing, and there is a line of boatsheds stretching for several hundred metres beside Midsummer Common. Fitzwilliam had one of these, and Rodney was trying to muster another couple of oarsmen to man an extra college boat which he would then cox. I could hardly say I didn't know one end of an oar from the other, and eventually succumbed to his persuasion, being duly installed as number seven in that boat. River rowing in a craft just over a foot wide and sixty feet long, wielding a twelve foot oar was utterly unlike paddling a dinghy around at home, and I had to learn a whole new way of rowing. Most rowing men started their rowing life at school, but the Fitzwilliam third boat crew was made up from a motley collection of individuals mostly leaned upon by Rodney who, no rower himself, fancied whizzing through the water shouting instructions at a line of sweating oarsmen. I was his latest recruit.

Rowing took place in the afternoons, a time for relaxation and recovery from the rigours of morning lectures. I was happy to do something more useful than pedal back to my dreary digs, where I would find Geoff stretched out on the settee having what he referred to as his 'creative contemplative meditation' prior to another spell on his drawing board, and a little convivial exercise was just what I needed. We rowed down to Baitsbite lock and back each day with a hearty coach from the Agricultural College racing along the towpath beside us on a rickety bike. He used some graphic agricultural descriptions of what he thought about our rowing which I would be too embarrassed to repeat here. Suffice to say we listened, heard what he said and put it all into practice. By the end of term we had a good crew that regularly beat our second boat.

By the end of my first term I was ready for a nice holiday. Unfortunately the Navy had other ideas. Not for us generous vacations swanning around doing nothing. We were expected to spend our time at various manufacturing companies around the UK who had sizeable Naval contracts. The first of these was for two weeks during our Christmas vacation period, where John Holmes, John Daly and I were allocated to the main employer at Rugby, Metropolitan Vickers, whose principal output was heavy electrical machinery. I already knew them as the main supplier of electric fans and generators for I had seen their makers' plates around H.M. ships, but I didn't appreciate the extent to which these companies were already swallowing each other up, even in the fifties. I discovered British Thomson-Houston, my favourite manufacturer of theatrical and cine equipment, was one of their companies, and lamp bulbs were made at Rugby, going out under several different names and prices. They also made huge electrical supply equipment, transformers weighing hundreds of tons, and had a research facility that specialised in heavy transmission equipment. A company this size had its own apprentice school, and it was this that we joined.

I arrived straight from Cambridge to find I had been put into digs even more downmarket than Mrs Smudge's. The other two were better off, in a largish house where they shared a bright airy room. My place was in a mean row of terraced houses, down near the station and within easy walking distance of the Works. We reported on our first morning to the supervisor of the apprentice school and were quickly disabused of any ideas we might have about drifting in at staff hours. We were issued with clock cards, warned of the dire consequences of clocking someone else's card, given overalls, and treated like undisciplined school kids; no doubt that being how they treated their normal apprentices. We accepted this for that first period as it was only for a couple of weeks, but it was not a happy time. Fortunately we all stayed together, attached to mentors in the noisy fabrication shop. Nowadays the noise levels in such places would not be permitted, but this was years before the Health and Safety at Work Act came into force. Our time there was spent sitting about for, as new 'apprentices', we had no skills to enable us to do anything else. It was 'sit with Nellie' training and only memorable for its uselessness. Apart from the ear-splitting racket of metal-bashing reverberating around this huge echoing fabrication shop, there was also the blue-white flicker from innumerable electric arc welders. Looking back from the safety-conscious times of today, the potential dangers in that place were quite frightening, with virtually no precautions taken apart from being advised not to look directly at the tip of a welder's rod when he was about to strike the arc. What with all this and probably poor nutrition, I had one of my rare migraines, only this time there was no opportunity to lie down somewhere to sleep it off. No headache appeared, but my vision began to go and I had the flashing lights that accompany a migraine. As my vision contracted until I was left with only tunnel vision with a flashing centre, I grabbed a surprised John Daly and told him I could not see, and would he guide me to the locker room. The next thing I knew I was lying on the ground amongst bits of metal and old welding rods looking up at a sea of worried faces, among them a man with a first aider's badge, also the fabricator with whom I worked. Apparently I had been out cold for nearly a minute. Surprisingly I felt completely all right then, my vision totally restored, and just wanting to get away from the noise. The first aider suggested I go outside in the fresh air, asked one of the others to accompany me, and said I should perhaps take the rest of the day off. Needless to say, both Johns came with me and we spent the remainder of that day wandering about Rugby town. Thankfully I have never had a similar experience again, though fairly often the jagged light would appear, almost always at a time when I was relaxing after a stressful week so that I would wake up on a Saturday morning with the beginnings of a migraine.

Towards the end of the first week I returned to my digs at lunchtime for something I'd forgotten, to find the place locked up and no answer to the bell. I looked round the back and discovered an open window. Climbing in I went upstairs to my room, to hear the landlady rush out of some back room downstairs where she had been all the time and start shouting at me to come down and how dare I break into the house like that. I ignored her, opened the door to my room to find someone else in the bed. The penny dropped. This was a hotbed letting whereby some poor bloke on nightshift had the room while I was out during the day. It explained a lot of things, such as why I could only use a certain part of the bedroom cupboard, why when I went there in the evenings none of my things were where I'd left them that morning, my pyjamas had been put away in a drawer instead of being left under the pillow where I'd have expected to find them. I told the landlady what I thought about her, said rather haughtily I'd report her to the Works for this, packed up my bag and stomped off. I lugged my suitcase round to the other two Johns, and we discussed what to do next. Their own landlady came to the rescue with some addresses of various acquaintances. John Daly offered to take my card with him and clock me in so that I could take the afternoon off to find somewhere to live, an offer gratefully accepted.

"If I get caught, they can't do anything," he argued. "The can't sack us because they don't employ us in the first place, and they can't create a scene with the Navy because they'd be scared of losing contracts." We couldn't fault the logic.

An hour later I found a middle-aged couple in a lovely house opposite Rugby School. It was an Edwardian house with huge rooms, comfortably furnished, and they couldn't have been a nicer couple to meet. Both in their late sixties, their own children married and living away, they were happy to have someone live in with them. We got on really well, and I couldn't believe my luck. The old boy was completely deaf, but we communicated fairly successfully. His hobby—or more accurately, his full time passion—was rebuilding a pre-war Morris Twelve tourer, bolt by bolt. He'd reached the stage where the engine, still out on his workbench, was being run in using gas, a procedure that would take several days. He was so pleased to meet another engineer although I didn't know a lot about the internal combustion engine, and his wife was so pleased to have someone who kept her husband interested. It was perfect. I spent the rest of the afternoon exploring Rugby seen in daylight for the first time.

That evening John Daly told us how he'd punched my card in a different clock in a different building where he would not be known, and reckoned no one would be any the wiser. So next day it would be my turn. I took John's card, adopted the same procedure while he had a lie-in. We met up for lunch as usual, elated that we'd apparently beaten the system. John Holmes cautioned us not to overdo it. For the rest of our stay one or other of us would have a morning off while the others went to work. Should anyone ask where the missing person was, then we could say they hadn't been well that morning and at lunchtime when we met, the missing person would be briefed. But the absent person was never missed, and as no one seemed particularly interested, we carried on like that until the end.

The Lent term at Cambridge is renowned for fogs, the icy east wind blowing in off the North Sea over sodden Fens. I was always cold outdoors, so to combat that I cycled everywhere at breakneck speed. Only once did I come to grief as I was going back to the digs one night when I skated across the road on a sheet of ice, just missing a bus that slithered to a stop in time. Rowing in the cold weather was hell for the first half mile; but we soon warmed up and by the time we returned to the boathouse for a hot shower, were usually glowing and sweaty whatever the weather. Then it would be back to somebody's rooms for tea stopping en route to buy a packet of crumpets to toast over their fire. One of the undergraduates was mad keen on Marx Brothers films and persuaded a cinema manager to put one on in exchange for free publicity. The cinema would then be full on the evening in question to everyone's satisfaction. I generally went to the pictures at least once a week, and often saw the Marx Brothers movie. After he'd graduated, the undergraduate bought that same cinema and started by projecting double Marx Brothers programmes, changing them midweek. His cinema was continuously full and he did so well out of it that this became his fulltime occupation. Some years later I noticed he had a film revue column in one of the national dailies.

Rag day at Cambridge was really quite something, at least it seemed so to us students; no doubt the townspeople thought otherwise. I reckoned we kept in sight the objective of collecting for charity, and had lots of fun doing so. Geoff Barge with some of his cronies set up a roadblock on the Madingley Road, stopped all cars coming into town and sold them stickers to put on their windscreens that would give them immunity against further bother from rag day students. They paid up happily and sped off, no doubt to be stopped just round the corner by another lot. Geoff collected several hundred pounds during the day which all went towards the Fitzwilliam total. The Strathspey and Reel Club put on a travelling dance display in the evening that was immensely popular. Marching down the centre of the street came a couple of pipers and a drummer, followed by eight dancers doing a sort of progressive jig which enabled them to keep up with the pipers. These were followed by half a dozen more dancers holding a big sheet between them into which coins were tossed. It was exhausting for the dancers who changed places from time to time with the sheet carriers, but by the end of their march they had collected more than any college, so it was well worth it. The local brewery donated a firkin of ale to the college who collected most, we expected one of the large colleges such as St. Johns would win, but no: it was our dear little Fitzwilliam with a total of £600—a lot in those days. A few days later the firkin was delivered and the junior common room assembled round a piano to drink it. Considering about half of Fitzwilliam men at that time were overseas students who were inclined to take no part in any college sports or social activities, we reckoned the rest of us had done pretty well. When it came to demolishing the firkin, there was an awesome quantity for each of us to drink, and I have to admit we ended up just a little bit legless. All in a good cause, of course. Someone was playing that musical limerick tune on the piano where the refrain goes:

> That was a wonderful song,
> Sing us another one,
> Sing us another one,
> Sing us another one, do!

whereupon someone else gets up and sings his verse and so on. Most people sang limericks that were so naughty we were all left holding our sides with laughter hardly able to join in, when the door opened and in came the Dean, an extremely prudish straight-laced sober-sided temperance-minded cleric. The singing died away, all except for the pianist who had his back to the door and hadn't noticed. The party ended rather abruptly after that.

I attended various CICCU gatherings, including the Sunday evening do at Great St. Mary's where the congregation neared a thousand. Generally I accompanied Malcolm Seymour and went to his rooms one day for coffee. He, like me, had started off in somewhat miserable digs far out of town in Cherryhinton but had now moved into a splendid place in Warkworth Terrace, just off Parker's Piece, and fairly central. He could walk from there to both Fitzwilliam and his

Geography Schools, also into the centre of Cambridge. There were eight rooms, mostly occupied by graduates. Malcolm had installed a piano in his own palatial room. He was an accomplished musician with a real gift and I envied him. Later, when one of Rodney's boat crew left, I persuaded Malcolm to join our boat. Like me, he was poor at ball games but liked the idea of trying his hand on the river. After that we often met in his rooms for tea, and I asked his landlady, Mrs Arnold, whether I could move in as soon as she had a vacancy. She booked me in for the start of the next term, and there I stayed until I graduated. The greatest asset about Mrs Arnold's was the back door. In those days, landladies had to lock their doors at 10.00 p.m. and record any student returning home after that time, something Mrs Smudge did most diligently. If the student did not come back until after midnight, the landlady had to inform the college, whereupon the unfortunate student would be on the carpet. Too many 'after ten' occasions also resulted in a carpeting. Mrs Arnold avoided all this hassle by leaving her back door unlocked, so no one was ever late. To get to the back door meant groping one's way down an unlit narrow passage and past the house bike shed, being careful not to trip over dustbins and suchlike; altogether a splendid arrangement.

Although each room at Mrs Arnold's had its own washbasin, not usual in digs then, there was just the one bathroom. This had an elderly copper geyser over the bath, gas-fired through a penny-in-the-slot meter. We all discovered how many pennies needed to be put in the meter to run a bath of one's chosen depth; in my case it was four. One of the other lodgers was a thin middle-eastern gentleman whom I seldom saw, but when I did he always seemed to sidle along with his back to the wall instead of walking normally, as though he wanted to avoid being seen, He would take his bath during the quiet of an afternoon. One such day there was a monumental explosion, rattling every door and window in the house, followed by a frightened wailing from the direction of the bathroom. I rushed out to find this terrified man, stark naked and covered in soap, sitting on the floor in the corridor outside the open bathroom door with bits of black sooty debris floating down around him. Afterwards piecing together what must have happened, what we think he'd done was to misjudge how many pennies to put in the meter, the geyser had shut down while he was in the bath still running in water, and he must have fed another penny into the meter and then struck a match. Possibly he'd dropped one or two matches before he could get a lighted one near the gas jets by which time enough gas had been pumping out to generate an explosive mixture. We never did discover how the poor chap landed in the corridor, still with his eyebrows intact. Apart from cracking a bathroom window and covering the room in soot, no harm was done, and the geyser seemed to work better afterwards; probably the explosion had effectively decoked it.

During the Easter vacation it was back to Metro-Vick for another spell. This time we were all three allocated to the small motor testing room, a development area where electric motors up to about five horsepower size were harnessed to electric brakes for extended spells of load testing. The room had a metal floor with slots in it, into which clamps could be bolted and slid up and down in the slot to hold a piece of equipment. A motor would be clamped to the floor thereby, its brake (usually a generator which absorbed the energy produced by the motor) would be clamped beside it and the two joined by a flexible spider coupling to take up any misalignment. About thirty such motor generator pairs would be under test at a time, making quite a noise. Above all this machinery was a small gantry crane for moving motors around, hand operated by means of a chain winch, the loop of the winch dangling down somewhat unsafely to just above the motors. Being a development area, no guards were fitted over the whirring couplings. Our job was to take load and temperature readings and record all this on some chart in the next room. From time to time the motors would be lifted off, placed on a trolley to be transported elsewhere and a fresh motor fitted. It kept us all fairly active, and was quite demanding work albeit somewhat boring after several days. At least it was useful work and something we were able to do. At last Metro-Vick was beginning to recognize we were not just boy apprentices.

It was during this spell that we had a visit from the Naval Liaison Officer from the Admiralty responsible for these factory training spells. On the appointed day we made sure we were all present and correct with plenty of interesting results to show him. We were just having a short tea break in a little cubbyhole next door when someone rushed in to say he was approaching, escorted by the apprentice supervisor. We leapt to our feet and busied ourselves over the equipment, but unfortunately John Daly managed to knock the dangling chain of the crane, which then swung around. Normally this was no danger, as it was a few inches above everything, but on this day we had on test a larger than usual machine whose coupling was high enough for the chain to touch. It did this and was caught by the spinning coupling bolts just as the door opened to admit the visitors. What happened next was all over in a second or two, but made a quite spectacular greeting: the chain stretched and broke, several links opened up and were hurled through the air in a frightening manner. Fortunately nobody stood in their way, but two of the links shot straight up and broke panes in the skylights above with a noise like a machine gun. Broken glass then descended and could have been lethal had any of it met one of the couplings. Everybody ducked, but by this time all the fireworks were over.

One other event occurred during that spell which would have rather upset the Metro-Vick apprentice supervisor had he been aware of it. There were two methods of entering the Works. One was through one of the gates passing the security staff, and we reckoned was only safe during normal shift changeover times. If one of us was coming in late having had our clock card punched by one of the others, it was necessary to adopt the alternative entry method, which was to march brazenly through the main administrative offices entrance, smile sweetly at the receptionist who came to know us after a while, and get into the lift. I don't know whether the receptionist realised who we were, but obviously she must have thought we were legitimate staff employees or whatever. Two floors up in the admin building there was a footbridge across into another building from where one could get back to ground level within the factory. Entry achieved! We often used this route on our 'non-duty' days. John Daly was in the lift with a couple of office girls one day when the lift broke down, and it was over an hour before they were released. He had no business to be anywhere near the admin building, and our escape route might well have been blown, especially as somebody had been asking for him all that morning and the two of us remaining had no good alibi for him. It was cloak and dagger tactics like this that made our dreary factory life more bearable, and we felt so sorry for the legitimate workers who came in every day all day with no thought of another life.

During this time Noggin and one other had spent time at the Lawrence Scott factory in Norwich, and I visited him there one weekend. He'd found lodgings in a big house run by a large and welcoming lady who, when opening the door on his arrival, greeted him with "And what instrument do you play?" Apparently she enjoyed evening soirées sitting in her commodious kitchen astride a 'cello with other lodgers who included a flautist and a violin. Noggin's musical expertise was nil, but he made up for it by his eccentricity, so was readily accepted. In one of the rooms I noticed several half empty bottles of milk, and peering round the door I saw about twenty more, all with the soured remains of their contents. I think I preferred where I was in Rugby!

~*~

Summers at Cambridge were idyllic. We found time for relaxing afternoons punting up and down the backs, or sometimes venturing up the Granta through the meadows. Punts for both sections of the river were hired from one of two firms by the weir at Silver Street. There was also a favourite pub just there that sold a particularly lethal brew of scrumpy which one drank by the half pint with devastating effects. It was rather easy on a hot day to down a glass or three of lovely cold beer, and it could quickly become a habit.

The Engineering Faculty buildings ran beside a large field named Coe Fen with the river running to one side of it, a piece of common land popular with dog walkers. Every summer groups of surveyors could be seen bent over theodolites, carrying out a meticulous survey. These were engineers doing their practical survey course, accurate to inches horizontally, but to a vertical accuracy of a tenth of a foot—not inches, strangely. No doubt it's all done in metres nowadays. The course we completed then has stayed with me all these years and I still have my surveyor's notebook with the readings recorded. Our supervisor for that course was a don who normally lectured on lubrication, and he came round to each group on a typical Cambridge battered bicycle. You could hear him coming from the tortured squeaks and groans of the bike chain as he stood on the pedals attempting to achieve forward motion, clouds of red rust rising from the chain area. "Got to keep fit somehow," would be his reply if we suggested some oil might be needed.

We worked towards mini exams at the end of term, the results of which would determine whether we would be allowed to continue into our second year. Percy Hammond pooh-poohed our concerns about this, saying that nobody failed these exams unless they were complete asses, and we didn't quite come into that category. Much more importantly I was working towards the May Bumps, a peculiarly Cambridge event whereby rowing eights set off down the river at set intervals, the object being to catch up the one in front and 'bump' it. This required only a feather touch, but sufficient to result in both boats withdrawing from the race, the one doing the bumping then going up a place for the following day's event. If one bumped on all four race days, the crew won their oars. This procedure was no doubt devised to overcome the problem of one boat passing another on the narrow Cam. Normally this could only be done safely by the boat wishing to overtake calling out to the one ahead for "permission to come by, please Sir!" whereupon the boat being passed would draw in their oars to allow them to do so. Following close behind the May Bumps came the social event of the year— the May Balls. Fitzwilliam had no facilities for a Ball, but many other colleges held them, and one was free to go to whichever event one wished. For the Naval people with friends in most colleges, it was fairly straightforward to join a party for a particular college Ball; all one needed was a partner. Some people imported their partner; others were lucky with a partner from either Girton or Newnham, the only two ladies' colleges at the time. Women at Cambridge were outnumbered ten to one by men, so the likes of me were usually unsuccessful. I went anyway, joined a party and had a dance with each of the girls in it. The dancing was a hotch-potch of different types, but with some of the top London dance bands, it was all great fun. The Balls took place in huge marquees erected in a college's court, students' rooms surrounding that court being used for a party's base. The Balls started late, were open to all comers after midnight, and fizzled out sometime next morning in time for breakfast. Some people with Herculean stamina managed a second ball the following night, spending most of the intervening day punting up and down the Cam.

The end of full term came, with the prospect of three months before the start of our second year. One or two people would be coming up for the long vac term, but I was not one of them. Instead, a goodly part of that time would be spent once again at Metro-Vick. The three of us spent it profitably in buying an old pre-war Buick that we garaged behind one of the Rugby pubs, then set to to do it up. It was a proper gas-guzzler, but petrol was cheaper than beer, so that didn't worry us. We had to put our time spent at work on a proper footing, so drew up a rota for duty clocker-inner, standby duty man and off duty man, the latter two spending much of their days on the car.

For one of our early runs we took the Buick to a somewhat well-to-do part of Warwickshire where some ex-Polsue guests lived, a couple with a truly beautiful daughter. I hadn't appreciated how well heeled these people were until we motored up their long approach drive to a superb pad with a large stable block on one side. They invited us to stay for a meal, and their daughter joined us to take a boat out on the Avon at Stratford nearby. She ignored me also the handsome John Daly, making a beeline instead for John Holmes. Now John Holmes had become engaged during the Easter vacation, the first of our Long Course to do so, and therefore had no right to encourage her. But he must have had something, I know not what. I was so murderously jealous, that my special day designed to impress my two friends was completely ruined.

At last Metro-Vick were realising we might be fairly responsible people, and gave us work this time that was more in keeping with our abilities. I was seconded to a research physicist developing a mechanical device for changing high power alternating current into DC, his 'contact rectifier'. It consisted of a bank of enclosed rotating switches being driven at an exact speed, controlled precisely from the mains supply. As the voltage went from positive to negative through zero the switches operated, thus reversing the current, so that the voltage always remained positive. Enormous currents of some thousands of amps were involved, but the switchover was carried out in that brief instant when the current was zero. Theoretically it was safe enough, but like all such experiments, when it goes wrong the results can be impressive. This did happen while I was there, when someone (could have been me, but I'm not admitting anything) threw a switch that connected everything up out of phase. The resulting bang took out the electrical supply to the whole research building, causing huge machinery trials that had been running for several weeks to slow down to a stop. In the ensuing silence angry shouts from other research scientists could be heard echoing round the vast testing hall.

The only picture I have of Long Course 6, taken on a visit to the submarine battery works at Bakewell. I am in the back row fourth from the left. Noggin is sitting cross-legged on the ground, second from right.

John's wedding in Southampton was the next main outing for the Buick, which at a pinch held nine sitting three abreast in three rows. All of LC6 were invited, complete with swords so as to produce an impressive guard of honour. On the appointed day six others working at nearby Midlands factories rendezvoused at Rugby and the eight of us set off for the drive to Southampton in great comfort. On the way we stopped for a bottle of beer and a pie which we consumed whilst driving along, stopping just once more for another bottle of beer each. The empties were rolling around at our feet, over a dozen of them. Perhaps it would have been sensible to have brought a crate to put them in. We arrived about the same time as all the other guests, having been warned it was a nonconformist church and there'd be no alcohol at the reception in the adjacent church hall; in fact it seemed to be one of those temperance institutions where the very mention of the word 'drink' resulted in a paranoiac agitation—and here was one of the church daughters proposing to marry into the Royal Navy! When the Buick stopped outside the church on a slight camber, not only did eight uniformed naval officers tumble out clutching their swords, but so did sixteen empty beer bottles which proceeded to roll all over the place, landing at the feet of aghast wedding guests. The bride and all her side of the family were short people while all the LC6 men attending were tall, around six feet or over, so our sudden arrival like that must have been quite a shock.

That summer I joined a local sailing club based on a reservoir at Daventry. As is usual at such clubs most of the members had boats and there was always a demand for people to crew them. The appearance of a lightweight man who could sail was just what they wanted. We had lots of away matches that gave me a chance of reservoir sailing all over the Midlands. The day I best remember was our match with the Burton-on-Trent Sailing Club, whose clubhouse was a wartime Nissen hut. It had an entrance at the end, as is usual, but the club had built a long semi-circular porch onto it. This gave the whole building the appearance of a huge half-buried beer bottle lying on its side, and they had painted it all beer-bottle brown, complete with a label that ran over the top and down the other side, on which the name of the club was written. The final touch was a gold-painted outer door and frame with a crinkly edge, fashioned to look like a crimped beer bottle top. We got out on the water and, needless to say, I then discovered all the buoys we had to sail around were large bottles anchored by their tops. These must have been display ones, or maybe they were Jeroboams or somesuch. After the races we repaired to the clubhouse where copious quantities of Burton's best brews flowed. My driver took us back to Daventry in record time that evening and managed to avoid actually hitting anything en route.

At last the time came for a longish spell at Polsue, a proper holiday this time. During this period a Doctor and Mrs Stokes visited. Father was a bit miffed when they asked to stay for a week and "if they liked it would stay for a second week". He referred to some "crusty old doctor from Bexhill" and was prepared to behave accordingly, but when they turned out to be charming people, staying on for their second week when their younger son, Peter, was able to join them, father forgot he'd been miffed. Jane and Peter hit it off straightaway, while the two sets of hopeful parents discreetly looked on. Ever unobservant, I didn't notice any vibes between these two, and just carried on with my sailing and my other country pursuits.

A large ketch, the Saoirse, arrived at a mooring off Stone Quay. She was a very elderly vessel built for comfort rather than speed. We rowed past in the pram on our way to our own moorings, and soon got to know the owner, a Surrey wine merchant by name of Eric Ruck. He invited Jane and me to go sailing in his boat several times, probably because of Jane (Eric didn't appear to be hampered with a wife or family) and if Jane went, I suppose I would have to go too. Saoirse was a super vessel, slowish with lots of assorted headsails, and absolutely right for cruising. A previous owner, one Conor O'Brien, had sailed her around the world. Eric took her down and up the Channel single-handed each summer, and spent quite some time in and around the Fal estuary and its creeks. He asked us for supper aboard one evening, the boat on that day lying up the Truro river at Malpas. We duly set off with me driving the Land Rover which was now the Polsue vehicle. The last mile to the creek from the St. Michael Penkivel area is down a lane between high banks only a foot or so wider than the Land Rover. Eric was anchored out in the channel and came for us in a tiny pram that just held the three of us. Back on board we enjoyed a wonderfully convivial evening with a super meal and far too much to drink, while outside it got dark, very dark. Sometime after ten there was a hail from the Truro harbourmaster's launch. Would we move Saoirse because a large vessel was due to come up the river on the tide in about an hour or so. This rather brought the party to a close, so Eric rowed us ashore again. I couldn't help noticing through my inebriated haze that we only had an inch or so of freeboard, and should the boat tip over we'd probably all drown in the state we were in. However, we made it, said goodnight to Eric, and set off home along the narrow lanes without colliding with any of the banks. Remarkable.

Eric was still around when it was time for me to return to Cambridge, but I believe it was about then that Jane went with him on the first leg of his trip up channel, being put off at Dartmouth to make her own way back. My mother, bless her, always the practical one but completely out of her depth when it came to anything to do with boats, asked Eric quite seriously whether he knew the way!

~*~

John Daly never returned for his second year, having failed to pass the first year exam. He was duly discharged from the Royal Navy, and on the strength of his surveying course, landed a job surveying for a company that was building a railway to run from Uganda to the Kenyan port of Mombasa.

I had moved into a grander room in my new Warkworth Terrace digs, a room above Malcolm's. It was great to be able to cross Parker's Piece and be at Fitzwilliam in a few minutes on foot. Apart from Malcolm the other lodgers were all postgraduates, if indeed they were anything to do with the university. One of them, a quiet Chinese who never had breakfast in the big basement dining room, seemed to have a lady friend in his room most nights, and it wasn't always the same one. I was in my room one morning when one of Mrs Arnold's cleaners who was doing the Chinese man's room started shouting down the stairs,

"Mrs Arnold, ee's bin at it again. Another one in 'is bed. You must come an' move it." A few days after that the Chinese gentleman was replaced by a research chemist and things quietened down again. These lodgings were not 'licensed' ones, and strictly speaking us students were not supposed to live in such places, but Fitzwilliam didn't seem to object.

We were obliged to dine in College a minimum of two nights a week. This involved wearing one's gown and paying over the odds for a fairly indifferent meal, so I never exceeded the two nights. A number of Fitzwilliam's foreign students with English as their second language meant that sitting next to one of them could be heavy going, but they often provided interesting conversation. Norman St John Stevas, who later went on to become an authority on royalty issues, I found a great bore. I was there, of course, when the Duke of Edinburgh came to open a new engineering building. He arrived with Lieutenant Commander Parker, his ADC. They stepped out of the official car nearby where I was standing wearing my blazer sporting the Naval crown on the breast pocket. Michael Parker spotted it, sidled up and said "Psst! Where are the heads? The Duke and I have been dying for a pee for the last half hour!" Later, when they were touring the building and also some of the laboratories in the old one, they came across a model of the DNA double helix suspended by a string from the ceiling, quietly rotating in the breeze. This was very soon after the two Cambridge scientists, Watson and Crick, had announced the discovery of DNA so it was an appropriate object to have on display. It could be that engineers had built this one for the Cavendish Laboratory. As they passed I got a wink from Parker but the Duke ignored me.

Malcolm and I got on very well together. I envied him his musical talent and would spend ages sprawled on his settee while he played away on his piano. We went to concerts together, his musical knowledge a great help when discussing the items on the programme. One concert featured the young piano soloist Peter Katin, who must have been about my age. I watched his long-fingered pale hands as they scudded up and down the keyboard, so flexible, so white. I couldn't imagine him coping in a naval whaler with salt-encrusted sisal sheets. I clapped and clapped at the end of the concerto and Malcolm asked whether I'd now like to meet him in the interval just starting. I stared.

"No problem," he said with a grin. "Let's go!" He led the way up the side aisle and through a door to the backstage area where musicians were milling around the tea urn, most of them sweating profusely. We were told to wait. In a few moments Peter Katin arrived and held out a hand, that wonderful hand I had so admired. I hardly liked to squeeze such a priceless appendage, but the response was firm and strong. Malcolm had kept it a secret that he and Peter had been at school together!

Malcolm had an elder sister, Elizabeth, who was props manager at the Old Vic. This gave him another entrée and once we went together to see Murder in the Cathedral, not a production I would have chosen, but it was a good time for Elizabeth to show us around backstage earlier in the day. I was keen to meet Elizabeth, for if she was as pretty as Malcolm was handsome, she would be a sight indeed. We met up at the stage door where my wishes were fulfilled and she took us up to her domain, a poky little space dominated by a noisy parrot called Binkie Beaumont. This particular prop had been acquired long ago when staging Robinson Crusoe, had been taught to say "pieces of eight!" and carefully kept away from the mischievous stagehands all of whom wanted to teach it to say something extremely rude. Actually it would come out with "Binkie!" from time to time, but it was more than Elizabeth's job was worth if it let down the side by uttering anything more embarrassing. It was loaned to other theatres putting on productions that required a parrot, but in the end became too much of a tie and had to go. We repaired to the canteen for a coffee, where a group of thespians were having a break from rehearsing another production. One of these was Robert Helpman whom I instantly recognized by his eyebrows and the manner in which he stood in first ballet position. It was about the time I'd seen him in the film The Tales of Hoffmann so there was no mistaking him. He looked appreciatively at Malcolm, cup poised halfway to his lips. One eyebrow rose enquiringly. Malcolm had to be introduced. Fortunately I knew nothing about his peccadilloes and didn't sense the vibes flying around.

Malcolm invited me to meet his parents who lived in Eastbourne, so we went down for the weekend. His father was a concert pianist and his mother had been a professional singer. On the Saturday night we all went to a seaside theatre where an old trouper, Clarkson Rose, had a show featuring a group of six attractive showgirls he called The Rosebuds. They all came round to the house after the show, which they often did apparently, so I enjoyed that party especially. They were all nice wholesome girls, doing the show for a bit of fun and not at all like some dumb blondes whom I've always found boring in the extreme when trying to talk to them.

I went to lectures on acoustics given by an enthusiastic lecturer who pranced around in trousers that were several inches too short for him. He was a Hi-Fi enthusiast, one of the first in the country. At this time, music was played on a 78 r.p.m. hard bakelite disc using a steel needle. The first vinyl LPs were just coming into the country. To demonstrate what an improvement this made, he brought in some of his own equipment, including his own design of loudspeaker enclosure, and played at high volume a record of breaking glass. Within moments the door opened and a worried looking lab assistant put his head round. The demonstration was a resounding success. I was anxious to find out more about achieving better sound quality and badgered father to give me a Leak amplifier for my 21st birthday. Thus began an obsession that has lasted me well. Soon I had built a loudspeaker cabinet which would reproduce good clean bass, then went on to obtain the latest thing in reel-to-reel tape recorders, a massively heavy tape deck such as the BBC used. Finally I found a second-hand quality microphone and was in business. I went around recording everything that was being played anywhere, from an orchestral concert in the City Hall, to birdsong using a homemade parabolic reflector, right through to a prestigious concert in Kings College Chapel given by the CUMS (Cambridge University Musical Society, in which Malcolm sang tenor) with a live orchestra conducted by the legendary Boris Ord. This last was also being recorded by the BBC who spent the whole day setting up and balancing their equipment—shades of the time I had got under their feet when they came to Bradfield all those years back. I listened to the broadcast that eventually went out and reckoned, with my newfound critical judgement, that their recording was muddied by having too many microphones, whereas mine sounded so much cleaner even though my single microphone was dangling over where the percussion was positioned, giving a slight imbalance. Throughout this time I never thought about copyright and would simply turn up somewhere and start recording. The BBC people doing the King's concert were obsessed with copyright red tape as they would need to be of course, but by the time I realised I might get into trouble one day I had by then made a recording in the newly built Guildford Cathedral of a concert in which my LC6 friend Antony Corfe was singing. The authorities there were only concerned that my microphone stand didn't scratch their shiny new floor and never thought to ask what I might want to do with my recording. They needn't have worried. I still have boxfuls of tapes recorded in those times in my attic, now obsolete and unplayable.

Cambridge at that time sported two live theatres, The Arts in the city centre where excellent productions would be put on, often on pre-West End runs, and the ADC, a little theatre tucked in behind Sidney Street where student productions were produced. I went there to see a much talked-about undergraduate musical called *Salad Days*. My ticket was taken at the door by a young man who, when it was time to start, shut the door, then went across to the stage where he sat down at a piano and began playing. This was Julian Slade, the composer who wrote the music, and what music—and lyrics! I still have the LP record I later bought and reckon it beats anything written by Andrew Lloyd Webber or Rodgers and Hammerstein, but then I would say that, wouldn't I.

Noggin had befriended a man who collected vintage Rolls Royces. He had come across him one day when the man returned to his parked 1920s Rolls which Noggin was admiring, and proceeded to start the engine by moving a couple of levers on the steering wheel. He said this was the only one of his Rollers he could start in this way, and only then if the engine was warm. The man didn't look as if he had two pennies to rub together let alone possess more than one Rolls Royce; it transpired he collected spare parts, from which he rebuilt a complete car from time to time. He did this on a miniscule income derived from marking examination papers. Noggin was invited to see the collection and took me along too. The house was somewhere near the Rex cinema of Marx Brothers fame in a fairly mean street, the back garden more than half filled with tumbledown sheds and tarpaulins hiding beneath which was the Rolls Royce graveyard. We often visited and enjoyed getting our hands dirty 'helping' him. Then one day came a break. Noggin discovered a rusting car chassis blocking a hole in a hedge off the Madingley Road, which looked very interesting. He scrambled around finding more bits that were probably part of the same car. Then he came across the body, which was propped upside down with hens nesting underneath it. Finally he came across the owner upon whom he prevailed to let him buy them all. I think he let Noggin have the lot for £25 cash. At this point I joined in and together we set to work. Our Rolls man let us have a covered area in his fast diminishing back garden and we were off. Lectures forgotten, we spent hours stripping down, cleaning, machining bits and pieces, painting, rebuilding the engine, making upholstery and a canvas hood, and generally enjoying ourselves hugely. The car was an open two-seater with a 'dicky', manufactured by Clark

Cluley in 1924. That company originally made bicycles but started manufacturing a light car in 1920 and ceased production in 1927, along with several other similar makers such as the Clyno, ousted at the time when one of them—Morris Garages—went into quantity production eventually producing the first of the successful Morris cars. Our Cluley had an incredibly fundamental design, beautifully made but with some impossible parts that simply did not work satisfactorily. For example, it had brakes on the two rear wheels only, operated by a rod connected by levers to the footbrake. This rod had a couple of bends in it to get around obstructions, so when one stood on the footbrake hard all that happened was the rod tried to straighten out thereby negating the action. The whole thing was potentially quite dangerous to put on the road, but it was such fun to drive and there were so few other cars on the roads in the early fifties that we taxed and insured it and off we went. It had 3½" beaded edge tyres that could only be obtained from a garage in Yeovil, so we motored down there in another car to get them. No windscreen wiper, of course. When it rained, one lifted the upper half of the windscreen and peered through the gap, the rain passing harmlessly over the top. She was full of character, rather like Bella, our cow. So we called her Bella. The local traffic police were always stopping us in order to have a look at her close up, and were very supportive. They kept their police cars in a lockup opposite my digs, so quite often when I came out of the house I would find one of them peering underneath her if I'd parked outside.

Bella had one or two tiresome quirks however. There seemed to be no provision for a spring at the carburettor end of the accelerator linkage to shut off the petrol when one took one's foot off the pedal, so we used a rubber ring cut from one of her discarded inner tubes. This worked just fine, except when it did break or come off, it always did so at a tricky moment. It meant the throttle didn't shut properly—something you don't want to have happen if you need to stop. Her gearbox was also somewhat worn in parts, with sufficient play such that if one pressed sideways when selecting a gear, the selector inside the box could pick up reverse gear when attempting to engage first, thus locking up the box completely. When this first began to happen (always when starting off) there was nothing for it but to undo six nuts on the top of the gearbox, lift the top off complete with gear lever, and fiddle about inside the warm oily interior with one's fingers to free it up again. I can remember this happening when we were both on our way to a dance, attired in smart dinner jackets with white cuffs, and the position Bella chose was at a set of traffic lights with a lot of impatient drivers behind us. However, as if expecting this kind of happening, she had a drain cock conveniently fitted on the front of the radiator, so it was a simple matter to rub 'Dirty Paws' on one's oily hands and rinse off under the hot tap! Bella's battery was clamped down on the running board, the usual place with cars of the twenties, but as she had magneto ignition, a battery was really only needed for voltage stabilisation and lights when the engine wasn't running. No one ever pinched the battery, nor for that matter attempt to drive off in the car (there was no ignition key). People just didn't do that sort of thing then, even in London.

We'd had to get special permission to have Bella up at Cambridge with us, readily granted by the appropriate proctor who was an engineering lecturer and as intrigued by her as everyone else. Having her there opened up a whole new world for me, one of the first outings being when Noggin invited me back to his home for a weekend. His widowed mother lived on her own in a small house on the edge of a wood in Ashampstead, a few miles from Bradfield. We would set off from Cambridge driving through Bedford, Bicester and via country roads to Wallingford. Bella was happier on these quiet roads as her fastest comfortable speed was about 30 m.p.h.; above that she began to vibrate rather alarmingly. People would always wave at such an extraordinary sight, so we got into the habit of waving back like royalty. The last half-mile to the house was up a gravel lane then across a field. Mrs Brooke was a proper countrywoman, looked after a small herd of bullocks which she fattened up in her meadow, was virtually self-supporting off the land, had a log fire in her sitting room using wood from around the house, and conjured up magnificent meals from her Aga cooker. Food came from her own garden, her own poultry, or from the village butcher who obtained his meat from local farmers. She was wonderfully fit with the country complexion of someone many years younger, and always great fun to stay with.

Owning Bella led on to taking an interest in vintage cars in general. We went to the annual VSCC Silverstone meeting where we would meet the most exotic machines still around. On the left is Sam Clutton's superb Itala. After the race was over Sam would drive it home, overtaking everything else on the road. On the right is the equally covetable 30/98 Vauxhall. Usually the people were every bit as interesting as their cars.

Sometimes Noggin's elder brother John would arrive unexpectedly. He had been at Harrow School before Noggin and, on the strength of learning to use an oxyacetylene welding torch there, had started up a small business in metal furniture manufacture. He lived in a Chelsea bedsit and I visited occasionally when in London and needing a bed. John had gone rather native in Chelsea, and on myfirst visit I could hardly believe anyone could live in such a bizarre way. To get into the house one put a hand through the letterbox of the house next door and withdrew the key which hung on a string inside, then went upstairs, tiptoed through the room of some artist taking care not to knock over his easel or tread on a tube of paint, went out onto the balcony, then in through the window of John's room in the next house. I think this was a temporary arrangement because John had lost his key, and was always going to replace it one day but never did. There were sufficient beds, a sofa, cushions, etc, for us to doss down for the night, and next morning we washed in a communal bathroom where various strangers wandered in and out with a sleepy greeting, apparently unconcerned about our presence; maybe they too were just visiting. John's usual practice in the mornings was to walk down the Kings Road in his dressing gown to a little café where they supplied takeaway breakfasts, quite popular with the Bohemian folks around there. On the day of our visit he actually dressed first, and after breakfast took us along to his workshop. His style of furniture was quite popular at that time and he would supply Heals in Tottenham Court Road.

John had acquired an even more ancient car than Bella. This was a three-wheeler Morgan with a two-cylinder air-cooled JAP engine mounted at the front. It had a brake only on the single rear wheel, which would get almost red hot when descending a long hill. My job, sitting in the dicky seat, was to lean over and dribble water onto the brake to stop it all catching fire.

On one visit to Ashampstead, John turned up with a story I found hard to believe. He had gone out in his Morgan with an artist friend of his, who expressed a desire to go to Florence.

"All right," says John, "Let's go." And with that they packed a toothbrush apiece, a box of tools for the car and some paints for his friend and set off in the morning. They had just enough money to pay the ferry fare. They made their way down through France, stopping when they got hungry. The artist drew caricatures of spectators, which he sold to them, using the proceeds to buy food, pay for lodgings and petrol. They got to their destination and most of the way back. Unfortunately they had an argument with a Flemish fire engine, which apparently expects automatic right of way over everything else on the road, including three-wheeler Morgans, and were unable to get out of its way in time. They arrived home on foot, the remains of the Morgan appearing a few days later. On its side they had painted the names of every town they had stopped at. The final name, scrawled rather badly, read "Hampstead Norries Railway Station". An ignominious end to an extraordinary trip.

Noggin and I took Bella to London occasionally, which seemed a normal thing to do at the time. There was no means of locking the door, since she didn't have a door; nor could one disable the ignition for there was no ignition key. We left her parked overnight, in Chelsea usually, and she never came to any harm. On one occasion we drove to Euston to collect a trunk that had been forwarded by train, parking inside the station environs while we loaded it up, tying it down across the back of the dicky seat. Before setting off again, we stayed awhile having a cup of coffee, and when we did emerge from the station it was to find Euston Road peculiarly quiet. We were frantically waved on by a policeman and it was only then we realised there were quite a lot of people lining the road on both sides. Eventually Noggin, who was driving, noticed in his driving mirror a police car following us a couple of hundred yards behind. Behind it was a Rolls with a fluttering standard on the roof. By this time we were getting a cheer from the people waiting to see the royal party so we gave them royal waves. Eventually we were diverted off the road by the police, but the glory was fun while it lasted. It turned out that the royal personage was to arrive at Euston and while we were finishing our coffee there, the roads had all been cleared for her. Nobody had expected us to find our way onto the station concourse in Bella.

Back at Polsue for my vacations I was beginning to feel almost like a visitor myself, so many things seemed to have changed each time I went home. Jane and Peter had been seeing more and more of one another and in due course the question was popped. Their wedding took place on a glorious spring day in April at the little church on the water's edge at St. Just in Roseland, surely the loveliest setting imaginable for one's wedding. Mrs Tracey had been married there in the twenties and had the organ installed especially for the occasion. Peter's sister and her husband, also his two older brothers—all of them erudite doctors—were attired in full fig looking most distinguished, much to father's delight. The wedding was before we had opened for the season, so the reception could be at Polsue. Flowers were at their best, the rhododendrons lining our drive all flowering their heads off, and our local AA man had fixed yellow signs at the more obscure road junctions to help those guests from 'up country'. Down at the church an enormous group of Echium Pininana with towering spires of mauve flowers fifteen feet high dominated the east entrance to this most glorious spot. Rare magnolias and lush bamboos fought for space with unusual rhododendrons. The winding walk down from the lych gate through the granite headstones of past seafarers was idyllic.

So Jane finally left us to set up house in Wilmslow in Cheshire near where Peter worked. Peter was no learned doctor, but an engineer, a very competent one. Jane's place was taken by Jill who knew the area well since her special friend, Jim Hosking, had an uncle who farmed Fentongollan, near Tresillian on the way to Truro. Jill and Jim had trained together at Seale-Hayne agricultural college in south Devon, and her arrival marked a turning point in our staffing of Polsue. Up until now we had employed local people for our season, from Easter until the end of October. In this part of Cornwall tourism and agriculture are the main industries. Tourism is seasonal and those employed on this basis have to subsist for the rest of the year on their six months' earnings in the season. Thus they look for wages that will allow this. With Jill's arrival she suggested we offer work to Seale Hayne students who are on holiday during our busy period from July to September. This we did, so taking on a series of attractive young people who came to work for us each year from then on.

~*~

In my next long vacation period Noggin and I were sent to Barr and Stroud, the optical instrument manufacturers in Anniesland, a suburb of north Glasgow. Before going, we had a couple of weeks holiday, so I borrowed Bella and took a Fitzwilliam friend, Spencer Millham, down to Cornwall in her. Looking back, this seems a crazy thing to do. Bella was fine as a local runabout, but to contemplate a trip all that way in such a vehicle was foolhardy. But I was young and had no inhibitions about attempting anything. Spencer was reading Geography and was completely ignorant about how anything worked, nor did he show any interest in learning. For him it was a pleasant drive through attractive scenery in a funny little open car and he relied absolutely on his driver getting there safely. And we did. Not only did we drive nearly 300 miles with no mishaps, we did so on the roads of the twenties, even to the extent of taking the old road from Exeter to Tavistock over the Moors. Our safe arrival at Polsue was greeted with incredulity resulting with father proudly bragging about his 'clever engineer son'. Little did he know! I don't think Spencer went down too well at Polsue, since he seemed to have no practical abilities in any useful direction so far as anyone down there could see. He was an 'intellectual' if anything; something that has no useful purpose in a busy hotel-cum-smallholding world.

On the way back, we diverted to tour through some of the Cotswold country, calling off at Tetbury to look up Anstruther who had moved there when his wife died. We found him living alone in a town house with no garden; he'd aged tremendously in the ten years or so since I'd last seen him, was rather deaf, very bent over and shrunken. He was so pleased to see us and thanked me profusely for taking time out to visit a lonely old man. It was a rather sad meeting, but I was glad we had stopped there.

Barr and Stroud had a number of large Naval contracts, the main one being the specialised manufacture of submarine periscopes. They were also one of the companies that made the CRBFD (Close Range Blind Fire Director). These were fitted to ships as part of the main armament and looked like a gun turret with a radar aerial instead of a gun. Operators would sit inside tracking the target by radar then directing the ship's guns by means of complex electro-mechanical equipment that was a Barr and Stroud speciality. One unit, the 'tachy box' (tachometric box), essentially a large complex precision-engineered gearbox, was the heart of the Director. Barr and Stroud quality was renowned for this type of work, and for me working here would be a complete contrast to the heavy engineering at Metropolitan-Vickers.

Barr and Stroud seemed to be run jointly by two managers. I never discovered which of them did what, but both were very pleasant to us and seemed genuinely pleased to have us with them, going out of their way to make sure we were never bored. For example, when some enormous lens was being cast, one of them sent word for us to slip up to the glass furnace and watch it being poured. About a week later when the glass block had cooled sufficiently we watched while the first cuts were made. Several weeks later the lens was on the grinding beds, taking shape at last and many times smaller than the original block of glass. At lunch breaks we would sit outside the factory entrance on a row of benches eating our lunch and attempting to understand the really thick Glaswegian accents around us. The boys tried to teach us, but were none too successful. Just when I thought I'd mastered it, one of them said,

"The problem wi' ye' twa London lads is I canna understand a worrr'd ye say." Oh well, we did our best! On one glorious day one of the managers came up and suggested we might like to be away up in yonder hills, nodding at the gap between two tenement blocks where the distant mountains could be seen, misty mauve and beckoning in the sunshine. We nodded.

"Och, awa' wi' ye'. I'll turn your key!" Now that's what I call a great manager!

Most of the craftsmen seemed to be called Willie. Wee Willie was very thin, accentuated by being well over six feet tall. Big Willie, naturally, was a shorty though he was stocky with it. Then there was Happy Willie, Dreamy Willie (he was a young bachelor who seemed to be always in love, changing his affections to a new lass nearly every week), and I remember a quiet dark man called Hamish. He would appear a little late on Monday mornings clumping along in heavy walking boots, having been on the hills since Friday evening. He always went alone, and we never found where he did his walking. Wee Willie would talk of "shootin' doon haggi" with the CRBFDs, and how careful one had to be to only shoot haggi in season. They were always pulling our legs.

As the Edinburgh Festival drew near we discovered that during that time the Veteran Car Club of Great Britain would be hosting a rally starting from Edinburgh and finishing a week later at Goodwood racecourse, and would be joined by their opposite numbers from the United States. Noggin knew one of the competitors, a man who owned a Silver Ghost Rolls Royce, so we went over to Edinburgh, met him there and waved them off at the start before repairing to the Usher Hall for a concert. The following Friday there was another concert we thought would be rather fun to go to, so jumped on the Edinburgh train once more and went to that one too. During the interval Noggin said rather wistfully that the cars would be arriving at Goodwood next morning at ten.

"Well," I said, "Why don't we watch their arrival?"

"Why not! John, you have the most splendid ideas!"

The moment the concert was over we dashed along to Waverley Station and managed to board the London Sleeper, with no proper plans or idea how we might fetch up at the other end. We had just about enough money to get there and back. In the early morning we crossed London, caught the train to Chichester, arriving just in time to meet our friend in the Dolphin Hotel car park putting a final polish on his Silver Ghost before setting off on the four-mile drive to Goodwood.

"Want a lift?" he asked. And so we arrived at Goodwood in style, sitting in the back of this lovely old Rolls waving condescendingly to everyone lining the road. We swept in through the competitors' entrance, thereby saving the cost of an entrance ticket, and had the most wonderful day with several concours trips around the circuit in an assortment of cars. The sun shone, we lived for the moment and enjoyed it all. The cars lined up in alphabetical order at one time, and sitting high up in a huge Bentley looking in the mirror I could see a row of Bugattis following behind. Quite a sight. Ettori Bugatti had once commented rather disparagingly to W.O. Bentley that he made "Quite the fastest lorries on the road".

After such a day we had to think about getting back. As happens with young people who land on their feet without a care in the world, it went without a hitch. Someone gave us a lift back to London, then on to Chiswick where a cousin of Noggin's was prevailed upon to put us up for the night. Next morning, we went dinghy racing at Hammersmith. My memories of that race were the filthy Thames soup on which we sailed, and we did so downwind of the Bemax factory, the effluvia from which was revolting. Still, the racing was good. Then we made it to Paddington in time for a sleeper back to Glasgow. Walking in on the Monday morning seemed like coming back after a week's holiday, and we wanted to ask what had been going on in our absence.

One hot weekend we biked up to Loch Voil on Noggin's old Norton, felt like a cool-off in the loch, so found a quiet spot and went for a swim in our underwear. We were so cold afterwards we then needed to warm up (and get dry—we had no towels). So we danced an eightsome reel without music with six dummies to make up the eight. We didn't mind the curious sheep, but suddenly realised someone had stopped in the lane nearby and must have wondered what on earth we were up to. We camped on that site overnight before returning to Glasgow.

On another occasion we thought it would be more sensible to stay at a youth hostel overnight and, searching through the SYHA book we found the hostel at Loch Ossian the directions for which said, "There are no roads to Loch Ossian". Now, here was a challenge, so we packed our rucksacks and biked to Rannoch Station at the western end of Loch Rannoch. Leaving the bike there we set off to walk the eight miles or so to Loch Ossian. The map showed boggy ground everywhere, so we played safe and walked along the railway track, an exhausting business since one is constrained to shortening one's normal stride to the distance between sleepers. A train came every couple of hours or so and one of them stopped to offer us a lift, but we had plenty of time, so thanked the driver and carried on walking. The hostel was just a wooden fishing hut by the side of the Loch comprising a single room with a wood-burning stove in the middle, a table and a few chairs, and sleeping shelves in a partitioned area at each end. These shelves were just wooden slatted bunks onto which we unrolled our sleeping bags. There were a couple of taciturn Scottish fishermen staying there who cooked a nice salmon they'd just caught for the four of us to share for our supper. Water to drink came from a little burn running nearby and we had a loaf of bread. Bliss. Next morning the warden arrived, striding over the heather in his kilt, looking absolutely right for the occasion. He took our 1/6d fee (9p) and we set off back again, meeting the postman at Loch Ossian who also doubled as stationmaster and just about everything else in that tiny hamlet out in the wilds.

Back at Rannoch station we met a couple of American tourists who asked us the way. They were 'doing' Scotland, had booked in to a hotel at Kinlochleven for the night, and wondered how much further it was. They were using the AA book of the time, which had a map showing the full width of Scotland on the one page, the distance between Rannoch and Kinlochleven being about ¼ inch on the map. We explained it was indeed only 15 miles as the crow flies, but to get there on a road would mean a detour back through Aberfeldy and Crianlarich of over 120 miles. I think they were a little upset, especially as Noggin impishly offered to lead them across Rannoch Moor on foot if they'd rather.

It was while we were out in the hills one weekend that I learnt to respect the wide-open spaces. The occasion that comes to mind was when we were doing a ridge walk when the mist came down leaving us with no landmarks. On the map we could see that all we needed to do was to keep going with the ridge on our right until we came to where a burn tumbled down to our left and follow that. No problem. No need to unpack everything to find the compass. We just kept on walking until we came to the burn only to find it ran down to the right. The map showed no such burn, so at that point we did get out the compass. To our amazement we realised we'd gone round in a complete half circle and were heading back the way we had come. This was a burn we'd crossed hours earlier. After that we took more care.

On a particularly lovely summer's day we decided we'd climb the local Munro, Ben Lomond. We rode up the track on the eastern shore of Loch Lomond until we were under the mountain, then set off for a steep and arduous scramble to the top. The achievement was somewhat spoilt as we breasted the summit to find trippers in town shoes standing around amongst the orange peel and old bottles. We do like our mountains to be remote, as befits a proper Munro.

Noggin had a desire to visit Skye and set off by himself one weekend while I was doing something else. On the Monday he arrived at work late having discovered the previous night that he could not leave the Island because it was the Sabbath, and so had to wait until the first ferry on the Monday morning.

During my Cambridge time the First Fitzwilliam boat in which I rowed steadily improved to the point where, in my final year, we 'bumped' every boat in all four bumps races thereby winning our oars. This meant each member of the crew was presented with a re-furbished oar that had the names of the winning crew painted on the blade so that it could be hung in one's trophy room. (I took my oar down to Polsue and hung it in the bar.) This gave us the idea that perhaps we would be able to shine amongst rowing eights other than Cambridge boats, so someone entered us for the Reading Head of the River races that year. Along with a few other Cambridge college boats, ours was transported to Reading while we made our own way there, booking in at a dreary little temperance hotel, which was all we could find in that busy week. After a couple of outings on the river, mainly for the cox to get some experience in the comparatively swift stream that runs on the Thames, we duly took part, doing quite well and beating a number of Oxford boats.

The final days at Cambridge approached. Both Noggin and I invited partners to the Pembroke May Ball. Noggin's partner was Ruth, a game lass from Newnham with whom he had taken up, but for me I had to import my girl as did many other men. Some weeks earlier Ruth had been to a dance with Noggin and arrived back at Newnham after midnight to find the night portress had locked up. There was nothing for it but to climb in. Ruth managed to scramble up the high railings at the side of Newnham's main entrance, but her long dress prevented her from getting her leg over the top. So she took off her dress, pushed it through the railings and had another go. Unfortunately she still couldn't get over the top, but by this time her dress was on the wrong side of the railings and out of reach. There was nothing for it but to ring the bell. As I say, Ruth was a game lass.

I asked Belinda if she'd like to be my partner and, a little to my surprise and hugely to my delight, Mrs Tracey enthusiastically arranged with a cousin of hers who lived near the Leys School in Trumpington Street to have Belinda to stay over. In the preceding days the May Bumps had taken place. Exams had gone well and I felt pretty confident of passing, the weather was fine and warm and my special girl friend was coming to the Ball. Halcyon days indeed!

I met Belinda at the station and drove her in Bella to her relations' house. She'd heard about Bella, but hadn't met her during the trip I made to Cornwall that time. I took Belinda around to meet my friends, had a meal with some sailing chums and we spent a long time saying goodnight in the shrubbery in front of her relatives' house, being disturbed by an observant passing policeman who shone his torch at us, then apologised when he realised what we were up to. The Cambridge police must have been very understanding. In the morning we explored the city and spent the afternoon punting up the Granta. Lots of others were doing the same thing and it was all very social. The Ball went really well, and way past midnight the four of us visited several other colleges to sample different dance bands and meet other friends. Humphrey Littleton was blowing away at the Trinity Ball, where, by the time we got there, most other dancers had adopted a slow rhythmical sleeping-on-the-hoof posture, holding one another up. Eventually it got light, we went back to Pembroke, said our farewells and, still in our glad rags, drove out in Bella for breakfast at a transport café on the Huntingdon road. Lorry drivers scarcely gave us a glance.

We delivered the girls back to their bases, Noggin drove off home in Bella while I took the train from Cambridge station for the last time.

9

Collingwood and After

Long Course six met up together again at Collingwood a few weeks later, back in uniform once more, but now sporting a shiny gold stripe on our sleeve above the dark green one that denoted our specialist Branch. I rather liked this colour, green for GO, or 'go ahead' maybe. The steamy engineers wore a purple stripe that didn't appear to have any link with engineering. Doctors, of course, wore red which was fitting, but dentists had a brown stripe, congealed blood I suppose. Pussers appropriately sported a white stripe, all that paper they dealt with, whereas the schoolies had blue, no doubt representing daylight, eureka!

The man from the Portsmouth branch of Gieves came to measure us for our evening wear, quaintly named 'mess undress'. He got to work on the inside leg measurement which all such people seem to be so concerned about. And then,

"Which side do you dress, Sir?"

"Eh?"

He coughed discreetly, and repeated the question. It sounded as if these trousers were going to be somewhat tight. I had to think for a moment before replying, and was beginning to worry about the tailor's designs.

"Well, Sir," he said, as he started writing down figures in his little book, "Gentlemen don't usually give much thought to this, Sir, but the mess undress, now the trousers are cut very precisely. You will look very smart, Sir."

I believed him, remembering someone once telling me that persuasive people have a saying, "When you've got them by the balls their hearts and minds will follow!"

This appointment to Collingwood would last for 18 months, at the end of which time we would be expected to be up to speed on all aspects of Naval electrical engineering, the practical application of all we had learned at Cambridge. We started straight in with classroom lectures from an assortment of schoolies, rather like being back at school again, but this time whenever we left the building—

always with our cap on—there was a risk of being saluted by a passing sailor. Most of the sailors at Collingwood were themselves on courses of various kinds, the more permanent ones being those at the artificer apprentices' school which would turn out fully trained artisans at the end of their time. Looking round the wardroom at lunchtime we realised the majority of officers crowding round the bar were schoolies, closely followed by electrical officers with just a sprinkling of other specialities.

We shared two-berth cabins in a single storey accommodation block beside the wardroom, which were comfortable enough. Rather surprisingly Wrens ran the domestic side of the wardroom, from cooking and waitressing to cleaning the cabins. It seemed a gross misuse of high quality servicewomen to use them in this way. One would have thought this entire domestic operation would have been put out to local civilian contractors, but the Service mind creaks along in a peculiar way, and no doubt they had their reasons at that time.

I shared my cabin with Antony Corfe whom I got to know fairly well. He lived in West Meon about fifteen miles north of Fareham, where his father was the local GP, and he sometimes asked me home on a Sunday evening for a meal. He had a sister, Deirdre, and we all got along well.

One day I met a chap in his twenties dressed up in Scout uniform knocking around in a disused hut behind the Collingwood theatre, who said he was the leader of the Collingwood Rover Scout Group and was I into Scouting then? We got chatting, and I could see a number of advantages in joining his group. They went on expeditions here and there, were regarded very favourably by the Camp Commander and other authorities, it would be an opportunity to get to know the minds of ordinary sailors, and would be a change from the life I was becoming enmeshed in. I joined and never regretted it, though my contemporaries thought me a bit odd wanting to return to scouting at my age. The man I had been talking to was a petty officer electrician. Most of the others were artificer apprentices or ordinary sailors, with a sprinkling of National Servicemen amongst them, one of whom was a very ordinary lad by the name of Baden-Powell who never actually admitted to any link with the great Founder. I made it a condition that when I was with them I was to be treated as a normal person, not an 'officer' and certainly not as a leader. I wanted to be just one of them. This was fine, as that was why each of them had joined.

Noggin had found an exciting boat to sail. It was an airborne lifeboat kept down at Warsash on the Hamble. This was an Uffa Fox design requested by the Air Ministry during the war. It was a fast craft that could be slung beneath an RAF rescue aircraft so that it could be dropped into the water by parachute to a ditched aircrew, thereby enabling them to zip away from the area. The design he came up with was a moulded-ply eighteen footer with twin masts. She had buoyancy tanks all round (a new concept then) and he hadn't overlooked the secondary idea—that these craft should be easily convertible to civilian use after the war! She was light, very strong and enormously enjoyable to sail, though keeping her upright was sometimes quite a job. She would get up on the plane in the lightest breeze, outsailing anything else on the water. Capsizing was no problem, as she righted herself quite easily, whereupon one just clambered aboard and started sailing again. Within minutes the water in the cockpit would drain out of large self-drainers in the transom—another of Uffa's innovations. The first time we capsized, a very concerned cruising boat came over and insisted on giving us a tow, which it did at quite a speed. That was how we found how efficient the self-drainers were. Whilst being towed along we re-set the sails and took off once more, overtaking our rescue boat with a wave and a thank you.

We had really outgrown Bella, needing something more reliable and faster. I made one more visit to Cornwall in her, and she died on me somewhere near Moretonhampstead in the middle of Dartmoor, her quirky sense of humour active to the last. I had to abandon her by the side of the road, her clutch slipping so much I couldn't climb the hill I was at the bottom of. From then on I hitched as far as St Austell, then phoned home for help. Jane came and picked me up in the Land Rover, and next morning we drove to Moretonhampstead with a towrope. I had one more go at trying to climb the hill, and like a naughty horse which gets bored with playing up, she behaved perfectly, the clutch not slipping at all. It was on that visit that while she was parked in St. Mawes a couple of children came up to her, one of them tracing the name on the oval blue radiator badge, then calling out "Mummy, it's got Grandpa's name!" Their mother appeared, stopped as if she'd seen a ghost, grabbed her children and started to make off. I rushed over to her.

"Please tell me, what upset you about our car?"

Reluctantly she said, "It's my father-in-law. He built these cars in the twenties, but they weren't a success. He thinks there aren't any left."

Try as I did I could not get her to say more. Clearly this venture of her father's was one he had put behind him and wished to forget. She rushed off with her children still looking shocked. It occurred to me afterwards that maybe there'd been a fatality with one of them, the blame falling on the company that made them. Although Bella was car number 1064 we'd always guessed that it was really just 64, as we doubted whether there'd ever been more than about a hundred made, if that.

I drove all the way back up country before the clutch began to slip again, and this time I stripped it right down to find the huge spring that operated the cone clutch had cracked. A local welder mended it for me, but the temper couldn't be satisfactorily restored, and from then on the clutch often misbehaved. Reluctantly she had to go. No doubt she is still somewhere around to this day so if you come across a funny little open tourer with spidery wheels and the number DP5630, then that's her.

Noggin coveted a Vauxhall 30/98, the ultimate fast tourer of the twenties, but they were far too expensive; however he did manage to find a smaller version, the Vauxhall 14/40, and bought that. She was a proper four seater, with a reasonably weatherproof hood and was fast and safe. Bella had undoubtedly been a feminine car, but the 14/40 was quite different. He was called Harold and became the star of the wardroom car park, most of the others being somewhat tatty pre-war vehicles. The best cars were owned by the Chiefs and POs who were the ones with money. Probably only about a hundred people in the whole of Collingwood had cars in the fifties, most of the others depending on the good public transport of the day.

The first Tall Ships race was to take place, starting from Torbay. On the eve of the race on the newly acquired wardroom television set we saw the ships assembling off Torquay. Southern Television had fitted out a boat with an outside broadcast camera and transmitter, and it was this that was transmitting pictures back to a base unit on Berry Head to be broadcast live from there. This was state of the art television, outside broadcasts being a difficult and unreliable method of live news gathering, and it hadn't been tried before from a moving platform. The cameras were massive pieces of kit, normally mounted on specially built dollies complete with operator who sat on a seat behind the camera. Generally, news gathering was still done with film, the viewer seeing the results much later. It was a lovely evening with a low sun and the sight of some of these majestic sailing ships was too much for Noggin.

"Let's go and watch the start!" he cried.

"But it's tomorrow."

"Right, then we haven't any time to lose."

That's how we made decisions in those days. No planning, no preparations, no worries. We picked up two others and the four of us piled into Noggin's 14/40, each with a holdall which was stowed between the front mudguard and bonnet, two either side (she had no boot). We had decided to drive to Dartmouth, knock up Brett-Knowles whom we knew was now teaching there, and persuade him to take us out in one of the Dartmouth yachts. We wanted as good a view as the Southern Television boat was getting. We arrived late at night, found BK who suggested we bunk down in the gym, where we found about thirty other hopefuls rolled up in sleeping bags on the floor.

Good old BK had indeed obtained a boat, a six-metre windfall yacht with room for the four of us, and we sailed out from Dartmouth next morning on a lovely day, hardly believing we were actually there. We sailed around in company with about fifty other craft of various types, narrowly avoiding one another as we watched the really big ships setting sail. The TV boat was there, with its huge camera mounted on a fancy gimbals construction for'd, and an enormous directional aerial aft which an operator was continuously trying to keep pointed at Berry Head. All electronic equipment in those days used valve technology that was big and heavy and didn't like salt water. The BBC also had a boat, but were only doing a radio broadcast.

It was a cloudless sky with very little wind. After the start the big square-riggers piled on the canvas, something that took them twenty minutes or so, and then they began to pull away from us smaller yachts. Our six-metre was a fairly fast sailer and we were able to keep up with the leaders initially, but even we soon dropped behind. It had been quite a misty morning, but now a thicker sea mist was rolling in. Soon the hulls of the big ships faded into the mist and all we could see were their ghostly topsails until eventually everything had gone, like the Cheshire cat's grin. We were alone. In fact we were very alone, as at this point we realised nobody had any idea where we were. BK pondered over the chart and reckoned that if we steered northwest we should find land not too far from Dartmouth. I shuddered to think what our Devonshire instructors would have thought about such navigation, but it worked. An hour later, amazingly, we heard breakers and moments afterwards the Dartmouth Mewstone appeared out of the mist. Then the mist suddenly lifted and there was the entrance to Dartmouth in the sunshine. BK had to return the boat, so we were left with a day and a half before we needed to be back at Collingwood. What to do? I suggested we go sailing in Kestrel, so off we went in Harold once more, arriving at Polsue to find them flat out looking after visitors with no time to spare for the four of us. We managed somehow, dossing down once more, this time in the kitchen of what had been Dick Harris's cottage, now in use as extra rooms for guests. We followed this with a sail in Kestrel around Mylor Creek and Restronguet.

Every morning the whole of Collingwood was expected to attend a parade, whereby each officers course would fall in after breakfast in front of the wardroom, then march up the main road beside which the Commanding Officer would stand and take the salute, then on to Collingwood's huge parade ground where by this time the rest of the men under training would have assembled. We stood around as various petty officers shouted at everyone before we were all dismissed. It was an irritating waste of time, but probably necessary if only to ensure every class was 'present and correct' and properly awake. If we had a Royal Marine class amongst us they enjoyed a little fun showing up everyone else with their spotless drill, much to our annoyance. In due course we quietly altered our routine whereby LC6 would assemble in one of the drill sheds on the edge of the parade ground, then when everyone was present we took up our places on the parade ground proper, more in keeping with the dignity of senior sub lieutenants. Sometimes we were absent altogether when we attended a course in one of the other Portsmouth establishments, as happened fairly frequently. It was only a question of time before one of us, Rex Turner probably as he found it difficult to get up in the mornings, suggested only some of our course need actually be on parade, and no questions would be asked, provided there were enough to look convincing. After all, nobody actually counted us. So we took to assembling in the drill shed, took a count and, if we did not have a quorum we would slink away out of the back door without attending the parade. If he didn't see us there, the parade commander would assume we were away on one of our day courses. We kept this up for the rest of our time at Collingwood.

One of our number suggested we needed a third party to blame for all the things that went wrong or didn't happen when they were supposed to, so he invented a new member of LC6 whom we called Sub Lieutenant Barrington. Barrington was very useful on occasions, for example "Why has no one handed in all the workbooks?" "Barrington should have done that, Sir. He's off sick today," whereupon a willing volunteer would step in to do the job while the blame was neatly sidestepped. Barrington also came in handy whenever we wanted an 'extra' of something or other. If all this sounds a bit puerile for a group of responsible graduates, it did have its uses to relieve the tedium of being on a long course and gave us some light relief. Barrington existed alongside us for about a year, including the days when we visited other training establishments. Eventually he was rumbled by someone in the Pay Office wanting to know his details so that his back pay could be arranged.

I missed not having a half share in Bella, and looked around for another car, eventually finding a splendid Alvis beetleback, a 12/50 two-seater open tourer with a single dicky seat behind. It had a polished aluminium body with brass headlamps—not a very sensible choice for a car that would be kept outdoors only a mile or so from the sea—but it looked such a lovely vehicle my commonsense was easily overruled. I went by train to Salisbury to look at it, taking Antony Corfe with me for moral support. There was no question but that we must buy the car just on appearance, and when we examined it in detail, we realised the owner was a proper engineer who had looked after it carefully. It cost me £125, a tidy sum for an impecunious Naval Officer. On a glorious sunny day we drove it back to West Meon where I was to spend the rest of the weekend with Antony's parents, and discussed a suitable name for the lively beast as we thundered along the country roads. Antony pointed out a hare galloping across a meadow, and both of us together shouted out "Harvey!" and that's the name we gave him. Yes, 'him'—for here was another male car, one that would give Noggin's Harold a run for his money. I had a lot of enjoyment out of Harvey, and at last felt I had an adequate mount to meet members of the Vintage Sports Car Club at their monthly social meeting in a Hartney Wintney pub. Here Harvey (or sometimes Harold, as Noggin and I generally went together in either his car or mine) would be duly admired as it nestled amongst the Blower Bentleys or 30/98 Vauxhalls in the car park. We met such luminaries as Sam Clutton who owned a 1908 Itala racing car with an enormous 12-litre engine that he raced at the annual Vintage Silverstone races. Harvey was a super car, extremely reliable, fast and exciting to drive, capable of coping with all the west country hills with no trouble at all and a bit of a passion wagon as an attractive extra. By this I mean that he had a rather narrow bench seat for the driver and passenger. If one needed an excuse to stop in a layby whilst driving one's girlfriend home at night, then this was achieved by surreptitiously turning off the petrol tap with a left foot. After about a hundred yards the engine would cough, splutter and die convincingly, timed nicely to coast to a stop at the chosen layby. The tap was positioned where it was so that it could be turned to the reserve tank position, but it was certainly handy on several occasions for what I considered its main purpose.

Antony Corfe reckoned it was time he too acquired a car, so he bought a lightweight Humber tourer he called Martha. Unlike Harvey and Harold, this one was definitely female, and very fussy about not getting dirty or being asked to venture off the main road. Martha was the name of the Corfe family cat, which would seem to be in keeping. Antony was not quite into cars in the same way as Noggin and I, but he nevertheless had much fun out of his Martha. He even came down to see us at Polsue during one of our later leave periods. I took him out in Kestrel, together with the two Tracey girls. Belinda made a pass at Antony which made me murderously jealous, and later that evening when the four of us went for a night-time swim at Pendower, Belinda and Antony got into several giggly clinches. Mary, sensing my frustration, came to my rescue and I discovered to my delight that cavorting around in the sea with her was far more fun than it would ever have been with Belinda. Ah, the joys of youth!

I attended several VSCC Silverstone events with Noggin, meeting all sorts of interesting people and vehicles. The car park was a sight to see, with many people looking under one another's cars. I saw Sam Clutton's famous Itala in action, racing around the club circuit like an unsilenced tractor, pursued by screaming Bugattis, an unforgettable sight. I quickly realised the spectators were every bit as interesting to watch as their cars, and after a meeting many of the competitors drove home in the same machines that they'd been racing earlier. On the way down the A41 towards London on one occasion Sam came hurtling past us in the Itala, its mudguards and windscreen now back on the car but with the race number on its side still in evidence. Sam had once said that the Bell Inn at Aston Clinton was one of only six places in England worth eating at, and as we passed there we were met by the sight of half a dozen huge blower Bentleys lined up in the little car park. Alas, those days are now long gone. These vintage cars have become hugely expensive to buy and maintain and can seldom be driven around on today's overcrowded and unsafe roads.

One of my rowing chums suggested we might enter a Royal Navy boat for the Head of the River tideway race, the one that takes place from Mortlake to Putney—the same course as the Oxford and Cambridge boat race, but rowed downstream in the other direction. There were about 200 entries from all over the country, with the RAF boats usually near the top. But then I reckon they cheat, since anyone in the RAF with rowing ability would find themselves posted to RAF Benson which is on the Thames, where they could perfect their rowing. The same happened with RAF personnel who were good at sailing, which explained how they did so well in that sport too. For the Head of the River race we had to find a scratch crew as well as a boat. We assembled our motley crew, most of them from various Long Courses who'd enjoyed their three years at Cambridge, but we'd all developed different rowing techniques at our various colleges, so needed to practice in order to adapt to a common style. We found a set of oars— Oxford were due to take delivery of their new oars a couple of weeks before the boat race, so we managed to acquire their old ones, which was ideal as they were already painted dark blue (near enough to Navy blue). The boat was borrowed from Eton College. I collected the oars from the boathouse at Putney, personally relieving each member of the Oxford crew of his oar as he stepped ashore after a tideway outing, and strapped them on my Alvis in a row along the top of the windscreen with the blades pointing forward and the handles tucked into the dicky. I arrived at Eton and was given a splendid lunch at one of the houses, then shown the boat we were to borrow, which had dark blue fixings. A few days later the rest of the crew assembled at the Eton boathouse and we set off to row to London, hoping to be together and fully trained by the time we got there. The trip, which involved negotiating a number of locks, took us two days at the end of which we were exhausted but fairly fit. Being a new entry, our boat was placed at the end of the regulars, so we started well down the list. This race is one where boats start at half-minute intervals, so there was plenty of scope for catching up ones in front. It was an exhilarating race with our crew really pulling together, and we spent the whole of it overtaking one boat after another until we finished about 60th. That was the last time I rowed in an eight, as once away from the various training establishments I was never anywhere where it might be possible to assemble a crew.

One day I noticed the Kings theatre in Southsea was putting on a seaside show which featured The Rosebuds. I made enquiries and found they were indeed the same troupe I had met whilst staying with the Seymours in Eastbourne. I asked whether they'd like to join a few of us after the performance. I then recruited five other brother officers to come with me for the show, not mentioning that I was acquainted with the chorus girls. In the interval I suggested we take them out afterwards and, knowing my clumsy ways with meeting people, they laughed at me but agreed with some amusement. It was not much of a success, both sides being somewhat shy; however, it may have boosted my reputation just a little.

In 1955 the LC6 training at Collingwood was temporarily halted while we were all appointed to a spell at sea. My first ship was the Aircraft Carrier Albion, then operating with the Mediterranean Fleet. This involved being flown out from what is now Heathrow by a charter company that operated converted York Bombers. I was subjected to all the fuss and bull associated with Service travel at that time, first being required to muster at the Goodge Street Deep Underground Shelter—a bolthole left over from the war but still in use. I was issued with various documents, and then taken to London Airport (as it was then known) in a tired Service bus with hard seats. It's almost impossible for anyone who has passed through the Heathrow of today to believe how basic the facilities were in 1955. The departure terminal was no more than a group of temporary huts and a few tents. Our waiting aircraft was parked outside and we had to clamber aboard by means of mobile steps. The noise of the four petrol engines was deafening and it took over five hours to reach Malta where we landed at the RAF airfield. That was quite the most uncomfortable flight I have ever endured, but at least there were no delays.

I could see the Albion as we came in over Valletta, along with several other Naval warships in Grand Harbour. An hour later I was being ferried out in one of the ship's retained dghaisas by a nut-brown Maltese who stood facing for'd as he leant on the big sweeps in the Mediterranean fashion. In the Albion I was attached to the ship's electrical department, and was given a set programme of familiarisation and training to follow. It involved learning all about every type of electrical machinery in the ship, for which I was required to keep a logbook which I filled with technical information and sketches. I seemed to spend my entire Albion time below decks and after all these years have very little recollection of anything else I might have done whilst aboard her.

After three months I transferred to a battle class destroyer, HMS Aisne. It's customary when in a ship to say 'in' rather than 'on' which would be a landlubber's term, but in the case of Aisne one avoided saying 'in Aisne' which might well be mistaken for inane! On the day of my transfer, Albion was back in Grand Harbour while the Aisne was in Sliema Creek on the other side of Valletta. An Albion boat took me and my precious tin trunk around the Heads and into Sliema Creek where I was welcomed aboard. If Albion was huge, remote and impersonal, Aisne was the exact opposite. I was introduced to the Captain, Archibald Gray, almost as soon as I arrived, and one of the junior officers was deputed to look after me. As usual on small ships there is hardly any space for supernumeraries, so I was shown a couple of hooks in the deckhead of a passageway in the after part of the ship and given a hammock. I managed to get a single drawer in one cabin for some of my belongings, and another drawer in someone else's cabin for the rest, while my tin trunk (these things are four feet long so that they can accommodate a sword!) containing the things I could do without was stowed in the rum locker down in the bilges.

I was the only officer under training and had a go at everything, from switchboard watchkeeper (where my boss was a leading hand) to assistant officer of the watch on the bridge. The main problem was trying to get a good night's sleep. I slung the hammock as high as possible, but even so people passing along the passageway always bumped me as they went by, and as the petty officer's messdeck was in that area, I got bumped every hour or so through the night. Immediately over my head was a light which stayed on most of the night, and if the ship was rolling, then this light appeared to swing to and fro a foot above my face. After a week or two the captain discovered my predicament and offered me his sea cabin, which I gratefully accepted. This is a small cabin immediately under the bridge, there to be available for a ship's commanding officer when at sea, since he can be summoned up to the bridge in a moment should there be an emergency. He never used this cabin, preferring to sleep in his normal quarters another deck below. Above the bunk in this sea cabin was a speaking tube, the other end of which was on the bridge. This was the means by which the officer of the watch would summon the captain if needed. It had a polished brass hinged cover at the top to prevent salt water gushing down onto one's face should it be a bit rough up there. The only trouble I ever had was when one of the bridge watchkeepers absentmindedly dropped a spent match down the tube instead of into the adjacent ashtray. Apart from that I reckoned I had the best cabin on the ship, with a nice porthole and its own washbasin.

We called in at several places on our way to Port Said where we were to spend several days alongside the naval toehold Britain still kept there. This meant, thankfully, that we were spared the attentions of the gully-gully man and the bumboats, which pestered ships traversing the canal. By this time it was extremely hot and I really needed my stupid trilby hat, which I was still expected to wear when going ashore. I was somewhat circumspect when leaving the confines of the naval station after hearing about lots of unsavoury things that went on in Egypt, and never had the courage to do more than accompany some of the more worldly-wise officers on the usual bar visits which, for a virtually penniless midshipman, didn't amount to much. Our gunnery officer had been the target for some street trader trying to sell fezzes, and when he returned on board and removed his hat there, stacked inside, were two or three red fezzes he'd somehow acquired. They came in useful for parties.

Aisne took me to several other Mediterranean ports, notably Civitta Vecchia, thirty miles or so from Rome. From there three of us took the train to Rome, found a little pension close behind Rome railway station, then spent two most glorious days with a roving bus ticket exploring the great city. We visited the Vatican, the Sistine Chapel and St. Peter's, looked round churches, museums and art galleries, dropped our pennies into countless fountains, explored the Forum, clambered around the Coliseum and ate spaghetti with a spoon and fork Italian-style. Our pension provided comfortable beds with crisply laundered sheets (luxury for a hammock-swinging sailor) and in the morning gave us the most wonderful coffee washed down with hot croissants. Hardly had I returned on board than I was asked to take a dozen or so sailors up into the mountains for a couple of days. The was an early sort of 'MedEx'—Mediterranean Expedition, or what we would later call an Outward Bound expedition. A lorry was provided into which we flung camping gear, lots of food, and ourselves. It ground up zig-zaggy roads 6,000 feet into the mountains and left us on our own for three days. I organised us into a smart camp, Scouting style, and we spent the time walking in the crisp clean air. We found a tiny village some two miles from our camp where, with the unerring nose of all sailors, we tracked down a wine bar. This was basically a large bare room lined on one side by huge barrels of the local plonk, which after the first glass tasted just great. Fortunately none of us had much money, so the evenings were spent in a convivial way rather than drunken orgying.

Another visit was to Naples where several of us took a trip round Pompeii with a local guide, being shown some of the naughty wall paintings not normally seen by mixed-sex tourists. The whole destroyer flotilla was at Naples, and I met up with Noggin, then in HMS Duchess. Together we crossed by ferry to Capri and climbed the 777 stone steps to Anacapri, visiting San Michele, the enchanting home made famous by Axel Munthë. We returned to our respective ships late in the evening, overcome by the magic. I found that a group of Aisne officers had won first prize at some bawdy Italian party, and had brought it back to the ship. This prize was a month-old lamb. For the next few weeks poor Larry roamed around the ship being kept alive by a compassionate sailor who bottlefed it with pusser's powdered milk, but there was no way he could give it a proper diet and the lamb did not prosper. It attempted to lick the green painted deck, the nearest thing it had seen to grass, and probably ingested lead, which was in the paint of those days. One day a boat was lowered in which the first lieutenant took out a pathetic little bundle, returning empty handed. The following day a notice in Daily Orders stated "Larry died of lead poisoning shortly after midday, his body being committed to the Deep with due ceremony." I wondered whether the lead in question had emerged from the barrel of the first lieutenant's pistol, a humane end for a pitiable little creature.

We called in to Toarmina in northwest Sicily for a stay. Here we were able to swim over the ship's side, take out our various boats for recreational purposes, and generally relax. Three of us took a bus up into the hills behind the resort, and enjoyed a long walk in the foothills of Mount Etna, which was rumbling away uncertainly then, an eruption expected at any time. We stopped for a drink of water at a little homestead, the lady lowering a bucket down an immensely deep well and bringing up ice cold water with a superlative taste; a welcome change from the lukewarm ship's manufactured water which was really undrinkable. Two of us sailed the ship's naval dinghy around into the next bay and, while my chum was having a swim and I was alone in the boat, an attractive girl grabbed hold of the hull, hauled herself in over the side and introduced herself as a BEA air hostess staying over for a few days. My chum had to wait quite a while as the two of us sailed about chatting, before she dropped back into the water once more. That evening he regaled the rest of the wardroom and my street cred leapt up.

At anchor one evening, a heavily overladen dinghy, similar in size to the Naval fourteen footers, appeared round the headland and sailed up to our gangway. A thin suntanned bearded young man stepped aboard and asked whether we could sell him some toilet rolls! He was on a solo passage from his home in Hampshire to Africa by way of the French canals and Malta. He was such a colourful character that we invited him to stay for dinner, and enjoyed a fascinating evening hearing about his adventures to date. So far he had hugged the shore, conscious that his craft was quite unsuited to rough seas, but would soon have to make his longest sea passage to date: the hop across from Sicily to Malta. After that it would be an even longer passage to Tripoli, but by then the weather should be set fair and his problem would be lack of wind rather than too much. He was heading off next morning down the coast to Catania. I asked whether he'd like company for this next leg, looking hopefully at the first lieutenant as I did so. Approval was granted.

That night he lay off at anchor, coming alongside next morning to pick me up. Catania is only about 25 miles south of Taormina, and for most of the way there was insufficient wind for sailing, so we used the outboard, a tiny Seagull—noisy, smelly but reliable. It was such a relief when the breeze freshened and we hoisted our sail. His boat had a tiny cabin for'd, lockers under the thwarts on both sides, barely room for two in the remaining cockpit space, and a freeboard of only about ten inches. No wonder he was anxious not to set out on any risky passage sailing. He put me off in Catania, waved goodbye and was off to anchor a little further down in a quieter spot. I made my way through the strange smells and bustle to Catania railway station where I hoped to pick up a train back to Taormina, conscious that I had no passport, hardly any money and couldn't speak Italian. It was an uneventful trip, and I was back on board again for dinner, rather sunburnt and with my own tale to tell.

We sailed for Malta where Aisne was booked in for a two-week stint in dry dock. By now the weather was really beginning to hot up, and the thought of spending time in a sun-baked pit didn't appeal at all. Fortunately for me I was due to return to Collingwood during this time, so would not have to endure it for long.

I watched gangs of nut-brown Maltese dockyard workers settle Aisne onto the keel blocks, supported on both sides by great timbers to hold her upright, then later that day discovered some Naval windfall yachts available for loan. I met a famous ocean racing man, Commander Errol Bruce, and asked him if he would take me out in one of these lovely boats to give me a taste of proper sailing, and he very kindly agreed to do so, saying he would join the boat in Grand Harbour, if I would rig it, set sail and meet him at the harbour entrance. I took a couple of Aisne ratings with me to crew and we duly met the legendary man who jumped aboard from the harbourmaster's launch. He had us careering along slightly over canvassed, spray coming over the whole boat, and getting us to change headsails time and time again without falling in or getting injured. An exhilarating hour was spent whereby I learnt that perhaps a life of that sort on the ocean waves was perhaps not really my idea of comfort.

It was time to say my goodbyes. It is customary when leaving a ship to be given a 'flimsy' signed by the Commanding Officer. There are set words that indicate how one has performed: for example, "He has performed to my satisfaction" is one down from "He has performed to my entire satisfaction", which is what one normally receives, and what I got. I said goodbye to Commander Gray and thanked him for giving me such a good time. It wasn't until later I re-read the flimsy when I realised he'd written, "He has performed to his entire satisfaction". I never did discover whether he really put that on the official copy that goes back to the Admiralty, as well as on mine.

The next year or so was spent at Collingwood, dreary in the extreme. We all arrived from our various ships in time to start a course in radio design and engineering: all, that is, except Noggin. He had left HMS Duchess in the Mediterranean having elected to hitch back overland using the three weeks' leave to better advantage, something I certainly wouldn't have felt competent to attempt. A postcard arrived, written in smudgy pencil, to say he was enjoying the art treasures in Florence and would be back in a week or two. We looked at each other, appalled. One just didn't have such a cavalier attitude in a disciplined Service. What would happen? We continued for the next month without him, getting several postcards telling us how wonderful Florence was, and promising to be back in another week or so.

Six weeks later he ambled in as if nothing was amiss and was duly put on C-in-C's Report. By this time the authorities were treating him as a possible deserter, and were said to be watching the ports. Noggin, being Noggin, didn't come home that way. For the last leg of his trip back he'd bummed a passage in a yacht sailing from Holland to Harwich, and avoided the Customs on landing. Later he regaled us with how he had survived his interview, which meant having to report to the C-in-C's office in Portsmouth and receive a carpeting from the Chief Staff Officer, someone who turned out to be a sympathetic elderly rear admiral who rather envied him his exploration of Florence, finishing his telling off by saying, "Don't worry about it, old boy, you never know, it might do you some good one day. Get you noticed. They'll say Brooke? Who's he? Wasn't he the one who used a bit of initiative in his junior time? Must be all right! Care for a drink before you leave, eh?"

So ended our eight week radio course with only three of the class passing the exam with really good results, one of whom was Noggin. Life isn't fair sometimes.

Like a bad penny the terrible Brett-Knowles was back, this time with a teaching job at Collingwood. He organised a sailing weekend across to the Isle of Wight, using Collingwood's Naval cutters and a few dinghies which were kept at Fleetlands up the Fareham river. The little flotilla had about twenty apprentices and one or two others shared out between the boats, and we dropped anchor for the night in Osborne Bay, walking up to the house in the evening to see whether we could buy a crate of beer from the house, then being used as a convalescent home for Service officers. They regarded us with some suspicion, not at all amused that we had walked up through the hallowed grounds that were not then open to the public. They would have been even more not amused had they known that some of us subsequently slept on the floor of Queen Victoria's little pavilion on the private beach.

I took a dinghy out from the Collingwood trot quite often, but seldom made it to the entrance of Portsmouth harbour because of the tides. On one occasion I saw a Naval whaler crawling along and recognised the man clutching the helm as my old physics master, he who'd started the Naval section of the Bradfield JTC. He had five incredibly bored looking Bradfield lads with him, the boat tacking back and forth making little headway against the flood tide. I sailed across and made to closer so we could talk, but this struck terror into the master who shouted at me to keep clear, obviously not realising I had no intention of colliding with him. I sailed on, reflecting how they were sadly missing out on the fun side of sailing, glad I'd never joined his section whilst still at Bradfield.

On another dinghy sail, this one over to the Island, six of us in three boats planned to camp overnight up the Medina River near Newport. We arrived at Cowes with the last of the daylight, and by the time we began to tack up river it was inky black and raining slightly. Large slab-sided merchantmen were moored along one bank, and there were shallows with soft mud everywhere. I discovered one could avoid sailing into the moored vessels simply by listening carefully. A sort of dead sound came back if one was too close, and we succeeded in tacking just feet from the ships. We made it to our campsite without going aground and by morning the sun was out and we dried off before setting off home.

1955 was the 150th anniversary of the battle of Trafalgar, and the wardroom decided to put on a special Trafalgar night dinner to celebrate. We always did celebrate Trafalgar night with a dinner in memory of Admiral Collingwood who was Nelson's number two, but this one would be special, with some VIPs invited. I was asked to think up how we might embellish the somewhat dreary dining room in a suitable way. I decided it would look good if we built some scenery around the back and sides of the high table, and what better than to depict Nelson's quarters in the Victory. I marched aboard HMS Victory in her dry dock in Portsmouth, asked whether I might take some measurements and make a few sketches, and a little to my surprise was allowed into the sacred area to do so. I then made up three panels and managed to paint these so convincingly that from a few yards away the high table really appeared to be in Victory's stateroom. The local newspaper published a super photograph of the stage set and everyone seemed delighted with the result. I had to exaggerate the perspective considerably to obtain a realistic depth in a space that was in reality much shallower. This made someone appear to grow in size when they walked to the back of the set, but this went unnoticed.

About this time Collingwood had built some new facility that the Queen was to open, touring part of the establishment afterwards and staying for lunch in the wardroom. Needless to say, the royal route was cleaned and painted, a little-used toilet at the far end of the route was smartened up with a new seat fitted, to be locked until the special day when a Wren would be detailed to guard it until after it might be needed (it wasn't). The wardroom officers who would be lunching that day learned there would be fresh fruit to round off the meal, and wondered what to select that would make eating it with a fruit knife and fork a genteel activity. We discovered it is possible to eat a banana with a knife and fork provided it is slit from end to end on the inside of the curve so that the two halves lie flat on the plate, open side uppermost. The rest is easy. On the day we glanced furtively at the top table to see how HM managed. She did indeed choose a banana, and far from messing around with a knife and fork, peeled it back like you and me. So there you are; the common touch after all!

Antony Corfe and I went to some show in London. Whilst there we called in on spec to see Belinda, who was at this time doing some sort of secretarial course, living in a flat in Earl's Court. We rang the bell and ages later Belinda's head popped out of an upstairs window to see who it was. We carried out a conversation from across the road three floors below, eventually she came down to let us in, apologising for not being very presentable. "We were asleep," she explained. Alarm bells jangled. We? As we walked in, there sitting on the edge of her unmade bed, tousled hair and yawning, was a young man I'd briefly met while visiting the Tracey's. He was doing National Service in the Army, and that was about all I knew about him except that Both Mr and Mrs Tracey's body language had left me in no doubt that they didn't approve of his obvious interest in Belinda. Antony and I didn't stay long needless to say, and we were very quiet on the way back. I had been out of favour with Belinda for quite a while now, but Antony was still fond of her. We neither of us took to the current beau who, in my eyes as the jilted suiter, was loathsome, fat and horrible, and we just hoped Belinda would eventually escape before it was too late.

I met an Oxford man, a keen sailor, who had been in the Oxford team when they sailed against Cambridge in Falmouth, an event I'd have loved to have been in with my local knowledge. He suggested we knock up a couple of teams for an informal week's racing in the Gairloch sailing Dragons from the Mudhook Yacht Club just across from Helensburgh. He organised the event and collected together a team of Oxford people, while I searched around for a Cambridge team, all of them naval people. As usual, we were somewhat skint, but managed to do it very cheaply by persuading the naval authorities this was a prestigious sporting event that deserved their help, if only to allow us to have travel warrants to get there and back. Amazingly this worked, and I even managed to find somewhere to stay—a tired old LTC being used as an accommodation ship at Faslane at the head of the Gairloch. Faslane was then a sort of Admiralty breaker's yard where pensioned off ships were stripped of certain parts before being sold for scrap. We found the ship to be quite comfortable and were even provided with a launch to take us across the Gareloch to Mudhook, a couple of miles down on the other side. I had to share a cabin with a man who worked at Faslane, unfortunately for me one who spent much of his spare time practising the bagpipes. After breakfast in the morning I would have to rush into the tiny cabin to collect my sailing things with him playing there, the drones scraping against the deckhead as he walked back and forth. He had the scuttle open, but that didn't stop the sound ricocheting around the bare cabin. The noise was indescribable and left a ringing in my ears all the way across in the boat. When the boat put us off, leaving us standing on the foreshore in the quiet, I could still hear in the distance those wretched pipes across the water two miles away. The sailing itself was fun, but I didn't take to the Dragons which I found uncomfortable and very wet in spite of their size. I don't like getting wet when the water is so cold!

I discovered it was possible to have the loan of a Pusser's bicycle if ever I was feeling masochistic enough to want one (they are heavy, single-speed and hard work to pedal). I suggested to the Rover group that they might like to ride out to the unknown wastes of northern Hampshire, and fetched up leading some twenty sweating volunteers along country lanes in single file, each of them astride a bright red bike. We arrived 35 miles later near Burghclere at the farm of a girlfriend of mine who, unfortunately, was in bed with 'flu at the time. Nevertheless, we were all welcomed, given tea with homemade bread (they not only made the bread but also grew the wheat and hand-ground it) and finally slept in an unused turkey house. The girl, whom I shall call Fiona, was someone I had met at a party and we got along well. I visited the farm on several other occasions, but drove there in Harvey, which was much less exhausting. The last few miles to the farm were along a fairly busy road and on one evening I ran into really thick fog along that part. Harvey didn't have anything special in the way of foglights, but he did have a split windscreen, the top half of which one could tilt up to look through the gap. This was extremely handy when visibility was poor: no need for windscreen wipers, no condensation either. I crawled along this part of the road conscious of another car following behind, eventually turning in at the farm gate and proceeding several hundred yards to the farmhouse. It was only as I switched off the engine that I realised I had been followed all the way to the yard by not one but two other lost motorists!

Fiona was an artist and at that time attended further education art classes in Winchester. She was jolly and great fun, and her parents were extremely welcoming. I enjoyed my visits to the farm, and asked Fiona if she'd like to be my partner at the Collingwood Ball. Her parents brought her down to the house of an aunt in nearby Hillhead from where I collected her, delivering her back afterwards for what was left of the night. Noggin's partner was a girl he had met whilst still at Cambridge, who had been at nearby Homerton on a teacher's training course. The four of us got along well, and Noggin was intrigued at the thought of one's own breadmaking flour. The bread supplied in the wardroom was the usual white steam-baked pap which both of us found a struggle to eat. For the next few months Fiona produced the wheat, Noggin got it ground and we prevailed upon the Collingwood Commander, Maurice Head whose quarters were on the campus, to allow us to use the kitchen in his quarters for baking it. He agreed, probably because it must have become clear to him that he had a couple of LC6 eccentrics in his midst, which amused him. One of us would produce one of our loaves at mealtimes, much to the ribald hilarity of everyone else, but we had the last laugh.

Two of the most memorable of my weekend pursuits took place in the wintertime. The first of these was on a fine frosty January day when I took an eclectic group to Arundel where we left our two cars, and set off through the park to the high ground, walking along the ridge all the way to Chichester by way of the Downs and Goodwood. We set up camp in a remote farmer's field near Chiseldown, and my evocative memory is of waking in the morning, a hard frost on the ground and the early morning sun just up, to the smell of frying bacon. The other expedition was similar in its way. We decided we'd do a section of the Ridgeway Path starting somewhere near Harwell and heading west. Once again it was in January only this time there was a foot of snow on the ground. Two of us set off in the squeaky snow while the other two drove in Noggin's Harold to a point some twelve miles further on and began walking back. At the halfway point we met up and spent the night squatting in an empty cottage just off the track to keep out of a penetrating wind that had sprung up. We then continued our walk, to drive back in one another's cars. It was the first time I had done an extended walk in deepish untrodden snow and I found it exhausting.

For the summer period we were all once again sent around to various electrical firms. Both Noggin and I plumped for the Marconi factory in Chelmsford, and found a place to live near Little Baddow, some five miles away. This was no lodgings but an orchard with a static caravan in it. Here we set up home very comfortably, catering for ourselves and with access to the landlord's house once or twice a week for a proper bath. It was a good place from which to set off at weekends to the muddy Essex estuaries. For a week or two Noggin had Jill, his ex-Homerton friend, to stay, which left me feeling somewhat envious but it worked out all right. At Marconi we were both attached to research men and were able to do something both useful and interesting during our time. I was involved in the manufac-ture and further development of the giant BBC television camera of the day, a heavy monster that came with a cable nearly an inch in diameter and took two men to lift onto its dolly. Noggin's man was into colour television, still in its infancy, and had built a colour transmitter and successfully sent signals from the factory to his home ten miles distant. He was about the first to use the 3-colour tubes still in use today, and some ten years before they came into general use.

During this time father had been having a lot of trouble with his duodenal ulcer and had been advised to have an operation. There was no way he could agree to this since Polsue couldn't run without him, and reluctantly they decided it was really time to sell. With the money they bought a plot of land in St. Mawes and set about having a bungalow built. In the meantime they took a long let on a house belonging to the Traceys which was a few doors along from them in what father always referred to as 'Snobs' Alley', now more prosaically named Tredenham Road. Until some years later, roads in St. Mawes didn't have names, since the postman knew where everyone lived. My parents were several years beyond retirement age, and running a hotel is a younger person's job, so it was a huge relief for father to have the worry lifted from his shoulders. With no business to worry about, he worried instead about having enough to live on and whether his operation would be successful. He sent me the design for the bungalow to comment upon. They certainly had to be careful with the money as he had no company pension, so the only way it was possible to build a house was to go into partnership once more. This time it was with Alma Thompson, the widow of our pre-war Woking dentist who had been a friend in those days. Thus the house design was for a pair of similar small bungalows linked by a common 'sun room'. They would share the garden (which meant father would do all the work while Alma picked flowers). I remember seeing a number of minor problems with the design, which I suggested changing (and, to my surprise, they did), but did not appreciate the dangers of getting entwined with one-time friends in such a venture. Nor did my parents, and many years later the house had to be split.

That Christmas I spent at the Tracey's bungalow. Father had his operation at the small Falmouth hospital, while mother and I went over each day to see him and later brought him home to convalesce. Major abdominal surgery then, in his case having over half his stomach removed, was no small undertaking. It was three months before he was well again, and always complained thereafter of feeling 'old'.

Back at Collingwood once more, I set off on a round of courses at the various Naval schools in the Portsmouth and Gosport areas. We had sessions at the Damage Control School, where the course started with a film in which a dreary voice spoke over the picture of a model ship bobbing about in a tank, with the words "A ship is designed to float." We put out oil fires, and escaped from a smoke-filled steel compartment. We went to HMS Vernon and learnt all about torpedoes, and to HMS Dolphin across the water to be indoctrinated in the joys of becoming submariners. A whole week was spent at HMS Excellent, the Gunnery School on Whale Island, where all the instructors went clumping around in highly polished boots and shiny black leather gaiters, and shouted on the parade ground in penetrating falsetto voices. A pair of six-inch shells stood proudly either side of the wardroom front door. The following week they stood conspicuously outside the Collingwood wardroom front door. Nobody knew how they had got there, as they must have been extremely heavy. (I know they were heavy: Harvey's tyres were pumped up to 60 p.s.i. in an effort to give the impression he wasn't carrying a load…)

One Saturday evening I was driving through West Meon on my way back to Fareham, when I took the last corner leaving the village a little too fast and skidded on wet leaves. The camber at that point is poor, so Harvey gently left the road and ploughed through a wooden fence to fetch up in the front garden of the last little cottage. He made a terrible racket as he smashed the fence into smithereens, splintered wood flying everywhere. He came to rest in an attractive rockery, a sudden silence descending, broken only by the hiss of escaping steam, for one of the splinters had punctured his radiator. Apart from that he seemed none the worse. The cottage front door opened to reveal a slightly portly man with a monocle wearing a purple smoking jacket and with a wine glass in one hand; a sort of latter day Sherlock Holmes.

"My dear boy," he cried, "What a shock for you. You must come in and have a drink!"

I stood up and leaned over the windscreen. All I could think of to say was, "I'm so sorry, I seem to have destroyed your fence."

"Never mind. Never mind. It's always happening. Bad corner just there!" I jumped down, examined the radiator, and realised I wasn't going far that night. We went indoors and he poured me a large whisky. Just in time I thought I'd better not, just in case someone might think my accident had been the result of drinking. He agreed and with reluctance poured the spirit back into the bottle. We chatted for twenty minutes or so, until I said I really must be going. I explained my friends the Corfes lived just back in the village.

"Aha! The good Doctor! So you are acquainted."

I backed Harvey out into the road. The fence looked properly done for and I promised to come back next day and sort it out in daylight. We waved goodbye and I turned Harvey round to drive the hundred yards or so to the Corfe's house, where I left the car for the night. Doctor Corfe kindly drove me back to Collingwood. Next morning I phoned a contact in Gosport, someone who had been advertising a similar Alvis for sale. Yes, the car was still on the market. Could I have a test drive? Certainly.

In the event I had a sort of extended test drive that ended up in my hiring his car in return for publicising its availability to the vintage car-mad enthusiasts around. I picked up a chum and together we drove back to West Meon where we did what we could to tidy up the front garden. This time we did stop for a drink. Our host was somewhat fazed to find the Alvis parked outside was not the one I was driving the night before.

"There's yet another one like this," he said. "The farmer over the other side has a barn full of junk in that field," he pointed through the gap in the fence, "And I'm sure I've seen one of these in there somewhere. Let's go and meet him."

The barn was an Aladdin's cave of delights. Sure enough, right at the back under all sorts of discarded rubbish I could see the unmistakeable bonnet of yet another vintage Alvis. We cleared a space around it. There it stood on four flat and useless tyres, an almost identical model to Harvey. The odometer read 16,000 miles, a low mileage indeed for a vehicle nearly thirty years old. The farmer said it had been there ever since his own father had dumped it because his new wife wanted something enclosed. Yes, that would be the right mileage. Never been out since that day. Was it for sale? And there was the sticking point. The farmer had kept it all those years for sentimental reasons. He would never part with it.

We towed Harvey back to Fareham with the borrowed Alvis, laid him to rest in the Wardroom car park and I returned the Gosport machine to its owner, promising to be in touch. I phoned the secretary of the Alvis Owner's Club who promised to search out a replacement radiator for me. Amazingly he did, and brought it along a week later, spurred on by my story of the 16,000-mileage machine in the barn. I got Harvey back on the road, while the Alvis Owners Club man spent the next six weeks working on the farmer. Eventually the poor man cracked, and the car was towed away to be rebuilt. Two years later it was winning top honours in VSCC concours d'elegance events.

With Harvey back on the road and in fine fettle, I was able to use him to attend another wedding. This was at Charing in Kent, and necessitated a lovely cross-country drive across Sussex in summer sunshine. The bride was none other than our Polsue's Jill, now getting married to her Jim. I had been invited as the Reeve representative and would spend the night at her parent's place, so felt really privileged to be singled out for such an honour and at such a time! When I arrived and located the house I realised I wasn't alone. The house was a huge and elegant Queen Anne place with what they described as a 'barn' attached, which had been converted into an enormous extension with room for an army of guests. All the 'young' ones were allocated space here and I was treated as one of Jill and Jim's quirkier acquaintances, arriving as I did in this dashing vintage car. I had burnished Harvey's aluminium body until it dazzled, and wore my naval uniform complete with sword for the wedding.

We had a Church of Scotland padre at Collingwood during the latter part of 1956 who organised a Scottish Country Dancing social club in the Collingwood wardroom. Noggin and I, the only ones interested from the LC6 class, went along and danced as well as one can on a concrete floor. I met various girls who were very good dancers, but I had become somewhat rusty and had to be helped. There was one girl, blue-eyed with a long blonde plait, whom I definitely fancied, but she was in hot demand and I only managed to dance with her occasionally. Unlike the others she chatted happily and we got on well. Her father had been the Instructor Captain here at Collingwood before retiring a few years ago. The family now lived at Lee-on-Solent. Alas, our ways parted. When one is in the Services there are a lot of ships that pass in the night.

Our next course was at HMS Ariel, the Naval Air Electrical School at Worthy Down just north of Winchester, where we were to stay for six weeks. We were all lumbered with these enormous tin trunks, so as I was going straight from Collingwood to Ariel at the weekend while most of the others were dashing home for a couple of days I offered to transport everyone's trunk. By this time I had built a trailer for Harvey to tow, which I'd made out of an old rear axle and a roomful of duckboards that I'd found in one of the Collingwood storerooms. It was a lovely trailer and much later I sold it to the Collingwood first lieutenant, thinking as I did so that he probably had those duckboards on his loan list and would have been aware they had gone missing. Now he was unknowingly buying them back again.

Ariel had a completely different atmosphere to Collingwood, smaller and far less 'pusser', with no bull or people marching around or white painted kerbstones. Instead there were flowers, ratings grinned and saluted out of respect rather than because they had to, and we were not treated as incompetent trainees. The equipment was quite different too. No more great big motors, giant fuse panels or enormous cables. Instead we stripped down miniaturised electronics on a tabletop, everything much cleaner and easier to cope with. I was so impressed at the change from Collingwood that I thought I might well decide to volunteer for the Fleet Air Arm at the end of our course. Three out of the twenty-one would be asked to do so, and about three more would be going into submarines. Yes, the FAA seemed a good idea.

Ariel had just taken delivery of a prototype air-to-air missile, the first to be seen. It stood on a cradle in one of the classrooms behind a locked door. On the day we were to have a talk on it we suddenly had our programme postponed. All became clear that evening when a very shaky lieutenant responsible for the missile told us that he'd had a phone call, the voice at the other end saying rather tersely, "This is the First Sea Lord. May I call in this afternoon at 1400 to have a look at your missile?" He thought it was someone pulling his leg and said, "But of course, Sir, just ask for the Commanding Officer Missiles when you arrive," put the phone down, and thought no more about it. Of course the First Sea Lord wouldn't be interested in the nitty-gritty of what went on inside a bit of electronics, and anyway such people moved around in an aura of bullshit, a visit being preceded by the entire establishment being fell in wearing their best uniforms. Just a leg-pull, and not in very good taste.

"I was horribly wrong," he told us. "Bang on 1400 there's this black car coming up the road with an Admiral's flag fluttering from the bonnet, and the Main Gate had no idea he was coming! The Old Man was properly in the shit, not to mention Yours Truly. I'd forgotten the First Sea Lord is Earl Mountbatten, with his keen interest in these things. He was quite charming, asked lots of questions, seemed amused he'd caught everyone on the hop, and only wanted to call in for a few minutes on his way to Portsmouth."

Everyone was relieved the VIP visit had gone so unceremoniously, except the Captain who probably worried about his next job, but by the next day even he had recovered.

It was during our Ariel time that Noggin was invited by an instructor schoolie to spend the weekend with himself and his wife in their nearby married quarters. Afterwards he kept on about 'marriage being a good thing' to such an extent I can only hazard a guess at what went on; perhaps it was more than the intimate luvvy-duvvy behaviour of his hosts. Whatever, it was not long after that when Noggin happily announced he was engaged to Bella—no, not the car, but his latest girlfriend.

Back to Collingwood again for the last few months. While there it was suggested LC6 might like to go back to Ariel and attempt a break-in on the night they were having an exercise to test the establishment's security. With our knowledge of the place, we shouldn't have too much difficulty. Dressed commando-like with soft shoes, blacked out faces and denims we set about gaining access. I tackled the perimeter fence at a remote part of the site, and as I stepped on the barbed wire to climb over, the wire moved causing a squeak from the staple on every post for 50 yards either way. A keen young sentry, all of sixteen years old, came crashing through the undergrowth and waved a rifle unsteadily in my general direction.

"Who goes there?"

"Steady on, lad," I replied in my best authoritative voice. "It's only me. I heard someone trying to climb over just along there! Better have a look. Creep along quietly, or you'll scare him off."

"Aye aye, Sir," replied the sentry and dashed off. I made my way quietly to the rendezvous point (the Ariel defence control room) to find two members of LC6 in smart suits had got there before me. Further, they appeared to be in charge, with the Ariel people standing around uncomfortably. Geoff Hamer, a somewhat overweight middle-aged looking member of LC6 with one other had openly driven up in a car saying they were from the local police, and asked to observe the exercise. Geoff looked far more like a shady detective than a sprightly Naval Officer, and they had been admitted after flashing homemade forged identity cards and taken direct to the control room where they promptly 'arrested' everybody there. Later in the evening other LC6 men arrived, having entered the wireless site, an enclosed transmitter station on a hill half a mile away, which they found unprotected with an easily penetrated wire fence. From our point of view the evening was just a bit of fun, but it must have been a disaster for Ariel who realised their security was less than useless. They thanked us for coming, and thereupon set to improving matters.

The Tracey's had moved from St. Mawes. Almost an institution there, the very idea of them ever leaving seemed so unlikely. However, they were still in sight of the sea, just outside Lymington, so on one of my jaunts I called in to see them. They had moved in to a largish modern house a good half-mile inland and I was warmly welcomed. They had both aged and I was really shocked by the appearance of Mrs Tracey in particular who had turned grey and looked years older since I had last seen her. Over lunch they talked a lot about the girls, Belinda in particular, who had married her odious army friend after he'd got her in the family way. It was clear this was the reason for the Tracey's distressed state. Sadly Mrs Tracey told me how they'd been hoping so much I would marry her Belinda. I don't know how I answered that one, but that had certainly been my wish too. If only Belinda hadn't gone cold. She would have made a wonderful wife and we had so many things in common. I felt I had let her parents down, and left soon afterwards feeling dejected and responsible for the situation.

I'd been to a party with Noggin and Bella to celebrate the engagement of one of his Harrow friends. There I met the Harrow man's sister and instantly fell in love. Fortunately for both of us this was only a one-day wonder, but I also met another of Noggin's friends, Andrew Beamish. When the party ended late that night I had to find somewhere to sleep, and Andrew took me back to his place where there were several spare beds. The house, which was in a very posh part of Hampstead, appeared empty when we arrived. Andrew showed me a room containing an unmade bed which he assured me had only been slept in once or twice, but I was too tired to worry before falling asleep. In the morning I staggered down to breakfast to find one or two others from the party also there, a butler carrying in silver dishes, which he lined up on the sideboard. There were no signs of Andrew's parents who owned the place; apparently they were 'in the country' at one of their other houses. A few days later, when I phoned Andrew, the butler answered the phone with a somewhat classy "Chez Beamish, butler speaking". I wonder what today's telephone-marketing people would make of that? It was through Andrew that I met another girl, Dita.

Dita, who had a double barrelled surname, was slim and dark and seemed to like me almost as much as I worshipped her. We met several times after that. It was difficult because she worked in London and I was at Fareham so it meant a train journey. On one of my visits to see her in London she told me the two of us had been more or less commanded to attend at Fullers in Regent Street to meet her mother for coffee. Dita's home was in Grantham on what sounded like a large country estate, and her mother sounded terrifying. She was even more so in the flesh, very dominating, had all the waitresses in Fullers jumping around and quizzed me about my family and my prospects. Clearly I was being checked out and later she would no doubt instruct Dita to be more careful in future. Maybe her daughter was known to be attracted to anything in trousers (why else would she have cottoned on to someone like me?). I asked Dita to spend the day down at Fareham with me, and she came with alacrity. We walked along the coast, had a lovely but sad day, and although neither of us said what was in our minds, our farewell standing on the platform at Portsmouth Harbour station was long and very intimate. I've often wondered since how my life would have turned out had that romance prospered. In some ways I was relieved to break it off because I very much doubt whether I could have lived up to it, although my father would no doubt have been over the moon if he'd known. Running parallel with this affair was my blossoming relationship with the blue-eyed blonde girl from Collingwood Scottish Country Dancing. Her name was Patricia, and she had asked me to come round to meet her parents in Lee-on-the-Solent. The meeting took place the day after I had said goodbye so lingeringly to Dita, and I expect I was rather on the rebound. I liked everything about Patricia's parents. They were jolly and accepted me as I was; not at all like Dita's formidable mum. They lived in an 'upside down' house, the bedrooms and bathroom being on the ground floor and the sitting room and kitchen upstairs from where they enjoyed an uninterrupted view over the hedge (and over the traffic) across Browndown Common towards the Isle of Wight. Patricia's father, Leslie, had retired about five years previously. He was a meteorologist by training and a gadget enthusiast, in that he devised all manner of gadgets to solve problems around the home, and took great delight in showing me how all these worked. Patricia's mother, Elizabeth, was delightful, and I took to her at once. I was shown the walk-in larder full to the ceiling with pots of homemade jam, bottled fruit and Winchesters containing many different sorts of homemade wine. It was a very happy afternoon spent with them and really the first time I had been accepted on equal terms by the parents of any girlfriend. Patricia asked me out the next weekend. We met several times after that and hit it off well, but as is the way in the Services, their Lordships put a spanner in the works.

I received my next Appointment. Sure enough three of our number went to Dolphin and became submariners, to be forever after identified by the smell of diesel impregnated in their uniforms. Three more joined the Fleet Air Arm, one of whom was myself. My Appointment read, "You are hereby appointed Lieutenant, Royal Navy, and are to report on 3rd January 1957 to RNAS Yeovilton for duties with 766 Squadron at RNAS Merrifield." I had never heard of RNAS Merrifield and discovered later it was a small wartime airfield some ten miles from Yeovilton in Somerset, retained as a diversion airfield in the event of the Yeovilton runway being clamped by fog or whatever. Nobody could tell me anything about it.

I said goodbye to Patricia and her parents, went off home to St. Mawes for Christmas not much the wiser, but now sporting two gold stripes with my training behind me. From now on I would be earning my keep at long last.

~*~

Harvey had gone. With the prospect of spending much more time at sea and with no settled base, I had to find a home for him. The Alvis Owner's Club secretary readily found him a new owner, as he had done for the loan Alvis from Gosport. Once again I clambered aboard the train, this time for Yeovil.

I arrived at a remote airfield on a Sunday night. There were only a few people about and no one at all whom I knew. I felt lonely and extremely vulnerable, about to enter a world that I really knew very little about. The only time I had been near a naval aircraft had been a five minute trip I enjoyed whilst at Collingwood, when each of us in turn had a spin in a Firefly naval fighter, sitting in the front seat with the pilot's distorted and completely unintelligible voice coming over the intercom. I had just hoped he wasn't telling me to eject or anything important like that, and was intrigued to look down the three funnels of the Queen Mary, then steaming up the Solent like a tiny tin toy.

In the morning I was introduced to the squadron's engineer officer who showed me the several different aircraft that made up 766 Squadron, a second line squadron used mainly for training purposes. By this time piston engined naval aircraft were obsolete, the replacement being attractive Sea Hawks, and the twin-boomed Sea Venom, a strange design with a small central pod containing the engine over which was the cockpit and two smaller sections that went back from the wings to a tail section. Both aircraft were jets that ran on kerosene rather than the highly volatile aviation spirit, were considerably faster and theoretically safer. I spent two months there awaiting my permanent appointment hardly getting to know anyone, not fitting in at all well, and not really seeing anything much of that part of Somerset. About my only memory is of talking to one of the pilots over a drink before dinner one evening, where I commented on the exceptionally heavy shower that caught us all out at lunchtime.

"Oh really?" he said. "I wasn't here then. Had lunch in Rome." He wasn't pulling my leg either. Apart from that awful grind to Malta the previous year I knew little about air travel. It never occurred to me that Rome was within lunching distance if one had a fast enough mode of transport. I was impressed.

My next Appointment turned up. I was to report to HMS Daedalus at Lee-on-Solent to join 845, a front line helicopter squadron just back from action at Suez. What luck! I could hardly wait to leave this dreary place. My thoughts turned to developing my acquaintance with Patricia.

845 couldn't have been more different. The squadron had been allocated a hangar at the far end of Lee airfield, which had an apron to one side suitable for helicopters to land and take off without interfering with the normal runway. The helicopters in use at that time were large lumbering Sikorsky machines, fitted with an anti-submarine sonar device. This comprised a big winch fitted in the cabin with a transmitter/receiver dangling from a cable below. The idea was to hover over the water, with the cable extended so that the listening device was well down in the water, below the temperature layers that can cause diffraction and loss of signal when using asdic at surface level. Employing two choppers, a wide channel can swiftly be swept ahead of the fleet. At least, that was the intended modus operandi. In practise, it seemed we spent an awful lot of time stripping down leaky domes, which were full of electronics and therefore needed to be waterproof. They were horribly unreliable, though marvellous when they worked.

There were eight aircraft in total, several of them sporting a few bullet holes where trigger-happy Egyptians had had a go during the Suez operation. One or two new crew joined at the same time as me, and we were welcomed into the squadron; a close-knit family comprising only about sixty men, so all knew one another pretty well. The Commanding Officer, Murray Hayes, welcomed me as one of the team rather than a supernumerary. The Air Engineering Officer was Ron Price, a serious but professional man who was a great help. He taught me all about the vital importance of the A700, that essential aircraft logbook in which the complete aircraft history is recorded, every fault reported there in writing by the pilot returning from a sortie, and signed off when it is fixed by the ground crew. My team of air electrical artificers and others were certificated competent to sign the A700. I was not. My job was not so much getting my hands dirty as to run the department responsible for ensuring every radio and electrical device was serviceable. This job had a disadvantage, the consequences of which did not become apparent until many months later: when a pilot landed in an aircraft that had developed some fault, he was expected to write down the details of this fault in the aircraft log so that it could be rectified and signed off before the machine next flew. All too often the pilot would mention the fault to me, maybe it was something small that barely warranted being recorded in the A700. Ron Price warned me that such 'small' things might suddenly take on vital significance should the aircraft develop something far more serious on its next flight, therefore it was essential to record them all in writing. So I took to carrying a little book wherever I went into which all these items were carefully noted, with date and flight number. The consequences then started to become apparent when I began to find I was forgetting normal verbal messages. My poor little brain, clearly overtaxed with all this, began to be selective and obviously decided without my say-so that it was not essential to remember things because they got written down if they mattered. Ever since that time I have had a poor memory; not consistently poor, just unreliable. It is a most irritating handicap and started with me in my twenties, rather than in one's dotage which would have been excusable.

It was not long before I went up in one of these noisy machines, and enjoyed it hugely. I would happily have been a member of the aircrew, but probably quite unsuited for the work needed. There were to be several months of home service based at Daedalus before the next embarkation in October, so some of the aircraft were to undergo major refitting at the Naval aircraft works at Fleetlands, two miles up the Fareham Road. Fixed wing aircraft having work done there would fly in to Daedalus then be towed by road to Fleetlands. That explains why lampposts along the towing route were all set back from the roadside, and there were no overhead telephone lines. These aircraft, even with wings folded, were very wide and high, and somewhat alarming to meet when driving along the road the other way. The aircrew also needed updating, and went off in ones and twos for short courses here and there.

One evening I was chatting to a lieutenant commander who worked in the base office. We were talking about boats and I discovered he lived on a hulk up Wootton Creek on the Isle of Wight where the Portsmouth car ferry comes in. That seemed to me a somewhat tedious commuting run to make every day, involving the ferry to Portsmouth, another to Gosport then the bus. Only in wintertime or when the tides were wrong, he assured me. The rest of the year he sailed over. That afternoon he pointed out his boat, a small cruiser of a couple of tons or so, bobbing up and down on a buoy just off the Daedalus slip. He could row out to this, sail across and be alongside at his home within forty minutes.

"Come across with me one day," he invited. I took him up on his offer a few days later. He kept the oars for his dinghy at the gatehouse, so we picked these up on our way across the road. The dinghy, hauled up above high tide mark, was soon launched and a couple of minutes later we were aboard, the dinghy tied on behind. The sail across took twenty minutes or so, plus another ten minutes to sail up round the first bend in Wootton Creek where he tied up to another buoy. Then we rowed across to the hulk, a wooden hulled ex-MTB, engineless, lying in a mud berth where it only floated at the top of the spring tides. He had converted her into a most comfortable home in which he lived by himself. We enjoyed a drink or two, then he rowed me down the creek from where I could catch the next car ferry back to the mainland. I reckoned it must take a special sort of somewhat mad person to have a lifestyle like that. One was utterly dependent on the tides and weather, and leaving his boat off the beach at Lee-on-Solent was no place should the weather deteriorate during the day. It wasn't called 'Lee' for nothing! A few days later he introduced me to another sailing friend. This one had been lucky enough to land one of the plumb sailing jobs around, that of boatmaster, I think he called it, to Prince Philip. The job was to look after the various craft that Prince Philip seemed to be accumulating. This had been no problem when it was just a Flying Fifteen or even his Fairy Fox, but the Dragon, 'Bluebottle', was a deep keeled boat that had to be on a mooring, and then the Prince acquired Drumbeat, a lovely sturdy ocean racer which required a bigger crew. This chap told a story of when he'd been out one day in Drumbeat with the Prince who'd brought along his two elder children, then aged about nine and seven. They were sailing down towards the needles with him at the helm while the three Royals were below getting something to eat. Another member of the crew appeared with some concoction on a plate for him. He peered at it and asked, "What on earth's this?" "I have no idea," came the answer, "It was prepared by two princes and a princess of the realm, and one doesn't therefore query such things."

Living in the wardroom at Daedalus was somewhat dreary. Many members of the Squadron were married, so the evenings were extremely quiet. I met Patricia several times, and she picked me up and drove me to Collingwood for Scottish Dancing one evening, where afterwards I kissed her for the first time. Nice. I took her out sailing and she took me as navigator on a car treasure hunt, driving her father's Austin A40. She drove with great panache while I navigated, and we finished up with the leaders. What a girl!

At Whitsun I suggested a visit to my parents, who had now moved in to their newly built house in St. Mawes. Mother welcomed Patricia warmly, but father seemed a little wary. Over the years I'd brought several fellow students to meet my parents, but this was the first girl. Furthermore she was a girl I had mentioned several times in my letters. Mother saw her as an agreeable prospective daughter-in-law while father was probably worried she might indeed become a daughter-in-law one day thereby shattering his dreams of me marrying into the aristocracy or into serious money. We walked around the village, and took the ferry over to Falmouth and back. In the afternoon Patricia tackled the new garden with her weeding fork, earning praise but not respect from father, while mother warmed to her and asked her to come again. Father drove us to the station along the scenic route through lovely Lamorran Woods, a fitting end to a marvellous weekend. On the way back to Lee in the Plymouth to Portsmouth 'Naval leave' train, sitting across from one another in a carriage full of sailors, we leant forward and chatted quietly to each other, swapping life histories and what the next step would be. Actually what we said in so many words sort of amounted to a proposal of marriage and its acceptance. I don't think anyone else in the carriage realised what was happening in front of their eyes, and we often have a laugh when we look back on that train journey. Patricia's mother realised the moment she saw the glint in her daughter's eye, though she didn't let on just then.

The next two weeks were somewhat frantic, since the squadron had started a detachment to Portland, providing anti-submarine cover for ships 'working up' at the start of a commission. It meant they had to have a refuelling and front line repair base at Portland, the aircraft flying there on a Monday morning, returning on the Friday. I drove down with Ron Price's chief artificer and we surveyed the area, soon agreeing that the best place for a heliport was the sports field behind the NAAFI club. We organised several temporary huts and, in my case, a field WT station comprising a hundred foot portable aerial mast and a trailer full of equipment. I went down in one of the choppers and helped everyone set it up and commission it. In the ensuing weeks I made several trips to and fro between Portland and Daedalus, sitting up beside the pilot and navigating by means of a small AA Handbook that showed most of the roads. If we hit poor visibility and got lost, we either veered out to sea where there was little likelihood of flying into a hill, or more usually, we flew low, slowing down to read the road signs when necessary. In the fifties, road signs at all the minor intersections were small fingerposts, so one had to hover quite low in order to read them. One of our pilots, Dougie Hale, told a story of running low on fuel on one of these trips so, to get himself home, he stopped in a field behind a petrol station and bought ten gallons of the highest octane fuel they had. There was no air traffic control for this sort of flight, we just did what we wanted. Dougie Hale used to fly along the top of the Bournemouth cliffs from where one could wave at people in their private swimming pools. I loved sitting in the open doorway of the cabin, my feet out on the step and holding on with one hand while enjoying the view passing beneath us. This was a favourite place to squat, usually the 'off duty' perch of the sonar operator.

Our Sikorsky aircraft were being updated to the newer Mark 7 version made by Westland. These were fitted with an Alvis Leonides rotary engine, originally designed to be mounted horizontally on a fixed wing. This had been adapted to fit the Mark 7 helicopter mounted at 45 degrees, and had all sorts of teething troubles, one of which was that when the maintenance engineers 'dropped the filters' (inspecting the oil filters for any suspicious foreign matter that might be an early indication of troubles ahead), in one of them a broken off lump of aluminium casting was found. Ron Price immediately had all the other aircraft inspected only to find an identical lump in another one. He promptly grounded the whole squadron and went up to the Alvis factory with his two pieces of evidence. Clearly there was a major problem that might affect safety. The design engineer who met him looked with interest at the pieces of metal, then opened desk drawer and brought out several more identical pieces, telling Ron that it didn't seem to matter, as no harm would be done. They were redundant pieces of engine casting and the filters caught them quite safely. Ron was not impressed; unlike the fixed wing aircraft to which these engines were normally fitted, our helicopters only had one engine. If that seized up it would mean the chopper would fall out of the sky. The Alvis man assured him there was no danger of that happening, but as a precaution the helicopters were forbidden to fly below 400 feet just in case. Above that height it would be possible to auto-gyrate down to a safe landing, but didn't address the problem of what happens when one is taking off or landing— a time when the engine is working at its hardest. Our aircrew took the news with their usual equanimity, but they must have had concerns every time they went up.

Once the Portland base was up and running I only needed to visit occasionally. Without a car this really meant a train trip one way and a helicopter ride the other, which all took a long time. I really needed a car. I saw an advertisement for a 1931 chain-driven Frazer Nash two seater, a highly desirable and exciting sports car at that time, and the price was just within my budget. Throwing caution to the winds I set off for a little village in Norfolk, saw the car, loved it, bought it and drove off without stopping to think why the price was so low. Ten miles down the road this became obvious. It drank oil like a Scotsman drinks whisky. At ten-mile intervals I had to stop and put in another couple of pints. I arrived back chastened and not a little worried, and set about trying to find a set of piston rings for the meadows 4ED engine. I'd never tried re-ringing an internal combustion engine on my own before. Last time this was needed was during our Barr and Stroud time, when I had borrowed brother-in-law Peter's Austin Seven and driven it to Glasgow where it broke down and Noggin had fitted new rings to the engine while lying in the gutter outside the McDougal's house; I had merely passed down the spanners. At least here at Lee I had a nice workshop for attempting the job and a team of lads all keen to help. The task finished, there began the job of running in the engine, not easy in such an exciting motor.

Henry (yes, the Frazer Nash was another male, no doubt about it) had his gear stick on the outside of the car. The clutch pedal had a movement of about an inch. Easing one's foot back just a fraction produced a kick in the back and one would suddenly be bowling along the road at twenty m.p.h. with a comforting gnashing sound of chains coming from under the seat. Henry had little finesse when it came to smooth driving, and was quite difficult to handle safely. After a while I stopped using the clutch altogether except for starting off, changing gear by pulling on the gear stick to disengage, then blipping the throttle until the engine revs were about right before pushing the stick into the next gear. He had four gears altogether, the third and fourth ones being very close together. It was said that when a chain broke, as could happen with a careless gear change, bits of chain would shoot out all over the place rather like the occasion at Metro-Vick when the chain hoist exploded so spectacularly. I was always conscious of this since I sat right on top of it with only a thin piece of plywood for protection.

I took Patricia along the quiet lanes near Stubbington for her to have a go at driving Henry. I explained where everything was and warned her about the clutch. Seemingly unfazed, she cheerfully let in the clutch and with a sudden parting squeal of tyres and a scream of terror from herself, was gone. I stood alone in the now silent lane, wondering what to do. Five minutes later I heard the unmistakeable sound of Henry approaching at speed. Round the corner he came with a white-faced Patricia clutching the wheel.

"Help!" she wailed, as Henry shot past, "How do I st…..op!" and disappeared down the other way. In due course she appeared once more, managed to switch off the engine as she approached, and came to a halt. A trembling Patricia clambered out and stood beside me, visibly shaken.

"Wow, that was terrifying," she said, with an unconvincing weak smile. Some girl! I had to admire her. Little did I know then that she knew nothing about the insides of a car, nor the insides of anything mechanical, come to that. With a father like Leslie, she had little need to find out, even supposing she had the inclination.

Patricia and I had been meeting as often as possible. We went formal with the engagement a week or two after our St. Mawes visit and got out the diary. Panic set in. 845 Squadron was due to embark in HMS Bulwark at the end of August and it was now June. If we were to get married it would have to be very soon. We fixed a date for 10th August, and worked back from there. Time with Patricia was going to be short and there was a lot to organise! We searched unsuccessfully for a ring to make it all formal, then while I was at Daedalus, Patricia and her parents worked flat out on invitation cards, a notice in the Daily Telegraph, and all the fuss of organising a wedding. She gave in her notice at work, told all her friends, met all my friends, was welcomed into the squadron 'family', and we spent a lot of time round the dining room table at High Winds, her parents' home in Lee, organising this and that. We decided to be married at the Lee-on-Solent parish church with a reception afterwards in the nearby Daedalus wardroom. I met a special Naval friend of Patricia's, John Goudie, a Church of Scotland Naval padre, who was going to be away at the time of our wedding and momentarily threw me by saying how much he would have liked to marry Patricia, not immediately realising he meant conducting the service at our marriage!

In the middle of all this a sailing team to represent the Fleet Air Arm was being put together to sail against Portsmouth, Devonport, Chatham and Rosyth from a sailing club on the Forth, and I was selected to crew a mad dentist in one of the Naval 14 footers. Our mad dentist, being a captain, managed to pull rank and organise our own private aircraft to collect our FAA team from Culdrose in Cornwall, Yeovilton and Lee-on-Solent and deliver us in Scotland. We made our base at the quiet little airfield of Donibristle on the eastern side of the Forth road bridge, won our various races and came back again the same way; an ideal way of travelling around with no worries about timetables or tickets. One felt very important when we stepped aboard and the pilot requested "Permission to take off, Sir?"

Patricia and I had an interview with the Lee vicar, The Reverend Sills, who quizzed us to check there was no reason for him not to marry us, and we eventually found the ring Patricia had set her heart on. We attended matins at the church the next Sunday and heard our banns called. Nobody objected.

I drove Henry down to the Portland base where I was met by an idle maintenance team who greeted me with a "Wash and polish, Sir?" when they saw the car. I let them loose on him while I attended to my business, and drove off in the evening for the trip back to Lee to discover the tank had been filled with 110 octane avgas, the unmistakeable exhaust smell giving the game away to anyone who might recognize it. A bit concerned about the damage this might do to the engine, I filled up with the lowest grade of fuel obtainable once I'd used a gallon or so, hoping the engine would not be harmed.

I paid one last visit to St. Mawes as a bachelor, this time in Henry, not thinking very clearly why I felt I needed to do this. I was probably beginning to suffer from shock by now. On the way round the Southampton ring road Henry threw his top gear chain, bits of which were spat out all over the road, but not, fortunately, upwards into my bottom. This was not a particularly serious happening as there was so little difference between third and top gears, and simply meant my top speed was restricted to about sixty rather than seventy—quite fast enough for a car of that sort on the roads of the day. Jane and Peter were staying at the time with their new toddlers, twins Fiona and Judy. I said goodbye to everyone there and confirmed arrangements for the family visit to Titchfield Haven where we'd fixed up for them to stay at a quiet guest house the night before the wedding. On the way back Henry blew up just beyond Lostwithiel. This was more serious, with bits of piston rod scattered over the road. The fill-up of avgas was probably responsible. I was able to coast down a hill to a garage nearby who put the car at the back of their workshop for a couple of weeks (it was loaded up with all my stuff from home), and set off back to Lee by train.

We now had to quickly rethink our honeymoon arrangements, which were to have been touring in Henry. Patricia's father generously agreed to loan us their own car after the first weekend when they needed it themselves, and we fixed up to have a honeymoon mostly touring in Cornwall with the intention of towing the disgraced Henry back to Lee at the end of it.

We were married on 10th August 1957, at which point my life changed. Noggin, himself, now married to the lovely Bella, was best man. I had first met Bella who was living on a barge that lay at Chiswick Eyot when, needing somewhere to rest my head overnight, had stayed there with Noggin. I remember bathing was a problem because there was a beam that ran fore-and-aft over the top of the bath only a couple of feet above it, thus making it impossible to lean forward to wash one's feet while sitting in the bath. Then at low tide the barge grounded and heeled over to one side slightly. This was no problem provided somebody had remembered to pump out the bilges recently, otherwise mucky bilge water would come over the floorboards. There were tin cans hanging below each of the leaky bits of deck head, making it simpler always to walk about the boat in a permanent bent over position to avoid them all.

It rained of course at the wedding. A splendid Naval guard of honour assembled for us to walk between as we came out of church, most of the sleeves holding shiny swords sporting an impressive number of stripes. We all assembled in the wardroom at Daedalus for the reception, Patricia radiantly happy and me in a sort of daze throughout. I don't remember much about the champagne, but I do remember buttonholing the wardroom wine steward in his cellar a few weeks previously when I was asked by Patricia's father to order it. He showed me a bottle that he recommended, and me, not being a wine buff, muttered something to which the wine steward obviously took exception. He pulled himself up to his full height, put on a haughty look and said sniffily, "I obtained this consignment for the Queen's visit, Sir. She liked it, so I expect it will be appreciated by your guests, Sir."

During the reception we came across my parents with Jane. They had stayed at the Tichfield Haven guesthouse overnight along with about six other guests. The place was apparently being operated by a lone woman who only had help in the mornings. There had been no sound of breakfast forthcoming. In fact, there was no sound at all. Jane went to investigate, wandered around the private part of the house and eventually came across the proprietress's body in her bed, where she'd died during the night. They had all the trauma of contacting a doctor and getting the authorities alerted while Jane herself turned to and cooked breakfast for all the other guests staying there. Eventually one of the part-time helpers arrived and took over while the guests all beat a hasty retreat.

At this point the next phase of my life begins, so I will finish part one of this book here. The next part deals with the life of a married man in the Royal Navy.

Part II

Married in the RN

10

Our First Home and a Cruise

Compared with the sort of honeymoons people seem to have nowadays, ours really was a bit of a fiasco. We had ten days together which was the main thing. As we didn't have a car to start with, we spent a couple of nights at the Dolphin Hotel in Chichester to which we travelled by train in a compartment that filled up with shoppers returning from Portsmouth. As one, they quickly moved to another part of the train when one of them noticed confetti dropping out of the suitcase above our heads! We attended matins in Chichester's acoustically awful cathedral (music was lovely, but the words were lost amongst the echoes) and explored Itchenor and Bosham. Then, penniless as usual, we borrowed Patricia's parents' car, and set off for a few days touring around Cornwall. For a day or two we stayed with Noggin and Bella who were then living in Helford and took out their lively Albacore dinghy in which we sailed across to St. Mawes to visit my parents, also seeing Jane and family who were still staying there. While there the wind unexpectedly got up to a fresh westerly and we were unable to sail back, so had to borrow another car, father's this time, to get back to Helford by road.

On our last day in Cornwall, we drove through Lamorran Woods to Malpas where Jim and Jill Hosking were then living in the little waterside cottage there. We enjoyed a lovely relaxing time with them and their two young children. I can see now Jill lifting her youngest one onto the back of a pet sheep and holding on while the sheep bucked around the lawn trying to dislodge her. During tea in their front room we were chatting away when Patricia was startled by a little grunt from under her feet.

"Oh, it's only Henrietta!" cried Jill, dragging a cardboard box from under the settee and lifting out a diminutive little piglet, which then proceeded to gallop excitedly round the room. Visits to Jill always risked one being swamped with various pet farm animals; in that way she was much like Jane.

We set off once more, driving to Lostwithiel station where we met up with Patricia's father who had come down by train from Lee. We all went on to the garage where I'd left Henry and proceeded to tow the Frazer-Nash all the way back to Lee where we deposited him ignominiously at our local garage to have his engine rebuilt. The cost of the engine rebuild would take virtually all Patricia's and my savings so we would have to sell Henry afterwards to have something to live on. We had one day left to zip up to London and buy some cutlery, and then I had to go back to work. Honeymoon over!

A few days with the squadron at RNAS Daedalus while we prepared to embark for some serious work, a quiet weekend at High Winds with Patricia, and then the two of us went over to Portsmouth Dockyard where HMS Bulwark was waiting. Bulwark sailed with families aboard for a jaunt out in the Solent, before the families were taken ashore in one of the large paddle tugs after many tearful farewells, and I buckled down with the rest of the ground party to await arrival of our aircraft. These made the short hop, all eight of them, flying in formation from Daedalus a few miles away and landed noisily on Bulwark's flight deck, attended by much arm waving from the flight deck officer while aircraft handlers ran up to each one in turn to put large chocks either side of the wheels. Managing aircraft on a deck that might tilt over without warning requires a quite different approach to landing on the apron at Daedalus. 845 squadron also provided the safety chopper, the one that hovers on the port quarter while fixed wing aircraft take off and land. The rest of the choppers were struck down into the hangar and we steamed further out to sea where we could get up speed to embark the fixed wing aircraft.

The first to arrive were our squadron of Sea Hawks which came in one after another in quick succession, followed after a short interval by the Sea Venom squadron. Bulwark had been fitted with one of the first angled flight decks, which meant there was room ahead of the island for aircraft to be parked safely away from the landing area making the whole operation of landing a complete squadron considerably safer. Another new feature we had was the newly invented steam catapult. This was capable of accelerating ten tons of aircraft up to a flying speed of nearly 100 knots in the few seconds that it took to go off the end of the catapult. During this time the acceleration was so fast that the pilot would momentarily black out—not a nice thing to happen just as one is getting airborne. The pilot held his throttle open with one hand, jamming his elbow into the seat arm so that it would remain open even if he did black out.

We also carried a couple of propeller-driven Skyraiders, large lumbering machines full of radar equipment with a crew of two. These American aircraft did a free takeoff with the task of flying ahead of the ship where they sent back radar information to the air traffic control room on board, but had to land using the arrester gear the same as the jets. Very soon after, British Gannets, powered by a double mamba engine with twin contra-rotating propellers on a single shaft that made a wonderful sound, replaced the ageing Skyraiders.

Right from the start shipboard life then occupied most of my time and thoughts and, I'm ashamed to say, I had to push thoughts of my new wife to one side while I settled in.

Not so with Patricia, however. She was alone at High Winds for several days while her parents were away, which she spent tidying up after the wedding, writing thankyou letters to all the wedding guests for their presents, and tried to find somewhere for us to live. It was over a month before she was able to locate a suitable place, and that was a very fundamental two-up two-down in a row of terraced fisherman's cottages at Hillhead, a mile or so beyond Daedalus. During this period she met many other 845 wives, the squadron 'grass widows', and started to feel part of the family.

Bulwark's first stop was to Portland where we practised a full flypast, something we would be doing on our overseas flag-showing visits. It involved our two fixed-wing squadrons flying in formation over the town that was to be visited (in this case Weymouth), then landing back on before the ship entered harbour. It was necessary to have a headwind of over 30 knots across the flight deck in order to land an aircraft, and if it was a fairly calm day, then the ship had to steam into what little wind there was for the ten minutes or so that it took to get them all back on board. A bit of arithmetic shows we would need five miles of sea room, and on that first tryout I don't think we had quite enough! There we were, steaming flat out straight for Weymouth beach with the navigator rather anxiously calling out the depth while the last aircraft was still on its approach run. The instant it caught an arrester wire and stopped, flight deck crew rushed to put the chocks under, secured the aircraft, as the ship started her turn still travelling so fast that she heeled right over in an alarming way. Minutes later we crept in through the narrow entrance of Portland harbour with a sigh of relief. We spent a few days 'shaking down' then sailed off to Belfast for a quick docking period in the Harland and Wolff yard. I phoned Patricia and suggested she come over for a few days. She happened to make the crossing from Heysham on the eve of the Scotland-Ireland football match in the company of hordes of wildly inebriated Scottish supporters; quite an eventful trip for her first visit to Ireland. Ron Price and I had found some miserable digs in Belfast, not very salubrious but the best we could get in the time we had. Patricia and I shared a quite dreadful bed with a lumpy mattress, squeaky broken springs and several nasty little creatures that shouldn't have been there and didn't welcome our intrusion. We hired a little Morris Minor and set off for a drive down to the Mountains of Mourne on a gloomy overcast day, the day only enlivened by a party on board in the evening. Patricia was a little concerned to see police purposefully carrying guns, not something ever seen in England then. The long weekend was over all too soon; Patricia went back on the ferry, mercifully this time without any football supporters, while Bulwark steamed off for another exercise way up in the Arctic.

It was during this time that we lost an aircraft. One of our Gannets had an engine failure and was forced to ditch nearly a hundred miles ahead of us and out of range of any other shipping. It meant a DIY rescue without assistance. Fortunately conditions couldn't have been better. Though cold, it was brilliantly sunny with a deep ultramarine sea as flat as the proverbial pancake. We heard that the pilot had achieved a smooth wheels-up 'landing' on the sea, the crew being able to step out onto the wing and climb aboard their inflated life raft without so much as getting wet feet. They then sat down to wait, hoping they would be located by means of the SOS beacon with which they were equipped. Bulwark put on full speed to close the gap, but even so the ditched aircraft was well beyond the range of our helicopters. With full tanks, our SAR chopper could only get there and part of the way back if we closed the distance a number of miles. It meant delaying takeoff for a couple of hours—no great shakes in such fine conditions and nightfall not for many hours. It was a textbook rescue, all the crew being winched safely aboard the helicopter and arriving back with sufficient fuel remaining for a few more flying minutes.

HMS Bulwark, all her aircraft ranged on deck, shows off her paces.

A fortnight later we were back at Pompey and I paid my first visit to our new home. The little place had a tiny living room, stairs opening off it to two small bedrooms upstairs, one of which just had space for our meagre belongings piled high. There was a tiny kitchen at the back with a small bathroom opening off that. In the front a minuscule conservatory that was really uninhabitable, as it was level with the scrap of grass at the front, backed by a shingle bank with the Solent lapping against the other side of it. At high tide and a sou'westerly the sea came over or through the shingle bank

One of the lumbering Gannets about to hook a wire. You can just see the SAR helicopter hovering in the background.

and right up to the house. We used the conservatory for storing driftwood picked up all along the beach, where it sat in a salty damp pile smelling of rotting seaweed until we picked out the driest bits for our little open fire, the only heating in the house. The fire never burnt very well, but it did burn with lovely coloured flames, pink, blue, yellow and orange. The house was cold and damp the whole time I was there, but while I was away Patricia did have one or two sunny days, and then it was lovely. To get to it, we either walked along the beach, or clambered down a long flight of concrete steps, 37 in all, carrying our bikes; one way was a non-starter at high tide and the other somewhat unsafe on a dark wet night.

On our first weekend together the sun shone, and we took our bikes out on the Sunday to visit Patricia's folks in Lee. As we passed the end of Daedalus's runway I noticed gliders being winched up and circling overhead, a knot of people at the far end of the airfield waiting around for their turn. On an impulse I suggested we go in to see whether there was anyone we knew. A little later while Patricia was talking to some 845 families someone asked me whether I'd like a go. "You bet!" I replied. "Well then, jump in," he cried, "We're next," and helped me into the open cockpit of a very simple machine, which was at that moment being hitched onto the winch wire. In moments we were off, just as Patricia looked round to see her new husband soaring up into the sky at an angle of 30 degrees, giving her a last cheery wave before he was gone. I'm afraid I was enjoying the experience so much that I never stopped to think what might be going through her mind at that moment. At a couple of hundred feet it was absolutely silent except for a soft swish of wind, the ground noises seemingly left behind. Over the sea the hum of traffic gave way to beach sounds, and even that faded a hundred yards out. Not so the other way, though. I looked over the side as we came in to see one of my erstwhile Collingwood instructors fiddling with a lawnmower in his back garden and commented about this to the pilot. As I spoke, the man below looked up, saw me and called out "Oh, Hullo!" All too soon we came in to land on the single skid, a helper grabbing the end of each wing, and as I climbed out Patricia came rushing up, a look of alarm all over her face. I received my first dressing down!

For the next few months some of our aircraft went back to Portland and I had to go with them occasionally, so was away from home quite often. As our senior pilot lived a few doors along from us, whenever I could I would bum a lift back with him. We would fly along the beach, slowing down as we passed our respective houses watching to check that our wives had seen us and waved. Often that was the first inkling they had that we might be home that evening, so the sound of a low-flying helicopter was welcome music for them.

At long last it was time for some Christmas leave, and we went down to Cornwall to stay with my parents where it was much warmer and sunnier than the dreary weather they'd had in Hampshire. We spent our days walking, meeting lots of local people, did the rounds of the pubs on Christmas Eve where I introduced Patricia to more Cornish locals most of whom had rich Celtic voices, and we sang all our favourite carols. The watchnight service at the little church of St Just in Roseland, walking by the light from flickering candle lanterns down the steep path through rustling bamboos with the water shimmering in the moonlight beyond, was magical. We had a whole ten days at St. Mawes, longer even than our honeymoon, and enjoyed every moment together.

But there was a cloud on the horizon. The squadron was to re-embark on Bulwark in the New Year for a ten-month cruise. Patricia decided to go back to her old job, stoically saying it was only for ten months. In fact her life was subtlety different: whether she liked it or not, her new status meant she was no longer regarded by all the lads as 'available', but was relegated to the ranks of the grass widows with a very different social life. Because we were now married, I benefited from 25/- a day Naval Marriage Allowance which could be put towards starting a much-needed nest egg.

Back at Hillhead, we enjoyed a few last days together, then Patricia drove me over to Portsmouth where we had a tearful farewell on the jetty before climbing the gangway, sailing almost immediately. Patricia went round to Sallyport where she stood on the walls with several other Naval wives to wave as Bulwark majestically steamed out of the harbour passing just fifty yards away. The aircraft joined us out in the Solent and we were off, a purposeful feel about the ship as we headed out into the channel.

I managed to get a letter off to Patricia as we passed Plymouth and another as we went within choppering distance of the Azores when incoming mail was also received. I have the highest regard for the Royal Mail, which succeeded in getting mail to and from HM ships wherever they may be in the world. One letter Patricia posted on a Saturday was delivered to me two days later as we sped down the Malacca Straits. The Navy used to reckon that if you fed the sailors well and made sure their mail arrived regularly, there'd be no trouble, and I'm sure they were right.

A week later Bulwark arrived at Port of Spain in Trinidad. No messing around with mooring ship this time; she steamed in, dropped anchor and had all her boats out within half an hour. On the way over, I had noticed one boat slung in a whaler's davits, which certainly wasn't a whaler. It was a hot-moulded plywood boat, half-decked, looking from below like a huge dinghy. I was told this was the Captain's own boat, and not to touch. One day when the Captain came into the wardroom for a pre-lunch drink I asked him about it. His eyes lit up.

"You sail?"

"Yes, Sir. I have my own boat swinging round a mooring at St. Mawes." (A little exaggeration often helps!)

"Lucky man! But that's splendid news. I'm keen to get about six of us together to crew the Fairey Fox." And he suggested I might like to go for a sail that very day.

His boat, a Fairey Fox was—as its name suggests—a craft designed by Uffa Fox and built by Fairey Marine, rather like Noggin's airborne lifeboat. The story went that HRH The Duke of Edinburgh had approached Uffa saying he wanted a fast and exciting boat to have with him in the Royal Yacht, the limitation being that it would have to be under 24 feet in length, including all spars, so that it could be slung from Britannia's davits. The first one to come off the mould wasn't quite as Uffa wanted it, so they made another. Percy Gick, our Captain, had obtained the original one. She was like a large half-decked dinghy, about eight feet in beam. That first exhilarating sail in her frightened the life out of me. We set off, Percy Gick at the helm, his trusty lieutenant on the critical mainsheet, and four of us sitting out, two on trapezes. We needed all these people to keep the boat upright in anything like a decent breeze. As soon as we cleared the ship's stern the wind hit us and we immediately rose up on the plane and scudded off at about fifteen knots, faster even than our fast motorboats, and ten minutes later creamed past the Trinidad Yacht Club.

Sailing the Captain's own boat had a huge advantage over anything I ever sailed when in dear old Devonshire; it meant that in theory all we had to do was to walk down the gangway where we'd find the boat fully rigged and ready to set off. In practice, one or two of the crew would get her ready while lying at the boom, but she was such a gorgeous boat to rig that I enjoyed it. No horrible rough sisal ropes; the Fairey Fox's rigging was stainless steel and nylon throughout, with tufnol blocks. She was a wet boat to sail, especially if one was sitting for'd. Out on the trapezes wasn't so bad as only one's feet got wet, but who cared? We were in the tropics with seawater temperatures up in the seventies.

Whilst I was enjoying myself afloat, most of my fellow squadron friends were living it up ashore. They had discovered white rum, an innocuous looking fuel that went very well with Coca Cola, and the wardroom had dispatched their representative to the local distillery to negotiate a deal. After a couple of days' hard work he returned victorious having agreed to buy 12,000 bottles of VAT 19 for a price that worked out at something under 4/- (20p) a bottle. A lighter appeared next morning laden with cases, while the logistics officer got to work on the charts to see if there were sufficient Coca Cola bottling plants in those parts of the world we were visiting, or whether we might have to rearrange the ship's cruise to ensure we didn't run out. I must say I quickly acquired a liking for the stuff, ordering a S! tot of rum in a long glass topped up with ice and Coke. After a few weeks most of the hard drinkers were on T! rum-and-Coke, and it didn't stop at just one. I found aircrew tended to live in the fast lane and a goodly alcohol intake helped them to maintain it. I'm sure they thought me wimpish for preferring my more sedate slow lane.

Our helicopters were soon pressed into service collecting mail, taking VIPs ashore or picking up people who had missed the last boat. The one designated SAR aircraft (Search and Rescue) was the one normally used for such missions as it had no sonar fitted. The SAR role was never very popular amongst our pilots. All the time there were take offs or landings the SAR machine would be hovering just on the ship's port quarter, ready to come instantly to the rescue should one of the fixed wing aircraft go over the edge. Between sorties the chopper would come back onto the flight deck and wait until aircraft returned when once again it would take off and station itself on the quarter. Whilst fixed wing aircraft were landing, the whole active part of the flight deck had to be cleared so that if one of them missed a wire it could take off again without hindrance. Ten tons of jet aircraft hurtling in to an arrester-wire landing is an awesome sight, and the sound of such an aircraft on full throttle is truly deafening. The flight deck was not a healthy place to be at such times, and was strictly out of bounds to all except the operational people.

Bulwark was fitted with three British inventions, two of them fairly new at that time. One I've already mentioned was the angled flight deck resulting in space for'd of the island for a few parked aircraft, wings folded, and meant that a complete squadron could land one after another at half-minute intervals, which just gave time for each one to disengage from the arrester wire, fold its wings and taxi for'd to the parking area seconds before the next one touched down. Only after the last aircraft had landed was it possible to operate the lifts to the hangar below and get the aircraft struck down. When one realises aircraft might arrive back with only enough fuel remaining for a few minutes flying, any hiccup could have serious consequences. An aircraft that crashed on deck would have to be moved immediately if there were others still flying, and to that end there was a heavy mobile crane on standby to move the wreckage, pushing it straight over the side if necessary. I never saw it in use, but our pilots told me that they were always aware that should their engine falter during the approach the recommended procedure would be to ditch in the sea.

Then there was the steam catapult, but we also had one of the first mirror deck landing sights. Up until this time a 'bat man' would have stood on a small platform to one side of the landing area waving a couple of bats to guide the

A Sea Venom's nose collapses as the aircraft catches an arrester wire. Because of the aircraft design the arrester hook has to be well for'd putting a great load on the nose wheel.

pilot in on the correct path. The new sight was a projector with a stabilised mirror that sent a beam of reflected light towards the approaching pilot, showing him the correct angle to descend along. All the pilot had to do was to fly down the beam and he would arrive on deck at the third of six arrester wires. Only after his arrester hook had connected with a wire did he fully close his throttle, and within the space of a hundred feet would decelerate from flying speed to stationary; not a pleasant experience. His reactions had to be fast during this uncomfortable few seconds for, should he miss all the wires, he would have to open up to full throttle and take off again.The arrester wires unwound against a brake, decelerating the aircraft safely. The flight deck officer would wave the aircraft forward the moment the wire disengaged from the arrester hook, and the pilot then taxied on to the parking area. By this time the next one would be barely a hundred metres from landing, with little room to manoeuvre. If it was too close, a Verey light was fired telling the pilot to go round again, hoping he had sufficient fuel to make a second circuit. It all required superb teamwork, accurate timing and cool heads. Lives were at stake, and the aircraft were exceedingly expensive. They were our front line, the very reason for our being there. When exercising in peacetime we would normally do so within range of another carrier or a diversion airfield ashore, a standard precautionary procedure, but in real action the luxury of a diversion landing area was not often an option. But we weren't flying our aircraft now. We were on a flag-showing cruise, with relatively few opportunities for operational flying, and it was time to move on.

Next stop was Bequia, one of the Grenadines, a tiny island just south of St.Vincent. It is a mile or two long and half a mile wide, with the usual extinct volcanic peak in the centre. The small population all lived near the only jetty. Trading schooners were all they normally saw. The arrival of this operational British aircraft carrier with noisy helicopters circling overhead must really have interrupted their peaceful existence. For some reason, we wanted a vehicle ashore; goodness knows why, for there were only a couple of dirt tracks. Our ship's Land Rover was slung below one of our helicopters and flown ashore, to be lowered onto the jetty amid a cloud of flying sand, and it drove up and down the tracks for a while. I had organised a small group of us to have a 'banyan' on a remote beach over on the far side of the island, taking with us the bare necessities to sleep under the stars overnight. There were one or two lads from 845 squadron plus a couple of the ship's midshipmen, and it was okay until dusk, but then the fun began. We had intended to sleep along the top of the beach, but realised as the sun went down that the onshore wind became both stronger and appreciably cooler, so much so that we each dug ourselves a shallow trench in an attempt to keep out of this wind. With the dusk, out came the crabs. I remembered Arthur Ransome's book Peter Duck where the children dubbed their uninhabited Caribbean treasure island 'Crab Island'. Hundreds of these small crabs came marching up the beach, many falling into the trenches we'd dug and unable to climb out again. None of us had much sleep that night! Nevertheless it was a relief to escape the unending ship's noises for a few hours.

After Bequia we set off for Kingston, Jamaica. We arrived in Kingston's lovely harbour early in the morning and within the hour I was out in the Fairy Fox making for the Yacht Club. Here we were greeted by members who plied us with invitations to crew in their boats, and— Oh! by the way, could they have a go in ours? Here were a number of ex-pats, bored with one another's company, each with their own boat and probably bored with that too, especially as most of them were getting on somewhat and found the handling of their large cruising craft was getting too much for them. The appearance of a large Royal Navy ship was manna indeed. I spent much of our visit out in one or other of these lovely craft and met some really generous people. Fortunately the ship's tropical working hours meant we were free every afternoon, so could manage the time. My chief electrical 'tiffy, 'Bungy' Williams, tired of hearing me going on about it all while we were working together on the sonar domes, asked if he could join us. He was a heavy boat man, brought up on Naval cutters and the like, but had always fancied trying something a little more sophisticated. Soon he was a regular member of the Fairy Fox team and enjoyed his share of crewing for the local yachtsmen.

As usual on flag-showing visits the first evening was given over to a formal cocktail party, arranged by the local consul or Naval attaché's office who would ask all the people who were reckoned to profit in one way or another from such an invitation (or, we hoped, who would maybe reciprocate). Improved trade was usually an intended spin-off. It generally worked well and the ship's company would enjoy the rest of their stay far better. Normally somewhat starchy affairs, this one was not, as Jamaica seemed to be such a lively and laidback place completely lacking in formality.

I did have one or two runs ashore in the big throbbing town, full of noise and loud music and too many people, but it was not really my scene. Instead I put my name down to take up the invitation from a philanthropic resident who asked for about eight young officers to enjoy a day out at his expense on the north shore, based at a hotel in Ocho Rios. We never actually met our host; a couple of cars took us from the dockside across to the north shore where we were deposited in a rather bare colonial house and invited to change into beachwear. Then they took us to a large hotel spread along a private palm-fringed beach with clear azure blue water lapping the soft sand, a few small boats, pedallos, that sort of thing, and several small thatched huts that were bars dispensing cool drinks non-stop. No money changed hands. I asked for a soft drink and watched while the barman produced a huge glass, poured a couple of tots of white rum into it, followed by the juice of several oranges and a handful of ice. I kept going on these most of the day, in between swims and a buffet lunch. We met the hotel residents and the reason for our visit became clearer. To a man they were all wealthy Americans, elderly couples who had become too old and infirm to enjoy active life, able only to enjoy watching others such as ourselves having the fun. We spoke to many of them and I had the impression they were an unhappy lot, though they took care not to let it show. But it was sad to behold, and left a lasting impression on me. In the early evening we were all taken to Ian Fleming's home, where we were shown round by his housekeeper, saw the typewriter on which the original James Bond books had been written here in this room, and were given yet another drink. From the open balcony we looked down on dense rainforest, at this time throbbing with night noises. Hummingbird feeders on the balcony told us it would be different in daytime. Then we went back to the hotel and found we were expected to be the cabaret, dancing energetically to a wild West Indian band, and having great fun attempting to limbo dance.

Captain Gick did things a little differently. He had met some people living a little further along the North shore who had invited him to spend a day with them, suggesting they rendezvous on the beach. It so happened that one of our choppers was doing a mail delivery to Montego Bay further along, so he took a lift in that. The chopper flew slowly along the shore low down about a hundred yards out until he recognized his friends waving, whereupon he promptly dived in and swam ashore. They were a little alarmed that he'd arrived without so much as a towel, for they had a formal evening arranged later. Apparently surprised to have forgotten to bring any clothes to wear he said he was sure that wouldn't be a problem, he'd flag down the chopper on its way back. This he proceeded to do, the chopper then lowering his bag on the hoist, which they'd intended to do anyway. Percy enjoyed using the choppers for this type of fun, and why not? He was one of only two men I served under who knew how to maximise the enjoyment obtainable from the extensive Naval facilities.

Our visit to Kingston ended with the traditional cocktail party, an opportunity to thank all those who had provided hospitality during our stay. It was utterly different from the party held on our first day, which included a number of stuffed shirts—this farewell one was specifically for people we'd come to know. And then we sailed. Leaving Kingston was a little sad for we were saying goodbye to friends, but to be heading out to sea always had that feeling of expectancy and our next port of call was to be Bermuda.

Entering Hamilton harbour with its white-roofed little houses had a definite 'colonial' feel to it. Whereas Trinidad had felt Trinidadian and Jamaica felt Jamaican, Bermuda was like a little piece of England. The place names were English, so were the few cars we saw, although the surreys were definitely not! The famous post office was one of the first anywhere, and as for the yacht club, well, it gave its name to the almost universal Bermudian rig adopted by all recreational sailing craft today. I enjoyed a drink or two in the club's bar in town where they had a wooden spoon hanging on the wall behind the counter. This was no ordinary wooden spoon, but one about fifteen feet long carved from mahogany. Down at the harbour the yacht club flagpole needed a new topmast, but there was no means of fitting one without recourse to expensive scaffolding. Once again a chopper was employed, hovering overhead while the new topmast was lowered into place and secured. Another job well done. Surprisingly for me I didn't get out in a boat while I was here, but spent my shore time either on the lovely coral beach (this definitely required sunglasses, it was so glaringly bright), or wandering about the town. Some of us went to the cinema where the newly released My Fair Lady was being shown. I enthused about this in my next letter to Patricia, suggesting she tried to get tickets for the show when it opened in London later in the year.

Duncan Sandys, then the politician responsible for the Navy, was in Bermuda while we were there and was given a lift towards our next port of call, Halifax, Nova Scotia. Several days steaming north from the tropics to a very cold, wintery destination with the temperature hovering a little below freezing, damp and foggy with it, was a killer. We did some cross-operational flying with the United States navy on the way up, and several of their top brass came aboard to see our angled flight deck and mirror landing sight. Our detachment of Royal Marines provided a guard of honour of a standard which only the Royal Marines can put on, commanded by a wild scar-faced major who frightened everybody from the captain down. After the parade, he marched his men towards the aircraft lift which would take them below, scattering the VIPs as he went. A fearsome but much loved man.

In Halifax I met up with a Canadian service family who invited me to their clapboard painted house just outside the naval dockyard. I had always coveted a lumberjack's thick shirt, something Jane had worn for years, and this—my first visit to Canada though hardly anywhere near lumberjack country—seemed as good a place as any to try. I didn't find one, of course, but bought a leather golfing jacket instead which I still wear to this day, though being a short jacket I tend to wear it on occasions with my kilt.

Duncan Sandys had left us when we were working with the US navy, flying home from one of their bases, but he'd left behind his rather sumptuous overcoat. We considered keeping it as a wardroom trophy, but in the end returned it via the Canadian Air Force. I wonder whether he ever received it?

In my cabin, which I shared with four other 845 people, we had all the punkah louvres closed off tightly and electric fires burned continuously, but it made little difference; we were cold. Bulwark had no modern comforts in the way of air conditioning. Fresh air came in either through the open scuttle, which faced aft just below the flight deck (a highly dangerous place to be, incidentally, when aircraft were landing), or from the forced ventilation which took unheated air from outside. The only heating was from these electric bars. Two decks below in the wardroom area it was a little better, but crew comfort was not a high priority in one of our warships of the day. I was extremely glad when the time came to sail away once more, this time crossing the Atlantic for our next visit: Gibraltar.

Gibraltar felt like an old friend. Bulwark was due to spend a few days in the dry dock, so we had time to explore in more depth. This amounted to clambering all over the Rock, inside and out, coming across such sights as the public loo with a cubicle containing the eastern version of a toilet pan—a ceramic hole-in-the-ground with a thoughtful ceramic footpad on either side for those who prefer to do it squatting on their hunkers. We also discovered the private swimming pool of the Rock Hotel where a number of us spent far too much time, and we acquired a taste for 'sticky green' (crème de menthe) then unbelievably cheap at the Naval Club, which also served very acceptable grilled swordfish steak with chips.

While there the squadron had a visit from a couple of boffins from the Naval anti-submarine research establishment who wanted to do field trials of a new development they'd been working on. They needed to lower a heavy sonar dome to a depth of several hundred feet and spend about half an hour taking readings. This involved us having to strip out our equipment and mount a hand winch in its place. As I was having to host the visit, and all our aircrew suddenly found they were busy elsewhere during the few days this was going on, I found myself the poor muggins who flew with them to cope with the winch, not something I found at all easy to operate in the confined space of a helicopter cabin. It took a good twenty minutes cranking the handle to lift the weighty dome up from such a depth, while all the time the pilot had to hover just above the water surface. We did three sorties before they had all the readings they were after, but they went back to England apparently satisfied with the results, though I never found whether anything came of it all. Whilst in Gib there were several comings and goings, the result of which was that I moved my cabin to one a little for'd and in the centre of the ship, though still on 2 deck, immediately below the flight deck. 2 deck cabins had the advantage of having exceptionally high deckheads, nearly ten feet high, but to offset this, the deckhead was a slab of steel which would heat up tremendously once we were in the tropics, and the insulation was not all that thick. Still, there was plenty of room.

I haven't said a lot about the operational role of our helicopters, which was a very boring one for the aircrew. Basically all they were required to do was to take up station ahead of the fleet, two or three at a time, and hover fifty feet over the water. Once in position, the heavy sonar dome was lowered and an all-round submarine search made from a position deep down, so as to overcome the problem of blind areas due to water temperature layers. Once a search was completed, the chopper hoisted its dome, flew on to the next spot and began another search. They could not do this very safely at night since there was no accurate way to judge the height above water, yet submarines could be just as active by night as by day. I always found 845 aircrew most uncommunicative about operational activities, not

One doesn't venture onto the flight deck in these conditions.

expecting their technical support team to be involved, and I only found out about this night time requirement and their lack of ability in fulfilling it by chance. It seemed incredible that the Admiralty boffins could expect the squadron to operate at night without a proper height aid. I immediately thought of Barnes Wallis and the dam busters, where lights were fixed to the wingtips of the bombers to send narrow converging beams down onto the water, the point where they intersected being at the required flying height. Choppers didn't have any wings, so could we, perhaps, do something similar with lights fore-and-aft? I discussed this with our aircrews who tried shining powerful torches onto the water next time they went out at night. They found the light beams too faint and the water too choppy for them to see anything, so asked me not to bother any further. I then thought about a salt-water switch, a crude version of which you may remember I had used so dangerously in my teenage years for dimming lights at the Portscatho village play. I suggested this to the aircrew, but again they didn't sound too keen, possibly because if it worked well they might be expected to do far more night flying! Nevertheless I discussed the idea with my electrical people and we built a prototype rig. This consisted of two switches made of tufnol with brass contacts spaced half an inch apart. When a switch was lowered into the water, the current flowed between the two contacts and lit a torch bulb satisfactorily. We then fitted a couple of these switches ten feet apart on a length of weighted line and connected the wires to a light box that sat in front of the pilot above his control panel. If neither switch was immersed, then a yellow light came on to indicate the system was active, but the aircraft was hovering too high. If the lower switch dipped into the water then a green light came on indicating the aircraft was correctly positioned, but if the second switch was also immersed, then a red light lit up to show the aircraft was too low. It was simple, worked extremely well, but the prototype was rather impracticable for serious operational use. However the aircrew loved it, and I sent in a report to the Admiralty suggesting this be further developed and a proper operational version supplied. I heard nothing more after that, but it didn't matter much to 845 squadron for, as you will see, they didn't do all that much operational flying on this trip, the helicopters being mainly used for almost every other requirement than looking for submarines.

An incident occurred in Gib that I shall always remember. A particularly unsavoury rating, a seaman in the ship's company, returned on board one day a little the worse for wear. He was the sort who gets belligerent after a few drinks, and was well known for his normally aggressive behaviour already having been in trouble several times. On this occasion he was unwise enough to find himself face to face with the Captain in one of the gangways and attempted to push past, elbowing the Captain to one side. The next thing he knew, he was whisked away to the Master-at-Arms' office where he was told that he had gone too far, and was to report next day to the quarterdeck where a boxing ring would be set up in which he could work off his belligerence. News of the impending boxing bout quickly spread throughout the ship and everyone tried to guess who his opponent might be. He was a big man, and several potential challengers were suggested, one of them a Naval boxing champion. By next day he was shaking with apprehension and as the hour drew near, he was reported to be physically sick with fear. He duly appeared at the appointed hour to find to his astonishment that his opponent was to be his own ship's commanding officer. Percy played with him for two rounds, then knocked him out cold. After that he was a changed man, and the Captain, who had taken quite a risk in setting this up, was raised to hero status. None of us discovered whether the whole thing had been set up in some fashion, but it certainly worked and was Percy Gick's style of leadership.

Marseilles was our next stop, where Bulwark went alongside in the French Naval dockyard. Here was an opportunity to visit Monte Carlo, which I took up. The harbour was full of millionaires' motor yachts, huge gin palaces kept in dazzling order by their paid crew, spending most of the time alongside. What a waste! Just occasionally an owner would appear with his guests, and go off for a few days. There were also some magnificent sailing craft, and Bungy Williams and I wandered around the jetties coveting them all. We were asked by one of the crew whether either of us would like to sail in one of these craft back to the UK in a few days time, since he would need help for the trip. Bungy and I looked at each other. I know what was going through my mind, but no—no way could I jump ship and jeopardise my career, but it was a tempting offer. Next day Bungy said he had seriously wondered whether to go, but reckoned there must be other opportunities and he would hang around such places again when he was free. In the event, he did take up an offer to deliver a yacht to its new owners in America. Our little run ashore in Monte Carlo sowed the seed for the start of something big for Bungy.

Bulwark sailed the length of the Mediterranean for my first trip through the Suez Canal. As a warship we headed one of the convoys, conscious of about twenty large tankers strung out at one mile intervals behind us, none of them very manoeuvrable and unable to stop quickly should the need arise. The pilot was a local Egyptian man who wisely left the handling of this awkward ship to the professionals, calling out 'hard a-port' or some such which had to be interpreted by our captain for what was actually meant. A large vessel steaming within the confines of a canal tends to have a mind of its own when it comes to steering. The huge amount of water displaced as she passes along will build up in front of the ship, then surge down either side, which results in the ship being held fairly well in the centre of the canal with minimum need for steering. Our twin rudders were designed for optimum results when travelling far faster than the canal speed so had relatively little effect. However, unlike commercial ships, we had more than one screw and could steer very effectively by varying engine speeds. It was a team effort between the pilot and the ship's crew that worked well. Passing through the Bitter Lakes with the half-sunken ships rusting away we were reminded of the Suez debacle not that long ago, the older 845 aircrew remembering only too well their last visit to this place. We traversed the canal without mishap except that we struck some submerged object, which damaged a screw, resulting thereafter in a nasty vibration at higher speeds.

Once in the Red Sea we opened up and headed south at some twenty knots, the welcome breeze across our decks much appreciated in the dry sultry heat. That night we slept comfortably, but not for long. About two in the morning there was a tremendous jolt accompanied by a grinding, bumping noise. Most of us were half thrown out of our bunks, the sideways lurch of the ship being quite severe. I rushed out to the after platform to see a number of lights springing up in the water astern of us. Bulwark had stopped and was launching a boat. What had happened? Piecing the story together afterwards, it appeared that a smallish overladen ship full of pilgrims heading across the Red Sea on their way to Mecca had been trundling along without any lights. Bulwark's navigation lights were up on the island, the only place from where they can be seen all round. If the pilgrim ship had seen us at all, we would have looked to them like a small jet-propelled speedboat up in the sky, or an aircraft maybe. We never saw them. They went straight into us on our starboard quarter, opening up a twenty foot gash high on the ship's side and demolishing their bow in the process. We sent the boat over ostensibly to see whether we could offer any assistance, but in reality to check what damage had indeed been done. Experience had shown that damage resulting from collisions of this type were often hugely exaggerated by the time the authorities were discussing compensation. The officer who went told of appalling conditions aboard, and his photographer captured it all on a series of unforgettable photographs that, just as well, were not for public consumption.

As for ourselves, the damage was fifteen feet above our waterline, so was of no immediate consequence. At the point where the vessel struck us, our ship's side flaired out at quite an angle, the compartment inside being the Royal Marine major's cabin. His bunk was positioned several feet in from the ship's side because of this flair, so he was not hit by the intruding bow, but the noise of tearing steel plate must have been deafening. It was said that the damage control party rushed to the compartments on that side of the ship, burst in to his cabin whereupon he sat up in bed and shouted "What the hell do y'think you're doin', comin' in like that without knockin'? Get out!"

We proceeded on to Aden at a somewhat more sedate speed, signals flying back and forth to the Admiralty about the mishap. As we approached Aden harbour, a Tannoy announcement stated there would be leave for everyone, but as several cruise ships were in the harbour, the Captain wouldn't tolerate drunks staggering about on shore in uniform; if anyone felt they had drunk too much, then the patrols would get them back on board and no action would be taken. The result of this, following soon after the affair of the bully-boy's boxing debacle, was that the entire ship's company behaved in model fashion. At Aden we had a couple of days' delay while divers went down to examine the starboard screw, reporting that a docking would be necessary to put it right. It meant our operational ability would be hampered slightly until this had taken place. We had the choice of continuing on our cruise to the dry dock in Hong Kong, return to Malta, or go on to Sydney. We opted for Hong Kong, via Ceylon and Singapore.

The visit to Ceylon (now re-named Sri Lanka, of course) was not a flag-showing visit, but just somewhere to have a few days relaxation. We were joined by several ships of the Far East Fleet for some exercises, then proceeded to the huge natural harbour of Trincomalee on the eastern side for a week of inter-ship sports and fun. Though not the 'senior' ship (a ship's rank is dictated by the seniority of her Commanding Officer, and one of the others had a crusty old captain who held that position) Bulwark was sufficiently different and, with her charismatic skipper, was big enough to ignore a good deal of the formal activities. We did exceptionally well in all the boating events, although we had had very little chance to practice, as we also did in the field events ashore, but then we did have a crew twice the size of any other ship which must have been an advantage for the team events. It was while we were in Trincomalee that we discovered our party piece sailing the Fairy Fox. There was reputed to be a huge old shark that cruised around the harbour after any nice little titbits that went down the ships' gash chutes, so when we capsized the boat (easily done; she was, after all, just an over-canvassed large dinghy) we were none of us anxious to remain in the water any longer than necessary. To a man, we all scrambled onto the upturned hull causing it to roll over so that we were thrown off the far side just as she righted herself, dropping us neatly back into the boat again. We called this our 'slow roll' and practised it whenever we felt we needed to cool off, or show off, or just whenever the key man on the mainsheet felt like it. We also discovered we had so much power when planing along that we could tow a water skier and still keep on the plane! Nobody had any water skis, so we used an upturned canteen table that worked after a fashion. The first time we tried this, with the Schoolie Commander up behind, we capsized unintentionally and had to do our slow roll (which we'd found was the quickest way to get her up again), but the poor old Schoolie had to sit in the water surrounded by imaginary sharks until we were planing once more.

One evening the ship's electrical officers, headed by Commander Wykeham-Martin, had accepted an invitation to join the electrical team of a nearby cruiser. As an ALO, I was asked to join them, and we set off in one of our boats with Wykeham-Martin holding a hurricane lantern in one hand. As he said, "You can't trust the electrics in these ships, y'know!" I think we'd all enjoyed rather a lot of rum-and-cokes before we set off, but it was a grand evening. Someone had discovered a super palm-fringed sandy beach a mile or so away, so 845's choppers were pressed into service to take as many as possible ashore for a great banyan, with lots of swimming in crystal clear water. I had to keep pinching myself to believe all this was happening to me, and what's more, I was being paid for it.

I took a trip in our Land Rover along quiet metalled tracks through some swampy thickets to a village where the ship's postman was taking his mailbags. On the way back, we came across evidence of the recent passing of an elephant, as witnessed by a steaming heap in the centre of the road about three feet high. We couldn't leave the tarmac because of swamp on both sides, and it began to look as if we might have been marooned. We imagined headlines shouting "Elephant Poo prevents Royal Navy getting its Mail" splashed across the newspapers at home, but just then some laughing local people came by and cleared the mess in moments.

All too soon our holiday break was over and we were back at sea once more. On a particularly hot Sunday the ship stopped to allow us to sea bathe. This involved rigging scrambling nets over the side, a distance of some twenty-five feet down to the water, then lowering a motor boat to cruise around in case anyone got into trouble, and finally having a seaman standing on the flight deck with a loaded rifle just in case somebody saw a shark. From up there, it was comparatively easy to see down to quite a depth in the clear water. While I swam around, I was conscious that there was probably a mile of water beneath me, but it was so buoyant it would have been almost impossible to drown. After I clambered out and was rubbing myself down, the sailor with the gun managed to fire it (sailors seemed to be unable to hold any weapon without it eventually going off. Hopefully they're better nowadays). I looked over the side to see fifty or so men streaking across the water towards the ship so fast, leaving a white wake behind them, that they almost got up and ran!

The following day we entered the Malacca Straits and it was while we were here that we received the much welcome mail delivery that I mentioned earlier. It arrived in a canister dropped from an RAF aircraft flying low over the sea about a hundred yards from us. We had scrambled a helicopter all ready to pick up the canister, so moments later it was on board, and half an hour after that we were reading letters posted from home only two days previously. Patricia had seemed so far away, but a letter from her, in fact I think there were several in that delivery as we hadn't received mail for quite a while, was especially welcome. Quiet descended over the ship as everyone buried their heads in the flimsy blue airmails. Dear Patricia, chatting away about trivia, trying to find something interesting to say about a very humdrum life. We did miss one another so much.

216

We arrived in the Singapore Roads, threading our way through countless merchant ships all waiting their turn to take on cargo. The skyscrapers along the coast glistened in the sultry sunshine. Our destination was the Naval dockyard on the north side of Singapore island, some miles up the muddy river. I have several memories of Singapore, the first one being as we came alongside where, waiting on the jetty, stood a Naval commander most improperly dressed. Instead of the white shoes and long socks, he was barelegged and wearing bright red flip-flops; not only that, but he also carried an umbrella. I could quite understand this, as the heat and humidity were appalling, even to us who should have become accustomed to the change of climate on our slow progress. Once we arrived, we too reverted to our sandals, but no umbrellas! (I was reminded of the irreverent ditty I had read in the Yachtsman's Weekend book: "Four things thou shalt not have in a boat: a cow, a bicycle, an umbrella and a Naval Officer." Yachtsmen had little time for the professional sailors and thinking back to my Dartmouth days, I could understand why.)

Then there was the fried egg event. Someone had said the flight deck was so hot you could fry an egg on it. Rising to the challenge, the Supply Officer with one of his chefs, the Commander and the flight deck officer all stood in a circle watching a miserable egg sitting on the deck as it slowly cooked. It took about six minutes, but it did indeed 'fry'. Somebody won his bet. It was unbearably hot up on deck in the sun, but at least there was a tiny breeze. Any air movement at all was a lifesaver, and I dreaded going below where the temperature and humidity were even higher. Lots of people suffered from prickly heat, and attempting to work on delicate electronics without dropping beads of salty sweat into the works was very trying.

Most evenings I crossed the dockyard to the Naval Club, which was built on a little promontory overlooking the swirling river that we dubbed the Limpopo. There were only flyscreens around the sides of the club, no walls. By evening the temperature had dropped a tiny bit and there was a welcome breeze wafting in through the screens. When the rain came which it did most evenings while I was there, it fell in a great solid mass making a deafening noise, stopping as suddenly as it started. Amazingly I went to the club because the local padre had a Scottish Country Dance group running. When the effort of putting out a hand to lift a glass was sufficient for one to break out in a sweat (assuming one wasn't already perspiring profusely) it seems unbelievable that this group leapt up and down cavorting around to the foot-tapping music of Jimmy Shand and his ilk, but energetically dance we did, with much enjoyment. On the way back to the ship we passed a swimming pool into which we usually jumped to cool off, before squelching back to the ship even wetter. As I approached, the heat of the still-hot steel would hit me, and it required quite an effort to go below into an oven a good ten degrees hotter than the outside night air. By this time I had discovered a removable inspection plate in the top of the forced air supply that ran over my top bunk, and by unscrewing this I was able to enjoy a blast of air that helped cool my naked body as I lay there trying to sleep.

I didn't actually get the opportunity to explore Singapore town itself, but I heard of one exploit that probably became exaggerated with the telling. Apparently a group of officers which included the Captain had been at the very posh Tanglin Club one night, enjoying the amenities around the pool, becoming somewhat lit up in the process when one stuffed shirt (almost literally, as he was attired in full evening dress) complained about their behaviour, demanding to speak to the Captain. The next thing he knew he was lifted up and dropped into the pool by someone who said "I am the Captain!" It made a good story, but I don't think even Percy Gick would have gone that far.

All this time we had been living with the vibration caused by our bent propeller, so it was a pleasurable thought to think of our next visit, Hong Kong, where we were to go into the dry dock and have it dealt with. But steaming north through the South China Sea we were diverted to Manila where we were to join some American activity going on in the Philippines. Manila boasted the American equivalent of our NAAFI, where just everything was said to be obtainable, but I was saving my shopping for Hong Kong which sounded far more exciting. I did, however, get around Manila in one of those highly decorated colourful taxi-buses, squeezing in with lots of half-pint sized Philippinos. The noise, pollution and sheer numbers of people was all most exhausting and I only made the one trip ashore, thankfully.

And then it really was Hong Kong. We came in, threading our way past the considerable amount of shipping, with the Star ferries plying to and fro across to Kowloon in between the big ships, one or two ancient traditional junks (with sails of stitched-together BOCM grain sacks) and a tremendous reception from Jenny's side party, a band of gloriously dirty women who had been contracted to look after the ship during her docking period. Not only did they get down into the dock to clean and paint the whole of the bottom of the ship, but they also dealt with all the garbage, where it was put into lighters and towed off to goodness knows where, no doubt to be recycled and used somewhere else. We embarked a Chinese laundry, a band of energetic spotlessly clean emaciated-looking Chinese who worked non-stop in all sorts of strange parts of the ship. Whatever time of night one walked about, looking down a hatch one would see one of these men bent over an ironing board, working away in the heat. They slept on top of their ironing boards when they weren't working, and smiled all the time at everyone. We also embarked a shoemaker, who happily set up shop in a remote compartment somewhere down near the bilges. He handmade me a pair of wonderfully comfortable leather lace-up shoes which lasted me well, the only handmade pair of shoes I'll ever own, and all for a few shillings. I'd heard one could get a good uniform made as well, and made enquiries. Within hours a Chinese tailor arrived, took my measurements, to return next morning for a first fitting. On the second day he came for a final fitting, and the finished article, neatly packed and with lieutenant's stripes on the arms, was delivered that same evening. Total cost £10. Messrs Gieves would have charged more than that just for the stripes.

I sallied ashore with various friends most days for other items. I spent several days negotiating to buy a carved mahogany chest lined with camphorwood for our new home, also a nest of French polished mahogany coffee tables, both items being made to order and delivered within days. This was where being in an aircraft carrier had great advantages. Bulky items were no problem to transport home! My mother had always coveted a dressing gown of Chinese silk, having once seen the one owned by a lady in Byfleet, so I set about choosing a suitable design from the bolts of silk in one of the bazaar shops. The salesman sketched a figure of my mother then gave me the pencil to put in her measurements. Mother was probably about normal Chinese height, but appreciably wider! The resulting garment fitted her perfectly and she loved it, but the beautiful material wasn't very long-lasting. We took the Star ferry (cost: one penny, first class) to explore Kowloon with its elegant hotels, the red light district and airport where approaching aircraft came in low between skyscrapers to touch down on the runway almost in the middle of town. On Hong Kong island I was ashore every day around the shops, went up to the famous racecourse, visited the cemetery where paper effigies were burnt at the never-ending funerals, walked among bits of shanty town on the hills above, unbelievably tatty shelters crammed together with narrow muddy walkways between them, whole families living in one room and succeeding in keeping clean in spite of everything. We met no garbage; presumably everything had a value too good to be thrown out in the streets. We ate at Chinese eateries in Wanchai, the district in which the film The World of Suzy Wong was based. It was all very authentic and atmospheric. If we were caught out some way from the ship when one of the daily thunderstorms hit us, we just sheltered under a canopy until it passed, or if we didn't have the time, we would purchase a paper umbrella for 1/6 which got thrown away once we were back on board. We went sailing in the harbour using local craft and had to manoeuvre through great rafts of sampans, all with entire families living permanently aboard. We went over the hill to the famous harbour of Aberdeen, a somewhat yukky estuary in which a couple of large floating fish restaurants were based. A sampan took us to one of them at which we were greeted by a bowing Chinese waiter who invited us to select our meal from a tank in the centre of the boat where strange fish swam around unaware of their imminent fate. Trying not to think of the half million boat people living without sanitation just upstream of the restaurants, ten of us sat round a circular table and chopstick'd our way through innumerable small dishes, dipping bits of fish into various intriguing sauces, then trying to get them into our mouths before the chopstick grip failed, sending the morsel spinning up into the air.

By courtesy of the RAF I spent an interesting day circumnavigating Hong Kong island in an air-sea rescue boat, a large businesslike craft capable of some thirty knots. With the local Naval people I spent another day over on Stonecutters Island, a mile or two to the west and one-time armament depot, where we enjoyed watching wildlife.

I was invited to an English couple's home on top of the Peak, reached by the Peak tramway, a pair of rail cars tied together by a long wire cable which went round a capstan at the top. One went up as the other came down, passing halfway where the track split into two for a short stretch. At their house we sat out on the balcony sipping cocktails with a superb aerial view of night time Hong Kong ablaze with neon lights of every type. Up here it was a different world, with breathing space around every house. One assumes that millions of Chinese live on top of one another because of the size of Hong Kong island, but from the peak it was possible to see hundreds of acres of forest-covered hillside over towards the comparatively untouched part of the island.

The two-week visit was over all too soon, and it was time to travel back to Africa. We were due to call in at Durban, then Capetown and Accra before returning home. But on the way back we heard that the South Africa visit was cancelled due to apartheid problems, so we might have to return by the Suez Canal. But first we would call in to Mombasa. Like Singapore, Mombasa is also an island, the southern entrance being the way in for shipping, while the western and northern sides are really just a river, not navigable in anything seagoing. We were only to spend a few days here, but rather than go ashore, I was able to join a section of 845 squadron which would extend our flag-showing activities by taking three of our helicopters down the coast to Zanzibar, then on to Dar Es Salaam, stopping off to refuel at the little airfield at Tanga. Nine of us went, a pilot for each chopper, one observer, engineer Ron Price and myself, also three maintenance people. We flew down the main dirt road south of Mombasa, rather thoughtlessly going over the top of an elderly lorry at a height of about fifty feet, frightening the life out of the driver who almost crashed his vehicle. We discovered later that it was most unlikely anybody in those parts had ever seen a helicopter before, certainly not large ones such as our Whirlwind Mark 7s. Tanga was an experience. We stopped in front of the little hut on the edge of the field and went inside for a coffee and chat with some local ex-pats who'd seen us arrive, while a couple of fuelling men rolled a forty gallon fuel drum out to the aircraft and started laboriously transferring the avgas by means of a hand pump, a job which took a good hour. Our hosts made us promise to stay a little longer on our way back so that they could give us lunch at the Tanga Yacht Club nearby.

Nearing Zanzibar, we lowered a large white ensign on the end of a rope below the lead chopper, and flew in formation over the elderly sultan's palace and around the town before coming in to land at the airport. Cars took us to a comfortable hotel overlooking the Zanzibar Channel, from where we made a visit to the market. On the way the cars had stopped at a clove plantation to show us how cloves are grown and harvested, and several spice shops were in evidence in the market. That evening we heard on the local radio station that the British Navy had arrived in town and would be giving a display on the airfield next day, the result of an interview with Murray Hayes on arrival when he rashly agreed to 'do something' for any sightseers there might be next morning. That night, spent in a lofty airy room with a gentle scented breeze wafting through the open window, and not a sound outside except for the occasional owl and distant lapping of waves on a sandy beach, was dramatically different from the stuffy, noisy ship, and so welcome after all these months.

After breakfast we headed back to the airfield once again, having spent some time devising our 'display', which was to be a couple of helicopters doing a sort of dance to music, a quadrille in the air. Appropriate music would play over the airfield tannoy and relayed to the pilots who would fly towards one another, stopping and reversing, then pirouetting round to the right and coming in again, four times in all. It was a party trick they'd tried once before somewhere, and looked good from the ground. They also recruited me to play the part of a ditched airman, sitting on the tarmac while the commentator described my rescue by helicopter with a winchman being lowered to pick me up and lift me into the hovering aircraft. When we arrived there, we were amazed to find most of the population had trekked in from right across the island, and were lining the airfield boundary three deep. Our simple display sounded very inadequate for such a huge audience. The musical display looked ever so good and the audience loved that. Then it was my turn, and I walked out onto the concrete runway for my rescue. I was well used to noisy choppers hovering overhead, but had never been lifted aboard one before. The wire is only as thick as a pencil and looks woefully inadequate to lift two full-grown men. As we went up, I looked down at the concrete apron fifty feet below me, and couldn't help thinking about that wire. Not only did it seem so thin, but the hoist was equipped with a cutter gun that could be fired by the pilot by pressing a button on his joystick in the event of the wire snarling on an obstruction. I just hoped the pilot's hand was nowhere near that button! Afterwards we landed and fielded questions from the public about our role in the Navy. Then it was farewell to hundreds of waving arms as we took off, circled once round and made our way on to Dar es Salaam.

I don't know that we achieved much at Dar es Salaam. A fairly active airport, we had to land in a remote part of the airfield, were met by some ex-pats and whisked off in their cars to be entertained individually. There was no 'formal' activity, and I don't suppose anyone knew we were there apart from our hosts. However, it was nice for us to spend another night away from the ship, in my case with a family in a pleasant colonial-style house. The children showed me round their garden, introducing me to their pet chameleon with its swivelling eyes and one or two other exotic creatures they had around the place. Come bedtime, when their father was dishing out anti-malarial pills to the rest of the family he asked whether I'd got my own, and was aghast when I said I'd never taken such things. "But malaria is endemic here," he said, "You must never miss a single day without taking protection." He made me take one. In the morning we met up at the airport again, said goodbye to our hosts and set off back to Tanga, sixty miles up the coast. This time we were expected and while the aircraft were being refuelled, we all repaired to the yacht club for a beery lunch followed by a sail in their boats. These were Jollyboats, another Uffa Fox design, eighteen feet long and wonderfully fast. Percy Gick would have loved them. We creamed around the inshore lagoon, protected from the easterly onshore winds that blow up in the afternoons until it was time for them to prepare for their routine race. As we took off we banked round over the little fleet, resisted the temptation to disrupt the race by blowing them over with our downdraught, and waved goodbye.

Back at Mombasa we found the ship humming with activity. The Royal Navy had been called in to help ferry a detachment of the British Army then stationed at Mombasa up to Aqaba to assist the Jordanian army in some skirmish. They embarked in a series of lighters, our ship's crane lifting off innumerable trucks and other baggage, some hundreds of men taking over half the hangar while our aircraft were ranged on deck. Looking at all the khaki-clad soldiers, tired and overladen, I was glad not to be in the Army, never able to take one's home comforts along to the front. As usual, the soldiers felt squeamish at the ship's motion, even though we were only at sea for a day or two, and with fine weather throughout. We arrived at Aqaba just as it was getting light, and spent a couple of hours landing the detachment while the sky coloured up with the desert sunrise, before setting off once more. This time we returned to Aden where we had been asked to stand by for what might be a prolonged time, several weeks possibly.

I discovered the two swimming facilities on the seaward side of Aden's Steamer Point, a five-minute taxi ride from where the ship's boats landed. One was a rather nice club where we had been made honorary members, and boasted a couple of seawater pools, shaded by palms and serviced by waiters smartly attired in white uniforms topped by a maroon tarboosh and with a matching sash around the waist. The tipple I adopted was a half pint tankard containing a tot or two of Pimms filled with ice and fresh fruit juice, handed down to me while in the pool. All very civilised. For a change, I sometimes went to the public swimming facility nearby at Tarshyne where the bathing took place in the sea proper, a rough metal palisade supposedly shark-proof, enclosing a good-sized beach. A changing room ran down one side and a restaurant-cum-relaxing area the other. It was while there one day with some of my friends that a familiar face bobbed up out of the water. It was Jill, Noggin's one-time girlfriend who had stayed with Noggin when we were sharing the Chelmsford caravan, now married to a BP oil man and living out here with her young family. I abandoned my mates who looked on enviously as I spent the rest of that afternoon with this attractive suntanned blonde who later invited me round to their Company apartment in Steamer Point for an evening meal and to meet her husband. It fell very flat. Jill had changed of course, no longer the carefree, dashing, leggy beauty but now a humdrum housewife. Her husband was clearly most displeased to find she'd picked up this sailor bloke, and was surly and monosyllabic throughout the evening.

I went a couple of times to the souk in Aden town proper, a few miles away from Steamer Point, but everything was very expensive here, carpets especially. The presence of oil company employees clearly affected the prices. Likewise the prices in the shops down at Steamer Point were also high whenever a passenger ship came in for a few hours, but they dropped back again once the ships had gone, in fact the whole place sometimes shut down altogether. I thought their method of street cleaning was somewhat original: whenever the place quietened down, a herd of goats was let loose around the streets where they ate everything in sight, old paper bags, discarded food waste, everything except tin cans and bottles, leaving the town cleansing service with a comparatively simple tidy-up afterwards. All they had to do was deal with the goat droppings, something that didn't get done all that thoroughly. I can still recall the goaty smell of Steamer Point.

845 squadron's helicopters were involved with the only front line activities going on at this time. They had been up in the mountains a hundred miles away

operating from Mukeiras, a settlement some 8,000 feet above sea level on the edge of the Aden Protectorate, barely a mile from the Yemen border. There were always border skirmishes in these parts, and the British Army had a small detachment up here. One of our machines lost power during takeoff, and ditched, fortunately not causing any harm to the occupants, but it wrote off the aircraft. I was not really surprised when this happened, as trying to fly our helicopters at those altitudes was right at the edge of their operating ability, maximum power being needed to get off the ground. Once flying speed was achieved there was no problem, but those first few moments were critical. The crew returned to Bulwark rather sheepishly and then began the task of salvaging what we could from the aircraft. The airframe would be left where it was, but we needed to get at parts of the engine to determine the cause of the accident; likewise there were electronic parts that needed to be reclaimed if possible. The sonar, of course, was not installed at the time. So a motley detachment of ground staff comprising three engine fitters, an electrical man and with myself to look after them went along to the RAF station at Khormaksar airfield nearby and bummed a lift up to Mukeiras in an RAF Prince, a small twin-prop passenger aircraft, which an RAF sergeant-pilot offered to pilot.

We climbed laboriously for the best part of an hour until we arrived at the edge of a huge escarpment, then just over the top we came in to land on a flattish area of dirt that had been roughly cleared of boulders. The pilot skilfully weaved his way between the smaller rocks and came to rest beside a knot of people, one of which was an Army captain attired in a most suitable rig for those parts:

open shirt, desert boots and shorts, topped with a red and white checked kaffiyeh, kept in place with a knotted cord. He was accompanied by a few fierce-looking local men brandishing rifles and wearing splendid curved knives in the place where a Scotsman hangs his sporran. He had with him a 3-ton lorry and said he would take us to the wreckage, but warned we could only get within a couple of miles of it with the lorry. After that we would have to walk. Up here it was

One of 845 Squadron's helicopters flying over the dessert north of Aden. We always kept the cabin door open, taking it in turns to sit in the doorway with our feet on the step. I never strapped myself in when I did this...

gloriously cool with temperatures down to about 75 degrees, so a walk in the fresh air sounded quite welcome. We set off on atrocious tracks, the lorry slithering about all over the place covering us with choking dust until eventually it came to rest in a morass of boulders and dried mud. Disembarking, we set off in single file, the local levies to front and rear keeping their eyes open for any movement among the rocks that might not be friendly. Needless to say I treated this little escapade as I did any other adventure and had brought my camera. I nearly got lynched when we met some people carrying huge bundles of dried sticks that I thought would make a good picture. They turned out to be women (I must say I found it hard to tell) who reacted to the camera as I would had one of the levies pointed his rifle at me. One learns. Up and down a few hills and then we came to a tiny field with young corn bravely growing away. In the corner were the remains of our old friend 'Charlie', half on its side, the rotor blades buckled and the tail rotor crumpled up. It took us a couple of hours to strip out all the useful parts of the aircraft, about a ton of it altogether, then one of the levies went off for some means of getting it back to the lorry. He returned with half a dozen packhorses (amazing what seemed to be available in this barren place). With heavy pannier loads, the little ponies struggled up the stony paths, leaving behind the bare remains of the aircraft which our Army captain assured us would be well utilised by the chap who owned the field, presumably for his chickens. We stopped to give the ponies a rest, and I asked how good the men were with their rifles. "Better than you and me," came the answer, "They've had a gun in their hands ever since they were lads. Let them demonstrate." And with that he invited one man to shoot a stone off the top of a wall about fifty yards away. Having done that convincingly, the man picked up the empty cartridge case, balanced it upright on the wall and fired a round straight through the middle of it, again at about fifty yards. Impressive.

Arriving at the lorry, we paid off the packhorses and crawled back down the dusty track once more, this time going to the Army encampment. No more aircraft were expected that day, but there would be one or two next morning, so we were invited to enjoy Army hospitality overnight. I was shown a large bedroom in the wing of an extraordinary stone building they were using for an officers' mess, and asked whether I'd like to clean up. In came bearers with a hefty full-sized bath, which they put down on the stone floor. More bearers followed with cans of hot water, and I had the bath of a lifetime. I had to get back into my dirty old fatigues, but at least I now felt clean. I don't remember the evening, but next morning I certainly do remember the breakfast. They say the Army marches on its stomach, and I watched disbelievingly as one plump young officer sat down to fruit juice followed by porridge, then a huge helping of kedgeree, and only then to the main course of fried egg, bacon, sausages, tomatoes, kidneys, and fried bread. After that he settled down to several rounds of toast and marmalade before finishing off with an apple, finally leaving the table with another apple and an orange stuffed into his pockets. All this up in the barren Arabian wastes, miles from anywhere. Amazing.

I stood at the side of the airstrip as an elderly Dakota came weaving in, the pilot jumping out to ask whether anyone wanted a lift to Khormaksar. Several local women with their bags and baskets stepped forward.

"Have you room for six of us?" I enquired.

"Sure, Jump in," he said.

"We've got the remains of a helicopter here. Room for that?"

"Yeah, put it in." He went off to get himself a coffee, while we humped all the bits into the Dakota, which was stripped of any seating. We tied everything down on the floor, while the passengers (there were now about fifteen people) sat down either side on canvas fold up seats. When the pilot returned, he shut the door, clambered over the pile in the centre without giving it so much as a glance, and went forward to the cockpit. He turned and warned us one of the magnetos was on the blink, so not to get worried if it backfired a little when he did his mag tests. "And another thing," he said, "The moment we're airborne I shall have to do a sharp turn to avoid going over the border. They're a bit trigger-happy over there." With that he turned and started up the engines, one of which banged and coughed in an alarming way. With a maniacal laugh he slammed the cockpit door shut and we careered off down the runway missing the worst of the stones, heaved into the air and banked over until I thought we would slip sideways back onto the ground, but the pilot knew what he was doing. A moment later we were over the escarpment and it was then downhill all the way to Khormaksar. Phew!

This happened shortly before our departure, for we had been summoned to proceed to the Gulf of Oman to take part in assisting the Sultan of Oman's air force in suppressing some little problem he was having. We sailed at nine in the morning, Percy Gick as usual having some entertainment at the expense of his current hosts. He had spent the night at a rather grand house a little way from Admiralty House on the seaward side of Steamer Point. Enjoying his breakfast on the balcony his hostess suddenly saw Bulwark coming round the point.

"Isn't that your ship, Percy?"

"My goodness, so it is. I thought it was tomorrow we were leaving."

"What will you do?" His hostess began to panic. Percy poured himself another cup of coffee. "I can't do a lot. Let's hope they notice I'm not on board." He settled himself back in his chair and pretended to look worried.

Needless to say, this had been a planned event, with the Commander taking the ship out, and a helicopter arranged to come over the house to take the Captain off. Percy Gick glanced at his watch, went in to collect his things and came out again just as the chopper arrived overhead. He said farewell and lifted off into the sky. Much more fun than waving from a pierhead. We had a couple of days or so to prepare for the forthcoming operation. This would involve our squadron of fixed wing aircraft carrying high explosive bombs fitted beneath the wings. Gone was the laidback mood as a charged atmosphere spread through the ship. Moral had been dropping during our enforced stay in Aden, and this was just what was needed to get us up on our toes again. The first sorties flew off, a businesslike air evident as the heavily laden aircraft shot off the end of the steam catapult one after another and formed up into a formation overhead. An hour later they returned to refuel, and straightaway set off for another sortie. I never discovered quite what they had been up to, but the task was satisfactorily completed within days with the Sultan much pleased.

A few days later we picked up an SOS coming from a vessel about a hundred miles away. This was a fully-laden tanker, the Melika, which reported colliding with a freighter. Damaged amidships and leaking oil, she had caught fire and the crew were abandoning ship. We turned towards the bearing given, opening up to full speed. In a few hours we were able to scramble our first chopper and soon were getting reports back. There was a twenty-foot gash at the waterline and the ship was listing. The fire wasn't serious, but we would need to land a firefighting party to deal with it. Two men had been lifted out of the water suffering from oil ingestion, and there were said to be several more who hadn't been spotted. A second chopper was soon on its way to pick up the remaining men, all of whom were found. As soon as all the casualties were accounted for and back on board, we turned and raced back towards Oman, to within helicopter flying range of its airfield where an ambulance aircraft had been requested to rendezvous to meet them. This part of the rescue was satisfactorily completed and all the survivors eventually recovered. Bulwark could now turn her attention to dealing with the tanker. By this time signals had been flying to and fro between Bulwark and the Admiralty, and a number of other warships had intercepted these and were on their way. The word 'salvage' had been mentioned, a word that is music to the ears of any sailor and something too good to miss. This was where it was extremely helpful to have a senior officer like Percy Gick who could tell everyone what to do. A destroyer arrived and was despatched to find the freighter, which it did quite soon, taking it in tow. A cruiser appeared from somewhere anxious to get in on the action. Percy had to play his cards carefully to avoid too many people becoming involved, one of whom could well be the Flag Officer Middle East with whom Percy didn't see eye to eye. He sent a message 'Personal to First Sea Lord' describing the action so far, and received a supportive reply effectively putting him in charge of the whole operation.

We caught up with the Melika once more, now wallowing a little lower in the water, and came within a few hundred feet while we set about transferring fire-fighters across by helicopter. This was the first time anyone apart from the initial helicopter crews had seen her. A naval photographer standing on our flight deck took a superb action photo of a man dangling below a helicopter, caught just as a cloud of black smoke billowed out from the deck beneath him. It was immediately sent to Reuters, arriving fortuitously on a blank news day, so made the front pages of the Daily Telegraph. A dramatic-sounding report accompanied the photo and suddenly we were catapulted onto the world stage. Having seen the outgoing signal containing the information used by the Telegraph for its piece, I could hardly believe that the printed article when I eventually saw it was anything to do with us! But that's 'news' for you. Journalists know how to sell their newspapers.

With her list, rolling gently in a long slow swell, the tanker's split in the side caused a blow-hole effect, a loud roar sounding every time she came over on that side, ejecting a spout of water from an open hatch that shot fifty feet in the air. From the blackened deck nearby there had clearly been a fire in that area, but now it had blown itself out. The remaining fires were burning in the superstructure itself, none of them seemingly very big. About twenty people went on board, soon to discover there was no power and no means of pumping water. One of our portable damage control pumps was lowered onto the ship, and within hours the fires had all been extinguished. It was time to set about salvaging the vessel.

The rules say that salvage money will be paid out after a stricken vessel is brought to a 'safe port', so Melika would have to be towed somewhere, probably to Muscat over a hundred miles away. A seagoing tug would have no problem doing this, but nowhere in the Gulf area was there such a vessel. A small warship such as a frigate would be the next choice, but the only one around was currently dealing with the freighter, which they were towing to Karachi. It was going to have to be us, and we all looked forward to the next few days with much more interest than anything else on the cruise so far.

The first job was to get a line on board, easier said than done. Because of the swell and the size of the two vessels involved, passing a line by boat was a non-starter. It would have to be the faithful choppers again. We sent over a light line by helicopter, the men on board the tanker took it up through the hause hole and round the capstan on Melika's anchor deck, passing the end back to the aircraft hovering overhead. This was then brought back to Bulwark and taken to our quarterdeck where it was wound round our own after capstan. Many hours later we had succeeded in passing a tow, securing the end safely on the tanker. With such huge vessels yawing and rolling so much, it would clearly not be possible to secure both ends without a considerable 'spring', and it was hoped to use the tanker's own anchor for this. Eventually the towing line was hooked up safely, at one time the 'spring' being supplied by over a hundred men who hung on to the cable like a huge tug of war team, while our end was secured. During this time the Melika swung far too close for comfort, and at one moment her bow lifted up right under our stern, catching the platform that protrudes just below the flight deck and wrenching part of it off. Then slowly we took up the strain and the Melika, now lying across the swell about six cables away began to turn towards us. For most of the tow that took nearly a week, she followed way off to one side, and it was not until our boarding party had struggled to winch the rudder across that she followed more closely behind us. The electrical power to move the rudder took two days to provide, starting by passing fuel drums across, needed to prime a small generator the boarding party had located high on the upper deck. Once this was running, the power from it was used to start up the main diesel generator in the machinery space, and then we were in business. It was a weird experience bringing a dead ship to life without knowing anything at all about how it works. There were no convenient handbooks to show them what to do, but they did find quite a lot of individual manuals in the chief engineer's office, which was helpful. It looked as though the chief engineer and his staff would never have expected to start up the ship from cold, probably relying on shore power and maybe contractors ashore to get it up and running. It was rather like wandering about the Marie Celeste as one endeavoured to understand how these absent people worked their ship.

On one day I managed to get over to the ship myself, sliding down a rope hanging under the hovering helicopter onto a cluttered deck that would be twenty feet below me one moment, and within jumping distance the next. As I landed the thought crossed my mind that I'd have to get back somehow! Things had settled down by the time I made my visit, and I was clearly not particularly welcome, wandering about with my camera without a specific task. I felt like a reporter who flies over a disaster zone, taking up valuable space in the aircraft.

Back on the Bulwark the engineering people were having difficulty with our own main propulsion machinery, for the ship was not designed to spend all this time with virtually no water flow beneath the hull, which meant the cooling pumps could not work efficiently. Fortunately we survived and on a bright sunny morning arrived off Muscat and with much ceremony cast off the tow and anchored the Melika in a 'safe anchorage'. Our salvage monies were secure, or so it would seem. Months later by which time we had all left the ship I heard it had not been such plain sailing after all. The lawyers had argued that Muscat was not a proper safe anchorage all the year round, and the Admiralty had to send out a large seagoing tug which brought Melika back to some European port. Before this, a naval tanker had taken off all the remaining fuel so that the ship now floated far higher in the water, but the split in her hull went down from deck level almost to her keel, so it was a tricky business towing her through the Suez Canal. Everyone on Bulwark received a share of the salvage payout, amounting to about £20 a share. The Chinese laundrymen (who remained on board until the end of the cruise) received one share each, junior ratings got about five shares, CPOs about ten. I think I got around twenty and the Captain received over 100, plus various other payments. I received my share tax-free as I was not paying UK income tax at the time the money was paid out, so that was a welcome extra.

With the Melika off our hands our time in the Gulf was over, and it was back through the Suez for us as well, the South African part of our cruise having been abandoned. As before, we headed the convoy with thirty or so fully-laden tankers behind us, and set off along this blue ribbon through the sand. Beyond the Bitter Lakes we were negotiating a bend when the ship failed to respond to her helm quickly enough, and within seconds had continued the turn until she fetched up aground, the stern swinging round and going aground on the other side. We had effectively jammed ourselves across the canal in front of a relentless phalanx of underpowered laden tankers. With nothing much he could do, the Captain sat back and watched with interest the pilot's next move. Actually, I'd never seen anyone act quite so quickly and decisively. Sirens hooted, flags shot up along all the canal signalling towers, the ship-shore radio crackled frantically, and the entire convoy was brought to a standstill, the ship immediately behind us stopping with just room to spare. A tiny tugboat came speeding down towards us and began to pull our bow round, and with help from our own engines, we were soon out of trouble. The rest of the passage passed without incident, and I expect the Canal authorities were relieved to see us disappearing through the muddy Nile isthmus waters into the Mediterranean.

We stopped for a week off Famagusta where we had a few more surprises up our sleeve. Anchored a few cables away was the Flag Officer Middle East's flagship, a shiny cruiser, very smartly turned out. Compared to her the dear old Bulwark looked as if she could do with a good smarten up, but we were on our way home, and we had been in action, hadn't we? We anchored a few cables from the flagship and immediately signals began flying to and fro. There was no love lost between Percy Gick and the Flag Officer, who was known rather disparagingly as Crap Myers. There are ways of ignoring higher authority as I learned from such experts as Earl Mountbatten at one of his splendid after dinner talks, and Percy Gick was up to most of the tricks. However, the occasion I best remember was when Crap Myers sent a somewhat cheeky signal saying he would like a sail in the Fairey Fox, having seen her careering about at high speed one day. Percy called the crew together and we hatched a plot. Almost certainly the admiral would wish to take the helm and probably he would sail between the two ships so that everyone could see him, and where the wind would be a bit fresher as it funnelled between two large hulls. This would be the ideal moment for us to put on our party piece. We set off in Fairy Fox and the Admiral's barge came over to transfer him across. I noticed he was wearing the sort of rig we would have worn at Dartmouth; perhaps he didn't possess any comfortable scruffy things. Personally I was in torn shorts (shorts always get torn sitting on cleats in a dinghy), a striped shirt and barefoot of course.

The admiral took the helm as expected while Percy shifted up to the critical mainsheet position. Off we went for an exhilarating sail and on the way back we sailed between the two ships, both of which had plenty of onlookers. A wink from Percy and we started our slow roll. When he realised what might be about to happen, the admiral roared, "Steady on, you'll have her over!" But he was too late. We did one of our finest slow rolls, scudding across the upturned bottom as she turned, and getting in again on the other side, hardly any of us getting wet. I looked back to observe how the admiral had managed, to see him sitting there, soaked to the skin, hair plastered down over his face, still gripping the tiller and with a murderous look on his face. I think he must have gone right round with the boat. A loud roar of appreciation came from the onlookers on both ships. Was it my imagination or was the one from Bulwark a roar of approval whereas the one from the flagship a roar of derision?

I'd heard there was not a lot to do in Famagusta except spend money, something I was perpetually short of, and so much of my spare time was spent sailing around in one of the ship's dinghies. On one occasion I was out alone when a swimmer grabbed the hull and swung himself aboard. It was none other than Percy, enjoying himself as usual. We sailed around for a while, then he somersaulted backwards into the water when we'd got near some of his friends. It was here someone even tried a novel way to water ski. They set off in the normal fashion, skiing behind one of our fast motor boats, then the line was passed to a helicopter overhead which took over the tow, but the helicopter's downdraft made it difficult to stay up for long. Not a lot of people can say they've skied behind a helicopter but I have a photograph to prove it.

Eventually we had to move on. Our next visit was to Malta where in Grand Harbour we met another carrier of our class, the Centaur. Even two ships of the same class are never identical in all respects, the individual shipbuilders installing the services and placing minor fittings without the aid of detailed plans. Late one evening I joined a group of officers at the jetty waiting for a dghaisa to take us back to the ship, and was somewhat concerned at how many of us the dghaisa-man managed to pack into his boat. A number of them had heavy golf clubs and the freeboard was only inches. With great relief I clambered up the companionway steps, saluted at the top and made my way to my cabin just thankful I'd survived the trip across, for surely the dghaisa would have gone straight to the bottom had she taken in water with so many bags of golf clubs for ballast. Noting only that the passageway along to my cabin flat seemed to have been painted whilst I was ashore, I entered my cabin to find someone else asleep in my bunk. It was only at this point that it also registered in my mind that a number of ventilation trunks, big bulkhead-mounted switchboxes and other fittings all looked wrong. I had, of course, stepped aboard the wrong carrier. Sheepishly I had to wait for the arrival of another dghaisa to take me across to Bulwark not far away.

Our final stop was at Gibraltar for swordfish steaks and sticky-greens and the welcome collection of mail. Patricia, who had spent most of the year back at work, dreary and pedestrian, wrote to say since handing in her notice a second time when Bulwark was originally expected home, she had spent time at St. Mawes with my parents, also with Jane and her family. She was now home again and looking forward to meeting me on the dockside, ready to take me back to High Winds and some leave. I could hardly believe my life in Bulwark was about to come to an end and a more normal existence living in a quiet house would soon take over.

We went back to 'blues', the heavier uniform prickly and restricting. The sea changed colour to the murkier green-blue of the Channel and then, early one morning, we sighted St. Catherine's point and then were entering Portsmouth Harbour, a long paying-off pennant flying from the masthead. Standing proudly on the flight deck in my new Hong Kong uniform, in line across the ship up in the bows, I searched the faces on the jetty for a familiar one. It began to spot with rain and, within minutes, I could feel a constriction across my back. The shoulders of my new uniform were moving—the stitches beginning to shrink! I stood smartly at ease, hands behind back, desperately hoping we would be able to get below before my uniform fell apart. The first line was thrown ashore and secured. "Hands fall out" was piped. Moments later Patricia was in my arms and everyone was talking at once.

11

A Trip to Australia

We drove to High Winds to unpack and spent the day talking. Well, most of it. Next day we went by train to Cornwall. 845 squadron having disembarked to the Naval air station at Culdrose, near Helston, but in a few months my time with it would come to an end. Many of the aircrew would change and the aircraft were due for upgrading. It was an unsettling period.

During this time Patricia was installed at Sea Lanes and I was living in at Culdrose, getting back as often as possible. I found an early morning ferry, a workers' commuter launch, that left St. Mawes for Falmouth docks each morning, and from there to Culdrose by bus was possible. My parents went away for a couple of weeks, so we had Sea Lanes to ourselves. This was a truly relaxing fortnight with a proper place of our own, free to do as we wished and just enjoy one another. It was lovely being there without being continuously aware of disapproving vibes emanating from my father. When they returned, Patricia stayed at a guesthouse in Helston for a short spell, memorable only for the bath that had lost all its enamel on the bottom, so that it was painful in the extreme to slide up and down! I've seen better baths doing service as cattle drinking troughs.

I was wondering where my next appointment would be, hoping I would be due for a shore spell with a chance to live with my wife. I saw an announcement in the AFOs (Admiralty Fleet Orders) stating that volunteers for loan service in the Australian Navy would be considered. We talked it over. This would be an accompanied trip for two or three years. I applied, then spent the next few weeks wondering whether I'd done the right thing. Accompanied jobs overseas were few and far between, and it was unlikely there would be another opportunity. I was only too conscious of Patricia hovering around at home, unable to settle down to either one thing or another. She had been properly messed up over Bulwark's return to the UK having first expected us back in August, then having it delayed a couple more times until we at last made it in early November. Her own mother had spent much of her married life away from Leslie when he was serving for long spells at sea or unaccompanied on the China Station. A safe accompanied overseas posting sounded wonderful. But I would be two years or more out of the mainstream electrical branch, out of sight and probably out of mind. Promotion prospects would very likely be affected. Would this be a sideways move, one taken all too easily but a one-way move I would later regret? But those couple of weeks alone at Sea Lanes had been very special. We just hoped I had done the right thing.

One of our pilots had discovered where I was living. We often had helicopters fly along the coast, the other side of the estuary from Sea Lanes. One Saturday while I was there, Dougie Hale on his way back to Culdrose flew over the area, spotted me in the garden and turned to hover overhead waving. The smell of hot exhaust blasted down accompanied by the familiar deafening noise. I loved it, but my father certainly did not. He came storming out shaking his fist, yelling at me to send them away, (how? I wondered…). I glimpsed our dustbin lid bowling down the drive and across the road, followed by one of his newly planted rose bushes. Perhaps it was not a good idea to have told anyone where we were.

A letter arrived from the Appointments Officer. I was appointed to HMS Collingwood for courses, followed by HMS President for transit, then to HMAS Kuttabul (the Sydney base establishment) for loan service with the Royal Australian Navy. There was no going back now. Next day came a welcome pack from the Australian Naval Attaché's office in Bush House in The Strand suggesting we both visit in the week before taking up the Collingwood appointment. The wheels had begun to turn. After Christmas Patricia made her final visit back to Lee-on-Solent, and I settled down to a few days living in the Culdrose wardroom awaiting the arrival of my relief. Patricia had been rather unhappy these last few weeks, with lots of unexplained depressive spells and feeling weepy. It wasn't helped by my father's attitude, which had been to treat her as someone who was trying to share his son. Back at Lee she went to see her doctor who confirmed the reason for her emotions. It must have been initiated during that blissful fortnight while we had Sea Lanes to ourselves. In view of the impending voyage to the other side of the world we decided to say nothing!

The day for 845's embarkation drew nearer. My relief arrived and was to spend a couple of weeks with me before taking over. We had a few days at Culdrose before the Squadron embarked in Centaur for the Med. The passage to Gib in January plunging through the usual grey stormy seas of the Bay had my relief curled up in misery. This was a different breed of officer, one that had not enjoyed the rigours of Dartmouth and Devonshire. I felt sorry for him, his first time at sea. However we were soon in the Med and he felt better at once. Three days later I said goodbye and stepped into a Skyraider for my first fixed-wing takeoff from a carrier. As we circled briefly overhead I looked down on the tiny postage stamp that was Centaur's gently heaving flight deck and realised how it must seem to a pilot flying over the sea with fuel for just a few minutes flying time. Twenty minutes later we landed at Gib's airport, the runway huge in comparison with an aircraft carrier, and I said goodbye to my Fleet Air Arm friends for the last time. A few hours later Patricia met me at Gatwick.

At last we were together albeit in the spare room at High Winds, but we had time with one another, went shopping together, were able to socialise as a couple. During this period I came to know Patricia's parents really well, and remembering the adage that one grows like one's parents as time goes on, I was content with what I saw. If Patricia in her old age was like her parents were now, then that was just fine. I was a lucky man. There was, of course, a But; there nearly always is. This one concerned her father who laughingly showed us the High Winds attic bulging at the seams with all the useful junk that just might be required one day. My own parents never kept anything once it had ceased to be immediately useful with the result that they never had anything that was unexpectedly wanted. Not so Leslie. If a little job needed doing, then he would rummage around in the attic, in the back junk room or in the garage, until he found what he wanted. Then it would be adapted to suit and another makeshift solution would be provided, all without the need to go shopping. It seemed marvellous. We used to laugh as he inspected the dustbin each week to ensure nothing that might have a use in the future was about to be thrown out. Of course, I never realised the extent to which this trend might visit us in the future: Patricia had inherited the same trait.

I visited a seamstress in Portsmouth who made me a poor man's kilt for £11 (I still wear it), for we were now going Scottish Country Dancing once or sometimes twice a week. We called in to the Australian Naval Attaché's office and were warmly welcomed as one of his flock. He gave us a pile of information about the country and the RAN. While we were there, several visitors popped their heads round the door asking for 'the usual'. This turned out to be a case or so of Australian duty-free wine. The whole of one long wall of his office was a floor-to-ceiling cupboard full of wine, six bottles deep, and a lovely sight it was too. Clearly a vital part of his job was to dispense the indispensable!

The days dragged on until in mid March it was time to depart for Tilbury to take passage in the SS Orcades. Patricia by this time was over three months pregnant and her hormones were playing havoc with her. Nothing showed and she didn't want to worry her parents, so we had said nothing. The boat train left from Liverpool Street station on a gloomy damp day, and clattered its way slowly through the wastes of East London to Tilbury. I'd heard it said that Tilbury was the arsehole of London, that visitors should never arrive that way, and looking out of the window I could well understand how this saying came about. However, our arrival on board soon changed all that. Unaccustomed to walking up a covered gently sloping gangway with hordes of porters relieving us of all our luggage and met by smiling faces at the top, it very soon became apparent that here was the other face of 'cruising'. We were shown our first class cabin and found our way round this very comfortable carpeted accommodation. It would take us over four weeks to travel to Sydney, just about time to work our way through the dinner menu. Yes, this was going to be good. And free: once again the Navy were paying.

Initially it was not quite so good for poor Patricia who was soon confined to her bunk where she remained for several days feeling quite awful. We didn't realise this was probably as much due to her pregnancy as to the ship's motion, so ignorant were we as to what she should be expecting. Eventually she surfaced and we began to enjoy the cruise. We had been put at the table of the Deputy Purser, a useful string-pulling officer who had no doubt scrutinised the passenger list selecting anybody who looked as if they might be remotely interesting. A Royal Navy Officer sounded better than a plain 'Mr' so there we were. In three days we were at Gibraltar, and once again I went ashore there, but this time with Patricia by my side. We did a quick sortie through the town, then climbed steps behind the houses to get up onto the side of the rock, from where we followed the track to the top, spending a little time at the Barbary ape lookout where we met other passengers who had arrived in taxis. We then went over the summit and traversed the ridge, looking down onto the old water catchment area on the far side. On the way back we stopped at the yacht club for a drink. It was a warm sunny day, but as it was Good Friday the place was quiet with nothing much going on.

A couple of days later we stopped at Naples to embark a number of 'ten pound' immigrants. This was at a time when the Australian Government were wanting to increase the population, so would pay the passage for people wishing to emigrate from their own country and become 'New Australians', charging them just £10. From our secluded deck in the first class part of the ship we looked down on some of these people embarking, their total possessions tied up in bags or cardboard boxes, as they set out on the start of their new life. Later in the day we visited Pompeii and Herculaneum, sharing a taxi with a Greek couple and their bambino. Alas, we were unable to take the magical trip to Capri and climb the 777 stone steps to Axel Münthe's house at the top.

Next it was to Navarino Bay where we stopped for an hour to take on a lot more ten-pound immigrants who came out in boats. At Port Said, we were besieged by boat traders and embarked the inevitable gully-gully man who was allowed to take passage with us through the canal. During the night Orcades grounded briefly on some obstruction. I kept quiet. I wasn't going to admit being the jinx, but I did wonder how many more times I would have to traverse the Suez Canal before having a clear transit without hitting anything.

It was a hot sticky passage through the Red Sea, where by this time we enjoyed our days lined up on deck in comfortable steamer chairs. Apart from a couple of dolphins and lots of flying fish there was little to see. We had a brief stop in Aden in the evening, just time to visit Steamer Point to buy some duty free camera bits, then I took Patricia round to the Tarshyne Club for a drink. It seemed strange visiting all my old haunts with Patricia instead of the Naval lads. The places seemed quieter, and we were treated quite differently. I was reminded of an acquaintance who has a small hardware shop, also a market stall for two days a week. She tells me her customers are completely different in the two places, or rather she treats them completely differently, calling her market customers 'dear' or 'love' whereas the shop customers are 'sir' or 'madam'. It was like that at the Tarshyne Club where it was immediately realised we were two paying passengers off the big ship.

We now had several days on passage before the next stop, once more in Ceylon, although this time we would visit Columbo and come alongside. The Orcades first class swimming pool was small without much deck space around it, but most of the first class passengers were somewhat elderly and didn't wish to swim, so a few of the younger people had it to themselves most of the time. When in harbour, the pool was drained to reveal a large hatch cover at the bottom. When this was lifted it gave access to the main luggage hold.

We had contacted a Mr Pillai in Colombo, friend of a naval padre of our acquaintance who had been a Methodist minister in Ceylon before joining the Navy. We were invited to spend the day with his family and be shown something of the island. He was a Tamil with the splendid title of Chief of Prisons. He met us off the ship with his official car, a tall man wearing an absurd pair of shorts with such wide legs that they looked more like a skirt, his thin brown legs protruding below encased in smart white stockings and polished shoes. This visit was a great success, and we had time to go to the botanical gardens, where wonderfully colourful orchids clustered high in the branches of magnificent trees. We visited Kandi, location of one of Mr Pillai's prisons, and drove through savannah and well cultivated plantations. There were a lot of elephants, commonly used in Ceylon for moving or dragging heavy loads. From a river bridge we looked down on several who were enjoying their daily bath, mahouts splashing around in the muddy water with brooms to scrub their backs. At the Pillai's house, a large airy colonial-style building with mesh screens in place of glass in the windows, we met their two willowy children, exquisitely polite and attentive, and enjoyed a true curry meal made with the genuine ingredients, fresh and delicious. We returned on board in the evening to find a troupe of Kandian dancers was performing in the ship's ballroom, a lovely graceful performance.

Next day we crossed the equator, a humdrum line-crossing ceremony put on for the benefit of the children on board, not a patch on the wonderful shows arranged by the Royal Navy where the Chief Stoker or some-such appears with a great red beard made from teased out sisal rope.

Another naval man, Bill Owen, was travelling out with his family to live in Sydney, where he was to take over command of a submarine. We chummed up with them and were also joined by an Australian of about our age. This young man was on his own and returning back to what he described as his 'homestead' a few hundred miles north of Sydney. When we enquired what he did for a living, he said he looked after a few sheep, as one does in those parts.

"How many?" I asked, thinking of a Cumbrian hill farmer we'd met who managed eighty sheep.

"Dunno for sure," he replied, "About 77,000 at the last count. The sheep station is seventy odd thousand acres." Clearly they did things in a different way down under.

The ship arrived at Freemantle in Western Australia. Patricia was not feeling at all well that day and declined to go ashore. I went with one of the other passengers, taking a bus to Perth, all red corrugated iron roofs and a lot of Victorian-style wrought iron balustrading. We walked most of the way back through green parkland. The sun was blazing overhead, fiercer than I remember out in Aden.

Next stop was Melbourne. We crossed the South Australian bight pursued by albatrosses, an unforgettable sight with their enormous wingspan enabling them to soar inches above the wave crests without so much as a wingbeat. The wind got up in the night, and there was a most expensive sound of breaking crockery coming from beneath us. For the first time, Orcades rolled and creaked, with thumps from the heavy seas breaking against the side of the ship just outside our cabin. In the morning we discovered that an elderly lady had fallen and broken her leg attempting to go down the stairs during the night. She was the wife of the boss of Royal Doulton, the company which supplied the ship's crockery, and her husband was both distressed about his wife's accident but couldn't disguise his delight about the weather we'd been through which would be good for business. Entering Port Philip Bay involves going through a whirlpooly tidal disturbance at the narrow entrance, but in a ship the size of Orcades this was hardly noticeable. We spent the afternoon walking around the botanical gardens in Melbourne, a favourite park right in the centre of the city, with the River Yarra running around two sides.

The ship entered Sydney harbour in thick fog, so we were not to see the magnificent harbour until we were almost up to the bridge, where we docked at Circular Quay. No opera house in those days; just a somewhat rundown area where the ferries for Manly left and the occasional large ship such as the Orcades berthed.

A diminutive smiling RAN rating who answered to the name of LEM Jones met us with a large van bearing Commonwealth number plates. He was the driver and general factotum for a small naval unit at Woolloomoolloo, a Sydney waterside suburb half a mile or so from the main naval base at Garden Island. He took our meagre luggage and ourselves to a hotel in Kings Cross near to the naval unit, then later collected us to meet his boss who apparently knew what I was to do.

The hotel was quite awful. It was unbearably hot and airless, smelt of stale beer and old fried food, was dark and grubby and utterly soulless. We would stay there until we'd found somewhere more permanent. Jones duly arrived and took us to meet Commander Bleak, a passed-over RN commander who was seeing out the last of his time in the RN heading up this unit before retiring. He was a miserable sod, never smiled, mistrusted everyone and was the perfect example of how not to run an organisation if you need cooperation. All the men in the unit ignored him, which of course made him worse. Apparently between the time the RAN had asked for a Fleet Air Arm technical man for a two-year loan and my arrival they had decided to fill the post with one of their own people, so I was to be attached to Harry Bleak's unit instead, but only after a couple of months at Nowra holding the fort until the RAN man was installed. However, I would spend my first week in Sydney and that would give us a chance to find somewhere to live there. The Woolloomoolloo unit was known as the Electrical Equipment and Trials Unit, or EETU for short, their job being to oversee the building of RAN ships at either the Sydney builders' yard on Cockatoo Island upstream of the Harbour Bridge, or at the dockyard near Melbourne. Generally each yard had one frigate under construction and I was arriving just at the right time to become involved with them both. So, after all my Fleet Air Arm time, it looked as if I was now to transfer back to ships without any conversion or update courses. Perhaps it wouldn't matter.

Our second day in Australia was Anzac Day; quite a shock introduction to the country. It seemed the whole population spent the morning walking about in their best suits, medals pinned on breasts, attending memorial services around the city. By lunchtime they were exhausted so repaired to various drinking dens to recover. By late evening they were all, to a man, legless. Kings Cross, appeared to be the centre of all this debauchery. We returned to our horrible little hotel holding on to each other for safety, crunched over the cockroaches and locked ourselves in our stifling room. By next morning it was all over and normal life resumed. We were glad this only happened once a year.

Arriving more or less penniless in an unknown country on the other side of the world was somewhat daunting. I wasn't a free man, and was expected to start work immediately, so most of the trappings of finding somewhere to live, opening a bank account, finding one's feet generally, this fell on Patricia's shoulders. Our first visit was to Mavis, a remote friend of a friend of Leslie's who had come out to Sydney some twenty years previously, married and settled here. She invited us to her home on the harbour north shore where they lived in the garden flat of a largish block of flats across from Circular Quay. We met her husband Guy, a largish bluff Australian who, it turned out, owned the entire apartment block and lived off the proceeds. He was in the process of building himself a weekend bolthole thirty miles north, high up on a cliff-side overlooking the ocean. Mavis recommended her gynaecologist with whom Patricia signed up. When she visited his surgery in Macquarie Street for her first check-up, she was impressed by the opulence and the way they did things down under, not discovering until the bills started coming in that he was the equivalent of a private Harley Street consultant. The Navy swallowed hard when presented with these bills, and in the normal suspicious way would only pay the UK going rate so that we had the find the difference—not easy when we were virtually broke. Mavis's husband kept five Great Danes, so the visit to their flat was far from peaceful. When I asked what happened to the neighbourhood dogs when this lot were out for a walk, he seemed mystified. "Dunno. I don't think there are any neighbourhood dogs in these parts." I wonder why?

Harry Bleak's number two was a New Zealander I'd met at Collingwood years before, where he was one of the instructors. There was also a quiet RN branch officer there, John Brunger, who suggested Patricia and I should start house hunting on the north shore, where it was far more pleasant to live, and a good deal cheaper. The Royal Navy would only reimburse us with an amount equivalent to what we would pay for service quarters back at home, so we had to be careful with our pennies. It meant, in effect, that we were obliged to live over twenty miles away. It took us four days, starting at Manly, then moving up to Curl Curl, Dee Why, Collaroy and eventually settling for a ground floor flat in a well-built brick house in Narrabeen. The owners, the Dunbars, lived over the top, and the floors were of cast concrete, so not a sound was heard from above. We had to go through the strange ritual of signing a contract in front of a solicitor, who was required to make sure we understood what we were letting ourselves in for. At the time there was a law that landlords were not allowed to refuse to have tenants simply because they had children. If the landlord didn't want children in his house, then he had to make delicate enquiries about one's circumstances without actually asking the question. Mrs Dunbar did not want children, and set about quizzing us, not doing so very effectively. She should, perhaps, have expected two young people in their twenties to start a family some time. Throughout the interview Patricia held in her tummy convincingly, we were accepted and next morning thankfully set about moving in.

Two days later I was off to Nowra. I found it a dreary little airfield surrounded by eucalyptus forest with a few 'temporary' buildings clustered to one side. My job was to look after all the electrical ground installations, which included not only the runway lights and so on, but also electrics of the married quarters in the nearby town. I had the occasional use of a Land Rover and was warned to watch out for kangaroos when driving. It was June and mid-winter on this side of the world. We were twenty miles inland, just far enough for the temperature at night to plummet down to freezing and here I was, sleeping in an unheated, uninsulated wooden hut. By day when the sun shone it shot up to the late seventies, and was very pleasant. At weekends I joined a car pool where four of us raced back to Sydney early on a Friday afternoon, assembling on Monday morning at about six for the drive back. After a few weeks I found a second-hand Morris Minor and was then able to take my turn with the ferrying. If there's one thing we really liked about our new country it was the attitude to the weekend. Whatever happened, a good weekend, free from work, was always achieved.

We discovered a freshwater lake inland from our Narrabeen house, which became our special place. It had a good path all the way round, where for most of the way it was fringed with birch trees and fairly open. Towards the middle stretched a sand bar usually occupied by large white pelicans, and in the trees we would hear bellbirds and met all sorts of strange insects and flowers. Ants came in several sizes, from huge monsters over an inch long to little fellows that packed a punch so painful that one dared not safely sit down anywhere. Just as well, as there were funnel-web spiders and other nasties, not to mention a number of snakes, all poisonous to some degree. But it was quiet, very therapeutic after a hectic day, and remained one of our favourite places. Patricia had made contact with the Royal Naval Wives Association, an informal group formed to help new families arriving to settle down. It was too easy to think of Australia as just a little bit of England simply because they spoke English, but like Americans who also speak a sort of English, they are different and one has to realise this before dropping too many bricks. With her Naval upbringing, Patricia was adept at settling in to a new area quickly.

We drove up the coast about twenty miles north and called in to see Mavis's Guy. His new weekend retreat was a most ambitious building, cantilevered out from a near vertical cliff-face using great baulks of 'Ironwood', a fiendishly hard timber that will blunt just about any saw. He'd reclaimed this from a jetty that was being demolished (maybe it was Guy who did the demolishing, working at nights...) He'd reached the stage where it was safe to live in, and was in the process of fitting out the bathroom when we called. We noticed the remains of his lunch snack in the living room, the skeleton of a whole smoked salmon and a chicken carcass. In the corner of the room was a box with about twenty empty beer bottles. As I said, Guy was a big feller, really tough to have managed this project single handed, and made me feel extremely inadequate. Here we saw our first kookaburra, which came down to see if there were any bits of chicken going. It seemed quite incongruous that this bird, which is a kingfisher, should live off meat when it can find any and have the most ghastly raucous, laughing call. But that's Australia for you.

After a few weeks Patricia couldn't keep her pregnancy a secret from Mrs Dunbar any longer, and with some trepidation broke the news to her. Unexpectedly Mrs Dunbar sounded delighted, and offered to babysit for us whenever we might need it. She knew us by now, aware we were only here for a two-year fixed term, and maybe only disliked older children who might be disruptive and noisy. We were so pleased, and Patricia at long last started to wear her maternity clothes!

Mr Dunbar had a joinery workshop at the end of the small garden in which he made window and doorframes from Australian maple, an exotic, easily worked and durable timber. He gave me some offcuts and on Saturdays while his staff were off, I was allowed the run of the workshop to make small items for our flat. But most weekends, we were off exploring as far as we could in our little Morris, meeting 'tame' aborigines who sold us proper boomerangs made from ironwood and taught us how to throw one. We visited such touristy spots as the Katoomba Caves and took a ride on a terrifying looking cable car that went out over a gorge in the blue mountains, so named because of the blue haze that hung over them from the eucalyptus oil which scented the air. We passed a roadside beekeeper's apiary, the hives piled high with up to twenty supers on each one, the air thick with flying bees. He sold honey in 60lb drums at A£3 a drum, so we bought one which lasted most of our time out there. We also bought oranges by the sackful whenever we passed an orange grove.

At long last my early Monday morning trips to Nowra came to an end and I rejoined the boys at the EETU in Woolloomooloo (someone asked me once about how to spell that name; think about it...). I joined up with John Brunger and we took turns driving in on the dual carriageway and across the famous bridge, six lanes one way and two the other, a tidal flow system with the most ingenious way of altering the lane direction depending on the time of day. Harry Bleak did not improve on further acquaintance so, like the others, I just ignored him. Patricia had been having some very uncomfortable times with her pregnancy, and was visiting the Macquarie Street clinic every week now. Mr MacBeth, the gynaecologist, assured her all was well, and she could look forward to a normal birth in a couple of months. He never said anything about pre-natal clinics and Patricia never attended one. Perhaps there weren't such things in those days? Apart from visiting Mr MacBeth a few times, she spoke to no medical person about what to expect at childbirth. Her mother was on the other side of the world, and the only people she talked to were our Naval acquaintances who had children. Mr MacBeth went off on holiday unannounced and two days later, at 6.0 a.m. on 4th August 1959 to be precise, Patricia woke complaining of intense pains. The birth wasn't due for another six weeks, so it couldn't be that, could it? It was: two hours later Susan Elizabeth was born, weighing in at 4lb 8ozs, a tiny bundle, somewhat jaundiced, whom I was shown through the plate glass window of the hospital premmy ward. Patricia was sitting up in bed, a broad smile on her face, but at that point hadn't seen the baby. They kept Susan in an incubator in the premmy ward for ten days, Eventually the two of them were allowed home, and it was only then that Patricia was able to hold her new baby, breast feed her and properly 'mother' her. During this time Susan's weight had dropped to 4lb before picking up again. Fortunately Patricia hadn't wasted her time while I had been at Nowra and had sewn up large numbers of nappies, accumulated lots of baby clothes, many of them cast-offs from other naval wives, and acquired a lovely old-fashioned pram with large wheels and a hood. I made a parasol that could be positioned over the pram to keep off the sun.

We quickly found that in Australia a young family is welcomed anywhere. Wishing to cross the road with the pram, cars would squeal to a stop and wave us across with a soppy smile from the leather-faced Aussie driver. We were invited to spend an afternoon with a well-established English couple who had been living in the Sydney suburbs for some twenty years. It was a lovely place with a huge garden, shaded by an enormous jacaranda tree in full flower, under which we parked the pram with Susan, now several weeks old and looking more like a normal bonny baby now that her premature birth was behind her. We entered their large sitting room where the drinks were. At one end was a knot of young men whom Patricia naturally made a beeline for. I, equally naturally of course, made a beeline for a group of attractive young ladies at the other end. Amid hoots of laughter and cries of "Pommies!" we discovered too late that the men were clustered around a beer barrel and the women were around someone's baby. The situation was saved when Patricia wheeled in Susan, whereupon both groups joined up to coo at her.

Our milkman at Narrabeen, a youngish man with a sun-worn lined face, always wore shorts and ran everywhere, accompanied by a 'chink, chink' from the bottles in his metal crate, so we knew when he was coming. One morning the chinking stopped, so we looked out of the door to see him standing bent over the pram outside the back door, smiling with a soft dreamy look in his eyes. "Jeeze! Sweet little bugger, isn't he!" he said to us and chinked off on his rounds. He used to stop by every morning after that to gaze at our baby. I hope he soon married and had lots of bonny children of his own. Susan was feeding every couple of hours or so, leaving poor Patricia worn out. One advantage of breast-feeding from the father's point of view is that he doesn't lose so much sleep!

By this time we were regularly attending St. Stephen's Presbyterian church in Macquarie Street in Sydney. We had tried the local Narrabeen and Collaroy churches, but didn't find them very stimulating. We'd heard the St. Stephen's service broadcast quite often on the local Sydney radio station 2UE, and liked the sound of it. The minister at that time was Gordon Powell, a charismatic preacher who filled his large church to capacity, with another few hundred in the crypt below who joined in the service on CCTV. One had to be there half an hour before the start to get a seat. They had a crèche where we left Susan, but an hour away from Mum was almost an hour too long, and she exercised her lungs every bit as well as the loudest singers in the church above. During quiet passages in the service we thought we could hear the familiar bawling through several feet of stone walls. After a while we felt too guilty about leaving her with the patient but distraught helpers, so stopped going, but by this time she had been baptised and accepted into the church.

The frigate under construction at Williamstown Yard, near Melbourne, was reaching the stage where equipment was being installed which would soon need commissioning, so our unit was required to visit. I would catch the 'breakfast' plane from Sydney Smith airport, a nice quiet turbo-prop Vanguard, which left at 8.00 a.m., served a nice breakfast in flight, landing in Melbourne an hour later. A naval car whisked me to the dockyard where I spent the day in the ship and at meetings, returning on the 'teatime flight' in time to get home again at a reasonable hour. If the meetings were protracted, I would spend the night at the Commercial Travellers' Club in the centre of Melbourne, an extraordinary old-fashioned men's club left behind in a time-warp that hardly ever had anyone staying, but was extremely comfortable, cheap and would put on a good breakfast.

It was while staying here that I received a phone call from Patricia in the middle of the night telling me she'd had a telegram saying my mother had suffered a stroke from which she was unlikely to recover. It finished with 'Category A air travel recommended', whatever that meant, but it suggested I ought to travel to her bedside as soon as possible before she died. I phoned the duty officer at Melbourne headquarters who organised a plane ticket for me to pick up at Sydney's Kingsford Smith airport, then I arranged for Patricia to meet me there with some civilian clothes. It was not until I was sitting in a Qantas flight on my way to the UK via refuelling stops at Darwin, Bangkok, Singapore, Calcutta, Karachi, Cairo, Athens, Rome, Nice and Frankfurt that I realised firstly that I had completely forgotten to inform Harry Bleak, and more importantly, this flight in a tired converted Super Fortress Bomber was going to take three days and I hadn't got so much as a spare pair of underpants in my hand luggage. At Heathrow, the slick naval machinery swung into action, I was met off the aircraft, taken by car to Paddington station and handed a return warrant for the train to Truro. A very quiet father met me, and I found Jane also at Sea Lanes when I arrived. Mother had been taken to the small hospital in Falmouth but had not regained consciousness. They had been told she would be very unlikely to do so. This emerged after several daily visits when a bit more of the prognosis emerged. Thus after several visits we were fully prepared that another stroke any moment would in all probability carry her off. It happened a day later, just after the three of us visited, leaving us both immensely sad yet relieved that she hadn't recovered sufficiently to survive as a cabbage. Jane was pregnant again, two years after the birth of her twins Fiona and Judy. Peter had stayed at home to look after them. It was a very quiet funeral, with just a few friends and us three members of the family present. Afterwards I set off back to Australia, sad but resigned, remembering my father's drawn face as, looking extremely lonely, he silently bid me goodbye at Truro Station. I wondered perhaps whether he might also die before our Australian tour was over.

Patricia met me at Sydney Smith. I had in my luggage some tins of Lyons Ground Coffee, something we missed at Narrabeen; also some tape recordings and a tin of talcum powder. The customs man pored over these for some time, convinced I was trying to smuggle in something I shouldn't. He thought there might be pornographic material on the tapes, drugs hidden in the talcum powder and goodness knows what else sealed up in the tins of coffee. Patricia had brought Susan with her, wrapping her in a blanket and laying her, still asleep, on the back seat of the car. She left the window open an inch, but locked the car of course. This seemed safe enough at the time as she reckoned she only had to pop in, collect me and pop out again. This was years before baby snatching was something people did, so such a thought never entered her head. She had to wait quite a while until the wretched customs man had cleared me, then we groped our way through the poorly lit car park to the car, to see an empty back seat. No Susan. Panic gripped us. It was fully half a minute before one of us noticed a tiny bundle in the floor well. She must have rolled over and simply fallen off the seat without waking. Phew! That was the longest half-minute of our lives. We were so upset by that little incident that she forgot to tell me that when she called in to the office to explain about me going off to the UK, Bleak had gone for her with all his vitriolic nastiness. She took it on the chin, anxious not to upset me at such a time, but never forgave him.

A week or two later I was back in Melbourne once more, and on the return trip which my companion suggested we take with the alternative airline, Ansett-ANA, we had what I considered an uneventful flight, except that he went to the toilet at the back of the aircraft and was gone for nearly half an hour. He returned and took his seat without comment, but I noticed a slight secretive smile and wondered what he'd been up to. Much later it came out that one of the airhostesses fancied him, and on flights such as this one they often spent time together crushed into the diminutive toilet. Heaven knows how they managed…

On a future visit to Melbourne I came to know an English naval couple in the RAN who invited me to stay at their house in Frankston, a few miles south bordering Port Philip Bay. They had two young children who gave me an insight of what we might be in for in a year or two should we expand our own family. It was lovely to spend a few days with a normal family in their own home. In the hottest time of the year we went down to the nearby beach for a swim. You might think this merely involved picking up a towel and walking the couple of hundred yards but, Oh no! This had to be planned like a military operation. First one got ready for the bathe, flip-flops on feet, towel in hand, just inside the flyscreen door. Then the car was driven to the door, someone shouted "Go!" and we'd make a dive for the car, shut all the doors and start frantically swatting the hundred or so flies that had got in with us. On arrival at the beach which was deserted, we all leapt out and sprinted for the sea, frantically wading about fifty yards out into the muddy shallow water until we had left the flies behind us. This is where the other bathers were. The flies knew exactly how far they could safely travel over the water and still be able to return again, and clouds of them swarmed just inside this line ready for the first person to make a dash for the shore. The fly problem was always bad in summer, but for a few weeks in the hottest time of the year it was almost unbearable.

Later, the following year, I would stay here en route to the Naval Gunnery School at Crib Point where we sometimes had new gunnery equipment that required commissioning. My main memories of the wardroom at the gunnery school were in wintertime with the temperature outside below freezing, when the beer dispensing machine was still set to deliver beer at a temperature only a degree or two higher. How anyone managed to sink quantities of such a cold liquid in those conditions beats me.

As we neared Christmas back at Narrabeen so the temperatures crept higher. Ninety in the shade became the norm, and as we were right on the coast, it only fell away to about seventy at night. The main advantage of having the beach coming right up to the lane at the back of the house was the breeze. In the mornings it wafted offshore for a few hours before dying away at midday. Then in the early afternoons it got up again, a salty onshore breeze that became fresher as the day wore on, making the high temperatures quite acceptable. Patricia fell into the habit of completing her chores in the morning, then spending much of the afternoon on the beach with Susan and sometimes with one or two other naval wives and their children. I would finish work at about four each afternoon and join her half an hour later.

On one particularly hot day when it was heavy and sultry, the heat sapping any energy one might have, Harry Bleak who seemed to have nothing to do that day, announced he was going out and would not be returning that afternoon. To me that meant he was off home, so I gave him a half-hour start then left the office as well. On my way over the traffic-congested Harbour Bridge, creeping along in my lane, I noticed something familiar about the car in the next lane. As I got closer, I realised it was Harry Bleak's, and there was nothing I could do to avoid coming up alongside; worse, my lane then slowed and for a while the two of us were going along side by side. I kept looking straight ahead, but was conscious of his eyes boring into me as we drove along. Thankfully, the lanes soon diverged and I was out of range. I felt I knew what it was like to be a hobbit, the Evil Eye upon me. Needless to say, next morning I was at the office half an hour early but he was there before me, yelling as I tried to slink past, to come into his office. A month later he left rather suddenly and returned to the UK without so much as a goodbye to anyone. No one discovered what had happened, but we all hoped for the worst. He was replaced eventually by the nicest man one could wish to meet, and from then on the unit looked up and we all of us enjoyed our time together, working far better as a team.

I used to have lunch in the wardroom mess at HMAS Kuttabul, a smallish shore base attached to the dockyard. I first went there on the day I arrived to start work, to be introduced by our subby to the senior RAN officer, a rear-admiral. The admiral was very chatty and treated me as just another socially met bloke, which I found a little disarming, having been used to the RN reserve when speaking to officers of such high status. The admiral said something cheeky to the subby who responded with a "Why, you bastard, you wouldn't dare do that!" while I looked on aghast, wondering if I had just been a witness to the man's last act before being locked up. But no, the admiral grinned and gave him a playful punch.

At lunch one day, a somewhat loud-voiced 'old-and-bold' branch officer saw the RC padre come in. "Ah, here's the black bishop," he called out (the RC padre was always dressed in sombre black). "And how are your black sheep, bishop?" I quickly came to enjoy the banter and soon gave as good as I got. The problem was meeting people who weren't used to it and might take it the wrong way. This usually only happened when an RN ship was visiting. One such was a Type 15 frigate, which docked at Garden Island, and I swept aboard with a couple of my chums to introduce them to British beer. It seemed strange to be walking up the gangway boarding a Royal Navy vessel, with its different coloured grey paint (The RAN's grey is quite greeny in comparison) and to be met by a quartermaster with a Portsmouth dialect. In the wardroom my chum carefully inspected the can of Worthington best bitter. "Which end of the can do you open her?" he enquired.

Apart from looking after the two new frigates under construction, the EETU's other task was to assist when ships completed a refit, tuning up the fire control and electronics and going to sea with them for the first few trips. My chief ordnance man returned one day with a wonderful story. He was on one destroyer that was exercising a bombardment run using her main armament. This would normally be carried out with a tug towing a target on the end of a half-mile cable, but on this occasion the target was another ship on which one did a 'throw-off' shoot. The director sights actually aimed at the other ship, but the guns themselves were trained to one side. The target ship was deemed to have been hit if the shells landed within so many yards of a small float she was towing, and was much more realistic for the direction crew than aiming at a towed target. Unfortunately on this occasion it was too realistic. The throw-off deviation had not been applied properly and when the ship fired, they achieved a direct hit on the target ship, holing her amidships right on the waterline. It was a perfect shot. Embarrassingly the target ship was the senior one, and not surprisingly there was panic as water began gushing into the engine room through a six inch hole. This provided a good opportunity for the damage control party to plug the hole, which they managed to do quite quickly. Even so, the ship could easily have gone straight down. She crept back into harbour with all pumps working flat out, and a list to one side occasioned by pumping fuel from tanks on the damaged side to ones on the other side, thereby bringing the hole above the water. There was a post mortem afterwards, but nobody was court-martialled.

Patricia had been having difficulty finding a good butcher in Narrabeen, the same problem we had, and still have, in England. We had been searching unsuccessfully for a butcher who bought in good quality properly hung meat. One day, wandering through the 'city' part of Sydney amongst the skyscrapers, the pavements full of smart suits dashing out in their lunch hour, I came across a little butcher's shop sandwiched between a couple of banks with a long queue stretching right down the street. I joined the queue to find out what was so special. Once inside I found frantic activity, nine or ten men cutting up and dispensing meat at breakneck speed while a little fellow sitting at a cash desk on a sort of podium in the middle of the shop kept in his head a record of what each assistant was shouting to him. The queue advanced at a slow walking pace, and in moments I was outside again, clutching the best part of half a lamb. Back at the office, Jonesey relieved me of the parcel, putting it in the office fridge that had been acquired for precisely that purpose. That weekend we enjoyed the best meat we'd had since we arrived, and from then on never bought our meat anywhere else. We often join a long queue just to see why it is so long, often discovering something good at the end.

We were getting the hang of bathing from a beach onto which tremendous surf pounded continuously, learning how to get out through the breakers without serious injury which can occur all too easily, either from surfboards or from mountainous breakers or 'dumpers' that curl over as they are about to break dropping any unfortunate swimmer who happens to be on the top of one down onto the sand, then crashing down on top of them just as they're trying to stand up and run for it. With the swimming came the lifesaver boys, muscular bronzed young men poncing up and down the beach attracting admiring looks from scantily clad young ladies. Each main beach had its teams of lifesavers who paraded regularly with their surfboats in competitions. Ours was only a minor team, but at Dee Why a couple of bays further down they had a championship team which attracted big crowds on competition days. The surfboats, manned by beefy oarsmen would launch out into the massive breakers nearly broaching-to in the process, and row off fast to anyone in difficulties whom the duty guard spotted from his high seat. Having effected a rescue, the boat then came back at high speed, riding the waves until with great skill they arrived on the beach whereupon everyone leapt out and carried the boat up before the next breaker crashed onto it, sucking them all back into the undertow. Spectacular stuff, good fun to watch, and definitely not the place to be with young toddlers.

Patricia discovered she had become pregnant again, and we worked out there would be about 14 months between the two of them; a bit close, perhaps, but just right if we wanted to have two children established by the time of our passage home a year or two later. Emotionally, this second pregnancy was equally upsetting for her, with unexplained despondent spells, but by now she had a circle of friends most of whom had been through all this themselves, so she could talk it over with them. In the meantime Susan had our total attention. We put her in our washing-up bowl with a cushion to lean against and placed this on the kitchen table, so she was able to watch what was going on around her.

We'd met another RN naval couple with whom we got on well. Jeremy was an engineer, and had just built a dinghy that he wanted to sail somewhere quiet, and they had a daughter a little older than Susan. Naomi got on very well with Patricia, and we began to go out together at weekends. Often Jeremy would be at sea, but whenever we could, we would sail his dinghy on an inlet off the Hawkesbury River that had a nice sand bar for the children.

My father now decided he would visit us, so had set off in a slow cargo boat for the six-week passage to New Zealand, from where he flew the last bit. He spent nearly a month with us at the hottest time of the year with temperatures over 100 degrees, but enjoyed sitting on the beach in the sun in spite of that. It was back to the old days where he tended to speak to me about everything, ignoring Patricia. As for Susan, he found her tiresome as she diverted much of our attention. He never was much good with small children. Patricia found it all rather exhausting; she was weaning Susan at this time, there were lots of activities going on with various naval friends and I had to be away quite often during his visit. However, we managed to give him an insight into what it was like living in that country. I would pour him a sherry before dinner, and the first time he tried this he asked which one it was. "Very good," he said approvingly, "Harvey's, I presume?"

"Oh no," I replied, "It's better than that."

"Exceptionally good. Where did it come from?" Father reckoned he was a wine buff and knew all the best ones. However, he was also a wine snob and in those days New World wines hadn't penetrated as far as St. Mawes. "Expensive?" he probed.

"It is rather," I replied, "sixteen shillings a bottle." In those days the best Harveys was about 12/6.

"Wow, that is expensive. May I see the bottle?" I produced the one gallon Winchester in which we used to buy our sherry, reminding him that sixteen Australian shillings was only about twelve English shillings. I'm afraid we heaved a sigh of relief when he set off once more on his travels.

We'd been in Australia for a full year! A two-week holiday was allowed, but still very short of funds we had to do what we could on the cheap. We'd found someone who offered to take Susan for this time, so with some misgivings handed her over for her first time away from Mum. We spent the holiday driving north for a week, after which we drove south for the second week. Not very adventurous, but it did enable us to see a little bit more of this huge country, even though we only seemed to cover a tiny bit up the eastern side. We had borrowed a heavy tent, built some sort of box that fitted on the roof rack and set off for Queensland. On the way we had to cross some large rivers on unstable ferries, quite quickly the tarmac ran out and most of the driving was on dirt roads. The recognised trick is to drive fast enough to hit only the tops of the ridges, then the ride is smoother, rather like planing in a boat. But our little Morris with its big box on the roof couldn't go through the essential speed barrier, so most of the time it was an extremely bumpy ride doing no more than about 40 m.p.h. We found good camping spots, all supplied with a water tap fifty miles from the nearest habitation. We passed through the famous Surfers Paradise, a loud, brash place full of expensive shops and wealthy beach people, not our scene at all. We drove through Brisbane and eventually reached Rockhampton, a more pleasant watering hole with colonial style buildings, lots of verandas with Victorian cast iron balustrading and a railway line that ran through town along the main street. In Queensland the railway engines, mostly fired on wood with extra water-carrying tenders, were monstrously huge affairs probably seeming so because of the three foot rail gauge in that state. These enormous beasts seemed far too big to stay on such a small track. Out in the country our road passed close to the railway line at one point where the line crossed over a river on a rough timber bridge only as wide as the line itself, so that when the train came creaking over, it overlapped both sides in a most unsafe looking manner.

After a day spent on a lovely mile-long beach looking out towards the Barrier reef where we were the only ones, it was time to head back. A milepost said we were 1,259 miles from Sydney. On the way we stopped off at a gold mine, not sure what to find. It turned out to be a hole in the ground many hundreds of feet deep and half a mile across, where all the mucky brown rock had gone through a crushing plant before the tiny quantity of gold had been separated out. Our holiday took in lots of different types of country, all of it remote and virtually uninhabited with not much wildlife. We only ever saw a kangaroo in a zoo. On our last day or two the weather broke, so we pushed on for home, getting back exhausted late at night. We didn't stop to unload the car, but drove it straight into the garage and fell into bed.

During that night I was awakened by a roaring sound outside, and when I struggled to open my eyes I could see a flickering orange glow coming through the curtains. Staggering to my feet, I looked out to see sparks and smoke racing past the house in a strong wind. It took a few moments to register that there was something uncomfortably close that was going up like a tinderbox. I woke Patricia, struggled into a pair of trousers and went out the back to see the Dunbar's wooden joinery shop well alight. My first thought was our car that was garaged only thirty feet away, so I drove that out and parked it down the street. By this time a fire engine had driven up and a tired looking fireman was wandering about trying to find a fire hydrant. No signs of the Dunbars. I went up to their flat and after much banging managed to wake them. Mr Dunbar stood at the top of the steps looking down at what had been his livelihood rapidly disappearing up in flames, then went back in to find some clothes. He didn't seem to be particularly upset, except to call out to the fireman to put a hose on the little bungalow next door to stop that too catching fire.

In the morning there was just a heap of ash.The strong onshore wind had ensured the whole building had burnt completely, and the bungalow next door had all its paint charred on that side, but was otherwise all right. The couple who lived in it were away at the time. Old Dunbar chatted happily to us about a fire that destroyed their previous place out in the bush before they came to live in Sydney, and didn't seem too concerned. He said he would rebuild the workshop in brick and within a few weeks he started to do so, putting up a superb building that put to shame all the wooden shacks that passed for homesteads in these parts. We wondered whether he was insured so well that he made a habit of having the occasional fire when he wanted to upgrade his premises?

Patricia by this time was beginning to 'show'. Mrs Dunbar certainly noticed, and her dislike of young children began to niggle although, surprisingly, she was still happy to have Susan's cot brought up to her flat occasionally when we were out late. She flew off the handle when Susan once picked a flower, and started to make life uncomfortable for us. We were prepared to endure this for a while since we had no wish to move from this extremely well-built house into one of the tatty buildings we might otherwise have to live in; nevertheless, we began to keep our eyes open for somewhere else.

HMAS Yarra, the frigate under construction at Williamstown, was reaching the stage where I was required to spend several days down there at a time. Two roads converged on the Williamstown dockyard gates, and in the angle between them directly facing the gates was The Sailor's Rest, a typical dockside pub. At lunchtime and again at knocking off time in the afternoons the publican and his two bar assistants worked flat out to satisfy the healthy thirsts of a large number of dockies, who would arrive at a sprint about ten seconds after the hooter sounded. Several hundred schooner glasses would be lined up on the counter top and filled to the brim from a beer hose fitted with a trigger dispenser. Then, as the hooter went, they would open both doors and stand to one side. The well-established routine was for a man to snatch a glass in each hand, and get out of the way before he was trampled underfoot. Then he'd slurp down one of them, place his glass on the counter at the far end where it was refilled while he was drinking the second one. He'd then pay for all three and retire to somewhere a bit quieter. A considerable amount of ice-cold beer could be dispensed very quickly this way, and it was a sight to see. Ten minutes later things calmed down somewhat and refills became more relaxed, being paid for as they occurred. The universal signal that you required your glass refilled was to place it on the counter, still clutching it. No words or 'catching the barman's eye' were necessary. At the afternoon session customers had until six o'clock to drink all they could after which the pub shut. The idea of these licensing laws was to encourage people to go home before they'd spent all the day's wages and the period was known as the six o'clock swill. It meant, of course, that it was not sensible to be wandering about on the streets just after six, and certainly not on the roads where drivers might well be weaving all over the place. Amazingly there didn't seem to be many accidents resulting from that extraordinary drinking law, but it was abolished shortly after we'd returned to the UK so maybe there were more than I knew about.

My Chief 'tiffy who accompanied me to Williamstown used to stay at The Sailor's Rest when he was working on Yarra, and suggested I should join him there rather than trail back to Melbourne half an hour away on the train, so I did. That is how I witnessed the beer-sinking spectacle. After we'd stayed there several times and become known to the publican, we used to help out sometimes by reporting for duty shortly before opening time for glass-filling. However, once the doors opened, it was best to stay well clear of the action. The bedrooms were satisfactory and so were the breakfasts. The publican was usually out later in the evening, so we had the place to ourselves, which meant we searched around in the kitchen for something to eat. My abiding memory of that experience was the all-pervading smell of beer and fried food, and the flies. Flies settled everywhere, and in spite of their main diet of spilt beer that made them stupidly brave, they still just managed to avoid being swatted. Horrible things.

Susan by this time was getting much more mobile, so I made a playpen about four feet square in which we could place her with her toys. Provided one of us was nearby, she was quite happy with this. Quite soon she had learnt to pull herself up unaided by holding onto the side, and quickly got the hang of standing up this way. We conceived the idea of giving her something that would move forward if she held on to it, thereby encouraging her to take her first steps, so we bought a little red horse on wheels which had a handle at one end for her to hold on to. It was on her first birthday a day or two later that she pulled herself up on the handle then, discovering that it moved when she pushed it, she was obliged to follow, and within a few days was pushing her horse happily around the garden. She now weighed in at 20 pounds, a far cry from the little bundle of a year ago. Down on the beach she discovered she was able to crawl along the sand really fast, and the moment Patricia's back was turned would make a beeline for the sea. On one occasion we were just in time to see her rolling over and over in the backwash and whisked her up just seconds before the next roller broke with a thunderous crash all round us.

It wasn't quite all babies at home and we did manage to get out fairly often. We managed Sundays at St. Stephens whenever we could, and looked out for special speakers. One such was the subject of a film doing the rounds called The Inn of the Sixth Happiness, This was about a lady's maid from London who, in the thirties, set out for a more interesting life, finding herself in China where she settled. She was delighted to discover here were other people in the world who were of similar stature to herself, for she was barely five feet tall. This was Gladys Aylward, a born-again charismatic Christian who happily stood on a box in the pulpit so that she could see over the top and addressed the thousand-strong congregation without turning a hair, modestly and humbly talking for an hour or more. Even now, over forty years later, I can vividly recall that evening, the sound of her voice and her magnetic personality radiating across the church.

We managed to go to the cinema about once a week or so, or to a live show in Sydney, and even tried Scottish Country Dancing. There seemed to be just the one SCD club, which met in a small bare hall somewhere in the southwestern suburbs. Here serious sun-tanned Aussies in shorts tried to get their feet round the steps urged on by a teacher with the book in one hand and lots of enthusiasm. I'd long formed the impression that the further one gets from Scotland the more intense the dancing, and after having danced in so many places, my experience in Singapore and now in Sydney confirmed that hypothesis. Still, it was good to hear the foot-tapping music again, but it was a long car drive to get there and we didn't pursue it for long.

I met an ex-Harrow friend of Noggin's, Adrian Garrett, who was into ancient cars. He was living on the North Shore now, and owned a most splendid 1907 Rolls Royce Silver Ghost open tourer, a car I had last seen at the Goodwood veteran meeting many years previously. He invited us to sit in splendour on the back seat while he drove through Sydney in a Veteran Car Rally, Patricia and me giving royal waves to anybody ooh-ing and aah-ing by the roadside. Later, after the judging, I was allowed to drive the car a short distance across a field. I felt very privileged.

Back at home Mrs Dunbar had been getting more and more unsettled, and her husband told us she went like this sometimes, and the sight of Patricia in the last stages of pregnancy somehow triggered her off. At 5.00 next morning Patricia awoke with a tummy pain she thought was the pork chop she'd eaten, but within the hour decided number two had decided to arrive. This was the correct day, so it was expected. While I bathed and dressed Susan, Patricia got her things together and we set off once more for Crown Street Women's Hospital, dropping Susan off with the Brungers to look after for the day; all part of the Plan. Four hours after she was admitted a little boy arrived. We called him Paul Jonathan. He was a fine baby and gave Patricia a bit of a time on the way out, but it seemed she was able to give birth so swiftly as a routine. In preparation for Patricia's confinement the clinic had provided a list of licensed baby residential homes and we had chosen one about twenty miles away where we would be able to leave Susan while Patricia was in hospital, a stay of over a week then being the norm. Paul had apparently been delivered with his head tilted back, and at first had a very receding chin so he looked rather strange. Patricia brought him home on my twenty-ninth birthday and I couldn't have had a better present! The next day we collected Susan who was very subdued and didn't take much notice of her new brother. She was, after all, only 14 months old, so maybe jealousy did not assert itself at that age.

HMAS Parramatta, the frigate under construction at Cockatoo Island just upstream of the Harbour Bridge, was nearing the stage when she would be ready for sea trials. Cockatoo was a wonderful little shipyard. Being on a small island helped in that it had a 'family' atmosphere and many of the employees had been there all their working lives. There were one or two lorries that trundled round taking parts from one area to another. One of these, shod with solid tyres, had been on the island since it was new in the twenties. It never got out of bottom gear, of course, and would in all probability last for another seventy years or so. The ship, which had been in the building dock when I first saw her, was now alongside a jetty for the fitting out, while the keel of her successor was being laid in the dock. On the first day of sea trials, all the dockyard people arrived in their seagoing clothing, and the naval skeleton crew were there to work the ship by their side. It was a strange relationship, the ship still belonging to the dockyard and flying the defaced blue ensign, while the Naval captain on the bridge worked jointly with the senior construction officer from the yard. We adopted the Naval method of running the ship with such commands as 'Special Sea Dutymen close up!' coming from the Tannoy, yet we didn't go down the river under the Bridge and past Garden Island with any ceremonial, though a welcoming signal from the

Garden Island Naval base was received and replied to, and we dipped our blue ensign to the white ensign on Garden Island.

The next three months passed very uneventfully, with the two children progressing and Patricia seemingly spending all day surrounded by nappies either being washed or drying on the line. Naomi and Jeremy Strugnell had so much in common with our family that we saw a good deal of one another. They, too, were anxious to move from their let, and then we were lucky. Naomi found a somewhat tatty bungalow which was divided into two. This became available, so we decided to have it together. We gave notice to the Dunbars that we'd be moving out a month later. After that they were most charming, and we almost wondered whether we'd done the right thing. The new house was at Collaroy, just a mile or so closer in to Sydney, but with a different beach to go to. It was an old 'homestead', originally four rooms with a wide balcony all round. This balcony had been filled in making narrow rooms around the sides while the ones in the centre had no natural light, relying on doors being left open. We each had our own back garden, in which was a separate shed housing the essential washing machine. We never discovered where the waste water went from those machines, but when we emptied ours, a puddle formed in the middle of the lawn next door. As we'd been washing soiled nappies, this probably wasn't very hygienic. The house was built about a foot above the ground on stilts with an airflow underneath, nice for hot weather, but not a good idea for toddlers as there were funnel-web spiders living under the house which could be lethal. Probably more serious was a little fellow about the size of a Smarty called a red-back spider, a bite from which could certainly be extremely nasty, and I found a nest of these in the corner of our dirt-floor garage. Amazingly, nobody got bitten, though Susan did get a rather horrible tick that we couldn't dislodge. Eventually it let go after being soused with kerosene.

The first time it rained, we quickly discovered how lucky we'd been living in the Dunbar's downstairs flat in a sturdy brick building. Here it was like living inside a kettledrum. The sound made by every spot of rain that landed on the corrugated iron roof was amplified and in one of our frequent heavy rainstorms we couldn't hear one another above the noise, and not all the rain stayed on the outside, though fortunately it was only in the outer parts which were uncarpeted where we had big floods. However, the place did have an extremely useful asset: there was a scruffy tree about six feet high in the front garden that always had several luscious ripe lemons on it. We picked one most days and never had to hold back. A fairly common sight in the suburban gardens in these parts, and our house was no exception, was the 'glass wall'. Whoever had built ours had made the wall about ten feet long and three feet high, so quite modest compared with some. It stood in the front garden set back a little from the actual front fence and was made of beer bottles, the standard big ones about a litre in size. For some reason these were difficult to dispose of, and building walls of this type put off the day when some other disposal method would have to be found. Mercifully, we didn't come across many broken bottles on our walks, for with the hot sun and often dry scrub that would have been highly dangerous. We were told about an even better use for the bottles, whereby someone had devised a jig for cutting the base off a beer bottle after which they had then threaded the bottomless bottles onto a garden hose and wound this glass 'rope' backwards and forwards at the back of their swimming pool. By pumping water into the pool through the hose it arrived at the far end nicely warmed. These beer bottles were used for all sorts of things, notably fishing reels: we often came across fishermen standing on the rocks just above the surf with long lines, the inboard end wrapped around a beer bottle. The bottles were also used as a volumetric measure. For example, my Chief 'tiffy referred to his new car as having a '94-bottle boot' and our fridge was apparently a 30-bottle job, not a five cubic foot model.

Having Naomi next door was a wonderful boon. We babysat for one another of course, the two girls often went everywhere together, and when I came home in the afternoons I would find them both on Collaroy Beach. This beach was sheltered from the direct onslaught of the Pacific rollers by a headland making it a little safer than Narrabeen. To get to it we walked along the side of a golf course that extended all round the headland. One day I was down on that beach watching the antics of a collie dog that kept rushing inland then reappearing a moment later to deposit something by the side of its owner, a quiet man who sat incongruously amongst the families, gazing innocently out to sea. Eventually I realised the dog was calmly bringing golf balls to its master, who surreptitiously popped them in a bag before sending the dog back for more. After twenty minutes the pair of them trudged off, no doubt to try their luck near some other golf course. The bag seemed pretty full as they passed us.

In February with Paul just four months old we decided to take to the road and drive to Melbourne. I had to spend several days on the Yarra, now starting her own sea trials, and it would be an opportunity for Patricia to see a little more of the continent. It took us two days, with an overnight stop at a motel. Amazingly, part of that intercity highway was still a dirt road which kept our speed down somewhat. We met a large number of huge trucks, some of them vast road trains with several trailers hooked one behind the other. They would overtake us with a terrifying blast from their horn and come thundering by so close we were obliged to get off the road until they had passed. Then for the next few minutes we were in a sand storm, by which time there'd be one coming the other way. It was one of the most unpleasant car trips I've taken anywhere. We booked in at the nice-sounding Botanical Hotel, which turned out to be a seedy impersonal place smelling like the horrible dump we'd stayed in at Kings Cross when we first arrived, but it did overlook the botanical gardens which were lovely. We'd arrived in a particularly hot period with the temperature over 100 degrees with a humidity to match, made worse by countless fine sprayers all over the gardens. In the hotel, which kept every window firmly shut and had no air conditioning, it was stifling. We were ten days there altogether, and I was able to take the family to Williamstown to see the ship, down to Frankston to meet the Moores with whom I'd stayed when in Melbourne the previous year, then on to Crib Point near where the Gunnery School was situated. That last destination doesn't sound very interesting for the family but we had a reason, for nearby was a homestead where one branch of

Patricia's ancestors had settled, and Patricia wanted to meet them. They were an elderly couple living in a home-built mud-walled house buried in the country, with flowers and trees around, all very English. Nearby was a new house in the process of construction, which their son was building. He used a type of shuttering which enabled him to pour in wet clay and tamp it down. The hot sun soon dried it and the walls went up surprisingly fast. Provided the roof had a large overhang, such walls lasted forever. They were about 18 inches thick, plastered and painted on both sides, and made for a very cool and thermally efficient house. There were no foundations apparently. The husband owned a stone crushing plant, and a year or two later we heard that he'd come to a nasty end when he fell into the hopper one day while it was operating.

Sea Trials in the Yarra were a repeat of those we'd done in the Parramatta earlier, but with one difference: in order to get to a decent stretch of open sea we had to leave Port Philip Bay through the Heads which were only a quarter of a mile apart. Unlike the Orcades two years earlier which came in with no fuss, it was quite a different matter in a vessel of just 2,000 tons. The notorious whirlpool is about 300 feet across and dips noticeably in the middle. We closed up 'Special Sea Dutymen' whilst negotiating this hazard, with the ship's coxswain on the wheel and a running commentary kept between him and the bridge above[1]. As we approached the edge of the whirlpool the coxswain had to spin the wheel this way and that to maintain a straight course and the ship jerked quite noticeably as we fought our way through.

Our day for setting off to the UK neared. With only a month to go my chums in the office reminded me I could from now on park my car with impunity anywhere on the penalty areas in Sydney, just be careful to avoid any tow-away areas. Their reasoning was that it took up to six weeks for the authorities to issue a parking ticket followed by a summons if the fine wasn't paid, by which time I would be safely out of the country. My Aussie friends were doing their best to rid me of my tiresome British habit of keeping on the right side of the law.

We had arrived over two years previously, the two of us with just four trunks. Going home was very different. It took days to pack up the house, sell the car, obtain crates and pack our delicate items safely. In all we collected 21 pieces of baggage, which were whisked off by a removals firm leaving us in an empty house. Friends rallied round and took us to our ship, the Dutch liner that was alongside in the commercial part of town, Woolloomoolloo Docks, just a stone's throw from my EETU office. Along with our friends, most of the office turned out to see us off and we stood for ages hurling coloured streamers from the passenger deck to the wellwishers on the dockside below.

Willem Rhys was a completely different type of ship to the oh-so-British Orcades. The officers and crew were all Dutch, English being very much their second language, and there were few concessions to passengers of other

---

[1] Non-naval people may not be aware that in a warship, the steering position is not on the bridge but several decks below where it should be less vulnerable to being put out of action by enemy fire. Communication between the two is by an intercom.

nationalities. The signs round the ship were in Dutch. The ship's agents in Sydney had assured Patricia there would be fresh milk on board and so she had weaned Paul onto this in readiness. It was a big shock to find that the fresh milk only lasted the first 24 hours and from then on it was reconstituted milk, which the children wouldn't drink. The ship's refrigeration capacity was clearly limited, and they depended far more on dried goods. What with these restrictions and the Dutch palate that favoured stodgy food with little fruit and no fresh vegetables, none of us enjoyed the eating experience. We were put at the Purser's table. He was a large man whose English was none too good. He managed the words, but none of the nuances. We had little in common. There was a crèche and children's playroom, so that was a useful facility, but neither of the children was happy to be left there for long. The upheaval of transferring onto this moving monster full of strange experiences made them both somewhat clingy, not surprising at their age. However, the ship did have a very good swimming pool with ample deck space around it, and that was where we were to spend most of our time.

There was one other Royal Naval person on board, a tired old commander who propped up the bar almost the whole voyage. He was genial enough when able to converse in a sober state, but after all these years the only word I remember him uttering was 'Bulawayo' which happened to be the name of one of our fleet repair ships, but he got it out in place of an unseemly burp, a problem he appeared to suffer from most of the time.

Susan was well looked after in the pool by another family, and she loved it. Paul, though, was having difficulties as he was at the stage when he was doing his best to stand unaided then take a few steps—not easy on a rolling ship when the ground goes from under your feet. Nevertheless, during the voyage he did progress to walking fairly well with someone to hold on to. As for Patricia, poor dear, she spent a lot of time trying to feed one or other of them.

An advantage in returning home on the *Willem Rhys* was that she was going east about, so we would complete a circumnavigation by the time we got home. Our first port of call was to Wellington where we remained for a day and a half. We took a coach a few miles out into the country, all lush green grass and sheep. We hadn't seen lush grass like that since leaving the UK. That evening we attended a Maori musical concert. Waiting for it to start, we all talked amongst ourselves as the lights went down, then a couple of elderly people at the end of our row who clearly had no idea of the Maori's traditional welcome suddenly screamed. Not surprising, for the troupe had crept down the aisle and now their leader suddenly leapt in front of this couple with a bloodcurdling war cry whilst making the most terrifying face. They put on a good show and presumably did the same one every time a cruise ship was in harbour.

Then followed a long spell at sea with heavy overcast skies, in fact it stayed that way all the way across the Pacific. The ship next put down an anchor a mile or so off Pitcairn Island while all the islanders came aboard in their longboats and set up stalls in the ship's entrance foyer. Ship's staff guarded every door leading off the foyer, as the islanders were known to be a light-fingered bunch. We'd brought their mail and it was an important day for them as they only had a passenger ship call once or twice a year, and this was their only opportunity to trade. A week later we passed an island of the Galapagos group but, alas, we would not be landing. A couple of days later brought us to Bilboa for the start of our Panama passage where I remained on the upper deck all day, trying unsuccessfully to recognise some of the birds and mammals in the trees either side. We locked through and were in the Atlantic again as the sun came out. Passing Cuba some way off, our next port of call was Miami. We joined a coachload of passengers for a guided tour through the place, stopping off at the Seaquarium to watch dolphins and killer whales put on a performance. The coach driver went on and on about how this was the biggest skyscraper, that was the most expensive hotel, there lived some celebrity or other. It was all so tedious and so American. Still, the dolphins were good. After that it was Bermuda, where the ship stayed at anchor out in the roads (presumably cheaper for them to do that) and we went ashore in launches. We had a whole day there, so I was able to show Patricia most of Hamilton town, and afterwards we spent the afternoon on the lovely white coral beach. A week later we were sailing up the dear old Solent to dock at Southampton. It took hours to clear customs. Patricia's parents met us on the dockside and looked after the children who were tired and grizzly while we were ordered to open various crates while the customs people searched around. They pounced on two stuffed koala bear toys which they thought were probably filled with narcotics. Goodness knows what had put them up to this search. We were thoroughly fed up by the time they reluctantly let us go. Everybody else just sailed straight through without any searches. At long last we were off and half an hour later arrived at High Winds for lunch.

We had left, just a young couple on their own and now we were back; a complete family and two carloads of luggage. It had been an eventful couple of years, but now our trip to Australia was well and truly over.

12

Agincourt at Home

The Royal Navy are proud of the way in which they look after their sailors, but in my time didn't apply much thought to what it was like being one. An especially irksome aspect was the way in which 'leave' was so graciously allowed. We'd been away in Australia for over two years, with a couple of week's 'local leave' per annum allowed during that time, and as a supreme gesture the Admiralty now sent me on six weeks leave 'pending appointment', which might be anywhere. In any thoughtful organisation that six weeks could have been spent frantically trying to find somewhere to live in the area where one would be working, but the Royal Navy didn't work that way. We might well be kept in the dark until just a couple of weeks before the new appointment took effect, which meant we had, in effect, to kick our heels all that time while the whole family lodged with Patricia's parents at High Winds, a small two-bedroom house, with all our worldly possessions cluttering up every space therein. But it was good to be home again, Patricia's parents doted on their two grandchildren and virtually took them over, which suited us as for the first time we were free to get out and about.

The first thing we did was to buy a new car. During our time in Australia we had lived very frugally. My salary was the same as I would get at home, but it was paid in Australian pounds, worth four-fifths of an English pound, and to make up the difference they paid me an extra month's salary every fifth week, what the Aussies called our 'Pommies' Pittance'. We tried to put this away in an attempt to save, for it was easier to save in a country where we could live adequately on less than at home. So we now had nearly £800 stashed away, a veritable fortune. Before we left Sydney we had ordered a new Morris Traveller, for which there was a long waiting list in 1961. The colours offered were black, dark or light grey, or a somewhat nasty mud colour. After the brilliant colours of all the Australian Holdens, to be offered such a limited palette was dreary indeed. This was something I always noticed when returning to the UK after a trip abroad—

how drab everyone and everything looked. People seemed afraid to wear bright colours and the same went for the colour of their cars, their houses, everything that could be made colourful; it was as if the grey skies and pollution inhibited any wish to create brighter colours. So we selected the dark grey that went well with the pale varnished ash framework and collected it a couple of days after we got home. It was supposedly an 'export' model which meant it was fitted with a new concession to modern comfort—a rudimentary heater! It also came with the usual starting handle, but this was stowed under the boot floor along with the spare wheel and jack. Reliability was reckoned to be so good that the starting handle would seldom be needed.

My appointment came through: I was to join HMS Agincourt in Portsmouth dockyard where she was partway through conversion from a conventional Battle class destroyer to a radar frigate. We still had about a month before I joined, and as it meant I would be undergoing courses in Portsmouth before joining a Portsmouth-based ship, we could go ahead and find a house to rent in the area. There was no question of buying. For a start we wouldn't have the money to put down a deposit, and where would we buy? This Portsmouth appointment would probably be for only a couple of years, and then I might be posted anywhere. We first approached the authorities for a married quarter that could have been better, but they only offered one or two grotty places that no one wanted. We refused these but doing so precluded us being eligible for a 'hiring'—navyspeak for a private house which the Navy rented and then sublet to naval personnel. After much arguing that nowhere of a satisfactory standard was available we did manage to insist we should still be eligible. So our searches began, and after a couple of weeks we found a place in Alverstoke, just a couple of miles from Lee. It was the servants' wing of a large house on the front overlooking the Isle of Wight, with just a golf course between it and Gilkicker Point. It was a super area, but the house itself was incredibly shabby, with the tattiest of furnishings. The wing hadn't been modernised since the house was built in Edwardian times.

Having secured somewhere to live, we were able to whiz round the country visiting all our friends, which included a visit to my father. He hadn't changed, and treated me as a labour source for all the small jobs he was finding he was too old to manage himself, ignoring Patricia whom he expected to produce food when he got hungry. He'd sold Kestrel and acquired a slightly larger boat with a tiny cabin. Not so much fun as a St. Mawes one-design, but much more comfortable and more suited to an older person. He spent a great deal of time just sitting in the sun doing nothing, and our presence seemed to tire him. The visit was not a success.

At the other end of the south coast we visited Bexhill, where Jane and Peter and their family were staying with Peter's parents. This was a lovely visit and so different to the Cornish one.

With a new son to consider, we also drove up to my old school, Bradfield, to see whether we might try there for Paul in due course. The dapper Colonel Hills had retired and his replacement couldn't have been a greater contrast. Although he, too, had come from being an Eton housemaster, Anthony Chenevix-Trench was a charming approachable man with dirty fingernails who appeared in somewhat sloppy clothes (or so they seemed after my memories of Hills' formal wear). I showed Patricia as much of the school as possible but we came away with mixed feelings. Would Paul fit in? What would it be like in twelve years time? It looked incredibly tatty, but then a lot of the old public schools look like that. The biggest unknown was would we ever be able to afford it? I think both of us felt it would be a huge on-going expense that would considerably affect our lifestyle, and would it ever be worth it? In twelve years time Paul might very well turn out to be the type of boy who wouldn't necessarily benefit from such an education, and perhaps we'd be living somewhere where the local education was exceptionally good. We couldn't even afford to start an educational insurance scheme at this time, and so we put the whole educational subject on the back burner for a few years.

During this waiting period we also attended Antony Corfe's wedding at Handcross in Sussex. It was a lovely wedding, helped by glorious sunshine and they both looked so happy. About half the Long Course Six men were now married (we'd missed a few whilst overseas).

I joined Agincourt. She was in dry dock at the far end of the dockyard, with offices nearby. I was the second officer to join. 'Chief', the engineer officer, Tony Tucker, had been with her for several months. The key senior rates were already there, in my case my chief electrical artificer and chief electrician (the difference between the two is that the chief 'tiffy is technically better qualified and was responsible to me for the operational efficiency of everything electrical, whereas the chief electrician runs the department, looking after all the junior ratings and all things to do with personnel). The two of them took me round the ship that was still in an early stage of conversion, and introduced me to one or two key dockyard personnel. The one that really mattered at this stage was the constructor foreman, a dockyard officer of crucial importance whose job it was to build various parts of the ship to suit the drawings, install ventilation trunking, doors, portholes and anything done in steel or aluminium using rivets or a welding torch. He had the power to put a bulkhead up so that a compartment was a wee bit bigger than it ought to be, or to get ventilation trunking made in a certain way so that you didn't bang your head on it every time you went under. Compared to him, the electrical foreman was no problem. For a start, we were both electrical people so spoke the same language, and we both had to cope with the constructor's men. For example, I'd arrange for a particular switch box to be mounted on a bulkhead just here, and while our backs were turned, a sheet metal man would measure up for his ventilation trunk, go off to make it up and on his return find it wouldn't fit because in the meantime the electrician had got his switch box mounted. There'd be an argument, so they'd both go and complain to the constructor foreman, and if we were unlucky, a pipefitter would have come along and fixed some pipe across the front of the box so the door wouldn't open. It was an extraordinary way to work, but they muddled along fairly amiably and managed to extend the time needed to fit out the ship (and indirectly the size of their pay packets, because the need for overtime would soon arise). I noticed a man draw a circle on a bulkhead behind which was an office, and he said a scuttle (porthole) would be fitted there. Now, I had an electrical cubbyhole with no natural light and thought it would be nice to have a scuttle fitted to that space, so when no one was looking I drew a circle where I thought it would look good, and lo! and behold, next morning there was a nice shiny scuttle there. I reckoned one would need to be fairly circumspect doing this sort of thing, but the ship was being built for us to sail her, so we might as well try to have everything as we'd like it.

On my second day I called the two chiefs together and had what turned out to be one of my most important meetings of all time. I realised I had two extremely experienced men to run my department, whereas I was a one-time Fleet Air Arm man, with just a smattering of ship experience gleaned whilst out in Aussie and in Aisne all those years ago. No doubt they had already decided I was a Hooray Henry type who would just get in the way, and I felt very vulnerable with my lack of knowledge. But the knowledge was there; I just stumbled across the right way to access it.

"How would you like the department to be run?" I asked them. The chief electrician quickly cottoned on.

"Well, Sir," he ventured, "You leave us to run it the way we always runs a department, which we can do very well indeed, Sir, if you just keep the First Lieutenant out of our way and look after the paperwork, Sir!" I looked at the chief tiffy, who sat there hardly able to believe his ears. "Chief?"

"Absolutely right, Sir," he said enthusiastically. "And I'm sure the chief radio tiffy will agree with us when he joins. It'll be a fait accompli by then, anyway. Yessir!"

I was enormously relieved. This may have been unconventional, but if we all did the work we were best at, then it would be a happy department, and that was paramount. I'd learnt one thing from the odious Harry Bleak, which was a malcontent department is an inefficient one, but the opposite is also true. If I had a happy and motivated set of senior rates, I would be okay. Together we set about designing departmental duties and roughing out an organisation, which would in due course become my departmental orders.

Fitting out progressed, and the months passed. Patricia and I went to Collingwood every Wednesday for our Scottish Dancing. It was fun to be amongst our friends who were steadily growing in number, and we had a super evening on the night of the Collingwood Christmas Ball. Sometimes we went to the Nuffield Club in Southsea where there was also Scottish Country Dancing once a week, so we enjoyed plenty of it. Patricia's parents were only too happy to baby-sit whenever required, living just two miles away being perfect for this role.

I resurrected my old Cambridge bike (still with the Fitzwilliam number on the rear mudguard) and used this to get to work. I cycled down to Gosport and caught the pedestrian ferry over to the Harbour station, cost four old pennies plus 2½ pence for the bike. The whole foredeck, about a third of the ferry, would be stacked with up to a hundred bikes for the short crossing. Provided one left the boat in the reverse order from coming aboard, one's bike would be at the top of the pile when it came to collecting it. What with so many people going around on bikes, and a very efficient and frequent bus service on both sides of the harbour, there really wasn't the need for people to struggle all the way round by car, and very few did.

After Christmas the first lieutenant, Colin Marr, joined. He was a 'pusser' type, navyspeak for a correct and authoritarian officer, which was not a bad thing since the skeleton staff so far had become a group of chums with Naval discipline somewhat lax. Colin immediately started to tighten things up. He was a paper man, scribbling out notes all the time and putting them on people's desks even though some shared the same office with him. He'd been on the Greenwich Staff Course, was well versed in running a ship and probably reckoned he could run a Navy just as well. I saw my chief electrician raise his eyes to heaven with a sigh. Perhaps I was going to have my work cut out with Mr Marr.

Working in Portsmouth dockyard was interesting. It is steeped in Naval history, with many of the old original buildings still there. I passed HMS Victory in her dry dock every morning, and all over the place there were dockside bollards made by sinking an old gun barrel head down into the concrete roadway, where they made perfect securing points for large ships, though most unforgiving if someone was trying to back a car without checking it was clear behind. The bollard always won convincingly.

In those days there was a strict but unwritten dress code with the dockyard personnel. A chargehand would be recognised as he always kept his cycle clips on, since he moved around between his various gangs all day on his bike. He was the first one up the ladder and like his team he wore the brown dockyard overalls. His boss was an inspector, normally similarly attired but only with overalls if he chose to wear them, and with a collar and tie but no cycle clips. Next came the foreman, quite an important man with responsibility for gangs all over the dockyard and in total charge of all activities in his speciality field. He occasionally wore a bowler hat, though he usually had sufficient 'presence' not to need additional identification. His boss was one of the dockyard officers, a chartered engineer of some type. These last two didn't often appear in overalls, but wore white ones like Naval Officers should they need to do so.

I'd heard a story concerning one of the foremen, disliked by most of his men. Someone saw his bowler hat on the ground on the dockside and took a swipe with his boot, hoping to see it soar through the air and land in a mucky part of the basin. What he didn't know was that there was a billet of steel under the hat. He hopped around on one foot clutching the other one which, Tom-and-Jerry-like, was no doubt swelling up with a red pulsating bump on the end, until someone took pity and helped him hobble off to the first aid post.

We settled well into our Alverstoke house. I used the garage as a workshop to complete a chest of drawers that I'd started at Lee, also one or two other items of furniture, a cot for Paul and various wooden toys. The Morris Traveller was a delight, with its fold-down rear seats that were an innovation for the time. When we set off as a family, we would stack up the back of the car with all our luggage, with a mattress on the top. Then we'd lift the two sleeping children into the car at the crack of dawn and drive most of the way to our destination before they woke up. They both tended to be carsick, so keeping them distracted once they were awake was important. The tiresome seatbelt hadn't been invented at that time, but the low traffic density and relatively low speed of ordinary cars meant the roads were fairly safe without.

For day-to-day living we found all we wanted in the local village shops. There was a good bakery, a post office and a small grocer. Patricia tended to visit the shops she was familiar with in Lee-on-Solent, particularly Quick Turnover, a fruit and veg establishment which did a Covent Garden run every morning and kept its prices down in spite of it being a village shop. It was the perfect example of the adage 'A quick penny is better than a slow sixpence' and it thrived. We also preferred the Lee butcher, who hung his meat better than the Alverstoke one. Slightly less visited places such as a dry cleaner were to be found in Gosport, so we seldom needed to travel into a big town. Portsmouth was somewhere we visited in the evening for social functions, or maybe Patricia would occasionally go there for clothes.

We discovered the downside of living in a house with views of the sea. Although we were supposedly sheltered by the Isle of Wight, the winter gales whipped across the Solent and sometimes it was difficult to open the garage doors or struggle to the post-box just outside our front gate without being bowled over. Our bedroom curtains fluttered inwards in spite of the windows being tight shut. There was certainly no shortage of fresh air in the house. Our hot water, also the heat for the back room, came from a coke-fired boiler, one of those freestanding stoves with mica-windowed doors. The chimney leaked acrid fumes into the back room, which, because it was usually the warmest place in the house, was where the children spent most of the day. We often wondered if it was doing any damage to their health, but there was not a lot we could do about it. I tried my hand at brewing beer, and one of the bottles exploded, so the beery aroma helped disguise the choking fumes for a few days. At that time home brewing was not accepted practice. There were various excise restrictions about bypassing the duty payable on beer, so nobody tried. Then one of my ship's staff told me he brewed his own beer, and said he bought all the gear from a hardware shop in Fareham. I called in there and in an under-the-counter voice enquired about screw-top bottles, dried hops and the like. I was told that Boots the Chemist next door stocked brewer's yeast, more commonly sold for some health purpose, so I got that. My early attempts were extremely acceptable, providing a lovely flavoursome brew far more enjoyable than the watery pub beers, so I suddenly became quite popular.

My radio chief joined the ship. Like the other two, he was an experienced salt-of-the-earth type and completed my complement of section heads. I felt lucky to be so well served. The ship had now reached the point where the hull and superstructure was complete and she was moved from the dry dock to a berth in the adjoining basin for final fitting out. Tony Tucker would soon be able to light his boilers and test out his steam machinery. The Captain joined and a few days later most of the seaman officers. They all went off together on various courses to prepare them to man this new type of vessel. There were four under construction at this time, all converted battle class destroyers, and would be known as 'radar pickets', with the role of steaming ahead of the main fleet providing a sort of forward aircraft control point way ahead of the base carrier. In some ways this was similar to the role played by the old Skyraider aircraft in my Bulwark days. It was appropriate, therefore, that our new Captain, John Elgar, should be an ex-Fleet Air Arm pilot with an understanding of the technicalities of such operations. But he had limited experience of small ships and, to Colin Marr's disgust, was no great ship handler. He needn't have worried, for with Colin as his number one and another young 'pusser'-type seaman officer as navigator, he would be well protected. Nevertheless, it was the Captain who gave the orders when manoeuvring the ship and good judgment based on experience was needed for this.

A month later came the great day when Agincourt locked through one of the dry docks that connected the basin with the harbour, all ready for her first trip to sea. Steam was raised, our main engines were tested and the ship shed all the wires that had joined her to the fitting out jetty for so long. Huge cables were connected from the ship to large capstans positioned around the basin, and dockyard workmen pulled on various wires, dragging the ship across until she was lined up ready to enter one of the locks. The gates closed behind us and the ones at the other end opened. We went ahead on our engines, and gently eased out into the open water beyond, a fussy little dockyard tug nudging here and there. Half an hour later we were safely secured alongside at South Railway Jetty, next to the aircraft carrier HMS Eagle which dwarfed us by her bulk. Two days later the rest of the ship's company arrived, and shortly after that we began to store ship. Then we left for a short run up and down the Solent with the ship full of dockyard personnel checking everything was working, ship's staff beside them signing acceptance chits as each piece of equipment passed its trials. This went for everything from the ship's main engines to the smallest radio set, and included such mundane items as the wardroom kettle. One by one it all became 'ours', ready for the great day when the last of the brown-overalled dockies would leave, both sides breathing a sigh of relief.

The local wine merchant, Saccone and Speed, watched the build-up of wardroom officers from their offices on The Hard, just outside the Dockyard gates. When everybody had joined, we were delighted to receive a wine-tasting invitation one lunchtime. Off we went, myself not fully appreciating the reason for this (I do tend to be rather thick at times...). We started with some very expensive wines which all tasted superb, and made appropriate comments. Colin Marr reckoned he was a bit of a wine buff, made notes, talked in wine-speak and rolled the wine around his glass in a most professional way. Nobody spat any out, though. After a while we'd dropped down to some good, honest cheap stuff and by this time they all tasted good. At the end of an hour we were all happily inebriated, Colin placed a generous order for our forthcoming sea time, and the Captain placed his own order, including some quite expensive wines for entertaining any important guests he might have. We rolled back to the ship, happy.

HMS Agincourt shows off her paces off the Purbeck coast.

The ship's commissioning ceremony took place on the jetty, wives and families joining in and swarming on board afterwards to inspect us from top to bottom, both Susan and Paul running around managing to find spots where there was still wet paint for them to stick their fingers into. In the wardroom Colin clapped his hands and commanded the messman to produce bottles of 'delicious Liebfraumilch' for the guests (already he realised he'd ordered far too much of this one, found it too sweet for his palate, and hoped the rest of us would ensure we had none over by the end of our time).

We had our first proper run out to sea, down the west Solent and across to the measured mile course between Swanage and St. Aldhelm's Head where Chief put her through her speed trials, opening up to full speed while we creamed down the coast a couple of hundred yards offshore past the two huge masts that mark the measured mile, leaving a long white wake behind us straight as a die. Chief clambered up through the engineroom hatch clutching his slide rule and called out "Guess what our m.p.g. is at the moment!" I thought it couldn't be much. "About a quarter?" I ventured. "Seven!" he pronounced, "g.p.m. That is, seven gallons per mile." It made our cars seem frugal in the extreme, but they weren't over 2,000 tons pushing through all that water. The energy expended churning up such a huge wake accounted for much of our fuel consumption.

We returned to Portsmouth where John Elgar had the problem of trying to come alongside in our allotted space at South Railway jetty immediately behind Eagle's enormous slab-sided stern, with the added complication of a running tide. We didn't have overmuch room for there was another ship just beyond our berth, in fact it was rather like trying to park one's car in a gap not that much bigger than the car itself. He nosed his bows in to the jetty and got a line ashore, then slowly went astern on his outer engine and ahead on the other one to bring the ship round, but misjudged it and found he was heading for the vessel in front, so quickly increased his astern revolutions only to find he was now heading backwards too fast. We bumped the precious Eagle, though not too seriously. Still, it meant John Elgar had to go round to the Eagle as soon as we were secured and make a formal apology to her captain—not a good start for his first command. The dockyard quickly patched up both ships the next day and the incident was pushed under the carpet.

There were several more days of minor work to be completed, and then we embarked ammunition ready for our workup down at Portland. Little tubby lighters came across the harbour from the main ammunition jetty on the Gosport side, and we spent all day hoisting the heavy shells and cartridges aboard and stowing them in our magazine. Agincourt was fitted with just the one 4.5 inch gun, the other two having been removed during her conversion. One had been replaced with one of the early ship-to-air guided weapons systems, while the other had gone to make way for all the additional radar equipment and associated offices that the ship now needed in her new role. About this time I had applied for a grant from the Nuffield Trust for a small amount of 'recreation' money, which I said we could use to build three little one-sail sailing boats called Minisails, forerunners of today's sail boards. The money had been approved and I had ordered three home-assembly kits. Just before we sailed for Portland a tatty lorry arrived alongside and a large pile of skimpy lengths of wood were dumped on the dockside, like a load of oversize matchsticks. Was this it? The driver handed over a small cardboard box in which he said were the rest of the parts, and would I sign here, please.

Colin Marr was very dismissive about this venture, and told us we would have to find room for the kits on the roof of the Chief Stoker's workshop, just beside the funnel. Somewhat to my surprise, my friends the ordnance artificer and electrical artificer who had both agreed to build the boats with me, checked all the parts and found it complete. We tied everything down under a tarpaulin and wondered where and when we might ever find time to build the things. All I had seen in the advertisement had been a small photo of a prototype being sailed on an attractive reservoir.

The families came to see the ship off, and we sailed for our shakedown followed by a six-week workup at Portland. In Weymouth Bay we 'degaussed' the ship. This involved steaming back and forth across a network of cables laid on the bottom of the sea, while a TAS (Torpedo and Anti-Submarine) officer ashore in his control room took readings of our magnetic signature, then radioed us to make incremental changes to an electrical circuit on board that would minimize the ship's magnetism. Satisfied at last, we dropped anchor and the officer came on board to give us our certificate and to enjoy a duty-free drink. The captain joined us in the wardroom and we listened with some amusement while this hoary old salt, a commissioned CPO or 'old and bold' as they were known, went on about proper seamen during which he somewhat dismissively spoke of Fleet Air Arm men as a lot of petrol pigeons. At this point his eye alighted on Johnny Elgar's wings so he had to backtrack as best he could. Our own TAS officer was a similar type, and now I think of it, most of them were much the same.

We came alongside the jetty at the Portland Naval Base to be greeted by a signal as we arrived saying how scruffy the ship looked. This was the start of a gruelling period where we were subjected to the full force of FOST (Flag Officer, Sea Training) and his staff. The idea was that we should be subjected to a continuous bombardment of critical appraisal twenty-four hours a day, most of it at sea with FOST's staff embarked to keep us on our toes. At the end of that time we should have gelled as a ship's company, and become a smartly turned out ship and a quick response fighting unit. Every day we closed up at action stations, tested all our equipment, joined in exercises with submarines, other surface ships, helicopters (shades of my 845 days!) with bombardment exercises on towed targets or pilotless aircraft. The last of these was quite fun, the 'pilot' arriving on our bridge clutching his remote control box, for all the world like any model aircraft enthusiast. The aircraft itself was a somewhat larger model, about eight feet long with what looked like a lawnmower engine to drive it. It was launched from our deck with a catapult and flew around like an angry hornet controlled by the pilot who sent it off until it was a thousand feet up and several miles away, then turned to fly backwards and forwards while we loosed off at it with our 4.5 inch gun. The noise of this gun was appalling and I tried to keep below whenever I realised it might be fired, since I found the pain in my ears quite excruciating. The Navy used to laugh at the way gunnery officers and others subjected to gunfire went deaf while still serving but it was not until some years later when men tried to sue the Services for causing this damage that anyone took it seriously. Nowadays strict precautions are taken when firing any sort of noisy weapon, or working any noisy machinery for that matter.

In the evenings we came back alongside, and apart from one or two occasions when the staff sprung a sudden emergency on us, such as setting fire to the ship or telephoning to report that an enemy agent had been seen creeping aboard unnoticed, we were able to relax, though usually too exhausted to do much. However, I found a large boatshed full of bits and pieces of naval craft with a slip nearby, and took over a corner of this to build our Minisails. The three of us set to with pots of Aerolite adhesive and quickly assembled the framework of the first of them. One evening a couple of men in sailing gear came through the shed to leave an outboard motor there, when one of them saw me and came over. It was none other than Percy Gick, my Bulwark captain, now a rear admiral; with him was FOST himself, but unrecognised out of uniform. Percy chatted about old times, and showed much interest in the Minisail taking shape. My two fellow boatbuilders had no idea who these two men were, so treated them just like they would any other passer by, which was exactly what both the admirals would have liked. That chance meeting probably helped us with our workup, for it demonstrated we could play as well as work, something always approved of.

Our air direction officer, Dick Withinshaw, had been on a weekend to his home in Portchester, returning by train with his golf clubs to discover they had been offloaded in error from the luggage van at some previous station. He'd had notification they had been found and were now waiting at Weymouth station, so four of us set off from Portland one evening to collect them and have a few drinks. We'd left the car at the far end of the high street, so when the pub shut we walked back along the deserted street when Dick announced he could easily cover the full length in a couple of shots. Calling 'fore!' in his best golfer's shout, he tee'd off, and using a number two wood, sent his ball slicing down the centre of the road on a murderous head-high trajectory. How he never hit anything was a miracle. Back in the car and on our way along the Chesil Beach road towards Portland, the driver announced he could do the ton along that bit of road and proceeded to demonstrate. I was too scared to shout and the others too full of alcohol to be scared. It is not a memory I relish.

Next morning my electrical petty officer was chatting to me on the upper deck while we waited for morning colours.

"Good run ashore last night, Sir?" I told him about the golf.

"Might have seen you if it'd been a bit later."

"You ashore, then?"

"Oh yes, Sir, very good time." He was known as a bit of a ladies' man.

"What did you get up to, then?"

"Well, Sir, I ended up with this young lady, Sir. Very good she was." "Where?"

He smiled and said dreamily, "All over…"

"No, no, no. Where did you get to?"

"All the way, Sir. On the promenade, in one of the shelters, Sir."

"Oh, really, Slater! You'll give us a bad reputation."

"Not me, Sir. I was being very discreet. On the side facing the sea. But as I was going up I noticed a familiar backside through the glass in the other side of the shelter also going up."

"Did you really?"

"Yes, Sir. I'd recognize that arse anywhere. Chief Stoker's it was. I banged on the glass and called out 'How's yours, Stokes?' He nearly fell off. Quite put him off his stroke, it did, poor old sod."

Petty officer Slater was incorrigible, and I never knew whether to believe any of the colourful stories he told me. On another occasion when he was looking a bit shattered after a good run ashore one of the others said he ought to start a course of Phyllosan.

"You know," he said, "Fortifies the over forties and all that." Then he came out with a little ditty:

"Uncle George and Auntie Mabel fainted at the kitchen table.
Let that be a serious warning, never do it in the morning.
But Phyllosan has set them right, and now they do it morn and night.
And Uncle George is hoping soon, to do it in the afternoon."

Our own weapons officer, Frank Harris, was another with a one-track mind. When he was bragging one day someone nudged me and reminded me that some people talk about it whereas others stay quiet and get on with it. You recognize the latter by the secret smile, but they never admit to anything. I asked Frank Harris how he seemed to find a willing partner every time he went ashore.

"I'll show you," he said. "Next time you're going into Weymouth, I'll come too."

I didn't take him up specifically, but was sufficiently intrigued when I did notice him on his own one evening walking into one of the seafront hotels that I called his bluff and followed him in where he bought me a drink while the two of us settled ourselves at the saloon bar.

"There you are," he said, looking around and seeing a couple of women the other side of a fairly full room. "That one on the left, possibly both of them."

"How do you know?"

"Watch. See how she's glancing around? Her eye lingered on that bloke over there… Now her friend's turned to see what's taking her attention." The woman now glanced our way and I sensed a look pass between her and Frank. A minute or two later Frank nudged me and said, "C'mon, we're in!"

He got up and walked over to the two women. I followed somewhat reluctantly. I didn't want to be an actual witness, and I certainly didn't want to be part of a foursome. The two women seemed to me like a couple of friends, probably in their forties, stopping for a quiet drink at the end of a day out before setting off home. Frank began the chat-up. An hour later when the pub closed, he had persuaded them to drive us back to Portland naval base, which they did willingly enough. I sat in the front with the frumpier of the two endeavouring to make small talk, while Frank apparently got to work on the other one in the back seat, much to my embarrassment. He never admitted what they had actually got up to, but I couldn't help thinking of his nice wife alone at home with their family, a Plymouth girl with a delicious Devonshire dialect, whom we'd met at Agincourt's commissioning.

We finished the first Minisail, painted and varnished it and one evening launched her in Portland harbour. I was the first to set off, hanging on to what was little more than a hollow surfboard about ten inches thick in the middle with a fixed mast and a single sail. I soon had the hang of making it go forwards (rather than backwards, which it would do quite well) and set off across the harbour, conscious of the fact that it was only held together by glue and might open up and sink any minute. The other two had a go after me, then we celebrated with a drink at the harbour pub before returning on board. It had taken us three weeks to build in between evening duties and the occasional run ashore into Weymouth. Clearly we wouldn't finish all three before the workup was finished, but we might complete a second one.

At the weekend Patricia drove over with the children in the Traveller and took me out onto the downs looking down on Chesil Beach, where we enjoyed a picnic lunch. Then we drove on to Maiden Castle and the children ran all over the grass ramparts until they were so exhausted they had to be carried back to the car, where they slept most of the way home. I returned to the ship, refreshed after this brief outing on a lovely sunny day.

At six next morning we battled out to sea against a fresh westerly gale, taking green seas right over our bow. By mid morning several of our ventilation fans had burnt out, salt water having got into the works. The most serious one was the fan that supplied forced air to a ghastly design of oil-heated cooking stove in the ship's main galley. If the fan stopped, the oil supply did not, it merely burnt with a thick smokey flame, giving out little heat but filling the galley with sticky black soot. We were only the second Battle conversion to complete, so I felt justified in drafting a signal to the Admiralty design people who conceived the idea of such an unworkable galley saying what we thought of their efforts, in particular siting the fan in the spot most likely to be hit with a douche of seawater. Fortunately, the galley also had a deep fat fryer that produced wonderful chips, and if you feed sailors with chips they are generally happy. The problem was partly that the ship's electrical supply was DC, so all the motors had commutators and brushes, parts that wore and required regular maintenance, and as a lot of heat was generated inside the motors they couldn't be completely sealed against the ingress of water. Then to exacerbate this by siting about fifty of these motors in exposed positions on the upper deck and expect them to work for long was asking the impossible. I was naïve enough to believe that because Agincourt's conversion had been designed by so-called professional experts, it would have been done correctly, fool that I was!

We returned to Portsmouth for a few days before joining in some exercise in the North Sea, so I had a chance to nip home for the weekend. Walking over 'Pneumonia' bridge across Alverstoke Creek I looked down on several large yachts occupying the bays where the motor torpedo boats used to tie up a few years previously, the end one being where I had joined the twelve-metre Wol in my Collingwood days. In one of these was a familiar figure. I diverted down to the nearby slip and had a closer look. Yes, it was my old Chief from 845 days, Leslie 'Bungy' Williams, the heavy boat man to whom I'd introduced the idea of 'yachting'. He was busy with another man messing around with a complicated self-steering gear on the stern of a huge sixty-foot plus single-masted ocean racer called The Spirit of Cutty Sark. I hailed him and he invited me aboard. He had taken a long break from Yeovilton where he was now stationed in order to sail this monster in the forthcoming Transatlantic single-handed race. The other man, Blondie Haslar, was the designer of the self-steering gear and they were ironing out some operational problems it was having. Leslie was just the same; quiet, unflappable, wonderfully laidback and late as usual. He had to put in 600 miles of solo sailing in this boat in order to qualify to enter the race, and time was running out. The internal fitting-out was way behind, but most serious of all was the self-steering which kept breaking. I left them at it, but Leslie invited me to join him on a publicity fund-raising sail that weekend around the Solent. Could I bring Patricia? Yes, of course. I hurried home to give her the news.

We turned up on a gloomy gusty day for our trip on the Solent. Leslie was halfway through an interview, sitting in the cockpit with a cameraman crouched in front of him while a couple of TV people stood around. He called me over and asked me to get the mainsail ready to hoist, as they were short of time, then continued his interview. The boat was enormous, the boom itself a good foot across at its largest diameter. The interview completed, the camera crew departed to board a launch that would film us out on the sea. Leslie was to sit by himself while the rest of us hid below the coaming during the film sequences, so that it would look as if he were sailing solo. We had a TV man with us in radio communication with the film boat, and made several runs back and forth to the Island. Watching the film on Southern Television a few days later, it wasn't obvious that Leslie was not alone in the Atlantic, but the giveaway for those few people able to watch in colour was the soupy Solent.

Another sailing event about this time was the America's Cup. We'd seen the British entry launched and fitted out at Camper and Nicholson, watched on television the huge sails being made in Ratsy and Lapthorn's sailmaking loft nearby, and seen the splendid boat out on the Solent, Peter Scott at the helm. Peter would pass our front gate each day in his open car en route to HMS Dolphin from where he boarded the boat.

Agincourt joined in several exercises, always operating out ahead of the main fleet in our air direction role. This was nice in many ways, for it meant there was little opportunity for the usual fleet shenanigans of station keeping, with ships flashing lamp signals to one another and all the other tiresome activities. We preferred it that way, though Colin Marr always looked wistfully at other ships when we saw them. Maybe he had his heart set on upgrading one day. We called in to Plymouth a couple of times, then went round into the Bristol Channel and visited Tenby where the non-duty watch was granted leave. This was the first time we had been in company with our 'Captain D'—the senior captain of our four-ship flotilla. He was a real 'pusser', a stickler for correct protocol, came down like a ton of bricks on anyone who wasn't efficient enough for his high standards, and was generally a pain. One got the impression no one aboard his own ship, HMS Rhyl, ever smiled. Agincourt was at the other end of that spectrum. Not only did most of us really enjoy our time aboard, but John Elgar ruled his ship with compassion, humour, understanding, held the highest principles, yet brooked no slackness. He had the absolute loyalty of every man aboard. It could be done, but Captain D did not have the skill. Unfortunately the four ships were graded by the seniority of their commanding officers, and whereas Captain D was the senior, John Elgar was by a long way the most junior. 'Canteen Boat', they called it, and when together we tended to be given the jobs no one else wanted. Fortunately this hardly applied in practice since by their very role, the four ships seldom worked together.

During the night in Tenby the wind got up and Agincourt began bumping rather heavily against the jetty. Chief had reduced our notice for steam to four hours (which meant one of the boilers was fired up, with steam available, but the main engines were allowed to go fairly cold). The captain was rather concerned after listening to the weather forecast and deemed it advisable to prepare for sea, so we came down to one hour's notice, and sent patrols ashore to round up any sailors still not yet back on board. By first light the storm was even worse, so we sailed for open water, much to everyone's relief. At least we could ride out the storm without risk of damage. We'd left three sailors behind who, on finding the ship had sailed without them, had reported aboard HMS Rhyl. Rhyl signalled us that she too was proceeding to sea and would transfer the sailors back to us when she arrived at the point where we were weathering the storm in the lee of a headland. This was quite an interesting transfer, since it was clearly unsafe to lower a boat in such seas, and was achieved by the Rhyl lowering an inflated liferaft into the relative smooth water on her lee side, the men then clambered aboard after which Rhyl moved away to one side while we came in to the place where she'd been. Then all we had to do was to remain stationary, protecting the liferaft from the heavy seas, while we were blown down onto it when ropes could be lowered and the men hauled aboard. It was all over in twenty minutes, quite long enough for all of them to become extremely seasick in the bucking waves. We stayed at sea all day, and then just as it was getting dark we were requested to answer an emergency call from an Admiralty tug, which had been towing a naval hulk when her tow parted. The hulk (a Royal Fleet Auxiliary vessel on its way to the scrap yard) had drifted in towards the north Devon coast and was in danger of going onto the rocks. We couldn't really see what help we could give, but the tug asked us to stand by. By this time BBC radio was describing the saga taking place off "The ironbound coast of Hartland Point" where the wind was now blowing Force 10 directly onshore. No self-respecting seaman will approach a lee shore like this in bad weather, and John Elgar was quite rightly reluctant to come too near. The vessel by now was aground, and the tug, standing off a hundred yards away, had succeeded in floating a line down to her. There were a few men aboard in no immediate danger, but they were hampered by the extreme darkness of the night. This was where we were able to help. Turning round so that we were head on to the seas, we kept position as near as we dared and trained our twenty inch searchlight at the wreck, a searing focussed arclight which probably blinded anyone who looked at it. We stayed there all through the hours of darkness, and I spent that night with my chief radio tiffy in the radar office high up under our mainmast. We'd had trouble on our main radar, and together were frantically trying to diagnose the cause, and having done so we endeavoured to fix it. This was quite difficult, for every time one of us opened the door to get out, great sprays of salt water crashed in. At one stage, while fighting my way down to the comfort of the main part of the ship I heard shouts from our bridge and answering shouts from the water beside me. There, plunging wildly up and down in the swell, was an RNLI lifeboat, her yellow-oilskinned crew hanging on tight. They'd come to thank us for our assistance. What courage it must take for ordinary men to leave the warmth of their beds on such a night and risk their lives in those mountainous seas.

We visited Londonderry, relieving a frigate of the Londonderry squadron whose crew were due for some leave. Going along the northern coast and up Lough Foyle was interesting enough, but I found the town so depressing I wanted to get away as soon as possible. Several of my chief petty officers went ashore to sample the local beer and invited me to join them, so I felt obliged to accept, but only stopped briefly. To me the no-hope atmosphere hung over the town like a poisonous cloud, not helped by the weather that had clamped down, a light drizzle getting into everything, the town grey and colourless like the few people we saw creeping about. And yet this was in the early sixties, before the more serious 'troubles' had flared up again.

We had a maintenance period back in Portsmouth which included a brief docking. While there, the ship's company lived ashore in Portsmouth Barracks, except for the lucky married ones who escaped home. Patricia's life, dominated by the two young children, interminable housework in this old place with few modern conveniences, and lots of visits to and from other Agincourt grass widows, was relieved for a while. We'd heard that for the second part of Agincourt's commission we would be in the Mediterranean, away from home for a year. Hopefully, it might be possible for families to go out to our Malta base for some of that time. It was still a long way off.

The First Sea Lord, Admiral Sir Michael le Fanu, was rushing through on a flying visit. His staff officer phoned one morning to tell us to assemble on the dockside in an hour's time when the admiral wished to address the ship's company. A youngish energetic man, showing no signs of the leukaemia which was to carry him off a year later while still in office, leapt out of his car, pulled up a box on which he stood, and bade us gather round. He chatted about our jobs, the esprit de corps we enjoyed in the RN, wished us a happy time and was gone. It must have been like that for the men of the Eighth Army under Montgomery. Previous First Sea Lords I'd distantly come across had all been august, dignified looking men, chests heavy with rows of medal ribbons, surrounded by protective staff officers. What a breath of fresh air to meet le Fanu! Later, when I did get to speak with him, he told us how a couple of years previously as Second Sea Lord he'd been on a formal visit to HMS Ganges, the boys training establishment at Shotley. Ever the thwarted thespian, he'd arrived unannounced the previous day wearing old countryman's clothes, visited the Shotley pub where the establishment chiefs and POs would repair of an evening, mixing incognito with them and gleaning a heap of useful information about the place. He reckoned that was the most reliable way to really find out what a ship was like! No, he hadn't played that trick with us!

Back at sea again, we took part in some more exercises, then set off on our own for a visit to the German naval town of Flensburg close on the Danish border. We went through the Kiel Canal, an interesting transit passing from the North Sea to the Baltic through the flat lands in this part of Schleswig Holstein. I'd never been to Germany before, and didn't know at all what to expect, certainly not the warm welcome with which we were received. The visit was hosted by the local Naval training establishment who invited men of all ranks to visit different parts of the town, take part in sports and drink their wonderful beer. Flensburg itself was clean and smart and felt very 'safe' at night, when on the Saturday several of the wardroom tried out a few pubs. To a man we all became pleasantly inebriated, and so did everyone else around, everybody, friends and strangers alike, moving about in groups together. As usual when in a foreign country, I felt embarrassed that I hadn't a word of German, and had to speak to everyone in my own native English. But the Germans spoke English and did so far better than us so one hardly realised we were in a German-speaking country.

In the morning everyone awoke with a crashing hangover, feeling very delicate indeed. This was unfortunate, for most of the wardroom officers had been invited to visit The Princess Victoria of Saxe-Coburg-Gotha. She was a great granddaughter of Queen Victoria through her fourth son, the Duke of Albany. We were taken by coach through beautiful wooded country, all colourful reds and yellows in the autumnal sun on a desperately cold day with a hard frost, until we arrived at a fairytale castle built in the middle of a lake, a short causeway connecting it to the shore rather like Leeds Castle. The castle itself contained a museum which we were shown around, clearly as honoured visitors since we were escorted by a guide with a large bunch of keys who opened doors and switched on lights as we went from room to room. The place was totally without any form of heating, the stone walls icy to the touch. None of us were prepared for this extreme cold and wore no overcoats, so shivered our way round hoping it might do wonders for our hangovers. I saw a display of military hats, one of which was one of those splendid brass contraptions with a spike on the top, reminiscent of the Those Magnificent Men in their Flying Machines film. I tried it on for size and it fitted perfectly, rather to my surprise as I have a very small head. Putting it back on its stand, I read on a label that it belonged to Kaiser Wilhelm.

The Princess lived in a large four-storey building flanking the road back across the causeway. Thankfully it had some noticeable heating, and in a largish drawing room upstairs we met the Princess, a dignified lady in her seventies with a remarkable likeness to all the Victorian dynasty, most of whom were depicted in silver-framed photographs on the tables and piano top in this comfortable slightly untidy room. We were offered sherry and she asked us lots of questions about our stay, the perfect host. John Elgar was at his most charming in spite of an obvious—to me—sore head, had swotted up on his history and so was able to discuss the Victorian connection.

The Naval attaché had organised one or two other events, one of which was as guests of the Lubeck police who would show us the notorious iron curtain passing only a mile or two to the east of Lubeck town. They wore wonderfully smart uniforms made of a beautiful material which made us feel very drab, and drove about in pristine Jeep-like vehicles. One of the sinister wooden towers was visible across a ploughed no man's land. I was conscious of its 'evil eye'—Soviet guards looking at us through their binoculars.

The Naval attaché offered to take three of us in his car to Hamburg as he had business there. When I asked what happened in Hamburg, he looked at me pityingly and said I'd better come and find out. So I joined the Gunnery Officer and the Schoolie and off we went, scorching along a frighteningly narrow autobahn. By now I discovered the attraction was probably the red light area, the Reeperbahn, full of drinking places and night clubs, some of them a little questionable. We checked in to a clinically clean and uninteresting boarding house for somewhere to stay overnight, then set off to explore. Actually it wasn't quite so titillating as we'd been led to believe. I found it rather unreal to venture into the Winklestrasse where every house had a 'shop window' lit by the appropriate red light in which a hopeful lady sat reading until she noticed she was being ogled, whereupon she looked up from her book and made come hither signs. All these people were licensed; their licenses displayed in the window, and apparently had to undergo regular health checks if they wished to remain in business. It was all very clinical and unromantic, and only the Germans could put the oldest profession onto such a businesslike footing. At least it kept them off the streets. The striptease artist who performed in the bars and (in our case) came down to join us for a chat after her show seemed more interested in making a few honest bob than anything else. Late in the evening we had arranged to rendezvous with the Naval attaché in a large beer hall, which we duly did. We sat quaffing our beer from earthenware pots with lids, listening to a super oompah band until he arrived. The 'business' for which he needed to go to Hamburg was with him, a very delectable English lady who lived in the city.

Back through the Kiel Canal we eventually fetched up at Portsmouth where Christmas leave was granted. It was particularly cold that winter (the start of the 1963 big freeze). Patricia and the children more or less lived in the back room with the coke boiler and its fumes. Patricia's uncle had been a coal merchant in Felixstowe before he retired, so when he came to visit one day he made straight for our coalhouse casting a professional eye over the contents. Not a lot of visitors go straight to a coalhouse when they arrive. The children seemed to be growing so fast, Paul now extremely active and both of them together quite a handful. We were blessed with frequent visits from Patricia's parents, and often left the children with them when we went out, so our social life together was easy to achieve. We had our Scottish Country Dancing, with a choice of several venues to try, and now that I owned a kilt we even bought tickets for a Highland Ball at the Southsea Pier Ballroom where Jimmy Shand played for us. That was when we discovered we were quite unfit to dance in such exalted company, and with hindsight we must have spoilt any set we joined. But it was a start.

When Christmas leave was over Agincourt sailed for Greenock, a temporary base where we spent a month going to sea each day working off the Ayrshire coast with submarines whose skippers were doing their 'Perisher' training. Although cold, it was nothing like as bad in that part of Scotland as in Alverstoke. This seemed to be a good time for me to try to grow a beard, for we were out of the social scene for a while. The Navy is happy for its men to be seen in public suitably bearded, but not in the first week or two when the wearer just looks unkempt. Arafat had yet to come on the scene with his designer stubble. I had to formally request 'permission to grow' from John Elgar who enthusiastically granted it.

Back at home again, there was a foot of snow everywhere, and the children were having a wonderful time. Pavements were not gritted, so getting around was rather a problem, since Patricia was unhappy using the car with so much snow about. Salting roads was not in those days the accepted way to make them safe, though in a small way the local council used to spray seawater on the main roads which was cheap and quite successful. I fixed wooden sleds to the wheels of our pram which we then dragged along the slippery pavements, this being by far the easiest way of getting to the local shops. It seemed the winter went on forever, and even in March when I had my next spell of leave we were still deep in snow. My beard went down well with Patricia and her parents, so I decided to keep it, though when we next visited my father he said it was dreadful and commanded me to shave it off at once (I didn't).

We took part in a long NATO exercise off the Normandy coast with Dutch and French ships, about twenty ships altogether. During this time we entered Brest on several separate occasions, berthed three abreast. We were the middle ship on one occasion, with a French ship on one side and a Dutchman the other. The French tended to be somewhat haughty and their ship smelt rather odd, while the Dutch and ourselves got along well. The Dutch seemed to have a huge capacity for alcohol, with good beer and a frightening choice of lethal spirits which they drank as if it was water. We tended to visit the French for petty aperitifs and the Dutch for serious drinking (the French were too snooty to join us in the drinking). At one party where a voluptuous French lady was holding forth, she discussed how the British were so restrained, rather formal in their social intercourse.

"But eez not deeficult to know what they eez thinking," she said.

"What am I thinking?" I asked her.

"Ah, that eez easy," she replied with a seductive leer. "You speak viv your eyes, I know exactly what you are theenking!" Oh dear, I hadn't realised I spoke with my eyes. I really would have to be more discreet in future. Or maybe not…

During our Brest stays I made several visits around the town. The weather was much warmer now, and the boules were out on the dusty pitches in several parts of the town. I passed a shop with some lovely reproduction paintings in the window and went in. There were racks of prints to explore, and from a gallery above one could hear music wafting down which exactly matched the mood of my picture hunting. I went upstairs to find a record shop there, selling specifically classical recordings. Having the two together in one shop was very astute, and I ended up buying both pictures and records.

It hadn't escaped the attention of the French that our converted Battle class ship was named after a certain British victory when an army under Henry V thrashed the French at the Battle of Agincourt in 1415. Four of our sailors thought it would be an appropriate idea to go to the town of Agincourt and call on the mayor with our greetings. They bravely set off on red Service bicycles, in their uniform with the HMS Agincourt cap ribbon, returning four days later with a letter of greeting from the mayor and lots of photographs.

Colin Marr's promotion to full commander came through. He heard about it by signal while we were on passage after the exercises were over. This would mean he would be leaving the ship for a command of his own. We celebrated at ten in the morning with champagne, the occasion in the case of some of us being to celebrate his imminent departure. The supply officer and myself also received our promotions to lieutenant commander, routine in my case as I had done my allotted time as a lieutenant without any accelerated seniority—that was something that only happened to brighter people as a means of speeding their ascent to higher things.

We returned to Portsmouth for some leave and a change of first lieutenant. Colin's replacement was Jasper Crawford, a fast-living fun officer who depended greatly on his departmental heads and continued throughout the rest of Agincourt's commission in that way. For the first time I was able to operate the department without the first lieutenant's interference which made my job far more pleasant and I had more responsibility, which I preferred. Jasper got along with everybody, but the seaman departments missed Colin's professionalism.

The day neared when Agincourt was due to sail for the Mediterranean. A programme had been issued, which showed all sorts of interesting places the ship would visit, including a passage through the Suez Canal. Our base would be Malta where there would be short maintenance periods and a docking, so it was suggested the wives and families might like to think about spending a bit of time out there for their summer holidays. Such a prospect made the parting less awful.

13

Agincourt in the Mediterranean

Leaving Portsmouth was even more of a wrench than usual. This time I was saying goodbye for a longish time not only to Patricia but the two children as well. Patricia dropped me off at the gangway, then rushed off without waiting to wave. I knew she would be trying to hold back tears all the way home, and felt dreadful. We sailed swiftly out to Nab Tower, passing a line of waving wives at Sallyport. It was a busy few days, and I buried myself in my work.

Jasper, the new first lieutenant, started energetically, changing masses of things which affected every department in the ship. This could have been disastrous for morale but he knew what he was doing and the ship's company responded wonderfully. My chief electrician was really pleased as he used to upset Colin Marr by wearing his favourite pair of fluffy bedroom slippers when pattering around off-duty in the evenings, something which always sent Colin into paroxysms of suppressed fury. Being the man responsible for the personnel happenings in my department with Colin responsible for personnel matters overall, I was constantly trying to appease both of them. Those days thankfully were over.

I had some new electrical ratings, all of whom were seasick when we went through the Bay of Biscay. On our third day we reached Gibraltar and sunshine and they never looked back. In Gib I enjoyed some super sails in the Minisail, scudding about at breakneck speed. She was so small and light that it was simple for one person to control her in almost any sort of wind. As I said earlier she was a prototype for the first generation of sailboards, which developed from a similar design but with the great advantage of a hinging mast enabling the hull to remain horizontal. HMS Duchess came alongside during our Gib stay and we partied in one another's wardrooms. Her engineering officer turned out to be none other than Cecil Young, my brother-in-law Peter's best man.

We had barely one day in Malta, just long enough to get our mail and refuel and to drop off Jasper's car which he'd insisted on taking out there. He had every intention of bringing out as soon as possible Izzie, his wife, and she would stay for the whole year. Malta was just the same; ramshackle buildings, bad roads full of potholes with polished tarmac surfaces, appalling drivers, and portly policemen strutting about full of importance. Then we were off to the Aegean. Arriving there, we joined up with Greek and Turkish ships, exercised together and tried some cross-operating. Transferring personnel to the Turkish destroyer was a scream. This is an evolution which starts by the transferring ship firing a rifle above the receiving ship as they steam along side by side 150 feet apart. A blank cartridge is loaded in the rifle, down the barrel of which is pushed a brass rod with a thin nylon line tied to one end. The line, plaited non-kinking 'Costin gun line' is flaked down in a bucket so that as the brass rod zips away over the other ship it pays out without snagging. Once this is done, the other ship's deck personnel who have taken cover while the rifle is fired, emerge and grab the line, pulling across a thicker line to which is attached the main transfer cable. One end of this is made fast to the receiving ship while the other end is held by a 'spring'— essentially a line of men who take the strain. Thus when the distance between the ships varies, as indeed it will, the cable always remains taught. A bos'n's chair is slung from a pulley on the cable so that it can be pulled back and forth between the two ships. Personnel are then transferred one at a time. This works a treat with most navies, but the Turks seemed quite fazed by the whole procedure. They only seemed to have two commands for controlling their deck people, one being to have them fallen in as for a ceremonial entering harbour and the other being action stations. In every language we could think of we requested them to take cover while we fired the gun, but they just stared back at us. Finally, we just had to aim high, hoping nothing would snarl up in a rotating radar aerial. Communications were not helped by the Turkish ships employing different radio frequencies to everyone else, so we had to use Morse code and a signalling lantern. After the exercise all the ships dropped anchor in Suda Bay off the Crete coast, and then ships' boats went to and fro for the exercise washups to take place. This all sounds somewhat disorganised, but it was extremely valuable for getting Turkish ships up to speed operating as part of a NATO force. The Greek ships were already pretty good, and operated in much the same way as ourselves. On board Agincourt we had both a Greek and a Turkish observation officer, the Turk, oddly, being by far the easiest to get along with.

After this exercise was over, Agincourt detached and sailed for an informal visit to the Piraeus, where we tied up stern-to against the harbour wall like all the yachts strung along beside us. One or two rather superior gin palaces didn't do this but anchored out in the harbour, mainly because their owners were super-rich plutocrats who don't mix with ordinary sailing people and were probably worried about their privacy and security. However, we felt far more at home with the small boats, and it was fun to walk up and down the harbour wall chatting to all the boat owners we met. One such was 'Voyageur', a converted Looe lugger, lying three along from Agincourt, with a delightful couple who wanted some electrical advice about a wiring job. I sent my weapons tiffy over to help them and followed later. This was the start of a friendship that lasted throughout our time in the Mediterranean. The couple, David and Barbara, had sold their house back home in order to live on board this gorgeous old craft, earning enough to keep her going by chartering her to groups of people wanting to cruise in a fully crewed boat, all found. She could sleep six in great comfort and was booked up all summer. Just now, they were recovering between charters, with a very heavily pregnant Barbara expecting their first child in a month or two, and were wonderfully hospitable. Voyageur was a heavy craft, ideal for the Mediterranean conditions where it's either calm or blowing a hoolie. She was attractively fitted out with a large saloon and three double cabins, also a lovely galley and a bathroom complete with a proper bath. We had the usual ship's cocktail party on our first night, so I invited David and Barbara along. Afterwards they took myself and Ken, our schoolie, to a little taverna high on the hill overlooking the harbour where I had my first taste of the notorious retzina wine. After we had chosen what we'd like to eat, the owner went off to buy some vegetables while his assistant (who kept a butcher's shop) went back there to collect a suitable piece of meat. All very Greek. Next evening it was back to a more normal event when we attended a cocktail party at the home of the British naval Attaché, then had dinner afterwards in a colourless restaurant, before being driven around Athens, which reeked of acrid car exhaust fumes. That left me feeling quite ill; goodness knows what it was doing to all the ancient stonework. Next day on my run ashore I was behind the others leaving the ship, and found them on the jetty with a group of young ladies. They all went a bit quiet as I joined them, and later on one of the women asked me "Are you really a priest?" Well! With my dark colouring and black beard (at that time) my fellow officers had played a rotten trick on me by warning them, "Careful how you go with our visitor; he's a Greek Orthodox priest, but prefers to go ashore incognito; likes to be one of the boys."

The following day one of the British grass widows living along the coast who had been to our cocktail party aboard Agincourt took Frank Harris and myself out for the day. She drove us to Corinth to look at the archaeology, crossing the Corinth Canal which lay deep below the bridge, a narrow cut in the rock seemingly barely a hundred feet wide. That night it was supper in Voyageur with David and Barbara, and the following day I was accosted by an American who wanted to buy our Minisails, and would we provide him with half a dozen more, please. He gave the impression of being a particularly mean money-grabber, not interested at all in the boats, but hoping to buy some at a knockdown price to resell and that left a bad taste with me. However, the Piraeus visit was otherwise wildly enjoyable, and one of the best I was to experience. Not quite so with one of my youngest ratings, though. He had gone ashore on the first night with the purpose of getting drunk with his mates, took up the offer of some lady of the night, then another, then staggered back on board where fortunately he bragged about his exploits. His messdeck was ruled by a leading hand who was excellent at looking after such youngsters. Actually, he was a 'loner' in that he was our only medical hand, with responsibility for the ship's sickbay. He kept an eye on my rating who predictably went down with the clap a few days later for which he was successfully treated. In the Navy getting VD was considered a technical crime, resulting in automatic stoppage of leave until the disease is fully treated, so my lad missed his next shore run.

We left the Piraeus with David and Barbara casting off our stern warps just as they would with any yacht leaving the harbour wall, and several other boat owners stood waving and sounding their klaxons until we turned and headed out to sea once more. Agincourt had booked a passage through the Corinth Canal, which would be interesting. Travelling through this straight cut, the vertical rock walls rising way up on either side of us with the little bridge I'd crossed only a few days previously looking very flimsy, it seemed there would be little room for us. We must have had twenty feet either side at most, but it looked far less. We then headed back to Malta which was reached a couple of days later, stopping briefly at Marsaxlokk (MX), the large bay at the southeast end of Malta, to land the kits for the remaining two Minisails before heading for Grand Harbour where the ship was due to go into dry dock for a fortnight. Jasper had arranged for the ship's company to move ashore and live in the old naval airfield at Hal Far, not so far from MX, so it would be easy for us to pop down there of an evening to build the remaining boats. We'd been offered the use of a large empty seaplane hangar at Kalafrana in which to do the work, and managed to finish both boats in the time available. While out sailing our first one, we quickly discovered the fun of falling off it into the warm water when feeling like a dip. The boat would immediately tip over onto its side whenever the crew fell overboard, but it was always advisable to tie oneself on with a long piece of cord in case she blew away. When sailing these craft one always wore bathing trunks and went barefoot; in my case I tied my spectacles on with a piece of string round the back. Then I was ready for the inevitable capsizes when they came.

We found, slightly to the hurt of our national pride, that the dockyard in Grand Harbour, now privately owned, was far better run than the Portsmouth yard and far more helpful. It was also cheaper for the Navy to use it rather than their own facilites at Portsmouth. Our docking fortnight was soon over and the ship moved round the other side of Valletta to Sliema Creek, the traditional home for ships of our size. When such ships come in through the main entrance, they turn to face out of the creek ready to make a sternboard up the creek past a line of buoys until arriving at their moorings. We did this, tying up at both bow and stern. On our first day, our lines were taken by a waiting dghaisa-man who afterwards came alongside our gangway and introduced himself as Peter, pointing proudly to the beautifully painted nameboard on the back of his dghaisa which proclaimed this was Agincourt's private tender. All the time we were in Malta Peter waited upon us, assiduously looking after our every need. One only had to appear somewhere near the top of the gangway for him to come alongside in case a shore visit was wanted. Likewise ashore at the jetty, he would recognize any Agincourt people arriving there and pull across, leaning over his big sweeps as he propelled his extremely heavy boat forward. Sometimes he would let me work the sweeps while he sat in the back. I liked propelling a boat that way, one could see where one was going, and it was a far better way to power a heavy boat along as one's whole body could be used. Whenever I am faced with rowing a large boat, I like to use the dghaisa method.

In the next creek HMS Ausonia, a Fleet Maintenance Ship, was tied up permanently to one end of Manoel Island, her job to provide assistance to any ship requiring outside help short of major dockyard work. She had huge workshops aboard and could cope with most things. We were often to use her when we were in Malta. I paid a visit to find my old LC6 friend, Joe Snow, was there. He had married Peter Walwyn's sister and the two of them had found a lovely old Maltese house out in the country. Thus started the first of my social visits ashore, a vital need when confined in a small ship for a long time.

Jasper Crawford had bought a little speedboat powered by a hunky outboard, which he intended to use for water skiing. The two of us chugged around Sliema Creek, but it was dull and heavy until up on the plane when it went like a bullet. The speed limit in Sliema didn't allow that, so we went out to the open sea where we quickly discovered the engine drank a tankful of petrol in about an hour. Suddenly we found ourselves wallowing helpless half a mile out to sea with no means of propulsion. Fortunately a smart launch spotted us and came over. It turned out to be the C-in-C's barge, resplendent with crew dressed in spotless whites, who handed us down a silky nylon rope for our tow. They brought us back to Agincourt, much to the consternation of the warships lying in Sliema Creek who panicked when they saw the barge.

We hired an MFV (Motor Fishing Vessel, a heavy tubby craft of about 80 tons powered by twin Gardener diesels) for a day's aquatic outing up the coast. We loaded the wherewithal for a barbecue not forgetting plenty to drink, and towed behind us Jasper's speedboat and a couple of Minisails. Anchored in a lovely rocky bay which we had to ourselves we spent a day swimming, snorkelling, sailing, water skiing, and just enjoying the sun. The weather was perfect, and the only missing items were our families, except for Jasper's wife who had turned up.

Agincourt's next visit was to Rhodes, a difficult anchorage for a ship, as the bottom shelves steeply making it necessary to anchor too close to the shore for safety in all but fair weather. But the weather was fair, and we anchored about five cables from a stationary transmitter vessel belonging to Voice of America. This ship, about the size of a minesweeper but fitted with a huge mast towering up into the sky, transmitted 24 hours a day to anyone at this end of the Mediterranean who felt they needed to hear American radio. We weren't spared either. It came in over our tannoy whenever someone switched on the microphone to make a broadcast, the guardrails round the ship crackled and buzzed with induced static, my ship's radios and radars were affected, and heavens knows what it did to the health of the Voice of America's own crew. The trip ashore only took a few moments, though, and I was able to explore the old part of Rhodes, the Knights of St. John influence still very apparent. The sight of spherical stone missiles about two feet in diameter still protruding out of the battlement walls was a reminder of those days. There was a lot to interest me there, and there were no tourists in spite of Rhodes being a favourite holiday destination. Such tourists as there were seemed to spend their time on the beaches on the other side of the island.

We then moved on to the nearby Turkish coast in the bay of Marmaris, where we anchored for a day or two. This time I took the Naval 14 foot dinghy for a sail, but didn't go ashore. The main attraction of that area was the islands we had to weave our way through to find the large bay beyond. Then we moved on to Izmir for a slightly more formal visit. A formal visit meant a dreaded evolution for the lads in my electrical department under the chief electrician—floodlighting the ship. We were alongside a jetty from where the outboard side of the ship could be viewed from the town area, so floodlighting that side would look good. In their strange wisdom the MoD had supplied the ship with a kit for floodlighting, the official reason being for flag-showing purposes, but a secondary reason was no doubt that floodlighting was also desirable if one was in a dodgy port where there might be unwelcome frogmen having a look at our hull. At Izmir the evolution was purely for ceremonial purposes. The kit consisted of a number of aluminium booms that stuck out from the ship's side every twenty feet or so, on the end of which huge 1000 watt lamps were fitted, pointing back at the ship. When we first tested these on our Portland workup we quickly found that the lamps got extremely hot and a single drop of rain would result in them exploding spectacularly. Not surprising when you think about it. Tongue in cheek I suggested to my chief that there wouldn't be this problem if one could only keep the lamps cool, and what about water cooling; after all the lamp bases were well sealed against water ingress. With some trepidation we tried lowering one of the huge lamps straight into the water without its cumbersome housing, then switched on. The result was wonderful; not only did it stay alight, but would be safe to use in wet weather, and it was ever so much easier to rig up than the official way. On the first night we switched on at dusk and the ship looked as though she were floating in a soft turquoise cloud; quite magnificent. When we used this method in company with other RN ships we were often asked how we'd managed to be issued with such effective floodlighting.

On arrival the British Naval attaché had come on board with a list of activities he'd arranged, starting with the usual ice-breaking party on board and including a private visit to the archaeological site of Ephesus in which I was lucky enough to be included. We went in his car and one other belonging to his assistant, starting at four in the morning. Because of the daytime heat he insisted we visit the site as soon as it was light, with breakfast afterwards before the temperature soared to unpleasant heights.How sensible. He arrived to pick us up attired in bright red trousers, a huge sunhat and carrying a clipboard. On arrival at Ephesus, we established a base in a quiet spot just above the site in the shade of some nearby olive trees, and then he led us around on the most professional guided tour one could wish for. Breakfast several hours later was extremely welcome. When we got back to the cars we found the two wives had set up a proper barbecue, the smell of sizzling bacon wafting to greet us as we clambered up the hill. Champagne straight out of a coolbox added that little extra, and made a superb visit that must have been far better than one could hope for on the most lavish tour company itinerary.

Two other memories of Izmir come to mind: One was the presence of a detachment of the Greenjackets regiment that was there. They came through the main square one evening marching at 180 paces to the minute, much to the astonishment of everyone around since in that climate most people move as slowly as possible to avoid getting too hot. One felt proud to see the immaculate drill and precision of these men, and felt that should they ever be called upon to fight, this too would be every bit as professional. The other memory was Abdul. He was a merchant who adopted us as soon as we tied up, plying us with boxes of marshmallows, packets of sultanas and various other dried fruits, arranging taxis, newspapers, persuading the catering people to buy this and that food, and was generally a godsend. Sure, he had a thriving business in which he excelled, but we benefited greatly from a good and cheap service that we were happy to enjoy. Certainly I was overcome by his generosity with the gifts of dried fruit, which came the way of every officer on board.

Agincourt set off for a visit to Palma, where we had been warned we would come alongside the same jetty as our Captain D's HMS Rhyl. We embarked a probationary padre who was to transfer to Rhyl once we met up. He was a somewhat red-faced plump young man straight out of theological college and utterly unversed in all matters naval. It must have been extremely hard for him to adjust after a sheltered life in his college. He started disastrously by entering the wardroom and flopping down heavily beside Jasper who was holding a cup of black coffee in his hand, managing to spill it all over Jasper's clean whites, also the freshly laundered wardroom settee covers. Jasper, never too careful about his language, leapt to his feet and yelled "Fucking Hell!" The poor man didn't know where to look.

Palma was superb and would have been even better without Captain D. HMS Rhyl had arrived several days ahead of us and should have arranged our social programme, but hadn't, so we lost the first of our five precious days in getting things organised for ourselves. I went out in Jasper's speedboat for some water skiing, passing the 'Shemara', a particularly flashy gin palace belong to flashy millionaire Bernard Docker, a vessel quite unsuited to being anywhere near water and quite the most vulgar thing I'd come across. I suppose it takes all sorts. One of the crew, who resembled a no-nonsense bouncer, looked down with a sneer as we sped past. The schoolie and I were taken out for the day by an English resident who drove us around the south coast and up the west coast for some miles, then back through the hinterland. She produced a picnic lunch that we enjoyed on a quiet sandy beach. Back at the ship, we had to put on our 'ice cream suits'—a stiff button-up-to-the-neck posh white uniform with gold buttons and shoulder straps; something one tries to avoid wearing on all but the most formal of occasions. This had been ordered by Captain D, who required us to come aboard Rhyl to co-host his own official party. He'd managed to rustle up the dullest VIPs imaginable, so the party (if one can call it that) was tedious in the extreme, but no doubt good for trying our patience. A few days later we attended another party, but this time it was given by a group of English residents in a resplendent hotel with fountains and coloured lights everywhere, lovely tropical plants and a swimming pool, marble piazzas, a band and lots of champagne. It couldn't have been more different.

The next day the wind got up, and I tried planing around in a Minisail which was exhilarating. It seemed to go tremendously fast but being so small and near the water, probably this was just an illusion, like go-karting. Eventually I got tired of falling in the none-too-clean harbour and called it a day. I took over from one of the others as most of the wardroom were off to a party that evening, leaving me in charge of the ship. I quite enjoyed these duties, as I wasn't beholden to anyone, and usually spent some time chatting to the duty PO and rum bo's'un when we had all the mismusters call in during the evening. These were men who for various reasons had missed their rum tot at midday, and it was my job to oversee them drinking it suitably watered that evening. The idea of the water was to ensure no one stored his rum ration for some wild party, since once the rum had been diluted, it would become undrinkable within hours. Chiefs and POs were allowed to have theirs neat, but they were expected to be responsible about how they drank it. I must admit that I was occasionally given a tot when I visited the Chiefs' mess, probably out of pity. A year or two after this, the daily rum ration (one eighth of a pint, quite a sizable amount) was stopped. It was about a hundred years since the days of a hard life on a sailing ship, the reason the tot of cheap rum, was instituted. With steam ships and proper shelter, it was not before time to do away with the tot. On one of these mismuster occasions I was with the duty PO and rum bo's'un waiting for just two more men to turn up but they didn't appear by the time we shut shop. What was then meant to happen was for any remaining rum to be poured down the drain, witnessed by the officer attending, since it could not be returned to the barrel.

The PO looked at me. "Always a pity, Sir, to just ditch this, isn't it, Sir."

"Yes, petty officer. A great pity. Still, it has to be done, doesn't it."

"Of course, Sir. You don't get pusser's rum in your wardroom, do you Sir?"

"No, petty officer. Good stuff, is it?" I tried to sound suitably interested.

"Excellent, Sir. Now, there's just you, me and the rum bo's'un here, and it's going to be a long night, and we've got a couple of glasses right handy, and…"

"Wouldn't dream of it, petty officer, now would I?"

The rum bo's'un, who was a junior rate and not meant to witness this sort of conversation said, with commendable tact, "I'll just return the measures," and left us to it. The petty officer poured out the remaining tots and we drank to our future prosperity. Powerful stuff, that rum.

Late in the night one of the catamaran fenders capsized. These are the floating padded rafts about six feet wide positioned between the ship and jetty to hold the ship away and protect its paintwork, and usually cause no problem. But on this occasion the sea was quite choppy even in the harbour, and I was woken by the gangway staff to be advised that we'd have to right it, since the ship's side was starting to bump against one of the piles. Three of us stood on the jetty looking at the catamaran on its side below, wondering how on earth we could ever move over 2,000 tons of ship far enough away for it to right itself. One of them produced a twelve-foot oar from our seaboat, we put one end against the ship and leaned on the other end for all we were worth. After about two minutes we could feel her shifting, and a couple of minutes after that she began to move out quite well. Soon the catamaran popped back onto an even keel, and the job was done. I would never have thought that three puny men would be able to push a mass that big sideways through the water, but the laws of physics say it can be done and we'd just proved it.

We set off to steam the length of the Mediterranean, with a brief stop at Malta. The ship was headed for Port Said and a passage through the Suez. Plans for a short refit period in Malta on our return were firming up, so I arranged for Patricia to fly out by herself for a couple of weeks, when we would take a flat in Sliema. Several other wives were coming out then, and in August it would be hot and sunny, a good holiday for them.

Agincourt arrived at Port Said in the evening for a night transit of the canal. We anchored for a few hours until it was time to go, spending those hours repelling boarders. Being destroyer-shaped, with a freeboard of only about eight feet or so for half the ship's length, it was a relatively easy matter for bumboat men to scramble aboard. It was necessary to have a full watch closed up all round the ship to keep them off. Eventually, it got too much, and we had to resort to fire hoses. These can deliver a considerable pressure, and we only had to actually turn a hose on one bumboat, one that seemed to be purveying nothing but illegal liquor and pornographic literature, for the others to get the message. Later in the night shortly before sailing, one boat crept in close under our bows where it wasn't be detected, and they started to lift things out of an open porthole using a boathook. The sentry peeped over the rail just in time to see the back of the boat and someone's uniform on its hanger being stuffed into a bag. He knew that if he shouted they'd just hurl abuse at him, so he looked around for something to drop on them, finding a large lump of metal (a link from an anchor cable). He dropped this down to see it go clean through the bottom of the boat with a most satisfying smashing of timbers. The boat promptly began to sink, the two bumboat men rowing for their lives, stopping from time to time to shout at him.

At Suez we met HMS Corunna, another of our squadron, whom we were to relieve. Then we steamed down the Red Sea, 'steamed' being the operative word for once, since the heat and humidity were almost overwhelming. About fifty miles from the southern end, we picked up an SOS message about a ditched aircraft just off the coast of Ethiopia. They couldn't have chosen a worse spot to come down, the waters in that part being only a few feet deep, with jagged coral reefs lurking just under the surface for about five miles out. We diverted to see whether we could help. A Shackleton aircraft appeared out of nowhere as they seem to whenever there is a emergency at sea, and dropped smoke floats in front of us marking the position of the only channel they could see from the air. The channel was very narrow, and the floats drifted away from the channel, but it was a help. We launched our seaboat which went on ahead, sending radio information back to the ship to steer this way or that. We daren't use echo sounding, for that would involve lowering our sonar dome which would have protruded several feet below the keel, very vulnerable to damage. It took over two hours to reach the ditched aircraft, by which time it had sunk, the crew sitting nearby in their life raft. With them safely on board, we felt our way back to the safety of deep water and breathed a sigh of relief! The aircraft was American, a small private two-seater. We never discovered quite what they had been up to, but it was their Mayday radio signal that had attracted the assistance of the Shackleton. This had only been able to drop the life raft after which it cruised around overhead until its fuel ran low.

On arrival at Aden a couple of days later a television news unit came on board to film an interview with the two Americans before they went ashore. I had time for a quick canter round the shops where I located and bought an 8mm cine camera and projector, something I'd coveted ever since we were in Australia. It was amazingly cheap, and I wondered whether there was a snag. There was: a few months later the Super-8 format was introduced and overnight my 8mm format became obsolete. This is the story of my life. However, I had several months of happy filming which I wouldn't have been able to enjoy without it.

In Aden we picked up about forty inhabitants from a tiny island situated just across the water from the Horn of Africa, Perim Island. This lump of black rock with no fresh water has a population of 350, their only means of trading being to bum a lift on a passing boat. This they had done and as the island was a British dependency the Consul persuaded us to take them back home. They sat in a huddle on the upper deck leaning against our gun turret for the four hours it took us to steam back there as if they always travelled this way, then having taken them ashore by boat, we decided to stay a couple of days, for there was a wonderful coral beach with crystal-clear blue water lapping onto it; too tempting to pass up in all that heat and humidity. Almost the whole ship's company piled ashore in one way or another, some of them swam there, the two ship's boats ferrying the others together with the wherewithal for a great beach barbecue. We launched all three Minisails and Jasper took his speedboat out. Local islanders had lumps of coral they'd picked up when diving offshore, so did a good trade. The sea was full of fish, so a fishing competition was held. In the evening we all caught handfuls of hermit crabs and built a racecourse out of pieces of loose rock, then held hermit crab races. I filmed everything that went on, and still have that film but, alas, now have no projector with which to screen it.

HMS Hermes was somewhere East of Suez which is why we had been sent there to relieve Corunna. We would be needed as Hermes' forward eyes and ears, and were due to take part in some exercise. We sailed to rendezvous with her off the Maldives, and almost immediately got into serious trouble. Rounding the corner we hit the full force of a south-westerly storm, and three people who were roped together on the fo'c'sle whilst securing the cable deck for heavy weather were suddenly swept overboard by a freak wave. One of them broke a leg and another had a suspect broken ankle. We happened to be giving passage to a civilian doctor, a tropical medicine specialist, so he earned his keep that day! However, both men needed x-rays and hospital treatment, therefore we turned around and took them back to Aden. We only intended to stay long enough to drop off the two casualties, but one of our main electric pumps broke down and we discovered the spare we carried wouldn't fit. Apparently, the dockyard had originally installed an updated pump, but the backup spare was for a previous model. This sort of mistake very seldom happens, so efficient is the Admiralty spares organisation. The correct spare was almost immediately located and put on an aircraft, and in a couple of days it had arrived and was fitted. When an HM ship does break down, enormous effort is made to get her back into service again wherever she may be in the world, and I was impressed how swiftly this all happened. This was not the only thing going on behind the scenes. We were due to be getting our mail from Gan via Hermes, which would be sending an aircraft there to collect it. But magically it arrived in Aden just before we left, so we didn't even miss out on that. All we missed, in fact, was the exercise itself with Hermes. By the time we left Aden once more it was time to proceed direct to Mombassa where the ships were all due to meet up.

Agincourt hugged the coast all the way down to Mombassa, partly to minimize the effect of strong northerly currents. The coast looked flat and uninteresting and was mostly obscured by mist. As we neared the equator, the temperature and humidity dropped—a huge relief. We were two days on passage, one of which was a Sunday. The captain decided to hold 'divisions', the formal inspection whereby each department parades in their best uniform in spaces around the upper deck while the captain and first lieutenant come round and inspect each man. This irksome interruption to the enjoyable time we were having was an opportunity to look our best and to demonstrate that every sailor could do so when required, also a useful rehearsal for a formal event back in Malta later on. The only men excused were a small team closed up in the boiler room and engine room to keep the ship steaming. 'Chief' had a couple of his more lowly minions who were apparently incapable of retaining all their uniform, and so (to their huge relief) these two were put on watch below and excused divisions. They were delighted, and happily disappeared down a hatch in their grubby overalls while their messmates struggled into best whites. Usually one's white cap cover would become stained and dirty rather easily, so most of the officers were wearing new ones for the occasion, myself included. It was a pleasant sunny day with a gentle breeze and only a slight swell, and everyone looked exceptionally smart. Chief's two stokers were safely out of sight, and so it might have remained. However, just as they were incapable of finding all their uniform, so these two were incapable of doing the right thing in the boiler room. One of them managed to close off a valve that had the effect of depriving the boilers of air. In the few moments it took the petty officer in charge to rush over to correct the situation the damage was done. For a full ten seconds heavy black oil-laden smoke belched out of our funnel, dropping oily smuts all over the ship and all over every one of the men standing to attention downwind. I still have a couple of yellowish stains on my best cap to remind me of the occasion. The language of the chief bo's'un's mate, the senior rating responsible for the ship's appearance, was said to outdo even that of the legendary chief stoker.

At long last, with the ship cleaned up, we steamed slowly up the Mombassa river to our anchorage, Frank Harris standing on the bridge with a happy grin on his face. He took a deep draught of tropical African air, "Ah, you can smell it! Just wait till I get ashore!" Frank's idea of what sailors did when they went ashore was the usual one, but not mine. I was looking forward to a two-day trip to the Tsavo game reserve that four of us had arranged.

A large Chevrolet met us next morning and we set off on the Nairobi road which, like some of the intercity Australian roads, ran out of tarmac after several miles. For a hundred more miles we sped along a smooth dirt road, red in colour like Devonshire soil. Jasper had organised this trip, and with him were Chief, Dick Withenshaw the Direction Officer and myself. We were to spend that night at the Kibo Hotel, a large imposing place on the slopes of Mount Kilimanjaro, and hit our first problem: we hadn't appreciated the place was in Tanzania and it was therefore necessary to cross the border in order to get there! None of us had passports. I had travelled all over the world, but always in the care of the Royal Navy. If stopped, I would produce my Naval identity card and that was that. We arrived at the border at a time only months after Tanganyika ceased to be a British dependency. Renamed Tanzania, the country had immediately set about establishing proper border controls. A large, somewhat sleepy official who clearly had no intention of allowing four passport-less Englishmen across his border manned the one we arrived at. It took us nearly an hour to persuade him to climb down, after suggesting he phone up his 'higher authority' for the necessary permission. Jasper, used to bluffing his way almost anywhere, was a skilled operator and provided a model lesson in diplomatic skills. We were through!

The hotel was huge, log fires burning in a twenty-foot high lounge, bedrooms as big as the Polsue kitchen, and cool night air outside with no mossies. I washed off the red road dust in an enormous bath and slept like a log. Not for long, alas, for we left at 5.30 a.m. next morning for the serious business of big game watching. Dawn in Tsavo is magical, certainly the best time to see the animals. At one stage we turned a corner and there, straddling the track, was a large male giraffe standing as if inviting us to drive between his legs. The Chevvy was one of those vast gas-guzzlers with a boot lid large enough on which to land a small helicopter, so the giraffe graciously stepped to one side and looked down at us inquisitively as we crept past. There were many such moments. At one point, Jasper got out of the car to get a better sight of a pride of sleepy lions, which panicked our protective driver. At a waterhole in the centre of the park we came to a partially submerged viewing platform from which we could see hippos paddling about in the soupy water. A notice by the side of the path said 'no bathing' as well it might for there were several large crocodiles there as well.

In the afternoon we arrived at the Kilagumi Lodge where we had booked in for the night. Here we met the only other visitors we'd seen all day; it's not like that nowadays! Game watching from one of these lodges is a luxury indeed. We sat on a shady veranda twenty feet up, sipping drinks and watching a family of elephants take a bath in a waterhole in front of us. All manner of small animals, impala, baboons, masses of birds and a great variety of larger mammals all came and went from time to time. Behind the main building was a circle of grass-walled chalets; windowless but comfortable enough with clean rush matting and an iron-framed bed. During the night I heard lions calling, then something fairly big snuffling around just the other side of the grass wall. I soon dropped off again surprisingly, and next morning there on the dirt path on front of my chalet were big cat footprints. We completed a further day in Tsavo, and then drove back to Mombassa in the evening. What a trip! I was surprised how comfortable the soft-sprung Chevvy had been, expecting to feel carsick on the bumpy roads, but nothing of the kind. Probably the whole venture was so exciting I didn't have time for such feelings.

After that it was back to the Mediterranean again. We rounded the Horn of Africa, where the temperature rose from 75°F to nearly a 100 in the space of a few hours, the humidity rising with it. Then on to Suez where we handed over our 'duty' to HMS Diamond on her way out. A quiet Sunday transit through the Suez Canal, where I spent most of the day sitting on top of the gun turret with cine camera and binoculars. I missed seeing a couple of sharks swimming around in the Great Bitter Lakes, but later I couldn't miss seeing a couple of scantily dressed Egyptian men standing on the nearby canal bank flashing their tackle at the sailors. They really are the limit. Early next morning we went alongside in Haifa.

Haifa was superb and a complete surprise, and couldn't have been a greater contrast to our brush with things Egyptian. We were to spend four days there on a social flag-showing visit and every minute had been taken care of by our hosts. Aided by the British vice-consul who came aboard with him, a cheery Israeli naval lieutenant met us and explained how we could maximise the enjoyment of our visit. Central to the arrangements was the part played by the Israeli bus company, who supplied coaches for all the outings and free passes for travelling on all service buses. Outings were to Acre, where we toured the old part of town and were shown the somewhat gruesome museum where photographs and artefacts from the Nazi atrocities were displayed for all to see, a biblical tour of Nazareth and Tiberius and a bathe in the Sea of Galilee, most welcome as the air temperature there was 104°F (though with humidity below 20% I didn't noticeably sweat at all and had been advised to drink plenty), and we saw lots of biblical sights such as the actual cave where Joseph and Mary were supposed to have lived and brought up the infant Jesus. Although it was August, there were very few tourists about, so we felt privileged to have such places more or less to ourselves. An English-speaking guide took some of us to a couple of Haifa bus employees' homes to meet them and their families and obtain an impression of their way of life, something one seldom manages on a normal tourist visit. On an 'off' day I took the service bus down the coast road to a favourite swimming beach for locals, where it seemed everyone we met knew about the ship's visit, and came up and said how welcome we were in their country. I have never had such greetings in any country before or since.

The visit had started with the usual party on board with our cheerful hosts full of fun which helped enormously to get the visit off to a swinging start. The following day we were invited aboard an Israeli ship for a return party. This was moored next to a captured Egyptian frigate and they told us the story about how they had acquired it, which I found hard to believe. The Egyptians had apparently bought a paid-off British frigate which they had arranged to have refitted in Portsmouth Yard. By the end of this refit the Israeli-Egypt war was brewing up and they were anxious to be off to fight it, so they managed to fuel and ammunition ship in a great hurry immediately the dockyard workers left. I expect the government were none too keen to allow them to rush off and have it out with the Israelis who, at that time, were pro-British whereas Britain still remembered only too well the debacle over Suez just a few years previously. Due to some 'mistake' the wrong ammunition was supplied and this was not discovered until the Egyptians wanted to practise some live firings in the Mediterranean on their way home, when they found the ammunition wouldn't fit the guns. Only days later they were attacked by an Israeli gunboat before they'd even arrived at Alexandria and, rather than let their new ship fall into Israeli hands, they opened all the stopcocks in order to scuttle the ship and took to the lifeboats. After half an hour the ship hadn't gone down, and the Israelis who boarded her found that all that had happened was some sealed-off compartments had flooded. Victoriously they took her back to Haifa leaving the Egyptian crew to make their way back to port as best they could. This made such a good story as told by our hosts that I felt I'd like to hear the Egyptian version before believing one word of it!

On the last day at Haifa I was the duty officer, and the only one on board. There was to be a 'children's party' that afternoon, a bit of fun that is part of the hospitality repertoire of most Naval ships, which the duty watch on board reckoned they could cope with. I waved goodbye to the rest of the ship's company in the morning as their various hosts arrived in an assortment of taxis, private cars and the inevitable buses to carry them away, then set about preparing for the start of the children's invasion that afternoon. We usually hosted about a couple of hundred visitors at most with these parties and were totally unprepared for the 650 who arrived. The jetty was full of parked buses, and I stood at the top of the gangway with my gangway staff quickly becoming engulfed with gifts that many of them produced. At the end of a quite exhausting afternoon when every sailor in the ship really pulled his weight and the visitors began to leave, I was summoned to appear to receive a formal 'thankyou' from one of the grownups present. I was handed several more sizable gifts and managed to whisper to the bos'n's mate by my side to go up to the first lieutenant's cabin and bring down the painted ship's crest on its wooden plinth that was on the bulkhead, taking care to give it a quick dust first! I realised I needed something to give them, but couldn't think of anything else at such short notice. I made my speech to a largely uncomprehending audience (not that many spoke English), handed over the crest and we all waved goodbye. I noticed most of the sailors who'd hosted our visitors also waving from along the ship's rail. Marvellous men, our sailors. Then we all collapsed in exhaustion, only thankful there wasn't a ship's party on that scale too often.

Jasper was a bit miffed I'd pinched his crest but agreed I had to do something. We ordered another, but he'd have to do without one for the time being. These crests make a good memento to give to people, and we usually had a few tucked away.

In the morning we sailed, the jetty crowded with waving wellwishers, friends that we'd made in our too-brief visit. Looking back now, it is hard to remember the joy of that visit, the happiness and hope of all the people we met at Haifa. My brief experience of Israel now seems rather unreal when we hear about the unhappy state of that nation today.

Next stop was to Limassol for a brief stop whilst at that end of the Mediterranean. We'd brought across a detachment of the 1st Gloucesters who were landed there. The RAF at Akrotiri still had their fleet of Albacores at the sailing club and arranged a tri-service match which they won convincingly. Once again I managed to capsize in the Albacore I was helming, but the water was warm and the conditions nothing like so dangerous as the occasion when I'd sailed as part of the Bulwark team a few years previously. And then at last, we set sail for Malta where many of the wives would be joining us for a few weeks while the ship had a maintenance period. I'd managed to hire a flat in Sliema for Patricia, who would be coming out by herself, leaving the children with her parents. We had considered bringing them too, and I had discussed this in the wardroom with all the others who had families, the consensus being that for such a short visit the trauma of subjecting very young children to the heat and strangeness of Malta in August was probably not a good idea, much as we'd like to see our own children.

And so Patricia arrived in one of the new BOAC Comet aircraft, along with several other wives on the same flight. There followed several weeks of bliss, long afternoons spent on one of the few sandy beaches, days out in the MFV towing a train of assorted boats with swimming and picnicking and a fair amount of duty-free to help it down. We worked a tropical routine whereby work started very early and was all over by 1.00 p.m. after which we had time to ourselves. I hired a little car to get us about, we visited Joe and Ruth Snow in their country retreat—a lovely old Maltese house with high walls surrounding a tranquil courtyard, there were parties on board and in one another's rented houses. Early on I took Patricia out on the Minisail (I say 'on' for one sat on top of this surfboard thing, not 'in' it) and we sailed out to sea for a mile or so on a glorious day with a gentle breeze. While out there Patricia dropped her sunglasses overboard and I looked over the side to see them starting to sink ever so slowly. Calling to her to just sit still and let the sail flap, I handed her my specs and dived in after her sunglasses, which by now had gone several feet down. I caught up with them at last and shot to the surface, to see a panicky Patricia sitting very alone on a strange boat that might tip her off it at any moment into an empty sea miles from anywhere. I realised the stupidity of what I had done and breathed a sigh of relief that we came to no harm. This was before the days of lifejackets... All too soon the holiday was over, our wives were waved off from Luqa airport and we were back at sea once more.

More exercises. On one of these for which Agincourt was to be used for her intended role of forward air traffic control, we sailed from Sliema for a five-day spell off Italy, and during that first afternoon when setting up the main radar we had a burnout in the radar office. This radar, a comparatively low-frequency set, sent its considerable power along a big cable rather than the conventional waveguide. The aerial, a monstrous twenty-foot wide rectangular structure atop the mainmast quite spoilt the sleek destroyer-like lines of our ship, but it was the main aircraft control radar, vital for our role. A slight mismatch had occurred where the aerial cable was bent a little too tightly within the radar office, resulting in the central conductor getting warm enough to soften the polythene insulation, with the result that over time the conductor began to drift through the polythene rather like a hot wire will work its way through a block of ice. All this must have taken months to come about, but the burnout came just hours before the exercise, so couldn't have happened at a worse time. It took a couple of hours to discover what had happened, then there was nothing for it but to turn round and head back to Malta, radioing on ahead for a spare cable to be flown out from the UK. We were back alongside the Fleet repair ship Ausonia by midnight and overnight leave was granted to the rest of the ship's company while my radar boffins and myself set to to dismantle the aerial. Overnight leave was perhaps unwise, for one or two sailors who still had wives ashore arrived home unexpectedly to find the worst had happened, with their wives having it off with another man. Naturally I was blamed for this since it was me that asked for the ship to be turned back. With commendable efficiency the new cable arrived in the morning, was fitted immediately and we were away again that afternoon, catching up the Fleet in time for the exercise.

In November, with the summer holiday just a memory, we paid a visit to Malaga. Here Chief rather let the side down when, having come alongside and the bridge had rung down 'finished with engines', the boiler room team were left with too much steam. A delicate balance is required at times like this, for the ship needs to be in a position to respond rapidly should an emergency be required as one comes alongside, but immediately one is safely tied up, there is no further use for the head of steam which has to dissipate in its own time as it gets used on ancillary equipment such as my electrical generators. This time the steam pressure continued to rise until the safety valve blew. At the time various Spanish dignitaries were arriving and there was a decorated horse drawn gharry on the jetty. Not many people realise just how much power is dissipated when the safety valve lifts, certainly I didn't. It went off like an Atlas rocket launch, with a noise to match. The horse bolted of course, while everyone else leapt for cover.

The official reception ashore took an unusual form whereby, because the Spanish hosts had practically no English and we British naturally expected everyone to speak our own language, communication was very stilted and perforce had to be somewhat formal. They had arranged a lunchtime session whereby we stood behind tables arranged round the side of a large bare room while in the centre a couple of flamenco dancers gave a short performance. Then we remained standing while we sipped sherry and long speeches were made, after which we sat down to a rather strange lunch, very Spanish. None of us had set foot in Spain before, the tourist business was nothing like it would become in later years, and we found it rather a culture shock. The situation was saved the next day when we hired a couple of coaches for a visit to Granada and a tour round the incomparable

Alhambra palace. Alas, it rained hard all day, but that didn't spoil the magic. We were about the only visitors there and the tranquillity was wonderful.

On the way back to Malta we were swept along in a force 10 gale, with a following sea that almost 'pooped' us several times. The upper deck was put out of bounds, one of our boats hanging in the davits took a few tons of solid water aboard and was completely written off, and a fair amount of minor damage was also sustained. It was the first time the fiddles had appeared on the wardroom table, but even so we found it safer and easier to eat standing up, one hand holding on as best we could. The storm blew itself out after a day, and we made up quite a lot of time riding before it. Arriving off Malta, we had problems reversing in to the Sliema Creek trot due to a residual swell that affected all the boat traffic even high up the various creeks.

I found that Voyageur had arrived for the winter, tying up at a jetty in the next creek at Ta'Xbiex along with several large boats similarly bedded down for the winter. I had made my number with one or two of them already, and now it was a pleasure to welcome David and Barbara among their number. They now had a third member of their crew, a lovely little baby only two months old who lay in his carrycot gurgling happily at everyone who looked in. I spent much of my leisure time in one or other of the laid-up craft, helping with the two-man jobs, fetching and carrying, or just sitting on deck in the sunshine enjoying a drink or two. It was a good life. From time to time we had to go to sea for a few days. One such was for exercises in the Tyrrhenian Sea followed by a few days in Civitta Vecchia where, naturally, I set off for a day in Rome. At the time another padre was with us, and he came with me to give the Vatican a good going over, spending several hours in the wonderful museums and, of course, paying a visit to the Sistine Chapel. Rome in November was overcast and cool, somewhat different to that first idyllic visit when I was a subby in the Aisne. Back at sea the padre earned his keep by standing on the bridge during some lamp signalling between ships where, as brevity is needed, it was a naval custom to quote biblical texts to put over a point. Our padre with a detailed knowledge of the concordance bible was, as our Captain put it, a godsend. Whole books have been written on the signals flashed between ships over the years. The one I always remember being before the war when an Admiral of the Far East Fleet was accustomed to having his laundry collected each day by a local washerwoman who would come to the jetty and have a boat from the flagship sent across for her. The Naval signalman on the jetty sent a message which read "Please send boat for Admiral's woman", and moments later when he realised how that might be interpreted, he sent another: "Amend my last signal. Insert washer between Admiral and woman". Those were the days when wireless telegraphy was not quite so quick to use as the humble Aldis lamp.

News of the next three months of Agincourt's programme was emerging and it looked as though we might be spending quite a lot of time in and around Malta. Several of us talked about bringing the families out this time. I longed to see Susan and Paul again, and when I walked past the little playground at the head of the furthest creek and saw the happy Maltese children running around in the warm sunshine, I thought again of our tatty Alverstoke house and easily persuaded myself it would make sense for Patricia to bring the family out for Christmas. I telephoned her that evening. Telephoning from Malta to the UK could be a protracted business, sometimes taking over an hour for an operator to wrestle with a manual connection, and then the line could be faint and distorted and cost a couple of pounds a minute—a day's wage. Patricia was delighted with the idea and contacted the RAF at Brize Norton to find out whether she could obtain an 'indulgence' passage. A few days later there was a happy letter saying she couldn't get an indulgence passage but had booked a BEA flight in a week's time, just before Christmas. Frantically I set about searching for somewhere for us all to live, which I found in the shape of an upstairs flat not a hundred yards from the boat jetty where Voyageur and the other yachts were over-wintering.

My Chief EA drove me to Luqa, and there was Patricia with the children coming into the customs hall. I looked after the children, who seemed to have grown enormously since I had last seen them, Paul not too sure who I was, while Patricia was ages with customs being checked over. They looked in a very old-fashioned way at the pushchair loaded with all the paraphernalia needed to travel with young children, complete with a Christmas tree tied down on top. The Chief EA took her suitcases and waited for us outside the customs hall. At that point he realised he had bypassed the customs with half our luggage but luckily no one noticed. The flat was designed for the hot weather, with polished stone floors, rather dark inside since it was built around three sides of a small light shaft, but did have the huge advantage of a large flat roof that would be marvellous for the children to play on. But on first opening the door it was not at all welcoming. Never mind, we were all together once more and what else mattered?

Then began a wonderful spell when we enjoyed Malta out of season, the gregarious Maltese were even more friendly with people actually living in their midst than they were with visitors. Immediately on arrival we were swept up in Christmas activities, starting with a children's party in Agincourt to which I took the children while Patricia was getting the flat how she wanted it, the Christmas morning church service on the Ausonia, drinks and social visits in various yachts, then return visits to the flat for some of the people who had been so hospitable to me over the months.

We hired a Morris Minor and the children quickly started a game of 'spot the priest'. Malta seemed overrun with priests who came in three colours. They scored one point for the black ones who were the most numerous, two for brown ones who were, I think, some other sort of order, monks maybe, and a top score of three for the rare sighting of a white priest who, by the deference conferred on him by everyone else, was probably of a much higher standing. Police were another matter. They looked rather like Gilbert and Sullivan stage policemen, and it was all too easy not to take them seriously, but that would be a grave mistake. Several of our group had brushes with them, usually something to do with their cars all of which were in an appalling unsafe condition. There seemed to be no actual crime on the island, so the police had time to deal with all the administrative trivia that came their way. Patricia and I had to apply for temporary driving licences, which involved a sight test and answering lots of questions.

Right up until the New Year we enjoyed lovely autumnal weather. Our dghaisa man, Peter, took us around in his boat which the children loved. The playground I'd seen on my walks some weeks earlier became a favourite too. Paul found it fun to swing round and round on the railings bordering the play area, but if he happened to slip off while on the other side he would have plummeted straight into the sea below, so that had to be discouraged. Almost every day there was a tea party or drinks somewhere, people visiting us or us going round to theirs. Lots of trips to beaches, playgrounds, walks along the creekside, trips in dinghies and dghaisas; it was a busy, social time for the family and I joined in whenever I was able, but Agincourt did have to go to sea from time to time! The winter rains arrived, and without any heating anywhere the flat felt dank and cold, though outside we didn't need coats. Patricia found a source of babysitters in the nearby Wrens' quarters (known rather crudely as Tampax Towers) so we were able to escape of an evening for our Scottish Country Dancing. No nice wooden floors, though. It was dancing on polished 'marble', potentially both dangerous and damaging to the knees, though at our age we didn't appreciate that this would one day be a problem. Families were even able to join us out at sea one day to watch stores being transferred from an RFA by means of a jackstay transfer (a heavier version of the bos'n's chair method when transferring personnel).

Eventually our protracted stay around Malta came to a close, and wives began to pack and set off for home. This time we had successfully arranged for an 'indulgence' flight for the family, courtesy of the RAF. We were in the middle of a dinner party at the flat when a call came through from the RAF Movements people. Could Patricia and the children be ready to be picked up at 6.15 next morning? The dinner party came to a rapid close, and we set about clearing the flat and packing. A very smart RAF car arrived bang on time and I went too to see them off. As an officer's wife, Patricia enjoyed the VIP lounge where we waited until her aircraft (an RAF Comet) took on a detachment of Maltese soldiers on their way to the UK for training. Finally when they were all aboard and settled in, a steward came for Patricia, someone else carried the luggage and a third person took one child in each hand. Patricia told me afterwards she had been allocated the best position in the aircraft and the pilot had come back to make sure she was all right before asking permission to take off! Oh, for such a privileged position! It was a terrible shock for them to arrive at Lyneham in a snowstorm and the realities of a British winter.

A few weeks later and Agincourt was also heading for home. First we took part in yet more exercises, this time with a sizable fleet of assorted warships with a number of RFAs and including HM Yacht Britannia which had the Duke of Edinburgh on board on his way home after visiting Malta. We practised night time convoy work, steering a ziz-zag course without any navigation lights: potentially extremely unsafe if one ship got its starting point out of kilter with the rest and began zigging while others were zagging. It almost happened with us when a large cruise ship ploughed straight through the fleet with all its lights blazing. The exercise was halted for a while, all ships being ordered to switch on navigation lights when, no doubt, the liner's deck officer must have had kittens. After this panic we 'resumed' the zig-zag and indeed one ship did think it meant they had to re-start it rather than resume where we left off. The Navy doesn't do that sort of thing anymore, fortunately.

After a brief visit to Gibraltar which we left with our paying off pennant flying from the masthead, Agincourt set off for the final leg home. First landfall was to Plymouth where we were cleared by customs. I looked after the customs team, plying them with coffee and chatting between seeing their customers. It took several hours to clear the whole ship's company. I asked how they decided how much duty to charge for such things as a watch bought in Aden a year previously and brought in as 'used'. The answer was that as no duty had yet been paid, duty would still be payable but reduced as it was now no longer new. The wardroom liquor stocks were also mustered, and any unopened bottles had to be put in bond pending the ship's next voyage. By some terrible piece of misunderstanding the wardroom wine steward had managed to open quite a large number of one-gallon Winchesters of our favourite sherry before the fateful stock take, clever man.

At long last we came into Portsmouth with the paying off pennant still proudly flying, all 200 feet of it, and there were the families waiting for us on South Railway Jetty. My father was up for a couple of days, so he, too, joined us all in the wardroom for a welcoming drink from one of the opened sherry Winchesters. By this time Susan had started at a pre-school kindergarten just at the back of our house. The house seemed even tattier than I remembered it and I felt almost embarrassed that my family had had to put up with such a place for so long, but that was how it was: a colourful life (for me) but no money. It was back to the bicycle with the morning rush hour crossing over to Portsmouth on the Gosport ferry, a lovely way to go to work really, far preferable to standing jammed together on the London Underground for example. On our way back from Gibraltar Agincourt had been joined by a couple of dockyard surveyors who made an inventory of everything that needed to be done at her forthcoming main refit. They were particularly concerned at the state of the immense amount of cabling that passed though the boiler room where it had been subjected to temperatures in excess of 160°F for so long. We were the first of the Battle conversions to go in for refit, and there was doubt about her overall condition. We remained alongside for some weeks while various people left. I went up to the Admiralty to badger my Appointments officer about my next job, but all he would say was that I might be having a job based in Plymouth, that I would certainly need to go on one or two courses in the Portsmouth area soon, and he'd let me know. Once again I was in limbo, living in a house we might not have for much longer, dying to go on holiday somewhere for a couple of weeks, but unable to take more than a few days leave at that time, and also anxious to look around the Plymouth area for our next home. My relief arrived and I handed over to him, finally leaving dear old Agincourt on 1st May 1964. She looked rather sad, alongside with a new skeleton crew and no prospect of going to sea for several months.

We drove down to St. Mawes for a wonderful break, sunny every day, clean, warm air and those superb views wherever one looked. We visited all my friends of old, showing off our two lovely children, we walked to Percuil through woods full of primroses and bluebells, visited Towan beach where the children played happily in the countless rock pools, and went sailing in father's new boat 'Caprice'. This tiny decked boat with a small cabin was much drier to sail than the one-designs. We rowed over to Place House on the St. Anthony side and spent happy afternoons on that lovely deserted beach, while I rowed across to Caprice's moorings and fiddled about on her. Messing about in boats—definitely there's nothing like it. Father did his best to be nice to all of us, but he was unused to having people upsetting his bachelor routine, and became edgy after a while, upsetting Patricia which in turn upset the children. We escaped out on the water when we could.

Father's old one-design had been bought by Eric, an incomer, who asked us whether we would like to join him out sailing. It turned out that what he actually wanted was for us to take him out as he didn't feel at all competent on his own. So I took the helm and we had a lovely sail across to the mouth of the Helford River and on to the Manacle rocks where I showed him various passages one could use to avoid hitting them. He was obviously scared of getting close to anywhere dangerous, but then I spied the fins of a basking shark, something he'd never seen, so we sailed over, coming alongside as it were. It was creeping along with an occasional waggle of the tail, cavernous mouth wide open to filter water for its plankton diet, and must have been every inch of 25 feet long. It dwarfed the one-design, and Eric began to panic, so reluctantly I had to back off. That was one of those unforgettable moments like seeing one's first kingfisher, which stay with you for ever. We had a day in Plymouth looking at the various married quarter sites just in case we did get to live down there. Plymouth was so bright and clean, with sea air wafting in over the Hoe, the dazzling new buildings looking really good in the spring sunshine. We did so hope we would soon be living there.

Then it was back to the Alverstoke house where an OHMS letter was awaiting me. I tore it open: "You are hereby appointed Lieutenant Commander, HMS Excellent for short OE course on 22nd June 1964 and HMS Drake from 24th August 1964 for duties in HM Dockyard, Devonport."

HMS Excellent is the Naval Gunnery School at Whale Island in Portsmouth, the OE course being training in ordnance engineering, something I had missed out on since the electrical and ordnance branches had combined. HMS Drake is the Devonport Naval base. We had done it! We would soon be off to Patricia's birthplace, Plymouth!

14

Plymouth

Now we had the next couple of years planned we no longer felt at such a loose end. Another three months or so at our Alverstoke home, then the move to Plymouth by which time, hopefully, we would have found a new home, and it would need to be somewhere with a nice school nearby for the children. No longer were we quite so unconstrained about where we could live.

The early experimental hovercraft was often seen careering around on the Solent. It was an extraordinary looking contraption that made a noise like an angry hornet, unlike anything else on the water; but then it was unlike anything else on the water. A second one, the SRN6, much more like a proper vessel with windows down each side, soon joined it and began a regular passenger service across to the Isle of Wight. We became used to the sound of hovercraft speeding across the Solent, passing within a few hundred yards of the house. We were out with Patricia's parents one day, the whole family walking along the front at Lee-on-Solent, when the latest hovercraft, a huge beast with a suitably deep bass voice, came creeping out across the road between the Naval air station at Daedalus and the nearby beach. Daedalus, with a wide slipway down to the nearby water, had been the base for flying the early machines, though there was a lot of argument as to whether one 'flew' them or whether they should be considered as boats. As there was no actual contact with water, the flying lobby won, and so they were driven by pilots, not captains. When hovercraft did cross the road at that point, traffic would be halted for the few moments the machine went across, but on this occasion there were quite a number of people 'hovering' around, also several other models of hovercraft were out there on the water, zimming up and down. What was going on? I lined up with a number of others beside the slipway as the big one moved down passing within a few feet of us, sending stones flying out all round, and a press photographer asked me to step back for a moment. At that point I realised he was aiming his camera at a knot of people; one of whom I later discovered was the actual inventor of the hovercraft, Christopher Cockerell. One by one all the different machines that had been developed from his original prototype came past to show off their paces. We had stumbled right into a display to honour the inventor of these useful craft. It was not long before the Americans would be using them all over the world, calling them air-cushion vehicles, and in their usual way implying this was another American invention. Most people from outside Britain probably still think they are. So I feel privileged to think I was lucky enough to be present at that little ceremony at Lee.

I began a series of ordnance engineering courses, starting at Whale Island. This was where we were well positioned, for the venues for all the courses were within easy reach of Alverstoke. My commuter trip to Whale Island started with a short bike ride to Clarence Yard, the Naval victualling depot, where I parked my bike under cover and walked past the coopering workshop where rum barrels were repaired, to a jetty from which a routine dockyard steam pinnace ferried me across the harbour, putting me off at Whale Island's private jetty. What a wonderful way to commute to work. I spent my days at Whaley learning from naval personnel, mostly Gunnery GIs all of whom had loud parade ground voices and clumped around in shiny boots with gaiters. Whale Island looked after all Naval ceremonial as well as being the Naval Gunnery School. Here was kept the gun carriage used for state funerals, the most recent occasion of its use being for Winston Churchill's.

Field Gun crews for that highly dangerous event between the three Naval Commands had a training pitch at Whale Island used by the Portsmouth Command, while the famous parade ground, several acres of raked gravel, was the scene for many other 'bull' activities, also a few fun and games events such as a monumental fireworks display on Guy Fawkes night (where the bonfire was lit, naturally, by firing a distress flare into the fire), also a families day where a mini-tattoo was staged. The GIs told of all the usual pranks that men dreamt up, the one that I remember best being when the parade commander climbed onto his rostrum one day to survey the scene, only to see a tree apparently growing in the middle of the hallowed gravel. Shouting, "Remove that tree!" the results were wholly predictable. For two men hiding under the rostrum this was the signal to throw a switch, whereupon the tree blew up in spectacular fashion, leaving a neat hole in the ground and leaves everywhere. I actually enjoyed my few weeks at Whale Island, probably because I was a 'mature' student with 2½ rings on my arm, so was treated very kindly by all these noisy GIs. I cannot to this day remember whether I learnt anything about naval ordnance. What I do remember is being told by a chuckling instructor about a deaf gunnery officer well past retirement age, still retained in some testing capacity and used to map out the safety limits around a gun within which no personnel should be allowed at firing time. He did this by walking round the area while the gun was firing, putting his hand up if he could hear anything. The callous way in which men's hearing was permanently damaged wasn't thought at all unusual. I feel strongly about this, since I am sure my own hearing was damaged by Agincourt's gunfire, and I know my father's deafness was initiated in World War I during his time in the Royal Artillery. By the time I retired from the Royal Navy, they were taking much greater care of men's health, as well they might for the age of litigation was then upon us.

I also spent a week or so at HMS Vernon between Portsmouth Hard and the harbour entrance, at that time home to the Torpedo and Anti Submarine (TAS) School, and enjoyed an interesting day at the Naval depot at a hideaway in Wiltshire which stored all manner of equipment in vast underground caves created where Bath stone was quarried, an ideal location where temperature and humidity were constant year in and year out without the need for any air conditioning.

About this time the sad news came through that our lovely, cheerful, life-enjoying Jasper Crawford had crashed his latest sports car somewhere in Wiltshire, and was dead. Poor Izzie. She must have feared something of the sort could easily happen, for Jasper lived his short life right on the edge. Their children were a few years older than ours, but it would hit them really hard.

Eventually all the courses came to an end and I started a couple of weeks' leave before taking up the Plymouth appointment. We spent a day down there, calling in on the Married Quarters office at the Plymouth naval base, HMS Drake, where we learned there was a new estate of quarters being built in Plymstock, about three miles to the east of the town (the opposite side of town to Devonport, and therefore an obvious site for the Navy's extraordinary illogical thinking). This had great attractions, especially after the tatty house in Alverstoke, but they would not be ready for occupation for another month or two. We put our name down for one, and then went round to the nearby primary school where we could then legitimately enter Susan and Paul. It meant we had to lodge somewhere temporarily while waiting for the new quarter to be finished, and Patricia managed to find a sympathetic friend not far away with a husband away at sea, who agreed to take in her and the children.

So, back at Alverstoke, we gave notice to our landlord and left, all our possessions being put in store for some weeks. Patricia moved the family down to Devon and camped with her friend, a traumatic time, which I missed as by then I had started work in the Dockyard, living for those first few weeks in the bachelor comfort of HMS Drake.

I had joined the Electrical Engineering Manager's Department, or EEM as it was known. EEM himself was a senior dockyard civilian, one of half a dozen reporting to the Admiral Superintendent, an engineer rear admiral. Under EEM were several smaller departments, three of which were headed up by naval commanders. Mine was the Electrical and Trials Unit, E&T for short, and the officer in charge of that was Robin Owen, an old acquaintance from my long course time at Collingwood. He was a wonderful help to me and we got along fabulously well. I shared an office with a civilian dockyard man of foreman rank, Mr Chegwin, of a similar level to myself. Between us we had responsibility for the weapons control systems, his being the straight gunnery part whilst mine was all the associated electrics and fire control side. This final installation and commissioning was looked after by an inspector who in turn had a charge hand with a team of fitters. Also based in our offices was a team of diagnosticians who would equate in skills with the naval artificers, so the dockyard organisation was similar to the naval one, with the mixing of naval and civilian people working very well. I was impressed with the quality of the Devonport dockyard staff, who appeared to be far more efficient than those in the Portsmouth yard, all in a lovely relaxed west-country way. Mr Chegwin said that most of the inspectors and foremen had passed their examinations for higher positions and had been offered such positions in other yards, the favourite usually being an armaments factory in Alexandria at the southern end of Loch Lomond. None of them wanted to move away from their beloved Plymouth, so were soldering on in the lower rank. It sounded like the tactic the MoD played with us when we first tried to find a married quarter in the Portsmouth area.

Robin took me along with him to one of EEM's weekly heads of department meetings where we all sat round a table with EEM himself sitting on a much higher chair so he could look down in a threatening way at everyone. He would run through refit progress on each ship in dockyard hands and come down like a ton of bricks on anyone whose department was responsible for delays. Always the reason would be waiting for another department to finish, generally a Marine Engineering one which was outside EEM's jurisdiction, so that left him frustrated. On this first occasion, the drawing office manager was struggling to answer some problem which he couldn't offload when Robin hastily scribbled something on a bit of paper, which was then handed round the table to the unfortunate man who unfolded it gratefully. He looked at what Robin had written, put the paper in his pocket and stumbled on some more.

"Well, Mr Vaughan, do you have your answer?" snapped EEM testily.

"Not yet, Mr Simms, but I should be able to report this afternoon." He looked slightly less cornered.

After the meeting I asked Robin what he had written.

"It doesn't matter what one writes," he replied, "It's just a game. Gets Jimmy Vaughan off the hook, and EEM will forget about it by lunchtime." He called Commander Vaughan over and the scrap of paper was produced on which Robin had written: 'First tart: Do you smoke during intercourse? Second tart: I don't know; I've never looked."

A couple of weeks later Robin had to go away for a spell leaving me to represent him at EEM's meeting. I didn't get any beginner's treatment, and managed to answer the questions without recourse to being bailed out with notes passed round the table, but a few days before Robin came back we did have a minor crisis which I put firmly at the door of the design people in Bath. I went to see EEM about what to do, and he asked me to put it down on paper. I didn't hear any more for some weeks after which Robin showed me a docket which contained a number of letters to and fro between the dockyard and Bath, this time Bath making the excuses and trying to wriggle out. I realised the genesis for the whole subject had been my original letter to EEM, someone in the Yard having supported my complaint and backed it all the way up.

These dockets would contain the complete history of some activity, from the initial notes right up to an outgoing letter signed on behalf of the admiral, with comments from every interested party concerned. They would be a complete and unique record.

Robin told me of the time he took over a Bath job some years previously. He met his predecessor who said the handover wouldn't take more than a day or two (a week had been allowed) as the work was quite straightforward, so they spent a couple of hours going over the job details. After lunch they dealt with one or two dockets that came in. Next morning his predecessor looked hopefully at a bag of golf clubs standing behind the door, said there seemed no need for him to stay any longer, was Robin happily in the reins?

"Quite unsuspectingly I said yes and agreed to him buggering off," Robin told me, "I spent that morning wondering why the job demanded a man full time, when I heard a rumbling in the corridor outside. The door opened and a couple of porters stood there with a large trolley. 'Where would you like your mail?' they said, then proceeded to stack a huge pile of dockets down beside my desk. On every one had been written 'Bring forward 1st August'. None of them had even been opened by that lazy sod. Some even had 'TOP PRIORITY' stamped on them, referring to actions that required an answer several weeks previously. In fact he hadn't looked at any dockets for over a month."

Robin went on to say that it took him several weeks to clear the entire backlog. Eventually the day came when he could afford the luxury of standing up, wander about the office, and wonder what to tackle next. He had noticed a hardboard cover over the redundant fireplace which was bending out at the top, and with mild curiosity pulled it forward to find a whole lot more dockets all covered in dust that had been posted into the space behind.

I just wondered how such irresponsible people got away with it, and whether this simply proved that paperwork isn't really important and one shouldn't get hung up on it. I once asked some august Admiral while he was in our wardroom on an informal visit to Agincourt—I think it was the then C-in-C of the Mediterranean Fleet, Admiral Sir Ian Henderson—what he would have done in his early days had he been sent orders to carry out something he didn't agree with. I remember his answer:

"Send it back with a query, send it sea mail and if you can, send it via Mauritius. Then by the time it gets to the Admiralty the person who initially wrote it will have moved on and no one will know what you're talking about."

I've never had the courage to try it out; besides, the orders I receive are usually ones delivered personally or by signal. But I am digressing. I must return to my early days at Devonport Yard.

In dockyard hands were four frigates at the later stages of their refits, all awaiting the attention of Marine Engineering and EEM workmen, and all likely to need the services of the E&T section at the same time. Planning had gone awry due to a lack of money. The Yard had fully spent the budgets allocated to these ships and was awaiting the arrival of HMS Ark Royal which was due in for a major refit costing tens of millions. New plans were drawn up based on the day Ark arrived. Nobody seemed particularly perturbed that the Fleet was thus being inconvenienced, and no doubt by the time various ships' captains had heard about revised refit dates, the reasons for the adjustments would have been forgotten. Men's leave dates or courses or whatever would all have been put on hold, and all because of Ark Royal which, unaware of the impact it was having, had delayed its arrival in Devonport. Ark eventually came in, the budget for her refit was released and days later amid a flurry of activity the dockyard had the funds to complete all the small ships in its hands, which went on their way rejoicing. Ark's refit began with a big hole in the budget before a single spitting dockie had climbed aboard.

We had a date for moving into our new quarter in Easterdown Close, Plymstock, to take effect only a week after Patricia and the children had come to stay with her friends, so this wasn't too bad at all. Not only was the house new, but so was every stitch of furniture and all the equipment down to the last teaspoon. It had a coal-fired boiler for the central heating and hot water which, when you consider Plymouth is about as far away from a coal field as one can get, with the cost of indifferent quality coal higher than anywhere else in the country, fitted in with the convoluted official thinking. (Some years later I visited friends living in an identical quarter in Rosyth on the north bank of the Forth, right on top of a coal mine. Their source of heating? Why, electricity of course. Electricity prices in that part of Scotland are the highest in the country. But they did have an open grate in the living room for which they scrumped sufficient free coal from the roadside near their quarter.)

I set to work putting up shelves and all those little things needed to turn a new house into a home. We weren't allowed to put holes in walls but I chose not to be aware of that rule. Contractors were due to sow wall-to-wall grass seed in the back gardens which, on our side of the road, sloped down to a hedge bordering what had once been a field. The ground had already been prepared for seed sowing. Had I done nothing we would have been left with a somewhat useless back garden, but I wanted somewhere for growing vegetables and somewhere else for the children to play, and a level area for deckchairs in the summer. So I turned to with a spade to reshape the would-be lawn, finding quite early on that only a foot under the ground was rock, a lovely pink-tinged limestone. A pickaxe joined the spade and at the end of a hard weekend we had our level area, plus enough lumps of stone prised out to build an attractive drystone wall. The soil was much deeper at the bottom of the field and that is where I made our veg patch, having real beginners' luck with everything I grew. Father came over for a short stay and brought young plants to start us off. People moving in to the houses either side regarded married quarters as temporary places where they never stayed long enough to want to improve anything, but not us. Patricia had spent all her life moving every few years while she and her mother trailed round following Leslie in his naval career when possible, and she was keen to settle even if we were only there for three years. We set about improving the place inside and out, and very soon were having parties every few weeks.

Most people when they move to a new area take a long time to put down roots, sometimes never succeeding if the new area is way out in the country where folk tend to be wary of incomers. In the Navy we moved so often, and the housing was often intermixed with non-naval residential areas, that we learned to get those roots down within weeks. The usual way to start this off was for one's

CO to invite new people to his home initially, and Robin Owen did this with us, introducing us to several other officers and their wives. Then it was our turn, scouring the area for people we'd met in previous jobs for starters. A nice custom was that the local Commander-in-Chief would hold a formal cocktail party every few months, and officers joining his domain were expected to go to his residence and 'sign the book' whereupon in due course a classy printed invitation would arrive. At his party one often met other kindred spirits, and with all these social functions one's list of friends quickly grew. It didn't take us long to find the venue for a Scottish Country Dance club which met weekly at the officers' club in Devonport, and there we started to meet civilian people with no service connection, after which we were away.

We just loved Plymouth. It was so clean, there were no litter louts that one was aware of. The fresh sea breeze blew in from the Hoe. The shops were good, and all around us were those lovely Devonshire voices. It was home to Patricia who was born there, and very soon became home to me too. I had acquired a motor scooter, an early Vespa, one of those gentle commuting machines with a running board either side to put your feet on. I would go to work on it most days, as it was quicker than the car, leaving Patricia with a means of travelling about. My office was actually outside the dockyard gates, in the end house of a residential terrace that looked over the high dockyard wall across the Hamoaze to Cornwall. Robin described the building as being in a state of 'controlled dilapidation', to the experienced eye instantly recognisable as a government building. I parked the bike in what had once been the coal shed round the back, and was greeted by our elderly clerk, Mr Longshaw, who provided my first cup of tea and 'did' for the senior members of the E&T unit. He'd spent his working life as a railwayman, only coming to this gentle job after retirement, and was very content. He would talk about his life on the railways, at one time shouldering responsibility for a section of the GWR track in Somerset. His large pocket watch would be consulted from time to time as only an old-time railwayman knew how. He lamented the way the railways were being destroyed (Beeching was at his most active then). I'd had a letter published in The Daily Telegraph in which I said there was no point in only leaving main lines open, since one needed the branch lines in order to get to and from the nearest main line station. Therefore the number of lost travelling passengers would be hugely higher than Beeching's predictions. That's exactly what happened, and overnight I for one went from being a regular user of the railways to a once-a-year traveller, and not even that now that we had a car and a family. Don Longshaw and I would spend ages talking about the railways of his time, bringing back to my mind the funny little train I caught to my prep school at Charlton Marshall.

It wasn't long before I began to build my next boat. This was a nine-foot dinghy with a single lugsail built from plywood with ash ribs and mahogany thwarts. Some of the timber came from surplus dockyard wood that the local secondhand shop who had a contract with the dockyard was able to sell on. The boat was absurdly cheap to build, and when it was finished I bought a little Seagull outboard for it. To tow it around I also built a trailer, a general purpose box trailer, the box part built from old dockyard packing cases. The trailer chassis came from a man who bought and sold them from his home up at Harford, north of Ivybridge where we spent Christmas at the Bullaven Farm Hotel during the war. He said he might be out when I called, but would leave the trailer in his outhouse. He was out, so I left my cheque tucked under the telephone in his hallway. No doors were locked nor windows shut, nor would any passer-by dream of taking anything. He had a lovely gurgling stream running through his large garden, the water having been diverted from a Dartmoor stream a few hundred yards away, and passing through three gardens before discharging into the River Erme, itself only a modest stream at that point.

With our own boat we were now in business. Over the next couple of years we often went out in the dinghy, usually launching it from one of the deserted sandy beaches along the coast between Newton Ferrers and Bigbury. They were happy days, with the children splashing around on the beach or on the water. Getting down to these beaches with a boat was not easy, for there were only little Devon lanes for access, but we managed, and generally there would be somewhere large enough to leave the Traveller with its trailer while we manhandled the dinghy.

One of the Scottish Country Dancers was a Commander Hall, the assistant harbour master. When HM Yacht Britannia came in for a short informal visit with the Queen Mother on board, each day the royal barge disembarked her in the dockyard where a car would be waiting to whisk her off on her visits. Tim Hall met her on the steps, slippery with wet seaweed in the half tide, taking her arm to ensure she didn't take a pearler. He found himself more or less in a Scottish Country Dance promenade hold one time, and commented on it. "Oh, shall we dance then?" quipped the Queen Mother. At the club that night his talk was full of his newfound partner! Like so many people I always felt especially privileged if the Queen Mother should drive past since she would be certain to give one a friendly wave. It happened to me later that week when I was alone in a quiet part of the dockyard as she came by (I almost looked behind me to see who she was waving at, then realised it must be me!). It happened again when Patricia and I were walking along the seafront near HMS Dolphin during our Alverstoke days, and we received our special wave. Wonderful lady.

At the dancing class we met a charming middle-aged childless couple who lived in Plymbridge, found they were walkers, and organised a complicated walk along the Abbot's Way from its start near Buckfastleigh right across the bleakest part of southern Dartmoor to Princetown, leaving one car at each end which involved rather a lot of motoring before and after. We loved walking on Dartmoor, always with the children of course, where we would spend the weekends playing around in one of the many streams. Going by the back roads we would be up at Cadover Bridge by ten on a Saturday morning, returning home about one-ish just as the population of Plymouth were setting out. We seldom met anybody up on the moors at the times we would choose to be there. Of course, many of the convicts holed up in the prison at Princetown would have been Londoners, and it was said that the ones who escaped while on working parties outside the gates would be back before the night was out knocking on the door to be let in. They found it spooky. But we just loved the rocky tors, each one distinct, each one an objective to be reached and climbed. Just stomping around in the heather or bracken, walking on soft sheep-shorn grass finer than any lawn, coming across crystal-clear streams tinkling under one's feet or rushing down a cascade; it was all glorious. Even in winter, with a salty mist blowing in off the sea and testing one's navigation skills to the limit, walking on the Moor was always enjoyable.

My uncle Ted and Dot, his wife, motored down to see us. They drove a diminutive little Austin A30 and took two days for what they described as 'the long journey'. We took them up to Hound Tor north of Widecombe-in-the-Moor where I discovered Dot had a heart condition and was unable to manage the hill. They were both keen birdwatchers, so we also took them to the upper reaches of the Yealm estuary to look at estuary birds. There were lots of birds everywhere in those days. I cadged the shell of a whole Stilton cheese from the wardroom steward that I took home for our blackbirds to clean out. One of them was so absorbed with this luxurious bounty that it wouldn't fly off when I came over to watch until I put my hand out to touch it.

We went down on day trips to St. Mawes from time to time to see father and go out in a boat. Jim Eva, our erstwhile farmer neighbour from Polsue days, still had his fishing boat, and took us all out one day. Off Nare Head some five miles further up channel we watched while dozens of gannets plunged into the water all around us. We had been fishing mackerel and the gannets had spotted the shoal beneath the boat. That was a good day for we also saw seals and the fin of a basking shark. The children weren't so sure, being more concerned with the effect the swell was having on their tummies. People down there all seemed noticeably older, and just about all of them welcomed a crew for their boat, so we never looked far for something to sail. Father had befriended a man named Douglas Gordon, a somewhat eccentric man who owned a lovely elderly, wooden-hulled boat in which he took us out several times. He had an ogrish wife so he told us, so went out on the water to escape. We didn't meet her for some time but when we did, she turned out to be perfectly sweet but just didn't enjoy being out in a boat. I think he may well have deserved any ogre-like behaviour she displayed to him. Douglas's boat was a big slow yawl which he generally sailed single-handed, but seemed pleased enough to have us all aboard. One day as we were tying up we were hailed by a man waving frantically from another yacht who, as soon as we were on our mooring, rowed across to talk. It was none other than Noggin, now retired from the Navy partly as a result of anti-nuclear demonstrations at Aldermaston he'd been involved in, with a new job as a lecturer at Reading University. There he'd been instrumental in developing a driverless tractor that could be programmed to plough a field. It was early days for this sort of thing and the field had first to have wires laid underground for the tractor to follow, but it was a step towards automation on the farm which interested him. Quite a change from the life of a Naval Officer! I noticed immediately that he'd acquired a quite different speaking voice. He spoke like a BBC newsreader with exceptionally clear annunciation, no doubt a very good asset when lecturing. Maybe he'd always spoken like that, but then I hadn't seen him for many years and in our younger days clear speech didn't really feature in one's priority list. Father was always getting on to me about my own woofy speech, but then he was deaf and said he could never hear what 'young' people were saying anyway.

HMS Drake had an indoor heated swimming pool complete with PTI swimming instructor, which was available for families at weekends. We took both the children there for their lessons, the instructor taking wonderful care with them, teaching them the rudiments of swimming with tremendous patience. After a somewhat clingy start when they first went to school, the children were now much happier there. Unfortunately, just as Paul was starting school the government introduced a new way of teaching children to read using something they called the initial teaching alphabet. So far as we were concerned, this was a disaster, put Paul's reading skills back about a year, taking him ages to make the transition to the normal alphabet later. However, the school head, Francis Baldock, was a wonderfully understanding man, and really did his best to help the children settle.

We attended Mutley Plain Baptist Church where Patricia used to go when she lived in Plymouth in her late teenage years, meeting some of the people she knew in those days. One such family was the Hurrells who lived at Wrangaton in a lovely family house on the edge of Dartmoor. We visited them at their home where Harry Hurrell kept some special attractions. He used to have the occasional spot on local television, sometimes talking over a film he'd made on urban foxes, or otters. He'd had a couple of otters called Topsy and Turvy which lived in a piece of water he used a lot in his wildlife films. By the time we came along, both otters had gone, but HG (as he was called) had become well known as the local naturalist so when a fisherman caught a young Atlantic seal in his net which was injured, HG was asked if he could look after it. There began a twenty-year association with the seal, which he named Atlanta. He kept the seal in the family swimming pool where he taught it all manner of tricks. He had to visit the fish market every week for half a hundredweight of fish, so keeping Atlanta would have been a costly venture. Of course he made lots of films of her, and she became quite well known. He also had visits from schools, and that was where our children came in, for they were treated to a special performance by Atlanta whenever we visited. Once there had been a mink farm on the premises, but the mink had long since gone, the empty cages being used for whichever wild animal was undergoing recuperation at the time. Some stayed permanently. One of these was Black Rod, a splendid raven which, again, would perform tricks to order. His favourite was to obtain a chunk of meat that had been tied to a string from his perch when, on being given the order, he would pull the string up with his beak, hold one end under his foot while he took a fresh hold until eventually the meat was heaved up the five feet from ground to perch. He had a lovely deep bass croak with which he greeted us as we approached. There was also a pine martin that performed a similar set of tricks. The Hurrells lived in a comfortable family house with a lovely higgledy-piggeldy untidy kitchen with a bay window in which the dining table was positioned, enabling them to watch the birds feeding on the bird table outside during mealtimes. Whenever we were there, there would be anything up to a dozen different species all jostling for space, including all three woodpeckers on the British list, and even a peacock that was there on one of our visits. They had two sons and a daughter, the elder son Leonard also keeping various birds at his home in Plymouth. One day he produced a buzzard which we were all allowed to hold for a while, a great treat for the children. Once, when visiting Leonard at his home, Paul spotted a kestrel fly over and pointed to it. "Ah, that'll be Charlie, he usually comes at this time for his tea," said Leonard. Charlie had once been one of Leonard's avian patients, and had become used to meat being put out on the bird table every afternoon at four. It was now free, but returned daily to its old haunt. Not a lot of people have names for passing kestrels, now I come to think of it. We were privileged to know the Hurrells at this time, and it was wonderful for the children to meet all the animals and birds at close quarters.

As winter drew in, the children were getting excited about what they'd heard in school about bonfire night. One or two people locally were joining up for a combined children's party with a fireworks display, but we'd discovered the Navy were putting on a proper display for naval families, hosted by the apprentice training school at HMS Raleigh on the other side of the Torpoint Ferry. It sounded rather like the one we had been to at Whale Island, with the opportunity to give a decent send off to any out-of-date distress flares and such pyrotechnics, so should be good. We drove over there, and stood around the large football pitch while the rockets and bangs were set off by an eager team of instructor petty officers. I was standing there in the crowd, about six deep, all of us gazing up into the sky watching the spectacle, when a spent rocket stick came down with a loud thud about six feet away. King Harold must have felt the same as all the arrows flew around him at Hastings. After the show was over I attempted to rescue the stick, to find it had penetrated about a foot into the ground, a stout pole almost as thick as a broomstick and quite heavy. It must have come down at considerable speed and I worried about this all the way home. It could so easily have landed in the sea of upturned faces. I have never since enjoyed a fireworks display, worrying where all the spent bits and pieces might land. Nowadays I find them next morning on my roof and in the garden, yet we are quite some way from where the things have been let off.

One of the items that came under Robin Owen's aegis was the responsibility for all radioactive sources used in the dockyard. There were surprising quantities of these, all very small ones, but needing special care with their handling. They were used in the main for testing or calibrating various bits of equipment, including Geiger counters, and there were a number of tiny 'buttons' used by ships for decontamination exercises, which had to be returned to the dockyard and accounted for when a ship paid off. Individually, these sources were not all that dangerous as they were well-shielded when in their boxes, but collectively they were potentially harmful. A disused brick built hut in a remote part of the dockyard had been chosen for storing them in, the Geiger counter which we carried when in that area starting to crackle as we got near. One day I visited the hut and out of curiosity walked round the back to where another disused room opened off it. To my dismay I found that a dockyard matey had discovered this space and built his little 'nest' there, his donkey jacket hanging on a hook with a copy of the Daily Mirror sticking out of the pocket, and a thermos flask and sandwich box sitting on the table. Two feet away from his chair behind an innocent brick wall were all our radioactive sources. I told Robin of this and the man was quietly ejected, the door being sealed up. We never discovered what happened to him, but he would have been nearing retirement age at the time.

There are two parts to Devonport dockyard separated by the road leading down to the Torpoint ferry, the whole area being over two miles from one end to the other. In my day the way to get about was on the dockyard train, a wonderful Emmett-like transport system with standard gauge tracks laid around the big basins, and a tunnel beneath the Torpoint ferry road. The train consisted of several trucks pulled by a quaint little tank engine, each truck designated for specific people, for instance the posh truck at one end was carpeted with pictures on the bulkheads and a sign saying 'Principal Officers Only' whereas the one next door simply said 'Officers' and the one beyond that 'Foremen'. At the other end of the train were two open trucks for equipment with some unspecified cattle trucks in between. One was reminded of the Service instruction that is reputed to have said: 'Officers and their ladies, Senior NCOs and their wives, Other Ranks and their women.' The Services and the Ministry that look after them took a long time to come to terms with the democratisation of its personnel.

A ship that came through dockyard hands at this time was one of the three proper cruisers we still had, known as 'Tiger, Lion or Blake' since they looked the same and no one I knew was sure which was which. I think this one was Blake. She had three splendid six-inch triple gun turrets and looked like a proper warship. One morning when most of the ordnance members of E&T were down on the ship and I was just enjoying my mid morning cup of tea and a chat with Don Longshaw, there came a menacing deep 'BOOM' which rattled the windows. Definitely an explosion, and not far away either. Didn't someone say they were testing something in Blake's 'A' turret? We glanced out of the window to where smoke was wafting up from the jetty where Blake was lying, while flocks of dockyard pigeons flew around in a panic. "She's facing this way," remarked Don, "If they elevated that gun a bit more they'd get us with the next one…" An hour later a somewhat embarrassed foreman returned to the office (I'd seen him cross the road and was sitting at my desk wearing my motorbike crash hat all ready for his arrival). Apparently one of the lads in the magazine had mistaken the order to send up a trial cartridge for test cartridge (I may not have got the names correct, but they were very similar). One is a dummy, used when trialling the workings of the loading operation, while the other contains a reduced charge when carrying out test firings. They'd got the wrong one up the spout and nobody noticed. It was low tide at the time, so it was the nearby dockyard piles that took the force of the explosion. It made a most satisfactory noise, which would have frightened more than the pigeons had the gun been elevated. We were lucky.

During our Devonport time we were able to take a proper holiday. Until now we had, like most couples with a young family, been constrained to visiting one or other set of parents for our holidays. The parents doted over their grandchildren and looked after them while we had time to ourselves and, of course, it was cheap. We never had any spare money, so a cheap holiday was essential. However, we'd begun to scrape together a few pounds by now and reckoned we'd blow it on an overseas holiday like so many of our acquaintances seemed to be doing nowadays. Going overseas for holidays was still unusual, with the Costa de this-and-that still being built like frenzy to satisfy the growing demand. Sitting on a beach in hot sun is not our idea of fun, so we settled for a walking holiday in the Italian Alps with the Ramblers Association. In June Patricia's parents arrived to live in our house and look after the children while we trained up to London, had a couple of days with my uncle Ted, then went by train to Folkestone, crossed to Calais in a French ferry (dirty and no nice food), and boarded the sleeper to Basle. This train was awful, with neither food nor washing facilities and a grumpy attendant who refused to unlock and let down the stowed hammock-style bunks until we were almost too exhausted to sleep. At Basle we changed to a slick Swiss train for Innsbruck, then a three-hour bus journey through the Brenner Pass to Corvara, our base. Getting off the bus I looked around for our leader who was to meet us there, to see an older man approaching with the unmistakeable stride of the hardened professional walker. He introduced himself with a Yorkshire dialect, and it soon became evident Patricia and I were almost alone in our lack of experience of proper walking, and we were about to embark on two weeks of it. What had we let ourselves in for?

In the event, the holiday was superb. We stayed at a Swiss-type alpine hotel with basic facilities, but it was clean and the beds comfortable enough. Every day we would set out for walks up in the surrounding mountains, sometimes taking the chairlift 3,000 feet up onto a plateau just below the receding snowline. We saw lots of alpine flowers, not appreciating until then that one can cover both spring and summer flowers by how high up the mountain one is looking. Our equipment, particularly our boots, was quite inadequate for much of this type of walking but we survived. Most days were hot and sunny with a brief but heavy rainstorm at teatime, usually when we were on our way down. The timing was so predictable, we generally managed to be close to cover when it came. Half an hour later the sun was out once more. One very hot and dusty day towards the end of the holiday when the length of walk was into the teens, we rounded a bend to see in front of us an English couple just setting out their picnic table on which they placed a large teapot while the primus beside them hotted up the water. We hadn't had a cup of tea since leaving the UK, so it was a welcome sight indeed. They invited us to join them. By this time the rest of the party were so far ahead, we'd just about given up, so we gratefully accepted. The return journey was just as tedious as the trip out, but this time the cross channel ferry was a BR one with a splendid restaurant that served a full cooked breakfast with all the trimmings and did a roaring business. Bliss!

The children were growing up, and we could plan more ambitious days out on the Moor. In winter it was lovely to drive from a bright sunny Plymstock up the country lanes to Ditsworthy Warren which would often have a few inches of snow. One or two lanes in that area, free of traffic and steeply sloping, made wonderful toboggan runs that the children enjoyed. Afterwards, we could drive back down into the relative warmth and dryness of the coastal area leaving the snow behind. I must not leave the impression the weather was always fine. For days Patricia's diary entries would read "rained all day…" information one's memory chooses not to retain! Plymouth is on the windward side of high ground, so not surprisingly the prevailing wind having come right across the Atlantic has picked up a lot of moisture to deposit on that side. Go a few miles east towards Torquay, and it is considerably drier, probably only 30 inches of rain a year as against Plymouth's 60. We normally went out regardless of weather, kitting out the children with sou'westers and wellies. I had a set of fisherman's oilskins bought at a fishy-boaty shop in the Barbican for my motor scooter rides to work, and the whole family had anoraks of course. The anorak was standard wear in those parts, and when we returned up-country after our Plymouth time, I think we must have introduced it to the urban folks in the home counties.

My daily commuter run to work took me twenty minutes, about four miles altogether along fairly good roads. One morning as I was waiting for some lights to change a motorcycle traffic cop drew up alongside. He was sitting on an enormously powerful machine way above me, with clipboards, telephone and other bric-a-brac spread across the petrol tank, a big man dressed in menacing black. He looked down with a condescending nod. I nodded back and said, "Race you to the next set of lights?" His lip curled just a bit. The lights changed, he let in his clutch and had roared out of sight before I even began to move. I never saw him again. Traffic on the whole was no real problem, but then this was only 1965. Visitors pouring into town choked it up in the summer, and I would have to find rat runs to avoid being held up. If I was travelling home in someone's car as I did occasionally, the trip home could take forty-five minutes, thirty of them spent in needless traffic jams.

Recounting my amicable brush with the law that morning, one of my diagnosticians told of a sailor who picked up a Plymouth girl and took her for an evening run on his heavy motorbike. They parked at the bottom of Sheepstor, then set off on foot to the top where he attempted to have his way with her. However, he had misunderstood the sort of girl she was. Leaping to her feet, she grabbed one of his boots which he'd taken off, hurled it as far away as she could, then sprinted down the hill to the parked bike while her sailor hobbled after her, shouting. Arrived at the bike, she leapt onto it, starting it expertly with a single kick and shot off home, leaving him to find his way back as best he could in the last of the evening light. They don't breed girls like that nowadays.

Union Street, the street linking Plymouth with Devonport, used to be alternate pubs and brothels until the Luftwaffe cleaned it up. After rebuilding, it was far more respectable, and one evening I took Patricia to quite a high class Chinese restaurant there. The clientele were very proper and it was quiet and expensive, but we noticed just one misfit customer who didn't seem to know quite where he was. This was a sailor, in uniform, sitting by himself, swaying slightly, and not really enjoying his meal. He began to talk to no one in particular. I sensed the

310

management watching intently. Then I was suddenly aware of a couple of small but beefy Chinese bouncers who sidled up from nowhere, then with one on each side hitched the sailor out of his seat, and slid silently behind a curtain, my last sight being the look of surprise on the sailor's face as he vanished. It was all over in seconds. No one in the restaurant seemed to have noticed anything. A few moments later, one of the waiters picked up the sailor's cap and disappeared with it behind the scenes. No fuss, no sound, no scene. It was so perfect it could have been part of the cabaret, and we should have applauded.

Ditsworthy Warren is a lovely area for walking, spared the encroachment of bracken, the sheep-cropped turf short and resilient under one's feet. It has a stone row and several huge standing stones, there are the remains of tin mining activities all over the place, the River Plym, a little tinkling stream at this point, runs down through the warren, and there are many interesting objectives all within a few miles. With Susan not yet seven and Paul only five, our walks were naturally limited, but from Ditsworthy we did make the letterbox at Duck's Pool, just beyond Plym Head, which is seven miles there and back and took us all day with stops and distractions all the way. We signed our names in the book and posted our letters, collecting ones that had been posted there by previous visitors. On another occasion when Patricia's parents were staying, they took us all up to Lydford where Patricia and I set out on our own to walk to Cranmere Pool, and on to rendezvous with the car on the track that goes round Okement Hill just beyond. The route is over the firing ranges and appears quite featureless to the first time visitor. We took map and compass of course, but soon discovered we were walking in an area where the compass needle wouldn't stay still. In the space of a hundred yards the needle swung through 180 degrees. This quite destroyed my confidence in being able to navigate that way, but our boats were burnt, as it were. At the end of the day the parents would have enjoyed their walk with the children down Lydford Gorge, driven up through Okehampton, and be patiently waiting on the deserted moorland track at the rendezvous. We just had to go on. Actually, it wasn't too bad since all we had to do was to walk due east, but then the sun disappeared and it was guesswork again. We got horribly lost in deep peat hags, clambering in and out of six foot deep gullies, but we did in the end stumble across the letterbox at Cranmere, the only other one on Dartmoor at that time, going on to make the rendezvous without trouble. Only then did we discover the road on the map was actually a military track not open to ordinary vehicles, but Leslie had ignored the notices and driven up the road anyway. Later still I was told that compasses always read incorrectly in those parts due to the geology thereabouts.

We enrolled for a pottery course at Plymouth Technical College and in the course of a year or so made some quite nice pots. The studio used stoneware clay, and there were some wonderful glazes available. Our house is still full of our homemade efforts, mainly flower vases, all with 'Mon Evg' scratched on the bottom. So what with Pottery on Mondays, Scottish Dancing every Thursday, quite often a party on Saturday and the occasional Mess Dinner in Drake, there was no problem filling the evenings. We did, in fact, get our first television, a monstrously heavy black-and-white set which I bought secondhand. It often went wrong but I had an electronics chum who would diagnose the problem over the telephone, leaving me to replace the suspected faulty component. TVs in the sixties were built with discrete components, so getting at an individual part was possible. The downside, of course, was that there were hundreds of soldered joints, wires all over the place and individual components were far more liable to failure than potted ones. The age of silicon chips had not yet arrived. The children watched Bill and Ben, Crackerjack and Blue Peter. We watched The Pallisers (which confined us to the house on one evening a week for ages) while thankfully the BBC appreciated its responsibilities in not broadcasting programmes containing unnecessary violence and unpleasantness, something they fail to do nowadays.

We came to know the road from Plymstock to Lee-on-Solent very well, always travelling via Exeter and Honiton, through Axminster, Charmouth, Bridport and Dorchester, then Bere Regis, Ringwood, Southampton and Fareham. None of these places had bypasses, so it was the main road through the middle of town in each case, a long and tedious journey with the children in the back trying to sleep or fight off car sickness all the way. In wintertime, this road would often be foggy around the Charmouth area, the car's hopelessly inadequate lights being no match for the thick sea fogs that rolled in. But there was no problem with getting stuck behind slow moving vehicles on those comparatively narrow roads, though people in the long queues behind us would probably not agree.

I had joined the Institute of Electrical Engineers, mainly because my dockyard peers were all members, and EEM looked more kindly on his Naval personnel having an approved professional qualification. My Cambridge degree and subsequent experience were sufficient for the IEE to take my money and put me on its books. This gave me two more groups of letters after my name since I could now put C.Eng as well as AMIEE in between the MA(Cantab) and RN. It looked quite impressive, but I'm sure it didn't change me in any way. The local IEE Branch ran outings from time to time on which spouses were also welcome, as they tended to have a technical visit somewhere followed by a general interest one, thus making a pleasant day out. So off we went to explore the workings of the BBC North Hessary Tor television transmitter, the WT station at Start Point followed by a visit to Ashprington House where we had tea. We also visited various power stations, and other 'heavy' plants.

For much of my time at Devonport, the yard had been building a type 12 frigate. Portsmouth and Devonport both built warships to keep their hand in, the MoD being happy not to be totally reliant on civilian shipbuilders. On my arrival the Devonport frigate, to be named HMS Cleopatra, had reached the point where she would soon be launched and was in the building dock crawling with dockyard workers with several cranes swaying about overhead. We had an interest to ensure equipment that we would ultimately set up was installed correctly, our fitters moving in to check out all wiring soon after the installation teams had finished. As soon as she was launched and moved to a fitting out dock the keel for her successor was laid down. I thought this might be for the same reason that a builder starts a job the moment his client has engaged him, even if it is only to knock a hole in a wall, after which he's not seen again on site until ready to start work properly, maybe months later. He's establishing ownership for the contract, making it much more difficult for the customer to change his mind.

I found it fascinating to watch the week-by-week progress of Cleopatra as she slowly took on the shape of a frigate. Eventually I had quite a number of men aboard her and even invited father to visit her on a day he came with an elderly St Mawes friend to have lunch with me in the Drake wardroom. The two of them clambered around the ship, managing to go up and down ladders and avoided hitting their heads on all the protruding hazards everywhere. I shouldn't have allowed them on board really, since it contravened all the safety regulations, but I thought they might enjoy it and they did. We lunched at a small private table to one side of the main wardroom mess, where were we waited upon by obsequious stewards wearing white gloves. They loved all this, of course, especially when a steward asked whether they could manage a little Stilton to finish with, producing a whole cheese in perfect condition with a spoon to scoop out the contents. In a glass case beside our table was a cup made from a carved coconut shell encased in chased silver on a silver pedestal, also a naval sword. They asked what they were, not really believing me when I said the cup was one that Sir Francis Drake had presented to Queen Elizabeth, and the sword was Drake's too.

A month or two after this we were at home watching on television the return of Francis Chichester's Gypsy Moth IV after his solo voyage round the world. He was becalmed just outside the breakwater for some time, and it was after dark by the time he finally arrived at the Plymouth Yacht Club for a hero's welcome. As Gypsy Moth made it into Plymouth Sound, we thought we'd pop up to Dunstone Point a mile away and see her for real. All four of us dashed out to the car and I started the engine to drive up there, realising as I heard dozens of other car doors slam and engines start that all our neighbours had the same idea, in fact I think the whole of Plymstock thought likewise. We only managed a short distance up the lane before we had to abandon the car and went the rest of the way on foot. The boat seemed tiny, surrounded by all manner of welcoming craft, but it was a low key affair compared with the welcome that solo sailors receive nowadays. Francis Chichester was a pioneer in this type of sailing. Some time later he was knighted by the Queen who used Drake's sword. The day it was announced, I noticed the sword had disappeared from the glass case. No one was taking any chances.

Patricia had several opportunities to enjoy the exceptional facilities in the wardroom mess, when we held Ladies' Nights. These were long dress affairs, or in my case a white tie with boiled shirt and white waistcoat. The candlelit dinner was always of the highest quality and we have never since dined in such opulence. Drinks before, a little dancing afterwards, home well after midnight; they were wonderful evenings. She actually handled the fabled Drake's Sword so recently held by the Queen, as it lay in its stand in front of the Mess President's place. I attended other mess dinners not involving wives, for which there would normally be one or two VIPs and a guest speaker. Once it was Earl Mountbatten who arrived wearing a well-worn Admiral of the Fleet's dress uniform where the gold braid was beginning to tarnish. Not a common sight, for few admirals of such rank remain active in the Royal Navy for long enough for that to happen. He was actually on our books at the time pending his final retirement from the Service, (it is the custom for MoD to place an officer in his last few weeks on the books of a different Command to that in which he is serving, presumably as a check on correct procedures). Introducing him, the Mess President reminded him he would be expected to return his sheets before leaving! For some quirky reason sheets were regarded as 'on loan' rather than issued outright. Mountbatten told us about how he had recently organised a social for all the Admirals of the Fleet still alive, some twenty altogether. The first to come into the room was his predecessor, so naturally enough he kow-towed to him and called him 'Sir'. In turn this admiral did the same to the next until finally it was the turn of Admiral Power, well into his nineties and walking with two sticks, to have everyone in the room call him 'Sir'.

The very next Mess Dinner had Prince Philip as the guest of honour. Prince Philip's uniform looked as if it had only been made the previous week, no trace of tarnish there! Before the dinner I learned a valuable lesson in making conversation, or perhaps more accurately, extracting information. Prince Philip's host had just gone to refill his glass and for a moment he was on his own. Looking around he couldn't really avoid me as I was standing right in front of him, so he said, "And what do you do?" I prattled away about the dockyard and EEM and so on, while from time to time he latched onto something I said and asked me to expand. Within a few minutes he'd got the picture and was talking about dockyard experiences he remembered from his active days, when the C-in-C returned and led him away. My chums surrounded me wanting to know why the prince had appeared so interested in such a nonentity. I've always remembered that occasion and years later have used Prince Philip's technique to illustrate questioning skills when giving management courses. Compared to Mountbatten's talk, Prince Philip's was far less colourful, but he did allow himself to relax in the closed company of fellow Naval officers with no intruding Press present to misquote him. He commented on Keyham railway station smelling of wet paint, as all railway stations seemed to; had we ever noticed that? No? And they all seemed to have a carpet to walk on. After the dinner I was having a much-needed pee, standing at the centre stall of three urinals when the C-in-C came in with Prince Philip for a similar purpose. For a few moments I was between these two eminent gentlemen while their conversation went on over my head. Not a lot of people have been in such a situation.

The Tall Ships Race was to start in Falmouth that year. A number of them were assembling in Plymouth, so we went to have a look. The British Winston Churchill was dwarfed by some of the huge square-riggers with their crews of a hundred or so. We drove to St Mawes on the start day, taking out father's Caprice so we could follow the big boys after the start. It was a glorious day, perfect for filming, so there I was steering Caprice with one foot on the tiller while I tried to film the scene with my cine camera. We'd positioned Caprice off St Anthony's, so the square-riggers would sail past between us and the shore, the sun behind my right shoulder in the approved position. Filming turned out to be well nigh impossible as I was trying to avoid all the other spectator boats at the same time, but it was still a super day out. A week later the film came back from the processors, but the results were far too jerky to enjoy.

One day as I was walking through the dockyard HMS Undaunted, a fairly elderly Type 15 frigate, came up the river. The approved method for warships to come alongside is to proceed further upstream beyond the berth, turn round, then approach the jetty facing downstream. I stopped to watch as she turned, which ships normally do by going ahead on one engine and astern on the other. From where I was standing on the far side of the large basin, it looked to me as if she was going astern far too fast and heading for a collision with the dockyard wall. Clearly something had gone wrong, sailors were rushing about on deck and a moment later she struck, coming to a fairly abrupt halt. Later I heard what had happened. In the ships of that time the engine room telegraph by which orders were given to the engine room, was operated by a handle in the wheelhouse just below the bridge being turned until it pointed to the desired speed, 'slow astern' for example. Then by means of a mechanical linkage a repeater dial down in the engine room would show the same request. The engine room petty officer would then move the handle at his end to acknowledge the order. Useful when in action, far better than screaming down a telephone or relying on an electrical connection that might be shot to pieces. However, this mechanical linkage was vulnerable, and could jam if the ship sustained damage. In this instance a pair of socks was responsible. Down in the stoker's mess through which the linkage passed, some stoker had hung his socks to dry inside the protective wire cage that shielded exposed gears joining two parts of the system. A sock had become caught up with the open gearing which had the effect of allowing the shaft to turn one way, but not the other. When the order for 'slow astern' was given, the shaft rotated satisfactorily, but then when the bridge wanted to stop going astern, the handle on the bridge wouldn't move, so the sailor up there pulled it to 'half astern' preparatory to taking a good swing at it, but the handle then stuck at half astern. Instead of stopping, the ship began to accelerate, heading for the wall at an angle of about sixty degrees. One sailor was in the stern flat, a space in the extreme back of the ship where the rudder mechanism is located. He felt the engines speeding up and heard shouting above him, followed by the sound of running feet, and realised something was amiss, so decided to beat a hasty retreat. He was just coming up through the hatch when the ship struck, the stern crumpled in reducing the space he was leaving from twenty feet long to under ten feet, with a sudden rush of expelled air out through the hatch. As a result he popped up in the air like a champagne cork, ending up on the jetty where he landed quite safely on a pile of rope. It was an incredible stroke of luck that he sustained no injury at all. No one else in the ship was injured either, but the stern looked a sorry mess.

We had another type 15 in the dockyard at that time, an old ship in use as an accommodation vessel. The dockyard construction people arranged for the two ships to be put into dry dock together, stern-to-stern, and then proceeded to cut the back off the accommodation ship, swing it around and weld it onto Undaunted. This worked well, with an almost seamless join. Fortunately both ships were—unusually—the same size at that point, and the damage had only been to the hull. The rudder and propellers were far enough for'd not to have been damaged. Undaunted, true to her name, went back to sea a few weeks later none the worse.

A new head of the dockyard electronics workshop had joined EEM's department, a Commander Elvy. He was a kindred spirit whom I came to know well, and we invited him and his wife round for dinner one evening with some other guests. We hadn't met his wife previously, so were somewhat startled when she came through our front door, a largish lady dressed in a most unsuitable long knitted pink dress. I'd never seen a knitted dress like that before and it took all evening to get used to, but she was quite unconcerned. I believe she had been an actress and enjoyed being the centre of attraction. A few weeks later we had a return invitation to their house in Ermington, a little village just off the Kingsbridge road. We couldn't find the house for a while, the description given to us seemingly led only to a large manor in its own grounds. Eventually we realised the large manor was their house and crunched up the long drive to an imposing front door. Moments later we were joined by one of the junior dockyard officers and his wife, and then a third couple. We were warmly welcomed by the Elvys and shown around before settling in their drawing room for pre dinner drinks. Disbelievingly we went from the entrance hall to a morning room, the library, a large music room and finally into this huge drawing room with a decorated plaster ceiling. I caught the eye of the dockyard man who was gazing around him wonderingly. At dinner the meal was served up on priceless china, with silver cutlery so heavy that I had difficulty controlling it. It was the most extraordinary evening I can remember, like one of those mystery films, and the dockyard officer and myself would talk about it whenever we met thereafter.

A favourite spot for a day on the beach was Bigbury Bay. We would go early in the morning while the sun was shining into the little bays around Sharpland Point and where the sand was smooth, the River Avon flowing quietly past and sheltered from onshore winds, the main seasiders preferring to remain nearer the car park so we had it to ourselves. By afternoon the sun would have moved round, but by then we'd had our fill and would be heading off home. The well-known West Country naturalist, Tony Soper, lived in an isolated house on the hill above us somewhere, with a view across the estuary towards Bantham. We knew that because one of his television programmes showed him on the terrace demonstrating various types of bird feeder. He often did a spot on our local TV channel, apart from his national TV programmes. He'd been in at the beginning of the BBC Natural History Unit at Bristol. We liked his relaxed and friendly presentation technique and always watched his programmes. At this time he was heavily involved with the Torrey Canyon disaster, where a huge laden tanker had gone on the rocks off Lands End, polluting the sea with thousands of tons of heavy crude oil which came ashore on many of the West Country beaches killing enormous numbers of seabirds. Almost nightly he had a report on the latest bird casualty figures. I had bought his The Bird Table Book, and thought of him up there above us as we lay on the beach. So one day we rather cheekily called in to ask if he would sign my copy of his book. He was quite charming, invited us in, chatted about the best identification guide for beginners like us, showed the children how to attract the small birds to one's garden, and signed my copy, noticing that I had an early edition which had a mistake in it which he corrected by hand. We'd mentioned our connection with the Hurrells whom he knew of course, so maybe that went down well.

We also watched the independent Westward TV local news that often had a small wildlife piece, sometimes from HG. At the end of the programme would be a dreadful ten seconds of what we could expect in the way of weather for the next day, read out by the front man. The BBC did a far better forecast, so we would have to switch to that channel for our weather. I used to comment to Patricia that in the West Country the main industries by far were farming, fishing and tourism, all of which depended on the weather, and here was a local TV station unable to say anything sensible about it and worse still, not using that essential visual medium they had. I put my thoughts down on paper and sent them off to Westward TV. Somewhat to my surprise that elicited a phone call inviting me to call round before the evening programme and meet the producer and presenter. I went along; keen to see how it was all put together. On the night in question one of the reporters, David Mudd, was running through film of an interview he'd had that morning with the Tory candidate for a Somerset constituency by-election, trying to find something usable without embarrassing the candidate, for he had been drinking far too much for his own good and it showed. Minutes before the programme went out, they were splicing together the usable parts ready for transmission. The presenter, whom I'd already met, was anxiously amending his copy of the script, while right up to the last moment they were adjusting the running order. There was only the most rudimentary of autocues available in those early days, the presenter often having to rely on a nearby studio manager waving bits of card at him while a voice crackled away in his earpiece. After the programme was over, the producer asked me whether I would like to join them part time, turning the weather information they received from nearby RAF Mountbatten into something usefully visual. I would love to have taken up their offer, but it would involve a couple of hours every afternoon, and no way would I be in a position to accept. However, I put them on to a recently retired Naval Officer who lived in Plymouth and had been a meteorological officer in the Instructor Branch. He took it up for a while and then they started with a far better presentation fronted by a younger man who stayed with them for years, and whose forecasts were really valuable, with sailing and surfing information for all the main areas.

My time at Plymouth was running out. We'd had nearly three wonderful years in this most attractive area and my chances of getting a Plymouth ship or another Plymouth appointment were slim. I went to see my appointer in the MoD to find out what he had in mind for my next job. I found that he already had my successor arranged, and had also at one time planned my new job, but a series of problems had arisen and now the job he had arranged for me had fallen through.

"I shall have to move you anyway," he told me, "And it will probably be to the Portsmouth area, but I have some more moves to confirm before it is all set." More than that he wouldn't say. We felt unsettled, rather like buying and selling one's house with chains that have to be established by both parties. But I wouldn't know about that, as we'd never bought nor sold a house before. We had, however, noticed the way people's houses were going up in value fast, and we were not with them to enjoy being on the ladder. During our time in Plymouth the sort of house we would need had gone up from about £3,000 to over £4,000, and we only had a few hundreds in the bank... We would have to buy our own house before too long, but where? I really envied those people like the civilian Dockyard Officers who could safely buy their own place secure in the knowledge it would be possible to live in it.

Patricia and I discussed the problem, but without certain knowledge of my next job, there was little we could do. A few days later my Appointer telephoned me to say he'd had to go firm with my successor, and would be moving me to Portsmouth, attached to HMS Bellerophon. This was the umbrella name for all the bits and pieces associated with the Reserve Fleet, a conglomeration of vessels spread around Portsmouth harbour in various states of unreadiness, some of them in mothballs. I would be based in HMS Belfast, a wartime cruiser used as an accommodation ship alongside a large floating jetty off Whale Island. It didn't sound at all like a career move. Was I at the age of 36 already being pushed sideways? Would the Portsmouth area be the best place to buy our first house? What if I was given a job at the other end of the country as soon as we'd bought one? It was all very unsettling.

We had an invitation to lunch with the Admiral Superintendent at his official residence in the South Yard. The current Admiral Superintendent was a most approachable man with whom I got on well on the rare occasions we met. Both being engineers presumably helped. People in such positions certainly have excellent perks. In this case it was the luxury of living in a large and extremely comfortable house generously staffed by deferential personnel who attended to one's every need. A scratch on the glasslike finish of the mahogany dining room table would be seen to at once by a professional French polisher from the dockyard, a chip on the paintwork anywhere would be dealt with similarly. Step outside and a swish official car driven by a uniformed chauffeur was there to whisk one away. As he said during lunch, it was very easy to get used to such living, but it could only be temporary. He treated it as compensation for the tiresomeness of the job, the constant bickering of his heads of dockyard divisions, the impossibility with complying with the MoD's demands for this and that without adequate resources to provide the results he'd like. He had to listen to the irksome demands of the Unions who had a completely different agenda, interested in the short term benefits with little thought for their own future, something which would certainly be curtailed should those somewhat selfish demands ever be met. He said his next job would most likely be in London, sitting at a dusty desk in Whitehall with secretarial help only if he was lucky, still having to juggle to keep the bosses happy. I thought he was trying to be kind to me by pointing out life was not all about clambering up some precarious ladder to a non-existent Shangri-La at the top. No doubt the very top was fine, for then one was above the clouds of discontent, but it was a very small pinnacle and there was only room for one or two people on it. Lord Mountbatten had given us just a glimpse of life up there. We packed up the house, the Married Quarters man came to check the inventory and was so surprised we'd looked after everything so well without breaking or destroying much of it that he asked whether we'd like some of the fittings, since he was allowed 'breakages'. We accepted a coffee pot and a set of silver plated teaspoons and could probably have had more.

It needed a big furniture van to get all our personal possessions back to Lee-on-Solent where we would once again move in with Patricia's parents whilst finding somewhere to live. We set off on a beastly wet day, the rain sheeting down the whole way. Patricia drove our overloaded Traveller, with the box trailer on the back, laden with all the things we thought we might need until we received the rest of our possessions from the furniture store. I rode escort on my motor scooter, currently a Honda 90. Ten miles down the road one of the trailer's little wheels had a puncture. In the rain, I had to prop up the trailer, take off the wheel, and leaving the trailer and my bike at the side of the road, we drove on to the next village where I managed to have the tube mended. By the time we eventually arrived at Lee-on-Solent we were all exhausted and I was so stiff I had to be helped off the bike. Five days later we put down a deposit for our first home. The date was 30th June 1967 and we'd found a house in Alverstoke for £6,000, far more than we could really afford.

15

Belfast and Cochrane

Alverstoke had changed in those few years we had been away. There was more traffic, nearby Gosport seemed grubbier after Plymouth, the people dowdier. But at last we had our first proper home, set back a couple of roads behind the draughty letting we'd lived in last time, and it was a quiet road near to a good church school.

The school was a turn-of-the-century building built of brick and flint with a steeply pitched roof atop tall walls with the windows set high up so that the pupils would not be distracted by passers by. The teachers were competent, kind but severe and their charges knew that no time wasting would be tolerated. They were there to learn and time was precious. When we first arrived Paul was too young to go there and had to waste the best part of a year at an infants school learning very little. However he was soon taught to read using the proper alphabet, the experiment into that ridiculous ITA quickly forgotten.

We found lots of naval friends around, so were quickly established socially. There were also the family friends; mainly older retired naval people of Leslie's generation, and Patricia's parents were always available for baby-sitting. Altogether a good though unadventurous move. Patricia busied herself with equipping the house with furniture. She would search the shops during the week, shortlist items and on Saturdays we would go round together and finalise the choice. We didn't need to buy all that much, nor did the house require much preparation for living in. It was built in 1938, a sturdy, quality semi-detached. Its drawback was that it had been designed for owners who would probably employ a maid rather than spend time in the kitchen, thus the kitchen was a gloomy room with quarry tiled floor, a coal-fired central heating boiler and a small window which looked out onto the narrow side passage between our house and the next. There was a small garden, about thirty feet by forty, but this backed on to glebe allotment land, so one of my first jobs was to obtain an allotment and put a gate into the back fence so that I could get to it. There I grew all our vegetables while we kept the back garden for flowers and playing in.

We thought it would be a good idea if the children learnt to play the piano, so advertised for one, receiving a call from a widow lady who lived a mile or so away. She had an upright Broadwood, which hadn't been played for years, but was in sound condition. Would £5 be all right? I discussed this with a musical police sergeant acquaintance whom I had met whilst waiting at the school gates one afternoon. He offered to come and look at it with me. The instrument had been used as a piece of furniture for a very long time, but it seemed sound enough, so I bought it. The police sergeant then offered to have it transported to our house, provided the lady didn't mind if he did so fairly late one evening. "Why?" I asked him later.

"Because I shall borrow some of the lads off the beat to lift it, and we'll use the Black Maria for transport!" This seemed an excellent idea.

A couple of days later he set off from the station, rounding up four hefty constables from the Gosport streets and drove to the lady's house. Then with a fair amount of noise they lifted the heavy piano out onto the road and hoisted it aboard the vehicle, greatly to the interest of all the neighbours, all frantically curtain-twitching by this time, quite convinced the piano must be full of drugs or explosives or something equally illegal. It took the poor lady a very long time to convince them.

Out came the old bicycle again, and I resumed my daily commuting by bike to Clarence Yard in Gosport, thence across the harbour to Whale Island on the dockyard steam ferry. Tied up on the other side of a large floating jetty to HMS Belfast was HM Yacht Britannia, her gleaming deep blue sides painted by dockyard professionals with specially ordered gloss paint. The sailors hand-picked from volunteers wore spotless soft white shoes; a big contrast to the Bellerophon crew in the Belfast who seemed to me to be a rag-tag of oddments who couldn't be found a home in a proper ship. I began to wonder whether I had been thus categorised, but my Appointer kept telling me this was a temporary job, and it had to be done by somebody.

Only a few episodes of that time come to mind. One was when I was asked to be 'prisoner's friend' to a sailor who was under shipboard arrest pending his appearance at the Portsmouth magistrate's court. His crime—attempting to set fire to the law courts where he was caught red-handed whilst trying to escape on a stolen bicycle. I went to see him, a sad unprepossessing soul with very little intelligence, alas. He made my job almost impossible by not volunteering any information at all, and seemed to have just given up. There are usually a few such people in the Services, attracted there by the uniform and the knowledge that they will be looked after, thereby being able to drift around in a dream being told when to get up or clean their shoes or salute. Usually such men thrive with the discipline, never reach spectacular heights, and stay on as long as the Services will have them after which they will look around for somewhere else where a uniform is worn. This chap was beyond that; a failure. I am afraid I must have been a most unsympathetic 'friend', having no experience of such people and certainly none of the judicial system, but I tried my best. His case came up a week or so later and the charges read out. There was no question of him denying anything; he was there for the court to assess what they would do about it. The prisoner had put on his best uniform but his effort to stand tall and look smart was spoilt by a dejected appearance, his body language saying all. Three elderly magistrates looked down from the bench, their leader, a motherly lady, smiling kindly as she attempted to get him to tell his story. She turned to me. What could I say? I came out with the usual things about this episode being quite out of character and him going through an unhappy spell for which he would probably benefit from some sympathetic counselling, but this cut no ice. The chief magistrate nodded, then turned to the prisoner and fined him fairly heavily. I asked for the fine to be paid in instalments over a period, since his naval pay would not be sufficient for him to pay it any other way, and won that concession. I found the whole affair distasteful.

Not much happened on the occasions I was duty officer, a task that meant I was the only officer who remained onboard for the night. But one incident I do remember was the Fire. Late one evening somebody had walked past a ventilation exhaust outlet and smelt burning plastic. With difficulty it was discovered where the exhaust air had come from and the cause of the burning located (it turned out to be a faulty component in some piece of electronic equipment) after which the fire was quickly extinguished by means of a squirt from a CO_2 extinguisher. In accordance with the rules, we reported this over the phone to the dockyard fire department, presuming they would be in touch in the morning to write a report. We were not prepared for flashing blue lights and the wail of a siren minutes later, which announced the arrival of an appliance from the Portsmouth Fire Service. They could only get as far as Whale Island itself, since the jetty to which we were attached was fifty yards or so offshore, attached by means of a chain of small floating pontoons tied end-to-end. Anybody who tries dashing along these at speed soon discovers they begin to bob up and down alarmingly. The person coming behind has then to attempt to jump from one to the next as they start snatching at their chains, and by the time the third or fourth person negotiates them the movement has become so violent they are in real danger of being catapulted into the sea. By this time the top of the pontoons will be awash and extremely slippery. I watched with interest while several firemen attempted to hurry along this bucking snake in the dark without coming to grief. I gave them top marks for staying aboard, but they all fell over several times and were not best pleased to be told on arrival that there was no fire. We placated them as best as we could, signed a whole lot of forms, offered them a drink which they had to refuse, then showed them how to tackle the jumping snake safely for their trip back.

A couple of hours later in the dead of night a slow launch crept up to the jetty and three elderly men dressed in huge brass helmets and carrying axes clambered slowly up our gangway. These were the dockyard fire department duty shift who had been over in one of the reserve ships on the far side of the harbour at the time of our incident. I was so thankful we didn't have to depend on them had there been a proper fire.

One evening while duty officer I was on the quarterdeck chatting to the duty

PO when a couple of our younger sailors came back on board, one of them bleeding from a cut lip and with the beginnings of a black eye.

"What happened to you?" asked the PO, in one of those voices that made it clear this was a question that required a mandatory answer. The lad replied he'd been in the Tipner Arms with his mate quietly enjoying a drink when a group of loutish youths came in, one of whom pushed his face close up to our sailor, snarled "I don't like you," and punched him in the face. The PO nodded at the bo's'un's mate listening nearby, who swiftly turned about and went below. I was then asked if I'd have a look at something over on the other side of the ship, and he led me away.

"What are you up to, petty officer?" I enquired.

"Better you don't know, Sir," was his response. Moments later I became aware of half a dozen shadowy figures slipping down the gangway.

"Ah!" I said.

"Quite so, Sir," answered the petty officer. "We don't encourage those sort to have a go at our young sailors. They'll be back in ten minutes, Sir. I'll keep you informed. Unofficial of course, Sir." He gave me a knowing look.

Later he caught up with me in the wardroom. "All back safe and sound, Sir. We won't be having no more trouble from them! We have an understanding like with the publican. We keep his pub free of that sort, and he looks after us. Works well, Sir" He gave me another knowing look that I interpreted as an order to keep mum. So I thanked him, said nothing, and forgot all about anything I might or might not have seen.

One of the perks of being in charge of a large ship such as the Belfast is that at weekends one can, up to a point, treat it as a private yacht. During the summer I was duty one Sunday and invited Patricia and the children, also her parents, to come on board for lunch. I had access to a 45 foot picket boat with a crew, a vessel used to visit various mothballed ships around the harbour. This boat fetched the family from Gosport so they could arrive in style. Lunch was served in the Commodore's private dining room, and afterwards we enjoyed an hour or so on the quarterdeck, a personal playground for the children. We rounded off the afternoon by taking a trip around the harbour, called in at several big mothballed ships where the children clambered aboard and played around pretending to be in charge.

On the trot next to Belfast were four 'liberty' ships, armed merchant vessels that had been provided by America (with millstone-like strings) to get us out of trouble during the war. From time to time one of these would proceed to sea for a day to check it was still seaworthy and in satisfactory condition. Choosing a nice fine day, our captain and a skeleton crew of which I was one moved across to the chosen liberty ship and set off. It felt really strange leaving Portsmouth harbour aboard a fairly large slab-sided merchantman, while we exchanged courtesies with the various shore establishments on the way. The engineer found he could clearly hear the comforting thump of her single reciprocating engine while he was up in the wardroom having his coffee, so spent much of the day there. I had discovered how to get the lights on, and established a satisfactory tannoy communication, but would have been stuck had anything given trouble. Shortly after that outing the MoD decided it would no longer carry out these checks, and started to dismember much of the Reserve Fleet.

These liberty ships had large numbers of hatches all over the upper deck, their covers secured with big brass T-handles for screwing them down against a watertight gasket. These handles as originally supplied could be removed completely, and some docky had once tried to acquire several hundredweight of the valuable brass to sell on to a bent scrap merchant. With a friend, he'd rowed across the harbour at night, boarded the furthest ship and removed about fifty of the hefty handles, which they lowered down to their dinghy in sacks. They then began to row back to the other side. They were spotted by one of the police launches that came up to investigate. The men had expected this might possibly happen, their plan being to lower the sacks over the stern and tow them along until the danger had passed, pretending to be out for a spot of night fishing. Unfortunately they hadn't rehearsed this part of the plan, and when they tried putting the sacks over the side they found the boat almost impossible to row, her stern very low in the water, the sacks dragging like a sea anchor. The launch put a light on them and watched with amusement while they floundered across, not moving in for the kill until the water was starting to get shallow. By this time both men were almost too exhausted to talk.

Something similar in the way of concealing booty under water had occurred one day while I was sailing around at St. Mawes. A boat had come in overnight and anchored off Polvarth Point, cheerfully displaying the yellow quarantine flag thereby inviting the Falmouth customs boat to clear her. So far, so good. But the customs boat spent a good half hour alongside and was still cruising around nearby when I came back from my sail. The next thing I noticed was the customs had boarded the vessel once more and were getting the crew to hoist their anchor. What emerged out of the water were crate after crate of sealed boxes, all threaded with loops of rope onto the anchor chain. I never discovered what was in those boxes, but clearly the customs had been tipped off, and knew that somewhere on board would be a worthwhile catch. This type of smuggler later adopted the far less obvious method of landing their haul by dropping it first on the end of a buoyed rope in deep water outside the harbour, later to be retrieved by another, local, vessel which would not be suspected of any involvement. Nowadays traffickers don't seem to have the patience for that sort of thing, preferring to use innocent couriers on aircraft or the cross channel ferries.

My morning commuter runs on the dockyard ferry became birdwatching lesson time. I was really rather ignorant about all but the most common garden birds, but the Captain's Secretary also shared that boat trip, and he was an avid birder. We would stand with our backs against the warm funnel searching the flocks of noisy gulls for unusual ones. I learnt that the raucous black-headed gull doesn't sport his black (actually chocolate-brown) head in winter, winter being defined as from when it moults in late summer until about January/February time. He pointed out the quieter common gull, which is not at all common and often mistaken for one of the other species. In summer, we had the terns to enjoy with their swooping dives and graceful relaxed wing beats, or there would be the occasional wader to be seen.

A team of people from the Imperial War Museum arrived to look around Belfast with the idea of acquiring her for their collection. She was well overdue for the scrap yard, and some of the armament had already been removed, one of the 4.5-inch turrets only just before the visit. She was the last of her type, and it would be a pity if she were to be lost forever. A few weeks later, the 4.5-inch turret was brought back and re-installed. The sale was to go ahead. Belfast would be refurbished in the yard, and then towed up to the Thames for a new permanent home and a new role. We would all have to live elsewhere.

Throughout this time I had been badgering my Appointer. Here I was marking time. Where was this next worthwhile appointment? I didn't want to rock the boat in case I was sent off to sea for a couple of years unaccompanied in the Far East (something Patricia's father had endured when she was about the age of our two children) and that was the last thing we wanted. But nor did I want to rot here, although it was lovely to be able to get home every day, knocking off work at teatime and able to plan holidays and suchlike. Which came first, career or family? I consulted Commander Wykeham-Martin who had been our Commander 'L' (electrical) when I was in the Devonshire, and since then had been the Electrical Appointments Officer at the Admiralty some years back. Here he was now, with a desk job in the Belfast, seeing out his last few months before retirement. His advice was to keep up a running ticktack with the current Appointments chap who had all this juggling to do. He said it was all too easy to overlook people who had drifted 'up the creek' as he put it, when a plum job came up. "Drop in every time you're in London," he advised. Patricia and I talked about the options—and the risks. I arranged to just happen to be passing the Old Admiralty Building one day and duly 'dropped in'. What I needed to know was where I stood in the promotion stakes. Was I destined for high places (extremely unlikely) or had I reached the end? After all, the pyramid had a very broad base, coming in quickly to a narrow pinnacle. There was only room for one at the top and maybe two at the next level down. A lot of us would never make it that far, and there were an awful lot of uncongenial jobs around that would part a man from his family for long spells on the way. It came back to the question of career versus family.

We chatted about the problems for some time. The Appointer answered my unasked question in a roundabout sort of way, pointing out how the diminishing size of the Navy was making it difficult to find really satisfactory jobs for the bright people. Out came the sherry bottle. I saw this as his apology for not having any good news for me. So I broached the subject of early retirement. After all, if one was to move into civvy street it would be sensible to get one's feet under the table before the critical age of forty. I was just thirty-eight. He said he might be able to find me a personnel job, which would round me off nicely if I wanted to leave early and start a second career. He'd had lots of officers sitting in the visitor's chair wanting that, but most of them had come far too late. We parted with me feeling really quite hopeful. I had never thought about a job outside the somewhat narrow confines of my discipline within the Royal Navy. Maybe there was another life out there.

For some weeks Patricia and I talked it over. There were fewer and fewer what I called 'promotion' jobs going, all of them at sea in one of the newer ships, and there were a lot of men in my branch who were probably better suited for them than me. I had wasted some of those critical years out in Australia where no doubt I really had been forgotten. I didn't regret it for a moment, for I had seen what happened to the ones who put their careers before everything else, and none of them seemed to be content with life, though they would never admit it, even to themselves.

Soon after this I had a phone call from my Appointer. A vacancy had come up for one of the jobs in the Royal Navy concerned with resettlement. There was a resettlement officer in the Portsmouth Command and another in Plymouth. It was intended to open a third one covering the Scotland and Northern Ireland area, based at Rosyth. Would that be of interest? If so, he could put my name forward. It would be ideal if I was contemplating early retirement, since I would be in the best possible job for finding employment outside. Would I think about it and let him know soon?

Plymouth would have been ideal, of course, for surely I would want employment down there eventually? Portsmouth, even, as then we would be able to continue living in Alverstoke. But Rosyth? We hum'd and ha'd for days, discussing nothing else on our walks together. I saw a cartoon by that inveterate old car enthusiast Russell Brockbank, showing a motorist getting out of his squashed car having attempted to squeeze between two trams. The caption read "Oh well. Nothing venture, nothing win…" Should I just sit on my hands? Would anything else turn up? I was attempting to make a decision without all the facts needed to assess the risks. Eventually we decided I should go for it and accept the offer, at the same time putting in a formal request for early retirement at the end a year. A month later the appointment came through.

We had decided I would leave the family where they were, and live in the wardroom mess whilst in Scotland. Scottish schools were quite different to English ones then, and for little ones just starting out we reckoned it was essential not to subject them so soon to a completely different system. Scottish schools still used the tause at that time…! Maybe I could get home every few weeks, using one of my free travel warrants (we were allowed three a year), and perhaps I would be able to have 'official' visits to the south occasionally and thereby qualify for free travel. I could take the car sometimes, and maybe Patricia could come up there for weekends occasionally. It wouldn't be like being unaccompanied overseas.

My enquiries revealed that the naval base in Rosyth, HMS Cochrane, was having a new wardroom built, along with a lot of new married quarters and other accommodation. Rosyth was becoming a major submarine refitting base, and the new nuclear subs were our latest capital ships. Whilst all this was going on, an old cruiser, HMS Glasgow, was being used as an accommodation ship. I would have to live in that.

I finished my time in Bellerophon, then spent a couple of weeks on a course in London learning all about my new job. This would be a proper desk job, and I would need to be one step ahead of my interviewees as I started to gain experience and usefulness in the business of 'resettling' men, which meant giving them all the help possible to obtain suitable employment after they left the Service at the end of their time. I also enjoyed some leave, during which time Alec Rose returned to Portsmouth after his solo sail around the world in his boat 'Lively Lady', a much quieter reception than that given to Francis Chichester the previous year.

Eventually my time arrived. I packed up our little Traveller with everything I thought I might need for a life in Scotland, said goodbye to the family and set off North, with an overnight stop at Jane's near Macclesfield.

~*~

Two days later I arrived at Rosyth and negotiated the dockyard main gate (not easy when you're not known, nor expected. It was a Sunday with no one around for the Dockyard Security people to ask). The accommodation ship, HMS Glasgow, lay alongside. She was utterly different from Belfast. Sleeker and lower in the water than the elderly Belfast, she gave the appearance of being more of a serviceable cruiser, able to proceed to sea and knock hell out of the enemy. However, once I'd moved aboard, woken up a tired duty officer who found me a tiny cabin, and moved my gear into it, and found somewhere to leave the car, then clamber back on board, I was already wondering how long I would be able to put up with the conditions. We were enduring a July heat wave at the time, the cabin like a furnace with smelly hot air jetting out from the punka louvres. There must have been a good foot less headroom on all decks which perhaps accounted for the sleeker first appearance, but it made for a hot ship. The wardroom smelt like an old pub, and that weekend they'd had the pest control people in to spray everything to deal with a cockroach infestation.

Next day I found my way to my new office, a room set aside in the Education Department in an annex of the newly built admin building of HMS Cochrane. It had a good library, a couple of offices and a classroom for more formal teaching. The classroom was formed by partitioning off the congregation part of the Roman Catholic church which was also in the building, an area not used during the week. The RC padre had his room beyond the holy part of his church, but wasn't often there. I was given one of the education offices and quickly struck up a good rapport with Harry Wood, the resident schoolie there, who until I arrived had to cope with sailors asking about the sort of facilities I was to provide.

I was unusual in that I was only lodging in Cochrane, but was responsible direct to the local admiral, Vice Admiral Sir Ian McGeoch, whose main administrative centre was a couple of miles away at Pitreavie Castle. His title of Flag Officer, Scotland and Northern Ireland, or FOSNI for short (The RN loves all these acronyms), reflected his operational responsibility for Naval installations and ships operating all the way up the northeast coast of the country, over the top and down the west side as far as about Liverpool. My clients might be based anywhere around these coasts, so it was quite a big parish for me. There had never been any resettlement facilities in FOSNI's Command before, so I would be setting up something quite new for the people there; something needed, since the navy was 'downsizing', to use a horrible word which civilian organisations have become used to nowadays.

My first priority was to escape from HMS Glasgow and its cockroaches. At lunchtime on my second day I talked to a lieutenant branch officer, Bob Pearce, to discover he was a one-time TAS man, but now operated from a small self-contained unit, HMS Safeguard, at the far end of the Naval area, half a mile or so towards the Forth bridge on the edge of marshland. There were about a dozen officers there, only two of whom regularly lived in, and he suggested I join them. I went round to inspect and loved what I saw. Not only was there a spotless cabin block, but also the rooms were large and airy and had windows that looked out over the marsh. I would be able to wake up in the mornings to the sound of the curlew! I moved in next day, much to the annoyance of Glasgow's bemused executive officer who thought I had no right to cock at snoot at his facilities and wondered what he'd done to upset me.

The job itself was quite amenable. I invited anyone who was within a few months of leaving the Service to come along for a talk about getting settled outside, giving them assistance with finding somewhere to live, fix them up with a job, and arranging introductions where possible. I set up a regular interview panel comprising the local SAAFA man, a man from the Edinburgh labour exchange and myself. Between us we reckoned we would know about most of the openings in the Edinburgh area, and should be able to provide contacts elsewhere. I printed lots of useful handouts and advice leaflets, then waited for them to knock on my door.

My first customer was a leading seaman, a 'twelve year' man who had joined the navy at age 18, signing on for a twelve-year stint. He was a Scotsman but with no local connections, married with a young family, and hadn't the first idea how to go about obtaining his first civvy job. The ideal candidate. He said he would lodge with his wife's family while job hunting, but we managed better than that. I contacted the SAAFA man who knew of a school in his area where they were looking for a responsible caretaker. There was the option of a house too. My client thought this sounded just right for him. He had been used to turning his hand to just about anything, liked the idea of having total responsibility for the upkeep of a group of buildings (all sailors are adept with a paint brush after years of applying ship's side grey to their floating home) and was eager to give it a go. I suggested he practise going for an interview and arranged for the SAAFA man to pop in to conduct the interview with me. This turned out to be a wise course of action, for I quickly discovered that my clients had a lot to offer but with no idea how to sell themselves, and were embarrassed to talk about being good at anything. I'm pleased to say my man got the job, and over the course of the next year a couple of others landed school caretaker jobs as well.

On interview board days the three of us would repair to some hostelry for lunch together, and became good friends. I learnt a lot about all the employment opportunities in our area, and visited a number of new companies setting up in some of the new industrial areas. Glenrothes, a 'new town' a few miles to the east, was becoming established as the silicon valley of these parts, and there were lots of vacancies for electronics people, though local women in the town did most of the assembly work. I visited a couple of companies there and discovered they needed supervisors, dedicated people with a good sense of responsibility. It had not occurred to them that an ex-petty officer from the Navy would be a likely candidate. I fixed up one man whose home was in Kirkcaldy, only about five miles away. We were starting well!

Various employers would write to the Admiral asking for people, such letters being sent straight on to me to deal with. One day Harry Wood came in waving an envelope with a Portcullis logo on the front and a severe-looking 'OFFICE OF BLACK ROD' printed on the back of the flap. What had I been up to? was his comment. I tore it open, to discover a request from Black Rod's office for any senior men who fancied employment in the Palace of Westminster to contact the office. Black Rod at that time was a retired admiral, and he recruited a number of people from the Royal Navy. Just down the road from there was the new Shell building, lorded over by a retired Naval engineering captain whose workforce also had a number of ex-Naval people. He had suggested it was a rather like a carrier, employing lift drivers, porters, cleaners, maintenance men used to air conditioning and electrical plant, carpenters, and someone to hoist the flag each morning. None of my people wanted to know anything about working in London, so those ones fell on stony ground.

A big chunk of the Home Fleet had arrived for a break at the end of some exercise, and the wardroom mess in Glasgow where I still went for lunch was full of senior officers. FOSNI came in for a drink, accompanied by the labour government's new Under Secretary of State for the Navy, a fresh-faced young lad with over-long hair by the name of David Owen. He looked a proper layabout compared with the august appearance of the entourage that surrounded him. He also looked a bit lost, and as no one seemed to think it necessary to rush up and chat to him, I thought I should do so. I had an entrée, since I was aware he'd been at Bradfield about ten years after me, so I opened with that. He told me he'd hated being at school there, and couldn't leave quick enough. He'd become a GP in the rather downtrodden Sutton area of Plymouth where his socialist feelings really developed, and he went into politics as he felt so strongly about the fate of his patients and others like them. I found him easy to talk to, but before long he was winkled away by various senior people who wanted to bend his ear about important matters.

At the end of my first two weeks I was pining for home, and drove down on the Friday afternoon and evening. There were far fewer motorways and other fast roads in the sixties, my little traveller's top speed was only about 65 at best, so it was a long and tedious journey, going via Edinburgh, Hawick, to Scotch Corner, then down the A1 and M1, then round the side of London to Windsor, finally down the Meon Valley to Fareham. It was midnight by the time I got home, and it took most of the next day to recover. Four hundred miles; a bit far for weekend commuting.

I soon established a better routine. I would aim to do a couple of weeks' work in nine days, then have a long weekend off, sometimes getting the Thursday night sleeper, catching the Monday night sleeper back which made for a good spell at home. I would sometimes arrange to attend IEE meetings at Savoy Place, which qualified me for an official first class warrant as far as London, sometimes there was an official visit in the Portsmouth area I could make, and if nothing else came up then I used one of my three leave warrants (which entitled me to second class travel with no sleeper). When all else failed, I drove up and down in the Traveller. On train days an official car took me to the little station at Inverkeithing where the London-bound sleeper stopped, and I soon came to know the regular sleeping car attendant. On the occasions when I was travelling on a precious leave warrant, if he spotted me he would beckon me over, but I had to tell him I was having to pay my own way this time, so would be roughing it across a seat in the second class end of the train. After one or two of these less comfortable journeys he would greet me with a "Are we travelling in style tonight, Sir, or the other way?"

Bob Pearce, my chum in HMS Safeguard, was a youth leader and took lads up into the mountains at weekends. I asked to join him on one of these jaunts, but he looked at me, muttered something about my being a bit old for that sort of rough living, and offered instead to accompany me up Schiehallion. This is a fine mountain seen at its best from the Queen's View on the other side of Loch Tummel, one that fascinated me since I was familiar with a complicated Scottish Country Dance called Schiehallion. It's over 3,500 feet high, but the car park where we started is a thousand feet up, so it was an easy climb. It took a tiring tramp through tall heather for a couple of miles before we were above the tree line. The top five hundred feet or so is all moss-covered boulders that made the going difficult, but my companion gave me lots of help coping with the terrain. Other outings I undertook on my own were mostly in the Ochil Hills, the nearest wild area to Dunfermline, our local town.

Someone suggested I grow a beard again. This involved looking dreadful for a week or two and normally meant one stayed on board until the unshaven look had begun to look like a proper beard. Living at Safeguard made this easier, so I started growing one straightaway and I have it to this day.

I realised I was going to have a lot of time on my hands when I would be stuck in the Safeguard mess of an evening and at weekends, so I enrolled for an art class in Dunfermline. I chose the Life class since I wanted to improve my figure drawing, and bought some oil paints and an easel. Over the year I did lots of pictures, but mostly of the Scottish scenery since my Life work was not very good, though I learnt a lot about observation and colour mixing. A cartoon in the art school showed an instructor talking to one of his Life pupils who is trying to draw a line without his hand shaking too much. The model in front of him is young, attractive and very naked, and the caption reads "You're new to this class, aren't you?" The models we obtained would not have caused the most nervous of pupils to have a shaky hand.

I also discovered there was a Scottish Country Dance class every week in Dunfermline, so I joined that too. We had a teacher and live music in the form of an accordionist who also managed a drum which he operated with his left foot. There were about thirty dancers, nearly all middle-aged women, and it was deadly dull. The dancing was all right but socially I could not get any of the others to talk. Maybe I had been pigeonholed as a predatory male and, of course, I was not properly Scottish. It was called a 'class' rather than being a club, and most Scottish girls would have been taught the basics at school; maybe they'd never discovered it could be fun. What a pity.

I received an invitation to attend a reception at the Scottish TV offices, partly as a result of some investigating I had been doing about a job in television when I eventually left the Navy. I met several useful contacts, and was invited to go round the studios later. About the same time I was asked by one of the Pitreavie staff whether I would show a BBC radio man and his family around one or two ships in the dockyard. This was John Bridges, a producer in the talks department, and a pleasure to show around. It also gave me an opportunity to make enquiries about television work with the Beeb, where I received the impression I was far too old already! Anyway, he left with an invitation for me to stop over on one of my trips through London and have dinner. This I duly did, meeting up at his studio in Bond Street before going on to Knightsbridge where he lived. His wife kept calling me 'Jim' after a singer she'd come to know, and their two young boys kept harking back to various well-known people who'd also come for dinner. The previous evening they'd entertained Mary Stocks. It must have been a good education for them meeting many erudite people on their home ground. John kindly gave me an introduction to the BBC Engineering Recruitment officer who invited me to an interview. There I discovered they really only wanted fresh young graduates, so the visit was a waste of time, except that it enabled me to get a travel warrant as far as London. I also had irons in the fire for both Southern TV in Southampton and Westward TV in Plymouth. Finally I was advised to avoid setting my sights on a creative job with its yo-yo ups and downs, something not recommended for a staid married man with a family and mortgage.

The autumn was drawing in, and I quickly noticed the difference the higher latitude of these parts made. It was still pitch dark without a trace of light when walking in from Safeguard in the mornings, and it wasn't properly light even by the time of my mid morning tea break. By early afternoon it was already getting dimpsy. What a contrast to the summer when it never got fully dark even at one in the morning. I found another activity that kept me busy during the evenings. At the nearby Apprentices' School, HMS Caledonia, they were rehearsing for a play to be put on in their main hall before Christmas, and needed a stage manager. I joined them, to find the main requirement was to build and paint the scenery, which I happily did, aided by a couple of chippies from Caledonia's staff. This was hugely pleasurable as all such enterprises enjoy a camaraderie one seldom finds elsewhere. What with the Bradfield productions, the special Trafalgar Night dinner at Collingwood and the village play at Portscatho all those years ago, I was returning to a creative side of me that had been on the back burner for far too long.

There was a request for me to visit a 'boomer' (boom defence vessel), HMS

Laymoor, which was working buoys at the extreme southwestern tip of Scotland, in Luce Bay. They had three men who all wanted retirement advice. I was to flash them up from the lighthouse area at the southern tip of the Mull of Galloway and they would send in a boat. This sounded like an adventure, so I went for it with enthusiasm. A retired Church of Scotland padre, Jock Grant, whom Patricia's parents had known, now had the living at the little kirk at Kirkinner near Wigtown on the eastern side of the bay, and they offered to put me up for the night. It was a vast stone manse with no apparent heating, but they looked after me very well. I was surprised to see lush grass in all the fields (it was mid November) but Jock said the weather never dropped below about 50ºF, which was a surprise to me. It was ever so much milder than Gosport. Next day I drove down to the Drummore peninsula as instructed, pointed the car at the ship which I could see a mile or so away and flashed my headlights. No response. I called in at the nearby coastguard cottage to find they were in radio contact, so that solved the communications problem. A few minutes later a Zodiac boat came scudding across the wave tops towards me, sending great sheets of spray into the air. I climbed aboard.

"Hold on tight," cried the petty officer as he pushed off. He then opened up the throttle and we careered back, me feeling about as safe as if I'd been rodeo riding. The ship was working cables, a lot of clanging noise as, link by link, heavy rusty chains hauled along from over a roller on the bow and down the ship's waist to the stern. The Zodiac came alongside where, with a good swell running, I was at deck height one moment and fifteen feet below it the next. I jumped when told to, hanging onto the outside of the guardrail until someone grabbed me and hauled me aboard. It was a good day with all three men keen to listen to all I could tell them, and grateful for the handouts and pamphlets I'd collected, plus another three men who thought they'd take the opportunity while it was there. It was certainly fascinating for me to spend time in a working vessel of this type; something I never knew existed within the RN.

The day for moving into the new Cochrane wardroom mess approached. I'd already had a peek at the new building, now being furnished, and it looked wonderful. Usually when the MoD puts up a new building it does so just as the main establishment for which it was built is about to become obsolete, but not in this case. Like all civil works projects the days leading up to our moving in were a scene of frenzied activity with forty or so men doing the finishing touches, painting road markings, making final adjustments to doors, removing floor protection and a hundred and one other things. On the Monday I moved out of Safeguard somewhat reluctantly and installed myself in my new quarters. I would miss the peace and quiet of Safeguard, especially the birds on the nearby marsh. I was almost the first to walk through the door of the mess, the whole place smelling of new carpet. For the rest of my time in Scotland I lived in extreme comfort, with my own bedroom opening off a sitting room-cum-study, and a bathroom next door.

I had a request from RNAS Lossiemouth; they had several people who would like to have an interview. Would it be possible for me to visit? I set off in the little Traveller, comforted by the thought that this was a 'duty' trip so again I would be able to claim the costs. The MoD was pretty stingy when it came to reimbursements. They would prefer to lay on a chauffeur-driven car, even a helicopter on one occasion (when I was in 845 squadron), or provide a first class railway warrant, rather than fork out for one's petrol. And that was as far as they'd go. The petrol costs were only a small part of running one's car of course, but the MoD was adamant. It was so stupid as using my own car was the only sensible way to get about in the wilds of Scotland, and far the most economical with one's time. I set off one day to motor up through Perth and Braemar to Lossie on the north Morayshire coast. My host had suggested I might like to spend the night at his home, a most welcome change for me. Next day came the interviews, all youngsters none of whom were Scottish so the advice I was able to give was mainly concerned with the business of getting an interview followed by getting a job—two separate stages. I think all the interviewees found it of great value, and I was now beginning to perfect my spiel on these aspects of resettlement.

The Fleet Air Arm also retained a small airfield near Arbroath, and I had arranged to visit someone there on the way back. It provided an opportunity to drive through Aberdeen and Stonehaven, exploring an area I might not otherwise have bothered with. I had been asked by the Captain's secretary at Cochrane, Ben Purser, if I would bring back some Arbroath Smokies with me, so I dropped them off at his house in Dunfermline. This was the start of many visits I made to their home, where I became their preferred baby-sitter and was frequently invited to stay overnight or for meals at weekends.

Christmas approached, and with it the thought of leave. We enjoyed a couple of weeks as a family at last, decorations in the house, a normal family life for a time. We went carol singing with the St. Mary's church choir, about twenty of us each carrying a lighted candle and singing lustily all round the village with a stop for hot toddies and a special indoor performance at the old folks' home. And then it was the excitement of Christmas Eve with the children trying to discover whether Santa Claus had visited yet, then the Christmas morning church service while the turkey cooked, a traditional Christmas lunch joined by Patricia's parents, followed by a walk along the coast path to recover. On New Year's Eve I struggled back to Scotland with a stopover at Jane's, a dusting of snow on the roads that froze overnight, finally arriving at Cochrane absolutely exhausted.

The Army decided to put on a presentation to demonstrate to outside prospective employers what fine people ex-Army personnel are. They did it in style, hiring the splendid Glasgow Civic Chambers, all gilded friezes, marble staircases and a lofty painted banqueting hall. Some eighty industrialists listened to a bevy of senior Army men that included four generals, a brigadier or two and some colonels. They did a good job of 'selling' their wares, and the show was preceded by a tri-service presentation, which was where I came in. We had a superb lunch where I sat opposite a somewhat overweight chap in a business suit who proceeded to cut up his steak into small squares then opened the flap of his jacket pocket and scooped the bits of steak into it. The three of us sitting opposite stared disbelievingly, but he smiled when he saw us and explained, "Too many business lunches, pocket lined with plastic, two Alsations at home. Only way I can survive." With a curt nod he continued his conversation with the person next to him.

I had been practising writing a Curriculum Vita for myself, as much as anything to improve the style and presentation of these important missives so that I could then prepare some samples for the benefit of my clients. They had to be typed on an old fashioned typewriter, so the appearance could never be better than mediocre, alas. I had impressed upon my clients that the object of a CV was to obtain an interview; no more. If it looked good, was more intriguing than any others a potential employer might receive, gave a hint of something interesting underneath, then they might want to see more, they just might want to actually meet the writer. If that happened, the CV had done its stuff. The next stage, the Interview, was when the main selling took place, and before the interview one would in all probability be asked to fill in a job application. If the interview resulted in the offer of a job, then at that point and not until then should one discuss all the problems and worries that might be in one's mind. These are usually the negative aspects of a new job, and one never muddies the waters by discussing them until after one has the job in the bag. The interviewer will usually ask at the end of his initial interview whether there are any other things one might wish to discuss; never use this invitation to raise any of one's negative worries. They can wait.

And so I built up a job-hunting pack for issuing to my boys. But first I had to verify I was saying all the correct things, giving the right advice. I had gleaned a lot of the ideas from discussions with my opposite numbers at Devonport and at Portsmouth and knew I was on the right lines.

I sent a copy of my own finished CV to my father, since I was sure he was fairly ignorant of what my Naval career had entailed, and here it was, all on one side of a sheet of foolscap. He was obviously impressed for he asked for another copy, as he'd sent the first one off to a friend. Alarm bells rang. Who was this friend? It transpired he'd kept in touch with Michael Clark, now chairman of the Plessey Group, whom he'd met on his trip out to Australia ten years previously. The result of all this was that I received a call from the group personnel man who dealt with executive recruitment with a suggestion that I apply to various Plessey outlets direct. Presumably father's covering letter to Michael Clark must have said I wanted to join Plessey! The damage was done and who knows, I might do worse, so I set about a series of visits, the first one to a small research establishment housed in a one-time country house near Templecombe in Dorset. Many of the people were retired Naval electrical folk, since the work they were doing was concerned with Naval weapons. My actual interview went very well, but the personnel man made the mistake of rounding off my visit by walking me through the offices where these people were working, to give me an idea of what my working conditions would be like. Apparently the previous day Michael Clark himself had visited, storming through the building wanting to know what everyone was up to, and was seen as a nasty threat to everyone's secure job. Rumours were going around that a number of people would be out on their ear by the end of the month. I had left Patricia sitting in the car outside, and we stayed there while we had a sandwich lunch and compared notes. The wilds of Dorset would be a wonderful place to settle, but the downside was a job that sounded extremely insecure, there would be no alternative employment should they decide to kick me out, schools were non-existent (we certainly wouldn't be able to afford to send the children to the nearby Sherborne public schools) and there were no shops or other handy town facilities anywhere. Patricia, always the practical one, had compiled a far bigger list of what was wrong to offset my dream of what might be right. I was sort of offered the job but did not accept.

Next I had an invitation to visit a Plessey assembly plant near Titchfield, not so far from where we'd lived when we were first married. Here I met a pleasant personnel man who wheeled me in to my interview with the technical boss who was engaged in a noisy telephone argument with someone in Australia at the time. No sooner had he put the phone down and I'd had a chance to explain I was there for an interview, something he didn't seem to have in his diary, than the phone went again and this time he walked about the room talking to someone in Canada. He only listened with half an ear when he next had a moment when no phones rang, then said he'd have to go off to a meeting. Back with the personnel man I tried to find out if they really wanted someone. His response was that he'd been told to find someone like me, but look! Outside the window trooped a string of workers, mostly women, heading for home at the end of what looked as if it had been a truly boring day. "It's their last day," he observed. Apparently some hiccup had caused production to be stopped, and they had all been laid off for an unknown length of time. I thanked him, collected my expenses, and couldn't escape quickly enough.

In February I answered an advertisement in the Daily Telegraph for a professional electrical engineer's job at Kodak, to work in their Harrow factory. This was the right sort of job though definitely in the wrong area, but the interviewing experience could be useful, and I could do it on the way home one weekend. My application resulted in a phone call where I was invited to attend for interview. What day would be suitable? I plumped for a Friday. One more interview 'just for experience' which, hopefully, wouldn't be as awful as the Plessey ones.

I was first seen by a charming personnel man who covered all the non-technical points then wheeled me in to see the head of the engineering 'Field' department— a department that had men out in 'the field' around the factory looking after the day-to-day needs of each production area. An extremely competent and pleasant man, Tom Castle, who said he wanted to recruit several more engineers during the summer, interviewed me and he'd asked for electrical people because they seemed to be good at diagnostics, but what he really wanted was all-rounders who could look after any engineering discipline in a supervisory way. Specialists in all the individual disciplines were available in the design department to be called on when needed. He walked me round the factory to meet one of his Field Engineers who had an immediate need. On the way he stopped several times for words with a few of his men, some involved in civil works, one doing some plumbing, a couple in a machine shop and several also walking up and down the road. All of them hailed him, calling him Tom, and he called them by their first names. He said, rather unnecessarily, that Kodak was a good firm with a 'family' of employees with often two, sometimes three generations there at once. We entered one of the production buildings, ran up four flights of stairs (Tom Castle was a lightweight man who walked extremely fast on the level and ran up all stairs. I had a job keeping up, and tried to arrive at the top without panting, just in case this was all part of the interview—him checking I was literally fit for the job!). We dashed through a pitch-black lobby and along a dark passageway with me holding on to his shoulder while he called out "mind me!" as he swept along. From openings either side one could hear whirring machinery, but I couldn't see a thing. At the end we came out into the light once more and entered a workshop where the Field Engineer joined us. Tom excused himself and I spent a half hour being quizzed by this next man who, at the end, walked me back to Tom Castle's office where he left me for a moment while he had a word alone with Tom. As he came out he grinned at me and left.

I had lunch with the personnel officer who said his boss, the Company personnel manager, wanted to meet me. It turned out the boss was a retired Naval gunnery officer by name of Vaughan Turner, a man with such exceptionally deepset eyes that they were virtually hidden behind his huge wiry eyebrows. On his cheeks he sported 'bugger's grips' tufts of black hair and he had a nice cultured N.O. voice, unlike all the men I had so far met who spoke with variations of London or Midland dialects, albeit slight. It transpired he had been in the same Battle Class destroyer squadron at the time I was in the Aisne, and so we had something in common to chat about.

I returned to Mr Castle's office where he said, "Well, John, when will you be able to start?"

I was unprepared for this; after all I had only attended the interview to get experience in such things, never thinking for a moment I would impress them. I had been relaxed therefore, which probably helped, but must also have seriously overplayed my hand. I stammered that I had first to obtain my early release from the Navy, which might well take up to three months. He said he couldn't wait that long. Please would I see whether I could accelerate it? We left with me promising to move things along, and to keep in touch.

All the way back to Scotland I tried to analyse where we stood. I had only scratched the surface of available jobs, had met a blank response, sometimes rude, sometimes uncomprehending, always negative, right up until this day. Now I had stumbled upon a friendly, interested company which exuded stability, paternalism, fairness to its employees, a good atmosphere, a job I would be able to get on top of, BUT—and there's always a but—it was actually inside the Greater London boundary. Hadn't Patricia and I been saying all along that our top priority was to settle in an attractive part of the country and not within 25 miles of any big conurbation? We would have to re-assess our priorities.

I chatted to Harry Wood next day, in fact most of next day. He mumbled about a bird in hand and for somebody of my age that was important. I wrote to Noggin who, you will remember, had been at Harrow School about a mile from the Kodak factory; maybe he would have some knowledge of those parts? His response

336

from Reading University where he was now lecturing was "Get a job. Almost any job. This is the first and greatest. It is far easier to get a good job from a poor one than from the dizzy heights of a retired 2½ (unemployed)." He also recommended not pushing for too high a starting salary. Either it will be raised once one has proved oneself, or if not, one leaves. Then on the subject of area he was less helpful. I had suggested Amersham as sounding a good place to live, nicely out in the Chilterns. Noggin now lived in Brightwell just beyond Wallingford so might have knowledge of that part. He gave some very sensible advice about house prices and availability, which I heeded. Patricia and I also explored the possibilities with schools in Bucks, Herts or Middlesex, all of which seemed to be different.

While all this was going on I attended one more interview, which like all the rest except Kodak, was negative. The vibes as I walked through the door were unfriendly and I terminated it as soon as I decently could. This last one was worth the trouble for the experience I gained from the need to go in for interview with a positive frame of mind. One mustn't base too much on the personnel officer or even the main interviewer who may have got out of bed the wrong side that morning. However, it strengthened my resolve to go firm with Kodak. As I was pondering this I received a lovely friendly letter from them, reminding me they were extremely interested in my application and would be prepared to offer me a position within the Field Department, and would therefore agree to hold my application for a month or so. If I were still interested they would arrange for me to have a second interview where I could discuss details of the offer, salary, accommodation, etc. Well! I responded that I hoped to be able to confirm in a day or two.

I had become mess secretary of the Wardroom Mess at Cochrane, so was able to have some say in how the place was run; useful for me, as I was one of the few permanent livers-in. We organised a Mess Dinner to which I suggested we invite as guest speaker a retired Service officer, now Chairman of the Glenrothes New Town. This could be handy for my resettlement job, since quite a lot of light industry was setting up there. I sat next to him at the high table, and he seemed amused that the Church of England padre said grace at the start of dinner while the Church of Scotland padre said it at the end while the Roman Catholic man said nothing. (I should point out that Cochrane, being the base establishment for the entire Rosyth complex, housed the padres covering the whole area). Mindful of being in a Service Mess in Scotland, he opened his speech with a story about how, when the Moderator of the General Assembly of the Church of Scotland turned his toes up he was greeted at the Gates of Heaven by none other than St Peter himself. "Glad to have you aboard, Moderator," he said. "We have a number of your followers here. Would you like a little car to get you about to see them all?" So the Moderator set off along wonderful empty roads in his little car to visit his parishioners. After a couple of miles as he was rounding a bend he was hit by a huge Rolls Royce coming the other way on the wrong side of the road. When the driver got out to apologise the Moderator recognised him as the Pope. "So sorry," said the Pope. "I must be accident-prone today. Why! back there I just knocked the Archbishop of Canterbury off his bicycle."

Not only had I heard a useful after-dinner story but later I also fixed up a leading hand and a petty officer in supervisory jobs in two of the new Glenrothes factories then opening.

I chatted to the Portsmouth resettlement officer about Kodak. As the 'senior' one with by far the largest number of clients I valued his judgement. He said he was pleased to hear Kodak had offered me a job as they had an excellent reputation. I wrote off and arranged a second interview. I suggested Patricia come up to Watford, which seemed to have good railway connections, and I drive down from Scotland, we meet there and set off house hunting in the Amersham-Berkhamsted areas. On a map we had drawn the shape of a hand centred on the Kodak Harrow factory to represent a 30-minute door-to-door travelling time for me, which I reckoned was as far as I would wish to commute. The palm of the hand was the two miles or so around the factory, the fingers extending out to Gerrards Cross, Amersham, Berkhamsted and St. Albans. We would see what we could in the two days available, and try to get a 'feel' for a nice area to live. We must have been very naïve to expect to achieve anything so complex in a couple of days, but ignorance is bliss!

The next weekend Patricia duly met me at Watford and we toured the Chesham and Amersham area, becoming thoroughly bemused before the day was out. Next day we explored some more and visited the education offices in Amersham to find out about transferring from the Hampshire system to a very different one in Buckinghamshire—not at all easy. Our ideas of a place in the country rapidly became more impracticable when we realised this would mean two cars, no school within walking distance, a drive to get to shops, and a whole lot of other difficulties. Would it be more sensible to stick with our half-hour-to-work objective, something that would have to be done every weekday, and accept that a drive to the attractive Chilterns countryside once a week at weekends would have to do? We started compromising, our original list of objectives being modified as we went along. We went our separate ways with no decisions reached, this time Patricia driving while I trained back to Scotland.

During the following week I spent an evening with the Pursers who had a proposition. If they drove me to Edinburgh Waverley station on Friday afternoon for the train to London, could I perhaps take a small package for someone in Lee-on-Solent who would collect it from our house in Alverstoke next morning?

"Of course," I said, intrigued, "What's the package?"

"Ah, well, it's one of the pups actually. We've sold it."

So the package turned out to be a tea chest with holes punched in it, straw in the bottom and a frightened little bull terrier pup inside, which would travel in the guards van. Ben drove me in and I found a compartment next to the guard so I could pop in every hour or so and play with the pup. I had a warrant for this trip that got me as far as London, and splashed out on a taxi to Waterloo (I usually walked, or occasionally took the underground). It was nearly midnight by the time I got off at Havant where Patricia's father met me and it was only as I was leaving the unmanned station that I realised I'd been so engrossed with looking after my charge that I'd forgotten to get an onward ticket for myself from

Waterloo. There were no station staff about, so I left without paying, feeling ridiculously guilty. A couple of miles down the road with our tea chest sticking out of the boot a police car flagged us down. I thought I must have been seen leaving the station without dropping my used ticket in the box like everyone else. Caught! I sat there shaking while a ponderous police officer leaned in the window.

"Excuse me, Sir. Would you tell me what you have in that box, please?"

Next morning the puppy was collected by its new owner, much to the relief of Patricia who didn't like dogs in the house, particularly ones that hadn't been house-trained. On the Monday I paid another visit to Kodak and was formally offered the job, to start on 28th July, four months later. The interview went well. I was offered £2,300 to start with, apparently about the same as a Field Engineer was then getting, so that looked good. I had a comprehensive medical, stayed for lunch and afterwards saw Vaughan Turner again. Then I was whisked over to Rayners Lane, a couple of miles away, by another Field Engineer who said one of the administrators at this Kodak outpost also wanted to meet me. It turned out this next person was also ex-Navy and had joined a couple of years previously. He extolled the good points of working for Kodak, and said it was an excellent company to work for, provided you could put up with this part of North London. He himself lived at Great Missenden which he loved.

Three weeks later we were again house and locality hunting, starting with the Berkhamsted and Tring areas. Not surprisingly one had to offset the cheaper house prices further out against higher commuting costs. We spent a frantic couple of days next looking closer in around the factory, which we found far too claustrophobic and not at all to our liking, then saw Patricia's cousin Bryan in Watford who took us around showing us one or two nice areas near to them. We had no intention of settling in Watford since we thought it still too urban, but we were given details of a number of houses by a Berkhamsted agent, one of which was in Kings Langley, between Berkhamsted and Watford. They said their Watford office had the details of the Kings Langley one, so as Kings Langley looked to be a good compromise, we called in to the Watford office. The agent there said, "Oh, by the way, do have a look at this one on your way," handing us the details of yet another one, this time on the outskirts of Watford itself. "The owners are emigrating and are keen to make a firm sale soon; you might well be able to get a good price for it." So on the way back to Kings Langley we stopped off there. By now it was getting a bit dimpsy, it was also rather cold and we were tired. We knocked on the door of the Watford house and were warmly welcomed and shown into the living room where a bright fire was burning. It had a picture window with an outlook over a large garden with trees beyond. Not a glimpse of another building. The owner wheeled in a trolley of hot scones and tea, while we relaxed and recounted our day of frustrations. It transpired they already had a date fixed for their passage to Australia, counting on completion of an earlier offer for the house. This had just fallen through.

We looked round. It was okay so far as the house went, but this was Watford, for goodness sake. What about our dream of a place in the country? I recalled what Noggin had said in his letter, how four out of five people have that dream, but when practicalities are considered, they never achieve it. We thanked our hosts and set off for again, wondering...

We were soon back; found the nearby primary school and checked with the local planning office for any long-term developments in the area (the house was in a sleepy cul-de-sac; ideal: but it was also an obvious road that could be pushed through a further couple of hundred yards to join up two busy trafficky thoroughfares). We saw more agents including one who told us the Watford house was now sold. We rushed off to the one who'd first told us about it, who said it was still for sale confirming this by phoning the owners there and then. He then told us the owner remembered our visit, and would be willing to come down a little bit more. We went to have another look at it, tape measure and notebook in hand. Back to the agents, where we made a bid. The owners wouldn't come down quite that far. We pointed out that we, too, were desperate to move as I had a starting date for my new job in the area. We needed to get settled. Surely they, too, wanted to settle? Telling us to wait, the agent slipped into the next room and could be seen arguing on the phone. He came back, all smiles. "It's yours!" he said, "They've agreed. They liked you and felt confident you wouldn't let them down." Phew! It was done. We drove back to Alverstoke hugely relieved, but at the same time wondering whether we'd been too hasty and maybe had settled for second best. Only time would tell. We were also strangely elated we'd committed ourselves to buying something that we hadn't the money for. It was going to cost us £9,250 plus all the costs of moving and buying carpets, etc., and would mean I would have to commute part of my Naval pension in order to put down a large enough deposit to keep the mortgage payments within our means.

Patricia set about getting our Alverstoke house ready for sale while I went back to Scotland. Before going, we met the local Gosport solicitor to ask him to do the conveyance for us. We were shown into a panelled room lined with leather-bound books that looked as if they had been bought as a job lot at a house sale. There was a large polished table with a couple of visitors' chairs at one end facing an enormous executive plush chair at the other. In this chair sat a genial man in a smart pinstripe suit, in front of him a gold pen and a pad with 'Instructions' printed in a script typeface at the top of each page. As an ice-breaker I asked him whether house conveyancing was a large part of his activities.

"Neighbour disputes and divorce proceedings are my two main activities," he replied. "Usually there's a couple sitting across the table where you are now, spoiling for an acrimonious divorce, and I'm trying to point out to them that divorce is how I make my living. They don't stop to think who is paying, always assuming the other one will do that. It's sad." He shook his head. "Then people seem unable to get on with their neighbours and find themselves in a situation where they feel they have no alternative but to take their neighbour to court. It never occurs to them that the neighbour is still going to be living next door and may live there for the next twenty years."

I've never forgotten that first meeting with a solicitor, and that pad with the 'Instructions'. That memory has served me well in later years—solicitors always work to instructions, never take the initiative themselves, and so can never be blamed if things don't go the way you thought; at least, that was how I interpreted it. He passed us on to his clerk who occupied a tiny garret room with a wobbly desk, hard chair, and a mountain of dusty briefs each bound with red tape stacked up all over the floor. I've never forgotten him either. He was a huge help in delaying the completion of our Watford purchase—something we needed to do since we were unable to take possession until I was free of the Navy.

Back at Rosyth I was at long last able to talk about my future. It transpired that a submarine commander, whose boat was in dock and was living in the wardroom at this time, had spent his teenage years living on the same Watford estate where we were buying our new home so was able to tell me quite a lot about the area. He also told me that one of my current screen heartthrobs, Susan Hampshire, had lived there too at the time.

We had been planning for Patricia to come up to Scotland while I was still at Rosyth and spend a week touring. Various people had offered to put her up, but she really wanted to see the Highlands and Islands and all those romantic places she'd heard so much about. I booked a week off in mid May which seemed a good time to do such a tour and no sooner had I done so than an opportunity came for me to have a couple of tickets to a royal garden party at Holyrood House. This would happen in the middle of our week's tour, so it would be necessary to re-plan everything. I asked Patricia how she felt and, I'm afraid to say, she opted not to disrupt the tour. So we set off from Alverstoke as planned, stopping on the way at Watford to call on the people from whom we were buying the house and take more measurements for curtains, etc. We were able to reassure them that we had absolutely no intention of pulling out at the last minute, even if we hadn't sold our Alverstoke house by that time, and for that they were most grateful. Then we stopped off for the night with Jane in Macclesfield. Next day it was up as far as the M6 went (not much further than Lancaster) then on through Carlisle and over the border. We called in to see Jock Grant, staying the night, drove on next day through Glasgow and had a picnic lunch on the shores of Loch Lomond. Then on over Rannoch Moor to Glen Coe with its sinister atmosphere where we put up for the night at the Clachaig Inn. This was somewhat unpremeditated since the place where we'd planned to stop was not open. Behind the reception desk a notice stated 'NO CAMPBELLS' which didn't seem a very promising welcome. The atmosphere all around penetrated right through us, making me feel quite uneasy. We were given a very strange meal that evening with black pudding and lumpy potatoes; slept in an ancient well-used bed with a lumpy mattress, and there was lumpy porridge for breakfast next day. What with an earth floor in the bar (it was a barn adjoining the main house with a serving hatch opening into the kitchen from where the beer was dispensed) and no hot water, the place could hardly be described as welcoming. We hurried on next day to Fort William and turned off at Invergarry to Shiel Bridge and on to Glenelg, overlooking the Sound of Sleat. Here we found a really welcoming place for the night in a private house, and explored Gavin Maxwell's last home on the shoreside, the reason for this diversion. We'd both been reading his autobiography which had made it sound quite magical, but the reality was not quite so good. There'd been a fire at the house and with still a lot of rubbish everywhere. There was also, somewhat to our surprise, evidence of otters in the little burn that came out near the house, but we didn't actually sight one.

Back at our B&B we found that Gavin Maxwell wasn't liked in the hamlet of Glenelg, but then that is often the case where an author sets up home in some quiet spot and writes about it. (Years later we found the same attitude in Elgol on Skye where Lilian Beckwith, the pseudonym of the authoress who wrote about crofting in the Highlands, was living.) Also staying at the B&B was a young man who worked for the Ordnance Survey with a job that many would give their eye teeth for. He looked after and kept in good repair all the trigonometric points over a large part of the Highlands, most of them on the tops of mountains of course. His hobby? Climbing mountains.

We passed by Skye this time, carrying on north, crossing on the Strome ferry and on to Shieldaig and up Glen Torridon, with the white slab-sided Liathach mountain rising up into the clouds beside us. I'd made an appointment with a somewhat surprised Naval man at a little boom defence depot at Aultbea on Loch Ewe, to interview one of his men who was due to leave the service. He'd never heard of the resettlement service, but was quite happy to see me as he understood perfectly well without my having to say so that the main purpose of interrupting my holiday to see him was so I could claim travelling expenses. He also gave us the address of a lady in the village who would put us up for the night. After that we visited the famous Inverewe Gardens, marvelling at how Osgood MacKenzie in the 1800s had converted a more or less bare rock in this bleak spot into a lush semi-tropical garden, starting by carrying in soil into which he planted a windbreak of Scots Pines, behind which the rest of the garden slowly grew. At the overnight stop we met a young man who was on his way south, so gave him the address at Glenelg. He in turn gave us a contact in Balchreick, a tiny seaside spot about as far up to the northwest as one can go. "Just ask for Mrs Mackay, everybody knows her," were his instructions.

Next morning we passed along the shores of Gruinard Bay, with its sinister anthrax-contaminated island, before going through Ullapool and up to Inchnadamph. Here we diverted to drive round the Lochinver peninsula for no better reason than it looked so intriguing on the map, all bare rock and little lochans. Patricia saw a Great Northern diver, something I'd especially hoped to find after reading Arthur Ransome's book of that name in my boyhood. Otherwise it was just wonderfully bleak with the huge pinnacles of Quinag and Sail Ghorm rising up into the sky. We went across on a couple more ferries until finally we arrived at Balchreick. Patricia was wearing her Mackay tartan skirt, so expected to find no problem locating Mrs Mackay. We asked the first person we saw. "Aye, I'm Mrs Mackay," came the answer. After a bit of confusion we discovered virtually everyone in the hamlet was called Mackay, and we do not know whether we eventually stayed at the right house! We walked on down to a deserted beach, a perfect spot with golden sands and not a soul in sight. I have a photograph of this idyllic beach, the distant snowcapped peaks of Foinaven and Arkle rising up steeply some twelve miles away.

After that it was, as it were, downhill all the way, the better road cutting across to Inverness taking far less time than the scenic route. Our next stop was to Lossiemouth where the schoolie who'd looked after me on my last visit had offered to put us up for the night. In the morning I showed Patricia the route through Braemar to Pitlochry, took a little detour to the start of Loch Tummel for a look at Schiehallion which was standing magnificently in the sunshine. We finally arrived at the Purser's in Dunfermline for a couple of nights. Next morning I showed Patricia around Edinburgh where we came across the Queen a couple of times, once very close as she was leaving St Giles cathedral after attending the General Assembly of the Church of Scotland. There was far less fuss up here, a single policeman holding back the few pedestrians as the royal car came past. After that Patricia felt less guilty about cutting the Royal Garden Party (when, incidentally, it had rained). For our final night I had organised a dinner party in Cochrane's mess for Patricia to meet all the people who'd featured in my letters home over the past year. By this time Patricia's special friend John Goudie had arrived to become the base Church of Scotland minister, so he said a grace before the meal while the C of E padre had to be content with saying the grace afterwards. Late that night I put Patricia on the sleeper at Inverkeithing.

I found myself selected to sail for the Royal Navy at Seaview on the Isle of Wight, using the club's Redwing boats. To me, a Redwing is a fourteen footer which I'd sailed at St Mary's in the Scillies many years ago when I was a cadet in Devonshire, but these ones were similar to a dragon, low and sleek. It meant I was able to sneak another free trip to see my family! The races themselves were nothing special, but since they were being conducted under the aegis of Portsmouth Command it meant we were taken over to the Island in a swish launch and looked after very well. Back at home once more I was put to work doing all those big jobs prior to selling our house. We'd had it on the agents' books for a couple of months, but no serious takers had emerged. The most we could expect to get for it was about two thirds what the Watford house was costing. We would still be strapped for cash as usual.

The Army in London had arranged a tri-Service resettlement day. We had an all-day conference in an annex to the Ministry of Defence in Whitehall which I found most interesting, with a long lunch break at the Greenjackets' barracks along birdcage walk. This meant us all trooping out, crossing Whitehall then taking a short cut through the Horse Guards parade ground and across St James' Park. As we filed past the two Life Guards standing beside the Arch, I wondered how they succeeded in picking out which of us were Army deserving of a salute, as no one was wearing uniform. I decided it must be the way Army people walk, which is a giveaway. The guards got it right every time, stamping noisily to attention and chopping off a vigorous salute to the right men. As a naval man I was ignored, as were the RAF men.

My last month in Scotland. I had one more visit south; down by train then back in the car, dumping off a carload of household items with Patricia's cousin Bryan in Watford. My relief joined Rosyth a couple of weeks later and I took him round to meet everybody, surprising myself about how much I had grown the job into one that would be indispensable for some time to come. Rumours about the need to 'downsize' the Services were spreading, and the resettlement work would be in much demand.

Then it was goodbye to everyone, and a final drive south with a laden car which I unloaded in a long-suffering cousin Bryan's house, then back to Alverstoke for the final tidy up. Still no firm takers, so we were leaving the house empty. We moved to Watford, settling down very comfortably, though without the Naval connections it took far longer to put down roots in the comparatively stony soil here. I had been in the Royal Navy for almost exactly nineteen years.

St Mawes

The stricken tanker *Melika*. The seas washing over her had extinguished the oil fire but secondary fires in her superstructure were still burning. A chopper is landing the first of the firefighters well clear. The pilot has to take great care to avoid becoming entangled with the superstructure, while the ship may be going up and down in the swell as much as twenty feet making it difficult to choose a moment to let go.

Navigating the Corinth Canal which
seemed barely wider than we were.

David and Barbara's *Voyageur* which we met at
Pireas again over wintering in Malta

One of the minisails we built which were
such fun to sail in warm waters!

The *Fairy Fox* fully crewed
for some fast sailing.

Above: Father in his best suit talking
with The Queen.

Right: Father in his later years. He is
standing beside the trig point on
St. Anthony's, with the Carrick Roads
in the background.

Below: The clans gather to celebrate
father's 90th birthday.
From the left: Patricia, Peter, Father, Fiona
(with husband Hugh behind) and Iain.

My favourite picture of Patricia taken with my new long lens so she wasn't aware of a camera pointing at her...!

...any my favourite picture of my two children. Paul and Susan shortly after we brought them back to England. This photograph was taken by Leslie while I was at sea in Agincourt.

Patricia and me warming up for a splendid dance at St. Columba's in Pont Street, London. On the right are three past Chairmen of the RSCDS London Branch, Wilson Nicol, Owen Meyer and Simon Wales.

Part III

Watford Here I Come!

16

Learning To Be a Civilian Once More

A day or two later Patricia and I drove up to Watford to start our new life. A near neighbour came over to introduce himself, Cyril Sugarman, a manager of one of the Kodak divisions at Harrow. Word had got around our end of the estate that the new arrivals were Kodak people. I went in to the factory and met several people, and to discover how easy or difficult it would be to get there from home when I started work properly in a week's time. Although only seven miles away, I had to drive through the middle of Watford as there was no bypass, and this could take half my 40-minute commuting time. Cyril Sugarman assured me there were plans to build an inner ring road around the town, after which it would be far better.

The first weeks were spent getting to meet many of our other neighbours, finding out where the various specialist shops were and meeting the head teacher at our local primary school; a good school, but a most unprepossessing head teacher—one that had 'favourites' and probably only survived because the school was in a good area with all the pupils coming from homes where they were likely to do well. A good catchment area for schools had been one of our main priorities.

I began work, joining others starting on Monday morning for an induction programme, after which I found my way up to the Film Finishing Department (the FFD) to find Ray Plowman, the field engineer I'd met on my first interview. By the time I got there, everyone was in the canteen having their morning cuppa, and they all wore white coats and looked the same! However, there was one exception. When I had met first Ray on the day of my interview, a Chinese engineer, Ed Waller, had accompanied him. In the canteen, I picked out Ed immediately, and then realised the person next to him was Ray, whose features I'd forgotten over the weeks. I've always been bad at remembering faces as well as names, and still have no sure way of overcoming that deficiency. I've quizzed Americans about how they do it so well, but none of them admit to having any special method. That first day I must have met and spoken with about forty new people and knew very well that the following morning I would be seeing most of them again, and wouldn't remember who was who.

Ray gave me a mentor, which helped. This was someone who'd joined the previous year, so could still remember the problems he'd had himself. He took me round the whole building, a large four-storey block about 250 feet square, in which several separate operations were carried out. Elsewhere on the site acetate film base, or in some cases a home-produced estar film base, was coated with emulsion. This fetched up on huge rolls six feet wide weighing half a ton. It was light-sensitive by this time, so the rolls were each stored in a light-tight box on wheels until they were drawn off for one of the three finishing processes. One of these was to slit the roll down into strips, then chop the strips into squares and pack the squares into yellow boxes. This was done in the sheet film area, producing every size of sheet film used in the industry. My area finished motion picture film. We started with the big rolls as before, but sliced it down into strips either 35mm or 16mm wide, rolling this up afterwards for the next operation which put the perforations (sprocket holes) down both sides. Each roll was fed into a noisy machine that shuttled the film through a mechanism where five perforations at a time were punched, and code numbers photographically printed down the edge. After that the perforated rolls were either packed into cans for the film industry, or sent down to the third finishing area where they underwent a further process of being wound onto spools in five foot lengths or less, then placed into a cassette and packed in the familiar yellow boxes for 35mm still photography use. In our building we 'finished' all the film used throughout the UK and in many countries overseas. That was a lot of little yellow boxes or cans.

The three 'Areas' carried out all production work, with a maintenance engineering group attached to each. In the case of the motion picture area, the engineering group that was to be mine to look after also had a manufacturing workshop in an adjacent building where the precision punches and dies were made. Kodak's philosophy at the time was to employ its own specialist engineering people rather than put such work out to contract, the belief being that home trained engineers would be specially trained for the purpose and had the huge advantage of a company loyalty second to none. My initial impression certainly bore this out. Everyone I spoke to was fiercely loyal to the company that looked after them so well, even the workers' representatives who in another company would have been shop stewards. The company would be put before most other things, even family sometimes. In return they enjoyed superb recreation facilities, an excellent health centre, understanding personnel counsellors, a good canteen service and—being Kodak—a camera club on each main site equipped with excellent darkrooms, a studio and a certain amount of free film. I don't believe the employees appreciated all of this, for most of them had never worked anywhere else.

A fourth Area, in the Film Finishing Department, was a small odds-and-sods group comprising a technical manager with one or two technical specialists, a training officer, the department main offices and such people as janitors. On the top floor lived the department manager and his main cohorts. It was a happy family and I was so glad to have stumbled into it, even if it meant living in Watford!

For the first few days I used the Traveller, but I soon tired of the traffic hold-ups, so started riding the motorbike. I had my fisherman's oilskins from the Plymouth days which I found ideal for the bike, and donned these on wet days. My little bike was a genteel one with thin tyres and a windscreen, a commuter's bike, but I could keep dry behind that windscreen and still see whilst wearing my spectacles. I got a few laughs as I waddled into the office in my fisherman's gear, but that was nothing to the odd looks that we all got down in Watford when we wore our anoraks. Standard dress in the West Country, such apparel hadn't reached the home counties at that time, most people going around on a wet day wearing a raincoat and sporting an umbrella—something never seen in the windy west.

Eventually I came to grief on my way home late one evening, hit by a car being driven by two young Asians which, without warning, swerved right across the road while both of them attempted to steer at the same time just as I was passing. Fortunately they were only travelling at a fast walking pace (which was why I was passing them) so I escaped with a bruised shoulder, a few grazes and a dented front fork. I was extremely annoyed, and phoned the police who, having asked whether anyone was injured, sent a constable out to take details. He asked me to sit in his car while he filled in his forms, and when the lads began to talk both at once, he silenced them with an authoritative bark, ordering them to stand back and be quiet. He was ever so pleasant to me and advised me to have my shoulder checked at the hospital in case I might later have an insurance claim. He then brusquely ordered the two lads to explain just what they were up to. I crept off on my damaged bike, worried that I had witnessed what seemed to have been an exhibition of unnecessary racial prejudice. Sure, Watford had large numbers of coloured people, something I had not experienced elsewhere at that time, but I had found the ones I met at Kodak to be pleasant enough. I tend to acquire a prejudice only from actual experience and, whatever their colour or race, am happy to accept anyone for what they are until proved otherwise. Maybe the police had reason to expect a particular section of the community to behave in a certain way, and treated them accordingly. Later, I, too, began to build up certain prejudices, mostly to do with shifty or dishonest behaviour which some sections of the community exhibit. I learned to be extremely wary of certain people I met for no better reason than I had found a lot of them would be unlikely to have the same values and customs as myself. Is that wrong? The Race Relations Act that came in tried to make voicing such thoughts illegal if the person concerned is of a different race, so one has to keep them to oneself, but I cannot help having them. It turned out that the car that had hit me was being driven by a couple of teenagers neither of whom had a licence and therefore were not insured. The car they were trying to drive belonged to a friend who denied being aware they had taken it out; one wonders how they obtained the keys...

Next day I took the bike in to have new front forks fitted, and went myself to the Kodak doctor at Harrow because my shoulder was stiffening up and giving me considerable trouble. The doctor tut-tutted and said he wouldn't drive on the roads in our area without the protection of a steel box around him. I got the message and sold my motorbike, much to Patricia's relief. I soon found other people on our estate who worked at the Harrow factory, and we set up the occasional car sharing arrangements.

In the first few weeks at Watford Patricia had to go into hospital for a few days. Suddenly I had to cope with the children, so couldn't get in to work. Unlike the Navy who always expected work to come before family, Kodak were very understanding and told me to stay at home until I could get organised. "No point in coming in to spend the day worrying about your wife and family," I was told. What a refreshing attitude! The neighbours rallied round, one side doing a bit of laundry for me, the ones opposite taking both children off my hands for a few hours, and the ones the other side providing something to eat.

The house itself, being built in 1952 at a time of building restrictions and with materials hard to come by, was very noticeably of a far poorer quality than the Alverstoke house. The woodwork was full of knots; skimpy skirting boards only a couple of inches high, doors made of hardboard, the exterior brickwork a poor quality sand-faced brick. Neither was the workmanship at all good in spite of our group of houses having been built by a 'well-known local builder'. I wonder why he had been well known? It had cost half as much again as the house we had just sold, but that was the value of the land, the price for living on the outskirts of London.

The little garage adjoining the house was, like every garage on the estate, of a size that would only take a pre-war Austin Chummy or maybe a Ford Popular provided one got out of the car and shut the door before putting it into the stupidly small garage. Hence no one used their garages for keeping their car in, filling them instead with all their essential junk. Patricia found the traffic dreadful, so took to her bicycle that she left outside whichever shop she was calling at. At our end of town she found a branch of Caters, a local supermarket chain, and a modest Sainsburys at the far end, so grocery shopping was quite easy by bike. A market operated from a group of muddy back streets somewhere in the town centre hinterland, and there she found good fresh meat and vegetables, so was well set up. Having lived on or near the coast for much of our lives we had been used to wonderfully fresh fish so didn't go much on the market wet fish stalls. However, as time passed our palates adjusted and the quality of the fish improved, so in a year or two we started eating fish again.

Patricia's parents visited quite often, her father as usual so active helping everywhere, full of ideas for this and that, looking after our children and showing them all sorts of things, while her mother helped in all the domestic areas. We visited Lee-on-Solent when we could. The trip down was a pleasant run, going round Windsor on the bypass, then to Bagshot and eventually picking up the Meon Valley road. A visit to Lee and the seaside was always popular.

We made enquiries about Scottish Country Dancing, enrolling with the local class at Watford where we found they spent so long walking through extremely simple dances that we got bored, wondering whether we'd bother to remain with them. We found the occasional dance at Potten End near Berkhamsted very enjoyable, but were not free on their regular weekly social dancing evening. We phoned around some other nearby clubs, but they also had their weekly sessions on nights we weren't free, so we didn't pursue it. I had enrolled at an evening class in life drawing, which was perhaps a mistake since it turned out to be on an evening when the best dancing took place. The teacher was a professional local artist whom I found very helpful but he had great difficulty finding models. Just the once he came up trumps, having noticed a girl standing on the Rayners Lane station platform across the line from where he used to wait. After seeing her there for several days, he accosted her one morning and she agreed to sit for us. As for myself, I couldn't help noticing an attractive girl at Kodak who worked for a while in one of the manager's offices in our building. It was the time of 'hot pants' and she certainly had a super pair of legs. I cheekily asked whether she'd be prepared to sit for us and she agreed, having first checked out this wasn't an invitation to anything else. She came along for one or two sessions, but had not the slightest idea how to pose. She stood there, shoulders rounded, a glum look on her lovely face, and the class just couldn't work with her. Needless to say the lads at work teased me unmercifully for what they assumed was an 'association'. Patricia tried a daytime pottery course, but with a shortage of facilities and no decent glazes available, this was nothing like so good as the super class we'd enjoyed in Plymouth. Nevertheless she stuck with it, and I also joined in. My initial flare which came along so well at Plymouth simply wasn't there at the Watford class, and when I look round our house today at our homemade pots the ones I like best all come from our time in Plymouth.

My father announced he would come to stay, provided I would pick him up from the station since he didn't fancy driving all the way from Cornwall by himself. A few days before he arrived, we realised what he meant by 'the station' was Paddington. He was under the impression we lived about the same distance from Paddington as he lived from Truro, and so the ride home would only take about half an hour, wouldn't it? Oh well. I was able to park in the short-stay car park right alongside the arrival platform, so the old boy was most impressed by what he thought was VIP treatment. He'd dressed in his special London clothes going back to the days when he worked in town, though thankfully he left his bowler hat behind. During his stay we took delivery of a new carpet and attempted to lay this around him while he remained sitting firmly in his armchair. Father was not at all impressed with Watford, not surprisingly finding it overcrowded, noisy and polluted after St. Mawes. He went on from us to visit Jane in Macclesfield, which was more to his liking.

I was having difficulty learning the names of the various fitters and mechanics in my two workshops, something that never gave me a problem in my ships (was I getting old?). Being Kodak, the answer was to photograph them all, then annotate the photos which I then kept in my travelling notebook. One of the workshops— the one that looked after the perforating and slitting machines—worked shifts, so I joined a shift a few times to work with them. Day workers such as the technicians and other white-collar workers (also the workshop that manufactured the punches and dies for perforating) worked from eight until five. Shift workers started at seven in the morning, went on until three when the afternoon shift took over finishing at 11.00 p.m. When a part of the production operation was overloaded, they worked a night shift as well, but generally that did not include any of my people. As soon as the day workers had gone home, the building became strangely quiet and the evening shift workers seemed to relax. They had the canteen to themselves when they took time off for an evening meal, and seemed to achieve far more than during the day when there were meetings and all sorts of interruptions.

My group's work was to carry out a precision operation on a flexible plastic product. This caused all sorts of problems, and adjustments to the machinery were a constant requirement. The whole building was air conditioned to a precise temperature and humidity with the air passing through absolute filters in an attempt to keep the product stable and clean, but even so it sometimes failed to pass its testing stage. Testing was carried out by an independent testing department that took samples off every roll, processed them and checked them by projection and with microscopes for any mechanical defects. Before reaching the finishing stage, the product would have been checked for photographic perfection. When a deviation was found, various processes would have to be tweaked a bit until it came right. Rather like cooking, the manufacturing methods were not always accurate, so it was not possible to know in advance whether the process was going to be perfect every time. Thus there was a lot of wastage. In order to keep production departments supplied with product, it was necessary to have 'buffer' stocks between each stage of manufacture so that a continuous process like, say, coating emulsion onto a film base, would top up the buffer while next day the two-shift finishing departments would draw it off to feed their part of production. It took a clear-thinking accountant to point out that part-made product has a value, and if that value is tied up sitting in an expensive buffer store, then the company is missing out on selling it. At the time I arrived the company was just beginning its attempt to become more efficient, something that only happens when rivals start to produce cheaper and better goods. Kodak had had it their own way for too long, but now they started to target waste and unsold product in a big way. They didn't at the time have the means for doing that.

I was slightly surprised to discover that, unlike the Royal Navy, technical initiatives seldom came down from above. Senior management seemed to rely on people closer to the coalface coming up with the ideas while from their lofty offices they vetoed this and that if it didn't fit in with corporate strategy at the time. As we, the coalface ones, never knew what the corporate strategy was, a lot of time could be wasted. I drifted along with the others supposing life was always like this in industry, with the assumption that someone higher up on many times my salary would provide the answers.

I soon realised that my engineering life in the Royal Navy didn't have many similarities to an engineer in industry, except in the administration areas. As Gerard Hoffnung would have put it, this engineer was 'good with pen, not too good with spanner'. I had no need to worry, however, for all the other engineers I worked with were the opposite—good with spanner, but not at all good with pen, so we worked well as a team. My immediate boss, Ray Plowman, was very sensitive about his shortcomings with the written word but didn't like to admit it; he used me to help him out by asking me to do all sorts of administration tasks, getting things down on paper for his department to use. Ray was a great worrier. If he couldn't find anything to worry about, he used to worry about why! After I had been there about a year or so, he went sick, leaving me vaguely in charge, and it was at this time that the company's Workers' Representative Committee, or in-house union, decided to flex its muscles. A number of engineering workers had also become members of the national engineering unions, and their shop stewards decided the time was right to get the EETU and AEW unions recognised within the company. The labour government at that time was all for this, even though it might do tremendous damage to industry as a whole. But then governments never look to the future. The men arranged among themselves to hold a meeting in a large engineering area to get support to 'cease cooperating' with the company so as to bring pressure on them to achieve this aim. I never followed the details of how this all developed, but suffice to say my foreman discovered that the meeting was going to be held in our nice new workshop which we'd just commissioned. Each morning the slitting machines needed to be set up by an engineer, without which they wouldn't be able to run and production would not be possible. Fortunately the foreman realised one morning when several key engineers had failed to report for work that the rumoured union action was about to happen, so he himself set up the slitting machines and waited for the sparks to fly. Sure enough, about a hundred engineering workers from all over the factory arrived in our workshop, followed by their pompous union steward who strutted in and started to address them. I was standing at the back and, wondering what the penalty was in civvy street for mutiny, I climbed up onto a table and pointed out to them that they had assembled in a critical production area. If they interfered with production, well, that was their wages in jeopardy, since if production stopped the company would not be able to pay them, indeed they might not be able to retain them on its books. I was soon shouted down, but for a moment a lot of men, especially the ones who had been in the company's sheltered employ since they left school, looked quite worried. The action they eventually took was to give guarded support for their leaders to make representations while in the meantime they would restrict their services but not to the extent of causing actual production loss.

And so the unions crept in to Kodak and the cosy Workers' Representative Committee, which had looked after them so well ever since the early days, was disbanded. The engineering white collar workers had a visit from the leader of ASTMS, a genial little Welshman, Clive Jenkins, wearing a shiny much-worn suit, who stood up and, spying the industrial chaplain who had called in that day and had come along for the fun, said in his Welsh sing-song lilt, "I see we have a proper white collar worker, then!" None of us wanted to join, but with our WRC gone, we had no alternative if we wished to be represented.

About this time there was a change in top management employee relations people, Vaughan Turner retired and the new company personnel manager, Derek Ford, took over all union negotiations. He appreciated that the unions expected 'us and them' confrontations at their meetings, something that by definition meant both sides pulled in different directions. He knew he'd probably never succeed in getting the unions to pull in the company's direction, so his tactics were to pull in theirs, pointing out to them how much he agreed with their point of view and let's discuss how we can work with it. This was something the unions had not experienced before, and were unsure how to proceed. It worked quite well to both the management and unions' advantage, but the comfortable relationship of the company 'family' had been destroyed for ever, and later the company tightened up its beneficence to the workers' disadvantage.

All this was spread over several years, none of it obvious at the time. My life went on as usual, working a set routine, arriving at the same time each morning, entering the factory by the same gate and walking to the same building to sit at the same desk. It was a big change from my colourful life in the Royal Navy. I walked in with people who had been doing the same thing ever since they left school thirty or forty years ago. At least I'd enjoyed a lively first career before settling down like this. One day I commented to Ray Plowman with whom I was walking in how was he able to contemplate the same routine for years without going round the bend? He looked very uncomfortable. The seed was sown in my mind that it would be sensible if I kept my eye open for a change of job within the company after a few years in order to remain sane.

In my first six months I was confirmed in the position and given a fairly generous pay rise. It was at the start of the Wilson government's inflationary spell, so actually the rise was little more than keeping up with inflation. We had found we could live fairly comfortably within my salary, thanks to the lump sum I had received from commuting some of my Naval pension, which had enabled us to have only a modest mortgage. From this point on we were able to save a proportion of my salary that built up to about 30% as time went on. Prompted by Patricia I realised I would never become a top earner in the time left before retirement, and so would need savings to invest in order to ensure a comfortable retirement when it came. I was only too aware of father's straitened circumstances through his inability to build up sufficient funds on which to retire.

In the meantime I was part of a multi-discipline workforce, which was immensely useful for me when it came to getting our Watford house in good condition. Not for me the never ending problems associated with so-called 'tradesmen' who were not only expensive, but never turned up when they'd agreed and when they did eventually come, the job was not done right. All our neighbours had suffered from shoddy uncaring cowboy workers and I didn't want to join their number. Morning tea break was DIY discussion time. I discussed the current problem I had at home with a lack of anywhere to leave our bicycles under cover. Immediately I was bombarded with ideas for building a canopy behind the garage, which little specialist shops stocked the parts I would need, how to put up a brick pillar to support one end, which bits I could legally obtain from the Kodak scrap bins (offcuts of sheet stainless steel were always useful) and a whole host of other ideas, all extremely useful for someone like me with little practical experience of civil engineering projects and little money.

Back at home I built my canopy, and also took delivery of a small greenhouse kit. A greenhouse would be extremely useful for tomatoes and for raising early vegetables, since I was planning to put down a large part of our generously sized garden to growing our own produce. One of my technical foremen pricked up his ears when he discovered my interest in gardening. He was a smallish bent-over man with rough hands and reminded me of Bertie Doe, supervisor at that time of the RHS Wisley vegetable plot who later demonstrated his skills on gardening television programmes.

Susan only had three terms at the primary school before moving on to 'big' school. So began the rounds of visiting all the secondary schools in our catchment area to see whether we liked one another. We still had old-fashioned grammar schools in the town, one boys and one girls, but had reservations about both of them. In the end we plumped for a school on the far side of town called at that time Watford Technical High School, choosing this because we liked the headmaster and those of his staff whom we met, and it seemed the school had high principles, a reasonable academic record, and the other pupils didn't look too awful. It is quite an eye opener to sit quietly outside a school at going home time and see what the other children are like. After all, children do copy one another, and most of the behaviour we saw was not something we would like our own children to copy. We were under a handicap because the headmaster of Susan's primary school had not known her at all well, and did not give her a good recommend. He told us she was 'not grammar school material' and no doubt said as much in his report to the secondary school. What tipped the balance was the man who would be Susan's form teacher, David Iliffe, who also taught music and was the choirmaster and organist at a large church in Northwood. He would certainly be a desirable influence.

We started doing the rounds of the local churches in an attempt to find one where we felt at home. The small C. of E. church on our estate was so very different from our lovely Alverstoke church with its excellent choir and charismatic Welsh vicar. We searched in vain for somewhere similar, but did not succeed in finding one half as good as Alverstoke. We attended the local church, but were never helped to feel part of it. Every Sunday we were greeted at the door by one of the churchwardens who rather vaguely welcomed us as visitors. We felt cold-shouldered by established members of the congregation so eventually looked elsewhere. At last we found an excellent church in Clarendon Road, a Congregational church with a lively minister, but a year or so later this minister moved to Essex, the congregation combined with another one which in due course moved to a new building in Langley Road and became a United Reform church. The church building in Clarendon Road that was sitting on what had become desirable commercial land was sold to part pay for the URC building, and now there is a huge office block standing on the site. Paul wasn't old enough to join the Scouts, but we heard that our local troop had an excellent leader and there was a long waiting list. We put his name down. However, Susan joined the Guides and set about getting an armful of badges, soon becoming the top badgeholder in her troop. Having achieved that over several years she left to take up other interests, but attended a Guide camp first. These were usually held in Hatfield Park, the

Guides taking great pride in the way they organised their camp. She found this tedious and wanted to get out and do things, so didn't remain with the guides for long. Later she joined one of the young persons Christian groups at St. Mary's church. This group went off to Limpsfield near East Grinstead for a few days. On one of these she became ill, the leader giving us a phone call to check we would be in, since Susan's condition would need her to be cared for. It was a very white-faced girl that gingerly got out of the car and came into the house and we were worried. She assured us she'd be all right overnight, but we were not so sure. We wanted to call the doctor immediately, but she wouldn't have that. In the morning she staggered down to the surgery where the doctor thought she probably had a rumbling appendix and had her taken immediately to the small hospital at the end of our road where she had her appendix operation later that day.

As our first winter approached the weather closed in with frozen roads and snow to remind us we were no longer living near the coast. This was the first time since my Bradfield days that I had lived inland. A week before Christmas carol singers came down the road one evening—at least that's what it sounded from within the house, but we opened the front door to see a car driving slowly past pulling a trailer with a lighted Christmas tree on it. From a loudspeaker on the roof of the car came a raucous distorted racket of what was meant to be carol singing. Collectors in Santa Claus hats went from door to door shaking tins. They were from the Round Table and were collecting for good causes, but the contrast with our lovely Alverstoke church choir was so stark, the noise so horrible and the commercial aspect which treated Christmas as magnanimous time where one could more readily be parted from one's money so unpleasant, that it left me feeling sad and disgusted. The meaning of Christmas would seem to have been forgotten.

As part of their ongoing development training Kodak decided to send me and one other to a residential management course in Bournemouth. I drove down in the Traveller to the opulent Bath Hotel where a porter rushed out to carry in my suitcase and someone drove the Traveller off to the hotel garage where it would be washed and filled up with petrol for when I next wanted it. I was shown into a huge bedroom with a private bathroom, something I had not experienced before, and met up with about twenty other aspiring managers all soberly attired in dark suits, as was then the custom. We introduced ourselves round the table, myself and the Kodak man referring to one another by our first names, something just not done at the time. We pointed out that Kodak was an American company and followed the American tradition of calling everyone, even our managing director, by their first name. The others were shocked. In our brief off-moments I walked along the prom breathing in the sea air, wondering whether we'd really done the right thing moving up to the dirty cosmopolitan hinterland. I told myself that we had to eat, and at least all my tools didn't go rusty overnight as they would certainly have done if we'd been living by the sea. The only memorable thing from that week was one day while I was on one of my walks braving an exceptionally chilly east wind (it was only March) I saw a small film unit on the beach below me. They were filming two comely bikini-clad models splashing about in the icy sea. Between takes a wardrobe mistress enveloped their shivering bodies in huge fur coats. No doubt the results would appear one day in some advertisement for sunny Bournemouth or even in a brochure for a tropical paradise holiday, retouched so that the goose-pimples would not show. I silently wished them well and hoped they were using lots of Kodak filmstock.

After a while I began to get itchy feet about sailing. Here we were, about as far as one can get from the sea, the only sailing available being in dinghies on small muddy reservoirs. Remembering the marriage of DIY television demonstrator Barry Bucknell with boat designer Jack Holt resulting in the hugely successful Mirror dinghy, I bought a kit. The entire package down to the last coat of paint cost me £79, about the same as I was to pay for a proper towing trailer to carry it around on. Our car had to stay out of the garage for a few weeks while I assembled the kit, literally stitching together sheets of waterproof plywood with copper wire, and then 'glassing' over the joints inside and out using glass fibre tape and resin. I found the resin smell made me quite ill, but the result was a wonderfully light and sturdy hull. Painted outside in kingfisher blue and varnished inside, she looked wonderful with her set of red sails. We took her to the public lake at Stanborough, near Welwyn Garden City for her official launch. She sailed beautifully, and didn't leak a drop. On the new trailer, we towed her down to Lee-on-Solent and launched her from the beach. We'd bought life jackets for the children and simple buoyancy vests for ourselves and, as it was Cowes week, the four of us sailed over to watch the start of a race there. I found that with Patricia crewing beside me and the two children sitting well for'd, one each side of the mast, we could balance the boat adequately and she went surprisingly fast even with four up. We had a broad reach for the home run and she moved at a spanking pace. I had to be careful not to get in the way of a race that had just started, so sailed close under the stern of one yacht so as to sure of being well ahead of the one following behind her. Standing in the stern of his huge cruiser and looking down at us, whisky glass in one had, her owner called out in a talking-down-to-the-plebs voice, "A bit rash, aren't you?" Shortly after clearing the fleet I looked behind me to see the seas were getting up, white horses had appeared here and there with a dark grey cloud building up behind. We managed to get her up on the plane which was exhilarating, and covered the four mile crossing in about half an hour. I was quite relieved to be back as I knew I had three people in the boat who would have been in bad trouble had any of the gear failed or had I capsized. They were fortunately unaware of my concern and thought it had been a wonderful sail! After that we sailed the Mirror on one or two inland waterways around our parts, and we also towed her down to Cornwall on our next visit to see father.

A drive all the way down to Cornwall to visit father was becoming rather a duty instead of the carefree holiday we had enjoyed in earlier years. Jane reported the same sentiments. Father regarded both Jane and Patricia as their respective family providers, and therefore in the days leading up to one of the families coming down he stopped attempting to cook or lay in provisions for himself, expecting to join in with whatever we would be providing for our families. As a result Patricia had to take most of the food we would be requiring during our stay as well as all the paraphernalia needed for a young family. Shopping from St. Mawes was a difficult and expensive procedure, there being only one small grocery shop, and it really needed a trip to Truro, which ate into precious holiday time. Dennis Edmonds who ran the St. Mawes shop was a friend of ours whom I'd known since my teenage years, so we understood his problems. Like many village shops, his regular customers were mostly elderly people without transport, some living alone, who wanted goods in small packets. People in the village with large families would shop in the nearest town anyway, so Dennis could only cater sensibly for these elderly ones. Visitors would buy from him if they were staying in a self-catering place, but there were not a lot of those at the time. As a result Dennis had to obtain his goods from an intermediate wholesaler, the prices he had to pay being about the same as we would pay in a large supermarket. Therefore by the time he had added on his retailing expenses his out-of-pocket costs were much higher, and that was before he had put a few pence profit onto each item. He was in a slowly declining business and later, when he reached the age where most people retire, he still kept going for a few more years as a service to the village old folks, losing money on every item he sold. Eventually he had to call a halt to this magnanimity and stop trading in groceries. The shop now sells knick-knacks for the visitors who swarm down there every summer.

Nevertheless, in spite of the dreadful journey to get there and the grim accommodation when we arrived, once away from the house the surrounding area was so lovely one is soon immersed in it and tries to forget the domestic side. Father had rearranged the house to be suitable for just himself, the second bedroom now a junk room smelling of damp bedding. It had to be cleared out and the whole room cleaned before we could even take anything out of the car. Once we'd done that we took a dinghy over to Place House opposite Stone Quay for a walk all round the National Trust headland at St Anthony's, a visit to the lighthouse past the old army encampment on the top, or go down to Carricknath beach. Or we might walk down through the village and along the shore track to St Just-in-Roseland and spend time chatting to Benny the boatbuilder. Or again, we would just amble around Polvarth Point among the boats hauled up on the mud, calling in to see Frankie Peters who kept his boatyard there, and who'd built almost all the St. Mawes one designs. On one day we went out for the day to the Helford estuary in Holy Smoke, an excitingly fast cruising catamaran. Afterwards we saw the stone-polishing machine her owner had, and this prompted us to spend the next day beyond the Lizard at Loe beach where attractive semi-precious stones could be picked up. It was a lovely week, helped enormously by warm weather and the superbly clean sea air. A wonderful break from noisy Watford.

Patricia had settled in sufficiently to find time for a part-time job. Looking around she soon discovered she wasn't going to find anything congenial unless it was voluntary work. She decided the quality of what she did was more important than earning some money; after all, we were coping all right. So she signed up with the Citizen's Advice Bureau for two days a week. This was full of interest with all sorts of problems to sort out for the never-ending stream of people who'd got themselves into financial or legal difficulties. It was certainly an eye-opener to finding out what was going on in the town, but unfortunately for me she was unable to talk about her 'clients' since the work was necessarily confidential. Pity, as many of the stories would have gone down well at any dinner party. She also took a part time job looking after administration work at the Watford Baths, at that time the only swimming facilities in the district.

We had problems with the summer heat waves experienced in Watford. Temperatures would soar into the late eighties for a couple of weeks every summer, the weather forecasters happily saying there was no end in sight to this 'lovely weather', but for all of us it was a real trial. Used to the tempering sea air, we found it oppressive and airless inland, not helped by a house that we couldn't keep cool. Being built in the fifties down to a budget, heat insulation just wasn't a priority in those days. The government's Building Research Establishment was just a mile or two away at Garston, so we took the opportunity to visit on an open day and quizz their scientists about sound and heat insulation and a whole lot of other things. Then I set about insulating the loft as a first step. A year or two later the idea of squirting foam or dry mineral wool particles into house cavities took on, and we had our house done. This made a huge difference and we were not only warmer in winter, but also much cooler in summer. Summer coolth was also helped by keeping curtains drawn and windows closed once the outside temperature had climbed into the eighties. Even so we longed for a fresh airy breeze, but the only relief was to drive out to Ivinghoe Beacon and walk along the ridge where there just might be a waft of cooler air.

In that first year we also spent a lot of time hard-landscaping the garden, laying a large patio across the back of the house with a raised alpine bed. I hankered after a pond, somewhere near the patio so we would hear the tinkle of water from a gentle water feature. I would lie in bed dreaming up wonderful designs for this, then next morning look at the reality and realise my ideas just wouldn't work. There was an area further down the garden that wouldn't grow anything, and when I looked at the 1908 six-inch Ordnance Survey map in our reference library I discovered why. It was the site of a large marl pit. No doubt this had been filled in with subsoil when the house foundations were built, and about the only sensible thing to do with it seemed to be to make our pond just there. It was on a slope, so maybe we'd have two ponds and link them with a little cascade. We got around to this in about our third year.

Settling in to a new area within Naval circles is quick, as I have remarked earlier. Usually one built up a circle of friends within weeks, starting with a social invitation from one's commanding officer and the official invitation from one's Commander-in-Chief; they all help to get started. Arriving at Watford was quite a different matter. The neighbours around us were all very pleasant people, but we were all different. Not quite kindred spirits; not people whose houses we would be invited to enter if we called round—not until we came to know them considerably better. Likewise, one didn't call out a "Good morning!" when passing a stranger, though it was different out in the country away from any habitation. A

"Good Morning!" or a "Hello!" could be exchanged then. At other times people would avoid eye contact. Initially this upset us, not being used to townies, but then we came to appreciate the hugely variable strata of society all jumbled together in suburbia, and the need to tread carefully. When we first moved in we waited hopefully for the first move to be made by my boss, but it never came. Eventually we took the initiative and invited Tom Castle and his wife to dinner. Actually we took them out to dinner at The Bell, that legendary pub in Aston Clinton where the Vintage Sports Car Club people would spend the evening after a Vintage Silverstone, but sadly we found it had changed hands and had deteriorated into just another pub that happened to serve food. Next we invited Ray Plowman and another Kodak man with their wives. The evening was hard work for us as none of them felt as ease, indeed Ray, as he stepped over our threshold, actually commented on the novelty of being asked out to a meal! We stopped trying after that until we enlarged our circle of friends in other ways, and Oh Boy, did this take a long time—talk about putting down roots in stony ground!

I joined the local residents association's committee, which resulted in building up further acquaintances, one of whom was an elderly man living further down our road who was a keen fisherman. One evening, walking back home with him, he told me he'd been shot at.

"What!" I exclaimed, "You mean someone tried to shoot you? Here, in Watford? Whatever did you do?"

"Couldn't do a lot," he replied. "I was knee deep in the river, carrying out a fish count, when that crazy woman suddenly appeared at the end of her garden which runs down to the river just there and started to shout. 'Be off with you! I know you. You're always snooping around here!' And with that she suddenly raised a loaded shotgun and didn't give me a chance to get away. You can't move quickly when you're wading in a fast-flowing stream. Before I'd gone ten yards she loosed off a barrel, peppering my backside and the water all around me. Lucky I was wearing thick clothing or I might have been hurt."

"Did you report her?"

"What's the point? Everyone knows she's mad."

"Who are you're talking about?"

"That Fanny Craddock. Mad as a hatter. Her husband's all right on his own, poor sod, but when he's with her he shouts just the same."

Fanny Craddock was at the height of her fame, if that is the right word. Fame turned to notoriety a year or two later when she insulted Gwen Troake, a Devon farmer's wife who was a cook of some considerable local repute, on air in one of Esther Rantzen's The Big Time programmes. After that she faded out of the public eye. We used to watch her cookery programmes on television, and remembered her remarking that she was now talking to us from the kitchen of her wonderful new home in the Hertfordshire countryside. We had no idea she lived more or less at the bottom of our garden! It would have been more accurate had she said she lived in Watford, for her house was just within the Watford boundary. After that we noticed the Craddock Rolls occasionally when we walked down the nearby lane, and Johnnie would often be seen creeping out of our local

Victoria Wine shop clutching an armful of bottles. A man we came to know much later told how he'd been employed by the Craddocks as a gardener and Johnnie would be quite reasonable giving instructions about this and that. Then Fanny would suddenly pop her head out of a window and countermand what Johnnie had just said, whereupon he would almost turn violent.

"He sometimes didn't pay me if Fanny thought I hadn't done what she wanted," he told me. I thought this unforgivable. Here was a successful couple earning a lot of money, while this poor man was just scraping along on occasional casual work, doing his best within his capabilities. We also heard stories of the girls that attended cookery courses in her large kitchen who were expected to do all the dirty work, washing up, cleaning, etc, in addition to learning Fanny's way of cooking, and to pay a huge fee for the privilege. No wonder Fanny was able to appear on her programme in smart clothes without an apron.

~*~

We were having withdrawal symptoms from our beloved Devon. A whole year had passed since coming to Watford, and all we'd done was to visit Lee-on-Solent or St. Mawes. A holiday in Devon was certainly overdue.

So we booked in to a farmhouse near Ivybridge for a week just before school started in September. We drove down very early one morning while the roads were quiet, not meeting any traffic at all until on the outskirts of Exeter. We took the old road, the one I shall always remember when my dear little Cluley broke down in the wilds, but this time there were no such problems. An early picnic lunch beside a small clapper bridge near Manaton was so wonderful, the sun shining down, complete silence from traffic, the clean moorland air wafting over us carrying that nostalgic scent of heather tinged with sheep's urine, a buzzard calling overhead. Without doubt, this was our favourite area. Once again I wondered why we didn't live down here, but then how could we do so? The practicalities of needing money, finding good schools for the children, somewhere to go shopping soon crowd out such wistful thoughts. We climbed Hound Tor and walked on down to Great Tor with its mediaeval village, then moved on to Cadover Bridge, one of our other favourite spots, for a picnic tea and a dip in the River Plym, eventually arriving at the farm where the children had rides on a pony before the evening meal. What a day!

We walked from Didsworthy Warren to Duck's Pool letterbox and back, and saw a fox cub close up. Then a day to Soar Mill Cove and along the coastal path to Bolt Tail, followed by a day on Harford Moor where we ended up at the Hurrell's house to watch his seal Atlanta being fed in return for showing us his latest tricks. Elaine Hurrell was at home at that time, looking after a buzzard that had been injured, and which we were all allowed to handle. That evening Elaine joined us for a badger watch overlooking a much-used sett we'd discovered earlier in the day. A final day re-visiting all our favourite spots in Plymouth and it was the long drive back home again, back to the airless hinterland.

Talking about our holiday at morning break on the Monday with John Meunier, one of my workshop supervisors, I met a quite different attitude. John was a Londoner, had lived all his life in the Kenton area. His idea of a good holiday was at one of the Spanish coastal resorts with plenty of hot sun, cheap liquor and a lively nightlife. Had he been to Dartmoor? Yes, once. Never again. Spooky. He'd got out of the car to feed the ponies, but didn't venture onto the moor. I mentioned it used to be told that convicts who'd slipped off when outside the prison on a stone-breaking party would be back before midnight, knocking on the door to be let in. "I can well understand that," said John. "I'd be just the same." We mused on how people can be so different. When Patricia and I go on holiday we seek out the peaceful remote spots. We find it wonderfully therapeutic to just sit quietly somewhere with a lovely view, nobody in sight, and recharge our batteries. Even now when we're needing a break we find an hour's walk around our favourite birdwatching reservoir, spotting a kingfisher maybe, just sets us up for the day. John couldn't understand this at all. He'd hate that. But that's as it should be. If we were all the same, life would be intolerable. Why was it then, that I have no interest in watching grown men running about kicking a ball? John was an Arsenal supporter, so that started him off again. I was getting a name amongst my friends at work for being so different as to verge on the eccentric, so I cultivated that image for a little enjoyment.

One of John Meunier's main tasks for his team was to keep the set of 16mm perforating machines in tip-top order. These had a printing mechanism in them that put a photographic 'footage' number down one side, an operation achieved by the use of a mechanical counter that was lit by a flash as the film passed. The counters had been giving a lot of trouble and we'd found a firm in Axminster that promised a better quality counter. Their main business was counters for petrol pumps. I suggested the two of us visit their works, so we set off by train. We were met at Axminster station and driven to the factory that turned out to be a tiny place on a hillside in Coombe St. Nicolas a few miles away. All the workers were local folk with lovely Devonshire dialects, so I happily lapsed into the vernacular much to John's amusement. Away from Harrow, John himself sounded like a proper Londoner in comparison. I must say I do enjoy immersing myself in regional dialects, provided they're not Geordie which I am unable to understand. We were taken out to lunch by the boss, placed an order for twenty or so bespoke counters to be built for us and bought a pot of Devonshire cream for Patricia. John had no idea Axminster carpets were made in the factory we passed on our way back to the station, didn't know the difference between Axminster and Wilton or even know that those two names are those of west country places… Returning to London on the train, the same line on which I used to travel to my Clayesmore school, John was looking forward to returning to his familiar London away from all these alien green fields and quaint rural people, whereas I was sad to be leaving the glimpse I'd had of my lovely west country with its congenial scenery, clean air and friendly natives.

We'd joined the Herts and Middlesex Natural History Society (now the Herts and Middlesex Wildlife Trust), the whole family going on short country walks looking at anything that moved or grew. We joined initially to give the children some purpose in their walks, to teach them to be observant and to develop an interest in wildlife, but the spin-off was for us to discover lots of interesting spots to go at weekends. Patricia also enrolled in a further education course in Geology, and we met one or two new friends that way as well as exploring working gravel pits and other strange places. Round about this time we also joined the RSPB, though it was some years before we discovered the local members' group. However, we paid our first visit to their headquarters at Sandy in Bedfordshire, walking round the bird-friendly grounds and talking to various headquarters staff. When we returned home Patricia was standing at the sink when, out of the corner of her eye, was conscious of a large bird lift off the lawn and looked up just in time to see it flying away down the garden and into the trees at the bottom. She was sure it must have been a buzzard, but a buzzard in Watford for goodness sake? We phoned Elaine Hurrell, who was now living in Oxford who said it might well have been hers which had gone missing. This was too much of a coincidence, but we never saw it again and it was not until several years later that occasional buzzard sightings were reported over towards St. Albans.

When my RYA subscription expired, I decided not to renew it. I had been a member since before joining the Royal Navy, with a membership number somewhere in the early thousands, an élite little club. Now it numbered hundreds of thousands, had examinations for landlubbers who wanted to say they could take a boat out safely, ran navigation courses for potential skippers, and somehow didn't seem the same as the 'club' I had originally joined. Years later when I applied to take out the Kodak boat, a small cruiser the Company kept at Hythe in Southampton Water at the time, I was asked if I'd sailed before, where and in what, and which certificates I had. On my application form I said I had no certificates, listed places all over the world where I'd sailed and boats from little Mirrors and Fireflies up to ocean racers such as the Wal and her sister ship Marabu. I also listed the sailing clubs I had been a member of, starting with the RYA, then the St. Mawes Sailing Club, the RNSA (Royal Naval Sailing Association) under whose flag Portsmouth greengrocer Alec Rose sailed round the world, the Cambridge University Cruising Club where I crewed with Jack Knights, plus one or two more such as the Rugby Sailing Club. With some reluctance they let me go, probably not believing a word.

Art classes hadn't helped me in any way to become a better draughtsman. I can study a figure, noting all the places where it goes in and out, the proportions and stance. When seconds later I transfer my gaze from the figure to my blank piece of paper, I am unable to remember what I've just been looking at. Yes, I could draw cartoons with no problem, but they were very amateurish. I had a slide of a couple of swans that had come to us hoping for food as we walked along the foreshore at Hillhead shortly after we were married. I tried projecting this onto my canvas, then sketching round the edges to get the proportions right. Afterwards I set about painting the scene in oils, using a palette knife to lay on the swans' feathers. The result was most pleasing and we have it in pride of place above our fireplace at home. Another scene, this time from a photograph I took of Customs House quay at Falmouth on that occasion I first took Patricia down to meet my parents, I also painted in oils, using the print to copy from, and it too hangs in our sitting room. A further boaty scene copied from a photograph of boats laid up at Percuil also fetched up as an oil painting in the same room, and we have more general landscapes dotted about elsewhere in the house. People say they like these paintings, but I am only too aware of their amateurishness and wish I could have done better. Maybe I should have persevered, but I stopped painting after a few more years as I didn't feel I was progressing. I concentrated instead on capturing all our holiday activities on slide film, a format that can be used for talks, and from which I can make prints should I wish to keep them in that form. At Kodak I joined the factory photographic society, and received lots of help with my photography. Kodak published several little books to help amateur photographers take better pictures. I was able to go one better by actually talking to the people who wrote the books.

We still had a box of stones collected from Loe beach, so I made a stone polishing apparatus from an old washing machine motor mounted on a bench with a belt drive to a tumbler polishing drum made from a piece of plastic drainpipe. The idea was to fill the drum with roughly equal size stones, add water and a couple of spoonfuls of coarse carborundum abrasive, switch on and leave for a week. Since the motor put out a certain amount of heat, I kept it in the greenhouse where the heat could be captured and put to good use. After its week, the coarse abrasive was washed off and replaced with a finer one for a further week, eventually finishing with a week's final polish using the finest grit available. I processed several batches and made one or two trinkets by mounting some of the best stones onto silver clasps set into a bracelet, or a chain for wearing as a necklace. I then worked out how much electricity it was costing to keep a ¼ horsepower motor running continuously. It was expensive! So what with that and the problem of the distant rumbling sound coming from the greenhouse which we (and presumably the neighbours) heard all night, this became another seven days' wonder and the apparatus now lies in the attic with a whole lot of other one-time hobby detritus.

Beyond the bottom of our garden we have a belt of trees, a remnant of a wood from the original estate. On the other side of that the Sun Printers, one of Watford's two large printing companies (the other being Odhams) had their sports field with several pitches and a pavilion. Beyond that runs the Grand Union Canal from which we would hear the clatter-clatter as some canal boatman let down the sluice gates when negotiating one of the locks just there. On the other side of the canal are woods and open country stretching all the way into the Chilterns. Paul would nip into the woods beyond our garden sometimes, egged on by his friends, only to be quickly ejected by the groundsman who had unusually sharp eyes. This area was very precious to all of us who backed on to it, and was definitely a positive feature of our properties. From time to time the local paper reported scare stories about proposals for a school or maybe a housing estate to be built there. Collectively the residents sought reassurance from the Town Hall that no planning permissions were being contemplated. Nevertheless I began to take much more interest in how land use is defined and just how easy it can be to get it changed. That was partly why I became a committee member of our local residents' association, an association set up to protect the whole estate when it was first established, to prevent it deteriorating in quality.

Originally this part of Watford had belonged to an Earl of Essex (not the same line as the Elizabethan earl of that name), and when the family died out in the 1920s their land, which spread out north and west from the centre of the town, was sold off. Ours is one of two large housing developments that were built with a narrowing belt of parkland remaining right into the town. This and the rest of the park was acquired by our local council who constructed a golf course on one part of it and retained the extensive woodland around it which they have jealously guarded ever since. The big house was demolished, though not before several Grinlin Gibbons artefacts that included a magnificent staircase were sold off. That staircase is now in the Metropolitan Museum in New York. All that remains of the buildings is a part of the original stable block, which has now been absorbed into an old people's home on our estate. Various paths that have proper foundations and once would have carried horse drawn conveyances can still be identified in parts of the park. When Bridgewater was building his canal back in the 1700s he was obliged to put in several right angle bends to accommodate the demands of Essex, who wanted the canal to pass on the far side of his estate and Clarendon, his neighbour, who wanted the canal to be tucked into a shallow declivity so that it couldn't be seen from his pad on the top of a nearby hill. The canal's towpath had to be on the side furthest from the big house where it passed through these lands.

Both children were now having piano lessons from a lady who lived on the estate almost next door to the old stables. They would come back complaining of her halitosis, something that assailed me whenever I went there to collect one of them. Neither of them actually progressed very far, and we regarded piano playing as just another part of their education, enabling them to read music. It was a job to get them to practice, but they eventually worked their way up through the grades. Like myself, they enjoyed the music but had little natural ability with a keyboard.

During the war when everyone was expected to plant vegetables in their gardens a proper man-of-the-soil, Mr Middleton, would broadcast advice on a regular radio spot. After the war another gardening guru came on the scene, a pompous man by name of Doctor Shewell Cooper, who considered himself a cut above the average dispenser of gardening advice since he said he was professionally qualified in that direction. (He was called up nevertheless, but managed to wangle the rank of colonel and give himself the job of Horticultural Adviser to South East Command, much to father's annoyance.) I discovered he now lived at Arkley Manor just a few miles away, and held garden open days. Intrigued to meet him in the flesh I decided to visit and took Susan along with me. We were met by the great man who patted Susan on the head and said how important it was to teach children at a young age all about gardening, particularly how to garden with worms (he was advocating a 'no dig' method of gardening at that time). After we moved on

Susan said "What a self-important old windbag!" I had to agree with her. He'd craftily established a sort of 'Friends of Shewell Cooper' coterie which he called the Good Gardeners' Club, and it was members of this 'Club' who had been prevailed upon to run the Open Day for him, all sporting their club tie with a fancy logo on it. Actually, the visit was extremely interesting and I learnt quite a lot about soil structure and compost making. Even Susan after her deprecating remarks said it was good.

Back at home I eventually got round to digging out a pair of ponds in the old marl pit area, linking one with the other by a small cascade with a circulating pump in the lower one. Ten inches down I came across sticky red clay, a layer of it a foot thick beneath which were the remnants of a dark stony topsoil. No wonder nothing would grow there! I discussed at our morning DIY teabreaks how best to line such a hole, and how to anchor the lining at the top. We'd seen demonstration ponds at the Highland Water Gardens centre in nearby Rickmansworth and in all cases the edging stones, which needed to protrude an inch or so over the water, would be a bit wobbly. I thought I could overcome that problem by first of all digging out a shallow trench and filling this with concrete which would then become my 'hard edge' onto which the edging stones would be laid. I built it this way illustrating each stage with photographs which I then sent to the Highland Water Gardens manager together with some notes on its construction. Two days later I had a phone call from Bill Heritage, the owner of the garden centre, enquiring whether he could use my ideas in a book he was preparing on water gardening. We met up, and he said he would be pleased to do some planting around the back of the pond to make a good picture. He suggested I write an article to describe the whole project, for eventual publication in the DIY Magazine. I wrote the article, finished the pond, and Bill came round as promised with a carload of plants from his Centre and spent a happy day with us. A few weeks later I had a call from the magazine Art Editor wanting a few instant snaps of the feature, for which he sent round one of his team. After that they arranged a photographic session where he turned up in person together with a professional photographer with a large format plate camera, an assistant and two models who were all long hair and big bosoms. By this time it was mid September so our water lilies were over. No problem; Bill had provided water lily flowers which we floated on the surface with a little weight under them to keep them upright. One model lounged at the back of the pond while the other stood holding one of our old trays with drinks on it. The session took two hours for this one photograph, but they all seemed happy with the results. The Art Editor drove off with the sexier of the two models, a secretive gleam in his eye, and we settled back to our more humdrum life. The article duly appeared the following spring in the DIY Magazine as their lead story, with the picture complete with our tatty drinks tray on the front cover.

A few months later we received an invitation from Bill's wife to a Christmas party at their Chorleywood house. His wife, who must have been a somewhat thwarted social climber had pricked up her ears when she heard that the person whom her husband had been involved with was a retired naval commander. Maybe she pictured a crusty old salt with a chestful of medal ribbons. We went along regardless to discover it was one of those combined parties where the teenage children had invited their respective girl/boy friends while parents had asked along the people to whom they owed hospitality. The parents' list was unbalanced being short of respectable married couples, so I expect that was our role. I found a gloomy man sitting on the floor with nobody to talk to, so I joined him to discover he was a 'resting' actor by name of Jack Smethurst, temporarily employed in the garden centre. He'd been in a soap called *Beggar Thy Neighbour* that had struggled along for a while. Later he went off to Australia where the same show was attempting to get off the ground with a fresh audience. However, his wife Julie was good fun and we came to know her later when we were both in the same Scottish Dancing club.

The much-respected Whitefriars glassworks was just across the railway tracks from my Kodak building, and I discovered the neighbour of one of my workshop people was a 'gaffer' there, so managed to arrange a personal visit for the family. He took us all round, wandering about the working floor with furnaces roaring away, men dashing here and there with gobbets of semi-molten glass, noise and danger everywhere. The children found it exciting and we came away with bits and pieces that had been made especially for them, also a lovely paperweight which was a Whitefriars' speciality. Remembering those days now I shudder to think of the complete lack of any safety rules, yet so far as I know there were no serious injuries. Workers just took great care in this dangerous environment while visitors like ourselves jolly well did as we were told! Alas, the place is no more, gone like so many small family industries. A few years afterwards they were in the news just once more: a huge spherical liquid gas canister in the yard had sprung a leak, gas escaping around the neighbouring housing estate which had to be evacuated in the middle of the night while firemen made it safe. Trains on the Euston line that passed within yards had to be stopped for several hours.

That railway line was very different about a century earlier when George Eastman, founder of the Eastman Kodak empire in Rochester, New York, paid a visit to this country with a view to opening a factory over here. He had caught a steam train from Euston that soon emerged out of London's grime into open country with pleasant green fields and little villages. He alighted at Harrow and Wealdstone station, a mere twelve miles from the centre of London, and bought a thirty-acre site beside the railway line on which he built the first Kodak plant outside Rochester. The site had fresh spring water of a very high quality, which was an essential requirement for his manufacturing process. His original building is still there, but he would not recognise the rest of the site now, with large multi-storey industrial buildings crammed into every possible space.

Patricia had been a member of the local Young Wives on our estate but was becoming somewhat disenchanted since the only topic of conversation seemed to be children. She wanted to broaden her horizons and was getting nowhere. She joined the National Council of Women, a nationally recognised pressure group, which she found far more to her liking. Most of the members were professional people with wide interests, and the NCW organisation was respected by the government as a body to be listened to and consulted when necessary. Patricia became a member of their housing group as a result of which she was able to take me along on some of the outings that looked at new housing developments. Thus began the game of teasing the unfortunate salesperson manning show houses. We would be shown round a carefully presented show house, point out that the master bedroom was too small to contain a double bed and maybe that was why it had been furnished with a 'double' bed that looked alright until you measured it, when you found it was a purpose-built undersized one. Armed with our tape measures we would then discover lots of other pieces of furniture were also undersized, a slightly dishonest attempt to make the house appear larger than it was. Patricia always noticed how often the power points had been positioned in such places that a trailing flex would have to pass across a door threshold, for example, while I looked for poor joinery and suchlike. There was one house with a gap of over an inch beneath a door, which had to be so because otherwise the door wouldn't open due to an uneven floor. Really basic faults such as these would be seized upon and reported back up the line. As consumers rather than builders, such a group might well become customers, so it made sense for them to be listened to. Patricia felt she was doing something useful, much more rewarding than sitting with a gaggle of young wives talking about babies.

Paul's scouting was taking off. His new leader 'Doc', a.k.a. Neil Shave, was an excellent youth leader with a real interest in developing his charges, bringing them on to become responsible leaders. His influence was considerable and the local Scout troop much respected. Neil had a small pottery business in Market Street, a potter's wheel in the window, an electric kiln at the back of the shop. He himself was not a potter, but would have various friends drop in from time to time to throw things on the wheel, more as an animated window display than for any serious production work. I had a happy hour on his wheel occasionally, but my throwing was really too amateurish and I was embarrassed to perform in public. Neil spent far too much time planning his scout leading activities and a year or two later he had serious cashflow problems and was forced to give up. He found a buyer for the kiln provided he would deliver, a lady who worked from home a couple of miles away. But how to get a huge kiln weighing well over a ton to her house? He solved the problem by recruiting half a dozen scout dads. One of the dads had hired a van for another job which would be suitable, but this wouldn't be available until he returned from a day up country, probably about 11.00 p.m. And so we all arrived at the shop in the dead of night, backed the van across the pavement up to the front door, and proceeded to move the kiln on rollers with much pushing and shouting. It took us nearly an hour and throughout that time not a single person passed by, no local resident's curtain twitched, no sign of a policeman to see what we were up to.

Neil took his troop off camping from time to time, the camp itself being utterly different to Susan's Guide camps. Neil's idea of a camp was somewhere to live while the boys went off on expeditions of one sort or another, and they'd be quite happy to stand around eating cold baked beans out of the tin when they got back, whereas Susan's camps had been spent mostly around the site creating a domestic home under canvas. I suggested they should go camping together, the Guides running the campsite while the scouts just used it. Not surprisingly I was quickly shouted down. Usually the parents all joined in with the scouts' activities in that we provided transport and helped with any large humping jobs needed (such as kiln-shifting!) which we enjoyed since that way we got to know the other parents. But Neil found this too restrictive and eventually acquired a vehicle of his own. This was an ex-Army ambulance, a large four wheel drive truck into which all the camping gear plus a dozen boys would fit quite easily. After that the parents were no longer required except for specials. One of these was the cumbersome marquee. Neil had also acquired an enormously heavy ex-Army marquee that came with a huge pile of poles and lashings. It was invaluable at their camps, but spent the rest of the year in a mildewy damp lump at the back of the scout hut. As one of the dads (an accountant) had pointed out, it was as asset not earning its keep; they should hire it out from time to time, if only to give it the chance to dry out. And so one fine summer day the call went out for all able-bodied dads to assemble at the hut, load up the marquee and take it to a house in Stanmore where it had been hired for a bar mitzvah. We arrived to find the house empty and locked up. Apparently they would not be back until evening and expected to find everything in place then. Their back garden wasn't much larger than the marquee so we had to drive in the tent pegs at the backs of the flowerbeds where the soil was none too hard. We just fitted it in and left the hirers to worry about the evil damp smell that would pervade everything. I often wondered whether Neil ever got paid for this hire.

There was one further activity I remember all too well and that was a father-and-son camp in the local woods. I shared a tent with two other dads plus a million mosquitoes. One of the dads, the headmaster of a local secondary school, arrived complete with his old army camp bed and slept the night through with no trouble while the other one and myself didn't sleep a wink. My camping days, which I'd never enjoyed that much, were definitely over. However, I had recorded this event on 16mm cine film which I showed the troop when next they had a social gathering that included the parents, but had to borrow a projector in order to screen it. The short film hasn't been seen since then as movie film quickly became obsolete once camcorders came on the scene.

Susan was growing up. For her twelfth birthday she asked for a sewing machine of her own, putting up half the cost with her own money. Almost her first item was a wonderfully made shirt for her brother Paul, with faultless stitching and superb tailoring. She became a very meticulous needlewoman and made several articles of clothing for herself.

When Susan had started to go to Watford Technical High School, we expected she would be entitled to a bus pass since the school was well over three miles away—the defining requirement. However, the authorities measured this distance not from one's home, but as the crow flies from the nearest point of the road in which one lives. Our road was over a mile long and we lived at the far end of it, and they found we were not entitled. So she walked. By taking various shortcuts through the town centre she could get there in about an hour and I am sure she arrived fitter and mentally more alert than the ones who'd come by bus. We gave her the cost of the bus fare each week, but she saved this and after a few weeks was able to buy a bicycle though she still walked for most of the time. When Paul also started at the school, he walked too (though not with his sister who would make sure she set off before Paul was ready to leave, such are the concerns of girls anxious not to be seen having to look after their younger brothers). After a few weeks Paul, too, bought his own bicycle. The route they took was mostly along quieter roads, but even so it was risky for schoolchildren to cycle on any roads in Watford, though at that time we didn't appreciate just how risky.

Paul had wanted to play the trumpet, and was therefore keen to be involved with the school orchestra. He met David Iliffe in his first day or two, but David suggested he might find the French horn a more satisfying instrument and suggested Paul take home with him a school instrument to see how he got on. So this little lad came running all the way back from school one day lugging a huge battered case with the school's French horn inside. Actually Paul got on quite well, started lessons at school with one of the peripatetic teachers, David Iliffe now having another horn player which he needed to help balance the orchestra. At the end of his first year, Paul had to return the horn and we bought him one of his own. He also wanted to play the guitar, since several of his friends were involved in 'gigs' though we had yet to come across one that had any talent. We bought him a classical guitar hoping he might attempt to play it properly, but before long he was strumming an electric one that made lots of noise but didn't sound very nice.

Patricia's friend Peggy from her training days lived in Bath, so we stayed with her for a couple of nights as a base for a Slimbridge visit and the standard tour of historic Bath, a service at the Abbey, the obligatory drink of sulphury water from the pump room and a walk around the Roman Baths. I'd been to Bath before in order to visit the Admiralty people who were up the hill at Foxhill, but never looked round the town proper. Peg's house was part of a terrace built of Bath stone, with a dripping damp basement, rooms that were unnecessarily huge (compared to our modern Watford house) with ten foot high ceilings and ornate cornices, the whole place smelling of damp and feeling chilly however much one turned up the fire. But Peggy was a good hostess, fed us well and was pleased to be able to chat to Patricia of old times.

We made regular visits to Patricia's parents at Lee-on-Solent, the journey now much easier since the M3 had been built enabling us to take a different route via Odiham and Alton. For some time Leslie had not been his usual active self, needing to sit down more often and not able to join us in striding out on a walk. He was eventually diagnosed with a blood disorder that made him anaemic and was undergoing rather unpleasant injections every week. Walking into Lee village, we'd separate, Elizabeth pacing out in front with one of us while Leslie came along more slowly with the others. When with Elizabeth I found myself opening the conversation with "If anything should happen to Dad…" a euphemism for "If Dad should die", and go on to say that we would bring her up to Watford if she wished, building on a granny flat to our house. She was in such a state about Leslie's health, worried not only about him but also about how she could possibly cope in that house on her own. Leslie had designed the house, but in the early fifties houses had coal-fired boilers for water heating, open grates, lots of paintwork needing regular upkeep and, in this case, Crittal galvanised metal windows that were just not suitable with all the salt in the air. All the Lee houses were built of brick and like every brick house by the sea, they all had faulty pointing, the mortar being of a quality that did not stand up to the salt either, but at least Leslie had the forethought to specify a pebbledash finish, though this, too, was subject to extreme weathering. Access to the loft was by means of a heavy wooden ladder which needed a strong man to hoist into place, and that loft was a repository for enormous amounts of useful 'just in case' junk that Leslie had hoarded there. Altogether the house needed a man to manage it; Elizabeth was no substitute and right now looked quite frail with all the worry.

One Sunday afternoon in March of 1973 we received a phone call from a distraught Elizabeth. Leslie had collapsed in the church foyer at nearby Stubbington just after the morning service and had been taken to the Naval hospital at Haslar. He was unconscious and it was serious. Leaving our neighbour to keep an eye on the children we immediately drove down to Lee. I collected Leslie's car from outside the church and drove it back to Watford while Patricia remained with her mother. Leslie died the following evening. Then followed a harrowing time for Elizabeth who was expected to identify the body and answer questions from the police since Leslie had died unexpectedly in a public place. I went down and spent a couple of days getting organised with solicitors and bank managers, generally holding Elizabeth's hand.

In the following months we sorted things out, visiting Lee whenever we could. Considerable help was needed in the overgrown and overplanted garden, and we threw out enormous amounts of useless objects which no one would ever need. We made the decision that Elizabeth would move in with us as soon as we'd built on a flat, and I set about designing a house extension which one of the Kodak architects drew up for me. I designed it to have separate services from the main house, but sharing the same front door. Should we ever wish to sell off the flat in the future, it would just need to have its own entrance built, a relatively easy job.

Father now sensed he was being pushed to one side as indeed he was, for Elizabeth took Leslie's death very badly and needed all the help we could give her. Nevertheless we made our 'duty' trip down to St. Mawes as soon as we could. It was not a success. The beauty of that wonderful place, the sailing and walks, the local people, it was all tainted with the chilly atmosphere in the house with father spoiling for a row at every opportunity. All his rancour was directed at Patricia whom he blamed for usurping him for my attention. Sadly, we left with a nasty feeling that future St. Mawes visits would be less frequent and more of a 'duty' than ever.

It was ten weeks before probate was granted and we were able to proceed with the extension. The Town Hall took its time with giving planning permission and it was October by the time the plans were approved. In good old Kodak style

I invited tenders from several local builders, not hearing from any of them until after Christmas. The tender was for putting up the brickwork and roof of the new extension, leaving me to do all the services, the plastering, first and second fixings and decoration. Leslie's car was now occupying our garage, the little Traveller being kept outside. When the Traveller's MOT was due it failed due to rusty chassis members, a result of having spent a lot of its life near the sea. It was now twelve years old and needed constant attention to keep it on the road, so we decided to sell. It was a sad day when a quartet of young lads excitedly drove it away leaving me with £75 cash in exchange. That had been our first car, with so many memories. Leslie's automatic Austin was no substitute. I fitted a towbar onto the Austin and in preparation for the extension we towed our boat down to Lee and left it in Granny's garage.

On school Open Days we had toured the Art Department and met Mr Walsh, a big strong-willed art teacher whom every pupil respected whether they had any art ability or not. He ran a metal jewellery business in the art schools, with oxyacetylene torches, kilns, and all manner of potentially dangerous equipment, and brooked no nonsense from any pupil. I admired his ability to keep such strict order and one day—I was now attending evening classes in jewellery-making myself so had come to know him fairly well—I asked how he did it. His answer was simple: "On their first day here I keep a sharp eye on all the little terrors. Easy to spot the troublemakers. Pick the worst one, give him a bit o' rope with which he quickly hangs himself, then at the end of the lesson I take him into the back room and give him such a going over that he's terrified to come along to the next class. Needless to say it's all round the school next day and no one else dares to misbehave." I never discovered what his 'going over' involved, but there was no doubt he ran an excellent class and the pupils loved it.

Alas, that was not the case with Paul and his maths teacher. She was well qualified in maths maybe, but had no ability at all when it came to discipline. The class had half a dozen troublemakers and made her life a misery. Unfortunately that meant Paul was not learning any maths. It was becoming obvious that he was developing as a practical science-oriented boy for which maths was essential, so we took steps to arrange additional tuition to help him through his 'O' levels. Oh, that there were more Mr Walshes and fewer wimpy maths teachers! Sadly all the rules coming in to curb what misguided authorities called 'child assault' resulted in a proliferation of troublemakers, their parents becoming quick to blame the school for everything. They would in due course resort to the courts to stop anyone laying a hand on the monsters they'd brought into this world, never stopping to think that perhaps it could be themselves who were mostly to blame. When our two went to their 'big' school I had reminded them they'd be competing with lots of other children, that teachers got their kick out of bringing on a pupil and watching him or her progress through the school to leave at the end with honours. If ours were to get on, they'd require help from the teachers, so needed to get their attention early on and demonstrate they were worthy of the teacher's interest. Once they'd achieved that the rest was easy. I'm pleased to say they both took that to heart and sailed through school with good results.

17

An Extension, Beekeeping and Hassness

I secretly fancied myself at being able to put pen to paper, preferring to write rather than speak since speaking involves thinking on one's feet—something I'm not too good at. My writing is laborious with lots of alterations and crossings out, but at least I get my muddled thoughts sorted out and the result is far better that way. Tom Castle in one of his chats to developing engineers had said, "Speak your criticisms but write your praises". He practised this himself, being quick to stamp on any poor work by a good ticking off, but whenever he heard of one of his people performing well there would be a congratulatory letter, always copied to the man's immediate supervisor. Tom got results.

But I enjoyed writing everything from short stories to technical articles. I would write to the newspapers if I wanted to air some issue. I remember my first letter to The Daily Telegraph that they published. It was at the time Doctor Beeching was wielding his destructive axe at our then comprehensive railway network. I wrote "If the branch lines are closed leaving just the lines between main stations, how will I be able to travel by train any more, since I need a branch line in order to get to a mainline station? Surely Beeching will kill off half the passengers as well as half the lines, so what is he achieving?" That's exactly what happened, of course, but in the long run there was little satisfaction in saying so.

I enrolled for a weekend course in creative writing, a subject I'd not thought of actually studying before. It took place at a house in Gomershall near Dorking, a large house owned by an organisation called Holiday Fellowship. Patricia's cousins used to go on holiday with Holiday Fellowship, or 'HF' as it was known, and recommended their houses. I arrived at teatime, was shown my room, or rather my share of a four-bedded dormitory, and met the other aspiring authors for an introductory talk. At 6.30 the booming of a dinner gong interrupted us and immediately the place erupted with dozens of people all heading for the dining room. I was swept up with them and found myself sitting at a large table with arms flying everywhere snatching bread rolls, butter, the water jug. It was like being back at school. The noise of fifty people all talking at the tops of their voices was deafening, and yet these people had not met one another until half an hour ago. What sort of place had I come to? After supper the quieter writers escaped from this mob and retreated to a small lounge to spend the evening discussing our various creative efforts while from far away came the sound of the rest of the house party having a knees-up. Happily I found I was in company with people who had similar abilities to myself, which is to say that they had very little. We got along well.

I hardly slept at all that night, sharing a room with three other men who snored and two of whom smoked. I was awakened at 7.00 by the clanging of a bell in the corridor outside. It was reveille time! A tea urn stood on a table at the top of the stairs, bleary-eyed tousle-haired dressing-gowned people staggered out for their early morning cuppa. After an enormous noisy breakfast, most of them departed with their walking boots and rucksacks leaving the writers alone in a suddenly quiet house. I remember little about the course content except that I didn't reckon it had been worth the effort, but I do remember my first experience of HF. It was not an experience I felt I ever wanted to repeat.

At Kodak I was getting itchy feet. I had now been there for nearly five years, far longer than any Naval posting, and I was still going in each morning to the same building and sitting at the same desk with the same people doing the same work. I had reached a plateau and felt I was getting stale. I wanted a change and dipped my toe in the water by answering an advertisement for an electronics engineer to head up a small project at a Texas Instruments assembly plant on the outskirts of Plymouth. I went there by train, and found their works at the airfield. The place was small, a hundred or so people run by three youngish, impatient young men in what I could immediately see was a peremptory but poor manner. As soon as I walked through the door I realised I would never wish to be employed by such a team. Kodak had spoiled me. I went through with the interview followed by a tour of the production plant (they were making one of the first generation pocket calculators which would soon be eclipsed by Clive Sinclair's creations), after which I spent the rest of the day sniffing around dear old Plymouth for possible jobs, visiting the employment exchange, our friends the Stevensons from Scottish Country Dancing days there, and the Naval Resettlement Officer. A couple of days later Texas Instruments wrote to say they didn't think I would be any use to them (I think they worded it differently, but that was how I read it. It told me everything). I considered this interview time well spent and returned to my Kodak desk with not quite such itchy feet. I applied for one or two internal jobs that came along instead, then discovered that Ray Plowman would be informed if I applied internally which worried him a little and might have affected how I was perceived by him in the future.

In the meantime I had other things on my plate. One of our chosen builders for the extension, P&H, had responded to my tender by putting in a very good estimate of £2,500. This was followed a couple of days later by two other, much higher, estimates from other builders one of whom I hadn't even contacted. I accepted the P&H's one, remembering the times when removals firms would give quotes to Naval people transferring to another location. We were required to provide three competitive quotations to the authorities, who would pay us removal costs based on the lowest tender. When we asked our chosen remover to quote, he would do so and at the same time save us the bother of approaching any other firms by arranging for two slightly higher quotes to be sent in. Thus all the removal firms benefited from only one valuation having to be done instead of one from each of the three. It worked well. No doubt the builders were doing the same thing, only in their case I noted it was an estimate, not a quotation.

Two days after acceptance, a young lad staggered onto our drive carrying a couple of steel lintels. P&H had staked their claim. I busied myself rearranging our front bedroom. When we first moved in I'd split it down the centre with a partition, one half for each of our children, leaving the spare room available for guests. Now we put Paul in our spare room, took down the partition in the front room, re-erecting it the other way to create a passage leading to the side of the house ending in a brick wall through which I would soon be knocking out an opening to the flat. The resultant space now made a good-sized room for Susan. If Patricia's mother—Granny, came to stay before the extension was finished then one of the children would sleep in the dining room.

A two-week silence followed during which P&H assured us whenever we phoned that they would be starting in a day or two. It gave me time to build a temporary roof over our side passage so that we would be able to clear out our garage and put all the bicycles, etc, there. Then an urgent phone call. Could they start in the morning? Sure enough their 'groundman', a little Irish fellow with a large new Volvo, arrived followed shortly afterwards by the boss. By the end of the day they had virtually demolished the garage and filled the first skip. Then they vanished for a week or two. Paddy the groundman reappeared and dug out the footings three feet down into almost pure gravel. He may have been small but he was wiry, immensely strong and had the stamina of someone half his age. While all this was going on I had ordered and taken delivery of the plate glass sliding windows to match with the rest of the house, had given them a coat of varnish and also taken delivery of a set of kitchen units ordered from Trewins, our local Jonelle department store. With no garage, storage became a problem. A little later the bathroom suite, one with a super cast iron bath we'd had so much difficulty finding, was delivered and I wheeled it round the back. It would have to live out of doors for a while.

I found the reason for P&H's tardy start. They had pricked up their ears when they received my tender. It fitted in well with their spare labour, for Paddy would soon be free and needing a job for a few weeks, while the two bosses who ran the firm jointly would finish off their part of the previous job leaving sub-contractors there while they came on to us. I discovered small-time builders like these depend on dovetailing their assorted trades into the various jobs they have on the go (that's why they do more than one job at a time), they expect to have free use of handy little builder's yards dotted all over town, meaning customers' own front gardens, and their planning of materials deliveries has to be very precise so that the minimum of double moving takes place. They may spend half a hour getting a load of bricks put down in exactly the right spot so it doesn't have to be moved from there until it is carried up a ladder onto the scaffolding in a hod on Paddy's back. Both bosses, the bricklayer and the carpenter, appeared full time at last, the concrete was poured into the footings, a Town Hall inspector arrived to have a look, and the following week bricklaying started in earnest. Six weeks later they were up to eaves height and then they all disappeared for another week or two.

While this was going on Susan had found a new interest. She had been reluctant to join us in our weekend walks for some time now, preferring instead to remain at home engrossed in homework, a quiet girl who seemed to have few real friends. It was only much later we realised there were very few good kindred spirits to be met in the circles she moved in. Her first break was to become involved with the local Liberal party, whose agent lived in the next road. Through them she met various other people and got out and about more. She'd met people her own age at the St. Mary's young people's group, which went under the extraordinary name of 'Sunday Joint', and later when she moved on to the senior group, the 'After Eight'. We left her with one of these groups while we had a day out at Virginia Water just at the start of azalea time when it was at its most dazzling. I'd heard about this area and the nearby Savill Gardens from father who used to visit when we lived at Byfleet only a few miles away, but he'd never taken the family. P&H finished the roof timbers, nailed on the roofing felt and battens and the extension became weatherproof. While we were waiting for the tiler to appear I had a chance to paint the soffits and fascias from the convenience of their scaffolding, and I also put the heavy plate glass sliding windows into their frames.

We took time off for a stay in St. Mawes. The visit this time was far better than our last one. Father made a great effort not to upset us, helped enormously by his immediate neighbour in the other half of the house having been taken to spend her last year or two in an old people's home so we had the run of her house for our family's use. Susan accompanied father to the home in St. Austell to see her and, like father, found the experience sad and depressing. Father said he would never consent to being 'put away'; but should he have a stroke or lose his marbles then he might not have much option. Douglas Gordon took us out in his boat to the Manacles and showed us several little channels that ran through those dangerous rocks, and we also sailed up the Helford, anchoring at the foot of the magnificent Glendurgan garden though we never set foot ashore at that time. It was a glorious week of hot sun and we were out in boats every day, exploring the upper reaches of the Percuil River, Froe Creek, across to Falmouth and up the Carrick Roads. Even the trip down and back were painless, with very early starts on empty roads. It's remarkable how a spot of nice weather and a positive attitude can transform a week we had been rather dreading into one of such bliss.

Back at home, we found the scaffolding was down and the tiles in place. P&H called in to hang the garage doors and do a final tidy up and then they left. It had taken just under four months to complete. Now it was my turn. I stood on the ground where the old garage had once been and looked up at this huge hangar I'd had built. Now I had to put in ceilings and floor and convert the upstairs into a cosy granny flat. The first task was to get the heavy cast iron bath up onto the floor joists above my head and for that I would need the help of four strong neighbours. I'd left a floor joist out so that we could do the lift inside, using a block and tackle in the good old Naval way, my helpers pulling while I stood to one side and shouted "Two, six, HEAVE!" I then set about building internal partitions and began to install plumbing for a kitchen and bathroom. My morning tea breaks at Kodak took on a new importance as I consulted and received advice from lots of people who'd all built their own extensions before me. I doubt whether I would have had the confidence to tackle such a job without their support. From this point on for the next six months I worked most evenings and nearly every weekend finishing off the inside.

Patricia hurt her back holding up heavy firebreak boards with a broom against the garage ceiling while I womped in nails to hold them in place. We had twelve of these boards to fit after which I could then start boarding over the floor upstairs once the electrics were in. My carpentry bench came upstairs and bit-by-bit I constructed cupboards, fitted skirtings, ceiling covings, installed all the kitchen cabinets, and completed the plumbing which to my delight worked without any leaks. I'd rather hoped to put in some solar heating panels, but soon found they were so expensive that one would never get one's money back in a hundred years. I guess solar heating, which is a sensible thing to do from the point of view of economizing on non re-usable resources, will never catch on if it is left to individuals; it would need a government incentive, and governments with their lack of interest in anything beyond their five year term of office, are not known for such philanthropic gestures.

One of the Kodak plasterers took a couple of days off and came to plaster all the rooms, with Patricia and me taking turns preparing his mix to keep him supplied. Ten days later it was dry enough to apply a coat of paint, and for the first time the rooms began to look like a habitable flat rather than a building site. Elizabeth, or 'Mother' as we called her (when she wasn't being called Granny in the children's company) came to stay and to see the progress. She brought with her a special friend, Enid Price-Hill, a most interesting person who in her working life had been an archivist at Windsor Castle with offices in the Round Tower. She and mother clambered around the half finished flat getting quite excited.

By the end of August we felt we really wanted a holiday from all this building work, so booked in for two weeks at a self-catering apartment in Guernsey. We took mother with us, a tight squeeze in the little Austin, drove to Weymouth and watched with bated breath while a crane lifted the laden car and lowered it into the hold of an ancient cargo boat. We ourselves then boarded a tatty British Rail overnight ferry that took us first to St Helier in Jersey where we all had to wait about on the jetty while the ship was cleaned. Most of the passengers had been unpleasantly seasick everywhere. Eventually we arrived at St. Peter Port in Guernsey to be reunited with the car. The apartments were grouped around a small swimming pool and ours seemed to have been used by chain smokers who had never opened any windows. It was so smelly and grubby we almost turned round to go home again, but were glad we didn't as our week on the island turned out to be really good with glorious weather all the time. Mother was reasonably fit and enjoyed the cliff walks. For the trip home we filled up with lots of commodities that were in short supply at home. The death-wish Heath government at this time were locked in a fruitless struggle with power hungry unions, the outcome of which was inevitable. Everyone suffered, there were food shortages galore, hence our welcome carload of provisions from Guernsey, but the worst result was a series of power cuts that affected everyone, the notorious 'three-day week'. Fortunately, the Kodak factory generated its own power, so was unaffected. The results were serious enough to bring down the government, so something positive was achieved though not in the way Heath expected. I'd rigged up a car headlamp on our sitting room standard lamp, powered by a spare car battery, so what with that and a log fire in the evenings we were not inconvenienced by the power cuts. Hot water was heated by gas with no electrics involved, and the whole exercise re-affirmed the sense in having more than one completely independent means of heating, lighting and cooking. I scrumped all my firewood from the local woods, sawing it up by hand. It was a further ten years before I bought myself a small chainsaw, but by that time we had become used to keeping the house a bit warmer which meant we only needed a live fire on really cold evenings when our basic central heating was unable to cope.

In the New Year Granny had an offer of £18,750 for the Lee-on-Solent house, which she accepted. She'd been thinning out all her possessions, conscious that she would eventually be living in a bed-sit with only a small bathroom and kitchenette opening off it. We had several clearing out sessions down there, and eventually professional house clearance people came in to finish it off. I completed the flat and we brought her up to Watford followed by a half-full removals van with all the 'essential' things she reckoned would go into it. She also brought enough 'almost essential' things to completely fill the lovely big double garage that was under the flat, which seems to have remained full ever since.

With Granny installed under our roof we had a built-in child minder so were able to go out more often on our own for dancing, serious walking or just ordinary shopping. It was a great boon having the extra grownup, though by the time she arrived Granny had become almost crippled with arthritis, hardly able to walk about. The medics said it was probably a result of grief followed by a year's worry over her move and would clear in time. Six months later during a heat wave we were walking gently round Windsor and Eton with her when she suddenly collapsed whilst we were in the semi-darkness of Eton College chapel. She'd thought she must have missed a step in the gloom, but it transpired it was a momentary blackout. Some time later she commented on an inability to see properly from one eye and an investigation showed a damaged retina. This had been linked with her blackout, and a blood test confirmed an abnormality that would have caused both events. She was put on a cortisone drug, which controlled the blood problem but also had the magical side effect of completely curing the arthritis. In no time at all she was walking about at her usual fast speed delighted to be fully mobile once more, but with a worry about her eyesight perhaps deteriorating in the future.

We had the builders back again, this time to push out the end of our somewhat small kitchen and build a bay window a few feet further out. As before, I employed them to do the heavy building work, moving in afterwards to re-arrange the plumbing, install electrics and plaster the walls (which this time I did on my own, and it shows!). Then with new homemade kitchen units, a new sink and a vinyl floor covering the original quarry tiles we felt we had updated our 'fifties house to last us another ten years perhaps. During the few weeks this was going on Patricia had to cope with no kitchen, doing all her family cooking on our cooker which we'd dragged out into the hall, and washing up in a tiny corner washbasin in the cloakroom.

Patricia and I took a holiday at a farmhouse near Haverfordwest. We wanted to walk parts of the Pembrokeshire coastal path for which we were blessed with wonderful summer weather. We also explored the lovely area around Bosherton where we saw lots of waders and various rails scrabbling around in the lily ponds. The farmhouse turned out to be a working farm with a large accommodation block built onto the main building, so was more like a hotel really. Our bedroom window looked out onto a yard on the far side of which the farmer had his kerosene tank, which leaked slightly. Right beside this was a hayloft into which he had spent the day taking up bales of hay on an elevator driven by a stationary engine. Bits of chaff had fallen into the open-topped cooling water tank, so that the whole engine almost glowed with heat. This was nestling in about a foot of kerosene-soaked hay, the whole potential conflagration only yards upwind of our bedroom. That night I checked the emergency exit was not obstructed, and hardly slept at all. Working at Kodak I had become extremely safety-conscious so a sleepless night after what I had seen was hardly surprising.

Safely back at home once more, our local walks were becoming restricted due to huge road construction works that were taking place between us and the village of Sarratt—a favourite walk of ours. Sometimes we could clamber down an embankment and get across what seemed to be a hundred yard wide ditch to the other side, but most times there was work going on which made it unsafe. Six months later it was all finished, the new road becoming a section of the much talked-about M25. Positioned just inside this psychological barrier we felt trapped and no longer living on the edge of the Chilterns but dangerously near to outer London. Would the value of our property suffer? The sound of construction activities gave way to a continuous hum of traffic, the almost constant dust in the air remained, a nasty smell of traffic fumes joining it. This has got steadily worse until now, 25 years later, it's everywhere except in the few wild parts of the country still remaining.

Paul was becoming interested in electronics. He acquired bits and pieces of radio equipment, finally building himself a CB receiver for which we rigged a large aerial to the side of our house. His room smelt of soldering flux and warm electronics and his knowledge soon overtook mine.

I thought I would like to go in for beekeeping, since I enjoyed proper honey so much, so took delivery of a nucleus of bees, about 10,000 of them in a box containing four brood frames. The box had ventilation holes in it from which came an angry drone of agitated bees all anxious to get out. I collected it from the suppliers in Uxbridge during my lunch hour and it spent the afternoon on top of the filing cabinet, the noise getting ever more menacing until a deputation arrived headed by Ray Plowman who suggested I might like to go home early, "and take that box with you". Other occupants of the office then came back in looking sheepish and very relieved. At home I had made a brand new WBC hive of traditional design smelling of fresh sawn cedar, and installed it down at the bottom of the garden where I reckoned the bees would have an uninterrupted access. I had assembled a tray of brood frames, leaving room for the nucleus ones to be inserted into the middle.

I joined the local West Hertfordshire Beekeepers Association and every week or two I would go to their meeting in Croxley Green when we opened each of the Association's hives that were kept there. We were extremely fortunate to have as Chairman, Harry Riches, a well-known beekeeper who taught me a great deal about looking after these busy little insects. I spent fascinating afternoons watching him examine the hives, expertly lifting out frame after frame of crawling bees and pointing out which was the queen and which were drones or workers. I found it enthralling. I learned all about the extraordinary social behaviour of apis mellifera, how the queen controls the intricate running of her colony by passing instructions to her court followers in the form of chemical messages which are passed on in turn to other workers telling them to bring in more pollen, or build more drone cells or whatever.

At home I donned my new veil, unscrewed the lid of the travelling box and, much to my surprise, successfully transferred the bees into the waiting hive as if I'd been doing that sort of thing all my life. Next morning there they were contentedly flying in and out of their newly painted front entrance. I felt a proper beekeeper at last. One of the local beekeepers, Alan, went white when he heard how I had hived my bees, Apparently I'd done all the wrong things and it was only by luck I'd avoided a nasty accident. Suitably chastened, I peered over his shoulder and watched as he deftly manipulated frames of brood from the depths of his own hives. It seemed so easy and the bees so docile. When I got home I tried to examine mine in the same way. A few puffs of smoke in the entrance, count ten, and quietly lift off the lid. Carefully I peeled back the quilt and immediately fifty or so agitated insects scrambled out and started a determined high-speed war dance between me and the hive. The first frame that I lifted out to inspect was being built up nicely; new honey already glistened in some of the cells. Trying not to let my hand shake too much, and with thoughts of a lovely honey harvest in my first year after all, I gingerly lowered the frame back, squashed a bee as I did so, and was promptly—very promptly—stung.

Now, when a bee stings, it also releases a substance which alerts all the others in the vicinity. I knew this from reading my books and rather wished I didn't. My nervousness was obvious to anyone, and without doubt the bees were thirsting for revenge, pinging into the front of my veil in their fury. Quickly I shut up the hive and retreated, telling myself I would look at the rest tomorrow, This wasn't too promising a start, but I told myself it was prudent, as you can't beat a colony of bees into submission like you might a horse or some other intelligent creature. In those first days I spent hours crouched near the entrance to my hive, watching. I was always amazed at the aggressiveness of the guard bees, which will fly out and attack any intruder regardless of their own safety.

Over the ensuing weeks I realised one doesn't become a beekeeper without first learning a bit about the entomology. There is clear demarcation between members of a honeybee colony. The queen is boss in this matriarchal society. She lays eggs at the rate of up to 2,000 a day, almost all of them destined to become worker bees. These are undeveloped females and are the ones generally encountered. Guard bees carry out their task for a few days at the time when their stinging apparatus is at peak efficiency, as I knew from painful experience; they then leave the hive to become foragers. As foragers their lifespan is determined by the number of flying hours they clock up, which may be as little as three weeks at the height of a good season. When first hatched though, the young bee is given the more humdrum tasks, such as housekeeping. It starts by cleaning and polishing the cells, goes on to feed the grubs and in another week progresses to feeding and grooming the queen. It then spends a few days house cleaning by which time its wax-secreting glands have developed and it will turn to building up comb or 'capping' over filled comb. In these early days worker bees also undertake fanning duties, standing for long periods near the entrance with all their feet anchored to the ground whilst flying at full throttle, so to speak, to circulate fresh air around the hive. Fanning exercises the bee's wings, and it's about this time it first ventures outside the hive on its initial flight.

All this I learnt in my first season by watching, and by talking to my new beekeeper friends, and I found it completely absorbing, Various people found out I had become a beekeeper and I was promptly categorised as an eccentric and asked to deal with stray wasps' nests in house eaves. (I soon learnt to direct such requests to the council's health department). But I didn't care; my busy little insects had produced a modest surplus of honey in their first year and I went out to collect it. Avoiding the kamikaze guards I lifted off two heavy trays of filled combs one evening after most of the bees had gone to bed. We turned the kitchen into an impregnable bee-proof fortress (for when it comes to honey, bees will dispute ownership in a most positive manner), and set about the task of extracting.

I had acquired an elderly centrifugal extractor which spins the still-warm honey out of the combs with ease, but even so it was well into the night before our task was completed, and by that time there was honey over the walls and ceiling and on every door handle in the house. Little bits of wax clogged the sink, and a mixture of honey and wax was somehow trodden into the new sitting-room carpet. The delicious aroma of new honey permeated the whole house and we didn't dare open any doors or windows until late the next day by which time it was all securely bottled.

We presented a pot of this hard-earned (and very expensive) honey to our immediate neighbours as insurance to their continued tolerance and I began to understand why not everyone keeps bees at the bottom of their garden.

In the following year my bees swarmed, and then the fun began, By this time

I had a spare hive waiting for such an event, so when I was summoned home from the office by a panic-stricken voice over the telephone, I came as quickly as possible. Several neighbours stood around outside the house looking none too pleased as I arrived. Clearly more pots of 'sweeteners' would be needed at harvest time. No, they hadn't settled; well they had, but now they'd gone. Well, most of them had gone. Where? Over there, between those two houses. Then followed a frantic half-hour banging on doors in the next road where I thought the flight path might have been, "Excuse me, have you seen a swarm of bees?" If people thought I was a bit dotty before, now there was no doubt. I drew a blank.

In desperation I phoned the police who told me someone had reported a swarm of bees in their chimney. (Hmm, how the devil would one set about dealing with that?) I said I thought it most unlikely any bees of mine would settle in a chimney; they must be somebody else's. I studied my incident map. Oh dear, the house was bang on their projected flight path. I drove past it slowly. Two or three distraught people were standing about looking up at the house. I drove on. Afterwards I heard that disoriented sooty bees were emerging by the hundred in the living room and the owners had spent the night with friends. I wondered what my legal position was.

Alan phoned later to say he'd collected a swarm and did I want it? My troubles seemed to be over. He came round and delivered a large and vocal cardboard box tied up in a sheet. We carried this amorphous lump down the garden, untied the sheet, and watched fascinated while the whole swarm marched up a plank and in through the front door of my spare hive like an army of determined soldier ants. This might sound a bit hazardous, but it wasn't really. Before swarming, a bee will fill its stomach with honey in preparation for a trip which may last for a few days during which it may not be able to forage. In that state it becomes benign and dozy and is easy to handle.

In the meantime I had examined the original colony of bees, those that were left. Swarming is a natural process by which bee colonies multiply. It starts when the queen begins to lose her laying ability, maybe after a couple of years or so. A few drones are produced as a normal procedure. These are fertile males, larger than the workers, their sole purpose to be available should a new unfertilized queen appear. They do no work and do not even have a sting. They expect to be fed by the workers, and indeed they are. They spend the day in little coteries in some nearby tree, idling away the time until they get hungry when they return to the hive for their next meal. They are tolerated until autumn when, the breeding season over, they are unceremoniously kicked out and not allowed to return. When I looked at my depleted colony, I found a number of outsize cells. These were queen cells, all either empty or containing a dead queen. What had happened was that the workers had built these special cells as a response to the original queen's egg-laying ability falling off. The grubs inside would have been fed with a especially rich food known as royal jelly which enables them to grow into queens. In the meantime the old queen has her food restricted and she grows thinner and becomes able to fly. Eventually she leaves the hive followed by most of her workers and settles on the branch of a nearby tree. The process may take half an hour or so. From that temporary lodging scout bees set out to locate a suitable place to build their new home, which is often in a hollow tree, or even in an empty hive somewhere. As soon as they have located such a spot which may take a day or two, they return to the swarm and persuade it to follow them. Thus a new colony is established. Back at the old colony, the relatively few remaining bees would be leaderless, but not for long. The queen cells start to hatch, which can happen in as short a time as five days from when the cell was capped, half the time it takes for a worker to metamorphose. The first one to emerge quickly dashes round the hive eliminating all her rivals by stinging them through the sides of their cell, a task made easier by a queen that is about to emerge from its cell making a piping sound that can be detected by other queens. Then the new queen emerges for her maiden flight accompanied by the patiently waiting drones, mating takes place on the wing and the newly fertilized queen returns to the hive to spend the rest of her life as an egg-laying machine. The original colony will, in a matter of days, be completely rejuvenated.

Susan was reaching the stage when she was wondering what career to work towards. I took her to Kodak to spend an open day in our Research laboratories, which mainly employed physics or chemistry graduates, but she felt this would not be in her line. Her real interest was in biology, helped no doubt by an excellent biology teacher at school. After her GCSEs she spent part of her summer holidays working with John Free, the bee entomologist at Rothamsted Agricultural Research Station, which she found fascinating. I welcomed the opportunity to go to Rothamsted with her occasionally, mainly to meet Dr Free. Alas, Susan had discovered she was allergic to bee stings, so Rothampsted might have to look for a scientist in another department who would be willing to have her.

After a year or two as a beekeeper, I carried out a reconciliation of all the costs to date. When I had a decent surplus I sold a few jars of honey for 60p a pound, which was halfway between the price of the uninteresting supermarket stuff and the exotic brands sold in our health shop. I reckoned it cost much more than that to produce, and the hives took a couple of hours every weekend through the summer to look after, and on average I received one sting for every ten pounds of honey taken. I got a swarm or two most years and would spend an exciting day tearing round retrieving the things, and by this time had a new hazard— a green woodpecker that came into the garden in winter and chopped holes in the side of one of the hives. On the credit side I discovered a wonderful set of new friends, all as peculiar as me. Most years we bottled anything up to sixty pounds of honey, wonderful natural stuff with a superb flavour since it all came from a wide variety of blossoms within a mile or two from home. As a spin-off I found all my fruit and vegetables were far more successful, with huge crops of runner beans, large apple harvests and plentiful soft fruit. My bees earned their keep many times over. However, I was beginning to find I needed to spend time most weekends bent over my hives, time we didn't readily have. Then there was the problem of the bees' flight path that was low over the garden. They have a very basic compound eye, and stumble into obstructions (such as Granny's coiffure) all too easily. Our neighbours were very good about it, but they, too, were uneasy about so many bees all over the place. The final straw was when the craze for growing oilseed rape took hold, a crop which produces an immense amount of cabbage-smelling nectar that the bees love. Mine found a field of this about two miles away, and immediately abandoned everything else, making a beeline as it were, straight for the evil yellow crop. Within days they had filled all the supers with watery nectar that quickly set hard, almost impossible to extract. Not only that, but the smell was distinctly cabbagy. The quality of my honey plummeted. Examining the stock one could see the workers excitedly performing their characteristic figure of eight dance to tell the others they had located a prodigious source of food. I cursed MAFF or whoever it was for encouraging farmers by means of subsidies to grow this largely unnecessary crop. The final straw was when my colonies began to change from lovely placid Italian bees to a more productive but far more aggressive strain, and I started to become quite scared of my weekly inspections. I felt the time had come to sell up.

By this time, in addition to meeting John Free at Rothamsted, I had chatted to one of Brother Adam's acolytes at Buckfast Abbey about heather honey production problems, and even Alan, my local friend and mentor, had changed his methods. At one time he used to keep about twenty stocks, moving these around the country to where the best nectar could be found. Farmers paid him to bring his pollinating insects along to their orchards or wherever, and he was halfway to becoming a commercial beekeeper. He told of the occasion when he was returning one night with six stocks in the back of his builder's van when he was stopped routinely by the police wanting to know what he was moving at that time of night. Bees are always moved at night when they are all back in the hive, so he had no option but to be moving them then. The police demanded he open the back door, whereupon a loud roar assailed them.

"What have you got there?" they asked, stepping back smartly.

"About half a million vicious stinging insects all waiting for you to make the next move!" was his reply. They quickly got him to shut the doors and waved goodnight.

Alan had a friend wanting to start up, so one night I, too, set off in the car towing my trusty old trailer with the two hives aboard and a pile of accessories to go with them. In a way it was a sad day, but by this time I'd had them for about ten years, an experience I wouldn't have missed.

A year or two later the dreaded Varroa, a disease carried by Asiatic mites that live on honeybees, began to infect stocks all over the world, spreading like the black death. Many beekeepers had to give up as their stocks became decimated, so I only just got out in time.

~*~

We had some new neighbours down the road who had arrived from Edinburgh. The husband worked for Heinz and had been transferred to their Willesden Branch. They had retained a croft in a remote part of the Scottish Highlands which they used to visit regularly at weekends, but were now unable to go nearly as often.

They were quite keen let it to friends for a modest amount in exchange for keeping it aired. Were we interested? Were we! We discussed it for some days and eventually agreed to a fortnight there in July.

In the meantime Susan, now in the sixth form, was facing the decision of what to do after leaving school. Biology was still her favourite subject. She liked the idea of marine biology, but we thought it unlikely she'd find a job in that line since although there were plenty of marine biology degree courses, there were few openings afterwards. In spite of achieving a good set of 'O' levels and now studying three good science subjects, Susan was still unsure of her abilities even to the extent of being able to get the required number of grades for entry to a suitable university, and was wondering whether she'd have to settle for a lesser type of further education. I discussed this with one of my friends at Kodak who had a daughter doing biology at Harrow Technical College. He suggested Susan visit the Head of Biology there for an informal chat. This was a forbidding lady, Doctor Jarman, whom he assured me would be only too willing to help. He phoned her there and then, chatted for a few moments then passed the phone over to me. Yes, she'd be pleased to see our Susan.

I dropped Susan off for her chat on my way to a party, and picked up a very different girl afterwards. After talking to her for a while Doctor Jarman said she felt Susan could do far better than spend three years at Harrow Tech., and suggested she try for a Natural Sciences degree at Cambridge. A disbelieving and somewhat demure Susan could hardly believe her ears. Doctor Jarman was interested to hear about her spell at Rothamsted and suggested she go there for a further spell in the summer so that she'd have something really relevant to talk about at her Cambridge interview. No suggestion that she'd never get such an interview. She put confidence into our daughter, something that was certainly missing at that time. Susan applied to Rothamsted once again and was invited to have a spell there in the summer after our return from Scotland, this time working on nematodes with a Doctor Evans. Not quite marine biology, but certainly something interesting, and working with a proper research scientist too. This was good news indeed.

Before going to Scotland, we first headed for St. Mawes for a week's holiday. Setting off at the crack of dawn on a Sunday. These early morning Sunday drives were our favourite, for we were usually able to get down there without meeting any traffic to speak of. We towed the Mirror dinghy behind us, and on arrival found a place for it on Stone Quay, our favourite spot. A widow lady who lived on her own in a gorgeous house just above the castle with a cracking good view across the Carrick Roads had offered to put the children up in her spare room, which was a great help as there really wasn't the space for us all at Sea Lanes. We spent the week out sailing nearly every day, either in the Mirror, or in father's boat or with Douglas in his lovely old ketch; Paul sometimes took the Mirror by himself while Patricia and I sailed beside him in Caprice. Barry Bucknell, the joint designer of the Mirror, was now living in St Mawes and had his own Mirror there, so ours was in good company. When he saw ours he remarked how well it was built. Praise from the highest quarter indeed! In between sailing and walking the lovely coastal paths we tidied up the old man's garden to keep him ticking along until next time. Back in Watford it seemed hot, airless and enervating after St. Mawes.

The Scottish croft was near Rogart, a tiny place on the road between Lairg and Golspie, in Sutherland, and not at all what we were expecting. A 'croft' to us suggested a traditional thatched roof one-storey building with gable ends and a fireplace at each end. This building was the same basic design but was modern, on two floors and very comfortable. It stood in a field with a rudimentary gravel track that led from the nearest road and half a mile from the next cottage where a Mrs Macdonald gave us the key. Sheep kept the grass short right up to the walls of the house, ideal for a second home. We'd brought some fruit and vegetables with us, found wonderful wild raspberries by the roadside, and drove along a tiny track over the hills to Brora where we'd been told there was a fishmonger. This turned out to be in the village centre behind an unmarked door in a blank wall, giving no indication of what might lie beyond. Inside we found a fishmonger's slab with several wild salmon that had been brought in by local fishermen. That was all they had so we settled for salmon steaks, luxury indeed! Both Susan and Paul had a go at driving the car along the mountain track, a good place to try without any other vehicles to get in the way.

Rogart turned out to be a good centre for exploring the top end of Scotland. We tramped through the heather over the local hills on our first day, watched buzzards in a nearby wood and listened, entranced, to their mournful cry, and spent a long time chatting to a quiet shepherd who seemed eager to have someone to talk to. Then we drove up the side of the River Helm to Betty Hill on the north coast where we sat on an empty beach and had our picnic lunch. My photographs show a wonderful sandy bay with deep blue seas and white breakers. What it doesn't show is a piercing onshore wind of about 50 knots coming straight down from the Arctic. We returned down the side of Ben Hope, a super Munro, and through Lairgs. On another day we watched salmon leaping up the ladder at The Mound as our local burn entered Loch Fleet, where ospreys swooped down for fish. Then we had a day out to the west coast, driving through Inchnadamph and down the side of Loch Assynt to Lochinver and a grand little beach with rock pools full of interesting marine creatures. It was a wonderful potter round the Lochinver peninsula, all white granite rock with little lochans everywhere, somewhere I'd wanted to linger since the day we rushed along this same road on our first Highland tour. We came back topped up with sea air and satiated by the wonderful scenery wherever we looked. Ben More Assynt, the highest mountain in those parts at almost 1,000 metres looked interesting. A couple of days later we were back, parked the car at the Inchnadamph Hotel which seemed to be a fishing hotel and nothing else, then set off to climb to the top. This turned out to be another wonderful day, red deer on the braes and a relatively easy clamber up with no scrambling needed. The peak was in cloud and as we were standing on the summit with swirling cloud around us, a golden eagle came over, the sound of the wind in his wings clearly audible as he glided past. Golden eagles have a lovely supercilious gaze which they bestow upon mere mortals scrabbling about below them and we received this somewhat disdainful glare as he sailed over. Minutes later the cloud lifted and there was the whole world beneath us, with views for fifty miles in every direction. We picked bilberries on the way down and had bilberry pie for our supper. But all good things come to an end, and in due course we had to set off south once more, the roads and pollution getting worse the further we travelled, until eventually we arrived back at Watford where they were in the middle of a drought, hot fetid air with no oxygen leaving us exhausted.

~*~

Susan started her time with Doctor Evans and loved it. She had her seventeenth birthday while we were in Scotland, and was looking very lovely, something that did not go unnoticed by various young men. Paul went off for a week's canoeing with his Scout troop on the River Wye from Hereford down to somewhere near Tintern, with plenty of white water for excitement.

We found Paul would still be having the same maths teacher for the year leading up to 'O' levels, the one who couldn't keep control of her class. Helped by the private tuition he'd been receiving he eventually passed his exams the following year, but no credit to the maths teacher at all. Alas, with modern youngsters it seems the ability to keep the class under control has to take priority over the ability to teach anything. He really wanted to do electrical engineering with the idea of joining the BBC to start his career. I'm afraid it might have been my own interest in BBC engineering that started him down that road. I wrote to the BBC engineering recruitment officer on his behalf, and a few days later they replied direct to him in a fairly positive way, but suggested he contact them again when he'd got his degree. In the meantime he was building various CB receivers and we fixed up another large dipole aerial on the side of the house.

Susan started her university interviews during this autumn term, the first one up at York. Later she sat for some Cambridge exam papers, but the biology one didn't seem to go to her liking. She applied for interviews at one or two other universities as well as Girton College, Cambridge. So far she'd been told she'd need three 'A's or two 'A's and a 'B'; another way of saying they only wanted the most academic, and she felt her results might not measure up to those sort of levels. Her lack of conviction probably showed at the interviews. Then we drove her to Girton for her interview, and she also had one at Newnham after which I showed Susan and Patricia around the backs. Cambridge in January can be horribly cold and dank, but the sun did shine weakly, just a bit. As we walked around Susan described her Newnham interview at which the interviewer started by asking whether she'd done anything during the summer holidays. When she said she'd worked with Doctor Evans at Rothamsted, the interviewer clapped her hands with delight. "Wriggly Evans! Wonderful! How is she, haven't seen her for years!" after which the interview became a reminiscing chat, and Susan felt so relaxed she was sure she'd be all right. A week later Newnham phoned to say Girton wouldn't be interested in offering her a place, but they would.

"What 'A' level results do you want?" was her reply.

"Oh, nothing special, my dear," came the answer. "So long as you pass."

She was in! From that moment she redoubled her efforts at school. She wasn't going to let this opportunity slip away, and was determined to obtain good 'A's. Sue had one more interview arranged for the following day at The Royal Holloway College in Staines, which turned out to be quite a good one. She was so relieved her Newnham result had come out before she'd clinched a place somewhere else.

In April we had our usual spring visit to St. Mawes. No sailing at this time of year, but plenty of maintenance work for father who, though well, was finding the heavy tasks were beyond him. We laid out the mooring for his boat, a two-man job which involves one person manoeuvring the dinghy into the right place using sighting marks ashore while the other leans over the stern with a hundredweight concrete block on the end of a long chain. We sawed up masses of wood for his fire and cleaned the bits of his house that seldom saw daylight (most of it!). In between, there were all the usual visits to people, including this time a visit to Caerhays Castle on its Open Day. Unfortunately it was raining, so the paths through the magnificent magnolia and rhododendron woods were slippery with mud. We were guided round by John Williams, grandson of the famous hybridiser who bred such wonderful plants as Camellia Williamsii 'Donation'. I rather cheekily knocked on the big front door and asked if we might see his wife Delia, whom I'd known in my Polsue days when her family lived in St Mawes. She was a slip of a thing in our teenage years and had now become very much the Lady of the castle.

That summer my niece Judy, one of Jane's twins, was married. Father came up from St. Mawes and I met him off the train at Paddington for a short stay with us during which my uncle Ted came over to see him. What with father moaning about the tedious train travel 'with all those people' (he never knew how lucky he was in St. Mawes) and Ted going on about the 'journey' over from Surbiton (all of an hour's drive) I felt I had a couple of real old dodderers to look after. Then I drove father up to Manchester for the wedding at which the entire Stokes dynasty were present, Peter's elder brothers and sister looking very distinguished in their finery. Driving father home afterwards was exhausting. He had reached the stage when he needed to pee every hour or so which is not easy when driving on a motorway.

A couple of weeks later we set off for a week's walking holiday based at Hassness, the house on the edge of Buttermere owned by the Ramblers Association. We just had Paul with us, Susan having better things to do. On the way we stopped off at Malham Cove in the Yorkshire limestone area for lunch and a walk. It had been a cold and overcast June and we'd dressed accordingly, leaving our shorts at home. However, by the time we reached Hassness, the temperature had started to climb. The house at this time was run by a Geordie couple, the wife spending her days in the kitchen while her husband led the walks. There were twenty of us, so it was extremely hard work for them. Eric, the husband, was a large man with a huge corporation which he filled up every night with countless pints of beer at the village inn, but this didn't stop him pounding up the fells leaving us puffing and sweating behind him. On our first day, though, it was to be a gentle walk up to the village, across the spit of land between Buttermere and Crummock Water, then beside Mosedale beck to Loweswater village for our lunch, after which we would return down the other side of the lake. We had in our party a quiet man with his garrulous little wife. We were all looking at one another on the first evening while his wife chatted away in a penetrating voice for the entire evening, hardly stopping to draw a breath, and wondered whether we'd ever last a week in such company. Sure enough, next morning as we set off in single file we could hear her at the back still talking, and it went on like that for most of the morning until we were in the hinterland beside Mosedale beck. Then, suddenly, silence. We stopped and looked back. There she was, lying on the ground, her husband standing over her looking rather worried. We all turned back and formed a circle round her while someone tried to discover whether she'd just twisted her ankle or maybe broken something. Eventually our leader (who'd gone on) turned back and looked at her glumly. I seem to remember him rolling her over with his boot, but I doubt whether that actually happened.

"Are you hurt, lass?" he said.

"Yes," she moaned.

"Humph." He looked about him; then, "Reckon yonder crows will pick y' off if you're still here by t' weekend." And with that he turned on his heel and walked on.

We looked at one another, not knowing whether to follow or stay with the now silent invalid. I'm afraid we followed the leader, but then barely a couple of hundred yards ahead we turned a corner and there was the road, the Kirkstile Inn where we were to have lunch, and the welcome sight of a Park Ranger's Land Rover. Our leader had simply gone to get help. The story has a happy ending, for from that moment on we barely heard a word from the voluble talking machine and were able to enjoy the peace of those wonderful fells.

We graduated to clambering up some high stuff, the top of Robinson (2,400 feet) and along a lovely high-level traverse to Dale Head and then a steep descent to Honister Hause before returning home round the back of Fleetwith Pike. It was now glorious weather with cloudless skies and temperatures that crept up into the eighties. All the others had donned shorts and ever since then I've never gone on a summer holiday without mine! Patricia came down the descent far too fast in her effort to keep up, and damaged a knee which, alas, swelled up and kept her out of the running for the rest of the week. So the two of us followed this with a quiet day driving to Ennerdale, and the day after Patricia stayed behind and took all day hobbling around Buttermere while the rest of us went to the top of Grasmoor and back, about ten miles. It was appallingly hot, so we shortened the original walk a little. On the way we met some fell runners who seemed to thrive in the heat, but they were wearing light trainers rather than boots and had no rucksacks.

Paul and I went up Red Pike and along the mountain ridge of High Stile, High Crag and down the scree to Haystacks, finishing up at Gatesgarth Farm where we consumed gallons of tea. It was the hottest day yet, and quite exhausting clambering around on the fells. However, our leader, all twenty stone of him, was fit and as we returned home he received a call from the Mountain Rescue team of which he was a member, to return up the mountain again and help someone who'd got into difficulties. He didn't get back until the early hours, and next day was leading a walk onto Great Gable as if nothing had happened. Patricia was still hobbling, so we took the day off once more and drove into Keswick and discovered Fishers (where we bought a rucksack) before driving up the lane over Ashness Bridge to Watendlath for a quiet afternoon by the little tarn there. Her knee took several weeks to recover and she still has occasional problems with it twenty years later.

That first taste of the Lake District was wonderful, but I had my doubts about going there again on our own; I thought the fells could be somewhat scary in bad weather, and surely it must rain sometimes? If it didn't rain, there wouldn't be any lakes.

~*~

For our August visit to St. Mawes we towed the Mirror again, setting off at dawn as usual. There followed our customary week of sailing and walking, with a few extras thrown in. One of these was to go up to the Castle and watch HMY Britannia come in to anchor in the Roads while the Royal Barge came in to St. Mawes harbour to pick up the Queen and Prince Philip after one of their Silver Jubilee tours. Naturally we sailed out in the Mirror to have a close-up look at the Royal Yacht and admire the glossy deep blue hull with no trace of rust or dirt anywhere. Having spent that year in HMS Belfast tied up on the opposite side of the jetty which Britannia used when in port, I knew just what it cost to keep the ship in that immaculate condition. I felt the major cost should have been borne by a national fund promoting trade (which is what Britannia was mostly used for) rather than coming out of the Naval vote. The Queen arrived by car from Truro, so we lined up along the road at a narrow spot where we were only one deep and sure to get a good view. Father meantime had been selected as one of the old village fogies to sit in a row on the harbourside to meet the Queen, so he had dressed in his best suit and looked very smart. Using a long focus lens I was able to get a photograph of him talking to the Queen, at least that is what it looks like. Actually she was talking to the man next to him, but you'd never know.

In the few days leading up to the Royal embarkation, panic had set in when it was realised it would be dead low tide at the moment the Queen wished to step aboard, a time when there is only about six inches of water lapping at the very end of the harbour wall. Frantically a bulldozer appeared and spent an hour each remaining day at low water scraping away the sand until there was the necessary depth for the Royal Barge.

During that week Paul had lots of solo sails in the Mirror and the two of us entered a race for that class in the weekly Thursday evening club events, Paul at the helm. We didn't win since we had no spinnaker, but we were the first boat without a spinnaker to cross the line. I felt proud of my son. We also had a full day out in Douglas's old ketch when he showed us more safe passages through the Manacles.

Paul came to Kodak with me for a week's 'work experience'. He tagged along with trade electricians holding the tools and generally learning very little. He hated it, and it confirmed his desire to get good qualifications in order to go for a meaningful technical job, hopefully in design or development. His 'O' level results came through the following week: a mixed bag of ten passes; all either science or English subjects. Like me, languages didn't come easily.

As for me, I had been getting restless feet again. Ray Plowman had rearranged his three sections leaving me to look after his departmental administration. I'd been doing this for a couple of years now, and found it tedious and clearly leading to nothing. I contacted the group who looked after the budgeting and control of all company projects and asked whether they needed an admin man. The outcome? An advertisement appeared and I was phoned up and asked to apply! The resulting interview behind closed doors consisted of chatting about the improvements we'd make. This was when I discovered that when I had applied for previous in-company transfers, Ray Plowman had contacted the advertiser to say he thought I wouldn't be the sort of person they would want. In other words, he was unwilling to let me go. I was furious. Next time I saw him I announced casually that I was looking for something fresh and might be leaving his department, so maybe he should be thinking about a replacement. This got him going, as he jumped to the conclusion I might be leaving the Company. When he realised I was planning an internal move, he tried to block it again. What a man! I moved to my new department, which had offices in Rayners Lane, a couple of miles away, and a slightly easier commuter run for me. The offices were shared with branches of the Accounts and the Engineering Projects, so this provided more useful contacts for my various home activities. I had long realised I would never rise far in the Kodak hierarchy, as it appeared to be full of backs-to-the-wall politically-minded people whose agenda was firmly that of treading on anyone who got in the way of their own advancement, even if it was not in the Company's interest. Few of them made it and most of them were so overstressed their lives must have been miserable. My priority was for a congenial life with minimum stress, even if it meant sideways moves from time to time, and I reckon I achieved that with more success than most people.

Paul and I set off on a sponsored walk for one of his Church charities, a thirty-mile walk to Chesham and back. I hadn't prepared for this very cleverly, and realised by the time I was there and starting on the way back that I really needed a pit stop for a change of footwear, a reasonable rest and some food. Everyone else had met up with their families at the official stop, whereas I was on my own and beginning to hobble around with a blister on one of my toes. For the rest of the walk I tried to avoid making it worse with the result I walked awkwardly and put a strain on my knees. I staggered home almost on those knees, and took all next day to recover. I am very careful nowadays always to walk straight, since blisters mend quickly whereas knees can take months.

Later in September I took Susan up for the day to Newnham where she sorted out some loose ends and met various people. While that was going on I attended a two-part lecture in the Engineering faculty for past members of the Department. The first part was given by the Research Director of ICI talking about huge digesters that could be built to make proteins out of seawater and thin air. I remember him putting up a slide of the vast chemical works at Billingham stretching from horizon to horizon and sighing "Pure poetry!" This was to be followed after a break by a talk from Clive Sinclair on the difficulties of staying six months ahead with his new inventions, in this case a tiny pocket-sized TV. As the smallest television set anyone had seen to date was a heavy monster needing its own stand, such an invention sounded really revolutionary. When we got up for the break I talked to the man who had been sitting beside me and seemed to know a lot about the little set when suddenly he whisked one out of his pocket and waved it at me. I realised I had been speaking to Clive Sinclair himself, and only hope I didn't sound too non-technical for his bright mind. I'm always surprised when I meet one of these icons to find they are just ordinary people like the rest of us!

A week later we delivered Susan to Newnham for the start of her three years at Cambridge. One fledged and one more to go...

18

SCD, HF and KT

After an absence from Scottish Country Dancing for several years we were getting withdrawal symptoms. Somebody suggested we try the little class in nearby Chorleywood, which met on an evening we were free. We enjoyed it and stayed with them for a while. They would go en masse to Amersham for the bi-monthly dances that would be held there, and we joined them for the next one. Entering the room full of bright lights and people all dressed in their best, lots of kilts and tartan sashes, a lively accordion band tuning up, we were somewhat overawed, but the dance itself was just great. During the evening we were approached by one of the host club members who told us their normal weekly club night was on a Thursday and we would be made very welcome if free then. Some months later we were indeed free so joined them, and later on stopped going to Chorleywood which seemed so dull in comparison. It was suggested we would enjoy a special dance at Porchester Hall in London, so off we went, not realising this was many levels above our ability at that time. The top Scottish Country Dance band of the time, Jim MacLeod, was playing and many of the dances were ones we had not heard of and hadn't been able to try out. There were well over a hundred dancers, the men in dress kilts with Prince Charlie jackets and the girls in long dresses. It was a most glittering occasion, but frightened the life out of us. Now, years later, we attend such functions with no qualms, and are conscious of the new people creeping around at the back of the hall feeling like we used to.

After sampling the Ramblers Association house at Hassness, we tried one of their overseas holidays, choosing Corfu for a gentle spring walking holiday. This had been very successful, especially as we were there just after our Easter but just before the Greek Easter which is such a special time for them. We had a lovely leader who looked after us exceptionally well, and made sure we saw as much as possible. So we decided to go with Ramblers again, this time to Tenerife in May based at Puerto de la Cruz followed by a second week in Palma. The leader this time, Ted, who was flying out with us didn't make himself known until our arrival when we discovered we were a tiny party of just him and six others. Ted had only picked up the instructions as he boarded the aircraft and had spent the flight trying to discover where he was supposed to take us, not having been there before. He was at a great disadvantage and really had no hope of leading a successful holiday. It turned out he was a senior civil servant, heading up one part of an Inland Revenue fraud team that tracked down seriously big tax evaders. He himself was divorced, paying a huge maintenance to his ex wife, and spent his working life watching all the slippery fraudsters getting away with millions while he toed the line himself. Not surprisingly he had become a miserable fellow where leading a walking holiday of this sort should have been a nice opportunity to escape and enjoy it. Unfortunately he couldn't shake off his unhappy mood, so passed it all on to us which was not at all what we wanted. Looking around at the other members of the party, there was one elderly man who was stone deaf and trotted along happily at the rear of the group, but was not able to take part socially. There was a young couple, dedicated walkers with no apparent interests apart from tramping along behind the person in front. They walked unaware of the countryside around them, their only topic of conversation being boots, boots and more boots. Then there was a very pleasant middle-aged man on his own who'd come at short notice 'to get away from the stress'. It transpired he was a Harley Street psychiatrist and halfway through the holiday he felt he was going round the bend and returned home. That just left Ted, the leader. So, not a very inspiring group. Ted's problems were magnified by the constraints he felt were placed upon him by way of keeping to his budget come hell or high water. It involved depending on local buses none of which went anywhere near reasonable walking areas. Clearly the holiday had been poorly researched and we felt he had been badly let down by headquarters and didn't stand a chance. His final problem was that he spoke the Castilian version of Spanish with all that lisping, something the Canary Islands people couldn't understand, so communications with the locals was virtually non-existent. On Tenerife we quickly discovered the sun goes behind clouds that gather around the top of Mount Teide soon after breakfast, so most of our walks on the north side of the island in the region of Puerto de la Crux were in the shade. Our hotel was an older building on three floors surrounded by huge high rise hotels all under construction. A smell of cement dust hung over the town even masking the smell of camel leather from the 'gift' shops and suntan oil emanating from most of the tourists. Constant noise filled the town, but thankfully this died away in the evening and stayed quiet until crack of dawn next morning. The hotel had a pool on top of the restaurant wing surrounded by chairs all occupied most of the time by grotesquely overweight Germans.

Most of the walks were rather ordinary through banana plantations or similar, not really what I would call walking country. But we did have one or two highlights. One was when we took a rickety bus halfway up the mountain then struggled on foot through the cloud amongst trees enveloped in wispy Spanish moss to emerge

8,000 feet up on top of the plateau, Las Cañadas, a moonscape of red volcanic rock ten miles across, with the level rim of the crater several hundred feet higher all round, except for the volcanic peak of Teide which soared a further 2,000 feet on one side. This was wonderful, with cool fresh air and brilliant sun. We had hoped to take the cable car to the top of Teide from where all the other islands in the Canaries were reputed to be visible, but discovered it had been out of action for many weeks. So we set off across the wastes, the red dust sticking to all the damp bits we'd picked up on the way up, and in my case with the sole of one of my boots flapping with each step where it had become detached at the front. Striding towards us came a tall young man, the only living being in that entire wilderness. We stopped and exchanged a few words. He was immaculately turned out with the finest hiking gear, highly polished boots (how did he manage that in the dust?), a pair of Zeiss binoculars and a Leica camera around his neck. He looked down at our scruffy little group in that slightly supercilious way that Herr Flick of 'Allo 'Allo fame employed to survey the customers in Rene's café. He was German, of course, but spoke beautiful English without a trace of an accent. As we parted someone asked him where he was off to next. He glanced about him.

"I shall walk around the rim," he replied grandly, looking up at Teide, "and take the mountain at dusk."

We hoped for better things on the island of Palma but it was not to be. Even more did we depend on the local bus service to get to and from any walking areas, and were utterly stuck when the bus company went on strike, scuppering all Ted's plans. He tried various walks that looked all right on his somewhat inadequate map, but due to the steep-sided barrencos radiating out from the central mountain we were constrained to walking either up or down them through impenetrable scrub, and as he wasn't too good at his map reading we often found ourselves walking the wrong way. Eventually he gave in to our insistence that we hire taxis to take us through a tunnel into the central crater, a magically different world of thick verdant forest, bright sunshine and some lovely tracks to walk along with views right across the Caldera de Taburiente. That was good, but poor Ted was beside himself with worry that he'd overspent! When we crossed the runway to board our aircraft for the flight home we wore our anoraks, since the temperature that day was only about 12°C and overcast. The cheery British Airways hostess stared at us from the top of the steps and called out "You won't need those at home. We're having a heatwave there!"

I wrote to Ramblers telling them about the dreadful holiday to be told that it must have been my fault, since no one else had complained. That was the final straw and we didn't travel with them again for many years.

~*~

Then it was back to work. I had much more to do with large projects now, since I had an engineering project planning group to look after. The Company needed to expand its labour-intensive film finishing business and had been looking for premises in a low labour cost area. They'd taken an option on a new site in Milton Keynes but then found somewhere even better near Nottingham. Two hundred acres of farmland just off the M1 between junction 27 and the village of Annesley Woodhouse had been designated for light industry, and was available at a very reasonable cost. Kodak bought a chunk of it and was able to clinch a deal with a large motorway construction company to create two level ten-acre areas on this undulating site. This fitted in well with the contractors who would otherwise have had their earth moving machinery idle for some months, so we had it done at a modest cost. The intention was to put up a large warehouse-type building on part of one of the level areas with room to expand, and in due course let off the other. We also had to provide the infrastructure, roads, car parks, a sewerage plant, gas and electricity. It was all great fun for the project boys and interesting for me to be involved with the planning. This site is in a coal mining area on the edge of Sherwood Forest (though Robin Hood would never recognise it!), so the building design had to allow for possible subsidence one day, with jacking points below the walls.

The local inhabitants in Annesley were very wary about all this work going on half a mile from their village even though it was out of sight in a dip, so we put on a public relations exercise to reassure them. There was a public right of way running through the site which would need to be moved to one side, consequently the local Ramblers Association took an interest. Since the M1 had been built the right of way no longer led anywhere, but that didn't stop the Ramblers' representative objecting. We explained we would build a new path with proper foundations and attractive planting which would run through a far better part of the area to replace the somewhat soggy unused track that went through a squelchy osier bed, but that wouldn't appease them. At the public meeting for Annesley residents, many of whom were unemployed due to the closure of several coalmines, this issue was raised along with employment opportunities to come. The residents liked the idea of a pleasant path and the Ramblers reluctantly acquiesced. We also had to keep the local trout fishermen happy, for the stream that meandered through the site then fed a fishing lake half a mile further on, and we intended to move the stream and create another lake needed as a fire fighting water reservoir, also the effluent from our sewerage plant would run back into the stream. This all worked out extremely well, the sewerage effluent was channelled through a purpose-designed reedbed which cleaned the water so well that it was purer than before, and water flow could be better controlled. Everyone was happy. I paid several visits to Annesley, initially stumbling about in the mud in my wellies and a hard hat, then later when the facility was up and running I would go to the occasional meeting there, staying for lunch to enjoy the mushy peas that seem to be the speciality of those parts. This was a fine example of the way in which Kodak did its best to work with the local people (many of whom would join the company payroll) and the modest cost of so doing would be amply repaid by loyal and contented employees.

Paul had passed his 'O' levels fairly well, and spent several weeks working with Pye Dynamics, later to become Graseby Dynamics, in Watford, work relevant to his interests which he enjoyed. He'd had several driving lessons and a couple of tests which he failed. The driving instructor said this did tend to happen with her teenage male pupils, maybe because the examiner thought they'd be too immature to drive safely once they were let loose on their own. Next time he took the test it was in our new car with only fifty miles on the clock and still smelling of the showroom. The examiner was probably so impressed Paul had been thought fit by his father to use it that he passed at last. He'd approached Southampton and Bristol universities about reading electronic engineering. Both wanted quite high 'A' level passes. Newcastle was a less-preferred choice, but they did at least offer him a place and seemed keen. Then we had a lucky break. Patricia had taken her mother along to a small drinks 'do' in the next road, began talking to someone about which university would offer the best degree course for Paul and was pointed in the direction of a man on the far side of the room who was only too pleased to chat about this, especially when Patricia explained that Paul was dead keen on joining the design department of the BBC. She listened while the man expounded on the pros and cons of virtually every university degree course, then went on to say that the BBC Engineering Department had their own preferences, and quite favoured the course offered by Liverpool University. He finished by saying "Why don't you get your son to ask for an informal interview with the Engineering Recruitment Officer to hear what he would recommend, rather than take my word for it. Would you like me to arrange it?" It turned out Patricia had been talking to the then BBC Education Correspondent, David Smeeton.

The very next day there was a phone call from the BBC. When would it be convenient to come and see the Recruitment Officer? A few days later Paul had his informal chat and was indeed recommended to go to Liverpool. They said they would put the notes from the discussion on file and when he applied to join the BBC after his degree, it would be helpful to him that they had that record. He came away with a strong impression they liked what they saw and would do all they could to help him. Good news indeed, and this gave him lots of confidence. When he applied to Liverpool, he was accepted subject to reasonable 'A' level results, which he worked hard to get.

Our visit to St. Mawes that year found my father very shaky and not really able to cope on his own. He insisted he was all right, but the state of the house was dreadful—it took two days to get it clean and shipshape again. We contacted the social services who organised a home help to come in twice a week. Was this the beginning of the end perhaps? All his village friends rallied round when they heard he was not well and from then on he had lots of visitors. During the Christmas break I decided to fit in an extra visit to St. Mawes and took Susan with me. We had a pleasant run down together, the first time we'd been on our own and able to chat for such a long time. We found father now being well looked after and in good spirits and we enjoyed a lovely few days. Lots of the residents had little parties that we went along to. Then, the day before we were due to drive back and were out walking on Nare Head the temperature began to plummet. Unusually for Cornwall, we felt really cold and hurried back to crumpets and tea by the fire. In the evening the wind got up and it seemed we might be in for one of those damaging gales. But I awoke in the morning to a silent scene, snow piled up to windowsill height where it had blown around the corner of the house. All was quiet now, the sun shining on a sight I had never before witnessed in Cornwall. There was no question of setting off in this; we soon discovered the blizzard had resulted in four-foot drifts in many places all along the only road from St. Mawes. The village was marooned until a snowplough could get through. Did the Cornwall County Council even possess a snowplough? In the event we were stuck there for three extra days during which we went for lots of walks in the snow. The local children had never seen snow before, and nor had many of the older people. Several elderly folk living on their own would be unable to go out, for all the paths and roads were untreated, the steep hill down to the village especially difficult to negotiate. We called on Charles Pears' widow who still lived in the studio down on Percuil Creek, but she said she had no need to leave the house for several days. One or two people coped extremely well by putting a pair of old socks over their shoes thus providing a good non-slip grip. And then on the third day a small farm tractor came chugging down the road pulling a tiny agricultural broadcast seed sower modified to scatter rock salt at the rate of one speck every foot or so. Surprisingly, it worked. By the end of the day other vehicles had got through and next morning Susan and I set off. The main road as far as Exeter had just one lane open, but there was little traffic and we had an uneventful trip home. St. Mawes took a long time to recover from that cold snap. Many gardens had sad losses amongst their tropical plants, the full effects not becoming apparent until the summer. Back at home the cold weather lasted a couple of months.

One day at the end of May I received a phone call out of the blue from one of my friends.

"Is Susan all right?" was his anxious enquiry."

"So far as I know," I replied. "Why?"

"The accident sounded dreadful. I wondered how badly she was injured." At that point he realised he had heard something we hadn't. It had been on the News and in his morning Telegraph neither of which we'd heard or read. Anxiously we phoned Newnham and eventually they found Sue who sounded a bit surprised we'd rung. She assured us she'd just hurt an ankle. In the meantime I'd bought a copy of The Daily Telegraph and read the full story. Six undergraduates had been returning from a meeting at Girton College, which is some three miles out of town, all on their bikes cycling in single file since it is a fairly narrow road, very dark, and there was some modest traffic. A Trinity College undergraduate driving a car and in no fit state to be at the wheel managed to hit five of them, all of whom were injured to some extent or other. One poor lad had serious injuries and a pierced lung from which he died shortly after. The emergency services were soon on the scene, with Sue in addition to trying to help the others also finding herself comforting the WPC who was attending her first RTA, and who was extremely distressed at all the blood. The paper had reported the names of all those involved. When we went to collect Sue at the end of term we discovered her injuries had been far worse than she'd admitted. She had been hobbling about on crutches (actually a wonderfully fast way of progressing as I discovered) right up until the previous day, her bike was a write-off but otherwise she was by now mending well. But no more cycling; a definite disadvantage in a bike-oriented city like Cambridge. She had originally gone up to Cambridge to read Natural Sciences, some of her lectures being joint ones with the medical faculty, and so had met a number of medics. To our surprise and delight she'd changed her subject and was now reading medicine herself, reckoning there would be far more social intercourse through being a doctor, and her accident where she had to succour several injured people, reinforced her conviction that this was the way she wanted to go. However, it would mean going on to medical school after Cambridge, a somewhat lengthier route to becoming fully qualified.

Along with a motley collection of others I had been nominated to attend a course in problem solving being run by an American company, Kepner-Tregoe. It was a technique that had been introduced at Kodak's parent company in America. Some Kodak Limited managers had attended an acquaint course in Hemel Hempstead and decided they should introduce a pilot over here. It turned out to be a five-day course at a conference hotel in Beaconsfield run jointly by the boss of Kepner-Tregoe's British branch and a KT instructor from America. It involved homework every evening until midnight and was exhaustingly intensive. I understood the concepts, but didn't really latch on to how it might affect me in my current job. Like many such management courses, I never followed it through with practising anything new, and in a few months I'd forgotten most of it.

In the meantime we felt like another walking holiday, but not with Ramblers, so we decided to take the plunge and try HF, plumping for a week at their Scarborough centre which offered fairly low grade walks and would be a new area for us. On the way we spent half a day in York, walked the walls, climbed to the top of the Minster tower and paid a visit to the wonderful Castle museum which was the first such 'living' museum we'd been to. We were met at the HF house by a gushing hostess* with really powerful lungs. In her other life she was the manageress of an old people's home, so was well suited to look after us! The guests were mostly older than us, quite a few of them appreciably so, but certainly fit. The food was marvellous, huge amounts of it eaten to the accompaniment of 65 lusty voices all yelling flat out. Memories of my weekend at Gomershall for the writers' course came back. Down on the front at Scarborough we met hordes of holidaymakers and the stench of chips and vinegar, so didn't stay there long—after our huge supper it made us feel slightly ill! Later that evening we danced for an hour or two in the centre's ballroom before retiring to bed exhausted. Next day was the traditional introductory day, short walks morning and afternoon with a big house lunch in between. Our main leader that

---

*HF used to nominate one of the leaders, generally one who was more into socialising than walking, as the 'host' or 'hostess' for the week. That person, in addition to leading one of the slower walks, would organise and lead the events that took place back at the house after supper every evening.

week was a stocky 73-year old Yorkshireman, Rex Bradburn, known by most of the ladies there as 'sexy Rex'. As both Patricia and I were only nearing our half-century, we naturally assumed we'd have no problem keeping up with an old fellow like Rex, but we were innocents from the soft south, unused to wiry Yorkshire folk. However, by the end of the week we were quite fit and managed to cope with the top-grade party each day. (HF normally run up to three grades of walk from each centre, High or Long at one extreme and Low or Short for the older ones with dicky tickers at the other. It all works very well, especially if one half of a couple has different abilities to the other). Most of the walks were 11 to 14 miles and we went to such areas as Kirbymoorside and across Spaunton Moor to Lastingham, Falling Foss via Fylingdales Moor to Grosmont, and the coastal path to Whitby. Every evening there was either dancing or house party games culminating on the last night with a concert party, activities we thought we'd never get used to. When we first heard about this, our immediate impulse was to creep up to our room with a good book, but eventually we came to enjoy these shenanigans. The culture shock had just been too much for us to cope with initially. However, we enjoyed the HF experience sufficiently to want to try another of their centres, so booked up for a week at the Lyme Regis one.

This next holiday had many similarities to Scarborough in that we had the same knockabout evening entertainments, wonderful food but not such good accommodation for we had been put in an annexe—in this case a tiny room in a wooden chalet behind the main house. The walks from Lyme were nearly all coastal ones, and during that week we walked most of the South West Coastal Path between Bridport and Exmouth, with one inland walk, all of it in lovely country in a week of good summer weather. These were linear walks with the advantage of being dropped off at the start and collected from the finish.

A week or two later I was crossing the Kodak car park when I met my divisional boss coming the other way. We stopped and chatted.

"We're thinking of extending the Kepner-Tregoe problem-solving techniques throughout the Company and will need to indoctrinate upwards of 400 managers. How would you like to be one of the instructors?"

"Sounds great," I said warily, "I haven't actually lectured before, you know."

"I've heard you've given presentations once or twice and come over very well."

"Mmm. Those would have been on engineering subjects with an audience of engineers."

"The three of you will have to attend the full indoctrination course first."

"Who are the others?

"Bill Warren from the Film Finishing Department, and Dave Pavitt from Paper Finishing, both technologists. It would be a nice balance to have the third one from Engineering."

"Can I think about it?"

"Over the weekend, then? I need to know very soon."

"OK." I started to move on. He called after me, "Oh, by the way, the indoctrination course starts in a week or so… In America."

I had one week to get my passport updated and an American visa, and would be away three weeks. The day after I left, Paul was due to start at Liverpool University. Patricia, who hadn't yet driven our new car on her own would have to drive him there and come back by herself. Not the most confident person in charge of a car, I believe she was more worried about that than about me disappearing across the Atlantic!

At Kodak we frequently had visitors from the parent Company, also some key jobs were given to Americans, as indeed some key parent Company jobs were given to British managers, so during my Kodak time I had met a number of American people. Now I would have an opportunity to visit their country and experience the culture for myself. Not only that, but I was going with two friends one of whom, Bill Warren, had been before and knew the ropes. It was an exciting prospect.

This was my first such business visit, and considerably different from travelling at my own expense. Rather like the weekend rail trips from Rosyth back to Gosport when I would either slum it in a second class compartment or sleep between laundered sheets in first class depending on who was paying, so it was with the flight. It started with a black limo arriving at the door to take me to Heathrow where I checked in BA Club class and met up with Bill and David. One of David's neighbours was a BA pilot who had given him a letter to hand on to whoever was piloting our 747, asking for us to be allowed to visit the flight deck on the way across. We hoped this might be possible.

It was indeed. One of the airhostesses collected us and we went 'upstairs' to the swanky first class area, big upholstered seats, lots of room, whisper quiet and only one or two passengers who eyed us warily. Passing through the door at the front we found ourselves on the cramped flight deck, instruments everywhere, and lots of questions to ask. I was intrigued to discover there would be about 70 tons of fuel used on the trip, which explained why such a flight is so expensive. Our takeoff had been immediately after Concorde's, the sound of her huge engines at full throttle deafening us even inside our sound-insulated cabin as we waited on the tarmac right behind her. Now, up on the flight deck several hours after takeoff, our captain pointed up to where the unmistakeable sight of that same Concorde 10,000 feet immediately above us could be seen on her way back, having refuelled at JFK and taken on a new load of passengers. She would be turning round for yet another flight before we had even landed.

We had been booked in for a couple of nights at the Holiday Inn hotel across the Hudson River in New Jersey. The hire car that took us was straight out of some gangster movie, the driver a huge gum-chewing man in a greasy suit who dropped our puny suitcases into the cavernous boot of his enormous Lincoln. I remarked that the car's 'trunk' would be big enough for us as well.

"Yeah," came the response, "Room for six stiffs in there."

Somewhat uneasily I was pushed into the front seat beside him while the others spread out in the back. The driver kept up a running commentary over the radio to his base, which advised him on the best route to attempt through town. Passing a couple of New York cops with arms hanging down by their sides, presumably ready to snatch a gun should it be needed, he said that if there was trouble they'd turn and run faster than anyone. Obviously there was no respectful opinion of the Law here! The hotel was absolutely ghastly; no welcome of course, thoroughly rundown, dirty, and positioned in the middle of what looked like a brown field desert. Crossing this were a couple of busy expressways and a railroad on which huge Sante Fé-type trains with giant braying sirens trundled past at frequent intervals. Numerous smaller roads criss-crossed this waste area and the noise of it all came straight through the walls into my room. As there was no fresh air in the room I tried putting on the air conditioning unit, but that made a sound as though it was full of loose bits of metal and wailed like the wind in the rigging of a sailing ship, but at least that partly drowned out the racket coming in from outside. It was going to be a sleepless night.

But even if we felt it was bedtime, here in New York the time was only 4.30 p.m. so although it was a gloomy, rainy Friday evening we decided to take a bus into Manhattan to have a quick look round. Standing at the bus stop was an individual who expressed surprise that anyone would want to go into New York at this time, saying, "Everyone else is trying to get to hell out." We alighted at East 42nd Street, not the most salubrious area to start in. It was quite the filthiest street I had ever seen, dirt everywhere, dirty people, dirty sex shops, dirty buildings and dirty rain when it came. We had a look at Kodak's huge panoramic picture in grand Central Station which they put up there, changing it every few weeks. This is a backlit transparency about sixty feet wide, and quite a difficult thing to make. We grabbed a rather nasty meal of sorts, then with beefy rugger-player Bill walking behind us for safety since we had to negotiate a no-go area of town, we eventually found a taxi for the trip back. The driver checked we'd locked the door as soon as we were inside.

Back in my hotel room I discovered the external wall was a thin cladding outside with an internal partition inside, so no wonder every sound came through. The bathroom had foul tasting water, so I had to search around for some drinking water, eventually being reduced to collecting a jug of ice from a rattly machine in the corridor outside. The bath plug didn't fit, the shower didn't function properly and none of the towels supplied were bigger than a table napkin. Three of the four lights in my room did not work and the door lock stuck. All through the night police sirens wailed as some chase or other swept across the wasteland outside. I checked the time every half hour from 8.30 (when I fell into bed) till 6.30 next morning when I got up. This was my low ebb, and from now on everything got better.

We met up in a little bar downstairs which produced coffee and eggs sunny side up, and a bright cheerful little waitress who welcomed us. It was Saturday. All the people left in New York seemed to be there on holiday and the sun was shining. We decided to take the Circle boat tour around Manhattan Island, a proper tourist trip. The day was perfect for photography as we went down the Hudson as far as the Statue of Liberty, then up the East River and round the top along the Harlem River. Twenty-five miles of unforgettable, unique sightseeing. Our informative commentator never dried up: "If you get tired of looking at buildings, there's usually something interesting floating by in the water…" Everyone looked over the side half expecting to see a dead body, and as we arrived back at the jetty, "Make sure you haven't left anything behind—coats, cameras, children…"

Back on shore we walked and walked. From 6th Avenue we walked as far as Central Park and into a land of joggers, horse buggies, cyclists, roller skaters and power walkers. We then traversed the length of 6th and into 5th Avenue to the Empire State Building, which, of course, we had to go to the top of (more photographs). On the way down in one of the huge lifts that drop from the 80th floor to street level, the indicator showing every ten floors, some thirty of us all standing spaced apart as one does in a lift full of strangers, mesmerised by the indicator which, incredulously, went 80, 70, 60, 50, in as many seconds with all of us thinking to ourselves just how fast we must be falling and would we stop in time, when a man at the back said, "My God, Mary, do you realise the contract for this elevator went to the lowest bidder!"

We then walked on down to Greenwich Village, the buildings getting tattier as we left the midtown skyscraper area. Here we found a whole new atmosphere, like Chelsea used to be only more free and easy. Strangers chatted to one another and to us, we had a great meal and sat around for a while before walking up to East 41st and the bus back to the horrible hotel. This had been a really super day and an unbelievable contrast to the night before. It just shows what one's mood can do to one's perception.

We checked out in the morning, now recovered from the jet lag, for an internal flight to Buffalo. As we waited in the hotel foyer for our car I got chatting to a man up from Miami and remarked on the two pistols I could see protruding from the hip pocket of a New York cop who was talking to the reception clerk.

"Now there's something we don't have at home," I commented.

"Your don't? Gee, I wouldn't be without my gun. No way!"

"Do you have it with you?" I asked, edging away a bit.

"Nope. Not allowed in New York. It's in the glove box of my car, back at Miami airport."

I was thinking this was a very different country to home, and the worrying thing was that whatever happens in America seems to arrive in Britain a few years later. Certainly all the things I saw that weekend in New York can now be seen in London, and is one reason I very seldom go there even though it is only half an hour away by train.

At Buffalo we took another hire car to the Niagara Falls area where we were to spend the next two weeks incarcerated in a pleasant hotel on the banks of the mighty Niagara River, about three miles above the Falls. What a change! It was clean, friendly and welcoming. The reception desk was manned by college students working to pay off their student fees, and they couldn't have been nicer. My room was huge, had a super outlook and the food was excellent. All the plumbing and electrics worked. I would be happy here for a few weeks. This was shortly after some guests were trapped in a hotel that caught fire elsewhere in the States due to a fire escape door being padlocked, so the first thing I did was to explore the place to ensure there was a way out. Sure enough, I followed the escape route down to street level and, clambering over a lot of junk that had been piled there, found this fire door also locked. I tipped off one of the student reception girls about it and about three days later it was grudgingly cleared.

We settled down to a concentrated work session starting each day at nine with a break at five'ish. Then we knuckled down once more from after supper (which tends to be no later than 6.30 in the States) until midnight. In addition to the three of us Brits there was one from Eastman Tennessee, two from Kodak Colorado, and four from Kodak's main plant at Rochester. Our two instructors were the same two who taught me in England, Brian Bentley, the English manager of KT (UK) and Tom, the man from the KT headquarters in Princeton, New Jersey. We each introduced ourselves, the man from Tennessee explaining in a lovely Southern drawl, "My name's Don Boy….d. Down in Tennessee….ee we may speak slow, but we don't think slow….w". For some reason they all loved my English accent and sat entranced, not listening to a word I said but just enjoying the way I said it. A bit disconcerting, that.

In case you might wonder how it could possibly take two long weeks to teach us how to run a course, a luxury no school teacher would enjoy, KT realised we had to overcome a difficulty with all such management courses: that of having to indoctrinate seasoned managers and supervisors in a new technique which they think is irrelevant; only being there because their bosses have told them to come. Therefore we had to start with an exercise that would motivate them by showing how the technique would solve a problem they couldn't solve using their current skills. In short, we would teach by stealth; not easy with a roomful of managers who think they know it all, otherwise they wouldn't be managers, would they?

Actually, we were teaching several techniques: to solve problems, where something has gone wrong and we don't know why. This would be the case with such people as diagnosticians, maintenance men, and—yes, even managers. The next technique usually follows on from that: now that the cause of the problem has been found, what to do about it? What decision do we make? The whole rationale of decision-making would then be taught. That then led on to the next one, ensuring a decision made can be kept to, by forestalling any little problems that may occur in the future, an essential tool for engineers planning projects or marketing people planning a product launch. In between there were all those little skills like asking questions in such a way that the right answers come forth. Amazingly, none of these techniques seemed to have been taught formally before, people getting on with their managing simply by the seat of their pants. When it came to the asking questions bit and it was my turn to practice teaching this to the others I was able to recount my own experience about being quizzed by Prince Philip in the wardroom mess at HMS Drake, which happened to be extremely relevant to the techniques we were learning. This went down ever so well, since all Americans seem to be potty about our Royalty. I suppose they themselves would never get within a mile of their own President. They simply didn't believe that occasion when David Attenborough who was covering a Buckingham Palace reception for the BBC documentary 'Royalty' at the time, stepped back onto President Reagan's foot, whereupon Reagan as the true professional said 'sorry' and leapt out of the way of David and his film crew. They thought we were making it up. In the lectures on the analysis of potential problems—that is, ensuring problems don't occur in the first place—we worked through a mythical situation when we wished to ensure nothing could go wrong with an occasion when the Queen was asked to open some new building. We had to list every detail that might go wrong and suggest what could be done to ensure it didn't. One of the Americans came up with "The Queen's carriage gets a flat". Bill's response to this was to say icily "The Queen's carriage is a Rolls Royce, and Rolls Royces don't get flats."

These management courses tend to take place in a room with tables arranged in a 'U', with the course director and his easel or screen across the top of the U, the participants sitting around the outside. The course director can then walk around inside the U while speaking. This is reckoned to be more intimate and friendly. One tip I well remember was how to deal with the chattering participant who won't shut up, the solution being to perch on the table right in front of the offender with your back towards him. Our mentor tried this out on one or two people and it worked perfectly. I've used that trick in my own lecturing and it never fails.

Most days in our lunch break we rushed off to a fast food place, a new experience for me and one I have never wished to indulge in since that time. We piled into someone's car and drove a few miles. Nobody walked, since there was nothing much within easy walking distance. In the evenings we had a couple of hours to explore a bit more. Once or twice we went down to Goat Island, separating the two main Falls. This is a sizable park where some of the men went jogging while David Pavitt and myself walked to the edge of the Falls and looked over the many viewpoints at the noisy cauldron beneath. I wasn't expecting the Niagara river itself which, for the several miles leading to the Falls is dropping more than a hundred feet and is several hundred feet wide, to be so silent. All the noise comes when that mass of water hits the bottom. We could feel the effect of this wherever we walked on Goat Island with the ground trembling beneath our feet. Some power there.

Towards the end of our course we celebrated by going across the bridge downstream of the Falls to the Canadian side for a hilarious meal out at a German restaurant called The Happy Wanderer. We sat at one large table, drank copious amounts of beer with the occasional schnapps, enjoyed a good meal and everyone told their favourite stories. Brian Bentley was on good form with lots of Irish jokes told in an Irish accent, then a whole lot more told in a Birmingham accent which sent the Americans into hoots of laughter. Some of the Americans were slow with their jokes but laughed at ours. I tried one in Cornish, but that foxed everybody including my English mates, so I attempted upper crust English ones which they seemed to like, ending with a particularly naughty one I'd learnt in the Navy. Afterwards as we were leaving, a lady from a nearby table came up to me and said "You're English, aren't you? We're from Stanmore." I only hoped she hadn't heard the final punchline of my last story…

On the last day we went once again to the Canadian side, walked along the river bank to the point where the Niagara disappears over the edge, then had dinner in the Skylon restaurant, perched a few hundred feet up in the air on a slender stalk. It was my 50th birthday and a lovely way to celebrate it.

The three Kodak Limited members had been told to take some extra days whilst over in the States to visit our opposite numbers at Eastman Kodak in Rochester. Rochester is about a hundred miles away, and we got there in a hire car, taking the scenic route through Buffalo and on down the side of Lake Erie for some miles before turning east and stopping at Letchworth State Park, a picturesque area of woods and rivers. The sun shone, it was at the height of the 'fall' with wonderful colours everywhere, the scenery magnificent. We stayed at the Canandaigna Sheraton for the night, a swish, expensive country hotel right on the lakeside. Next day was spent exploring the area around the Finger Lakes. We stopped at Naples with its colonial style clapboard houses and toured a winery, explored a nature reserve and saw the appalling desecration that results from dam-building exploits of beavers (heavens knows why somebody wants to import beavers into Britain). Next day we went on to Rochester and checked in at the Marriott, an over-the-top upmarket business hotel which was to be our base for a couple of days before flying home. That evening we were invited by one of Bill's opposite numbers to their home, a huge timber house in a forest. Their fridge was the size of a large wardrobe, and the drinks four times more powerful than I could really cope with. The meal was super, the meat being barbecued outside and brought indoors when ready. They told us what it was like in winter when snow would lie five feet deep (which was why the house was built high, with steps up to the front door).

The day after was spent in the factory, in stuffy conference rooms, touring around, meeting people, and getting a headache. However, we escaped eventually for an evening with one of the men who'd been on the course with us, a lovely relaxing evening with a delightful family. They had a huge family room in the basement with a lounge, diner and kitchen above. This time it was barbecued chicken cooked in the 'back yard' and brought in for the meal inside. On the final day we three split up and I spent it with an international liaison manager with whom I had corresponded and spoken on the phone over the years. He wanted me to try and get some sense out of our neighbours, the French, whom they found extremely difficult to get to tow the line. I had to decline, admitting that we, too, had difficulty with them. This French attitude that I had thought was directed only against the English was almost certainly one reason why they were disliked the other side of the Pond. I wonder whom they blame? I had a lovely day, ending with a guided tour of the whole factory by car (it is several miles from one end to the other and even has its own railroad). I flew from Rochester to Toronto where I picked up an overnight Air Canada flight home.

~*~

Back at Kodak in Harrow the three of us then moved into another building and were seconded to a Personnel Department where we set about designing our own course, which we would give initially as a threesome, dropping to a two-handed one after a few sessions. We would spend one week teaching followed by a week preparing for the next one, until we'd taught all four hundred people due to partake. It was expected to last over a year, quite a chunk out of my Kodak time.

I found the job of instructing to be very much to my liking. Incredible as it may seem I'd never done anything remotely like this before, never had to stand up in front of a group of people except for being a sort of mandatory figurehead—the bloke 'in charge'—such as on parade in the Royal Navy. Sure, I'd chaired the odd small meeting, but nothing more. My baptism, I suppose, was when I jumped onto the table at the unofficial Union meeting in my workshop all those years ago when they were as surprised as I was to find myself up there. Teaching was something very different: I had a roomful of competent professional people who, after the first couple of hours, realised they needed something I was able to provide. It was wonderfully satisfying having at my fingertips the means for providing it. I suppose it is power one is wielding and it gives one a 'high'.

As the KT techniques spread through the Company, people started using various KT ways of describing what they had done or would do. For example, when submitting requests to the States for large capital expenditures, one of the options would be what KT called 'do nothing', in other words to get round the need for this expenditure in some other way such as putting on an extra shift rather than increase the capacity of the plant. Accountants airily discussed these options with their counterparts in America and discovered they all understood so much better. Engineers and technologists, who tended to be the ones at the coalface who first recognise the need to spend money, found that if they expressed their requirements in the KT form, they were better comprehended by our local management. For the first time we were all speaking the same language. Especially fruitful was to invite accountants and senior managers along to early development sessions, after which everyone was on the same side. In between running courses the three of us were being approached by people to help them through the defining stages of initiating a new project: we were hired as 'facilitators', a role new at that time. It didn't stop within the Company. Bill spent a weekend with a group of volunteers responsible for the work of one of the big charities. They had huge funds coming in and didn't really have a clear idea how best to utilise them. Bill had them all sitting round the table defining what it was they wanted to achieve, then designing how best to achieve it, the basic type of 'decision analysis' module that KT taught. His audience were delighted at how successful this was, and he was prevailed upon more than once to repeat the process with other organisations.

I quickly found that in my teaching weeks I'd seldom arrive home until after ten, thus scuppering all our social life. I could see this was going to be extremely disruptive, and it seemed unfair on poor Patricia who was on her own so much. However, looking back it was the best part of my time at Kodak and I wouldn't have missed it for worlds.

19

A Break From KT

Our Scottish Country Dancing had quietly advanced. Gone were the days when we crept into the Amersham hall to congregate at the bottom of the room, hoping our mistakes wouldn't be noticed by all the competent dancers who tended to avoid sets like ours. Most of these 'competent' dancers had drifted off. Now it was ourselves who were considered competent by the new people who had joined. We took our place at the top of the room. We had a new teacher, Wesley Harry; no Scotsman himself but with a Scottish wife and several grownup children one of whom had cultured a Scottish accent so pronounced I doubt whether Wesley himself could understand it that well. Wesley had been a teacher for much of his life with that rare gift of a good teacher—that of putting himself in the place of his students, and choosing his words to match their comprehension. Oh, that some hugely clever people who live on a higher plane were able to do likewise; how much we would all learn sitting at their feet! Wesley managed to teach Scottish Country Dancing to everybody who came along, the only exception being those folk who seem incapable of listening. Unfortunately we had a few of them; people who had been coming to the club since it was founded in the '50s, and still couldn't remember anything much. They didn't mind since they mainly came for the social side, but it was a confounded nuisance when too many of them got into the set we danced in with the probability they'd mess it up. The trouble was we'd discovered the enormous pleasure to be had from dancing to perfection, after which knocking about any old how seemed far less satisfying. Not that we managed to achieve perfection very often, but we strived to do so. It all started when we attended a Day School—an extended one-day event of quality teaching for dancers as distinct from beginners. There would be a formal class morning and afternoon, some sort of cabaret turn in the early evening ending with a full-blown dance later in the evening. Often this would be combined with a Day School for musicians, who'd spend their day rehearsing with a professional band, finishing by playing with them at the evening dance.

The first of these we attended was a small affair put on by our own club for our own members, with an imported teacher, dancing to records. After that we attended a school at Reading with classes covering several different levels of ability. One of the best-known London bandleaders played solo accordion for the classes at this one and brought his complete band along for the evening dance. Over the years we attended several of these, meeting some of the top gurus and musicians, watching wonderful displays all of which were danced flawlessly. The occasional snip one sees on television is not at all the same as the real thing seen close up.

Many of the dancing clubs within reach of Watford would put on a special Ball once a year, so we went along to these. I'd kept my old Naval mess undress uniform, the one with a 'bum-freezer' jacket, and by the simple expedient of taking off the gold stripes and replacing the brass Naval buttons with diamond-shaped silver ones, it became a passable Prince Charlie jacket. With a lovely new kilt I was now able to appear at such functions properly dressed. At the Harpenden Ball one year we met an elderly lady, Pat Batt, who was a dab hand at writing ditties which she published in aid of her local hospice. One of these concerned the problems experienced by women on the dance floor who, because a lot of husbands seem to be shy of going dancing and prefer to stay at home watching football on television, have to dance with one another. Pat had written a lovely poem which is so true I must (with her permission) share it with you. It goes:

I'm a two-sex dancer, and may seem rather dim.
But I never spend one evening as a fulltime her or him.
I change my sex from dance to dance, my corners always alter.
It's really not surprising I occasionally falter.

The old and simple dances I can manage very nicely;
And I can learn a new dance, and do it most precisely.
But when it comes to next week, I don't know if I can,
For I learnt it as a woman, and dance it as a man!

And so you men who have the luck
to always stay the same,
When female gentlemen go wrong,
be sparing with your blame.

I'll add a postscript to this tale,
one comfort I have got –
When both the women change their sex,
it doesn't show a lot.

For some years I had been going to St. Albans for regular meetings of a writers circle, where aspiring writers would sit round a table and discuss techniques, read out some composition and generally immerse themselves in their scribblings. We would have a speaker now and again, and on one occasion this was the editor of Ideal Home magazine, who spoke about the type of article she accepted from 'amateur' people such as ourselves, ending with a warning not to submit articles on wine or cooking as the magazine retained regular contributors to cover those subjects. As it happened I had just completed a short piece on making elderberry wine for which I was looking for a market, so that was not good news. Anyway, I buttonholed her in the interval where she kindly agreed to read it if I sent it in. I did so, and received a cheque a few days later. It was published about ten months after that at the correct season, so I felt I'd had a satisfactory baptism. Most of the group were busy writing journalistic pieces for the local Hertfordshire magazine, which was really a vehicle for the advertisements and took articles of a local interest in order to help sell it. Ideal Home was quite a different matter. However, one of our number had just had her first book published; one of those reminiscent autobiographies. She was Eileen Elias and her book, which I found later in our local library, was called On Sundays We Wore White. It was a good read.

One evening we had a new member, or rather a new visitor for she only came the once. She clearly regarded herself as several cuts above the other people sitting round the table, and talked down to us in a dreadful condescending manner which I think we all saw through. She introduced herself as an established authoress, and said she would be at home at three on the coming Sunday. She stayed for about twenty minutes and then with a patronising smile she rose to her feet and made a stage exit, head held high. We looked at one another and started to giggle, then some of us put our heads together and decided to take up her invitation. She'd given her address rather grandly as Brocket Hall which I knew was a large country mansion near Welwyn Garden City, so I was intrigued at the thought of visiting the place. I imagined a haughty butler leading us into the Presence. It all sounded rather fun. On the Sunday a number of cars converged on Brocket Hall for the visit. We drew several blanks until we cornered someone just coming out of the house who pointed to a door down some narrow steps on one side, past several dustbins. On this door was her name with a pencilled note saying 'At Home'. The door was ajar, so in we went. We found ourselves in the basement, pipes and electrical cables overhead, fuse boxes on the walls, chipped tiled floors and a long dark corridor. We had entered one of the 'below stairs' catacombs. Halfway down the corridor we found another door that led into a reasonably pleasant room with an outlook over the lake, though as this was a basement room, the windows were set fairly high in the wall with a gravel path outside at windowsill level. Sitting on a sort of dais at one end of the room was our hostess presiding over a silver teapot on one of those gimbal-like stands on a table in front of her. She grandly lifted a hand to be taken, though didn't rise from her throne. I wondered whether she was expecting the men to kiss it. Then followed an extraordinary solo performance while she told us about her many erudite publications, all of which were laid out on another table for us to see. We picked them up to examine. Most were mediocre poetry attempts all self-published, and not a patch on the amusing ones Pat Batt wrote. There were reprints of one or two articles from some very peculiar magazines one of which I read, but the grammar was so strange I was brought up all standing at every sentence. Was this it? Was this the extent of her prolific publications? The woman must have been nuts. We enjoyed our cup of tea and a biscuit, and compared notes when we emerged into the daylight once more. The budding journalists amongst us were thrilled: here was wonderful material for a hugely entertaining story.

I stayed with the writers' circle for several years. Most of my publications were technical articles, and I also edited (which meant I also wrote) an in-house quarterly magazine for the Kodak Engineering Division. That was in the seventies, when printing such things was quite difficult. I prepared all my material, had it typed and checked with my boss, took the photographs, then set off for the Kodak plant in Hemel Hempstead where the little yellow boxes were made, and where some small-scale printing was also carried out. Someone there had a high quality typewriter, a revolutionary IBM golfball machine, which only certain trusted people were allowed to use. All my copy was then re-typed on this machine. The headlines and other words that were to be printed in a non-standard size or font were set on a typesetting machine which produced bromides. Then a layout artist sat down at a drawing board with scissors and paste to set it out, a page at a time. Eventually the paste-ups were ready to be photographed, and printing plates made. Actual printing on an offset litho machine could then take place. It was hugely labour intensive to reproduce, but the costs were absorbed in-house, so that was not a worry for me. I have one of these magazines now, and it looks dreadful to anyone currently used to knocking out such things on their word processor. Times have most certainly changed.

The Health and Safety at Work Act had come in. Kodak already had an excellent record for safety in the workplace, the safety people considering that even one accident was one too many. They'd always worked well with the Safety Inspectorate, but this new Act gave us a lot of paperwork and needed people across the Company to be trained. We already ran sessions on such activities as how to lift safely, and even had lightweight office girls lifting a loaded box off the floor without noticing just how heavy it was and, of course, our operating staff were constantly heaving great loads around without rupturing themselves. Engineers worked on potentially lethal machinery so needed to take special precautions. To bring ourselves up to speed, three of us drove over to Harlow one day to visit the United Glass works, where safety at the workplace had to be a high profile concern. Here was a different world indeed. We crunched round the operations floor getting splinters of glass embedded in the soles of our shoes, stepping over cables and pipes while billets of molten glass emerged from the furnace high above and flew with unerring accuracy over our heads and into the jaws of a bottle press, which clamped shut while, with a fearful noise, a jet of air blew the glowing mass into another shiny new bottle. Finished bottles rattled down a conveyor line beside where we walked, looking so lovely that it was tempting to pick one up to study the perfection; there was nothing to stop one from doing so except the knowledge that the glass had been red hot only moments before. Amazingly, the accident rate in this noisy hellhole was remarkably low, and after our tour we sat down with the management people to see how they achieved it.

Back at Kodak it seemed very safe and peaceful in comparison and perhaps that was the real danger. Operators were complacent. And so began a series of safety days, short courses, films, all carried out low key until the whole attitude to safety had changed. It worked well, and our accident rate fell even further. But I do remember one incident that frightened us all at the time, back in the days when I worked in the Film Finishing Department. During a production lull one day a couple of my maintenance men were allowed access to one of the giant film guillotine machines to make adjustments. The machine was isolated from the power, of course, and they had removed the guards. One of them was inching the machine around by hand while the other sat on the top of it with a spanner. He managed to catch his sleeve in an exposed gear at which point they discovered they couldn't move the machine backwards in order to release him. So while he sat there, his mate phoned the main shop to discover how to reverse it. The message that was heard at the other end was that a mechanic had his arm caught in a guillotine, unable to move. This conjured up the gory picture of some poor man trapped with his arm partly severed and blood everywhere. In seconds the emergency call went out. I was walking back through the factory when a fire appliance came hurtling past, its siren wailing and lights flashing, followed by the factory ambulance. I wondered what had happened. By this time the fitter who had made the phone call found how to wind the guillotine backwards, had released his mate and they were just putting the covers back on. No one was more surprised than they were when the door burst open and purposeful-looking helmeted firemen came clumping in.

One day I had a phone call from the Factory accounting manager; could he come along to see me? I wondered what I'd done wrong, and why did he want to leave his cosy management office and tramp up through the factory to see me. He must want something. Sure enough, he was after someone to do some cartoons for a 'do' he was organising. Ray Plowman, who'd seen him come into my office, since his office and mine only had a glass partition between them, was worried that maybe one of our Capital Expenditure requests was flawed, but then Ray would work himself up into worrying about anything. Not a lot you can do when your boss is like that, so I used to ignore him. The next request was from Ed Waller, Ray's one-time equal but now the manager of one part of Engineering Design. He wanted a menu card designed and printed for the management Christmas dinner party. This was rather fun to do, for he wanted to have a photograph of three production managers dressed up as choirboys singing away in front of the factory manager himself who would be dressed up as their choirmaster conducting, or 'calling the tune'; but none of the four people concerned must know anything about it. Could I get some photographs of their heads and stick them onto a picture of choirboys in their surplices? I collected the factory photographer and we went to see each manager in turn, asking them to pose in a particular way for some trumped up publication (the three stooges with their mouth forming the letter 'O') and then I got him to take a shot of three real children dressed up as choirboys in our local church with our son, Paul, dressed in a surplus as the choirmaster. We then did a cut-and-paste job putting the managers' heads in the place of those of Paul and the choirboys, and produced a lovely picture that looked completely authentic. I particularly liked the smallest choirboy, half the size of the others, onto whose head we had stuck that of the smallest manager who was quite a short man, with him looking up in a most convincing manner. The finished menu card was considered a 'classic' being kept by everyone at the dinner and from then on I was required to do any cartoons and suchlike, almost on an official basis.

~*~

As a result of our two holidays at HF houses, we'd taken a liking to group walking. Not only was all the pioneering work done by the organisation so that we walked in the best places, but it combined walking with socialising on the hoof. At the centres we'd discovered programmes displayed in a rack for local HF groups, one of which was a Watford one. So, somewhat warily, we approached them and arranged to join them one Sunday. This first walk started at Chesham, walking over lovely Chiltern hills that were all new to us. The leader that day was Ron Joiner, a retired policeman who made us very welcome, the weather was fine and the ground just right for walking on with no mud. We enjoyed it so much that we joined, and walked with them most Sundays, usually covering about ten to twelve miles with a break at lunchtime.

In the summer we visited another HF house, this one at Selworthy near the Devon/Somerset border. Here again we enjoyed a lovely week with good walking in a new area, super food, and lots of social goings on. The only drawback was our room, which was in one of the chalets away from the main house. It was en suite and very well appointed but had a flat roof. At dawn a group of chattering starlings would land heavily on the roof and go pattering up and down until we gave up trying to get any more sleep. One of the leaders that week had damaged her ankle the day before the holiday started, so was unable to lead walks, concentrating instead on running the evening social activities. When only two of the three walks are led, then there is always the problem with the older walkers who cannot manage more than a slow or low-level walk, so the slow walk always has to be led, leaving only one other. It means the remaining walk is often over-subscribed and will have to be modified so that the middle-range people unable to cope with an exceptionally long one are still able to go. Thus the long one, often the most interesting, tends to suffer. On this week, I led one or two of the slow ones, thereby easing the situation a little, but shortly after this HF tightened up the requirements for their walking leaders and to have an unknown untrained leader such as myself would no longer be allowed.

Patricia was quite pleased when we downgraded our walks at Selworthy since she had not been fully fit for much of the summer. On our return home, she had to have an operation, one that she should really have had years ago. It took a long while for her to recover, during which time she was only able to go on short walks. Unfortunately, we'd already booked to go at the end of August to the HF house at Loch Awe, one of the strenuous mountain centres, so that was out for her. Rather than cancel, Paul agreed to take Patricia's place and we set off early one morning, dropping off loads of his things at Liverpool University on the way. This was a wonderful week for the two of us, a time to get to know one another so much better. We took turns with the driving, stopped for some touristy shopping in Callander, took photographs of the scenery as we went up the side of loch Lubnaig and detoured a mile or so down the 'wrong' side of Loch Awe so as to get a good view of the house from across the loch. I took a picture of it with a long lens and this was used by HF for their brochure the following year. On arrival we found our host for the week was Charles, the same man who hosted us at Lyme Regis a couple of years previously. The house itself is superbly situated, right on the edge of the loch with its own railway station on the Oban line right beside it. It was originally built as a Victorian fishing hotel, with extravagant architecture of an earlier age built in severe granite with little turrets all over the place. The entrance hall was panelled oak, with a heavy Jacobean-style staircase and a lovely soft tartan carpet up the stairs and along all the corridors, a poor man's Balmoral; all the bathroom fittings 'unimproved', and the rooms large and comfortable. It was a pity Patricia was unable to come, but maybe she would at a later date. It was a wonderful summer's evening with perfect views in every direction. It had all the makings of a super week.

Next day the whole party (there must have been about sixty guests) clambered up the local mountain, Monagh Driseig, on a perfect morning with a really hot sun. This was shakeout day, the object being to divide us up into high, medium and low groups depending on how we'd done. Seven of us made the top, and about twenty didn't get far at all. Our three leaders then knew where they were. Back down again, hot and tired, we soon discovered the pub, which served draught Tartan. A good start to the week!

As it turned out, that week could be divided into three. The first and last days when it was gloriously fine with the bit in the middle when it rained as only it can up in the mountains. We did attempt one of the peaks, but were soon up in the cloud with no view, so that seemed rather a waste of time. The following day Paul stayed with the 'high' party where, once again, he spent all day up in the cloud, while I sensibly joined the middle party on a good forest trail. In our party was a middle-aged German man with a close-cropped hairstyle and a heavy German accent. He marched ahead of the group and was very fussy about keeping to the instructions, commenting if the leader attempted to modify the route. This had to happen when we found our way was blocked by a river in spate, and it would have been foolhardy to attempt to cross. It was necessary to make a five-mile detour with George the German complaining all the way. That evening we were entertained to a type of *What's My Line* evening that finished with many people telling outrageous stories. Not to be outdone George stood up and proceeded to tell a long and involved tale in his wonderfully thick accent, ending with a "Ach! I forget ze punch line." After that we realised he had been playing us up all week, pretending to be a Teutonic version of Colonel Blimp. He dropped his German accent then and it was laughs all the way to the end of the holiday. George wasn't with us when Paul and I went with the high party on our penultimate day where we took a launch near the Tainault ferry right to the top of Loch Etive, a glorious loch with seals hauled out on one side, red deer on the braes and with the sun just peeking through the clouds. The idea was to walk from the top of Loch Etive over the bealach on the west side, crossing a little burn to drop down to the shores of Loch Linnhe for a rendezvous with the coach which would also pick up the low party. At the top of the bealach the rain started up again, driving horizontally with such force that it went through all our waterproof clothing in a matter of minutes. Then we found the burn had turned into a dangerous torrent of peaty brown water making it quite impossible to proceed any further. By this time the launch had gone and we had no other means of getting back. We had our picnic lunch standing up in the rain, then slithered down the side of the hill back to the little lane at the head of Loch Etive, from where we started to walk up Glen Etive pursued by midges. We found a lonely telephone box there so were able to contact the house who organised a minibus to drive all the way over Rannoch Moor to Glen Coe where we would meet them. That slog up the road was pretty grim. We were really tired, but if we went too slowly the midges caught up and got us going again. After ten miles or so we met the minibus and thankfully collapsed into it for the trip back. The coach in the meantime had waited for four hours before giving up, with everyone in it upset at missing their hot supper. Nowadays everyone has mobile phones so this sort of problem happens less often, but mobiles don't always work in the mountains. At last the sun came out properly for our final day, the day we walked up a service road to Cruachan reservoir and onto the braes beyond. Loch Awe was a memorable week and I was only sorry Patricia had missed it. I liked my first taste of a mountain centre, and hoped to bring her along when she was well.

Back home again to find Patricia much improved. She and I spent a gentle exploratory week based in Bournemouth, from where we toured the eastern part of the Purbecks. We thought this would be an excellent area for an HF holiday, and as they had a house in Swanage, we made a note to go there one day.

We heard that my uncle Ted, whose wife had died a year or two earlier and was now living alone, had had a stroke which left him without coherent speech. Apart from that he seemed well enough in himself, but his sudden cessation of the means to communicate must have frustrated him terribly. We drove over to Surbiton as often as we could for a few hours with him. He chatted away just as usual, but the only intelligible word he was able to get out was 'Yokel', the name of his devoted beagle. He attempted all ways, but eventually just smiled and shook his head. We tried asking him questions requiring a 'yes' or 'no' answer, suggesting he nod or shake his head, but his comprehension was affected. He either didn't understand or was not able to do as we suggested. His regular contacts, the postman, his local newsagent, his cleaning woman, all understood and looked after him remarkably well, so he was perfectly able to carry on living alone. His cleaning woman in particular had no problems, for she herself was totally deaf and they'd always communicated by sign language with no difficulty. Sometimes we combined the trips to Surbiton with a visit to the Isabella Plantation in Richmond Park, or the Valley gardens in Windsor Great Park. On other occasions we would visit Kew Gardens and pay our penny entrance fee, and occasionally we went on from Ted's to the Royal Horticultural Society's garden at Wisley. It was two years later we had a phone call from Kingston Hospital in early January. Ted had been found in his unheated house sitting on the stairs shivering in the cold, having been there all night. We rushed over to visit him. The hospital were not concerned by the hypothermia which they were dealing with, but it seemed he had suffered another stroke and had lain unconscious all night. He was conscious by the time we got there but appeared less comprehending than usual, though otherwise quite bright. His main worry was for Yokel. I think I was able to reassure him that Yokel was being looked after by the cleaning woman and he was clearly pleased to hear that. A week later he had a far worse stroke and died shortly afterwards. I had the difficult duty of phoning my father to give him the news. His elder brother Bernard had died after the fire in the old people's home many years ago, and now his younger brother had gone. Father, marooned down in Cornwall, was the last surviving member of that generation. He must have felt terribly alone even though he hadn't seen Ted for a number of years. Since having his morning help two days a week father had perked up no end and had been well and moderately active for a man in his middle eighties. I was worried that Ted's death would make him depressed and affect his health long term. As Ted's Executor I set about dealing with his affairs, to find he had probably anticipated his next stroke, for he had tidied up and put everything in order. Jane and I went through the house after the funeral and in the ensuing weeks prepared it for sale. The house with all its fittings and services was utterly unimproved since the day it was built at the turn of the century, even down to a really early gas cooker and a geyser for heating the water. There was no central heating, just a coal fire in the front room and old-style electric radiators elsewhere. They had lived very simply on a modest pension. On one of Jane's visits to clear the house, she told me she'd had a breast lump examined which had turned out to be malignant. She and Peter had already booked the holiday of a lifetime in Sri Lanka a few weeks later which she was determined not to miss, after which she would be going into hospital for a mastectomy.

~*~

Sue had started her three-year medical training at Guy's Hospital, which she found very demanding. There were medical people there with definite misogynist tendencies who would mutter about it being a waste of resources training women to be doctors, since all that happened was they got married and left. She must have had to restrain her feelings about such opinions. She had found rooms in a block of flats about a mile away in Dulwich, so we took her there with her gear. We wandered round nearby Dulwich Park before returning home, leaving with the impression that she'd found a nice area, though one was conscious of Brixton just the other side of the railway line where there had been recent riots. But a railway line is a great divider.

Our neighbours, Norman and Margaret Jarritt, had gone to the States for three years leaving their house with all its furniture in the hands of an agent. Norman was a senior bank executive and his job in America was to start up a branch over there, so they would no doubt be discovering a big difference in living standards. This was at a time when UK tenants had just won the right not to be forced to leave at the end of their agreed time if they had nowhere to live. Not surprisingly this had quickly resulted in homes to let disappearing off the market. However the Jarritts assured us theirs would be an 'executive let' to business people staying for a fixed time, and should this be for over six months, then the contract would be renewed for a further spell. Apparently this then did not give the tenants the right to remain there indefinitely. There followed a fascinating array of new neighbours. We started with a Dutch family, with two teenage boys, all sporty people. Every day they would hurtle off in their running kit to keep themselves fit. When in a neighbourly way I chatted over the fence offering to show them the local area, they said they would look at a map if they wanted to know. Miffed, I left them to it. The agent had arranged for a contract gardener to keep the place looking reasonable, but no one looked after the house fabric, so when bits started to fall off the house or the water tank overflowed it was usually us that noticed first, and reported it via Norman's brother to the agent. We had two more lots before eventually a Japanese family arrived. On their first evening there was a knock on our door and there, standing in a line, were four little people, father and mother with two children, who grinned broadly and all bowed together. The father, who was the only one to speak much English, handed me his card. We shook hands and I did my best to respond in a Japanese way, but probably failed dismally. After that we often saw them, always busy, always smiling. The garden started to look much smarter and there was a hum of efficiency about the place. The father had come to manage a Mitsubishi factory in Watford making electronic products and I went next door one day to hear his Hi-Fi equipment, kicking off my shoes in the approved fashion as I stepped over the threshold and into the sitting room where every piece of polished furniture shone with the results of loving care. After ten minutes or so chatting to him and listening to music the sitting room door opened and in came his wife, on her knees! She was carrying a tea tray and deferentially crawled across the room to place it at my feet. They were a delightful family to have as neighbours and when it came to leaving they held a Western-style party for all the nearby people, which was very well received. The contrast with the next tenants couldn't have been greater. This was a family of Ugandian Asians, kicked out by Idi Amin, on a six-month visit. They never spoke to anybody so we never discovered what they did, but they certainly didn't seem short of funds. Several men visitors in large Mercedes cars would call from time to time, but we never saw the womenfolk leave the house. Extraordinary smells emanated from the kitchen, not always very appetising. No washing went up on the line and we never saw anyone in the garden. One day I was asked if I would fix a broken electrical contraption in the kitchen. What I saw was too awful for words. The lovely clean house nurtured so well by the Japanese had deteriorated into a grubby pigsty. The walls were dirty, paper peeling off in places where children had discovered their little fingernails could easily lift it. A couple of buxom middle-aged women in saris stood around helplessly while I fixed the fuse and tested the appliance for them. The kitchen was absolutely filthy, walls, ceiling and floor all spotted with bits of food. On the floor was a paraffin cooking stove; the electric cooker had part of a packing case across the top of it on which was a pile of dirty cooking pots. It would seem they didn't use it at all but preferred to crouch on the floor cooking over their oil stove. No wonder we'd had such horrible smells coming over the wall. We contacted Norman's brother to tip him off about the state of the house. A month or two later these people succeeded in setting fire to the kitchen which they soon put out but not before sticky black smoke had permeated all through the rest of the house. Then, in the middle of one night, they suddenly left. Norman's brother arrived with the agent to assess the damage which amounted to thousands. The entire house had to be professionally cleaned and redecorated and most of Norman's furniture needed to be replaced. We found the whole business extremely worrying but not so the Jarritts. When they returned they laughed it off with a "Well, it's only money!" as though that were the least of one's problems. I suppose that for a successful banking family it was only a minor problem. Norman's job in the States was his last before retiring, and after a few months they found a lovely retirement home near Ipswich and moved in there. We still visit from time to time and whenever they are in Watford they always come to see us.

Patricia and I felt we'd like another overseas holiday, a Mediterranean spell in the sunshine. We'd gone through one of the coldest and wettest winters ever, leaving us with that feeling that there would never be any sunshine again. But who would we go with? Could we trust Ramblers after our Tenerife experience? I had a long chat with them over the phone and voiced my concerns. We rather fancied their 'Crete in the Spring' tour, a series of weekly departures at the best time of year for spring flowers after the end of the cool rainy weather, at a more gentle pace with time for photography. Reassured that the leader was a middle-aged Army man who'd been leading that holiday for years we booked.

~*~

We had a few weeks at home to recover, look after the garden, get re-stocked and ready for our next venture which was with HF once more. We'd opted for their centre on the Isle of Arran, a little bit of Scotland with a mountain or two thrown in, all on a compact island. It had the advantage of being easily accessible from Watford using a cheap rail ticket available through HF. The Glasgow train stopped to pick up at Watford, so it was a very easy journey for us. Approaching Glasgow Central it became apparent we were running so late we might well miss our connection to Ardrossan, so we walked the length of the train with our luggage until we were in the front coach, ready for a speedy takeoff. The train came in at exactly the same time as our Ardrossan connection was due to leave, so we leapt out the moment it stopped, sprinted across the concourse heaving with the Saturday crowds, dashed onto the platform at the far end past a ticket inspector on the barrier who shouted to us that the train was moving, and just managed to leap aboard as it gathered speed. Phew! Picking ourselves up we looked around to find we were the only ones from the Euston train who'd managed it. The next train would not be for another couple of hours, and the ferry for that would get them to Brodick too late to clock in at the HF house in time for the traditional welcoming tea!

This house is based in Lamlash at the southeastern end of Arran looking out to Holy Island across the bay. It is a comparatively small centre with some of the rooms in a group of chalets round the back. We'd opted for one of these since they seemed to be better appointed, and someone had assured us they had pitched roofs with no likelihood of early morning starlings pattering about overhead. As a centre it was only average in those days, but the walking was good. We enjoyed walks of all types, gentle heath rambling, some coastal tramps, and mountain walking. We had a lovely dreamy day on Holy Island, hiking from one end to the other over the top, enjoyed our picnic lunch in a sheltered spot on the south side looking out to Ailsa Craig, and came back to the landing stage along a pleasant grassy track. Here there were wild Soay sheep, a breed that obtains much of its nourishment from brousing the seaweed on the shore. On one of the days the cloud level was below the tops onto which the high party was going so we opted to join the 'geriatric group', a choice we regretted later when the sun came out. There were quite a lot of much older people staying at that centre who were not really walkers at all, and we wondered why they'd come. The answer seemed to be with the type of group holiday, the 'house party' atmosphere that they enjoyed, and some of them had first come to HF for a special interest holiday such as painting or birdwatching, and had been coming ever since.

On one day we attempted a 3,000 foot 10 mile walk up Beinn Bharrain on the other side of the island. There was one spot where it was necessary to do some scrambling to get round an obstruction, with a sharp drop to one side. As the rock was wet and quite slippery, we found it somewhat hazardous. I helped one of the others who was the spitting image of George Formby from teeth to dialect. As his fingers failed to latch onto anything to grip and he began to slither off the edge, looking behind him with considerable alarm at sheep grazing several hundred feet below, he wailed "Eeeeh! I wish I'd stayed at home!" But we all made it, and the highlight of that day was when we saw our first red-throated diver on one of the mountain lochans.

Then there was our Glen Sannox day. This was one of those memorable occasions with hot sun, cotton wool clouds, no midges and glorious scenery. The going was sublime, with springy peaty turf beneath our feet; a day that more than makes up for the dull or rainy weather that can so easily spoil a holiday. On our way down afterwards we espied in the far distance what looked like a huge humpty-dumpty egg, pink on top and red underneath. As we approached, we could see it had legs beneath it. Closer still, it resolved itself into a somewhat rotund man wearing nothing but a swinging red kilt and a pair of walking boots. He had a fiery red flowing beard and was bright pink all over, either from exertion or too much sun. He called out "A grand day! Aye. Thanks be to God!" and stopped for a chat. What a lovely way to be greeted.

There were days walking high (well above midge level) with superb views across Kintyre to the Paps of Jura, and north to the Grampians with Ben Lomond clearly visible. We saw lots of wildlife, which we weren't expecting. No golden eagles, but while sitting on the beach below the centre we had a raft of eiders, a nursery of little ones shepherded by two adults that came within feet of us, and a heron fished only yards away. Out in the bay we saw the fin of a basking shark, and in the nearby hedgerow were yellowhammers. We had no binoculars, but the wildlife was so unconcerned about our presence that we managed without them. I've noticed since then that humans seem to be less feared out on the islands, which makes for far betting birding.

We loved Arran, but have yet to return there for a second visit. There are so many other places we haven't been to yet, and the cost of rail travel has shot up so much and the complications of trying to buy a reasonably priced ticket are so difficult, not to mention the unreliability of such travel, that we don't use the train nowadays, so Arran will have to wait.

~*~

Back at home I was summoned to attend Jury service, an experience I found fascinating. About thirty potential jurors hung about for half the morning at the St. Albans Crown Court waiting to be called—what a waste of our collective valuable time—and it was not until the second day I was appointed to one of the juries to try a well-known slippery villain who'd been sailing a bit too close to the wind. It started by all of us being humiliated, one by one, while the defending counsel tried to ascertain whether he considered us suitable to try his customer. I felt as though I were being doubted about my honesty and impartiality, which I resented. The police prosecution waffled on about how the prisoner in the dock had done this dastardly deed, and backed up their exposition by showing the court video clips of a man getting out of a car, videoed from a distant viewpoint.

Out in the jury room the twelve of us looked at each other and waited for someone to speak. Eventually I muttered something about the gloomy room we had been locked in, whereupon all the others rounded on me as the one with a voice who would make an admirable foreman. I didn't really want this as I was new to the game and never watched any courtroom dramas on TV, but acquiesced for the sake of getting on with it. We sat down and debated the issue before us. We all agreed immediately that the shifty looking bloke in the dock, smartly dressed with slicked down hair for the occasion, was without any doubt as guilty as they come; then proceeded to say why we thought so. From time to time I reminded them what it had said on our jury summonses—what evidence do we have? As the afternoon wore on it became apparent that the police had provided no actual evidence at all. It was purely their knowledge of the man's activities and, although they had been following him for some time before they pounced, there still was no actual evidence. Two jury members were adamant we could not convict without proper evidence, while the rest of us reckoned we had sufficient circumstantial evidence. After a few hours we filed back into court, everyone there waking up as if from a scene in The Sleeping Beauty. I was asked for our verdict. When I said "Not Guilty" the judge sat up, looked at his two barristers below and exclaimed "Well! There you are, then!" I thought maybe he'd had a bet on the case going the way it did.

As we trooped out, the one-time accused was standing outside in a huddle with his underworld cronies, all smiles. He caught sight of me, smirked and said, "Anytime, mate," and gave me a big wink. Was this an invitation to benefit, if I wished, from contacts on his side of the Law...?

Back at Kodak my time teaching the KT course was running out. This was not before I'd spent a few days at The White House Hotel in Cirencester on a short update course with them, and a full week at a swish country house hotel outside Lymington on one of their 'public' courses learning some new techniques they were introducing. I don't know how much Kodak were profiting from me attending these courses, but I certainly enjoyed swanning around the country staying at such smart places. Like the train trips I had whilst in the Royal Navy from Rosyth to Alverstoke and back, so it was at these hotels. If I had Patricia with me and we were paying for ourselves, then I'm afraid it meant a cheapish B&B so poor Patricia never got to see the posh side, but then she said she'd never want to stay in such places.

Kodak had discovered a new guru, another American, of course. This was Tom Peters who at the time was telling the big international corporations all about looking after customers. We had to have an in-house indoctrination on the subject, and such phrases as 'Nobody ever won an argument with a customer' and 'The customer is the only reason you're in business' were plastered up in Head Office lifts and such places where they could be seen by everyone several times a day. Throughout the Company we were reminded the customer not only meant the person in the High Street who bought our product, but we all of us had customers: in the case of a production worker, his customer was the next person down the line who would do something further to the product that he was involved in.

I found myself in demand as a 'facilitator', the natural development of the KT technique where a group of people are trying to knock out the best way of doing something. In my case this was usually in the early stages of some engineering project, and there would be technologists who were the ones who wanted the project, engineers who would build and install it and accountants who would try to keep them focussed on the need to ensure there would be a payback. We would include various managers as necessary, mainly to ensure we kept them on our side (though they came along thinking they would keep us on their side). All these people collectively had lots to offer and it was the facilitator's job to work through a fairly formal procedure to ensure the group—who would soon become a team—explored every way of achieving the object and obtaining consensus on the best way to do it. We might start with several exhausting all-day sessions with regular follow-ups while we worked up the project; all this before applying for money and launching it. Such an operation was expensive to set up, but could be cheap compared with the cost of not making the best decisions. I found my role a very rewarding one, even though as facilitator I was not involved in the content of what they were all talking about. Indeed, I had to be careful not to become involved, though it was helpful to know enough to understand the technical jargon. We would work through all our deliberations using flip charts, pasting sheets of paper round the walls so that everything that was discussed was visible to everyone. Then I would write it all up and issue a report. This is where I found my Naval background of staff work to be extremely useful. The people I came across in industry were naturally enough focussed on their primary job, and disliked the administration side of it. They welcomed my presence to look after that for them. So I was part of the team but not deeply enmeshed in the nitty-gritty of the detail; just what I liked.

All Kodak departments were told to become more efficient. One of these was the medical department where they had to take notice of the sickness statistics. Their vision, intertwined somewhat with the safety people, was to reduce the numbers of employees who became sick for whatever reason, and resulted in all sorts of fringe activities to keep people healthy; not a bad aim really. A dour medical orderly at the Harrow factory by name of 'Mac' (inevitably, since he was a Scotsman) used to take our blood pressure and so on at our annual health check, also a full sized chest X-ray. In the case of the X-ray it was probably useful for the Company to do these in order to confirm their X-ray film was up to scratch. After a while Kodak marketed a blood analysing machine and so we also had a simple blood test, which gave Mac a chance to use the machine. The result of this was that I was summoned to the medical department one day to be told I had a high cholesterol reading and was advised to lower my fat intake. Chips with everything were out; so was all that other fried food I so enjoyed. From now on I was told to eat more sensibly. Within a year or two this message was getting about the general populace and there were healthy eating pieces appearing in magazines and on television and radio programmes. Kodak was ahead of the game. Occasionally Mac was even seen standing quietly in the canteen by the checkout as people came out of the servery with their trays. The look on his gloomy cadaverous face spelled the end of my enjoyable bingeing. At Christmas time there he was with other members of his department with a bar they'd set up, dispensing non-alcoholic 'wine'. It was an attempt to curb people's desire to have a little alcoholic fling at such a time and, hopefully prevent accidents as a result. It worked up to a point, but what a spoilsport! I commented to him "You're depriving me of all the good things in life. You'll be telling us next we mustn't have sex any more."

"Ah!" was his reply, "We shall be coming to that!"

Poor Mac. A few years later he himself fell ill resulting in an early demise. I hope it wasn't brought on by worrying about our health.

Our daughter Sue had come home one day with a young man also called Paul to whom she was attracted. In fact it had got beyond that stage. This first visit was to introduce us to someone whom she wanted us to get to know well so that in due course (as we realised much later) they would be able to tell us they were engaged without it being too much of a sudden surprise for us. Paul was another medic, a quiet and very nice young man whom she'd met at Guys. By coincidence he had been at Cambridge also reading medicine at the same time as Sue, but they hadn't known one another at that time. Somewhat to our concern Sue was now back on a bike again, a proper sporty job with lots of gears. Paul's influence no doubt. She would cover the few miles from Dulwich to Guys hospital, which meant negotiating the awful Elephant and Castle interchange, far quicker than on public transport and seemed happy to be back amongst the traffic after her accident.

We were now going regularly on long Sunday walks with our local HF group, and were getting to know the numerous paths in the Chilterns quite well. We loved the area, which could have been made for walking, with 2,000 miles of footpaths criss-crossing all over it. The scenery constantly changes as one climbs out of one valley or 'bottom' as it is locally known, up over a wooded ridge and down into the next one. There are lots of picturesque villages nestling attractively in the valleys and plenty of good pubs. Being relatively close to London with a great many walkers, means most paths are in good condition, though the conflicting interests of horse riders do tend to churn the shared bridlepaths into a muddy morass for part of the year. Watford, we were discovering, was an ideal place to live. Not only could one cycle into an excellent shopping centre within a few minutes, but we were right on the edge of these Chiltern hills making our weekend jaunts into that area so easy. Also it was only half an hour door-to-door to my work and, as if that were not enough, there was an excellent network of roads to get us further afield when needed. The M25 was now complete and we used this to cover quickly the thirty miles to the RHS gardens at Wisley, which we now proceeded to visit much more regularly. These gardens are a real inspiration to budding gardeners such as myself, and I felt really privileged to be able to wander round seeing everything growing to perfection and to be able to stop and ask one of the experts how to achieve such results in my own garden. And those experts really are experts, the top professionals in the country. I well remember discussing pruning our soft fruit with Harry Baker, author of 'The Fruit Garden Displayed', TV presenter of a super series on fruit growing, and one of the top fruit growing experts in the country, who took time to explain and demonstrate on one of the precious blackcurrant bushes growing nearby. One could just turn up to formal demonstrations without additional charge and without having to book ahead— something I hate doing in case of bad weather on the appointed day. Membership of the RHS was small enough in those days for such demonstrations. Now it has escalated to such numbers that one can no longer enjoy that freedom and it is always necessary to book ahead.

Alas, it was not long after its completion that everyone else started to use the M25; that brief honeymoon period when the road was underused soon over.

Worse, when the last section was built joining up 'our' bit with South Mimms and connecting with the all-important M1 we had non-stop traffic all the time though it did ease up in the early hours. Lying in bed I would guess the time by the noise coming over the fields at the back of our house, which increased markedly just before my getting up time. If I awoke to an eerie silence, then it was either foggy or there had been an accident.

We had a weekend break with our local HF group. This was a springtime visit to their HF Crowlink house on the Sussex downs just inland from the Seven Sisters. Ron Joiner, who knew the area well through having led the long distance South Downs Way for years, was looking after us for the three days we were there. The weather was kind and our small group walked from the house both over the downs and inland through Friston Forest to the Wilmington Long Man area. We explored Alfriston and Westdean and found a good pub in Eastdean. The house itself lay in a shallow hollow down a narrow gravel track, a small place with a row of tiny double rooms over a communal ablutions area. It was one of the few remaining houses which HF owned, that had been okay in its day but was now only really suitable for use by school parties. It lacked almost any facilities, but was conveniently positioned and cheap. The trip down there through lovely parts of Surrey gave me the opportunity to go through Holmbury St. Mary and show Patricia the Guinness model farm where Jane had worked all those years ago.

This was Paul's graduation year. He'd approached the BBC once more and was given his interview. They offered him a place, hugely to his relief. In his long vacations he'd worked locally in a couple of electronics firms, and felt the BBC Engineering job would be exactly what he wanted, so the offer was wonderful news. In the meantime I had completed dealing with my uncle Ted's affairs, and had seven principal beneficiaries to send cheques to—Jane's four children, our two and a nephew of Ted's deceased wife, Dot. For all of them the arrival of a sizable cheque at the start of their adult life was extremely welcome.

The year was moving on. It was time for our proper holiday, a late spring one walking in the Snowdon area, based at the HF Centre at Conwy. We drove via Shrewsbury to Machynlleth to have a look at the Alternative Technology Centre en route, but we found it full of hippies which was most disappointing and not at all what we expected. I had been hoping for something fairly helpful for my new interest in energy saving but this place looked a bit of a dump and I could find no one who could talk technicalities. Then it was on through Dolgellau and over the slatey top of Blaenau Ffestiniog. Whenever we drive anywhere Patricia always checks to see whether we can take in any interesting places en route. Over the years we must have travelled through many places we'd never have discovered if we'd stuck to the fast main roads, and this trip was no exception. We were especially lucky in that we seemed to have chosen a fine week for our holiday, which is such a vital element of a good walking week.

This centre was going through a transformation. It had been somewhat rundown and was far too small for the purpose. Half the bedrooms including ours were in a modern annex, but that left the public rooms crowded. The manager was obviously struggling and his worries were reflected in the lackadaisical way his staff addressed their duties. However, we were not there to bemoan the facilities; there was all this lovely country to explore! On the first day we climbed the local Conwy mountain, Allt-Wen, and paid homage to the plaque commemorating the work of the HF founder the Reverend T. Leonard, with lots of stops to sit in the breeziest spot we could find and enjoy the hot sun. The following day was a little more adventurous: we went by coach to Llanfairfechan some seven miles away, then walked back over the top of Tal-y-Fan over glorious sheep moorland with superb views all round. Then it was up to the Snowdon area proper. The weather now was really hotting up, and the main walk was over Tryffan which we opted out of as it sounded somewhat severe, so we climbed Snowdon instead. I say 'climbed' but we started up the Miner's Track with loads of others so it was more of a steady uphill tramp than any pretence of climbing. I did something I'd always been warned against—I set off with nothing more in my rucksack than a bottle of water. With the temperature creeping up to ninety, the thought of carrying even a jersey was too much to contemplate. Most of the way I just wore a pair of shorts and a sunhat, and was extremely glad to have nothing else. We went up the Pyg Track to the saddle where we were joined by hordes of holidaymakers who'd walked up beside the railway from Llanberis. The whole mountain was alive with people like a huge anthill; everybody in talkative mood as people are when on holiday. At the top we searched for a spot of breeze but found none. If anything it seemed even hotter up here. We'd fully intended to come back round one of the ridge walks, but in the end we just returned the same way as we went up because it seemed the coolest option. We heard and saw our first ring ouzel, which was a thrill for me.

Only three or four miles from Conwy is Bodnant, home of the then RHS President, Lord Aberconway, so we spent a day going round his garden at what was probably the very best time of year. Everything was in flower, glorious colour from one end to the other, such exotics as a superb embothrium looking quite magnificent and the famous laburnum arch at the height of its splendour. It was worth the trip from home just to visit this one garden. We nearly spoilt this day by detouring back through Llandudno, which wasn't our scene at all. The place was full of trippers shuffling about in their own litter and nowhere to park. We didn't stay. A day was spent with the middle rambling party walking from Lake Ogwen up the lovely grassy slope to Craig Yr Ysfa and on up to Carnedd Llewelyn, only a few metres less than Snowdon itself and blessedly empty of people. And there was a breeze that helped! We went on to Carnedd Dafydd enjoying the most wonderful all-round views before dropping back down to Lake Ogwen. Our final day was to have been another strenuous day up in the mountains, but it was hotter than ever, so we just walked up from Beddgelert to the nearby mountain of Moel Hebog and abandoned the idea of tackling two others, choosing to come back through lovely forest trails, paddled in a lake we found there, and discovered somewhere selling ice creams. On the way back we noticed the roads were full of puddles; we'd narrowly missed a monumental thunderstorm where we'd been. That holiday will always bring back memories of intensely hot, humid enervating days. I've never seen Snowdonia in the rain.

Returning from Conwy we called in at the Christie Hospital in Manchester where Jane had been admitted. Her mastectomy had been too late to stop the cancer spreading and now she was being treated with massive chemotherapy sessions that were the best that could be offered. Peter and my niece Fiona joined us for a few quiet hours with Jane. I said a poignant goodbye to her, leaving her smiling and laughing like the old days, putting on a very brave face, and was very conscious I might never see her again, glad this last visit was a happy one to remember. A month later Peter phoned to say that Jane, who was now being nursed at home, was slipping. It would only be a matter of days. Would I warn father? It was a difficult phone call for me to make and I was wishing we lived a little closer at that time so that I could be with him. I phoned the next day, but his voice sounded terribly old and shaky. Only the day after that Peter phoned me to say Jane had died that afternoon. I spoke on the phone to father's best friend in St. Mawes and told him. I asked if he would visit father in the morning at the time I planned to phone, so that he could be there to comfort him. Poor father. He was alone. He'd lost all his family now except me, and I lived 300 miles away, unable to visit that often. On the day of Jane's funeral I was unsure whether to go to Manchester to attend it, or to visit father and comfort him. In the end we went to St. Mawes and had a quiet but peaceful day wandering about and talking with father. The following day Peter arrived with his youngest son Iain. Paul and Iain spent most of that week sailing around together in one boat or another, we all went for walks over the super National Trust headlands across the other side of the Percuil River, father coming down to Stone Quay to watch the boys sailing and to help them get their various boats ashore or secured on the mooring.

Back at home we'd joined the Chiltern Society to better explore some of the lesser-known footpaths criss-crossing the hills. The Chiltern Society's aim is to preserve the beauty of the area, and has several sections. One of these comprises landowners and tenants to involve them all, and another one, the Rights of Way Group, is there to keep all the rights of way walked and in good condition. So we had a situation where the landowners and walkers were both members of the same Society, which made it much easier to resolve conflicting interests. It worked well. We usually went on a five-mile walk on Sunday mornings, getting to know lots of others and discovered paths we would never have walked just from studying maps. The Society published its own footpath maps and worked with the County Council to ensure they did their bit as well. The Ramblers Association also had a similar interest in keeping the Chiltern footpaths in good condition, and a lot of people were members of both organisations. Even the seemingly remote and unapproachable Ordnance Survey took an interest whereby some small features first highlighted by the Society crept onto the larger scale OS maps. Like all such organisations, walking leaders were always required. Patricia didn't feel happy about leading since she has problems knowing in which direction she is walking and would soon become lost, not a good idea for a leader; however, I led a number of walks. That presented me with the usual problem in that walks programmes would be published up to six months ahead—longer than my inflexible work commitments were planned, and always further ahead than the holidays we would be wanting to book. Several times we'd booked our holidays to avoid a day I had agreed to lead a walk, only to find that on the day of the walk it poured with rain and no one turned up. This was exacerbated when we found the holiday itself was not so good because of the alternative dates we had been obliged to choose. Things came to a head on the date of one of the Chiltern Society walks which I had been pressurised to lead, the Company putting me on a course at short notice with the result that the man who'd pressurised me suddenly found he was stuck without a leader and had to do it himself. There was a lot of bad feeling about that occasion; the man concerned having never been in a situation where he was unable to drop everything whenever needed. So we stopped going with them since they didn't welcome walkers who were unwilling to lead. Impasse. The local Ramblers group were different, and welcomed everybody. It meant they had large parties, for a number of older women who didn't feel comfortable walking on their own were happy to do so in a group and those walks would often have as many as fifty people on them; the leader having to adopt a shepherding instinct to ensure he lost no one on the way!

In August that year we returned to the Crowlink HF centre to join one of their 'Special Interest' groups, this one on visiting Sussex gardens and led by a one-time professional gardener. We drove down via Newdigate in Surrey, stopping for lunch with Janet, my brother-in-law Peter's younger sister. Unlike Peter's two elder brothers who became eminent senior members of the medical profession, I believe Janet had been a consultant in oncology. She'd married a delightful but somewhat eccentric medical man who later went on to become the Surrey county pathologist. They were both retired now, living in a huge rambling house with a lot of outbuildings at the back where Raymond, her husband, was able to pursue his hobby of stripping down and playing with large bits of machinery. The house had a basement in which resided heavy rusting hunks of metal waiting their turn for his attentions. It is only six miles from Gatwick airport, so most of their more trusting friends would leave their cars with Raymond while they went off on holiday, Raymond chauffeuring them to Gatwick in his vintage Rolls after which he would service their car all ready for the return. It was this Rolls that Raymond had used for Jane's wedding at St. Just-in-Roseland. On the day we arrived, Raymond was buried under the bonnet of someone's car, and stood up when he heard our approach, his hands dripping with thick black oil, holding them out as a surgeon does after he's scrubbed up. Clearly old habits died hard. His eye alighted on our Vauxhall with interest; maybe he was short of a part for the job in hand, and I wondered whether it would be safe to leave it there while we had lunch.

We then called in at Nymans, but it was going through a bad spell and did not look all that well cared for. However, one always learns something visiting such gardens and this was no exception. On our first day from Crowlink we went by coach to Borde Hill garden, but like Nymans it was disappointing. Both gardens were really spring gardens, and we asked our leader why he'd chosen August for these visits. "That's the date they offered me," was his reply, so we wondered whether he or they knew what they were doing. The following day he'd planned to take us round Churchill's garden at Chartwell, which seemed a wonderful idea as it is closed to the public on Mondays and we would have the place to ourselves. Getting suspicious I enquired how he had managed to arrange for our party to visit on a closed day. Oh dear! —he didn't know the garden was only open on certain days of the week. From then on I checked all his arrangements. In the event we visited Wakehurst instead which we loved. Our leader had worked there when he was an improver, and showed us various trees and shrubs he'd planted twenty years previously. On our own after lunch Patricia and I walked the entire Wakehurst estate, right down to the extreme far end. It made a great day out.

The two of us found time to explore Lewes, a town full of historical interest. We went round the old town, castle gate, the ruined Abbey gardens and Anne of Cleves house. We also discovered a little vineyard tucked into a dip in the nearby chalk hills at Breaky Bottom and bought some of their wine. This was my first taste of English wine, which with the shift in climate has been getting better ever since. We also visited Herstmonceaux and Battle and fetched up at Bedgebury arboretum.

We visited Sissinghurst where we spent much of the day after a pleasant stop in the old town of Rye. I've tried to analyse why Sissinghurst has that touch of magic, which is not evident in such gardens as Hidcote, for instance. Is it just the ghosts of Vita Sackville West and Harold Nicolson?

Finally we spent a day at Hever Castle and Penshurst Place. Hever had a lovely homely atmosphere, presumably imbued by the Astor legacy, which made Penshurst dull and soulless in comparison. On the way home we stopped off at Wisley to find those wonderful gardens full of colour and interest. Looking back at the Sussex gardens, none of them were geared for summer visiting and would have been so much better in the spring. This was a holiday where HF let us down, mainly because the leader didn't seem to have planned his week nor realise he should have put his foot down about the dates. We learnt that one must not assume the organisers will get things right, and we now always check for ourselves when planning our holidays.

A month later Sue and her friend Paul arrived on their bikes to join us for a walk in the Chess valley to Chenies and Latimer (our favourite local walk) after which we had lunch and sat on the patio chatting. This was when they announced they were getting engaged, though it was another few weeks at their next visit before we saw the ring actually there on Sue's finger. They had decided to get married in St. Mary's in Watford, but not until the following summer when they might both be a little more settled. But with junior doctors only able to have six-month contracts in the NHS would they ever be settled? Shortly after, Sue landed a job at York District hospital as a junior houseman, the start of a long and arduous climb up the National Health Service ladder. Meanwhile her Paul was off to Malawi for a spell there.

Our own Paul had now started at Wood Norton, Evesham, a one-time country house now the home of the BBC's Engineering Training Department, and was loving it. There was an elderly man who danced at the Amersham club whose name was Ken Sturley. He lived nearby in Chesham Bois in a house he called 'Wood Norton' and I knew of him as the author of several erudite textbooks on aerials and transmission theory which were the standard textbooks of my day. He'd written these when he was the chief engineer at Evesham, after which he went out to one of the African third world countries to start up a television service there before retiring in Chesham. After three months at Evesham Paul started at the BBC Television Centre at White City, with a bedsit in a pleasant house in Acton only a mile or two away. His job involved coping with a ponderous video recording machine for Grandstand where he had to be ready for sudden requests to replay selected clips. The equipment was not only very complicated but tended to be somewhat temperamental which was why the production people felt happier with the thought of a proper engineer at its controls. This was in the mid eighties and now, twenty years later, it seems incredible to think that television in those days was so rudimentary behind the scenes.

Father had to go into hospital for an operation and took a long time to get better again. Several weeks later we heard he'd been moved to a small nursing home in Truro to convalesce, so we took a couple of days off and drove down to see him. He was not at all well, with a buildup of fluid, slight cardiac failure and no appetite. For a man who normally enjoyed a fit outdoor life he looked all in and very frustrated. He was 88, so it wasn't too surprising he took a while to recuperate. He spent over six weeks there and the manager told me they thought they'd lost him at one point, but he was so determined to get back home again and plant his potatoes before they all sprouted too much, they reckoned that was what kept him going. Ever the market gardener! I visited him again a month later by train, doing the return trip in one day, and while I was there he ran through a list of his effects he'd like me to have or pass on to various people, clearly thinking he'd never make it. But he did—he was a tough cookie.

All too soon it was summer and only a month to go before Sue and Paul's wedding, a month spent dashing around hiring morning suits, arranging flowers, seeing catering people, getting the cars organised and generally getting in a flap. On the night before her wedding Sue was sewing up the hem of her wedding dress. Her new in-laws were due to have supper with us, but had forgotten to bring the Watford map and my route suggestions, so not surprisingly they got lost. Perhaps they were in a spin like we were. The day itself dawned bright and sunny with every prospect of it being seriously hot by midday. A friend of mine from Kodak appeared in his silver Rolls, wearing a smart grey uniform complete with peaked cap. Neighbours all down the road came to their gates as we glided past with a royal wave. It was a wonderfully happy occasion. They had invited about a hundred guests and the vicar almost jumped out of his skin when the first hymn started. He'd not reckoned on everyone present all singing at the tops of their voices. Apart from half a dozen oldies of whom I numbered myself and Patricia, just about everyone else was of Sue's generation, most of them doctors, a number of them from Cambridge and mostly churchgoers used to singing lustily. I must say I was slightly concerned when I looked into the back of the going away car that they'd hidden in a side street to find it full of ropes and all the paraphernalia needed for serious rock climbing. The thought of our precious Sue clinging on to some slippery rock by her fingernails looking over her shoulder at a thousand foot drop was not easy to dispel. I needn't have worried and didn't dare let on to Patricia. All too soon they returned from their honeymoon, Sue going back to her job in York and Paul remaining in London where he was now working at Greenwich hospital. Perhaps it was not such a good idea for two doctors to marry one another if they had to work 200 miles apart. We hoped this would just be until the training phase was complete. Little did we know...

A few months later Patricia and I went down to Pembury near Tonbridge in Kent where Sue was now a junior houseman in the hospital there. Her husband, still working at Greenwich, was able to join her most nights so at last they were able to live as man and wife, albeit in a little hospital flat. We took Sue with us to Bedgebury arboretum for a long walk, dropped her off at the flat then went on to Leonardslee gardens which were at the height of their flowering season, with rhododendrons, azaleas, magnolias, and acres of other flowering shrubs to wander amongst. This was the finest such garden we'd been to, but then we hadn't at that time 'done' the great Cornish gardens.

We'd joined a WEA (Workers Education Association) class on birds, our tutor being a lovely man, then head of education at the RSPB, David Elcome. We started with illustrated talks on the basic garden birds, but as the evenings got lighter, the lectures continued on the hoof, as it were, with walks around local areas while David taught us how to spot birds without sometimes getting a clear sight of them; in other words, to recognize them by their 'giss'. He had the real teacher's skill with an ability to teach dunderheads such as us all the basics without it ever seeming exasperating for him, as indeed it must have been. His slides were superb, for he had access to a huge RSPB slide collection. As we became more adventurous, so we extended our outings to some of the reserves, nearby Fowlmere in Cambridgeshire, Elmley Marshes on the Isle of Sheppey, Farlington Marshes at the head of Langstone Harbour just to the east of Portsmouth, and eventually to Minsmere (where we were greeted on our arrival at the car park by a nightingale singing its heart out only yards away). We'd spend hours crowded into hides with David standing behind us, pointing out all the birds feeding out in front, his teacher's penetrating voice clearly heard by us all. I shudder to think now how it must have felt to have our somewhat rowdy class descend on some dedicated birdwatcher, alone in a hide quietly trying to enjoy his birds in peace. I well remember one of the Minsmere hides built up on stilts overlooking the reedbeds where we came across two such men who had spent their whole morning in silence, one at each end of the hide waiting for a bittern to appear. I imagined them sitting there peacefully when a sound like an approaching party of rumbustious schoolchildren with the penetrating loud voice of their teacher would have shattered the peace. Then, oh drat! They're coming here! The whole hide would begin to shake as noisy feet clattered up the steps, the door swung open with a crash and moments later the hide was full, not with children but lively chatty adults, their exuberant mentor calling out, the two men having to hold on to their telescopes before they were knocked over, and moving their sandwiches away before someone sat on them. And then, after ten or fifteen minutes, the whole party got up and stomped off like a flock of geese taking off, the terrible noise diminishing until once more peace descended and the birds began to come back. Yes, we must have been a dreadful group, but it was a good baptism for us and we certainly learnt a great deal. Sorry, chaps. We're now quiet birders like you, and can only apologise for our unruly behaviour in those days!

In the early summer we went to Andorra with Ramblers, flying from Gatwick in a new HS146 to Perpignon. As we were going up the escalator at Victoria Station I noticed a label on the rucksack of the man in front of us which told us he, too, was flying to Perpignon, but with the CHA (the walking company that broke away from HF many years previously, and usually regarded by HF as a poorer relation). We got talking: he was the leader of his CHA party where they were staying on the French side at Villefranche. We would meet up again at the airport in two weeks time. At the airport we were met by our own leader, Jon Salabera, a young Basque man who loved Andorra and led for Ramblers as a way of improving his already very good English. It was a tedious four-hour drive as night descended, finally arriving at the hotel in Encamp at two in the morning. We staggered into our room and—as we always do when arriving at a foreign establishment—pulled back the shutters and opened the window for some air. Instantly our ears were assailed with a roar from the darkness outside. We were too tired to investigate at the time and it was not until the morning when we awoke that I looked outside to find our hotel was perched on the edge of a fast flowing white-water river. That was about all I could see, for thick fog obscured the far bank through which flakes of snow came down relentlessly. I could scarcely believe my eyes. Here we were, in early June on the borders of Spain, here for a walking holiday and it was snowing?

The fog lifted as soon as the sun came out and after breakfast Jon took us for a local walk around Encamp, and as it began to snow again after lunch we spent the afternoon catching up on our sleep and spent a pleasant evening looking at some lovely slides Jon had brought with him. When we looked out of the window on our second day, the sun was shining with the snow already beginning to melt, and we had a full day out along pleasant tracks up in the mountains. Encamp, a small town on the main road right in the middle of Andorra is at an altitude of some 5,000 feet, so the sight of snow shouldn't have been that much of a surprise. Jon said they'd had bad weather all the previous week, but it should be fine from now on; and it was. Every day we went for glorious walks, either in the local valleys amongst spring flowers and lush meadows, or up in the mountains sometimes as high as 10,000 feet, with wintry snow conditions under foot, but with a hot sun beating down. Jon had negotiated a good deal with the local bus company to use one of their little school buses after the school run to take us to our walking area, picking us up again in the late afternoon after the return school runs had finished. It meant we started and finished a good hour later than perhaps we'd have liked, but the cost was so low that it was well worth it, and gave Jon extra spending money to enhance our holiday somewhat. Oh that our Tenerife leader had as much gumption! We were able to spend one day down on the Spanish plain some 3,000 feet lower visiting the old market town of Sao de Urgel with its huge cathedral and little dark streets. In the course of the fortnight we explored every valley in Andorra, walked miles and miles, saw quantities of wild flowers and large numbers of birds many of which we didn't recognise as we had no reference books with us.

By the end of the holiday it was high summer in the valley bottoms, but still with snow on the tops, and on the last day we walked from winter heights all the way down to Encamp, starting with crocuses and dactylorhiza orchids pushing through the snow, to alpine meadows and down through some lovely tracks amongst trees (where a capercaillie erupted right under our feet and flew off with a wild raucous call, frightening the life out of us) down further to wild tulips and gladioli in the riverside meadows; from the bleak snow slopes above the treeline, through springtime trees just coming into bud or into blossom, to the woods in the valley in full summer foliage. We'd not been prepared for such a profusion of wild flowers and should have brought our flower books as well. Jon proudly took us to 'English' valley, which was high up at about 8,000 feet and completely carpeted with lovely delicate narcissi. It was a perfectly glorious holiday and, thanks to Jon's lovely personality, we 'gelled' from day one and became inseparable by the end of our fortnight.

Arrived back at Perpignon airport for the flight home we gathered around Jon in the departure area, chatting away, a united coherent group, when I noticed one or two other rambling types creep in and sit down in various parts of the lounge, followed after a while by the CHA leader we'd spoken to on the Gatwick train two weeks previously. He sat down somewhere else on his own looking years older. I went over to him.

"What happened?"

He shook his head. "Sheer hell! I never want another experience like that again." He looked just about all in, "That one over there." He nodded towards an elderly lady who'd just come in. "How old would you say she was?"

"She looks about seventy," I guessed. (I was 53 at the time, so anyone over seventy looked pretty ancient to me.)

"She's 82," he hissed between clenched teeth. "She put down 74 on her booking form because, as she well knew, CHA don't accept people over 75. Made our lives hell." He sighed.

"Couldn't she cope?"

"Nope. On the first day after we'd gone about a mile she said, 'Is it much further?' Then she just stopped, and I had to walk her back to the village and leave her. Every day she said she'd be all right, and every day she keeled over after a mile or so. We all took it in turns to walk her back while everyone else had to wait. Eventually after about four of these abortive starts I read her the riot act and told her she'd have to amuse herself in the village while we went on our walks. After that it was all right, except that I'd been relying on the little mountain train to get us to the start of some of the best walking country, and it had broken down."

I thought about our Tenerife holiday when the bus company went on strike. The leader is on his own, and can be in deep trouble when depending on public transport.

"And then the wretched woman amused herself in the village by eating something that disagreed with her, caught a really nasty strain of enteritis and passed it round to everyone in the party. The last of us is only just getting over it." He groaned. I glanced across at the guilty party. She was happily digging around in her rucksack for a book to read. I felt really sorry for him. He wouldn't have been far off 75 himself, and having to cope with that sort of situation would have been the last thing he needed. It wasn't as though he was being well paid to look after the group. Such leaders are more or less volunteers. I guessed CHA had lost a good leader as a result of that experience.

Back at home they'd had a heat wave and it took us several days to recover from our holiday. We were greeted with the news that our Paul had been offered a better job at the Beeb, in studio equipment design. Looking after broadcast equipment at the beck and call of a frantic producer where the programme is going out live could be very stressful and not really why he joined. This would be much more in his line.

The following week Patricia and I set off for St. Mawes, stopping on the way for a walk on Dartmoor to clear our heads. Friends from Polsue days, the Wallaces (the ones who'd allowed me to drive their new triumph car a few weeks before my seventeenth birthday, bless them!) were staying at The Rising Sun. He'd been given a knighthood having held one of the top positions at the British Motor Corporation for some years, so could afford to stay there! Peter Stokes and my two nieces arrived a day or so later so it was a nice reunion. We'd all arranged to be present for father's 90th birthday party which was held at the house of one of his friends who had a large enough sitting room. He was on excellent form, delighted to have about fifty people all come to wish him the best and made a lovely speech which was something I'd never heard from him before.

As usual father had been having difficulty with his new neighbours, whom he reckoned should be more understanding since it was he who'd had the house built and planted up the garden, including some fairly fast-growing trees on their half. These were now interfering with the jointly owned cesspit and in desperate need of attention. This had been okay when mother's friend Alma Thompson lived there, but when she died and sold up, the new neighbours didn't recognise father as having any interest in their side and resented his interference. Father had stirred things up, then waited until I came along to smooth all the ruffled feathers, claiming he was too old to do so himself! We didn't stay in St. Mawes very long this time since it was the height of the soft fruit season, and we needed to pick nearly every day. Also the runner beans were ready, and we had to drop everything to pick them too. All this produce gets sorted out into portions and put in the freezer to last us through the next year. When we bought our freezer at the time when our family was four hungry people we got the largest one available and now, with just the two of us (plus Patricia's mother who had a tiny appetite and didn't really count), one would have thought the freezer was far too large; but our garden is very productive and by freezing so much down we were practically self-sufficient in wonderful tasty organic produce. Being at home in late July and August was therefore almost essential, and as far as we were concerned we would prefer not to be on holiday while all the schools were shut down, so that suited us fine.

As soon as this harvesting eased up the two of us went on a short break to East Anglia. We took the scenic route through Long Melford and Kersey to Beth Chatto's garden at Elmstead Market where we spent the afternoon—a real education in choosing the right plant for the right place!, then fetched up in Westleton near Minsmere for the night. We'd intended to visit Minsmere the next morning, but discovered it was closed that day so we explored Framlingham, Southwold and Blythburgh, finishing up at Dunwich for a coastal walk. This was my first visit to some of the wonderful Suffolk churches, which I'd only known about from a book I'd studied at school, The Parish Churches of England. My Bradfield art master used this when giving us some fundamental teaching in architecture. Then the next day we spent at Minsmere, sighting all sorts of unusual birds, including close up views of a wryneck. How is it that birds all seem to know places like Minsmere are theirs and they can strut around there in safety? When we were sitting in one of the hides and mentioned there was a wryneck back at the car park, the hide emptied in seconds, the other people all dashing off to see it for themselves leaving us alone in the hide where we sighted our first bittern. We came home via Lodden in Norfolk where we bought a lemon tree, then went on to Bressingham Gardens, near Diss, for their Open Day. It was the gardens I'd been wanting to see and didn't realise Alan Bloom was also a steam fanatic. He drove us round the nursery fields on the narrow gauge steam railway used commercially for the business. It didn't stop there, for there was also a full size working steam-driven fairground carousel complete with pipe organ which attracted crowds of visitors and, curious to see what lay in a huge shed off to one side, I opened a door and found myself staring up at an enormous steam locomotive—the Black Prince, complete with a hundred yards or so of railway track. We explored the ruins and church at Bury St. Edmunds on the way back before finally arriving home exhausted after a three-day break that seemed like a fortnight. Patricia's ancestors all came from around those parts and we planned to take her mother there for a drive around one day.

Sue and her Paul both landed a six-month spell together at Poole Hospital, so they had taken a rented house within walking distance. We stayed with them one weekend, exploring Radipole Lake RSPB reserve in Weymouth sort of on the way, then enjoyed a lovely sunny day walking in the Lulworth and Durdle Door locality without the summer crowds who normally swarm all over the area. We do like the Dorset coast; it's a pity it's such a tedious drive for that last hour or so. A few months later it was all change. We endured a miserably cold winter back at home with deep snow, roads unsafe for Patricia to cycle on and her mother stuck indoors for weeks on end, while Sue and Paul had completed their Poole time and were now living in Leeds. This was their second job together and they had decided to buy, having found a fairly attractive place on the northern fringe of Leeds, fairly close to the ring road. It enabled them to escape to the

Dales at weekends, and was not too far from either Leeds District Hospital or St. James'. We went to see them there, and I got talking to a man in the next-door garden frantically digging over a fairly unkempt border. He didn't somehow look the gardening type to me, and from the state of the garden, he clearly wasn't. It transpired his elderly mother lived there and he'd come over for the day to do the odd jobs that had been piling up, taking a break from his job as the bishop of Wakefield. I suppose bishops are entitled to do the gardening like anyone else. While I was writing this, we had a break in Cornwall and were wandering around Burncoose nursery when we espied another bishop in his gardening togs, only distinguished by his purple vest, which like most of the rest of him at the time, had got rather muddy. This was bishop Bill, the charismatic bishop of Truro. Whilst in Leeds we had outings to some of the nearer parts of the Dales country, and some super walks in the Wharfedale and Litton valleys. We were conscious of being 'soft Southerners' and felt we'd maybe not like to overwinter in these parts even though it was so lovely in summer.

My nephew, James Stokes, was getting married to a local girl at Mold, an area we'd never been anywhere near before. The entire Stokes dynasty appeared for the wedding, somewhat overwhelming the younger ones. Patricia and I found ourselves categorised as oldies and put at a table at the wedding reception with Peter's elder brother, an eminent doctor attired in a bespoke Savile Row suit. He had been the ethical man at the BMA and I found him very interesting to talk to without admitting our own family tree was beginning to fill up with doctors. James was not very academic and after school had become a physical fitness instructor. Now he was about to join the police force, a career he would find interesting and fulfilling.

In the spring we went to Majorca with Ornitholidays for the cheapest tour they had in their brochure. Our leader was Carl Nicholson, the Midlands area officer for the RSPB, taking a busman's holiday. This all came about from the WEA classes we'd been attending with David Elcome for about three years now. We'd also been along to the RSPB local members' group in Watford where we enjoyed wonderful illustrated talks from a wide range of birdy people, a number of them professional wildlife photographers, and inevitably some of these talks were about birds of other countries. We pored over the brochures set out on tables there and were recommended to try Ornitholidays. Most of their tours were to exotic spots all over the world and way beyond our means, but the Majorca one looked about okay for us, not too far away, the birds mainly familiar ones on migration and as I say, cheap. This was our first experience of flying en masse to a popular holiday destination. From Gatwick we flew in a wide-bodied jet for the relatively short flight. At Palma we were whisked away from the crowds to a waiting bus, almost at once spotting exotic (to us) birds such as black-winged stilt and avocet in a marshy spot just outside the airport. This was going to be good! The bus quickly took us north and into the quieter countryside where eventually we arrived at a small hotel virtually on the beach at Puerto Pollensa, a pleasantly quiet resort with few other holidaymakers—it was, after all, only April.

Next morning our first outing was the lovely walk up Bocquer Valley, still completely unspoilt in 1985, where we saw our first hoopoe and lots of other European birds not found north of the English Channel. We were the only people in the valley, the birds seemed remarkably approachable and we had wonderful sightings of all of them with, for us, many 'firsts'. Then followed quiet days in the Albufera and Albuferator marshes that were teeming with all manner of waders and scrub birds, with the big stuff overhead like marsh harriers. We enjoyed a glorious day right on the tip of the island at Cape Formentor, a day with a keen breeze on which Eleanora's falcons wheeled and swooped, taking little things like red-rumped swallows with practised ease. We had another day on the southeast coast, near Port Colom from where we were so close to the not-very-common Audouin's Gulls that some people managed to get good photographs without special lenses.

And then there was a day at some quiet Salinas in the far south where more waders were found. Here we had our first brush with local people who were unwilling to let us onto the site. Carl's Spanish was rather rudimentary, but he had prepared for this by carrying with him a letter from a well-respected local ornithologist explaining we were serious birders, people whom the Majorcans needed to encourage to visit their country. It worked and we were grudgingly allowed in. On a future visit to the same Salinas at the weekend we met no workers and had no problems entering, but we saw why they were wary to allow us in the first time. While we were at the far end on one of the narrow strips between two saltpans a couple of hire cars briefly careered into the area, full of noisy youngsters who chased each other over all over the place, shrieking and blowing their horns. They did a great amount of damage, frightened off the birds needless to say, and completely spoilt the tranquillity of that peaceful spot. I'm afraid they were in all probability drunken British lager louts, and we felt deeply ashamed that such people could behave so dreadfully whilst visiting a foreign country. Thankfully that was the only incident we encountered, and as we only went to the quieter spots on the island, we were just unlucky to have met any of them. Up to a point I blame the Spanish for encouraging the more unpleasant 'tourists' by providing the sort of attractions—cheap booze, all-night discos, facilities for endless rave-ups, to which the sun, sex and sangria types will flock. It is understandable since such people spend plenty of money, but is it all really worth it for the indigenous population who have to endure it?

We went up in the mountains. Lluc Monastery is a quiet reflective spot and we carried on from there to the Cuber Reservoir for a glorious day of really superb birding. We were joined by Pat Bishop, widow of Eddie Watkinson, author of the authoritative A Guide to Birdwatching in Mallorca. Pat had taken over her late husband's weekly get-togethers for birders in one of the Puerto Pollensa hotels. She lived for part of the year on the island and was therefore most interesting to talk to. She also joined us on another day when we walked from Pollensa town to the remote promontory of Castell del Rev at the end of the Ternelles valley. This was a great help to us, for it meant going over private land and passing 'KEEP OUT' notices. Pat assured us we were on a path that led direct to the coast thereby giving us the right to travel on it regardless of any notice. Sure enough we were not stopped, and nor did we meet any other tourists.

A number of the those we saw in Puerto Pollensa were older British people who were living there for several months. We talked to some in the little supermarket and were told they found it cost less to spend the winter and early spring in that more benign climate than to hibernate in their centrally heated house back at home; but then they had no garden nor any pets, so it was an easy choice for them.

All too soon our tour was over and it was back home to work. Soon the birds we'd seen in Majorca that had been holed up there by strong northerly winds during our stay would themselves be arriving, if they didn't get shot by trigger-happy Frenchmen on the way. Our taste for overseas birdwatching had been awakened and we would go on further such trips. One of the people we'd met on the tour had told us where we could find Dartford warblers, an elusive little bird we'd never seen that was prominently on the danger list, only being found in a few spots in southern Britain. A week or two after we returned home we went to the spot he'd described down in Surrey and within half an hour we'd seen one; moreover it popped up and down on its favourite gorse bush, singing its heart out, and we had the most marvellous close sighting. I thought what a remarkable thing it was to be told of an exact spot, an exact gorse bush perhaps, by talking to someone a thousand miles away and be able to locate it immediately. The same thing happened on the occasion when we'd stumbled across a lovely specimen of a large butterfly orchid deep in some Forestry Commission land in the Chilterns, which we mentioned to a flower photographer of our acquaintance. From our rough description he found it for himself the next day with no trouble.

That summer Granny had another fall. This time she tripped whilst walking with us in Osterley Park where we'd stopped on our way back from a visit to Paul in his Acton house. Although Granny was only a very lightweight person, she was clearly suffering from osteoporosis and her arm snapped as she landed. We took her to the nearby hospital where they x-rayed her and strapped her up temporarily and next day she was inspected from head to toe at our local hospital for any damage elsewhere. She found she was unable to walk and they weren't sure whether it was just the extensive bruising she'd received. The drug to control her blood condition which she'd been on ever since blacking out that time in the Eton College chapel had side effects, one of which was to make her blood vessels very thin, so almost any slight bump would produce a huge bruise which could be very painful. Poor Granny, she looked so old and vulnerable as she lay in bed with us fussing over her. The compensation was a non-stop stream of friends who called in to chat for the next week or two. Soon she was back to her normal sprightly self and Patricia had time to get on with other things. This little episode made us realise what a tie it might be if Granny were to become permanently crippled or bed-bound. As it was, we had to cancel a planned visit to St. Mawes since we didn't feel it was sensible to leave her on her own at this time with her arm still in a sling. Instead of going to St. Mawes we took her off for a few days to a B&B in Chichester, exploring on the way the Wildfowl Trust reserve at

Arundel. A day in Southsea followed, after a walk around the perimeter track of Farlington Marshes; then home via Wisley. It was a lovely break for us and Granny coped very well with the walking, well on the way to full recovery. Father had reacted most unpleasantly to the cancellation of our visit to him, saying that he had been preparing for it for weeks and how thoughtless it was to just cancel at such short notice. With hindsight it was clear he had felt and resented all our attention going to Patricia's side of the family leaving him as just someone to stay with when we felt like a holiday. Maybe he was jealous of all the attention Granny received. But as he refused to budge from lovely St. Mawes, we didn't have much option but to only visit at holiday time.

20

More HF and The Royal Caledonian Schools

Our late summer visit to St. Mawes was one of the best. Father was in fine form, a bit stumbly in his gait and not seeing too clearly because of cataracts, but mentally very alert and pleased to see the two of us. He'd arranged for us to have the loan of a St. Mawes one-design for the week, which is a boat I love and feel absolutely at home in after having sailed Kestrel from the age of fourteen. It is the ideal craft for those waters. Together we went out almost every day, way up the Percuil river on the top of the tide, across to Helford, up the Carrick Roads to above King Harry Ferry, and just sailing around off St. Mawes itself. There were seals, lots of sea birds, buzzards over St Anthony when we went across to our favourite beach of Towan (what we called the 'local's' beach as not many visitors discovered it), and throughout the week the weather was kind. To return home to airless Watford was always such a contrast, and I longed for the time when I retired and would be free to move down west permanently. However, that might not be possible for a long time, since Patricia's mother had put down lots of roots in Watford and certainly wouldn't want to leave.

We visited Sue and Paul in their Leeds house, where Sue took us to Fountains Abbey and Studeley Royal, on to Ripon. We also visited Rievaulx Abbey and Thirsk (one of Sue's contemporaries who'd become a vet was working there, his boss being none other than Alf White, better known as James Herriot). Sue was working the most appalling hours with a duty weekend that started at 9.00 a.m. on a Saturday finishing at 9.00 a.m. on a Monday, at which time she was expected to be bright and cheerful for the start of another gruelling week. I don't see how any doctor can be capable of making critical decisions when deprived of sleep for all those hours, but that's what her employers must have thought possible—if they thought at all. It seemed she'd gone into the most impossible career imaginable and it wasn't just in her current position. This was expected of all junior doctors (which means anyone below consultant) right across the NHS. People in other professions might assume she got huge overtime pay for a 100-hour week, but overtime pay wasn't time-and-a-half or double time as in most such situations, but a fraction of normal time. It really hurt her when sometimes she was confronted by ungrateful patients for whom she had tried her hardest to look after. Fortunately there were few of these.

In the autumn we went with our local Watford HF group for a weekend at Swanage. We drove down a day early as we wanted to explore the Purbecks while we were there, an area Patricia knew from living in Weymouth during the post-war days of petrol rationing before she met me. We found the HF house and enjoyed a lovely welcome. Their Centre was in fact three large terrace houses that had been knocked into one, end-on to the outgoing one-way road in the centre of Swanage. Thus there were three front staircases with three less salubrious ones at the back. It was a largish place though didn't hold that many people and had nowhere to park a car. The establishment opposite was a nunnery with masses of car parking space, so HF had a parking arrangement with them but one had to be parked before 10.00 p.m. when the nunnery gates were locked. The Centre was clearly quite unsuited for its purpose but then a number of HF Centres were similar at this time. It would take a big shake-up in HF management before things got better.

On that first afternoon Patricia took me to Durlston Head via Peveril Point for a breath of fresh air before supper and my first impressions were good. We had the following day to ourselves before the rest of our group arrived that evening so we went down to Studland Heath and walked the nature reserve looking hopefully for Dartford Warblers. I stood on the top of a little rise scanning around the dunes on the seaward side with my binoculars when to my complete surprise I caught sight of a tall thin man standing on the top of another dune not so far away. He was completely naked, a beanpole with one bean hanging from it. What a shock! Nobody had told me there was a naturist area adjacent to the reserve. We quickly retired in the other direction and had good sightings in this promising habitat of lots of little birds that we didn't get at home, such as pipits and stonechats, but no Dartfords, alas. We enjoyed our picnic lunch beside the road at that wonderful viewpoint halfway up Nine Barrow Down, looking across to the whole of Poole harbour and I recounted to Patricia my one overnight stop there in my Collingwood sailing days. Some ten of us had taken out Wal, the 12 metre windfall yacht in which I'd had my first cross-channel trip and which BK borrowed from time to time, on this occasion sailing her from Gosport down the West Solent for a superb passage across Bournemouth Bay, coming into Poole Harbour to anchor for the night off the area of Lilliput (now a marina) which, from where we were looking, was hidden behind Brownsea Island. When we'd left next day the wind had got up and we had a hard beat back in a rising sea with increasing swell. Most of us were seasick, but the huge yacht was so exciting to sail in those conditions that it didn't really spoil our day. My lasting memory of the occasion was arriving back at the berth in Haslar Creek absolutely ravenous since we'd not eaten all day and were full of sea air. We sat round the cabin table tucking into huge helpings of a fine beef stew that our talented cook had prepared, with potatoes that had been boiled in a pressure cooker containing sea water scooped up whilst sailing back up the West Solent. Never had anything tasted so fine.

Patricia and I then drove on to the RSPB reserve at Arne, a lovely area of heathland stretching down to the shores of Poole Harbour at Shipstal Point, but again—no Dartfords. Never mind; the birding was otherwise fine and the area lovely for a good walk. Later that day we walked through the Purbeck Forest conifer plantation to Wytch Farm, hoping to get down to the foreshore, but the track ran out. We looked at the small group of nodding donkey pumps in their unattended enclosure, quietly and relentlessly extracting low-grade oil from the shale area beneath our feet. The whole area had an unpleasant atmosphere and we didn't stay.

At the house other members of our party were arriving. Ron Joiner was once again leading. He and his wife Margaret were at this time away from their home leading HF weeks for about half the year during which time they met masses of other HF'ers, so when Ron was put up for election to the HF Board he was known and easily voted in. He told us that evening about all the petty infighting which I suppose one always gets with a volunteer group like that where everyone wants to have their say. The Chief Executive at the time was an honest do-gooder (he eventually went into the Church) and not particularly tuned in to the commercial holiday business. HF, after all, had been founded by a Congregational minister to provide cheap, wholesome, healthy holidays for the disadvantaged working classes of the day, and the ethic hadn't changed all that much. Ron told us of the arrival of Peter Brassey, a young dynamic executive recruited from the holiday business to take over as our new Chief Executive and make it prosperous. His vision was to retain the group walking holidays, add many more 'special interest' weeks and to open it up to a far wider, more upmarket clientele. The old guard of traditional HF'ers didn't like this at all. They could see their cheap walking weeks becoming swamped with unnecessary extras like ensuite rooms, and seemed oblivious of the need to survive commercially. Peter Brassey was as good as his word. He needed to spend considerable money updating all the centres, which would enable him to attract fresh blood by way of lots more holidaymakers from 'outside' who would finance it. He set to with unbounded energy. Ron told us he welcomed this but the old guard were too blinkered to appreciate the need.

We woke in the morning to relentless rain blown in on a westerly gale. Swanage itself is sheltered from the westerlies and we'd arranged to take the local bus to Corfe Castle and walk back along the top of Nine Barrow Down. The weather forecast suggested the rain might ease during the day, so off we set clad in our noisy so-called waterproofs, dragged down to the bus stop by our leaders. By the time we clambered out of the steamed-up bus at Corfe it was, if anything, raining even harder. There was no going back now, so off we tramped, slithering around in the slippery marl up the side of the ridge for the long walk back. At the top we felt the full force of the wind that blew us along so that we had to hang on to one another to keep upright. The rain, of course, had penetrated our innermost garments in no time at all and most of us had squelchy wet boots as well. We did not enjoy that walk in the slightest, but the experience was a useful one, if only to teach us how not to dress in such conditions. Next morning was a little better. We walked up over Ballard Down heading for Old Harry Rocks, a chalky outcrop with isolated stacks going out over the sea, a continuation of the Needles seen across the bay. But the rain came down once more and we cut our walk short. After lunch we said goodbye and drove down to Studland, went walking over Newton Heath (the rain had gone by now) then drove on over the ferry to South Sands, through Bournemouth and back home. It had been an eventful weekend, the first of many visits to the Purbecks. But all our subsequent visits would be in wonderful sunshine.

We had noticed one of the 'Special Interest' weeks offered by HF was Scottish Country Dancing at the Loch Awe house, led by a certificated teacher who did a lot of this sort of thing. It looked promising, and I'd remembered the ballroom at Loch Awe had a good floor, so we booked up for the following April. Hopefully this time Patricia would be able to enjoy some of that superb scenery at last. We went there by train—by far the easiest way, as the Glasgow sleeper from Euston picks up at Watford. Two of the coaches went all the way to Fort William, so we would be able to stay on the train to Crianlarich, then change for the Oban train that passed directly below the HF house. I love these journeys where you get on in dreary suburbia and wake up next morning in a magical new country. So it was with this one, as we pulled the blinds back whilst passing the top of Loch Lomond with the early sun glinting across the water, fresh damp birch woodland by the track just showing the beginnings of bright new leaves. Our Euston coaches had been shunted onto the back of the Glasgow to Fort William train pulled by a diesel with no facilities for providing the electric power, something needed in a sleeper for heating and hot water. Therefore we had to ourselves a unit called an 'Ethel' which one of my train-spotting friends told me stood for Engineless Train Heating and Electricity. All this involved a lot of thumping and shunting at Glasgow which woke everybody up of course. At Crianlarich we had a couple of hours to wait for our Oban connection, but the station buffet was geared for such things and provided a much-appreciated welcome breakfast.

On arrival at the HF house we met up with most of the others who would be on the dancing week and one of the ladies joined Patricia and me on a walk up to the Cruachan Reservoir, too late for us to discover she was no walker, the climb almost finishing her off for the week. I've always assumed right from the days of my wimpish inability to play games at school that I'm not as good at physical activities as other people, but more and more I was discovering I was way out in front when it came to dancing, hill-climbing and general walking. We were really in pretty good shape for such a week as we were about to enjoy. That evening after a dram or two and a good HF supper we had a lovely informal dance with all our favourites. Our room was one of the finest with views out across Loch Awe and the sun woke us up next morning so we could enjoy it at its best. Where was the relentless rain Paul and I had endured on our last visit? Was it still down at Swanage? We had all the day to do as we wished, for the dance instruction proper did not start until the next morning, so once again we took to the hills, this time on our own. We found large numbers of cuckoos had arrived and were hungrily gobbling up hairy caterpillars, something most birds are unable to eat, but cuckoos obviously tuck into them with relish. They seemed quite unconcerned with our gawking at them through binoculars at a range of fifty feet, the closest I've ever been to a cuckoo. No doubt some poor meadow pipit would soon discover an over-size egg filling its nest, and instinctively take over the unenviable task of feeding a monster chick that would quickly become many times bigger than itself. In the afternoon our whole party walked to the castle ruins at the head of Loch Awe and came back along the railway track. These single track lines in the quieter country areas are often used by walkers needing a dry path, so we weren't too concerned and had been told there were no trains on a Sunday anyway.

Next morning promptly at nine we assembled in the ballroom for our first class. The week had been billed as dance instruction in the mornings with optional walking in the afternoons, and social Scottish Country Dancing in the evenings. We met Eleanor Warburton, our teacher, and her pianist. Eleanor taught Scottish Country Dancing as laid down by Dr Jean Milligan, the lady who founded the Royal Scottish Country Dance Society in the 1920s and put Scottish Country Dancing on the map. Eleanor had a large framed portrait of Jean Milligan that she displayed for us all to pay obeisance to each morning. We began to feel that maybe we'd come to the wrong sort of class, but we needn't have worried. Her technique instruction was excellent and brought us along no end. Unfortunately when it came to learning new dances she had nothing like the skill of our Amersham leader, Wesley. Nevertheless, we really felt that by the end of each morning's instruction we had achieved a lot. The weather all that week was sublime, with enough cotton wool clouds scudding along to enhance the photographs I took and a light enough breeze to enable us to really enjoy the warmth of spring sunshine coming down from a clean unpolluted sky. I always fret when stuck indoors in such weather, but at least we were able to get out in the afternoons. We'd have a break mid morning for coffee on the terrace and one morning while I was sipping my coffee gazing across the loch I became conscious of a coach that had stopped in the road nearby. I glanced up to see a horde of camera-clasping American tourists all scrambling down for the shot of a lifetime. One of them called out over his shoulder, "Quick, honey, there's the laird himself!"

I looked around for this laird and then realised they were all was pointing their cameras at me. From where they were standing looking over the wall they had a super shot of this Scottish castle with its baroque towers, water reflecting the mountains beyond, and there on the terrace in front of the castle a man in a kilt. I could just imagine the pictures being shown to the folks back at home.

The week followed a set routine. We'd have Eleanor's classes each morning, break for a couple of drinks and a great HF lunch, then off we'd go up into the mountains for our afternoons, a bath and change when we got back, a dram and a huge HF supper followed by dancing until late evening. We don't like sitting around, and there was little time for that!

Actually, our afternoons weren't all mountains; on one day we all took the boat from Taynuilt up Loch Etive to look for seals. I drove the boat which I love doing, the boatman keeping a wary eye on me. I regaled Patricia with a description of the conditions the last time I'd been on this boat with Paul. This time we were not only able to creep within yards of lots of seals, some of them hauled out, but I also spotted a golden eagle over Ben Meean to the southwest, and again there were red deer on the braes at the back of Ben Cruachan. We disembarked to walk back down a track for four miles or so to where the bus would pick us up, and at this point discovered we had no other 'walkers' in the party except the leader (designated by HF headquarters) who was no leader in the accepted sense. He'd not sussed out the walk with the result that when the track ran out he had no idea where to go, and he had no map. At least I was able to come to the rescue with an OS map, and we eventually managed to fight our way to the road through impenetrable conifer forest criss-crossed with little streams.

The next day some of us went to Cruachan Power station for the tourist visit, being taken from the reception area on the edge of the Pass of Brander down a slope in a minibus to the power station itself which is several hundred feet below the level of Loch Awe and some 2,000 feet or so underneath the reservoir. In the turbine hall we saw massive electricity generating machinery whining away and heard how the water falling down a huge pipe from the reservoir overhead has sufficient energy after driving the turbines to run uphill to the surface from where it runs gently out into the loch. Judging by the size of the National Grid pylons marching across the landscape, this is a sizable contribution to Scotland's hydroelectric power. Our party also took a trip on the loch in a couple of boats, one of which was driven by the boatman and the other by me. This time I was appreciated for my ability to handle a boat! On the other days Patricia and I walked in our favourite valley near to the house, usually doing this before breakfast when there were more birds to be seen.

~*~

In case you are wondering if I ever found time to go to work, let me assure you I had to do that as well, but it would be boring to talk too much about it. My routine had settled down to the point where I had a permanent arrangement for car sharing with Peter Prosser who lived in the next road. We would take turns with the driving and in the process came to know one another very well. Peter is a competent do-it-yourselfer and I learnt a lot of tricks from him. The car sharing also meant we had to keep regular hours, which I am sure was a sensible habit for both of us. Far too often people found they needed to work on in the evenings to get the work done, something the Company turned a blind eye to but probably welcomed in the same way that the cash-starved NHS appeared quite happy to turn a blind eye to junior doctors working 120-hour weeks for virtually no additional pay. Sooner or later something would give—usually the victim's health.

Way back in 1981 my department had acquired the latest thing in computers. Until then we employed two or three people who looked after all the engineering budgeting and control paperwork, and I remember those desktop calculators with big keys and a handle on one side that you pulled every time a figure was entered. Then there was the Roneo machine, which used methylated spirits and a horrible purple dye that got all over one's hands and on the carpet. One day a little computer arrived which was to do away with all that. It was so small that it fitted onto one of the office tables and didn't need an air-conditioned room all to itself like other computers we'd been used to around the factory. It was one of the first IBM 1088 PCs and cost about £5,000. Needless to say it turned out to be completely inadequate for the job, but did prove to be a most useful tool for us to learn what one might be able to do with such a machine. Once it was realised it was inadequate no one in our department wanted to play with it except me, as I find such things fun, and—to be honest, I often had time on my hands. I spent hours learning to use spreadsheets and plot graphs. I also learnt something about the early word processors. This put me light years ahead of most of my contemporaries and as computers improved over the years I was able to keep up to speed with them. Now, five years later, I had a useful 386 machine to myself and was able to knock out posh-looking reports with graphs and tables for the other engineers.

I was doing this whilst still looking after the project planning boys, since that job didn't fully extend me. Fun as it was, I was somewhat vulnerable. A minor reorganisation had left our unit with a new manager, one that was universally unpopular and, as I soon discovered, was not a very pleasant person to work for. We guessed he had been put there in the role of hatchet man. The Company were in the throes of one of their terrible 'downsizing' exercises and I knew the work I was doing was hardly essential, that if the accountants wanted to find activities around the Company that were not profitable, then most of my tasks would come into that category. I was firmly out of front-line engineering and thought it might be more sensible to jump rather than wait to be pushed, at least one would then have a chance of jumping in the right direction. I could probably jump sideways whereas if I was pushed it would almost certainly be down or even over the precipice. I wondered whether any administrative job might be needed somewhere completely different. Without going up the line within my own engineering division, I asked my local personnel man if he'd keep his ear to the ground, and the very next day received a telephone call from someone in Head Office who had been looking for a person to do employee relations work, in particular handling the administrative side for those people who were on assignment overseas but still on the Company's books. Would I like to come along for an informal interview?

An informal interview meant they would assess me and give me a chance to look at the job before my boss found out. I went to Head Office (the same distance from home as the factory, but in the opposite direction) and met a number of relaxed and laid-back individuals. I would be working in a tiny unit of only half a dozen others in great comfort and in a relaxed atmosphere. It would be a one-year assignment with an opportunity to extend it if both sides wished to. I couldn't make up my mind. I'd be leaving a congenial technical group of friends and starting again from scratch. Did I want to do that in my mid-fifties? When faced with decisions of this type I have been known to recall one of the Brockbank cartoons, the ones featuring old cars and their eccentric drivers. This one showed a little man who'd attempted to drive his rickety vintage car between two trams, the car emerging the other side squeezed into a tall thin shape. He's standing beside the wreckage and the caption reads, "Oh well, nothing venture, nothing win!" I'd spent most of my Kodak time not venturing very far. I accepted the job.

Within a few weeks I discovered beneath the surface of my new managers a desperate underlying insecurity, all of them suspecting everyone else of trying to push them off the ladder. They went round, backs to the wall, desperate to look after number one at the expense of giving their all to the hand that fed them. The atmosphere was charged with political intrigue. It was a complete shock for me, having spent the last twenty years or so in an environment where everyone pulled in the same direction. I was so naïve I hadn't appreciated that Peter's Principle (the one that says people get promoted until they reach their level of incompetence) was any more than a joke. These people had been struggling up the ladder, kicking down all the opposition, until they'd reached a point where they had risen too high, and there they'd stuck, unable to cope and with everyone else baying for blood. To me it seemed they were all in it. At meetings nobody said anything without first considering the effect this might have on their position. Nobody pulled together.

There were lighter moments. In a nearby office the wife of the then president of the Berkhamsted Strathspey and Reel Club where I'd first met her, had a part time secretarial job. She was a well-built lady, who proceeded along the long Head Office corridors like Joan Hammond dressed up for her role in Aida. One day as we found ourselves approaching one another I did a little entrechat as we neared, whereupon she turned about, grabbed me in a promenade hold and together we danced a reel-time promenade down to the far end, beautifully in time and using our best demonstration quality steps. It was only as she turned to walk back again that we noticed one of the managers staring disbelievingly after us. The word must have got about for we were both regarded somewhat warily after that.

My immediate workmates were pleasant enough, the unit worked satisfactorily and the comfort of a carpeted restaurant instead of the works canteen was agreeable, but the job did involve meeting managers of other divisions, also some of the directors. These were the people who were so jittery. I endured it for a year, then there was some shuffling around and the Company Personnel Officer asked me if I would read up on trade union law and become his right hand expert at trade union meetings. I pointed out that an engineer is ill equipped for such matters and no way would I be able to be any good at that! I hate going to 'Us and Them' meetings where, almost by definition, there are two sides negotiating for their own ends whilst pretending to go along with the opposition. It's all so unproductive and neither side ever wins. To be part of the negotiating machine would be anathema. It was an opportunity to bow out gracefully and return to the comfort and relative safety of my engineering friends.

In my absence the little unit I used to work in had more or less folded, as I had thought it might. A new job was readily found for me. Most engineers were, to use Gerard Hoffnung phraseology, 'good with spanner; not too good with pen', or in other words, they'd concentrated at college on the science subjects, ignoring completely the written word. In their misguided wisdom the Government had decided to take English grammar off the school curriculum which meant that younger engineers educated at state schools (and that included all the people with whom I worked at Kodak) had only the vaguest notion how to string a sentence together. The chickens were coming home to roost. I found myself in the unofficial and unexpected role of English mentor for anyone needing to write a report. All project engineers had to write reports from time to time, and the senior ones wrote important reports that found their way to top management and sometimes to the international top management. These people would creep up to me: "As someone not close to the project, John, please could you just give this the once-over and see whether it all makes sense?" What they meant was, would I also knock it into grammatically correct English suitable for sending up the line. As, relatively speaking, I was good with pen but nothing like so good with spanner, this was an ideal arrangement, work I enjoyed doing and was much appreciated. It was a natural follow-on from Kepner Tregoe training where, usefully, I had met several of the International Head Office personnel at the end of my KT course in Niagara Falls; contacts that turned out to be very useful when helping these lads.

So began a new life for me. My work concerned with engineering planning and budgeting died down and I became the engineering project departmental paper man. This role I carried out for several years, spending my spare time working with another engineer, Brian Wareham, making videos for the Division. As a hobby he had all the gear and would do his editing at home, shooting originals and editing the results on Super-VHS, after which he'd run off copies on normal VHS. He'd been dabbling in wedding videos and club motoring events until now, but our enlightened divisional manager liked to give an annual review to his troops (it was an ego trip for him to stand up in front of several hundred employees and front a 'show'—the more razzmatazz the better) and he welcomed video footage of the major multi-million pound projects being built. Hence my backdoor involvement. Once again I had found a role I enjoyed, and had accepted by the simple process of taking it up and ignoring my normal deskwork. Project managers would ask one of us to shoot various stages of their project in case it might be needed in the future, and—importantly—they had the funds to pay for it. Just before I left the FFD a few years previously that group had acquired a video camera, supposedly for training purposes. It was looked after by the training officer who allowed me to use it occasionally and taught me the rudiments of editing. It was a monstrous affair really too heavy for handheld use, and the viewfinder was not very good so we always used it with a little monitor which meant several cables to trip over in addition to the tripod legs. However it had been a useful introduction to video making and, of course, it was fun.

Brian and I worked as a team, Brian calling himself the technical director with me the artistic director. My slight artistic talents and general interest in watching television programmes had led me to ponder how some of them were made; how did they get the camera into that position, was this interview filmed with one camera, the interviewer doing 'nodding' shots afterwards, to be inserted into the interview from time to time? and Wow! What an introduction! This will be a programme that I must see, and so on. Brian felt the same way, and together we'd plan a shoot and try to make anything we did come alive. I recalled the time when in the Navy I had been subjected to a course in ship damage control, and we'd had to watch a dreadful training film that began with a model ship bobbing about in a tank, the voiceover speaker droning in a boring voice, "A ship is designed to float…" We would never make a film like that! The two of us set to with enthusiasm, and produced a ten-minute roundup of project work around the Company which we back-projected onto a huge eight-foot high screen in a large auditorium. While we were at it we put a camera onto the speaker and projected his image on the screen behind him, just for good measure. What with fading lights up and down, playing suitable music between items and inserting small cutaways to fit in with slides other speakers were using, the whole event became well worth turning out for, and we repeated it again the following year. We soon became known around the Company, and the Harrow Fire and Safety people commissioned us to make a training video of a mock accident in one of the production buildings. This involved the local emergency services that were keen to have this done, so we attended several planning sessions before the big day. The resulting video was well received and our Fire Officer asked for several copies to be made for use by the Harrow Fire Service.

A year later we were asked by the Hertfordshire Fire Service to do the same for an exercise, where a fire would be staged on the upper floors of our 17-storey Head Office in Hemel Hempstead. The building would be evacuated, all three emergency services would be involved and we'd use several cameras, one of them carried by a fireman at the scene of the 'blaze'. In great secrecy a date and time were fixed, the local news media were informed half an hour before zero hour, a team of 'accident' actors with gory makeup were smuggled into the building, and one of our own people in a wheelchair looking for all the world like JR just 'happened' to be on a visit to an office on the 6th floor. Then while I filmed her, one of the secretaries took off her shoe and smashed the little glass window on the nearby fire alarm.

Smoke bombs were set off as the bells began to clatter, and the other cameras rolled. We'd chosen a quiet day, the sun was conveniently shining, and few of the office workers realised this was not the real thing, especially when noisy fire appliances soon surrounded the building, the police arrived to divert traffic, ambulances came in to take away the volunteer 'injured' as they were discovered and the Head Office maintenance manager bawled at everybody through his loud hailer to stand well clear. One of my chums spotted me crouched behind my camera and guessed it might be a set-up job but couldn't be sure.

Half an hour later the show was over, people trooped back inside, the firemen rolled up their hoses and we went along for the washup meeting. A week later Brian and I had produced a half-hour training film for the Hertfordshire Fire

Service, and our Managing Director asked to see it. However, he said he could only spare ten minutes, so would it be possible to edit a version for him? Wise man—he more or less forced us to re-edit the whole film, cutting out all the unnecessary bits and tightly editing all that remained. The result was a much more professional film that raced along, and that was the version which was used most of the time.

~*~

Along the Aldenham Road beyond the Watford Technical High School which our children had attended were two of the bigger secondary schools for Watford, Bushy Meads and Queens School. Also along there was another building, a turn-of-the-century red brick place called The Royal Caledonian Schools. I first went along there back in the 1980s when our Watford Club held one of their periodic dances in the main school hall, as it had a good floor and—of great importance to any Scottish organisers—it was cheap! Donald Wallace, a member of the Watford Club and a retired RAF Group Captain padre, was something to do with the schools and persuaded the Watford dancing club members to help in an annual fund-raising shindig that took place every year. The first year we went along to find what appeared at first sight to be a huge up-market jumble sale, but it was more than that. A couple of Scottish traders had come along, one to sell haggis and the other was a fishmonger who specialised in Arbroath Smokeys and Scottish wild salmon. We were recommended to try the fish which we did and enjoyed very much, and we sat through the big auction where most of the items that hadn't gone earlier were sold off for very high prices, altogether netting many thousands of pounds for the Schools. The children were running around helping or just enjoying themselves, dressed in their smart red kilts with green jerseys, and they seemed a well run and happy bunch. To round off the day we all sat down in the school hall while the children put on a display. They had a pipe and drum band which played exceptionally well in a military way, and then on came groups of children who danced some lovely pieces, choreographed Highland dancing. I was quite spellbound by their enthusiasm and the quality of their performance and wished I had brought the Kodak video equipment with me on which to capture it. This occasion took place the year before I met Brian Wareham and the equipment I am talking about was the early hefty camera and monitor I'd first used. Home videoing was still in its infancy with no accepted standards, and not many people possessed the wherewithal to make videos.

The following year we were back. This time I came prepared with the borrowed equipment and set it up on the balcony commanding a good uninterrupted view of the stage. Donald Wallace was dashing around earlier and I asked him where the power point was. He was wearing his dog collar and all the children were rushing about at his beck and call. At this point I discovered he was the Schools' padre and ran the establishment jointly with the Master (who was a retired Royal Navy captain). Donald helped me get organised and said the schools would like to see the video afterwards. The formula was much as last time, so I filmed it all without the need to do any editing, besides I was not at that time into inserting 'cutaways' and similar devices to make a more coherent video for watching. They were shown my resulting video, seemed to like it, and things went quiet for a while.

In 1988 the Schools were to have a grand opening of their dining hall, which had been refurbished and was now hung with a lot of regimental pictures and had been rather grandly re-named The Hall of the Regiments. They had arranged for Her Majesty Queen Elizabeth The Queen Mother to perform the opening ceremony. Donald contacted me: would I like to come along and video the occasion? Would I! How was it the Schools were able to attract royalty to come along? Over time I found out.

It all started in 1808 when the Highland Society, chaired by Queen Victoria's father, the Duke of Kent and Strathearn, started to raise funds to establish an Asylum (a word more correctly used in those days to denote a simple sanctuary, or place of refuge and safety) for the many destitute Scottish children roaming the streets of London. This had come about as a result of their fathers having enlisted into the army, many of whom did not return. And so, in 1815 an Act of Parliament was passed to create the Caledonian Asylum. It began with just six boys and some premises in Hatton Garden. In 1826 new premises were built in a quiet rural part of Islington known as Copenhagen Fields. The road that led out to that spot from the Liverpool Street area becoming known as the Caledonian Road. The new building had accommodation for 100 boys and was extended a few years later to take in girls as well. By 1852 the name was changed to The Royal Caledonian Schools after it received Royal Patronage. By the latter part of the century the countrified nature of Islington was changing fast and the Schools found they had a new neighbour—Pentonville Prison! So it was decided to move, and in 1902 the current building was put up in the rural area of Bushey, where it still is. It was probably at its most active in the years after World War II when many British forces personnel were serving overseas in Germany, so that the need for boarding education was great. However, with good state schools adjacent and the Caledonian buildings bulging at the seams, it was decided in 1947 that the children should receive their education in the local schools, the Caley building itself remaining as their home during termtime. This is how it was when I came on the scene.

On the day of The Queen Mother's visit I turned up in my best kilt and set up my camera on a huge tripod at one end of the hall, myself standing on a table so I could command a view over everyone's heads. Donald, looking very grand in a scarlet cassock (a legacy from his time as a Queen's chaplain during his service years) rehearsed the last details, then we all trooped out to the school entrance to welcome the Royal party. The Schools' president, the Duke of Argyll, was there to introduce the other main players. The Queen Mother came into the hall, The Duke of Argyll made a short speech, Donald read a prayer and The Queen Mother pulled the string that parted curtains to display the plaque that had been affixed to the end wall. I thought that was it, but oh no! The Queen Mum, bless her, spent the next hour and a half going round the room, speaking to the representatives of every Scottish regiment present, and talked to every single child in the school. After that she went into the Master's rooms to sign the book and have a short break while everyone else moved next door into the main hall and took their seats for the dancing and band display. I'd had my problems with the arrival just before the event started, when a somewhat pushy film crew from ITN wanted a short piece for the news that night. They stayed for the entire morning and the problem for me was their crew included a lighting man who manned a powerful floodlight that completely spoilt the homely atmosphere and frequently pointed it at me, making my own videoing difficult. We also had present a man from a local Watford shop that sold and hired video gear who had been persuaded to come along and do some videoing for free (Donald's main role was evidently to be persuasive in the nicest possible way. He would succeed not only in extracting money from every Scottish business around, but extended his skills to getting anyone who could be useful to help the Schools in other ways. I suppose that was how I came to be there as well).

The Schools' Chairman, Bill Heeps, a retired newspaper owner, presented Her Majesty with a superb specially commissioned cut glass bowl and made a lovely little speech which he introduced with the unforgettable words "With the magnanimity for which the Scots are well-known…" That, of course, brought the house down.

The ITN crew went off at last, their morning's work wasted since that evening's bulletin was full of other matters leaving no time for it, while the man from the Watford shop eventually produced his shots for me to incorporate into my little video, which I had great fun editing. I showed the results to Donald and was invited to come along to show it again to the members of the Board at their next meeting at the Schools.

This Board meeting was combined with a social visit to the Schools, the meeting itself being held in the Boardroom while the Directors' wives together with myself and Patricia met and chatted in another part of the building. All the children had once again dressed in their kilts (I'd never seen them dressed otherwise, so had presumed they always wore kilts) and there was to be an opening of their newly refurbished swimming pool. When it came to the video, I found myself seated beside someone who introduced himself as a retired Captain RN who would shortly be taking over as Master. After everyone had seen the video I was presented with a School plaque (similar to the Agincourt ship's plaque that I had presented to our Israeli hosts all those years ago, and probably made by the same company) and afterwards Donald said they'd like to invite me to become one of the Schools' directors.

For the next few years I attended the Board meetings, which were normally held at the Caledonian Club in Halkin Street just behind Buckingham Palace. Sometimes I went by underground, but usually bummed a lift with Donald. Donald was a great name-dropper, and I had the impression he may have been at school with some of the rich and famous, referring to our august President whom he'd known for years as Jimmy Cameron, and told a story of a time while he was staying at Inverary Castle, the Duke's seat. The two of them were planting a shrub in one of the borders near the visitors' entrance when a visitor came up supposing them to be a couple of gardeners, and asked about some aspects of the castle. The Duke chatted away to her, answering all her questions and wished her a pleasant day. She trotted off, Donald thought, quite unaware to whom she had been speaking. Many of the Schools directors, and there were a great number though only a few attended Board meetings, had titles or senior military ranks, and had no doubt been recruited for the help that would give to the Schools. In my case, I had no abilities in the decision-making activities particularly when it came to financial affairs, but found it interesting to be part of the team. My contribution was mainly to lay out and print their annual colour brochure, a task I found most enjoyable, and to be available for any more video making that might be required.

Every year Donald organised an event he called 'Kirking of the Tartan' whereby he would arrange for one of the Clan Chiefs to visit the Schools for a special service where that clan's Tartan would be paraded, the address being given by the Moderator. It took place in November when the Moderator had business in London, a regular annual occasion. I was asked to make a video of one of these, the tartan that year being the Macdonald. Lord Macdonald, who ran an up-market hotel in southern Skye with his wife Claire (a renowned cook), would be up in London at that time. His full title is Macdonald of Macdonald, Paramount Chief of the Clan Donald, quite a mouthful for such a pleasant and unassuming man. Donald Wallace called him 'Godfrey', though not in other people's presence. We contacted our local Macdonalds takeaway establishment and suggested they might like some publicity being seen with the Chief of the Clan from which their name came. We suggested their American headquarters would be thrilled, since Americans love that sort of thing. The result of this was that the shop provided every child with a Big Mac, and Lord Macdonald was photographed biting into a Big Mac himself with feigned relish. All the children in the schools whose name was Macdonald were, naturally, introduced to their Chief and duly recorded on the video. My son Paul attired in my other kilt joined me with a second camera, and we made a lovely film of the whole occasion, one of my best which I still treasure.

When it was time for Donald Wallace to retire, the Directors' Meeting at that time was a special affair followed by a party to which all the wives were invited and the Duke of Argyll came along as well, and chaired the Board meeting. He chatted to Patricia and myself, but we didn't get an invitation to plant any shrubs at Inverary. Donald said later that the Duke could be very formal when necessary, and quoted the time he'd been present at some function when a gushing American lady had discovered there was a real Duke present. She pushed her way over to where he was standing, started talking away with "Oh my, are you a real Dook? What do I call you, Dook?" to which he replied very seriously with a slight tilt of the head, "Your Grace will suffice, madam," and turned to continue the conversation he had been having.

After Donald retired he was replaced by Roger Dean as padre. No military man, (although his initials were R.A.F.) Roger was more of a down-to-earth padre, and it was unfortunately during his time the schools went into a decline.

The numbers had been dropping over the years, from a high of over a hundred down to just over sixty when I came on the scene. About fifteen of these were the children of Black Watch fathers who were overseas in Germany. Then the British Army presence in Germany was terminated, the Black Watch came home, their children returned to their families and went to school elsewhere. The Schools were now below breakeven strength. Part of the premises were let to a Montessori School who used them for classes during the day when the Caley children were away at local schools, but the cost of maintaining the crumbling premises was huge, and Roger found looking after these premises had become his main responsibility, taking most of his time. Then, out of the blue, our Chairman Bill Heeps died unexpectedly. Shortly after that one of the Schools' housemasters had to leave under a cloud resulting in several children being withdrawn, and crisis talks began about the Schools' future.

It was decided to wind up the Schools, the remainder of the children returning to their parents for them to be educated at other establishments, to sell the premises and with any remaining money and the proceeds from the sale to invest this in an educational trust for the benefit of the children of Scottish Forces personnel.

A recently retired social services man, also retired from local politics where he'd just had a spell as Watford's mayor, came in to look after the children and run the establishment while the rundown took place. I was able to give a lot of help with publicity material, for it would still be necessary to keep the funds rolling in, and I made a final rather sad video of the end of the Schools, with some footage of now empty dormitories still echoing with the ghostly shouts and chatter of past children.

The school buildings sat forlornly empty for a year or two until the Purcell School of Music took them over and they began a new life with a new purpose. All the Schools artefacts collected over the years were dispersed, some to the Bushey Museum locally, and some to Inverary Castle.

I was glad to have been involved with the Caley Schools during its heyday, but its raison d'être was over. I met lots of interesting people during my time there, and have memories (not to mention videos) of some of the good times.

21

Home Once More

They do say that you can recognise cars owned by mechanical engineers because of their poor state of repair, and I shall never forget the rusty bicycle owned by the Cambridge don who lectured us in lubrication. As I am an electrical engineer, it would not be surprising for you to know that the wiring in our house was verging on the dangerous. But then I was aware of this and replaced bits and pieces to keep ticking along in reasonable safety. Eventually even I began to get concerned that it was becoming hazardous, so asked a couple of Kodak electricians who did house rewiring for their weekend moonlighting activities if they would like to do mine. I approached them, as there is all the difference in the world between a professional engineer who may well be all fingers and thumbs, and a tradesman whose job is to do the actual work. They gave me a frightening quote and admitted it was messy, very messy.

"Floorboards up in every room, can't help the dust I'm afraid, spoil the decorations too. That's inevitable. Chasing out the plaster for new cables will mean bits of plaster fly all over the place. Even found some inside someone's fridge once. Best to do a job like this when the house is empty, really."

I thanked them and said I'd think about it. The wiring had originally been done very well, everything encased in metal conduit, but it was rubber insulated, and the rubber had perished where it was exposed at the few inches leading into every fitting. When the old 15-amp round pin sockets had been upgraded to modern 13-amp sockets, insulating tape had been used to keep the exposed live wires from touching. I thought about it some more and decided to do the job myself, bit by bit, slowly, and without the mess in every room, or in the fridge.

Actually the job turned out to be remarkably straightforward. I installed a new consumer unit (that box with all the fuses in it) in the garage, which I connected up with a temporary lead. Then I began running a ring main from there, starting in our dining room where the lack of a proper power point had been annoying us for years. I completed this, connecting it to my new consumer unit so that we were back in business, filled the holes in the wall and redecorated just those bits and that little part of the job was done. I went from room to room taking a day or two with each one, and in a couple of months of evenings and weekends I'd completed the whole rewire. When I had the electricity board in to connect me up the engineer commented on how neat the wiring looked and which firm had I used? In the whole process I'd found lots of the original wiring had been extended at some time by various 'little men' and was far more dangerous than I'd suspected. Now at last I had a proper ring main installed in compliance with the latest IEE Regulations and was able to sleep at nights once more.

While all this was going on I had a call one day from a rear admiral phoning from a MoD establishment in London. It turned out he was one of my old Long Course mates who'd stayed on longer than the rest of us and reached the dizzy heights of flag officer while everyone else fell by the wayside. He himself was retiring soon and had been in touch with several others from our entry about having a reunion before we all lost touch or turned our toes up. Several of them lived in and around Bath, since they had bought houses there way back when they'd had a shore job at the Admiralty design offices in Bath, so that was where the reunion was to be. Patricia and I set off and were put up for the night, together with six others, in the house of my friend David Allgood. Surprisingly for nowadays, only one of the twenty or so original members had a different wife to the one he started with. The others were married in the good old-fashioned way, though I didn't know more than a few wives, having lost touch with most of the others when we set out for Australia. One of our number had retired early and gone into the church and another one was reputed to be a monk in some enclosed order.

When we arrived for the reunion proper I was in for quite a shock. My memories of our Long Course days were of twenty slim young men bursting with fun and energy. I now walked into a room full of stout grey-haired old gentlemen, some with quite a stoop, several now sporting spectacles, but all vaguely recognisable. It was their voices that hadn't changed at all and the mannerisms were the same. I found it quite fascinating. What about me? I hadn't changed at all, had I? One of them pointed out that I, too, had an old man's walk, was bald and sported a beard that was going white here and there. Well, at least I hadn't got too rotund. I'm rather proud of the fact that I weigh the same as I did when I joined the Royal Navy at age nineteen, and I can still get into the suit I had made just after our wedding.

I noticed amongst the classes offered by our local authority an evening course in horticulture working towards the RHS exams and decided to give it a go, as it seemed to be covering the subject in an academic way. Maybe I'd learn the right way to do things from a professional, rather than just pick it up, so I joined. I'd always felt I'd have liked to attend horticultural college in my young days, but one can't do everything. Maybe this would be a poor man's substitute. Alas, most of the others turned out to be the usual folk who attend such courses— they'd come along for the social side and weren't too fussed whether they learnt anything or not. The teacher appreciated this, so took it along at a slow rate.

Unfortunately he was also teaching the same course at another venue, and sometimes gave us the same lecture twice having got the two classes muddled up. Nevertheless, I did indeed learn something and got to know one or two others, one of whom worked at our local garden centre.

That winter father was taken into hospital with a serious problem to do with his digestion tract. He'd never been completely well in that department ever since his duodenal ulcer operation, and suffered a lot of constipation. We had a phone call to say he was having a barium meal as part of the investigations. When we contacted the hospital, they told us he would be having an operation. Two days later we phoned again to hear that the operation had been postponed, since he was not well enough. Perhaps we should go down? Father had been so unpleasant when we postponed our regular visit to see him that time when granny had broken her arm, and had virtually accused Patricia of taking me away from him. He'd gone so far as to write me a letter saying he was fed up with what he called my behaviour and would alter his will in favour of Peter's side of the family. Well, if he was going to do that, there was nothing I could do about it, but as a result we'd not gone to St. Mawes for some time now. Patricia had been dreadfully hurt, but kept her true feelings to herself. I now felt very guilty that I hadn't kept up to date with his deteriorating health, and was still wondering whether I should rush down to Cornwall when the hospital phoned to say father had died. It was cancer of the bowel which had spread to his liver; the end being very swift.

A week later we went drove down for the funeral at Truro, then carried on to St. Mawes where one of the neighbours had laid on a lunch for all of Peter's family, also Patricia and myself. Afterwards we called in to see the solicitor and found that father had indeed cut me out of his Will entirely. Peter was rather embarrassed and said afterwards he would go halves with everything that came his way, which was unlikely to be very much. He was as good as his word, wonderful fellow, and a very generous gesture on his part since I believe he wasn't particularly well off. Some years previously father had already made over the house jointly to Jane and myself, so it was only father's other assets which would be involved. These turned out to be modest, so modest that he must have been living very simply out of necessity rather than choice, although he always said he preferred the simple life. He'd bought a £20 premium bond when they first came out and ever since had been saying "I'll do so-and-so when Ernie comes home." Maybe he really needed a big premium bond prize? We drove home in contemplative mood, sad but relieved in a way that father's eighteen years as a lonely widower were now over.

Our Paul had wanted to move out of the room he had in the Acton house and get onto the first rung of the house owner's ladder before prices went up any more. He was searching in the Acton area which would make commuting to the BBC television centre easy for him, but London prices are horrendous. We would need to help out, and we went along to look at lots of places with him to give what advice we could. Patricia is adept at seeing through estate agents' rosy marketing hype and would quickly spot problems (and there were plenty). As for myself, I was at that time working in an office with Jim Wise, the Company quantity surveyor, and a most competent one at that. Countless people would ask Jim for house-buying advice and we too asked him to look at one or two for Paul. Jim warned us of all the usual problems with multi-occupancy, and none of the houses Paul had found came anywhere near to being in even passable condition to satisfy Jim. I didn't need Jim's advice about one of them which was an end-of-terrace house where the owner had stripped out the redundant fireplace and chimney, making a pleasantly large room downstairs, and more space in the room above. However, when I looked outside and lined my eye up along the blank end wall where the protruding chimney had been, I could see the entire wall with no longer any chimney structure to stiffen it had now begun to bow. We crept away from that one and advised Paul it was probably not safe even to enter.

That spring we signed up for an HF holiday, this time a 'special interest' one at their house in Alnmouth. The house borders a lovely golf course right by the sea, and many of the holidays there were for golfers, but they also had a couple of birdwatching ones in May which is the ideal time to see nesting birds on the Farne Islands. Our leader was Peter Hawkey, then the National Trust warden for the Farnes, so we couldn't have had a better person. The house was the usual rambling HF one, but being in the town of Alnmouth without any grounds of its own, it rambled over the tops of some other buildings. Various passages meandered around upstairs with groups of rooms here and there, but the public rooms were all downstairs along the front of the building and were very pleasant. HF also had a bridge party there for the week which we had to put up with. Bridge players spend their days indoors round their card tables and when we returned from our day's birding we would enter the house to find all the windows tight shut and the place full of foul smoke which made our eyes run. I don't know how they could put up with it! In the evenings they went on to play more bridge and the only time we saw them was at mealtimes when they were clustered in a group of their own all deeply involved in post mortems of the day's activities. There couldn't have been two more disparate groups. We spent our evenings watching Peter's slide shows, or talking about the next day's outing, or just talking amongst ourselves. It was unlike the usual HF house party where all groups (usually a predominance of walkers) all muck in together for dancing or communal games.

Peter was a superb leader, one of the best. We started gently with a morning walk round the local estuary which took in some sea cliffs, then in the afternoon walked in Hulme Park in Alnwick which was most interesting, for this is a keepered area with not a crow or magpie to be seen; instead there were masses of small birds the like of which we hadn't spotted for years. Was this the result of no predation from the crow family? During the day Peter told us the highlight of our week would be a full day out on the Farne Islands, and he would select the best day for weather which would mean he wouldn't know until the night before. Sure enough that very same evening he phoned in to say we would go to the Farnes next day, and the coach would pick us up early in the morning. HF were obviously used to this and organised early breakfast. Peter was not only able to arrange a coach at almost no notice, but he also managed to commandeer one of the tripper boats for our exclusive use. This was easier than it sounds, as being the Farne Islands warden he had control over the number of people visiting the islands over the nesting season. Too few and the boatmen were deprived of their living, too many and the birds were unduly disturbed. Peter had been experimenting over the years and found that 25,000 visitors a year was the maximum the birds could tolerate. The numbers could be increased by only allowing half-day trips, which also benefited the boatmen, and that had been established for some years. Peter, naturally, was extremely important to the boatmen, and they would always respond instantly if he wanted a boat at short notice, and in his case he was able to have one for a full day. We felt very privileged to be one of his party, even more so when we met one of our Majorca birdwatching acquaintances on the jetty who had only been able to get a booking for the afternoon, so was obliged to kick his heels all morning.

The day was perfect with a dead calm sea, no swell, cloudless sky and warm, and the birds were superb making it one of our most memorable birding days of all time. The Farnes lie about four miles out from Seahouses where we embarked, and when we were within a mile or so of the first stacks the unforgettable reek of guano wafted out to us. Around us in the water guillemots and razorbills. Puffins and shags bobbed around filling the air with their cries, diving if we came too close. It was just magical. First of all the boat took us to one of the furthest islands where a number of common seals had hauled out in the shallows. We were told the story of 20-year old Grace Darling and her lighthouse-keeper father who, in 1838, rowed out in a wild storm to rescue the crew from the ship Forfarshire which had foundered on the rocks. Conditions on that day were frighteningly hazardous, but they succeeded in their mission and Grace Darling became a folklore heroine, but dying some four years later of TB. To hear the story whilst actually on the spot where the rescue took place gave it great realism. We inched our way within feet of some of the Outer Farnes rocks on which were crammed nesting birds, with kittiwakes clinging to the narrowest of flat surfaces where they were able to establish their rudimentary nest. Many birds had newly hatched young and the tension in the air was strong. Being so close to guillemots we were well able to see that some of them were bridled guillemots, which have a white eye ring and white band around the neck making them look as if they are wearing spectacles.

We then landed on Staple Island, stepping ashore right beside nesting shags which became extremely agitated as we walked past them. There was a roped off walkway to prevent sightseers treading on nests, and Peter assured us the birds which chose to nest right beside the walkway did so with a purpose: it might be stressful having humans so close, but their principle foes were the predatory greater black-backed gulls; these humans kept the gulls off and the birds had discovered the safest place to nest was almost under our feet. Out came the camera, and I obtained lovely close-ups of the shags but, alas, their vivid viridian green eye did not come out at all well. We'd recently watched a television programme, one of the watching wildlife ones where the cameras return to the same spot several times in the course of a day. This one had been on the Farnes and had been hosted jointly by well-known wildlife presenter Tony Soper with Peter Hawkey as the local expert assisting him. The television cameras had picked out the viridian eye perfectly well. Peter told us how the two of them were sitting together on a rock with birds all around, introducing short excerpts from scenes that had been shot earlier. To do this they were watching in front of them a TV monitor behind which crouched the cameraman. As they talked, they noticed a shag had come waddling up to the cameraman and taken a fancy to his shoelaces which it was deftly unlacing with its bill. The cameraman felt something nuzzling around his foot but couldn't turn to see what it was as he was filming at the time; all he was able to do was lash out with his foot somewhat unsuccessfully. Both Peter and Tony had to try not to laugh at this bizarre sight.

On the other side of the island there was no walkway and we ambled across a rocky level area and almost stepped on a nesting eider. So convinced is the female eider of its camouflage that it will not move a muscle if a potential predator comes near. We were able to stand right over it, a foot or so away, and it remained there immobile.

We moved on next to Inner Farne which has a lighthouse at one end and a small chapel at the other with several buildings nearby, the base for the research staff and wardens. This is a very different island, grass-covered so therefore with a different bird population. The moment we landed and began to walk up the roped-off track to the chapel we were viciously attacked by screaming terns and I can assure you they have extremely sharp beaks and don't hesitate to jab one on the top of the head as one negotiates the path. The wardens were okay—they were all wearing hard hats, a useful gift from the BBC film crew who'd needed them a few weeks previously. These were mainly arctic terns and, like the shags, they'd chosen to nest close to the walkways but not so close as the shags. Every so often all the terns, numbering many hundreds, would rise up in the air together with raucous screams, a strategy to frighten off the more adventurous gulls that wheeled continuously overhead. Further away were nesting fulmars, the 'albatrosses of the north' which soar over the waves on fixed narrow wings so efficient they hardly ever need to flap them. Also on the island were thousands of puffins with their underground holes in which the females would be sitting. The males were the ones we saw, clustered in little social groups, their deep growling voice quite bizarre for such a small bird. There were also many eider nests, and Peter was able to show us the way they are lined with soft feathers plucked by the female from her own chest—eider down—and how she covers the eggs when briefly leaving them to forage for a meal. He lifted off the down from a nearby unattended nest and invited me to feel how warm the eggs were. I found them hot rather than warm. No wonder eiders are farmed for their wonderful insulating down. Peter quickly replaced the down and said that the instinct to sit on eggs is so strong that a female on her way back to her nest will sit on the first one she sees. This is not as silly as it sounds for, as soon as they hatch, all the chicks are led down to the edge of the island from where they jump off the cliff and float down through the air into the water where they are rounded up into a crèche by other females, probably ones that have no mates themselves. The male takes no part in sitting and he is so highly coloured it would draw attention to the nest if he did. In spite of that we saw some males sitting around a few yards from their mates, which must have defeated that object somewhat. All the activity on Inner Farne was possible because of the foot or two of soil covering the island, unlike Staple Island which has virtually no soil at all. That evening Peter showed us some magnificent bird slides he'd taken during the time he'd been warden, and I bought some of his spares. Like all wildlife photography one has to be there a long time for the opportunities to present themselves, and no way could I ever obtain some of the shots Peter managed to take.

We enjoyed a day up in the hills behind Wooler and saw pied flycatchers. This was during our picnic lunch stop where we not only had the pied flycatchers at their nest, but ten yards away a pair of greater spotted woodpeckers was also feeding young at the nest. As we'd found some nice logs nearby to sit on it occurred to me that Peter had planned this lunch stop most carefully.

And then there was the day we crossed the causeway to Lindisfarne when it was low tide at midday with little likelihood of being marooned there. We attempted to walk round the island but a northerly onshore wind made it almost impossible to remain upright on the exposed northern coast. No camera or binoculars were safe from the danger of being sandblasted and they remained firmly zipped up inside my innermost cagoule! At the other end of the island we came across a gardener tending a small patch of vegetables on the level area beside the castle which just there was remarkably quiet and wind-free. The patch, carefully chosen by Edward Lutyens, was surrounded by a waist-high stone wall for those occasions when the wind is in the east. Behind the village we found a warm spot in the priory ruins to have our lunch, time for a quick visit to the priory shop and then back aboard our coach where we crossed the causeway just as the tide was lapping at the coach's wheels.

There followed a sea-watch on the beach near Newton, a few miles south of Alnmouth, and on a spare day Patricia and I returned to Hulme Park where we walked for about eight miles right into the hinterland, seeing red squirrels in the conifer plantations, goosanders on the River Aln and were frightened out of our wits while enjoying a peaceful picnic by a shatteringly loud screaming bird which erupted almost at our feet. It was only an oystercatcher, but the adrenaline rushed to my heart causing it to thump for several minutes.

All too soon our wonderful week was over, the Edinburgh to Kings Cross train stopped at Alnwick to pick us up and in no time at all we were back in grubby old London, and home soon afterwards. Back at home the weather was exceptionally hot and we went on a walk in the Wendover area with the local HF group. About a couple of miles from the end I suddenly became conscious of my left knee making clicking sounds every time I put that leg down on the ground. Something clearly wasn't right. In a couple of weeks we were due to go on our first CHA walking holiday, this one in Eskdale west of the Hardknott Pass in the Lake District. I asked the Kodak physiotherapist whether she could get me fit for what would be an arduous week. She did her best, but something had slipped inside my knee, and the clicking sounds were caused by the joint knocking as a result of the muscles which hold the knee together having slackened off. It would be necessary to tighten up those muscles by lots of strengthening exercises before I would be fit enough to walk without a stick. Alas, it was only days before our trip.

We went anyway, having such an early start from home that we left the M6 at junction 36 before 8.00 a.m. What a wonderful time of day to travel on that dreadful motorway. We had a pleasant morning birding overlooking the Duddon estuary, then went north over the fells and spent the afternoon at Muncaster Castle and on down to the Ravenglass estuary hoping to find natterjack toads.

The CHA house is right opposite one of the Li'le Ratty narrow gauge railway stations, the means of transport we would use several times during the week. The house was somewhat tatty, the emphasis seemingly on cheapness rather than quality, and did it show! They had a new manager, recently retired from the catering branch of the RAF, who was coming to terms with looking after an establishment considerably different to anything he'd met before. We tried a couple of 'B' walks, the second one being a gentle route up the back of Coniston Old Man, but not gentle enough for me. My knee began to play up badly and we had to opt out of serious walking for the rest of the week. So next day just the two of us drove up over Hardknott Pass while I regaled Patricia with the story of my last visit there during the night in January 1963 while I was still a Cambridge student. We went for a very gentle stroll by the side of Blae Tarn with the Langdale Pikes behind, and moved on to Tarn Howes to go round the tourist track. There were lots of people wandering along this track and not one of them noticed a family of crossbills, the males bright red and their mates bright green, which came down to drink from the beck beside the path. It was our first sighting of these colourful birds and for half an hour we sat entranced sitting on a nearby bench watching them.

The next day we took advantage of our runabout train ticket and went once more to Ravensglass, this time seeing a natterjack, also red-breasted mergansers on the river. After that we drove up the side of Wastwater for some photographs, but attempting to walk along the track that leads up to Great Gable was beyond me. I felt a proper oldie. However I did manage a walk from Ravenglass over Muncaster Fell all the way back to the house the following day.

The house itself was not without incidents. On our second night we were awakened by a lot of commotion outside. Opening my eyes I saw a blue flashing light reflected on the ceiling and, with memories of the fire at the Dunbar's house in Narrabeen, I was out of bed in a trice. I parted the curtains and looked down on the roof of an ambulance with its back doors open and a couple of men loading on a stretcher. Next morning we found that one of the guests had been taken ill and would probably need an urgent operation at the Cockermouth hospital. Later that same day the chef went berserk and started setting about the place with a particularly lethal-looking meat cleaver. Our manager managed to disarm him and the chef, too, was then carted off never to return. Now our manager had to turn to and do the cooking himself. Fortunately an RAF catering man is well trained for such exigencies and he coped very well, though had a great deal of difficulty with the enormous cooking pots which CHA had presumably deemed necessary for this establishment.

When we left Eskdale we went via Cockermouth and Hadrians's Wall stopping at the Vindolanda museum, on our way to Leeds for a couple of nights' stay with Sue and Paul, where we joined them for a splendid concert in Leeds Town Hall. We'd seen television broadcasts from there when the Leeds Piano Festival was broadcast, but didn't realise the majestic malachite pillars either side of the stage were, in fact, plastered with a patterned paper finish. Sitting right beside one of them round the back of the orchestra I could see the join all too clearly! The following day we went to Harlow Carr gardens and to Roundhay Park, then next day Sue drove us out to Grassington for a gentle walk among limestone pavement outcrops, and explored the well-known Leeds market (I was particularly amused by a stall, the overhead sign painted a dark green with gold lettering which proclaimed it to be 'Arrods. Not a lot of resemblance to its illustrious London counterpart.) This visit was a couple of weeks before they moved to their new house in Dunnington, about five miles from York, where Paul had already started his next spell in York District Hospital as a registrar, and would no longer have to commute from Leeds while Sue would start a GP job at a York practice.

A few weeks after that I went down with some strange complaint, a tummy pain that was intense on and off, and was unable to keep my food down. This came on suddenly whilst in the office alone with our motherly clerk, Rita, a martyr to diverticulitis herself and immediately diagnosed that I must be suffering from the same trouble. I was groggy for about two weeks, took time off work and my GP had no idea what it could be. He booked me into the hospital for a barium meal x-ray examination as he thought it might possibly be a twisted bowel or something similar. It eventually went away on its own still remaining a mystery. Six weeks later I was summoned to the hospital for the x-ray examination. Not surprisingly they found nothing, and the radiologist muttered something about wasting his time. As I had needed to postpone a meeting involving ten other people in order to trail in for the examination, I told the consultant I had wasted my time as well and suggested the hospital needed to pull its administrative socks up. No doubt my fruitless visit there had put back the examination of some other needy patient requiring an urgent x-ray. He was not amused and I certainly wasn't either.

In the autumn that year Patricia and I took a quiet holiday with HF at their Freshwater Bay house. My left knee still played up from time to time, and the gentler pace of the Isle of Wight holiday seemed sensible. We drove there, crossing on the car ferry from Southampton to Cowes. After checking in we walked the length of Tennyson Down in lovely autumnal sunshine with clean sea air wafting across. On the first organised walk we crossed the Island to Yarmouth on the old railway track to the east of the river Yar, then back along the west side. The estuary was teeming with birds, as was the scrub along the way. It was altogether a good birding day, but as we were with a walking party we couldn't stop for a proper birdwatch. During the week we walked in all parts of the Island, discovering areas we'd not known about before. When we lived in Alverstoke we used to take the ferry over for a day's outing, getting about on the Southern Vectis buses which were cheap, frequent and reliable. Later we'd take our bicycles over and find some of the lesser-known tracks, and once or twice we went across on one of the early hovercraft ferries that left from the beach at Stokes Bay within a few minutes of where we then lived. The Island seemed to have stood still in the intervening years, the roads quiet and narrow, finger posts the only signage, the villages sleepy and the people relaxed and unstressed. Not much had changed, and it was a peaceful week for us. What with red squirrels and all the birds it was a good wildlife-spotting week too. After we checked out on our last day we spent the morning down at Newton for a final birding spell and then went on to visit Osborne House, now very different from the time I had gate crashed all those years ago when we'd sailed across from Collingwood with BK and his lads. We even had time to visit Hilliers arboretum on our way home.

Our son Paul had moved out of his Acton flat and spent some months lodging with friends nearby pending the conversion of a three-storey warehouse in Ealing into a number of self-contained flats, for one of which he'd put down a deposit. He'd been searching all year for a place of his own, watching house prices creeping up all the while. Once on the ladder he felt he could relax, and wasn't too concerned that his first home would be quite tiny. In fact the place he'd selected was really only suitable for one, but was new (except for the building shell) and considerably better than some of the dreadful places we'd seen during the year. Our own house was filling up with his belongings, but at long last he'd been given a completion date for moving in. While all this somewhat unsettling business had been going on, his BBC work had been unsettling for him as well. First he'd been moved to a building behind Broadcasting House where the remnants of the design department were housed, but the department itself was being downsized once again, only the research side being retained with the development part likely to be put out to contract. He had been feeling vulnerable for some time and had put out feelers for a job elsewhere. A BBC trained engineer is a good catch, and he received several offers. Now, just days from moving into his first house, he accepted one of these and handed in his notice to the Beeb. His new firm was one of those that had sprung up when the BBC started using contractors more, and were manufacturing one-off pieces of television and radio equipment. They were very keen to have Paul, and were located not that far off, so the commuting would be straightforward.

I hired a large van and we took all Paul's gear to his new home, where Patricia set to with a bucket of soapy water to wash the place from top to bottom, after which we moved him in, and did those little adjustments that always need doing when run-of-the-mill builders consider they've finished and move out. This included planing the bottom off several doors so that they would shut, trying to get the hot water system to work and making some of the light fittings safe. We left Paul on his own to settle in.

Sue meanwhile also had a job change. In her case it was to move from the GP practice in York where she first started, to a small country practice with a surgery in Escrick, a ten-minute country drive from their home in Dunnington, where she joined two men GPs and soon became very popular with the other patients many of whom wanted to be seen by her particularly when it came to women's problems. She eventually became a partner there and was very content. In many ways it was rather like the James Herriot adventures in that some of her patients were those unbelievably eccentric Yorkshire farmers, complete with farm gates that fell to pieces when one tried to open them. She'd arrive in a muddy farmyard, hoot her horn for someone to come out and chain up the dogs, only then deeming it safe to get out. She kept a pair of wellies in the back of the car, and also a drugs cabinet so she could do her own dispensing since many of the farms were way out in the sticks. Nice as this type of practice was, it was hard to make a good living, especially when the government changed all the rules and made GPs the fund holders, where the more patients there are on one's books the better. One cannot operate like that in a country practice where it might well take an hour just to see one patient.

~*~

In early May the following year we had another tour with Ornitholidays, coincidentally led by the same leader as the Majorca one, Carl Nicolson. This one was to the southern end of Montenegro a few years before all the upheaval in Yugoslavia. I knew little about the Balkans and their inability to like one another which was perhaps just as well, as there was plenty of unease just under the surface. We had a change of aircraft at Zagreb with an hour to kill, so spent it wandering around the scrub just outside the airport which was full of nightingales. Not a bad start. Although we were transit passengers, it seemed we were perfectly free to wander outside the small airport building and could have escaped into the nearby housing estate had we so wished. Maybe the authorities thought it so unlikely anyone would ever want to enter illegally that they didn't worry.

The second flight took us on to Dubrovnik, which, from the approach road high up, looked quite lovely nestling on its island surrounded by the deep blue Mediterranean sea. My memories of the eastern Mediterranean were in my Agincourt days when it was far hotter and drier than our Malta base, and I was unprepared for the cold air that greeted us as we stepped out of the plane. Perhaps we'd arrived on an unusually cold day?

We met up with our coach and driver for the week, a large coach with a big brusque Montenegrin driver who didn't give a hoot for the State, and in particular, the police. He came with an interpreter, a young girl with her friend (a trainee perhaps?) who stuck to us like limpets from the moment we arrived; a mandatory official requirement apparently. They were certainly a great help to Carl who spoke no Serbo-Croat, but they were as frightened as rabbits every time we came anywhere near any State official. They simply could not understand our laidback British attitude to foreign authority; maybe if we had been subject to the same regime we might not have been so laisser-faire ourselves. The coach set off for the two-hour drive to Petrovac, a small coastal town with a number of somewhat severe, large hotels in one of which we were deposited. It was cold; not only the atmosphere but the temperature, which was not helped by the place having been built for summertime heat with no means of warming it up at any other time. We had chosen to come at this time because it was plumb in the middle of the migration period, so would just have to put up with the cold marble floors and draughty rooms. The corridors leading down to the public areas were all external, so one needed one's outdoor clothes (including a cagoule) in order to get to the dining room. Here we met the ridiculous attitude of people in such a strict communist country when dealing with foreigners. The waitresses had seemingly been trained by numbers and were unable or unwilling to use any initiative, so would not deviate at all from the way they'd been taught (were they afraid of being whisked off to some terrible detention centre if anyone caught them fraternising?). Thus we were obliged to sit at the same seat at every meal or otherwise we wouldn't be served. We got round this by pretending we were someone else, but this left them extremely suspicious. Of course, we treated this as a game, and deliberately muddled the staff when we wanted to have some fun. Alas, they were devoid of any trace of a sense of humour. It was all very sad, really. So, with much form filling and selecting the menu for the following meal before we started the current one, we were eventually allowed to eat.

The first day was spent walking around extensive scrub along the nearby coast. There were several British holidaymakers braving the nearby beach for the sake of an exceptionally cheap seaside holiday, but they didn't venture into the hinterland at all. There were nightingales in almost every bush, along with all the usual small Mediterranean birds, various warblers, shrikes, flycatchers and the like. A good day for us with several 'firsts'.

Our coach with its two wimpish girls took us to Lake Skadar, a super spot the other side of the mountain. Our driver, whom we called No Problem since they were his only words of English and was his reply to anything anyone said to him, was an adept hand at manipulating his large coach round the hairpin bends, blasting his horn authoritatively at any other vehicle that might not get out of his way in time. It really was quite exciting to be driven with such panache provided one didn't think too much about coming off the road. No Problem reached for something out of a locker beside him just as we were passing a slow lorry, and I saw it was a none-too-clean bottle of something from which he took a swig, then wiping the top on his shirt he passed it on to Carl nearby. The girls explained that it was to be passed round to all the men for them to sample. "Very good. Is Slivovitz," —a potent plum brandy made in those parts. Carl had met this before. "Nice and warming," was his comment. When it was my turn I cautiously took a tiny sip, feeling the spirit travel down my gut until it exploded in my tummy a few minutes later. Yes, it was certainly warming. With some alarm I saw No Problem had the bottle back again and was emptying the rest of it. His driving became more deadly and we hung on tight.

The lake was fed by a wide fast-flowing river over which our road went at the narrowest part, alongside a railway bridge carrying the line to Ulcinji. Here were lots of large waders and marsh birds, so we got out for a walkabout and met our first obstacle. In addition to binoculars most of us had cameras, and it was forbidden to photograph any military installation or any strategically important structure, which included all railway bridges. The wimps flew into a panic as they saw the first camera being levelled at an egret standing some fifty yards away from the rusty bridge. The lake was a really fascinating place, deep at one end and shelving gently at the other, with a water level that would rise or fall some ten feet depending on the season. At the time we were visiting it was high, still in flood from the snow melt many miles up stream, and the shallow end had overflowed over many small meadows and areas of scrub. This was all full of waders, masses of little egrets, pygmy cormorants, squacco herons, a few glossy ibis and a fair number of Dalmation pelicans. It was a fantastic birding day.

On another day we returned to the lake, as Carl had been tipped off about a fish eagle that came for its lunch at the same time and same spot every day, near to a vantage point from where we could stop for our own lunch and enjoy the entertainment. He made the mistake (unlike Peter Hawkey in Northumberland who just appeared to stumble upon wonderful sightings) of telling us about the sea eagle, and then spent half an hour staring at his watch since the eagle that day was late! It turned up in the end, scooped up a huge fish and flew with it over our heads before setting off, presumably to its nest somewhere.

On our way back over the mountains that day No Problem had gone to town with his bottle of Slivovitz and was happily tucking into a second bottle as we came down the hairpin bends and caught up with a large road tanker that was crawling down in a low gear with much hissing of vacuum brakes. This was too much for No Problem who gaily gave it a devastating trumpeting from his horn and proceeded to pass on a blind corner, meeting a police car coming the other way which only just managed to avoid going over the edge. We sat, holding on tight, and waited for the inevitable turnaround of the police car while the coach thundered along, but it never appeared. Maybe the driver was changing his underwear, or maybe they'd caught sight of No Problem's shaking fist and decided they had more congenial things to do than confront him.

One morning Carl came rushing into our room just before breakfast shouting to us to come at once and bring our 'scopes. There, overhead, were masses of honey buzzards wheeling around the edge of an updraught gaining height. We counted 47 altogether. Later that day we went to some saltpans which were right alongside a military airfield near Tivat where it rained heavily for much of the day. Fortunately there was a nice restaurant nearby in which we were able to shelter for a couple of hours, and from where we had wonderful close-up sightings of little bitterns, clinging in hundreds onto the reeds close to us. There seemed to have been an eruption of them, as they were just everywhere. Exploring on the far side of the salt pans later on when the rain stopped, we found lots more interesting birds and, stalking these, aroused the interest of some guards from an airfield on the other side of a high fence. A small detachment of them clambered into a truck and set off to come round by road to investigate. The wimps were beside themselves, while Carl calmly gave us our instructions.

"If they ask any of you for your name, tell them it's Carl Nicholson, right? And don't any of you allow yourself to be led away. If one goes, then we all go. They can cope with one or two, but not a whole coachload. There would be too much risk of an international incident and their commanding officer could be in trouble."

It worked. Through the two girls they asked us what we were doing, saw all the bird books Carl had in his rucksack, looked through someone's telescope at a little bittern, the girls with much prodding told them how rare they were and how we'd come all the way from England to see this wondrous sight, and they left somewhat mystified and with a fair amount of muttering about mad Englishmen.

We had a glorious day of hot sun after that, and I was able to dismantle my telescope which had steamed up inside and dry it out in the sunshine. We spent most of the day in a little gorge looking hopefully for wall creepers and other gorge-type birds, a relaxing day with not too serious birding. Then, for a change, we took the tourist trip to Dubrovnik and spent the whole day there, walking around the walls and exploring that lovely ancient town with all the other tourists. Someone even found a tee shirt with 'Nemo Problema' emblazoned across the front which he bought for something to give our driver at the end of the holiday.

There was the day we spent up in the mountains at 6,000 feet for a quite different selection of birds, after which we took a long ride through extremely difficult mountainous scenery to Cetinji and on to the dreary communist town of Titograd for various unusual larks. That trip was memorable for the sight of several coaches like ours which we looked down on, rusting away upside down at the bottom of ravines. Would they have had drivers like No Problem perhaps? Would they have been full of tourists when they went over? That was also the day when, as we were a hundred yards or so from joining another road, there was a traffic holdup with officious-looking police stopping everyone. No Problem sat impatiently in the queue for a while, then decided to circumvent the blockage which he proceeded to do by leaving the tarmac, driving down a shallow bank and across a sports field to join the other road further up.

Then we had a really lovely day in a sandy area near the Albanian border, saw bee eaters, a magnificent roller with its blue colouring showing well in the sunshine, and came across a beautiful little green tree frog sitting in a bush beside our track. As we were clustered around photographing it I became aware of some people behind us craning to see what we were looking at. They were border guards, dressed in fatigues and carrying rifles. But they weren't interested in us, just wanted to see what we'd found. I stood back to let them have a look and was joined by one of our number whom we called the brigadier (not to his face). He was an ex-Army man and rather strutted about talking with a Sandhurst voice which reminded me of Graham Chapman doing his Monty Python sketches, hence the sobriquet. He nudged me.

"Look at all that dust on those boots. Not seen any polish for ages. Damned scruffy. Wouldn't have had that sort of thing in my regiment!" He thwacked his side with an imaginary stick.

I looked. The lads must all have been in their early twenties if that, and their badly fitting uniform just hung off them adding to the scruffy appearance. It was really poor quality, and I expect they were paid a miserable wage. The cost of the army must have been a drain on meagre national resources, and everyone universally hated them since their raison d'être was to hold their own uneasy nation together, not to defend it. The two wimps had remained in the coach while we'd been looking at the frog, and made no attempt to get any nearer. Later we went for a brief sea watch, since the Adriatic was only just over the hill, but we found little there, except for what appeared to be a lot of pink seals hauled out on a sandy tree-covered island half a mile away. A closer look through the telescopes identified them not as seals, but over-size Germans enjoying a naturist holiday. Terrible sight.

The nearby town of Ulcinji is in a mostly Moslem area, the women with their faces veiled. We took photographs (with care) in the bustling market and went on afterwards to some marshes where we saw our first pratincole (which someone referred to as an Arthur Scargill bird), and stopped to photograph a spectacular Paulownia Tormentosa tree in full bloom, its scented mauve foxglove-like blossoms looking quite magnificent.

All too soon the two-week tour was over, and it was back home to catch up with the chores, and return to normal. It had been a superb holiday, all the objectives achieved, a large number of birds seen in a wide variety of habitats, an interesting though unhappy country to remember. A few years later Yugoslavia collapsed and they were at one another's throats once more.

~*~

The rainy summer gave way to a fine spell, the weather forecaster with a smile for once predicting several days of warmth. We phoned the HF centre at Swanage and booked a room for the Saturday night, driving down early on Saturday morning for a full day's walking, with another on Sunday before returning home after dark. It felt as if we'd been away for a whole week. We walked our favourite coastal path to Whinspit, and on the next day continued the walk from Kimmeridge to Tyneham and back along the ridge to Swyre Head. What wonderful walking country this is. Back home again, we walked what we call 'The Chequers Round', a lovely part of the Chilterns circling the Prime Minister's Chequers country residence, and up onto Coombe Hill with splendid views right across the Vale of Aylesbury. Apart from not having the sea, this is pretty good walking country too. What we like about the Chilterns is the way in which the scenery changes every time the path goes into a wood and emerges on the other side in another valley. And although we do like remote areas to walk in, the Chilterns does have the advantage that every footpath is well used and in good condition.

Sue and Paul had asked if we'd like to bring Granny up to see them in Dunnington. We took the scenic route, stopping at Rutland Water, then having a look round the attractive town of Stamford (a favourite location for historical television dramas), then on to Lincoln with a walk round the cathedral and on up the Roman road until we neared Scunthorpe, stopping eventually at the RSPB reserve at Blacktoft Sands at the confluence of the Trent and Ouse rivers. There, surprisingly, we saw a spoonbill amongst other more usual waders, then after driving through Goole, which we found had an eerie atmosphere, we continued on to Beverley where we looked round that cathedral as well before fetching up at Dunnington. It was an exhausting day, but even so Granny was recovered by the next morning and wanted to go round York Minster, and even walked round some of the nearby city walls.

Generally when Granny took a holiday she liked to go with one of her elderly widow lady friends. They often stayed at one of the Methodist Holiday Homes, where we would take the two of them, collecting them at the end of their week. Patricia and I would listen to them chatting away in the back seat and I remember one snippet. They'd been talking about some film they'd seen starring Flora Robson.

"That was a long time ago," said one. "She must be dead by now."

"Yes," said the other. "Well maybe not, or we'd have heard. But she must be nearly dead, surely?"

Granny sometimes went on a coaching holiday which she enjoyed as these were geared for older people who liked to be looked after. Although her little suitcase only seemed to weigh a few pounds, she never had to lift it, the coach or hotel people ensuring the luggage was delivered to one's room on arrival.

We haven't reached that stage yet, and the next holiday for Patricia and me was to South Wales for a short visit to the Brecons, an area our Paul had enjoyed very much and recommended to us. We approached via the strangely quiet Merthyr Tydfil valley and did the Brecon horseshoe walk, starting from Neuad reservoir, climbing Cribin, Pen-y-Fan and Corn Dû on a lovely day with magnificent views from the tops, after which we drove on to Crickhowell where we were booked in for the night at a spooky one-time vicarage complete with four poster bed and rooks cawing in the trees outside. We spent the next day walking in the Black Mountains from Llanthony Priory with cracking good views across to Hereford, and the day after that walked the lovely valley around Grwyne Fawr reservoir. We returned home via the falconry centre at Newent to watch them flying all the usual birds. I was intrigued that caged monsters, for example condors and some of the large eagles, should get very agitated when a small falcon such as a kestrel flew overhead. It was rather like my family's little Scots terrier going for an Alsation which turned tail and fled.

Then in October we went to our first proper HF mountain centre together. The one we'd chosen was the Loch Leven house at North Ballachulish, certainly the toughest centre at the time. It was an easy place to visit by train since, like the Loch Awe visit, we could board at Watford on a Friday evening, with a sleeper all the way to Fort William. As I've said earlier I do like the feeling of adventure when one goes to sleep in one place, waking up next morning somewhere utterly different, but although I achieved that on the occasion I first went to St. Mawes by overnight train during the war, with advancing years I find it not so easy to sleep. Patricia, especially, was quite claustrophobic shut up in a small two-berth compartment with windows that would not open. She hardly slept at all and looked awful in the morning! The last part of the journey from Crianlarich to Fort William goes over Rannoch Moor, with memories of Noggin and my visit to the Loch Ossian YHA hut all those years ago.

A bus took us the 12 miles to the HF house where we'd have a quiet day exploring locally before the rest of the party arrived, either in cars throughout the afternoon, or on the evening train. Next day was fine and we bravely chose the 'A' walk for a fast 8-mile tramp over the hills to Kinlochleven, and back on a service bus. Then we tried a more gentle walk through the lovely Glen Nevis, going through woodland down to Fort William.

Leaving Patricia to walk with the slow party up to the Lost Valley (a mysterious hanging valley just above the Meeting of the Waters in Glen Coe), I joined the middle party the following day and went up Buachaille Etive Beag, a fine mountain at the head of Glen Coe with superb views across the Mamores to the north. We encountered some loose scree which frightened the life out of some members of the party, but I rather enjoyed coming down on the stuff, moving forward an extra yard or so with each step I took. I was lucky not to take a pearler, for I didn't understand the dangers of scree walking. We got back to find Patricia's party never reached the Lost Valley because some of the slower members were unable to cope, and had spent several hours at the Glen Coe visitors' centre being regaled with an embellished story of the Massacre of Glen Coe.

Then it was back to Glen Nevis, only this time we walked up the glen. In our party we had a somewhat spindly fairly elderly lady who wore an extraordinary waterproof trench coat. We'd all crossed the fast-flowing river at Steall on a tight wire with handholds either side, not as frightening as it sounds, for the wires were quite thick and extremely rigid, and were inching our way back again, the trench coat lady looking quite out of place as she wobbled her way across. Some young people approached me as I stood at the end waiting for the others. They asked who we were, meaning who on earth were these fuddy-duddies attempting such antics. I explained we were an HF party, and there were more of us, some of the really ancient ones, who had gone to the top of Ben Nevis, waving my hand up at the clouds that obscured the mountain just to the north of us. They clearly didn't believe a word, but were full of admiration, for they had looked at the wire bridge earlier and decided they wouldn't attempt to cross on it!

On the final day we awoke to the sight of snow cover down to the thousand-foot level and our 'B' leader abandoned any idea of the official walk that would have taken us up into the wet snow in long grass for much of the way. Instead he put together two 'C' grade walks end-to-end to make an 18-mile tramp across Rannoch Moor and eventually all the way to Kinlochleven. This, he said, would be straightforward and not at all strenuous provided we took all day over it. The coach dropped us off in the middle of the Moor, about level with Loch Bà in a particularly wet area, and we struggled across this to the West Highland Way which along this part is on a good track with proper foundations, the General Wade Road. The weather cleared up and it was a lovely walk as far as the Kings House Hotel where we stopped for lunch, an extraordinary place on its own in the middle of nowhere, surrounded by the only trees in sight. Not surprisingly it is a haven for ramblers who all pass through this spot, and on the day we stopped by there must have been fifty visitors, but only two cars. After that it was down the old road for a mile or two, then over the witches' staircase across the glen from Buachaille Etive Beag and down to Kinlochleven. Here we persuaded the

Highland Bus Company to take us back to the hotel, as one of the drivers lived at Kinlochleven and had his bus with him.

On our last day we left Loch Leven, still in the cloud, but by the time our train reached Glasgow the sun had come out. It was an expensive 90 minute wait at Glasgow Central for our Watford train, since Patricia and I left our baggage in the care of one of the others while we rushed off to the shops to buy a beautiful blue tartan skirt for Patricia and a bottle of Glenmorangie for me!

22

Last Years at Kodak

Paul had quickly become disillusioned with his work at the company that manufactured bespoke television equipment, finding the people running it had little interest in their personnel, so after only a year started looking around for a better, more rewarding, job. He found just what he was looking for not far from us, at Radlett on the old airfield site. This was a small offshoot of GEC Medical, American owned, making specific medical apparatus for the world market. They took Paul on for development work concerned with gamma ray camera equipment used in diagnostics; one-off hugely expensive equipment but with great potential. So here he was, working back in Hertfordshire, but with a house in London. At least he would be commuting the 'wrong' way, though he'd still be using the horribly overcrowded Central Line underground each day.

He came over for a meal one day with a girl in tow. This was Alison, who lived in Luton, and was suggesting he should move to Luton which would be an easy run for his work in Radlett! She was quite a bit older than him, and we didn't sense any vibes from him towards her, though she was clearly hoping she might be able to generate some. She seemed a nice enough girl, with parents who lived in the northwest.

Paul started his job with a two-week visit to a plant in Denmark that was making some of the equipment and who had been doing development work in which he would be involved, managing to fit in a pleasant weekend across in Sweden before returning. He enjoyed his work with GEC Medical and was much happier working for a larger company with a proper personnel structure. A few months later he was thinking more seriously about moving house, and the search was on. We'd made him a loan to buy the first place, but he'd done so on the top of the market and now, a couple of years later, it might well sell for less than he paid for it.

A few weeks later we heard, much to our surprise, that he'd put in a bid for a house in Harpenden. Harpenden is a lovely town, but—so we thought— prohibitively expensive. We drove over there to discover it has a less salubrious side where the house was located. We took him on a round of other houses for sale in Hemel Hempstead, Abbotts Langley and Kings Langley, but he didn't like the atmosphere of any of the areas we visited. Harpenden was what he wanted.

It was a couple of months later that he phoned us to say he'd had his offer accepted and a few months later he moved in. We went over to see the house and I have to admit I was not too impressed, but then, I suspect, nor was Paul. He'd probably done the right thing by getting a poor house in a good district, rather than the other way about. From this position he could always move up when he'd accrued more funds, yet remain in the same town, and in Harpenden he would be able to move up a very long way. His choice of Harpenden was clearly influenced by Alison, who had fancied living in Harpenden herself one day.

Later in the year he brought over a different girl for supper. This was Gill whom he'd met at one of his churchy social meetings. And then he produced a somewhat pushy girl, one Sue Little, the four of us going for a walk in the Chenies area. Sue talked non-stop as if she was just filling in the details with us about her cementing relationship with Paul, one that would soon result in the announcement of an engagement. Patricia and I looked at one another in some dismay; the thought of having such a chatterbox as a daughter-in-law was not one we relished. Besides, she was too incompatible in every respect and it would never work. Paul didn't seem at all fazed and a few days after this meeting we had a letter from the girl to say she'd enjoyed meeting us and how sorry she was that she and Paul couldn't be continuing the relationship. We wondered whether meeting us was the last straw! By this time Paul had done the coast-to-coast walk with Alison from St. Bees on the Cumbrian coast across to Whitby and had met up with Alison's parents on the way, somewhere near Ambleside where they'd arranged to stay for the night. After that Alison began to fade out of the picture: maybe Alison's parents had disapproved of Paul. Certainly, Alison's father had taken the opportunity to quiz Paul about his prospects!

Our holiday this year would be with HF once again, this time at Derwentbank, their large house on the side of Derwentwater in the Lake District. Since our Hassness holiday several years previously, followed by the one at Eskdale, we'd felt further visits to the Lakes were inevitable and were looking forward to this one very much. We went via York, spending a couple of days with Sue and her Paul, from where we drove cross-country via Brigham Rocks, a slow but very scenic route. It was the May Bank Holiday week with the house fully booked and humming with activity. Two of our leaders were HF directors and had been staying at HF houses all their lives, so we expected great things this time! We got off to a good start with lively dancing on the first evening, then had what was to become one of our favourite walks next day, circumnavigating Derwentwater via Walla Crag and Ashness Bridge on the eastern side and returning through lovely Manesty Woods, where rhododendrons were in full bloom in many of the secluded gardens we passed.

The following day our party enjoyed a super walk from Gatescarth at the head of Buttermere. The enjoyment was for two reasons: the glorious weather and our leader. He had in the party someone who said they'd never been up a mountain before and was afraid they wouldn't be able to manage it because of a weak heart. "No problem," he'd said, "I will take you up there and you'll never realise you've climbed it!"

He was as good as his word. We had the whole day for a comparatively simple walk, so his technique, very simply, was to go extremely slowly. We went up Haystacks, on top of which we had our lunch. At only 1,900 feet it is not a proper mountain at all, but the nervous party member thought it was just great. As for me, I took lots of stunning photographs that day, which is perhaps why I remember it so well. Our leader had with him one of Wainwright's guidebooks, and that was my first introduction to the Grand Master of the Lakes. He told us how Wainwright had singled out Haystacks as his favourite mountain, and showed us the passage in his Guide where AW waxes lyrical with his lovely poetic prose on the perfection of this one. We saw a peregrine falcon zooming around in the sunshine close over our heads which just added to our pleasure, and then we walked along the side of Innominate Tarn, and onto the top of Fleetwith Pike from where our leader pointed out all the other summits we could see from there. I was impressed with his knowledge of the whole area, little thinking that in a year or two with my own essential copies of the Wainwright Guides in my rucksack, I, too, would be doing the same thing.

Next day it was up Green Gable. We'd intended to go on to Great Gable, but both summits were in thick cloud, so instead we went down Aaron Slack to Styhead Tarn and the sunshine below, missing out Great Gable which is not much fun in the fog. On our off day Patricia and I drove over the Kirkstone Pass and went up onto High Street from Hartsop hoping to see the golden eagle that we'd heard was around those parts, but no luck this time. Never mind; it was all superlative country and made a lovely day out.

Back with the group once more, we coached to Glenridding from where Patricia did the walk along the east side of Ullswater from Patterdale and up onto Place Fell while I joined the party that went up Helvellyn. Again, I took lots of photographs, so my memories of that day, like the Haystacks day, are renewed every time we show the slides. Once again the weather was kind, and we had great fun clambering along Striding Edge on our way up. My party had over forty people in it, so the going was rather crowded, but by this time we were all friends so that just made it more enjoyable. Once over Striding Edge and onto Helvellyn itself we were joined by lots of people who'd walked up from the other side on what could almost be described as a road. These were what we rudely called the sandals and orange peel brigade, who will get just about anywhere if there is a reasonably easy path within reach of their car park. Noggin and I had met them on the top of Ben Lomond all those years ago when we worked together at Barr and Stroud. Perhaps that is why I preferred remote places with no nearby roads.

Our final day was a walk from the house up Newlands Valley and onto High Spy, where it rained briefly, unfortunately while we were sitting on the top having our lunch Then the sun came out and we had that wonderful drop down the Maiden Moor ridge walk to Cat Bells and on back through the woods to Derwentbank house.

On departure day we went via Pooley Bridge to Haweswater, parking our car at Haweswater head, and trying once again for a golden eagle, once more with no joy. We hadn't at that time known about the flooded village of Mardale Green lying at the bottom of Haweswater where, in a dry year with the Manchester Corporation water board having taken their fill of the waters of Haweswater, a broad white beach appears all around the reservoir and one can look down on the water and just make out where the village stood with its church. We made our way back to Shap, crossing the old A6 which I remembered so well from my student days, and joined the M6 for that thundering hell through the overcrowded midlands back to Watford.

Next day it was a complete contrast for a day out with our local bird group led by David Elcome to Minsmere, where we had a huge list of wonderful sightings, including bearded reedlings, a 'first' for us.

Later the same summer we paid a return visit to Loch Leven, once again taking the sleeper from Watford to Fort William. This time the weather was completely different, and we spent our first evening sitting quietly at the end of the garden on the beach overlooking a little island with the Pap of Glen Coe behind, watching a red-breasted merganser, black guillemots, arctic terns and some eider. We'd already had a golden eagle on the ground on Rannoch Moor that we'd seen from the train as it passed very close, and had seen red deer and buzzards as well. We were undoubtedly back in Scotland! Bravely we attempted the high level walk on our first day (HF had stopped calling their walks A, B or C, preferring High, Medium and Low at the mountain centres, or Long, Medium and Short at the others). This went off all right, and we opted for another high level walk next day, to Stob Ban and Mullach na Coirean, a couple of Munros in the Mamores range. Our leader that day was a gentle elderly man by name of Jack Tibbs, who was leading a walk up his favourite mountain the following day, Bidean nam Bian, at 3,700 feet the highest one in the Glen Coe area. Would we be joining him? I explained we were not really mountain people; would he think we could cope from what he'd seen of us so far? "You'd have no problem," he replied, "It's no more difficult than today's walk." Reassured, and comforted by the fact we were a good fifteen years younger than our leader, we agreed to go.

The coach took all three parties next day, dropping off the Low party at the Glen Coe visitor centre, then proceeding another mile for our High party. We got out and the coach drove off with the Medium party. I looked around us. Apart from Jack, there were seven others, all big strong purposeful youngsters in their twenties. Patricia and I gazed at each other in horror and glanced up the road the see the back of the coach disappear round a bend. We were committed. Jack set off, marching up a steep slope at such a cracking speed we were left huffing and puffing way behind in the first few minutes. He did stop, though, but only to don waterproofs as we were about to go up into thin wispy cloud that hung around the rocky mountainside above us.

"I thought we'd do one of the more interesting routes today," he announced.

"We go up 'dinnertime' buttress just up there," he pointed up into the murk, "and it's an easy ascent after that, right to the top." He turned and set off. With a last look down at the little lochan by the roadside below us we followed. Neither of us had done any proper scrambling before, nor we had no idea how to set about going up a chimney. The others helped as best they could, but quite a lot of loose stuff was dislodged by several people and came bouncing down all round us. Conditions weren't improved by the drizzle which made everything quite slippery, and really we should have been roped up. One slip and any one of us would have lost their footing and brought down everyone else below them as well. Every so often I glanced down, occasionally getting a glimpse of the lochan way, way below, with tiny ants crawling up and down the ribbonlike road beside it, which I realised were the tops of cars. It was a long drop. The next hour was a quite frightening experience that I'd rather forget, and as for Patricia—she was so terrified it coloured her memory of the whole day, which was pity for most of it was very memorable.

Eventually I realised I was no longer needing to hold on, and the next moment I found I could stand up straight and take some forward steps. We'd come out onto a plateau, and there in front of us were a couple of surprised-looking ptarmigans no doubt wondering what on earth we were doing there. We'd made it! The top of Bidean was only another forty minutes trudge away, and that's where we stopped for lunch, unfortunately still in cloud so we were unable to enjoy the tremendous views from that point. I remembered when I'd slogged up the road from Glen Etive all those years ago when Paul and I had stayed at Loch Awe, Bidean was in view then looking very grand. After lunch we descended several hundred feet to a wide bealach where Jack stopped while we all caught up. If anything he went downhill faster than he went up, sure footed as a chamois. Even the youngsters in our group were stumbling about by this time. From here one could look down onto Glen Etive to the south, and to a hung valley to the north.

"The Lost Valley," he announced, waving at the northern vista before us, and proceeded to tell us about the feud between the Campbells and the local Macdonalds, when the Macdonalds hid their cattle up in this secret valley and were never discovered. I remembered that grim night we'd spent at the Clachan Inn on our first tour of Scotland with that stark notice behind the reception desk stating 'NO CAMPBELLS'. Today, with the sun at long last breaking through, the huge valley with its immense rock fall blocking the exit looked wonderful. Suddenly Jack disappeared. One moment he was standing beside us talking about a fun bit of scree, and the next he had stepped off the edge and gone. I looked over to see him about a hundred feet below careering downhill over the boulders. Carefully we all followed. This was no fun scree, far from it. The boulders were mostly the size of a football, covered in slippery moss where the sun never penetrated this steep northern slope, and the going was fraught with ankle-spraining opportunities. Gingerly we crept down, placing each foot with care before trusting our weight on it. It took a good hour to get down onto a proper track from where we could at last walk with some enjoyment. Quite a large burn was opening up, fed by numerous smaller burns, filling the whole valley with sound as it tumbled down waterfalls. The only other sound was the echoing cronk from ravens soaring around the peaks. There was no wind.

At the bottom we came to a shingly beach into which the river flowed, vanishing underground. Here we stopped awhile, shed our waterproofs and enjoyed the sunshine which was now quite hot. For the next part we had no accompanying rush of water to break the silence. Then we started the last descent down to The Meeting of the Waters where the coach was waiting. When we arrived the other two parties were standing outside the coach looking up into the sky. Following their gaze we saw a family of four golden eagles soaring quietly overhead on massive outstretched wings, barely a hundred feet above us. What an end to an action-packed day!

The following day was the 'off' day. Some of the group were arranging to climb Ben Nevis, a mountain they'd never otherwise do since it was not on this week's programme. However, after yesterday Patricia and I looked forward to a change from mountains. Besides, the weather forecast was for low cloud and rain. We opted instead for a trip to Mull. A public coach ran from Fort William to Fionnphort, where the little boat crosses to Iona. We picked it up where it crosses Loch Linnhe at Corran, less than a mile from the Centre. This is a strange ferry where the vehicles board from the side of the boat at one end, leaving from the same side at the front of the boat when it comes alongside after the crossing, so it required a lot of backing and filling to get the huge coach on, while everyone else had to wait for us. The driver assured us the weather would be just fine once we'd crossed the mountain range in front of us and he was right. Looking across to the Glen Coe area as we drove off, lowering clouds covering every peak, I was glad we'd taken this soft option. The drive is a magnificent one, Munros wherever one looks. We dropped down to the shores of Loch Sunart, a sea loch with the first of the huge salmon farms well established opposite the village of Strontian, then over another massive range until we descended to Lochaline for the ferry crossing over the Sound of Mull to Fishnish. At this point everything stopped for an hour, as the ferry had broken down, a copper fuel pipe having fractured. It always amazes me that the need for an emergency repair, in this case for a fitter to arrive and braze on another piece of pipe, can be done so swiftly out in such a remote area, but it was. Back in Watford it would have taken a week to find someone with the skill and interest to come to one's rescue.

The trip across Mull was another we remember so well. We were sitting in the front seat beside the driver, far and away the best place for the superb views that opened up around every turn, and were the only ones to see the two short-eared owls beside the road that flew off as we passed. I'm never sure why many coach passengers choose to sit further back and miss the best views; are they worried about the coach crashing, maybe? We often find the front seat empty.

At Fionnphort there were frequent crossings over to Iona. Here we experienced that ethereal light one gets in these parts, a light that turns the sea a clear ultramarine instead of the usual greeny-blue further south. There were a lot of visitors to Iona, and they all made a beeline for the Abbey, which nestles solidly a few hundred yards from the village. We too went there first, but with so many visitors and a fair sprinkling of weirdies, the atmosphere was spoilt for us. Quickly we escaped and went to a higher part of the island for the views. We'd come over here hoping it would be possible to get over to Staffa, some seven miles to the north and just visible from our viewpoint, and had booked a seat on a boat leaving later. The trip over was unexpectedly good for we were surrounded by masses of seabirds all going about their business; guillemots, razorbills, little whirring puffins, lots of assorted gulls, gannets and cormorants. They were everywhere.

Approaching Staffa, one could see the huge flood basalt pillars rising up fifty feet out of the water with a turf capping, an extraordinary geological feature that echoes the better known Giant's Causeway just across the sea in Ireland. We approached the entrance of Fingal's Cave, famously visited by Queen Victoria who was rowed over to see it, and with a permanent memorial from Felix Mendelssohn's evocative overture of the same name after he, too, had been to the island.

Back at the HF centre we all swapped stories. There was no doubt we had made the best choice. The ones who'd tramped up the soggy track to the top of Ben Nevis in the rain had had an exhausting 4½-hour walk and seen nothing from the top, but they'd been there! Plans for the next day were made. The forecast was once again for rain and cloud, so we opted for the Low walk which, coincidentally, was a coach trip across the Corran ferry once more and over to Strontian for some walking around the village, along the beach and over some moorland on the way back. We went to the little museum in the village and read about how in 1808 Sir Humphrey Davy first isolated the metallic element strontium from the mineral strontianite first found hereabouts and named after the village. As it gives off a brilliant red colour when burned in air it is mainly used for flares and fireworks, but is probably better known in its radioactive isotope form for the detection of bone cancer.

We awoke on our last morning to look out of the window and see a pine marten galumphing across the lawn towards the kitchen area. The only other pine marten I'd ever seen was one kept in captivity by H.G. Hurrell at his house on the edge of Dartmoor, where he had taught it to perform simple tricks for the visitors who came to see the menagerie. It was a rare privilege to see one in the wild. Later that sense of privilege was shattered somewhat when one of the kitchen staff said they put out food for it every day.

Back home once more, and now we were given a lovely coffee table book from Sue with evocative photographs by Derry Brabbs of the Three Peaks area of Yorkshire. It looked enticing. It was time to see for ourselves.

We booked in for one night at a small hotel in Austwick, just off the Settle to Kirby Lonsdale road. On the way we visited at the RSPB reserve at Leighton Moss, explored this from one end to the other including going on down to the coast for a seawatch, then drove around the Silverdale and Arnside areas. This top end of Morecambe Bay is not well known to most visitors to Cumbria, who usually scorch up the M6 on their way to Kendal or Penrith. We found it an attractive peaceful area and well worth a further visit one day.

The week was to be one of exploration, starting with the climb up Ingleborough. We started off from nearby Clapham, struggled up through the gap of Trow Gill and set off across the moors, conscious of all those ominous marks on the map showing shake holes and all manner of other holes any one of which we might, perhaps, fall into and never be seen again. We followed a good track that brought us to Gaping Gill, a dip in the ground with a goodly sized beck running down to it. However, the beck vanished down a large hole at one end and was seen no more. There were a lot of people around, and it transpired we'd arrived on a day when the Clapham Caving Club had their open day and anyone visiting would be able to go down into the huge cave beneath us. We'd been following a lone man with shiny brown boots who was walking the track ahead of us, and as we looked over the edge of Gaping Gill, there he was being strapped into a sort of bo's'un's chair above the roaring waterfall that took the river underground. With a signal from the strapper-in to someone manning a powered winch, brown boots suddenly dropped into the abyss, our last sight of him being a look of terror as he peered over his shoulder, clutching the rope, white knuckles clearly visible. We waited for a while and as no one emerged from the hole, we stopped and asked what happened to them. Evidently there is an exit some half mile downstream to where the visitors would be guided, and from where they would be able to climb out with ease. We believed it, and carried on our way to Ingleborough. Alas, we didn't make the top, for the sun went in, clouds rapidly appeared and we found ourselves groping around in thick mist. So we dropped down out of the cloud and headed off to the east, past magical limestone outcrops amidst sheep-cropped springy turf, returning on the far side of Clapham Beck; a lovely scenic day out.

After checking out next morning we'd hoped to climb Pen-y-Gent en route to our next planned stop at Dufton, but once again were foiled by imminent rain so explored Settle instead, discovering a rabbit warren of lovely outdoor gear shops. Then we paid a brief visit to Stainforth Force, a waterfall on the River Ribble marked on the map in blue, which was in spectacular spate, huge volumes of peaty brown water hurtling past at twenty miles an hour; not surprising after the heavy rain they'd been having for many days. It cleared by early afternoon when we drove on to Dent Head and down the lovely Dentdale to explore the village. By now we were virtually in Sedbergh where relatives of Patricia's cousin Bryan lived, so we phoned them and were asked to stop by for tea. We arrived to find Bryan and his wife, Judy, staying there. Afterwards we all went up onto the Howgill Fells, an open area which Patricia didn't like much as there were no distinguishable features, and the hills were dreadfully steep! Then we drove over the tops and down through Brough to Dufton. We'd chosen Bow Hall, a farm a mile or so out of the village and on the Pennine Way, which we'd found in our Ramblers Accommodation book. It turned out to be a good place for food but perishing cold. There was a blazing fire in the little sitting room, but upstairs it had no heating and the stonebuilt house was damp. It was only late August, for goodness sake, so shouldn't have been as cold as that. After supper we sat with one or two others in front of the blaze, the room smelling strongly of scorched socks hanging out in front of the fire to dry.

In the morning it was raining so we decided to visit the Bowes museum near Barnard Castle, which we enjoyed very much and found good value. The costume displays are excellent, I loved the famous silver swan automaton made by James Cox in 1772, and was also intrigued by a stuffed two-headed calf in a glass case in some gloomy back room, rather macabre. Then to Middleton-in-Teesdale and a walk up the river to Low Force and High Force. Still the rain came down and we got fully togged up in cagoules, waterproof trousers and umbrellas. Once we'd left the farmhouse, the temperature was mild as could be, so it must have been the damp that made us so cold the previous night. The meadows beside the river were wonderful, and apparently had we been there a month or two earlier we would have found many wildflowers for which it is famed. Coincidentally we met once again with Bryan and Judy also exploring the same area. The two waterfalls were great with all that rain (the water the colour of milky stout), and we wondered whether to venture further upstream to Cauldron Snout, but Wainwright in his Pennine Way guide had dismissed this once-lovely waterfall as not worth going near, for the Cow Green reservoir now filled the valley above and the water no longer tumbled down as it should, but emerged out of a large rusty pipe. So we gave it a miss.

At supper that night we met a young family from an Army outpost in the Outer Hebrides en route to Aldershot. This was about as far as they could get in one day. We felt sorry for them if their beds were anything like as damp as ours had been. In the morning the sun came out and, as we were so near to those beckoning hills of the Lake District, we drove over there to Haweswater which is quite easy to get to from this side of the county, then walked round to Riggindale where, at long last, we saw our golden eagle and also a juvenile. A volunteer RSPB warden had a 'scope for us to get a better view, and explained the whole valley has to be protected all through the summer in order to stop egg thieves. These people are an absolute menace and waste a huge amount of police time and precious RSPB resources, with all the resulting costs incurred; money which has been donated for conservation. They don't care a damn about this but seem to be driven by a selfish compelling urge and are, in my opinion, just as objectionable as some of the perverse religious fanatics. For inexplicable reasons the courts are unable to fine them sufficiently to even begin to repay the costs, and certainly not enough to deter them. Back at the farmhouse, we had time to walk up to the top of High Cup Nick, an interesting geological 'punchbowl' on the edge of the Pennine escarpment just above Dufton. Next morning we once again went over to the Lakes, this time driving down the south side of Ullswater all the way to the far end of the little lane. It is a beautiful spot and would make marvellous walking— if only the rain would stop! In several places the water lapped over the road. We continued round the other side of Ullswater, parking in Patterdale at the head of the lake for Patricia to show me the walk she'd done on the day I climbed Helvellyn. One crosses the Goldrill Beck which flows down from Brothers Water, then walks across a meadow to Side Farm. This meadow was flooded to within an inch of the top of our wellies. With great care we stepped gingerly along following a line of posts that marked the track and halfway across met a Landrover coming the other way, creating a fine bow wave that would certainly swamp us. With commendable courtesy the vehicle stopped and waited for us to pass before getting under way again, like one does when meeting a frisky horse on a country road. Once on the other side we were able to do our walk without any problems, but did wonder whether the lake level could have risen even further by the time we got back. It hadn't. That evening it was fresh wild salmon for supper (the landlord had a part time interest in a fishery on Ullswater).

On next day for the scenic route to York to stay a couple of nights with Sue and Paul, via Swaledale where we stopped for a walk by the river at Muker, then on to Richmond to explore the castle and where we had a look inside the little theatre, before driving down to Harlow Carr gardens just outside Harrogate which we found extremely muddy with not a lot to see at this time of year.

In the morning Sue took us on a drive to the North Yorkshire Moors near Pickering where we walked in the sunshine through acres of glorious heather, driving home the next day. That was an exhausting week but strangely, as I write this, the memories of all that rain are swamped—if that's the right word—by the far better memories of the lovely walking and superb scenery.

~*~

We had been enjoying having Granny live with us all these years. She was a tie, of course, in that we were now rather stuck in Watford since she'd put down lots of roots which, if we uprooted her, she'd now never establish anywhere else at her age. So we were stuck as it were until the end. We'd originally thought of Kodak and Watford as a ten-year option intending to think again once I'd passed the 50-year old watershed. Now here I was going on sixty and we had been in Watford nearly twenty years. We now had a most productive garden, full of vegetables and soft fruit, all of which required nurturing through the early part of the year and time-consuming harvesting through the summer. Without Granny remaining at base camp while we went gallivanting around the country, there would have been no one to look after things.

For her part, she dovetailed her own holidays between ours, generally going with various friends of her own generation. Initially she'd been quite adventurous, and enjoyed several cruises in the S.S. Uganda, a ship that put on educational cruises for children. The first class section took some older passengers who joined in the lectures on the places they were about to visit but otherwise did their own thing, and she'd met several interesting people that way. Later it had been some coaching holidays around the UK, and latterly she'd gone to these Methodist Holiday Homes holidays I've mentioned. Now approaching her nineties she was getting too old to really enjoy the hassle of uprooting even for a week.

There was one thing she did want to do though, and that was to revisit the places of her youth in Suffolk. The Pendals and Carters had been farming folk and until the 20th century had never wandered far from where they were born, a ride to the next village being considered quite far enough. We took her off for a few days to have a look round, starting with a visit to Felixstowe where her cousin had lived, but—as we'd feared—it had changed for the worse, with the genteel nature of the place she remembered replaced by bawdy seaside tat and, of course, the whole Felixstowe docks complex wasn't even a gleam in anyone's eye when she knew it. We drove through the villages to Waldringfield and on to Woodbridge, and a couple of villages on the other side of the river Deben. These were the holiday stamping grounds of her youth where not a lot had changed. After an overnight stop we went on to Framlingham and met up with a cousin she'd lost touch with who, interestingly, not only looked very like her but also had many of the same mannerisms. We left her there chatting away while we slipped off to explore Framlingham Castle. Afterwards we went tombstone hunting in the churchyards of Dennington, Tannington and Horham and then on to Instead Manor at Weybread where the original family farm still is, and found the churchwarden who showed us ancient church records with many of the names she recognised. This was a nostalgic trip for her which she really enjoyed. By this time we were near Bungay Otter Trust, so stopped off there to see at close quarters these delightful creatures gambolling about. We finished the day at Southwold. A couple of hours later we were back at home after what seemed more like a week away.

On the outskirts of Watford strategically situated near Junction 5 of the M1 the Hilton group have put up a large hotel with conference facilities for up to 400 people, and the RSPB had decided to use this venue for their AGM. Patricia and I are not 'AGM people', but decided we would go on this occasion since it was on our doorstep. We were glad we did, for we met all those luminaries whom one normally only reads about in the 'Birds' magazine. Magnus Magnusson was President at that time and conducted the meeting in his usual lovely way, we bumped into Carl Nicolson again, also David Elcome. Somewhat to our surprise, none other than Jeffrey Boswall whom we'd last seen presenting a lovely television series on Ethiopia opened the conference room door. Here he was looking after the RSPB film unit. The hotel failed dismally to feed the 400 in the time allotted for lunch, much to the irritation of Tony Beach, a mate of mine from Kodak who was the catering manager at our Head Office. He told one of the RSPB organisers that next time they wanted to have an AGM in the area, he would like them to have it at Kodak where he would show them how it should be done!

~*~

Our friends, John and Catherine Dolman, arrived for dinner one evening full of repressed excitement. We had first met them at Amersham Scottish Dancing evenings, John being the mainstay when in later years Catherine only came to the occasional main dance since she'd become very involved with lecturing on Fine Arts, also on Scottish history. Over dinner it emerged they had just bought a second home at Strachur, on the banks of Loch Fyne. Would we like to join them for Hogmanay?

This was a lovely invitation to receive. Our children were now flown, Christmas was becoming a quiet affair and we'd never celebrated Hogmanay except for the occasional local function. We left home early on the 28th December stopping off at the recently opened RSPB reserve at Caerlaverock on the shores of the Solway Firth for masses of geese, mainly Barnacle, and lots of waders. We went up through Dumfries thereby avoiding the Locherbie area which was still reeling from the aircraft disaster of only a week or so previously. The M8 winding through the middle of Glasgow spared us the usual snarl-ups one used to experience in that city, and then it is not far to Gourock from where the ferry took us over to Dunoon. From there it is a lovely quiet drive through the Argyll Forest Park to Strachur.

I had been half expecting a 'holiday home', a sort of chalet but built like a croft. It was nothing of the kind, but a pleasant family house on a new estate, beautifully appointed and furnished. The Dolmans had themselves arrived only an hour before us, but were so organised that they had the house up and running by the time we turned up. They'd also brought with them another Catherine, also from the Amersham Dance Club, so it was a party of five. Next morning the Catherines went off to the hairdressers while Patricia and I walked along the shore birdwatching. Then we all went up the local mountain getting stuck in great boggy swampy bits near the top, returning to the house in the dark pursued by mosquitoes. We had a day in Glasgow where Catherine Dolman gave us a splendid conducted tour of the Glasgow Museum, which under her tutelage we found absolutely fascinating. I very much doubt whether we would have got much out of it had we visited on our own. We rounded off the day with an evening at the Theatre Royal where Scottish Opera were presented Iolanthe, a performance of quite exceptional quality, somewhat spoilt for me by someone we'd never heard of who had a main speaking role which he delivered in a thick unintelligible Glaswegian accent. It turned out he was Billy Connolly, an important member of the cast as he would ensure every seat was sold. Sorry, Billy, but I hadn't come across you before with my somewhat restricted interests.

Then on the big day we left John's Catherine to prepare for the evening while the rest of us walked locally, and in the afternoon we all went for a drive to Tighnabruaich on the Kyles of Bute and back along a lovely lane through Glen Lean where we saw a buzzard on the ground tearing to pieces a rabbit. We stopped right beside him without frightening him off. We stopped in Dunoon for tea with friends and to meet 'Cousin George' a relation of Catherine's and a great larger-then-life character. We met again later on, at about 2 a.m. to be precise, when Cousin George appeared at the house in full Highland dress for the traditional Hogmanay greeting.

Morning service next day at the little Kirk in Newton was somewhat subdued, most of the congregation having been out on the tiles the previous evening, but it was nice to have the traditional Church of Scotland service once more. Next day was our last, and we spent most of it out walking. John's Catherine dropped us all off at Lochgoilhead, at the head of an offshoot off Loch Long, then went on to

Glasgow while we set off to walk back over the tops to Strachur. Almost at once we found ourselves in difficulties, with the main forest track several inches deep in soft peaty mud. This degenerated the further we went but there was no turning back, so we just had to struggle on as best we could. When we emerged out of the forest onto the open hill, we found we were on the wrong side of a biggish burn that then had to be crossed. Patricia slipped on a wet rock whilst crossing and cut her leg, while the other Catherine also slipped, succeeding in falling in.

The journey home, plus a half-hour delay passing the restricted area at Locherbie, was long and extremely tedious; really too far for the likes of us to manage in one day. It had been a good break, and considering it was mid winter, the weather had been kind: very mild all the time and only occasional rain.

~*~

In the summer it was time for another visit to the Lakes. Now we had discovered Wainwright we felt no need to go with a leader, so booked in to a B&B on the village green at Grasmere. For several weeks leading up to the holiday I happily studied the Wainwright Guide covering that area, and worked out several half-day and all-day walks. My main concern about wandering about on the fells on our own had been the danger of bad weather closing in and the need to get off the tops safely. Too many of the best fells had sheer drops which it would be easy to stumble over in bad visibility, and one needed to be aware exactly were one was. Wainwright's wonderful Guides resolved that concern.

So, after a couple of days stop in York to see Sue, we made our way to Grasmere with a visit en route to Haweswater for eagle-spotting. It was a perfect day, and we went anticlockwise round Riggindale, seeing the eagle in the distance, up Kidsty Pike and on to High Street for a half mile or so before coming down via Blae Tarn back to the car park at Haweswater Head. That was the plan; however, while we were on the exposed top of High Street a bank of cloud suddenly rolled in, the temperature dropped like a stone, the wind got up and in moments we were caught in heavy driving rain. Lightning was crackling within the clouds all around us and it didn't seem at all a good place to linger. Yet it had been so clear when we started off that we'd left our heavy waterproof gear behind in order to have room for the telescope and tripod in my rucksack, so were utterly unprepared. Within minutes we were both soaked and shivering, unable to feel our extremities and by the time we got back to the car and tried to unlock it my hands were so cold I couldn't grip the key, I'd learnt several valuable lessons about fellwalking which I very much hope we shall never forget. Ruefully, I knew that had we been with a leader, he would never have let us go up on the fells without adequate gear however heavy that made our rucksacks.

While our wet clothing steamed from the clothes drier above the B&B's Aga cooker, we wandered around the village (in sunshine once more). It was early evening and Grasmere was very quiet, yet we'd heard it is a visitor honeypot, people coming from all over the world because of the Wordsworth connection. Where were they? "You'll see," we were told, but had to wait to find out. Next

489

morning we drove round to Patterdale where we left the car and climbed Helvellyn 'by the edges', as I had done with the Derwentbank HF Group on the day Patricia went on her 'C' walk. We took the day over it and Patricia coped with all the scrambling around on Striding Edge with no problems. Once up on the plateau we met lots of people who'd walked up the relatively gentle path from the Thirlmere side, and that could explain why Helvellyn is so popular—anyone can get to the top with comparative ease. We came down by Swirral Edge, which meant we had to wander around on the top peering over the side to see where the track down to Swirral Edge started from. There were no cairns or other marks to suggest which way to go and I could well imagine the problems one might have in the mist. Go off a few yards to one side, and it would be all too easy to find oneself slivering down the scree all the way to Red Tarn nestling up against the side of the mountain 500 feet below. It was a lovely walk that day with superb views all the way and, forgetting yesterday's rain, a wonderful beginning to our week in Grasmere.

We started a little later next day after going round the village shops and soon discovered why Grasmere was so quiet and peaceful. At about 10.00 a.m. the cars began to arrive followed half an hour later by the coaches. Soon it seemed to be standing room only. We were told they all started back for the fleshpots of Ambleside and Windermere before 5.30, so if we returned after that we would find a parking space outside our B&B with no trouble. Well, that day we left our car where it was and walked up Easedale, a gorgeous valley with a tarn perched halfway up it. We carried on to Stickle Tarn, a popular spot nestling at the foot of Pavey Ark, one of the Langdale Pikes, and returned over the fells with the Langdale valley below us to our right until we reached Silver Howes from where we dropped down to Grasmere, a grand walk of about nine miles with (if my calculations are right) about 3,000 feet of ascent in total. After Helvellyn the previous day we were pretty tired by the time we reached the village (now quiet again after its invaders had left), but were beginning to feel fit.

The next outing was a circular walk starting from Ambleside which I'd had great fun planning after studying several Wainwright mountains from his pocket guide and linking them together. I found out later that the same walk is described in his Fellwalking with Wainwright book, which he calls 'The Fairfield Horseshoe'. This was a very strenuous day for us, some 12½ miles and, once again, about 3,000 feet of ascent. But the weather was sublime and we had the whole day to do it, going up via High Sweden Bridge and returning through Rydal Park, the last couple of miles telling us with every step they were two miles too far. About halfway round ascending Hart Crag on a tricky bit of near-scrambling we were overtaken by a couple of fellrunners, and spoke to one of them (he wasn't even puffed when he stopped to chat!). How long did it take him? About 1½ hours… He stood there in singlet and running shoes looking fit and relaxed, and probably would not have been much younger than us. With a "cheerio" he sprang lightly off and in a moment had vanished. Patricia and I looked at one another dressed in our heavy clothes, rucksacks on our backs, perspiring and dishevelled, and suddenly felt extremely old and past it.

Restored again after a good night's sleep we surveyed the weather prospects next morning and decided to make the most of it, so attempted another similar walk, this one a bit further over towards Kendal. We parked the car in the sleepy little hamlet of Kentmere and walked round the top of that valley, from the northern end of which we found ourselves on the summit of Mardale Ill Bell with a view down to Haweswater. As we approached the peak along that part of the High Street ridge, the temperature dropped, the wind got up and the sun went in. Shades of our recent sousing on our eagle walk a few days previously! However, the rain held off and we completed the round walk quite grateful for the cooler conditions. Once again we'd completed another 12-mile walk, and decided to take it quieter the following day. Already we'd completed all the walks I'd planned, for I assumed we would never have a whole week of fine weather and had only expected to be up on the fells for four days of our week.

So, after breakfast we wandered down the lane past Dove Cottage (Japanese pilgrims were already starting to congregate there waiting for the house to open), then sat on the top of White Moss Common, a hill between the two lakes of Grasmere and Rydal Water and enjoyed the views. Then we returned round the other side of Grasmere along Loughrigg Terrace where we met a CHA party with one of our Watford acquaintances at the head of it, and came back to Grasmere village over Silver Howes once more. A much gentler day and, given such superb and hot weather, one that we really enjoyed.

But our last day was also fine and sunny, so we couldn't just not go up on the fells. Off we went once more to Easedale, this time walking over to the next valley, Far Easedale, from where we went up onto the plateau and had our lunch sitting on top of a little pile of rocks known as Sergeant Man. On the way up we had our best view yet of the Cumbrian eagles, two of which were soaring gently along the ridge beside us near Helm Crag when a pair of peregrine falcons who presumably had a nest nearby went for them, and we watched a dramatic aerobatic display from the peregrines and the disdainful way in which the eagles ignored them. All very exciting and it made a fine ending to a really excellent week and undoubtedly our best Lake District holiday yet.

Back at home once more we had to set to, harvesting early crops and dealing with urgent house maintenance (I never called in any 'little man' for this sort of thing, considering my own skills were adequate for all jobs around the house except, perhaps major plumbing work like fitting a new boiler). During this time Sue and Paul spent the night with us on their way to the French Alps for one of their dangerous climbing holidays (they all seemed dangerous to us, but Paul was an exceptionally careful and competent man on the rocks, and I am sure Sue was in the safest of hands). They left their car with us while continuing the journey by rail, so we took them down to the station next morning. I attempted to lift Sue's rucksack and could barely get it off the ground, and Paul's was even heavier. I could not get his off the ground at all. Poor things—they would be back-packing for much of the time, travelling from hut to hut.

And next thing we knew it was off for our next jaunt. We'd booked in to a B&B at Hope Cove in South Devon. As usual, we'd found the place in the Ramblers

Accommodation Guide, happy that all the places we'd heard about through that guide would be okay; the main criterion being that they did an evening meal. This would eliminate 80% of them and, of course, we avoided the big hotels which would cost twice as much and lack the personal touch.

As usual on such journeys we looked around for a nice spot to visit en route, stopping on this occasion at the Exminster marshes, then on to Dawlish Warren where we picked our way through all the seaside brigade wandering about in their own litter, emerging onto the warren itself for some birding on the tidal flats, with the unexpected bonus of lots of wild flowers.

Hope Cove is a little seaside village reached by the narrowest of Devon lanes from the Kingsbridge to Salcombe road, and we were to get to know that road well by the end of our week. The house had six lovely double rooms with superb views, and the 'personal touch' was almost too much this time! One couple were old regulars and at dinner the first night initiated lots of banter between us all, with the result we became a close-knit group almost immediately. The husband and wife team who ran the house chipped in, treating us all like a rather tiresome family, which sounds dreadful but turned out to be good fun. We have lovely memories of the Hope Cove house and visited it again a few years later.

Hope Cove is tucked in behind Bolt Tail, the westernmost point of one of South Devon's most glorious bits of coastline. We 'did' the walk on our first day while the weather was perfect, six miles or so to Bolt Head, then inland to Salcombe where we searched out a homemade ice cream vendor, then returned to Hope Cove by the inland route; a lovely, though exhausting day. We next had a day over at Slapton Ley, then after some birding we explored the coastal area around Prawle Point, another excellent stretch of coastline with a good path all the way. After that it felt time for our Dartmoor fix, so spent the whole of the next day on one of our favourite walks from our Plymstock days, over Ugborough Moor from Bittaford north for some six miles or so, then back to Harford and a paddle in the little stream to cool off. It had been a hot day with relentless sun and no shade, and even the cattle were standing around in the breeziest spots they could find.

After that we spent a day east of Salcombe, going over on the little passenger ferry to Portlemouth and walking the cliff path to Prawle Point approaching it from the west this time. It was far too hot for this sort of thing, no whiff of a breeze and very humid. The weather forecast suggested a thunderstorm before the day was out, so we returned to the house a little earlier than usual and just made it before the heavens opened. Hooray for the accurate forecasting!

What else could we do from here? We decided a morning visiting old haunts in Plymouth would be fun, and found the Sutton Harbour areas had received a makeover, the dockside fish market that had been such a colourful part of the harbour having been moved to the other side, away from the touristy part. Tourists were having their photographs taken standing by the Mayflower Steps, where the Pilgrim Fathers are supposed to have set off for their adventures. Presumably unknown to the tourists, the actual steps the Pilgrims would have used are some ten feet below the modern ones, and can only be accessed by entering a small church nearby and asking to be allowed down into the crypt.

On the way home to Watford we went via Dartmouth, always a favourite of mine, especially as I no longer have to wear Naval uniform and behave in a dignified Service fashion. We reached home to find Sue and Paul back from their French Alps holiday so spent the evening relating one another's experiences. A couple of months later Paul landed a job for his next 6-month contract in his chosen discipline—infectious diseases. Unfortunately it was in Glasgow, so once again they would be living apart. No wonder the NHS is always short of doctors. I wonder whether they ever think what it must be like trying to have a family life with a job change every six months? Various politicians talk about everything except the medical people at the coalface who do the work, and feign surprise when they leave for a career somewhere else.

~*~

Two of my Kodak friends were celebrating their silver wedding anniversary. Alan Bruce, a technologist in one of the production departments, and Olive, a research scientist, had first met at the Glen Coe HF house. Alan (also my friend Greg Child) were ardent members of the 'Puss-Puss' Society, which after some time I discovered was actually 'PSPS', short for Paddle Steamer Preservation Society. At Kodak lunchtimes they would talk interminably about the PS Waverley's visit to wherever (the Waverley was one of only two Clyde paddle steamers still running, now only used for short trips around various resorts). I would chip in with my reminiscences of the big paddle tugs used by HM Dockyards, which also doubled as tenders for some of the larger ships since they could take a couple of hundred sailors ashore in one go. Patricia and I now received an invitation to celebrate the Bruce's silver wedding anniversary with a trip down the estuary from Chatham on board the Kingswear Castle, another paddle steamer now beautifully restored and ideal for such an event.

We drove down early enough to have a look at nearby Rochester Castle before going on to Chatham which, since my last visit in the '50s when it had been a proper working Naval Dockyard, is now an empty lifeless maritime museum. We spent a happy day with about fifty others sitting around on deck talking and watching the shore slip by, with every now and then a peer down into the engineroom where big pistons thumped back and forth driving the paddles on either side which went "Splosh, splosh, splosh" in a pleasantly soporific manner. I didn't mention to any of the others that this type of propulsion was phased out rather quickly when it was discovered the quickest way to capsize a paddle steamer was to go ahead on one paddle and astern on the other; to do this might give the boat wonderful manoeuvrability when being used as a tug, but was not safe. The Mississippi style of paddle steamer with the paddle at the back was probably the best sort, but they all suffered from poor manoeuvrability compared with screw propulsion. The paddle steamers still in use had fixed paddles driven from a shaft with no means of stopping or reversing one without the other, so they were not dangerous. Most of the other guests were also Kodak people so, not surprisingly, the event was well recorded on film, cameras clicking away all afternoon. It was a lovely way to celebrate their wedding anniversary.

The last time I mentioned my Kodak work I talked about my involvement with putting together reports for my project engineering contemporaries. This had expanded further in that I developed an interest in artistic layouts, the use of different typefaces, eye-catching headlines and all the paraphernalia of the newspaperman. I read Harold Evans' excellent book written when he was editor of The Times, and any other books I could find on the subject. Though nothing to do with writing and presenting technical reports (where the reader is usually only concerned with the content, not noticing nor caring how it is presented) it was nevertheless a skill in which I had an interest and one I wanted to make use of if the opportunity presented itself.

Microsoft had brought out Windows Version 3—a big advance over the somewhat basic earlier versions—and independent software companies were writing useful applications to go with it. Through one of my project engineering chums I was introduced to an acquaintance of his who was employing three young programmers to develop a computer drawing package. I went along with him to meet the team who operated from smart offices in Acton, and they showed me what could be done. I watched, fascinated, while one of them worked on the P&O logo, which depicts the company flag fluttering in the breeze. It was so realistic it seemed to stand out from the screen and one could almost hear the bunting flapping as it moved. Nobody had created anything like this before without a camera. Was this the beginning of the end for Kodak? I asked them whether it would be possible to use their techniques for generating the 35mm slides I currently used for our engineering annual reviews, at this time being made tediously by a graphic artist sticking down Letraset, letter by letter, the resulting artwork being photographed in the conventional manner. But of course it could! They generously offered to let me have the programme (which came on several floppy disks) to see how I got on. Yippee! I spent many happy hours playing with it, and received lots of help over the telephone from these people. This offer was not so magnanimous as it sounds, for they wanted the program trialled by ordinary users such as myself. They realised they'd spent many man-years of expensive programming time to bring it to the state it was in, and were now needing to either market it or even sell the rights. Would Kodak be interested? I asked around, and with some reluctance, the Research Division at Harrow agreed to host a demonstration and see whether it should be something the Company ought to be involved in. The demonstration duly took place followed by discussions, with the result Kodak showed some cautious interest, but the whole venture was later vetoed by Eastman Kodak back in the States. However, their time was not entirely wasted, for the team gained useful contacts and subsequently visited the States and discovered several other software companies also developing something similar.

Shortly after this I found that a Canadian company, CorelDraw, had a better program that was considerably more user-friendly, so acquired a copy of it for my Kodak work. Unfortunately it was really too big for the computer I was currently using, so I was unable to employ its full potential. It started me thinking it was time I had my own computer at home, to which I would then be able to add additional memory. The project engineer who had introduced me to the Acton team was also thinking about a home computer; we egged each other on and eventually bought two machines, one for each of us.

Round about this time the latest round of downsizing figures were being bandied about. At one of our departmental meetings our manager said there was no need for us to worry. Out of his sixty-strong department they were asking him to 'lose' just two people by the end of the year. Maybe one or two might want to retire early, and in any event this was not a mandatory requirement; perhaps another department would lose more than their quota so that we would need to take no action. Unwittingly (or perhaps not) he sowed the seed. For some weeks I wondered whether I would be able to retire early (I was 59 and the 'normal' retirement age had recently dropped from 65 to an optional 63); would I be able to manage financially? From my work at Head Office I was familiar with all the redundancy packages, and was fairly certain I would hardly notice the difference in income. Sure, my pension would be half my current salary, but that difference would be considerably reduced if I invested the redundancy money and took into account the costs of actually going to work. Why, I might never need to buy another suit! All those canteen lunches would be a thing of the past, and what about the petrol savings from the daily commuter run? It was quite an attractive proposition.

A couple of months later I walked in from the car park one morning with our manager (why is it all the important meetings in my life always seem to take place in the car park?).

"Morning, David," I ventured. "Have you found your two people yet?"

"Not yet, John. Why? —Are you volunteering?"

"Not me! One thing I learnt in the Services; Never volunteer for anything."

He sensed I had a reason for raising the subject. "But?"

"Well, David, I suppose if the redundancy terms were right, I could allow my arm to be twisted…"

He laughed. "Your Head Office time wasn't wasted! I'll see what we might be able to do."

A week or two later we met once more (in the car park as usual). "Well, John," he said, "I can say that we would not be replacing you, nor the job. The lads will just have to learn to do their own Capital Expenditure reports. All the tasks you currently do would either cease to be done at all, or would be spread around the others. Does that answer your question?" He looked hopeful. I said I'd think about it over the weekend.

Our mortgage would become fully paid up in another year, so instead of regular outgoing mortgage interest payments we would receive instead a one-off lump sum as a result of our endowment mortgage having done exceptionally well over its life. Then there would no longer be National Insurance contributions, nor contributions into a pension fund. Various retired friends said they had over-estimated the living costs of being retired, worried that too little income would be coming in, and although they had intended to find some congenial paid work after they retired, they'd never got round to it because there was no need. It sounded just great. A few days later I said I would probably volunteer to be made redundant and could I see the redundancy terms, please? These turned out to be better than I expected, so I put in my application (or rather, my manager put in his request for me to be made redundant). The machinery took over and I started the rundown, lasting about three months. During this time I passed over various jobs to others and went on a redundancy course, which was a bit of a joke as I had originally been one of the people who'd helped get the course up and running during my Head Office time.

My peers were frantic about coping without my services, so I happily offered to keep providing any writing and presentation services they might need, only I'd do it mainly from home and, of course, for real money rather than as part of the job. Thus when the time came to leave, I took with me a small amount of work, and kept returning once or twice a week for a month or two; a gentle let-down to the new life of leisure that I expected. Needless to say, no life of leisure materialised; I seemed to be busier than ever but with jobs I wanted to do instead of jobs that Kodak wanted me to do. Within weeks I was in a position where I certainly would not have had time to go to work as well!

My final connection with Kodak was to make two more videos with Brian Wareham. The first one was a safety training video to be shown to contractors who worked on our factory site. People watching it would not want to waste time, and we had to get the message over in about 10-15 minutes if we had any hope of holding their attention, which provided quite a problem with presenting what was needed. We achieved this by putting it over in a fairly lighthearted manner, and this went down well. The other video was a safety-awareness one concerning movement of heavy product in some production areas. The corridors where trucks and forklifts dash about with loads of several tons is a potentially extremely dangerous area, and the object of the video was to demonstrate what could happen if one didn't take care constantly. We used one of the training officers in his other life as a thespian, the storyline being that a few months after retiring he returned to meet one of his chums, to discover his friend now worked in a different area. His adventures going around to find his chum's office involve him in a number of narrow escapes. At last he sees his friend walking across the end of a high-rise warehouse bay and runs to catch up with him, but gets knocked down by a forklift truck. The final scene shows him arriving at last in his chum's office, but by now he is on crutches with his head bandaged.

My only other visits to Harrow were to the Staff Shop where I handed in my films for processing but, whereas in the old days it would take me a few moments to cover the hundred yards from the gate to the shop, I now took half an hour, meeting friends on the way and talking to them all. Everyone wanted to know how I found it 'outside'. Over time I met fewer friends but was passed by younger bright-eyed bushy-tailed people who were the new generation. Oh well— I needed them to help pay my pension! My Kodak days were definitely over.

Tailpiece

It is now seventeen years since I retired. Patricia hoped when that happened we would then be able to go off whenever we liked and do far more things together. But of course things never work out like that. I came away from Kodak with an interest in creating artwork for publications and found I was in demand from a number of small organisations that wanted brochures or syllabuses or just tickets. The main break came when one of my dancing friends told me the London Branch of the RSCDS were looking for another printer for their quarterly newsletter, then a four- or six-page affair rather crudely printed. I put in an offer and was accepted. It is now sixteen to twenty pages with lots of pictures and adverts, and is eagerly awaited by the readers, and I do all the layout and artwork (but not the editing!) while a local printing firm runs off 2,000 copies which fetch up all over the world. As time went by I developed my printing hobby as by so doing I found I was meeting people from all walks of life, some of them most interesting, a few not.

We have visited masses of gardens, been on many more walking holidays, two or three a year, usually with HF, also one or two more specific birding ones to exotic places such as the West Indies and Central America, tried a culture cruise in the Baltic and another visiting islands and culture ports between Dover and Malta. During this time our children have not been idle, our Paul married his Gill and between them the two families have produced five grandchildren for us to dote over. Granny had a stroke in her 94th year, followed by two years of failing health until in her 96th year she went to join Leslie. The house is now very quiet with just the two of us, but somehow we fill it all, largely with junk. (A variation of Parkinson's Law might well state: The accumulation of junk continues for as long as there is somewhere to put it.) We have now reached the state where we would find it very difficult ever to move from this house because of the insuperable problem of down-sizing.

Many of our friends are retired professional people, and amazingly quite a few have never adjusted to retired life, seemingly unable to slow down and enjoy the pleasures of a life without stress. I used to joke that I married Patricia because she was a fine cook and an expert housewife, while she joked that she married me because unlike her I could mend a fuse and was able to cope with gadgets about the house, thus making for a contented couple. Life has become very much more contented as we wake up each morning and decide how to spend the day, with an eye on the weather perhaps. I am sure that Patricia's distrust of many packaged foods, always insisting she prepares our meals from fresh ingredients with a known provenance, fruit and vegetables from the garden whenever possible, has contributed hugely to our health and long may it continue.

Over the last seventeen years we have done so many things together that I have probably sufficient material for another book.